# JUST AND
# LASTING PEACE

# A JUST AND LASTING PEACE

In 1862, as Union and Confederate soldiers continued to wage war, plans for the future of the country had already begun, set down in competing proclamations, essays and manifestos. After the South's surrender, throughout the harrowing and chaotic process of Reconstruction, Americans voiced their hopes and grievances in private diaries and from public pulpits; brought court cases and launched bold new experiments in governance; hatched vicious plots to undermine order. It remains the most controversial and least understood period in American history. Through a selection of primary documents, *A Just and Lasting Peace* portrays the full scope of attitudes and conflicts that drove, threatened, and eventually won the modern union.

**John David Smith** is the Charles H. Stone Distinguished Professor of American History at the University of North Carolina, Charlotte. He has been a fellow of the American Council of Learned Societies and received the Myers Center Award for the Study of Human Rights in North America. He currently serves as contributing editor for the *Journal of American History* and on the editorial boards of several scholarly journals. Among the books he has authored or edited are *Black Voices from Reconstruction; Slavery, Race and American History;* and *Black Judas: William Hannibal Thomas and "The American Negro,"* which won the Mayflower Society Award for Nonfiction. He has appeared on the History Channel, as an authority on the U.S. Colored Troops, and on Voice of America, as an authority on conservative racial thought during the Age of Jim Crow.

# A
# JUST AND
# LASTING
# PEACE

## A DOCUMENTARY HISTORY OF RECONSTRUCTION

### EDITED AND WITH AN INTRODUCTION BY
## John David Smith

SIGNET CLASSICS

SIGNET CLASSICS
Published by the Penguin Group
Penguin Group (USA) Inc., 375 Hudson Street,
New York, New York 10014, USA

USA | Canada | UK | Ireland | Australia | New Zealand | India | South Africa | China

Penguin Books Ltd., Registered Offices: 80 Strand, London WC2R 0RL, England
For more information about the Penguin Group visit penguin.com.

Published by Signet Classics, an imprint of New American Library,
a division of Penguin Group (USA) Inc.

First Signet Classics Printing, May 2013

ISBN 978-0-451-53226-8

Printed in the United States of America
10 9 8 7 6 5 4 3 2 1

ALWAYS LEARNING                                                    PEARSON

*To Peter Coveney—friend and editor extraordinaire*

# ACKNOWLEDGMENTS

I wish to acknowledge the support and research assistance of several persons who helped me in various ways in preparing *A Just and Lasting Peace*: David Blight, Ann Davis, Mary Dougherty, James J. Harris, Kathleen Johnson, Jane Knetzger, Charles McShane, Leigh Robbins, Sylvia A. Smith, Lois Stickell, Stephen Wrinn, and Andrew Zimmerman. Tracy Bernstein kindly asked me to undertake this project. Through the years, I have enjoyed working with a number of people at Penguin, including Charleen Davis, Michael Millman, Stephanie Smith, and Naomi Weinstein.

# CONTENTS

# Chronology of
# Reconstruction

| | |
|---|---|
| April 16, 1862 | Slaves in the District of Columbia emancipated. |
| September 22, 1862 | Preliminary Emancipation Proclamation issued. |
| January 1, 1863 | Final Emancipation Proclamation issued. |
| December 8, 1863 | Lincoln issued Proclamation of Amnesty and Reconstruction and announced the Ten Percent Plan of Reconstruction. |
| July 2, 1864 | Wade-Davis Reconstruction Bill passed. First Freedmen's Bureau Bill passed. |
| July 8, 1864 | Lincoln issued pocket-veto proclamation on Wade-Davis Bill. |
| August 5, 1864 | Wade-Davis Manifesto issued. |
| January 31, 1865 | Thirteenth Amendment passed by Congress. |
| March 3, 1865 | Freedmen's Bureau established. Freedman's Savings Bank incorporated. |
| April 14, 1865 | Lincoln assassinated. |
| April 15, 1865 | Johnson succeeded to the presidency. |
| May 9, 1865 | Johnson recognized Pierpont government in Virginia. |
| May 10, 1865 | Jefferson Davis captured at Irwinsville, Georgia. |
| May 29, 1865 | Johnson issued Proclamation of Amnesty and inaugurated Presi- |

| | |
|---|---|
| | dential Reconstruction in North Carolina. |
| July to December 1865 | Former Confederate states (except Texas) reorganized under Johnson's plan. |
| December 4, 1865 | Congress reconvened and refused to admit Southern members-elect. |
| December 6, 1865 | Thirteenth Amendment ratified. |
| December 13, 1865 | Congress established Joint Committee on Reconstruction. |
| February 19, 1866 | Freedmen's Bureau Bill vetoed by Johnson. |
| April 9, 1866 | Civil Rights Bill passed over Johnson's veto. |
| May 1866 | Ku Klux Klan organized. |
| May 1–3, 1866 | Memphis Race Riot. |
| June 13, 1866 | Fourteenth Amendment passed by Congress. |
| June 20, 1866 | Joint Committee on Reconstruction recommended that the former Rebel states were not entitled to representation and should remain under Congressional authority. |
| July 16, 1866 | The second Freedmen's Bureau Bill passed over Johnson's veto. |
| July 24, 1866 | Tennessee's representatives readmitted to Congress. |
| July 30, 1866 | New Orleans Race Riot. |
| August 28 to September 15, 1866 | Johnson's "swing around the circle." |
| January 7, 1867 | Johnson's impeachment proposed in Congress. |
| January 8, 1867 | Black suffrage granted in District of Columbia. |
| January 25, 1867 | Black suffrage extended to the territories. |
| March 2, 1867 | First Reconstruction, Tenure of Office, and Army Appropriation |

|                          | Acts passed (first two over Johnson's veto). |
|--------------------------|----------------------------------------------|
| March 23, 1867           | Second Reconstruction Act passed over Johnson's veto. |
| July 19, 1867            | Third Reconstruction Act passed over Johnson's veto. |
| August 12, 1867          | Johnson suspended Stanton and appointed Grant secretary of war. |
| October to November 1867 | Democratic victories in various Northern states. |
| December 7, 1867         | Resolution for impeachment of Johnson failed. |
| January 13, 1868         | Stanton restored to office by Senate. |
| February 21, 1868        | Covode Resolution impeachment resolution made against Johnson. |
| February 24, 1868        | Johnson impeached. |
| March 11, 1868           | Fourth Reconstruction Act passed. |
| May 16, 1868             | Johnson acquitted. |
| June 22–25, 1868         | Arkansas, North Carolina, South Carolina, Florida, Alabama, and Louisiana readmitted to the Union. |
| July 6, 1868             | Freedmen's Bureau continued by Congress. |
| July 9, 1868             | Fourteenth Amendment ratified. |
| November 3, 1868         | Grant elected president. |
| February 26, 1869        | Fifteenth Amendment passed by Congress. |
| January 26, 1870         | Virginia readmitted to the Union. |
| February 3, 1870         | Fifteenth Amendment ratified. |
| February 23, 1870        | Mississippi readmitted to the Union. |
| March 30, 1870           | Texas readmitted to the Union. |
| May 31, 1870             | First Enforcement Act enacted. |
| July 15, 1870            | Georgia permanently readmitted to the Union. |

| | |
|---|---|
| February 28, 1871 | Second Enforcement Act enacted. |
| March 3, 1871 | Civil Service Law enacted. |
| April 20, 1871 | Third Enforcement Act (Ku Klux Klan Act) passed by Congress. |
| May 22, 1872 | General Amnesty Act passed. |
| November 5, 1872 | Grant reelected. |
| September 18, 1873 | Panic of 1873 began. |
| March 1, 1875 | Civil Rights Act passed. |
| November 7, 1876 | Disputed presidential election. |
| December 1876 to March 1877 | Congressional deadlock leading to Compromise of 1877. |
| January 29, 1877 | Electoral Commission established. |
| March 2, 1877 | Hayes declared victor over Tilden. |
| March 5, 1877 | Hayes inaugurated. |
| April 3, 1877 | Federal troops withdrawn from South Carolina statehouse and abandonment of state Republican administration. |
| April 20, 1877 | Federal troops withdrawn from Louisiana statehouse and abandonment of state Republican administration. |
| October 15, 1883 | *Civil Rights Cases* decided. |
| May 18, 1896 | *Plessy v. Ferguson* decided. |

# INTRODUCTION

The bloody American Civil War ground to a halt in April 1865, abolishing chattel slavery, establishing the sanctity of free labor, and maintaining the integrity of the American union. Despite the internecine struggle that cost possibly as many as 750,000 lives, the nation had survived.[1] As historian Eric Foner, the foremost authority on postwar Reconstruction, has explained, "The Civil War changed the nature of warfare, gave rise to an empowered nation-state, vindicated the idea of free labor and destroyed the modern world's greatest slave society. Each of these outcomes laid the foundation for the country we live in today. But as with all great historical events, each outcome carried with it ambiguous, even contradictory, consequences."[2]

In his Second Inaugural Address, delivered March 4, 1865, President Abraham Lincoln looked ahead to the reunification of the Union. He urged Americans, north and south, "to finish the work we are in; to bind up the nation's wounds; to care for him who shall have borne the battle, and for his widow, and his orphan—to do all which may achieve and cherish a just, and a lasting peace, among ourselves, and with all nations."[3] Lincoln, whose life would be cut down by a Southern sympathizer on April 14, just five days after Confederate General Robert E. Lee's surrender at Appomattox Court House, Virginia, had hoped to restore the Southern states to the Union smoothly and expeditiously. Months before his assassination the president had taken steps to ensure the constitutionality of the Emancipation Proclamation by supporting the passage of the Thirteenth Amendment (ultimately ratified on December 6, 1865). In his last public address, Lincoln referred to his 1863 "plan of re-construction (as the phrase goes)" and supported conferring the vote "on the very intelligent"

African-American men, "and on those who serve our cause as soldiers."[4]

War-weary Americans, however, soon learned that their much sought-after peace led to a bewildering array of constitutional, economic, and social problems. White Southerners, for example, struggled under the new order of things: life in a world without mastery over slaves. Though many feared retribution by their formerly "loyal" slaves, in fact most of the freedpeople sought to find loved ones separated by slavery, stabilize their families, find jobs either as laborers for wages or on "shares" of the crop, and create lives for themselves and their children. A former plantation mistress recorded in her diary late in 1865 her surprise at the behavior of the ex-slaves. "They are orderly & subordinate but incorrigibly lazy. Occasional acts of insubordination by the returned negro soldiers occurs here & there, but in this neighborhood we are exempt from all the ills of Emancipation save those which spring from Laziness & Theft."[5]

Modern historians increasingly expand the traditional beginning and ending dates of Reconstruction. "If we come to regard emancipation as a protracted national process," writes Steven Hahn, "we must also take a new look at the dimensions of what we call Reconstruction. Either Reconstruction must be seen as a similarly extended phenomenon, initiated in the Northern states well before the Southern (and thus almost coincidental with American nation building more generally), or we have to acknowledge a great many 'rehearsals' for the large-scale Reconstruction of the Civil War era: rehearsals that suggest different and more wide-ranging political dynamics (involving class, ethnicity, gender, and culture as much as race) than we are accustomed to recognizing."[6]

Some scholars interpret the postwar years as a continuation of the war, as Americans north and south confronted the obstacles of restoring the Union, generating new battles over sovereignty, representation, and race relations. Though armed conflict between Union and Confederate forces ground to a halt in April 1865, over the next dozen years new forms of violence—including murder, mob beatings, urban race riots, and guerrilla warfare in the countryside directed against blacks and Unionists—vexed the period that historians term Reconstruction. "The belligerence of Southern leaders did not end with Appomattox," explains historian John Stauffer. "They neither laid down their arms nor accepted the terms of their unconditional surrender. Instead they went home and engaged in a terrorist war for the next twelve years."[7]

This book is the first major documentary history of Reconstruction since the early twentieth century when historian Walter Lynwood Fleming published his popular two-volume *Documentary History of Reconstruction: Political, Military, Social, Religious, Educational, and Industrial, 1865 to 1906* (1906–7).[8] Fleming, trained in Professor William Archibald Dunning's famous Columbia University history seminar, underscored slavery's righteousness, the inherent inferiority of African-Americans, and what historian Robert D. Reid termed "the noble purposes of the white South, and the deleterious effects of Reconstruction."[9]

The documents in *A Just and Lasting Peace* reflect all sides of the Reconstruction experience—constitutional, economic, legal, social, and, above all, the pull and tug of human adjustment during the post–Civil War years. But whereas Fleming's excerpted texts combined to depict Reconstruction as an exceptional, extreme, radical moment in American history, the documents in *A Just and Lasting Peace* highlight the inertia and the limitations on politicians and reformers determined to remake the South and, in doing so, to transform the nation into a biracial representative democracy predicated on true freedom and citizenship. The historical texts included in *A Just and Lasting Peace* also reflect Foner's "rejuvenated revisionism" captured in his path-breaking and influential *Reconstruction: America's Unfinished Revolution, 1863–1877* (1988).[10] As historian Gregory P. Downs has noted correctly, Foner, without dismissing the ideals and contributions of white Northern reformers and Republicans, showcased the agency and experiences of the ex-slaves during the postwar period. Foner and those historians who have followed him, most notably Steven Hahn in *A Nation Under Our Feet: Black Political Struggle in the South from Slavery to the Great Migration* (2003), have emphasized the emancipated slaves' determination for full freedom, including economic autonomy and citizenship on a par with whites. They un-

derscore Reconstruction as a nonlinear historical process
with many twists and turns, but nevertheless identify a leitmotif in the hopes and dreams of blacks, who, during the
dozen years following the war, acted as agents of their own
economic, political, and social freedom.[11]

Reconstruction, a critical period of American history
that began during the Civil War and continued into the
1880s, remains an amazingly complex and complicated historical epoch, a watershed in American political, social, cultural, and economic history. For scholars, the period
presents a many-headed hydra. Reconstruction signified an
end to the Civil War and, after a stormy interlude, led to the
readmission of the former Confederate states to the Union.
But it also represented an experiment in economic, social,
and political democracy—America's first civil rights movement—and, ultimately, it launched a new beginning for
Americans north and south. Significantly, Reconstruction
marked the end of an era: the end of slavery, the end of the
so-called "slavocracy," and the end of the serious idea of
state interposition and secession in American politics. Yet,
as much as Reconstruction signaled a termination point, it
also marked a new beginning. With Reconstruction, Americans commenced a period of experimentation in interra-
cial democracy—a period of civil and political rights for the
freedmen, a period of strong federalism, and a new nation-
alism. Each was tested.

Revisionist scholars of the 1940s, 1950s, and 1960s, responding to the traditional, or "tragic era," interpretation of
Dunning-era historians like Fleming, approached the period sympathetically and optimistically. These historians
highlighted Reconstruction's triumphs. "If the era was
'tragic,' revisionists insisted, it was because change did not
go far enough, especially in the area of Southern land reform," Foner explained, but Reconstruction was still "a time
of extraordinary social and political progress for blacks."[12]

Disappointed by the slow pace of racial change during
the Second Reconstruction of the 1960s, historians in the
1970s and 1980s, whom Foner terms "postrevisionists,"
viewed the so-called gains of Reconstruction skeptically
and went to great lengths to describe the period's essential
conservatism, whether in terms of land distribution, in the
courts, or in the persistence of white planter economic, ra-

cial, and social control. According to Foner, "The postrevisionist interpretation represented a striking departure from nearly all previous accounts of the period, for whatever their differences, traditional and revisionist historians at least agreed that reconstruction was a time of radical change."[13] Prior to the appearance of Foner's book, most scholars emphasized the limitations of reuniting the nation occasioned by Northern racism, capitalism, and politics.

Foner, as Downs points out, revitalized the 1950s revisionist interpretation by privileging not only the accomplishments but also the struggles of the freedpeople. Reconstruction did not signify a triumph of egalitarianism over entrenched racism, state-rights particularism, and economic control by wealthy agricultural and urban capitalists. But Reconstruction nonetheless was not a totally failed experiment.

The Thirteenth Amendment (ratified 1865) freed the slaves permanently by law, not by military order; the Fourteenth Amendment (ratified 1868) defined American citizenship to include African-Americans and included penalties for states that denied citizenship rights; and the Fifteenth Amendment (ratified 1870) enfranchised black men. Beyond this, probably as many as 1,800 blacks held public office — as congressmen, state legislators, constables, trial justices, and other local officials — during the Reconstruction era.[14] Many African-Americans served in all-black militia companies while others began commercial and communal enterprises that served their communities, some continuing today. That said, even before the 1870s, many of the early gains of Reconstruction began to wither away, returning former Confederates to power, ushering in white racial control, and rendering most of the freedmen and -women to the status of landless peasants.

Ironically, as white Southerners reentered the Union, they seemingly captured in peace what had eluded them in war: newfound racial control, not by slavery, but rather by controlling the region's capital and land. Farm tenantry, sharecropping, and peonage replaced the racial control of slavery without providing the freedpeople with any of the alleged benefits of chattel slavery. Whites fashioned so-called free labor into an effective mode of labor and racial control. In 1879, Albion W. Tourgée, the Union officer–

turned–North Carolina carpetbagger, lawyer, judge, and leading novelist, critic, and racial radical, remarked, "In all except the actual results of the physical struggle, I consider the South to have been the real victors in the war. . . . The way in which they have neutralized the results of the war and reversed the verdict of Appomattox is the grandest thing in American politics."[15]

This story and many others play out in the documents presented in *A Just and Lasting Peace*. The texts, arranged chronologically, provide insights into the ebb and flow of the emancipation process, debates over programs of "restoration" versus "reconstruction," Presidential Reconstruction and its reversal, then Radical Reconstruction and its eventual retreat. The powerful first-person accounts document the oft-sidetracked project of reuniting the nation after a blood-soaked civil war and the construction of new nationhood. The Civil War and Reconstruction freed the slaves, included African-Americans as citizens, and enabled blacks to vote and participate in political activities. Even though black agency sparked obstructionism by whites at every turn and culminated in decades of racially motivated violence, Reconstruction nevertheless settled the question of state rights versus federalism, establishing the ultimate locus of power in the United States in the federal government, not in the states. Concomitantly, Reconstruction witnessed the enormous growth of central state government authority in the North, what historian Richard Franklin Bensel appropriately termed the emerging "Yankee Leviathan."[16]

Despite Reconstruction's gains, and the courage and conviction of reformers black and white, North and South, the postwar period fell short of true biracial justice and representative democracy. State centralization had little direct impact on the day-to-day lives of the South's ex-slaves. No sooner had the smoke of battle between Northerners and Southerners cleared but proscription, intolerance, and racial tension began to hover over the Reconstruction South like a miasma, choking the freedmen and -women as they marched determinedly ahead toward true freedom. The Black Codes of Presidential Reconstruction first blocked their path. Then extra-legal violence threatened the exercise of the freedmen's newfound political rights. De facto segregation circumscribed their social interactions. And finally, starting soon after Reconstruction ground to a halt in 1877, Southern states began codifying Jim Crow–era segregation laws. "The destruction of slavery," notes historian Edward L. Ayres, "a major moral accomplishment of the United States Army, of Abraham Lincoln, and of the enslaved people themselves, would be overshadowed by the injustice and poverty that followed in the rapidly changing South, a mockery of American claims of moral leadership in the world."[17] Reflecting in 1935 on the gains and losses of Reconstruction, the great African-American historian and sociologist W. E. B. Du Bois explained: "The slave went free; stood a brief moment in the sun; then moved back again toward slavery."[18] Universal freedom and equality proved elusive.

*A Just and Lasting Peace* uses period documents to introduce Reconstruction's complex history and long-term meaning to a new generation of readers. Writing in 2000, Foner remarked, "Reconstruction remains perhaps the most controversial and least understood era of American history." Understanding the postwar years remains essential for Americans, however, as "long as the issues central to Reconstruction remain unresolved—the balance of power in the federal system, the place of black Americans in national life, and the relationship between economic and political democracy."[19]

# A
# JUST AND
# LASTING PEACE

# PART I

# WARTIME RECONSTRUCTION

The Reconstruction process began years before Confederate defeat. In fact, President Lincoln took steps to prepare for Reconstruction as early as 1862. In that year, Lincoln proclaimed emancipation for bondsmen and -women in the District of Columbia and, after issuing his Preliminary Emancipation Proclamation in September 1862, on January 1, 1863, he issued the Final Emancipation Proclamation. This order only freed blacks then in Confederate-held territory, but nonetheless signified a radical first step in the experiment that became Reconstruction, suggesting civil and political equality for people of color and allowing blacks into the military to fight alongside white soldiers. By war's end, roughly 200,000 black soldiers and sailors wore the Union blue. Historian Eric Foner notes that African-Americans who served in the army and navy during the Civil War composed a leadership class during Reconstruction. They held at least 129 public offices in the postwar years.[20]

Foner also observes that the Final Emancipation Proclamation created a turning point in the course of the Civil War, but it did not immediately address the divisive question of Reconstruction. Rather, the Proclamation created more problems, as it ensured that after the war, the political social structure of the South would be fundamentally and dramatically altered forever. The questions thus raised included who would mandate the changes in Southern society and what shape they would take. What would be the role of blacks in Southern society once they became freedmen?

Lincoln took the first step in reconstructing the Union when, on December 8, 1863, he issued the Proclamation of Amnesty and Reconstruction. He declared that insurgents who agreed to swear an oath of loyalty to the U.S. Constitution and who would accept emancipation would receive

3

full pardons. Once ten percent of a rebellious state's 1860 electorate had agreed to these terms and took the oath, Lincoln specified, the state could reenter the U.S. after re-establishing a republican government. This offer of amnesty excluded certain classes of individuals, including Confederate military officers, high government officials, and members of the U.S. government or military who had resigned their posts to aid the slaveholders' rebellion. Lincoln proposed a conservative Reconstruction plan, hopeful that it would attract moderate former Southern Whigs and make the process of restoration occur smoothly. The president purposely avoided the question of black suffrage in his so-called Ten Percent Plan, hoping that allowing Southern Whigs to oversee the process of transitioning from a slave economy to a free-labor economy would serve as a viable concession to Southern Unionists. Although the provisions of Lincoln's Proclamation of Amnesty never came to pass, it set a precedent that the Executive branch of government, not the Legislative branch, would regulate and direct the Reconstruction process.

The Radical Republicans, the wing of the president's party that had shunned compromise with the Confederates before secession and that pressed for emancipation following Fort Sumter, considered Lincoln's Ten Percent Plan too accommodating and lenient. Determined to reorganize the South and implement black equality, in July 1864 two leading Radicals, Senator Benjamin F. Wade of Ohio and Representative Henry Winter Davis of Maryland, passed a congressional bill as an alternate to the president's Ten Percent Plan.

Under the terms of the Wade-Davis Bill, Reconstruction and the reintegration of the rebellious states into the Union required that once hostilities ceased in a state, a majority (*not* ten percent) of the state's citizens take a loyalty oath. Those persons who could attest to past and future loyalty to the Union could then elect a convention to amend their state constitutions to abolish slavery, disfranchise Confederate military officers, and declare their state's war debt invalid. Lincoln, determined to lead the Reconstruction process and to provide a smooth transition for willing former Confederate states to rejoin the Union, pocket vetoed the Wade-Davis plan on July 8, 1864. He hoped that the restoration (including the abolition of slavery) of Union governments in Louisiana and Arkansas under his Ten Percent Plan would establish a model for reconstructing the remaining Confederate states, and also that a Constitutional amendment would end slavery permanently. Lincoln's veto exacerbated the growing rift between Congressional Radicals and the president. Responding to his pocket veto, on August 5, 1864, Wade and Davis published a manifesto in the *New York Tribune*, condemning Lincoln for overstepping his authority regarding Reconstruction. Wade and Davis insisted that Reconstruction was the province of the Legislative branch, a concern solely within the scope of congressional authority. They implored the president to execute and obey, not make laws. Yet, as Foner notes, "Despite the harsh language of the Wade-Davis Manifesto, these events did not signal an irreparable breach between Lincoln and the Radical Republicans. The points of unity among Republicans, especially their commitment to winning the war and rendering emancipation unassailable, were far greater than their differences."[21]

In assessing the rival wartime Reconstruction plans, historian James M. McPherson notes that in reality, among the Rebel states only Tennessee could have met the prerequisites set by Wade and Davis. According to McPherson, "The real purpose of the Wade-Davis bill was to postpone Reconstruction until the war was won. Lincoln, by contrast, wanted to initiate Reconstruction immediately in order to convert lukewarm Confederates into Unionists as a means of winning the war."[22]

# "An Act for the Release of Certain Persons Held to Service or Labor in the District of Columbia"

## (April 16, 1862)

For decades, abolitionists and other critics of slavery underscored the shame of slavery existing in the nation's capital. On April 16, 1862, President Abraham Lincoln signed a bill ending slavery in the District of Columbia. It provided for immediate emancipation, compensation of up to three hundred dollars per slave belonging to loyal (Union) masters, and for the voluntary colonization of the freedpeople outside the United States. The bill suggests that notwithstanding Lincoln's denials that abolition was to be an outcome of the war, almost nine months before he issued the Emancipation Proclamation the president had established freeing the slaves as one of his war aims.

*Be it enacted by the Senate and House of Representatives of the United States of America in Congress assembled,* That all persons held to service or labor within the District of Columbia by reason of African descent are hereby discharged and freed of and from all claim to such service or labor; and from and after the passage of this act neither slavery nor involuntary servitude, except for crime, whereof the party shall be duly convicted, shall hereafter exist in said District.

Sec. 2. *And be it further enacted,* That all persons loyal to the United States, holding claims to service or labor against persons discharged therefrom by this act, may, within ninety days from the passage thereof, but not thereafter, present to the commissioners hereinafter mentioned their respective statements or petitions in writing, verified by oath or affirmation, setting forth the names, ages, and personal description of such persons, the manner in which said petitioners acquired such claim, and any facts touching the value thereof, and declaring his allegiance to the Government of the United States, and that he has not borne arms against the United States during the present rebellion, nor in any way given aid or comfort thereto: *Provided,* That the oath of the party to the petition shall not be evidence of the facts therein stated.

Sec. 3. *And be it further enacted,* That the President of the United States, with the advice and consent of the Senate, shall appoint three commissioners, residents of the District of Columbia, any two of whom shall have power to act, who shall receive the petitions above mentioned, and who shall investigate and determine the validity and value of the claims therein presented, as aforesaid, and appraise and apportion, under the proviso hereto annexed, the value in money of the several claims by them found to be valid: *Provided, however,* That the entire sum so appraised and apportioned shall not exceed in the aggregate an amount equal to three hundred dollars for each person shown to have been so held by lawful claim: *And provided, further,* That no claim shall be allowed for any slave or slaves brought into said District after the passage of this act, nor for any slave claimed by any person who has borne arms against the Government of the United States in the present rebellion, or in any way given aid or comfort thereto, or which originates in or by virtue of any transfer heretofore made, or which shall hereafter be made by any person who has in any manner aided or sustained the rebellion against the Government of the United States. . . .

Sec. 10. *And be it further enacted,* That the said clerk and his successors in office shall, from time to time, on demand, and on receiving twenty-five cents therefor, prepare, sign, and deliver to each person made free or manumitted by this act, a certificate under the seal of said court, setting out the name, age, and description of such person, and stating that such person was duly manumitted and set free by this act.

Sec. 11. *And be it further enacted,* That the sum of one hundred thousand dollars, out of any money in the Treasury not otherwise appropriated, is hereby appropriated, to be expended under the direction of the President of the United States, to aid in the colonization and settlement of such free persons of African descent now residing in said District, including those to be liberated by this act, as may desire to emigrate to the Republics of Hayti or Liberia, or such other country beyond the limits of the United States as the President may determine: *Provided,* The expenditure for this purpose shall not exceed one hundred dollars for each emigrant.

# ABRAHAM LINCOLN, "PRELIMINARY EMANCIPATION PROCLAMATION"

## (September 22, 1862)

In June 1862, Lincoln began drafting an emancipation decree designed to prevent European powers from recognizing the Confederates, to satisfy radicals in the Republican party who favored emancipation, and to placate border state slaveholders who professed loyalty to the Union as long as slavery remained protected by federal law. At a strategic moment, following the Union Army's success at repulsing Confederate General Robert E. Lee at the Battle of Antietam (September 17, 1862), the president issued the Preliminary Emancipation Proclamation. This document promised freedom to all slaves held in territory still in rebellion one hundred days later (January 1, 1863). Lincoln hoped that the threat of his emancipation edict would convince the Confederates to lay down their arms.

I, Abraham Lincoln, President of the United States of America, and Commander-in-chief of the Army and Navy thereof, do hereby proclaim and declare that hereafter, as heretofore, the war will be prosecuted for the object of practically restoring the constitutional relation between the United States, and each of the states, and the people thereof, in which states that relation is, or may be suspended, or disturbed.

That it is my purpose, upon the next meeting of Congress to again recommend the adoption of a practical measure tendering pecuniary aid to the free acceptance or rejection of all slave-states, so called, the people whereof may not then be in rebellion against the United States, and which states, may then have voluntarily adopted, or thereafter may voluntarily adopt, immediate, or gradual abolishment of slavery within their respective limits; and that the effort to colonize persons of African descent, with their consent, upon this continent, or elsewhere, with the previously obtained consent of the Governments existing there, will be continued.

That on the first day of January in the year of our Lord, one thousand eight hundred and sixty-three, all persons held as slaves within any state, or designated part of a state, the people whereof shall then be in rebellion against the United States shall be then, thenceforward, and forever free; and the executive government of the United States, including the military and naval authority thereof, will recognize and maintain the freedom of such persons, and will do no act or acts to repress such persons, or any of them, in any efforts they may make for their actual freedom.

That the executive will, on the first day of January aforesaid, by proclamation, designate the States, and parts of states, if any, in which the people thereof respectively, shall then be in rebellion against the United States; and the fact that any state, or the people thereof shall, on that day be, in good faith represented in the Congress of the United States, by members chosen thereto, at elections wherein a majority of the qualified voters of such state shall have participated, shall, in the absence of strong countervailing testimony, be deemed conclusive evidence that such state and the people thereof, are not then in rebellion against the United States.

# ABRAHAM LINCOLN, "EMANCIPATION PROCLAMATION"

## (January 1, 1863)

When the Confederates refused to surrender, Lincoln issued his Final Emancipation Proclamation declaring free all slaves in areas still in rebellion against the United States. This document made clear that the Civil War had become a war to end slavery and to keep the Union intact. Lincoln's decree mattered because it brought freedom to slaves as federal armies enveloped the hitherto unoccupied Confederate states while leaving bondsmen in the loyal slave states—Delaware, Maryland, Kentucky, and Missouri—untouched. The proclamation exempted slaves in Tennessee and in occupied portions of Virginia and Louisiana. The document also authorized the recruitment of African-Americans as armed soldiers. Lincoln, worried that the legislative or judicial branches might eventually overturn his proclamation, pushed for a Constitutional amendment permanently outlawing involuntary servitude.

Whereas, on the twenty-second day of September, in the year of our Lord one thousand eight hundred and sixty-two, a proclamation was issued by the President of the United States, containing, among other things, the following, to wit:

"That on the first day of January, in the year of our Lord one thousand eight hundred and sixty-three, all persons held as slaves within any State or designated part of a State, the people whereof shall then be in rebellion against the United States, shall be then, thenceforward, and forever free; and the Executive Government of the United States, includ-

11

ing the military and naval authority thereof, will
recognize and maintain the freedom of such persons, and will do no act or acts to repress such persons, or any of them, in any efforts they may make
for their actual freedom.

"That the Executive will, on the first day of January aforesaid, by proclamation, designate the States
and parts of States, if any, in which the people
thereof, respectively, shall then be in rebellion
against the United States; and the fact that any
State, or the people thereof, shall on that day be, in
good faith, represented in the Congress of the
United States by members chosen thereto at elections wherein a majority of the qualified voters of
such State shall have participated, shall, in the absence of strong countervailing testimony, be
deemed conclusive evidence that such State, and
the people thereof, are not then in rebellion against
the United States."

Now, therefore I, Abraham Lincoln, President of the
United States, by virtue of the power in me vested as
Commander-in-Chief, of the Army and Navy of the United
States in time of actual armed rebellion against authority
and government of the United States, and as a fit and necessary war measure for suppressing said rebellion, do, on
this first day of January, in the year of our Lord one thousand eight hundred and sixty-three, and in accordance with
my purpose so to do publicly proclaimed for the full period
of one hundred days, from the day first above mentioned,
order and designate as the States and parts of States
wherein the people thereof respectively, are this day in rebellion against the United States, the following, to wit:

Arkansas, Texas, Louisiana, (except the Parishes of St.
Bernard, Plaquemines, Jefferson, St. Johns, St. Charles, St.
James[,] Ascension, Assumption, Terrebonne, Lafourche,
St. Mary, St. Martin, and Orleans, including the City of New
Orleans), Mississippi, Alabama, Florida, Georgia, South-
Carolina, North-Carolina, and Virginia, (except the forty-
eight counties designated as West Virginia, and also the
counties of Berkley, Accomac, Northampton, Elizabeth
City, York, Princess Ann, and Norfolk, including the cities

of Norfolk & Portsmouth[)]; and which excepted parts are, for the present, left precisely as if this proclamation were not issued.

And by virtue of the power, and for the purpose aforesaid, I do order and declare that all persons held as slaves within said designated States, and parts of States, are, and henceforward shall be free; and that the Executive government of the United States, including the military and naval authorities thereof, will recognize and maintain the freedom of said persons.

And I hereby enjoin upon the people so declared to be free to abstain from all violence, unless in necessary self-defence; and I recommend to them that, in all cases when allowed, they labor faithfully for reasonable wages.

And I further declare and make known, that such persons of suitable condition, will be received into the armed service of the United States to garrison forts, positions, stations, and other places, and to man vessels of all sorts in said service.

And upon this act, sincerely believed to be an act of justice, warranted by the Constitution, upon military necessity, I invoke the considerate judgment of mankind, and the gracious favor of Almighty God.

In witness whereof, I have hereunto set my hand and caused the seal of the United States to be affixed.

# "PROCLAMATION OF AMNESTY AND RECONSTRUCTION"

## *(December 8, 1863)*

Lincoln's first of several proclamations of amnesty offered to pardon all Confederates agreeing to take an oath to support the U.S. Constitution as well as acts and proclamations pertaining to the states. The proclamation further stated that when ten percent of a state's 1860 legal electorate had taken the oath, this group could form a new loyal state government (one abolishing slavery) to be recognized by Congress. Lincoln was careful to exempt from his amnesty plan six classes of insurgents, including high-ranking Confederate officials and military officers, members of the U.S. armed forces who had resigned their commissions to enter Confederate forces, former U.S. congressmen or judges who had resigned their seats to join the rebellion, and those persons who had mistreated African-American prisoners of war or their white officers. This so-called Ten Percent Plan went into effect in only two occupied Confederate states, Louisiana and Arkansas, where the military, working with Unionists, was able to reestablish loyal governments. Lincoln's lenient Reconstruction plan raised the ire of Radical Republicans, who objected to the president's leadership of the Reconstruction process.

Whereas, in and by the Constitution of the United States, it is provided that the President "shall have power to grant reprieves and pardons for offences against the United States, except in cases of impeachment;" and

Whereas a rebellion now exists whereby the loyal State governments of several States have for a long time been subverted, and many persons have committed and are now guilty of treason against the United States; and

Whereas, with reference to said rebellion and treason, laws have been enacted by Congress declaring forfeitures and confiscation of property and liberation of slaves, all upon terms and conditions therein stated, and also declaring that the President was thereby authorized at any time thereafter, by proclamation, to extend to persons who may have participated in the existing rebellion, in any State or part thereof, pardon and amnesty, with such exceptions and at such times and on such conditions as he may deem expedient for the public welfare; and

Whereas the congressional declaration for limited and conditional pardon accords with well-established judicial exposition of the pardoning power; and

Whereas, with reference to said rebellion, the President of the United States has issued several proclamations, with provisions in regard to the liberation of slaves; and

Whereas it is now desired by some persons heretofore engaged in said rebellion to resume their allegiance to the United States, and to reinaugurate loyal State governments within and for their respective States; therefore,

I, Abraham Lincoln, President of the United States, do proclaim, declare, and make known to all persons who have, directly or by implication, participated in the existing rebellion, except as hereinafter excepted, that a full pardon is hereby granted to them and each of them, with restoration of all rights of property, except as to slaves, and in property cases where rights of third parties shall have intervened, and upon the condition that every such person shall take and subscribe an oath, and thenceforward keep and maintain said oath inviolate; and which oath shall be registered for permanent preservation, and shall be of the tenor and effect following, to wit:

"I, ———, do solemnly swear, in presence of Almighty God, that I will henceforth faithfully support, protect and defend the Constitution of the United States, and the union of the States thereunder; and that I will, in like manner, abide by and faithfully support all acts of Congress passed during the existing rebellion with reference to slaves, so long and so far as not repealed, modified or held void by Congress, or by decision of the Supreme Court; and that I will, in like manner, abide by and faithfully support all proclamations of the President made during the existing rebellion having reference to slaves, so long and so far as not modified or declared void by decision of the Supreme Court. So help me God."

The persons excepted from the benefits of the foregoing provisions are all who are, or shall have been, civil or diplomatic officers or agents of the so-called confederate government; all who have left judicial stations under the United States to aid the rebellion; all who are, or shall have been, military or naval officers of said so-called confederate government above the rank of colonel in the army, or of lieutenant in the navy; all who left seats in the United States Congress to aid the rebellion; all who resigned commissions in the army or navy of the United States, and afterwards aided the rebellion; and all who have engaged in any way in treating colored persons or white persons, in charge of such, otherwise than lawfully as prisoners of war, and which persons may have been found in the United States service, as soldiers, seamen, or in any other capacity.

And I do further proclaim, declare, and make known, that whenever, in any of the States of Arkansas, Texas, Louisiana, Mississippi, Tennessee, Alabama, Georgia, Florida, South Carolina, and North Carolina, a number of persons, not less than one-tenth in number of the votes cast in such State at the Presidential election of the year of our Lord one thousand eight hundred and sixty, each having taken the oath aforesaid and not having since violated it, and being a qualified voter by the election law of the State existing immediately before the so-called act of secession, and excluding all others, shall re-establish a State government which shall be republican, and in no wise contravening said oath, such shall be recognized as the true government of the State, and the State shall receive thereunder the benefits of the constitutional provision which declares that "The United States shall guaranty to every State in this union a republican form of government, and shall protect each of them against invasion; and, on application of the legislature, or the executive, (when the legislature cannot be convened,) against domestic violence."

And I do further proclaim, declare, and make known that any provision which may be adopted by such State government in relation to the freed people of such State, which shall recognize and declare their permanent freedom, provide for their education, and which may yet be consistent, as a temporary arrangement, with their present condition as a laboring, landless, and homeless class, will not be objected to by the national Executive. And it is suggested as not improper, that, in constructing a loyal State government in any State, the name of the State, the boundary, the subdivisions, the constitution, and the general code of laws, as before the rebellion, be maintained, subject only to the modifications made necessary by the conditions hereinbefore stated, and such others, if any, not contravening said conditions, and which may be deemed expedient by those framing the new State government.

To avoid misunderstanding, it may be proper to say that this proclamation, so far as it relates to State governments, has no reference to States wherein loyal State governments have all the while been maintained. And for the same reason, it may be proper to further say that whether members sent to Congress from any State shall be admitted to seats, constitutionally rests exclusively with the respective Houses, and not to any extent with the Executive. And still further, that this proclamation is intended to present the people of the States wherein the national authority has been suspended, and loyal State governments have been subverted, a mode in and by which the national authority and loyal State governments may be re-established within said States, or in any of them; and, while the mode presented is the best the Executive can suggest, with his present impressions, it must not be understood that no other possible mode would be acceptable.

Given under my hand at the city of Washington, the 8th. day of December, A.D. one thousand eight hundred and sixty-three, and of the independence of the United States of America the eighty-eighth.                    ABRAHAM LINCOLN

By the President:

WILLIAM H. SEWARD, Secretary of State.

# THE WADE-DAVIS BILL

## *(February 15, 1864)*

Radical Republicans led by Senator Benjamin F. Wade and Congressman Henry Winter Davis challenged Lincoln's Ten Percent Plan of Reconstruction, substituting their own plan, the Wade-Davis Bill, in its stead. Under their program, a Confederate state could not reform until fifty percent of the white male registered voters took an "ironclad" loyalty oath guaranteeing past and future loyalty to the U.S., and the new state convention abolished slavery, disfranchised leading Confederates, and repudiated the state's Confederate debt. The Wade-Davis Bill underscored the stark difference between the Radicals' hopes for Reconstruction and the president's. Though the bill passed Congress on July 2, 1864, Lincoln killed it with a pocket veto.

## A BILL TO GUARANTEE TO CERTAIN STATES WHOSE GOVERNMENTS HAVE BEEN USURPED OR OVERTHROWN A REPUBLICAN FORM OF GOVERNMENT.

Be it enacted by the Senate and House of Representatives of the United States of America in Congress assembled, That in the states declared in rebellion against the United States, the President shall, by and with the advice and consent of the Senate, appoint for each a provisional governor, whose pay and emoluments shall not exceed that of a brigadier-general of volunteers, who shall be charged with the civil administration of such state until a state government therein shall be recognized as hereinafter provided.

SEC. 2. And be it further enacted, That so soon as the military resistance to the United States shall have been suppressed in any such state, and the people thereof shall have sufficiently returned to their obedience to the constitution and the laws of the United States, the provisional governor shall direct the marshal of the United States, as speedily as may be, to name a sufficient number of deputies, and to enroll all white male citizens of the United States, resident in the state in their respective counties, and to request each one to take the oath to support the constitution of the United States, and in his enrolment to designate those who take and those who refuse to take that oath, which rolls shall be forthwith returned to the provisional governor; and if the persons taking that oath shall amount to a majority of the persons enrolled in the state, he shall, by proclamation, invite the loyal people of the state to elect delegates to a convention charged to declare the will of the people of the state relative to the reestablishment of a state government subject to, and in conformity with, the constitution of the United States.

SEC. 3. And be it further enacted, That the convention shall consist of as many members as both houses of the last constitutional state legislature, apportioned by the provisional governor among the counties, parishes, or districts of the state, in proportion to the white population, returned as electors, by the marshal, in compliance with the provisions of this act. The provisional governor shall, by proclamation, declare the number of delegates to be elected by each county, parish, or election district; name a day of election not less than thirty days thereafter; designate the places of voting in each county, parish, or district, conforming as nearly as may be convenient to the places used in the state elections next preceding the rebellion; appoint one or more commissioners to hold the election at each place of voting, and provide an adequate force to keep the peace during the election.

SEC. 4. And be it further enacted, That the delegates shall be elected by the loyal white male citizens of the United States of the age of twenty-one years, and resident at the time in the county, parish, or district in which they shall offer to vote, and enrolled as aforesaid, or absent in the military service of the United States, and who shall take and subscribe the oath of allegiance to the United States in the form contained in the act of congress of July two, eighteen hundred and sixty-two; and all such citizens of the United States who are in the military service of the United States shall vote at the head-quarters of their respective commands, under such regulations as may be prescribed by the provisional governor for the taking and return of their votes; but no person who has held or exercised any office, civil or military, state or confederate, under the rebel usurpation, or who has voluntarily borne arms against the United States, shall vote, or be eligible to be elected as delegate, at such election.

SEC. 5. And be it further enacted, That the said commissioners, or either of them, shall hold the election in conformity with this act, and, so far as may be consistent therewith, shall proceed in the manner used in the state prior to the rebellion. The oath of allegiance shall be taken and subscribed on the poll-book by every voter in the form above prescribed, but every person known by or proved to, the commissioners to have held or exercised any office, civil or military, state or confederate, under the rebel usurpation, or to have voluntarily borne arms against the United States, shall be excluded, though he offer to take the oath; and in case any person who shall have borne arms against the United States shall offer to vote he shall be deemed to have borne arms voluntarily unless he shall prove the contrary by the testimony of a qualified voter. The poll-book, showing the name and oath of each voter, shall be returned to the provisional governor by the commissioners of election or the one acting, and the provisional governor shall canvass such returns, and declare the person having the highest number of votes elected.

SEC. 6. And be it further enacted, That the provisional governor shall, by proclamation, convene the delegates elected as aforesaid, at the capital of the state, on a day not more than three months after the election, giving at least thirty days' notice of such day. In case the said capital shall in his judgment be unfit, he shall in his proclamation appoint another place. He shall preside over the deliberations of the convention, and administer to each delegate, before taking his seat in the convention, the oath of allegiance to the United States in the form above prescribed.

SEC. 7. And be it further enacted, That the convention shall declare, on behalf of the people of the state, their submission to the constitution and laws of the United States, and shall adopt the following provisions, hereby prescribed by the United States in the execution of the constitutional duty to guarantee a republican form of government to every state, and incorporate them in the constitution of the state, that is to say:

First. No person who has held or exercised any office, civil or military, except offices merely ministerial, and military offices below the grade of colonel, state or confederate, under the usurping power, shall vote for or be a member of the legislature, or governor.

Second. Involuntary servitude is forever prohibited, and the freedom of all persons is guaranteed in said state.

Third. No debt, state or confederate, created by or under the sanction of the usurping power, shall be recognized or paid by the state.

SEC. 8. And be it further enacted, That when the convention shall have adopted those provisions, it shall proceed to re-establish a republican form of government, and ordain a constitution containing those provisions, which, when adopted the convention shall by ordinance provide for submitting to the people of the state, entitled to vote under this law, at an election to be held in the manner prescribed by the act for the election of delegates; but at a time and place named by the convention, at which election the said electors, and none others, shall vote directly for or against such constitution and form of state government, and the returns of said election shall be made to the provisional governor, who shall canvass the same in the presence of the electors, and if a majority of the votes cast shall be for the constitution and form of government, he shall certify the same, with a copy thereof, to the President of the United States, who, after obtaining the assent of congress, shall, by proclamation, recognize the government so established, and none other, as the constitutional government of the state, and from the date of such recognition, and not before Senators and Representatives, and electors for President and Vice President may be elected in such state, according to the laws of the state and of the United States.

SEC. 9. And be it further enacted, That if the convention shall refuse to reestablish the state government on the conditions aforesaid, the provisional governor shall declare it dissolved; but it shall be the duty of the President, whenever he shall have reason to believe that a sufficient number of the people of the state entitled to vote under this act, in number not less than a majority of those enrolled, as aforesaid, are willing to reestablish a state government on the conditions aforesaid, to direct the provisional governor to order another election of delegates to a convention for the purpose and in the manner prescribed in this act, and to proceed in all respects as hereinbefore provided, either to dissolve the convention, or to certify the state government reestablished by it to the President.

SEC. 10. And be it further enacted, That, until the United States shall have recognized a republican form of state government, the provisional governor in each of said states shall see that this act, and the laws of the United States, and the laws of the state in force when the state government was overthrown by the rebellion, are faithfully executed within the state; but no law or usage whereby any person was heretofore held in involuntary servitude shall be recognized or enforced by any court or officer in such state, and the laws for the trial and punishment of white persons shall extend to all persons, and jurors shall have the qualifications of voters under this law for delegates to the convention. The President shall appoint such officers provided for by the laws of the state when its government was overthrown as he may find necessary to the civil administration of the state, all which officers shall be entitled to receive the fees and emoluments provided by the state laws for such officers. . . .

SEC. 12. And be it further enacted, that all persons held to involuntary servitude or labor in the states aforesaid are hereby emancipated and discharged therefrom, and they and their posterity shall be forever free. And if any such persons or their posterity shall be restrained of liberty, under pretence of any claim to such service or labor, the courts of the United States shall, on habeas corpus, discharge them.

SEC. 13. And be it further enacted, That if any person declared free by this act, or any law of the United States, or any proclamation of the President, be restrained of liberty, with intent to be held in or reduced to involuntary servitude or labor, the person convicted before a court of competent jurisdiction of such act shall be punished by fine of not less than fifteen hundred dollars, and be imprisoned not less than five nor more than twenty years.

SEC. 14. And be it further enacted, That every person who shall hereafter hold or exercise any office, civil or military, except offices merely ministerial, and military offices below the grade of colonel, in the rebel service, state or confederate, is hereby declared not to be a citizen of the United States.

# LINCOLN'S RESPONSE TO THE WADE-DAVIS BILL

## (July 8, 1864)

Lincoln issued a proclamation describing the Wade-Davis Bill as "one very proper plan for the loyal people of any state choosing to adopt it," but he nevertheless was unwilling to sign it. Lincoln explained that loyal citizens in Louisiana and Arkansas already were at work reconstructing their states along the lines of his Ten Percent Plan. Lincoln added that he doubted Congressional authority to emancipate slaves and looked forward to a Constitutional amendment to abolish slavery throughout the country.

## BY THE PRESIDENT OF THE UNITED STATES
### A PROCLAMATION

Whereas, at the late session, congress passed a bill to "guarantee to certain states, whose governments have been usurped or overthrown, a republican form of government," a copy of which is hereunto annexed;

And whereas the said bill was presented to the President of the United States for his approval less than one hour before the sine die adjournment of said session, and was not signed by him;

And whereas the said bill contains, among other things, a plan for restoring the states in rebellion to their proper practical relation in the Union, which plan expresses the sense of congress upon that subject, and which plan it is now thought fit to lay before the people for their consideration;

Now, therefore, I, ABRAHAM LINCOLN, President of the United States, do proclaim, declare, and make known, that while I am (as I was in December last, when by proclamation I propounded a plan for restoration) unprepared by a formal approval of this bill, to be inflexibly committed to any single plan of restoration; and, while I am also unprepared to declare that the free state constitutions and governments already adopted and installed in Arkansas and Louisiana shall be set aside and held for nought, thereby repelling and discouraging the loyal citizens who have set up the same as to further effort, or to declare a constitutional competency in congress to abolish slavery in states, but am at the same time sincerely hoping and expecting that a constitutional amendment abolishing slavery throughout the nation may be adopted, nevertheless I am truly satisfied with the system for restoration contained in the bill as one very proper plan for the loyal people of any state choosing to adopt it, and that I am, and at all times shall be, prepared to give the executive aid and assistance to any such people, so soon as the military resistance to the United States shall have been suppressed in any such state, and the people thereof shall have sufficiently returned to their obedience to the constitution and the laws of the United States, in which cases military governors will be appointed, with directions to proceed according to the bill.

In testimony whereof, I have hereunto set my hand, and caused the seal of the United States to be affixed.

# THE WADE-DAVIS MANIFESTO

## *(August 5, 1864)*

Senator Wade and Congressman Davis found Lincoln's pocket veto and his accompanying proclamation infuriating and published the vituperative Wade-Davis Manifesto in the *New York Tribune*. They charged that the president brazenly disregarded the will of Congress and that his lenient Reconstruction program was a bid to win votes in the November election. Though the manifesto signaled loud and serious opposition to Lincoln's approach to Reconstruction within Radical Republican ranks, it proved unsuccessful in denying Lincoln the Union party nomination and ultimately victory in the presidential election. Their politically indiscreet manifesto ended Davis's political career (Marylanders failed to renominate him for office) and tarnished Wade's reputation.

## PROTEST OF SENATOR WADE AND H. WINTER DAVIS, M.C.

*To the supporters of the Government:*

We have read without surprise, but not without indignation, the proclamation of the President of the 8th of July, 1864. . . .

The President did not sign the bill "to guarantee to certain States whose government have been usurped, a Republican form of government" — passed by the supporters of his Administration in both Houses of Congress after mature deliberation.

The bill did not therefore become a law; and it is, therefore, nothing.

The proclamation is neither an approval nor a veto of the bill; it is, therefore, a document unknown to the laws and Constitution of the United States.

So far as it contains an apology for not signing the bill, it is a political manifesto against the friends of the Government.

So far as it proposes to execute the bill which is not a law, it is a grave Executive usurpation.

It is fitting that the facts necessary to enable the friends of the Administration to appreciate the apology and the usurpation be spread before them.

The proclamation says:

"And whereas the said bill was presented to the President of the United States for his approval less than one hour before the *sine die* adjournment of said session, and was not signed by him—"

If that be accurate, still this bill was presented with other bills which were signed.

Within that hour the time for the *sine die* adjournment was three times postponed by the votes of both Houses; and the least intimation of a desire for more time by the President to consider this bill would have secured a further postponement.

Yet the committee sent to ascertain if the President had any further communication for the House of Representatives reported that he had none; and the friends of the bill, who had anxiously waited on him to ascertain its fate, had already been informed that the President had resolved not to sign it.

The time of presentation, therefore, had nothing to do with his failure to approve it.

The bill has been discussed and considered for more than a month in the House of Representatives, which it passed on the 4th of May. It was reported to the Senate on the 27th of May, without material amendment, and passed the Senate absolutely as it came from the House on the 2d of July.

Ignorance of its contents is out of the question.

Indeed, at his request, a draft of a bill substantially the same in material points, and identical in the points objected to by the proclamation, had been laid before him for his consideration in the winter of 1862–1863.

There is, therefore, no reason to suppose the provisions of the bill took the President by surprise.

On the contrary, we have reason to believe them to have been so well known that this method of preventing the bill from becoming a law without the constitutional responsibility of a veto, had been resolved on long before the bill passed the Senate. . . .

Had the proclamation stopped there, it would have been only one other defeat of the will of the people by the Executive perversion of the Constitution.

But it goes further. The President says:

"And whereas the said bill contains, among other things, a plan for restoring the States in rebellion to their proper practical relation in the Union, which plan expresses the sense of Congress upon that subject, and which plan it is now thought fit to lay before the people for their consideration—"

By what authority of the Constitution? In what forms? The result to be declared by whom? With what effect when ascertained?

Is it to be a law by the approval of the people, without the approval of Congress, at the will of the President?

Will the President, on his opinion of the popular approval, execute it as a law?

Or is this merely a device to avoid the serious responsibility of defeating a law on which so many loyal hearts reposed for security?

But the reasons now assigned for not approving the bill are full of ominous significance.

The President proceeds:

"Now, therefore, I, Abraham Lincoln, President of the United States, do proclaim, declare, and make known that, while I am (as I was in December last, when by proclamation I propounded a plan for restoration) unprepared by a formal approval of this bill to be inflexibly committed to any single plan of restoration."

That is to say, the President is resolved that people shall not *by law* take *any* securities from the rebel States against a renewal of the rebellion, before restoring their power to govern us.

His wisdom and prudence are to be our sufficient guarantees! He further says:

"And while I am also unprepared to declare that the free-State constitutions and governments already adopted and installed in Arkansas and Louisiana shall be set aside and held for naught, thereby repelling and discouraging the loyal citizens who have set up the same as to further effort—"

That is to say, the President persists in recognizing those shadows of governments in Arkansas and Louisiana which Congress formally declared should not be recognized—whose representatives and senators were repelled by formal votes of both Houses of Congress—which it was declared formally should have no electoral vote for President and Vice-President.

They are mere creatures of his will. They are mere oligarchies, imposed on the people by military orders under the form of election, at which generals, provost marshals, soldiers and camp-followers were the chief actors, assisted by a handful of resident citizens, and urged on to premature action by private letters from the President. . . .

Slavery as an institution can be abolished only by a change of the Constitution of the United States, or of the law of the States; and this is the principle of the bill.

It required the new constitution of the State to provide for that prohibition; and the President, in the face of his own proclamation, does not venture to object to insisting on that condition. Nor will the country tolerate its abandonment—yet he defeated the only provision imposing it.

But when he describes himself, in spite of this great blow at emancipation, as "sincerely hoping and expecting that a constitutional amendment abolishing slavery throughout the nation may be adopted," we curiously inquire on what his expectation rests, after the vote of the House of Representatives at the recent session, and in the face of the political complexion of more than enough of the States to prevent the possibility of its adoption within any reasonable time; and why he did not indulge his sincere hopes with so large an instalment of the blessing as his approval of the bill would have secured?

After this assignment of his reasons for preventing the bill from becoming a law, the President proceeds to declare his purpose to execute it as a law by his plenary dictatorial power.

He says: "Nevertheless, I am fully satisfied with the system for restoration contained in the bill as one very proper plan for the loyal people of any State choosing to adopt it;

and that I am, and at all times shall be, prepared to give the Executive aid and assistance to any such people as soon as the military resistance to the United States shall have been suppressed in any such State, and the people thereof shall have sufficiently returned to their obedience to the Constitution and the laws of the United States—in which cases military governors will be appointed, with directions to proceed according to the bill."

A more studied outrage on the legislative authority of the people has never been perpetrated.

Congress passed a bill; the President refused to approve it, and then by proclamation puts as much of it in force as he sees fit, and proposes to execute those parts by officers unknown to the laws of the United States, and not subject to the confirmation of the Senate.

The bill directed the appointment of provisional governors by and with the advice and consent of the Senate.

The President, after defeating the law, proposes to appoint without law and without the advice and consent of the Senate, military governors for the rebel States! . . .

Whatever is done will be at his will and pleasure, by persons responsible to no law, and more interested to secure the interests and execute the will of the President than of the people; and the will of Congress is to be "held for naught," "unless the loyal people of the rebel States choose to adopt it."

If they should graciously prefer the stringent bill to the easy proclamation, still the registration will be made under no legal sanction; it will give no assurance that a majority of the people of the States have taken the oath; if administered, it will be without legal authority and void; no indictment will lie for false swearing at the election, or for admitting bad or rejecting good votes; it will be the farce of Louisiana and Arkansas acted over again, under the forms of this bill, but not by authority of law.

But when we come to the guaranties of future peace which Congress meant to enact, the forms, as well as the substance of the bill, must yield to the President's will that none should be imposed.

It was the solemn resolve of Congress to protect the loyal men of the nation against three great dangers: (1) the return to power of the guilty leaders of the rebellion; (2)

the continuance of slavery, and (3) the burden of the rebel debt.

Congress required assent to those provisions by the convention of the State; and if refused, it was to be dissolved.

The President "holds for naught" that resolve of Congress, because he is unwilling "to be inflexibly committed to any one plan of restoration," and the people of the United States are not to be allowed to protect themselves unless their enemies agree to it.

The order to proceed according to the bill is therefore merely at the will of the rebel States; and they have the option to reject it, accept the proclamation of the 8th of December, and demand the President's recognition!

Mark the contrast! The bill requires a majority, the proclamation is satisfied with one-tenth; the bill requires one oath, the proclamation another; the bill ascertains voters by registering, the proclamation by guess; the bill exacts adherence to existing territorial limits, the proclamation admits of others; the bill governs the rebel States *by law,* equalizing all before it, the proclamation commits them to the lawless discretion of Military Governors and Provost Marshals; the bill forbids electors for President, the proclamation and defeat of the bill threaten us with civil war for the admission or exclusion of such votes; the bill exacted exclusion of dangerous enemies from power and the relief of the nation from the rebel debt, and the prohibition of slavery forever, so that the suppression of the rebellion will double our resources to bear or pay the national debt, free the masses from the old domination of the rebel leaders, and eradicate the cause of the war; the proclamation secures neither of these guaranties.

It is silent respecting the rebel debt and the political exclusion of rebel leaders; leaving slavery exactly where it was by law at the outbreak of the rebellion, and adds no guaranty even of the freedom of the slaves he undertook to manumit.

It is summed up in an illegal oath, without sanction, and therefore void.

The oath is to support all proclamations of the President, during the rebellion, having reference to slaves.

Any government is to be accepted at the hands of one-tenth of the people not contravening that oath.

Now that oath neither secures the abolition of slavery, nor adds any security to the freedom of the slaves the President declared free.

It does not secure the abolition of slavery; for the proclamation of freedom merely professed to free certain slaves while it recognized the institution.

Every constitution of the rebel States at the outbreak of the rebellion may be adopted without the change of a letter: for none of them contravene that proclamation; none of them establish slavery.

It adds no security to the freedom of the slaves; for their title is the proclamation of freedom.

If it be unconstitutional, an oath to support it is void. Whether constitutional or not, the oath is without authority of law, and therefore void.

If it be valid and observed, it exacts no enactment by the State, either in law or constitution, to add a State guaranty to the proclamation title; and the right of a slave to freedom is an open question before the State courts on the relative authority of the State law and the proclamation.

If the oath binds the one-tenth who take it, it is not exacted of the other nine-tenths who succeed to the control of the State government, so that it is annulled instantly by the act of recognition.

What the State courts would say of the proclamation, who can doubt?

But the master would not go into court—he would seize his slaves.

What the Supreme Court would say, who can tell?

When and how is the question to get there?

No *habeas corpus* lies for him in a United States Court; and the President defeated with this bill the extension of that writ to his case.

Such are the fruits of this rash and fatal act of the President—a blow at the friends of his Administration, at the rights of humanity, and at the principles of Republican Government.

The President has greatly presumed on the forbearance which the supporters of his Administration have so long practised, in view of the arduous conflict in which we are engaged, and the reckless ferocity of our political opponents.

But he must understand that our support is of a cause and not of a man; that the authority of Congress is paramount and must be respected; that the whole body of the Union men of Congress will not submit to be impeached by him of rash and unconstitutional legislation; and if he wishes our support, he must confine himself to his Executive duties—to obey and execute, not make the laws—to suppress by arms armed rebellion, and leave political reorganization to Congress.

If the supporters of the Government fail to insist on this, they become responsible for the usurpations which they fail to rebuke, and are justly liable to the indignation of the people whose rights and security, committed to their keeping, they sacrifice.

Let them consider the remedy of these usurpations, and, having found it, fearlessly execute it.

B. F. WADE, Chairman Senate Committee.
H. WINTER DAVIS, Chairman
Committee House of Representatives
on the Rebellious States.

# HENRY HIGHLAND GARNET,
## "LET THE MONSTER PERISH"

### *(February 12, 1865)*

In February 1865, the Reverend Henry Highland Garnet (1815–1882), a former Maryland slave, a leading black abolitionist, a recruiter for the U.S. Colored Troops, and a proponent of Pan-Africanism, preached a moving sermon in the House of Representatives to commemorate the passage of the Thirteenth Amendment. The first African-American to speak in Congress, Garnet called for a national atonement, praised Congress, and made an eloquent statement in favor of equal rights. The Reverend Garnet ended his life as U.S. minister to Liberia and died and was buried in Africa.

For they bind heavy burdens and grievous to be borne, and lay them on men's shoulders, but they themselves will not move them with one of their fingers. — Matthew 23:4.

In this chapter, of which my text is a sentence, the Lord Jesus addressed his disciples, and the multitude that hung spellbound upon the words that fell from his lips. He admonished them to beware of the religion of the Scribes and Pharisees, which was distinguished for great professions, while it succeeded in urging them to do but a little, or nothing that accorded with the law of righteousness.

In theory they were right; but their practices were inconsistent and wrong. They were learned in the law of Moses and in the traditions of their fathers, but the principles of righteousness failed to affect their hearts. They knew their duty but did it not. The demands which they made upon others proved that they themselves knew what things men ought to do. In condemning others they pronounced themselves guilty. They demanded that others should be just, merciful, pure, peaceable and righteous. But they were unjust, impure, unmerciful—they hated and wronged a portion of their fellowmen, and waged a continual war against the government of God.

Such was their conduct in the Church and in the state. We have modern Scribes and Pharisees, who are faithful to their prototypes of ancient times.

With sincere respect and reverence for the instruction, and the warning given by our Lord, and in humble dependence upon him for his assistance, I shall speak this morning of the Scribes and Pharisees of our times who rule the state. In discharging this duty, I shall keep my eyes upon the picture which is painted so faithfully and lifelike by the hand of the Saviour.

Allow me to describe them. They are intelligent and well-informed, and can never say, either before an earthly tribunal or at the bar of God, "We knew not of ourselves what was right." They are acquainted with the principles of the law of nations. They are proficient in the knowledge of Constitutional law. They are teachers of common law, and frame and execute statute law. They acknowledge that there is a just and impartial God, and are not altogether unacquainted with the law of Christian love and kindness. They claim for themselves the broadest freedom. Boastfully they tell us that they have received from the court of heaven the Magna Charta of human rights that was handed down through the clouds and amid the lightnings of Sinai, and given again by the Son of God on the Mount of Beatitudes while the glory of the Father shone around him. They tell us that from the Declaration of Independence and the Constitution they have obtained a guaranty of their political freedom, and from the Bible they derive their claim to all the blessings of religious liberty. With just pride they tell us that they are descended from the Pilgrims, who threw themselves upon the bosom of the treacherous sea and braved storms and tempests that they might find in a strange land and among savages free homes where they might build their altars that should blaze with acceptable sacrifice unto God. Yes! they boast that their fathers heroically turned away from the precious light of Eastern civilization and, taking their lamps with oil in their vessels, joyfully went forth to illuminate this land, that then dwelt in the darkness of the valley of the shadow of death. With hearts strengthened by faith they spread out their standard to the winds of heaven, near Plymouth Rock; and whether it was stiffened in the sleet and frosts of winter, or floated on the breeze of summer, it ever bore the motto, "Freedom to worship God."

But others, their fellow men, equal before the Almighty and made by Him of the same blood, and glowing with immortality, they doom to lifelong servitude and chains. Yes, they stand in the most sacred places on earth, and beneath the gaze of the piercing eye of Jehovah, the universal Father of all men, and declare that "the best possible condition of the Negro is slavery."

In the name of the Triune God I denounce the sentiment as unrighteous beyond measure, and the holy and the just of the whole earth say in regard to it, Anathema maranatha.

What is slavery? Too well do I know what it is. I will present to you a bird's eye view of it; and it shall be no fancy picture, but one that is sketched by painful experience. I was born among the cherished institutions of slavery. My earliest recollections of parents, friends, and the home of my childhood are clouded with its wrongs. The first sight that met my eyes was a Christian mother enslaved by professed Christians, but, thank God, now a saint in heaven. The first sounds that startled my ear and sent a shudder through my soul were the cracking of the whip and the clanking of chains. These sad memories mar the beauties of my native shores and darken all the slaveland, which, but for the reign of despotism, had been a paradise. But those shores are fairer now. The mists have left my native valleys, and the clouds have rolled away from the hills, and Maryland, the unhonored grave of my fathers, is now the free home of their liberated and happier children.

Let us view this demon, which the people have worshipped as a God. Come forth, thou grim monster, that thou mayest be critically examined! There he stands. Behold him, one and all. Its work is to chattelize man; to hold property in human beings. Great God! I would as soon attempt to enslave Gabriel or Michael as to enslave a man made in the image of God, and for whom Christ died. Slavery is snatching man from the high place to which he was lifted by the hand of God, and dragging him down to the level of the brute creation, where he is made to be the companion of the horse and the fellow of the ox.

It tears the crown of glory from his head and as far as possible obliterates the image of God that is in him. Slavery preys upon man, and man only. A brute cannot be made a slave. Why? Because a brute has not reason, faith, nor an undying spirit, nor conscience. It does not look forward to the future with joy or fear, nor reflect upon the past with satisfaction or regret. But who in this vast assembly, who in all this broad land, will say that the poorest and most unhappy brother in chains and servitude has not every one of these high endowments? Who denies it? Is there one? If so, let him speak. There is not one; no, not one.

But slavery attempts to make a man a brute. It treats him as a beast. Its terrible work is not finished until the ruined victim of its lusts and pride and avarice and hatred is reduced so low that with tearful eyes and feeble voice he faintly cries, "I am happy and contented. I love this condition."

> *Proud Nimrod first the bloody chase began,*
> *A mighty hunter he; his prey was man.*

The caged lion may cease to roar, and try no longer the strength of the bars of his prison, and lie with his head between his mighty paws and snuff the polluted air as though he heeded not. But is he contented? Does he not instinctively long for the freedom of the forest and the plain? Yes, he is a lion still. Our poor and forlorn brother whom thou hast labeled "slave," is also a man. He may be unfortunate, weak, helpless and despised and hated; nevertheless he is a man. His God and thine has stamped on his forehead his title to his inalienable rights in characters that can be read by every intelligent being. Pitiless storms of outrage may have beaten upon his defenseless head, and he may have descended through ages of oppression; yet he is a man. God made him such, and his brother cannot unmake him. Woe, woe to him who attempts to commit the accursed crime.

Slavery commenced its dreadful work in kidnaping unoffending men in a foreign and distant land, and in piracy on the seas. The plunderers were not the followers of Mahomet, nor the devotees of Hinduism, nor benighted pagans, nor idolaters, but people called Christians, and thus the ruthless traders in the souls and bodies of men fastened upon Christianity a crime and stain at the sight of which it shudders and shrieks.

It is guilty of the most heinous iniquities ever perpetrated upon helpless women and innocent children. Go to the shores of the land of my forefathers, poor bleeding Africa, which, although she has been bereaved and robbed for centuries, is nevertheless beloved by all her worthy descendants wherever dispersed. Behold a single scene that there meets your eyes. Turn not away either from shame, pity or indifference, but look and see the beginning of this cherished and petted institution. Behold a hundred youthful mothers seated on the ground, dropping their tears upon the hot sands, and filling the air with their lamentations.

Why do they weep? Ah, Lord God, thou knowest! Their babes have been torn from their bosoms and cast upon the plains to die of hunger, or to be devoured by hyenas or jackals. The little innocents would die on the "middle passage," or suffocate between the decks of the floating slave pen, freighted and packed with unparalleled human woe, and the slavers in mercy have cast them out to perish on their native shores. Such is the beginning, and no less wicked is the end of that system which Scribes and Pharisees in the Church and the state pronounce to be just, humane, benevolent and Christian. If such are the deeds of mercy wrought by angels, then tell me what works of iniquity there remain for devils to do?

This commerce in human beings has been carried on until three hundred thousand have been dragged from their native land in a single year. While this foreign trade has been pursued, who can calculate the enormities and extent of the domestic traffic which has flourished in every slave State, while the whole country has been open to the hunters of men?

It is the highly concentrated essence of all conceivable wickedness. Theft, robbery, pollution, unbridled passion, incest, cruelty, cold-blooded murder, blasphemy, and defiance of the laws of God. It teaches children to disregard parental authority. It tears down the marriage altar and tramples its sacred ashes under its feet. It creates and nourishes polygamy. It feeds and pampers its hateful handmaid, prejudice.

It has divided our national councils. It has engendered deadly strife between brethren. It has wasted the treasure of the Commonwealth and the lives of thousands of brave men, and driven troops of helpless women and children into yawning tombs. It has caused the bloodiest civil war recorded in the book of time. It has shorn this nation of its locks of strength that was rising as a young lion in the Western world. It has offered us as a sacrifice to the jealousy and cupidity of tyrants, despots, and adventurers of foreign countries. It has opened a door through which a usurper, a perjured but powerful prince, might stealthily enter and build an empire on the golden borders of our south-western frontier, and which is but a steppingstone to further and unlimited conquests on this continent. It has desolated the fairest portions of our land, "until the wolf long since driven back by the march of civilization returns after the lapse of a hundred years and howls amidst its ruins."

It seals up the Bible and mutilates its sacred truths, and flies into the face of the Almighty, and impiously asks, "Who art thou that I should obey thee?" Such are the outlines of their fearful national sin; and yet the condition to which it reduces man, it is affirmed, is the best that can possibly be devised for him.

When inconsistencies similar in character, and no more glaring, passed beneath the eye of the Son of God, no wonder he broke forth in language of vehement denunciation. Ye Scribes, Pharisees, and hypocrites! Ye blind guides! Ye compass sea and land to make one proselyte, and when he is made ye make him twofold more the child of hell than yourselves. Ye are like unto whited sepulchers, which indeed appear beautiful without, but within are full of dead men's bones and all uncleanness!

Let us here take up the golden rule, and adopt the self-application mode of reasoning to those who hold these erroneous views. Come, gird up thy loins and answer like a man, if thou canst. Is slavery, as it is seen in its origin, continuance and end, the best possible condition for thee? Oh, no! Wilt thou bear that burden on thy shoulders, which thou wouldst lay upon thy fellow man? No. Wilt thou bear a part of it, or remove a little of its weight with one of thy fingers? The sharp and indignant answer is no, no! Then how, and when, and where, shall we apply to thee the golden rule, which says, "Therefore all things that ye would that others should do to you, do ye even so unto them, for this is the law of the prophets."

Let us have the testimony of the wise and great of ancient and modern times:

> *Sages who wrote and warriors who bled.*

Plato declared that "Slavery is a system of complete injustice."

Socrates wrote that "Slavery is a system of outrage and robbery."

Cyrus said, "To fight in order not to be a slave is noble."

If Cyrus had lived in our land a few years ago he would have been arrested for using incendiary language, and for inciting servile insurrection, and the royal fanatic would have been hanged on a gallows higher than Haman. But every man is fanatical when his soul is warmed by the generous fires of liberty. Is it then truly noble to fight in order not to be a slave? The Chief Magistrate of the nation, and our rulers, and all truly patriotic men think so; and so think legions of black men, who for a season were scorned and rejected, but who came quickly and cheerfully when they were at last invited, bearing a heavy burden of proscriptions upon their shoulders, and having faith in God, and in their generous fellow-countrymen, they went forth to fight a double battle. The foes of their country were before them, while the enemies of freedom and of their race surrounded them.

Augustine, Constantine, Ignatius, Polycarp, Maximus, and the most illustrious lights of the ancient church denounced the sin of slave-holding.

Thomas Jefferson said at a period of his life, when his judgment was matured, and his experience was ripe, "There is preparing, I hope, under the auspices of heaven, a way for a total emancipation."

The sainted Washington said, near the close of his mortal career, and when the light of eternity was beaming upon him, "It is among my first wishes to see some plan adopted by which slavery in this country shall be abolished by law. I know of but one way by which this can be done, and that is by legislative action, and so far as my vote can go, it shall not be wanting."

The other day, when the light of Liberty streamed through this marble pile, and the hearts of the noble band of patriotic statesmen leaped for joy, and this our national capital shook from foundation to dome with the shouts of a ransomed people, then methinks the spirits of Washington, Jefferson, the Jays, the Adamses, and Franklin, and Lafayette, and Giddings, and Lovejoy, and those of all the mighty and glorious dead, remembered by history, because they were faithful to truth, justice, and liberty, were hovering over the august assembly. Though unseen by mortal eyes, doubtless they joined the angelic choir, and said, Amen.

Pope Leo X testifies, "That not only does the Christian religion, but nature herself, cry out against a state of slavery."

Patrick Henry said, "We should transmit to posterity our abhorrence of slavery." So also thought the Thirty-eighth Congress.

Lafayette proclaimed these words: "Slavery is a dark spot on the face of the nation." God be praised, that stain will soon be wiped out.

Jonathan Edwards declared "that to hold a man in slavery is to be every day guilty of robbery, or of man stealing.". . .

Could we array in one line, representative of all the families of men, beginning with those lowest in the scale of being, and should we put to them the question, Is it right and desirable that you should be reduced to the condition of slaves, to be registered with chattels, to have your persons and your lives and the products of your labor subjected to the will and the interests of others? Is it right and just that the persons of your wives and children should be at the disposal of others and be yielded to them for the purpose of pampering their lusts and greed of gain? Is it right to lay heavy burdens on other men's shoulders which you would not remove with one of your fingers? From the rude savage and barbarian the negative response would come, increasing in power and significance as it rolled up the line. And when those should reply, whose minds and hearts are illu-

minated with the highest civilization and with the spirit of
Christianity, the answer deep-toned and prolonged would
thunder forth, no, no!

With all the moral attributes of God on our side, cheered
as we are by the voices of universal human nature—in view
of the best interests of the present and future generations—
animated with the noble desire to furnish the nations of the
earth with a worthy example, let the verdict of death which
has been brought in against slavery by the Thirty-eighth
Congress be affirmed and executed by the people. Let the
gigantic monster perish. Yes, perish now and perish forever!

# "AN ACT TO ESTABLISH A BUREAU FOR THE RELIEF OF FREEDMEN AND REFUGEES"

## *(March 3, 1865)*

The establishment of the Freedmen's Bureau by Congress in March 1865 constituted one of the most revolutionary results of the Civil War and Reconstruction because it created a large-scale federal bureaucracy to provide relief for the freedpeople and white refugees. Led by General Oliver O. Howard, the agency began a controversial policy of leasing plots of land to the displaced freedpeople. After Lincoln's successor, President Andrew Johnson, ordered the restoration of all property, including land, to pardoned insurgents, Howard's bureau directed its efforts largely to the legal relief and protection of the freedmen and -women. The Freedmen's Bureau remained a lightning rod for Johnson and for the Radical Republicans' critics. In 1869, as Northern interest in Reconstruction waned, Congress eliminated many of the agency's functions. Its educational work terminated in 1870, and the Bureau ceased operations entirely in 1872.

*Be it enacted by the Senate and House of Representatives of the United States of America in Congress assembled,* That there is hereby established in the War Department, to continue during the present war of rebellion, and for one year thereafter, a bureau of refugees, freedmen, and abandoned lands, to which shall be committed, as hereinafter provided, the supervision and management of all abandoned lands, and the control of all subjects relating to refugees and freedmen from rebel states, or from any district of country within the territory embraced in the operations of the army, under such rules and regulations as may be prescribed by the head of the bureau and approved by the President. The said bureau shall be under the management and control of a commissioner to be appointed by the President, by and with the advice and consent of the Senate, whose compensation shall be three thousand dollars per annum, and such number of clerks as may be assigned to him by the Secretary of War, not exceeding one chief clerk, two of the fourth class, two of the third class, and five of the first class. And the commissioner and all persons appointed under this act, shall, before entering upon their duties, take the oath of office prescribed in an act entitled "An act to prescribe an oath of office, and for other purposes," approved July second, eighteen hundred and sixty-two, and the commissioner and the chief clerk shall, before entering upon their duties, give bonds to the treasurer of the United States, the former in the sum of fifty thousand dollars, and the latter in the sum of ten thousand dollars, conditioned for the faithful discharge of their duties respectively, with securities to be approved as sufficient by the Attorney-General, which bonds shall be filed in the office of the first comptroller of the treasury, to be by him put in suit for the benefit of any injured party upon any breach of the conditions thereof.

SEC. 2. *And be it further enacted,* That the Secretary of War may direct such issues of provisions, clothing, and fuel, as he may deem needful for the immediate and temporary shelter and supply of destitute and suffering refugees and freedmen and their wives and children, under such rules and regulations as he may direct.

SEC. 3. *And be it further enacted,* That the President may, by and with the advice and consent of the Senate, appoint an assistant commissioner for each of the states declared to be in insurrection, not exceeding ten in number, who shall, under the direction of the commissioner, aid in the execution of the provisions of this act; and he shall give a bond to the Treasurer of the United States, in the sum of twenty thousand dollars, in the form and manner prescribed in the first section of this act. Each of said commissioners shall receive an annual salary of two thousand five hundred dollars in full compensation for all his services. And any military officer may be detailed and assigned to duty under this act without increase of pay or allowances. The commissioner shall, before the commencement of each regular session of congress, make full report of his proceedings with exhibits of the state of his accounts to the President, who shall communicate the same to congress, and shall also make special reports whenever required to do so by the President or either house of congress; and the assistant commissioners shall make quarterly reports of their proceedings to the commissioner, and also such other special reports as from time to time may be required.

SEC. 4. *And be it further enacted,* That the commissioner, under the direction of the President, shall have authority to set apart, for the use of loyal refugees and freedmen, such tracts of land within the insurrectionary states as shall have been abandoned, or to which the United States shall have acquired title by confiscation or sale, or otherwise, and to every male citizen, whether refugee or freedman, as aforesaid, there shall be assigned not more than forty acres of such land, and the person to whom it was so assigned shall be protected in the use and enjoyment of the land for the term of three years at an annual rent not exceeding six per centum upon the value of such land, as it was appraised by the state authorities in the year eighteen hundred and sixty, for the purpose of taxation, and in case no such appraisal can be found, then the rental shall be based upon the estimated value of the land in said year, to be ascertained in such manner as the commissioner may by regulation prescribe. At the end of said term, or at any time during said term, the occupants of any parcels so assigned may purchase the land and receive such title thereto as the United States can convey, upon paying therefor the value of the land, as ascertained and fixed for the purpose of determining the annual rent aforesaid.

SEC. 5. *And be it further enacted,* That all acts and parts of acts inconsistent with the provisions of this act, are hereby repealed.

# ABRAHAM LINCOLN, "SECOND INAUGURAL ADDRESS"

## (March 4, 1865)

In his famous Second Inaugural Address, Lincoln
reflected more on the spiritual meaning of the
Civil War than on plans for what became his tragi-
cally short-lived second administration. Simple in
language and direct in purpose, Lincoln's speech
defined the war as the crucible for a new American nation, one fashioned from the sacrifices of
Northerners and Southerners ("this mighty scourge
of war"). Slavery, Lincoln informed his countrymen, was the nation's great sin, and he hoped
that the reunited nation would live in a world
"With malice toward none; with charity for all."
The racial violence of Reconstruction and the almost century-long history of Jim Crow betrayed
the president's dream.

At this second appearing to take the oath of the presidential office, there is less occasion for an extended address
than there was at the first. Then a statement, somewhat in
detail, of a course to be pursued, seemed fitting and proper.
Now, at the expiration of four years, during which public
declarations have been constantly called forth on every
point and phase of the great contest which still absorbs the
attention, and engrosses the eneregies [*sic*] of the nation,
little that is new could be presented. The progress of our
arms, upon which all else chiefly depends, is as well known
to the public as to myself; and it is, I trust, reasonably satisfactory and encouraging to all. With high hope for the future, no prediction in regard to it is ventured.

On the occasion corresponding to this four years ago, all
thoughts were anxiously directed to an impending civil-
war. All dreaded it—all sought to avert it. While the inaugural address was being delivered from this place, devoted
altogether to *saving* the Union without war, insurgent

agents were in the city seeking to *destroy* it without war—seeking to dissol[v]e the Union, and divide effects, by negotiation. Both parties deprecated war; but one of them would *make* war rather than let the nation survive; and the other would *accept* war rather than let it perish. And the war came.

One eighth of the whole population were colored slaves, not distributed generally over the Union, but localized in the Southern part of it. These slaves constituted a peculiar and powerful interest. All knew that this interest was, somehow, the cause of the war. To strengthen, perpetuate, and extend this interest was the object for which the insurgents would rend the Union, even by war; while the government claimed no right to do more than to restrict the territorial enlargement of it. Neither party expected for the war, the magnitude, or the duration, which it has already attained. Neither anticipated that the *cause* of the conflict might cease with, or even before, the conflict itself should cease. Each looked for an easier triumph, and a result less fundamental and astounding. Both read the same Bible, and pray to the same God; and each invokes His aid against the other. It may seem strange that any men should dare to ask a just God's assistance in wringing their bread from the sweat of other men's faces; but let us judge not that we be not judged. The prayers of both could not be answered; that of neither has been answered fully. The Almighty has His own purposes. "Woe unto the world because of offences! for it must needs be that offences come; but woe to that man by whom the offence cometh!" If we shall suppose that American Slavery is one of those offences which, in the providence of God, must needs come, but which, having continued through His appointed time, He now wills to remove, and that He gives to both North and South, this terrible war, as the woe due to those by whom the offence came, shall we discern therein any departure from those divine attributes which the believers in a Living God always ascribe to Him? Fondly do we hope—fervently do we pray—that this mighty scourge of war may speedily pass away. Yet, if God wills that it continue, until all the wealth piled by the bond-man's two hundred and fifty years of unrequited toil shall be sunk, and until every drop of blood drawn with the lash, shall be paid by another drawn with the sword, as was said three thousand years ago, so still it must be said "the judgments of the Lord, are true and righteous altogether."

With malice toward none; with charity for all; with firmness in the right, as God gives us to see the right, let us strive on to finish the work we are in; to bind up the nation's wounds; to care for him who shall have borne the battle, and for his widow, and his orphan—to do all which may achieve and cherish a just, and a lasting peace, among ourselves, and with all nations.

# PART II

# PRESIDENTIAL RECONSTRUCTION, 1865–67

As the Civil War ended, the question of who would direct Reconstruction remained unanswered. Unsettled too was the status and role of the South's four million ex-slaves, now freedmen and -women, in postbellum society. Lincoln's assassination added a dramatic new twist to the Reconstruction story.

With Lincoln's passing the responsibility of reconstructing the nation fell upon a most unlikely man: the Tennessee ex-slaveholder Andrew Johnson, whom Lincoln had added to his Union Party ticket to gain the support of conservative Republicans, moderate Democrats, and border state voters who had voted for Constitutional Union Party candidate John Bell in the 1860 election. Not only a former slaveholder but a lifelong conservative Democrat who believed in limited government, Johnson nonetheless was a vocal nationalist who condemned secession, and especially large planters, whom he held accountable for disunion, which he considered treason. Johnson remained loyal to the Union during the secession crisis, becoming the only Southern U.S. Senator to retain his post. To reward Johnson's loyalty, and to provide a strong presence in Unionist east Tennessee, Lincoln appointed him military governor of the Volunteer State in 1862.

Despite his strengths as a stump speaker and his loyalty to the Union, Johnson proved an unfortunate successor to Lincoln, especially when confronted with the immense task of restoring the Union in the aftermath of a horrific civil war. Such a task required diplomacy, patience, and tact, qualities that Johnson held in short supply.

Many politically astute Americans assumed that Johnson, whose bellicosity toward secessionists was legion, would commence a harsh Reconstruction policy toward the Rebels, dramatically transforming the South. Yet as president, Johnson declared his intention simply to restore (as op-

posed to reconstruct) the defeated Confederate states. He
also made clear his unwillingness to side with Congressional Radicals, objecting loudly to their determination to institute political equality for the freedmen. Instead, Johnson
attempted to carry forward what he considered to be Lincoln's plans for Reconstruction, first appointing provisional
military governors in the former Rebel states, then offering
lenient terms to white Southerners, allowing them to reenter the Union quickly and with minimum political rancor.
Johnson's plan for restoring the Union called for the granting of amnesty for most (all but fourteen exempted classes)
former Confederates, once they had taken a loyalty oath
and after their states had abolished slavery and ratified the
Thirteenth Amendment (passed by Congress in January
1865 and ratified in December). Johnson requested too that
the former Confederate states repudiate their Confederate
debt and nullify their secession ordinances.

Johnson formally announced his Reconstruction program in two proclamations on May 29, 1865. These documents stated clearly his animus toward the antebellum
planter elite, his sympathy toward Southern white Unionist
yeomen, and his uninterest in the freedpeople. Though the
Radicals hoped to work with the new president, they soon
realized that Johnson's hostility toward blacks—shrouded
in states' rights rhetoric—would block cooperation and
progress. "Throughout his Presidency," Eric Foner explains,
"Johnson held the view—not uncommon among Southern
yeomen—that slaves had in some way joined forces with
their owners to oppress nonslaveholding whites."[23]

Johnson's antiblack bias and celebration of working-
class whites initially won him supporters among various
Northern political factions. Moderate Republicans supported Johnson's interpretation of the essential supremacy
of states' rights over federalism and of limited racial reform. Northern Democrats looked to Johnson to help revive a party riven by sectionalism and civil war. Northern
capitalists, eager to increase profits, considered a speedy
restoration of the Union as good for business. To their
minds, political union would help restore the rich antebellum cotton trade, stimulate domestic and international
commerce, and, in turn, profit businessmen north and south
through the repayment of war debts. Former Confederates

judged Johnson, though a combative and fiery east Tennessee Unionist, one of their own, at heart a Southern Democrat. The Radical Republicans quickly took note.

Confederate defeat in the Civil War essentially ended the question of secession as a legitimate political solution to questions of state versus federal sovereignty. The legal and Constitutional status of the freedpeople, as well as African-Americans residing north and west of Dixie, however, remained far less settled. To be sure, Lincoln's January 1, 1863, Emancipation Proclamation had theoretically freed roughly three million slaves living in territories in a state of insurrection, but in fact his military edict emancipated only around 50,000 slaves.[24]

But what would be the status of all Southern blacks after Union forces finally suppressed the rebellion? Would Lincoln's decree stand up in the courts? Would the freedmen and -women be citizens? Could black males vote?

During the last months of the war, the U.S. Congress resolved the question of chattel slavery in American life once and for all by abolishing it in the Thirteenth Amendment. The process of ratifying the amendment began in several border states even before Lee's surrender. The necessary three-quarters of the states, including eight former slave-holding states, ratified the amendment on December 16, 1865, and it became part of the Constitution.

Congress took another step in helping to define the future of the freedpeople when on March 3, 1865, it established the Bureau of Refugees, Freedmen, and Abandoned Lands (generally known as the Freedmen's Bureau), a temporary agency designed to aid freedmen and -women in the transition to a free labor economy and society, a daunting task. The bureau, according to Foner, became one of the first large-scale federal agencies. It gained responsibility for "introducing a workable system of free labor in the South, establishing schools for freedmen, providing aid to the destitute, aged, ill, and insane, adjudicating disputes among blacks and between the races, and attempting to secure for blacks and white Unionists equal justice from the state and local governments established during Presidential Reconstruction."[25] Though criticized by contemporaries and by later historians either for overstepping legitimate bounds of government or for not providing enough relief and as-

sistance to the ex-slaves, the Freedmen's Bureau nevertheless did achieve limited success in bringing short-term
relief to blacks in the immediate aftermath of the Civil
War, particularly as white Southerners resisted the growth
of the free-labor system. Freedmen's Bureau agents distributed food and clothing to those struggling to survive at
war's end, adjudicated disputes between former slaves and
ex-masters, assisted in the drafting of labor agreements, and
served as liaisons between the African-American community and the federal government. The Bureau, often in con-
junction with Northern Protestant missionaries, established
primary schools for the freedmen. Though confronted with
an overwhelming task, the Bureau remains one of the un-
derappreciated triumphs of Reconstruction.

Johnson's eagerness to restore the Union quickly and
unilaterally (especially while Congress was on recess during the summer months of 1865) and his sympathy for
white Southerners (as evidenced by the leniency that he
showed former Confederates) ultimately led to the failure
of Presidential Reconstruction. During the summer and
fall of 1865, one former Confederate state after another
took steps to meet Johnson's requirements, eager to gain
readmission to the Union. Their representatives abolished
slavery, repudiated secession and their Confederate debts,
revised their constitutions, and conducted elections for
governors, state legislators, and members of Congress.

North Carolinians, for example, met on October 2, 1865,
to put into place Johnson's Reconstruction plan with hopes
of expeditiously restoring their state to the Union. Delegates to the state convention repealed North Carolina's
Ordinance of Secession, declared slavery abolished, repudiated the state's Confederate war debt, and established
the mechanism to elect a governor, state legislators, and
representatives to the U.S. Congress. According to one unhappy North Carolina woman, "The N.C. Convention has
prostrated the State so low and I doubt if she can find more
dust to lick up. Their declaration that the Ordinance of Secession was null & void & their Repudiation of the War
debt is I should think abject enough to please even a Yankee Conqueror!"[26]

Though the Southern states met Johnson's stipulations
to rejoin the Union, Northern observers noted how white

Southerners radiated contempt for U.S. officials, seemed unrepentant for their role in what late-nineteenth-century historians termed the War of the Rebellion, elected former Confederates to high office in the fall 1865 elections and, most egregiously, refused to treat ex-slaves as freedmen and -women in deed as well as in word. "Recognizing the most limited meanings of emancipation," explains historian Steven Hahn, "state constitutional conventions and then legislatures under Presidential Reconstruction did make provision for blacks to marry, enter into other contracts, own some property, and gain highly circumscribed access to the courts. But no state gave even fleeting consideration to any form of black suffrage."[27] In what historian Stephen Kantrowitz considers "emblematic of this version of Reconstruction, the newly re-formed legislature of Georgia elected former Confederate vice president Alexander Stephens to the U.S. Senate."[28] Not only did white Southerners assume that they would be led by their former leaders, but they took for granted that their former slaves would work on their farms and plantations, either for wages or for "shares" of the crop. Whites expected blacks to act as subordinates, to defer to them socially, and to retain the racial etiquette of the former "peculiar institution." To define the conditions of their work and ensure this behavior, during late 1865 each Southern state passed ordinances specifically designed to control the blacks' mobility, their deportment, and their labor. These were the notorious Black Codes, laws so blatantly reactionary that they quite nearly nullified the spirit of the Thirteenth Amendment.

Southern state legislators fashioned the Black Codes much like the antebellum slave codes, determined to regulate the economic and social relations between whites and blacks. The codes signify as much a determination by white Southerners in the aftermath of emancipation to retain the legal and social control mechanisms of slavery as a belief that white Northerners would simply acquiesce to them. In practice the Black Codes proved so restrictive that they imposed upon the recently freed African-Americans a legal status as close to slavery as possible, what Hahn terms "a new system of group dependency."[29] The new laws denied the freedmen the right to vote or hold office and circumscribed their economic freedom and mobility, leaving them constrained in terms of finding new employers or owning their own land. The laws also restricted the types of jobs blacks could hold.

Mississippi's infamous Black Code of November 1865 exemplified the restrictions imposed in the laws generally and served as a model for the other Southern states. The Mississippi laws prohibited blacks from leasing or renting land except in preselected black sectors, owning firearms without police permission, and selling or receiving alcohol. Moreover, vagrancy laws mandated that persons of color sign written contracts for poorly paid long-term agricultural labor, rendering them akin to peasants. Workers caught violating their labor contracts could be forcibly returned to their employer.

After months of observing affairs in the South, Northern congressmen responded to Johnson's conservative Reconstruction plan, the Black Codes, and the growing defiance by Southern state government by asserting control over Reconstruction. When the Thirty-ninth Congress reconvened in December 1865, it refused to seat the newly elected Southern congressmen, a move led by Thaddeus Stevens, a Pennsylvania congressman, and Edward McPherson, clerk of the House of Representatives. The Congress established a Joint Committee on Reconstruction, composed of six senators and nine representatives, and led by Stevens. Its mission was to report on conditions in the South and to judge whether any of the former Confederate states were entitled to representation in Congress. In 1866, the Joint Committee conducted extensive hearings, gathered voluminous testimony, and interviewed numerous Unionists, former Confederates, and African-Americans. The committee reported that Johnson's Reconstruction program fell short of protecting the freedpeople or ensuring Southern loyalty. Its findings helped usher in congressional control of Reconstruction.

# Charles Sumner, "Right and Duty of Colored Fellow-Citizens in the Organization of Government"

## (May 13, 1865)

Massachusetts Senator Charles Sumner (1811–1874) ranked as one of the most consistent and forceful opponents of slavery and champions of equal rights. During the Civil War, he implored Lincoln to free the South's slaves immediately, thereby weakening the Confederacy. Sumner, a leading Radical Republican, maintained that by seceding the Southern states had committed treason ("state suicide"), thereby forfeiting their Constitutional rights. In this correspondence between members of Wilmington, North Carolina's Colored Union Leagues and Sumner, he admonished the freedmen to demand full civil rights, including the vote.

Wilmington, N. C., April 29, 1865.

Hon. Charles Sumner, *Washington*.

DEAR SIR,—We, the undersigned citizens, Executive Board of the Colored Union Leagues of this city, respectfully ask your attention to the subject of Reconstruction in this State, and for a few plain directions in relation to a proper stand for us to make.

We forward also a copy of the *Herald*, containing an article on Reconstruction, which causes us much anxiety, in connection with other facts that are constantly pressed upon our attention in this Rebel State, although much is said concerning its loyalty that is unreliable and untrue. Many of us have done service for the United States Government, at Fort Fisher and elsewhere, and we shrink with horror at the thought that we may be left to the tender mercies of our former Rebel masters, who have taken the oath, but are filled with malice, and swear vengeance against us as soon as the military are withdrawn.

We are loyal colored citizens, and strive in all things so to conduct ourselves that no just cause of complaint may exist, although we suffer much from the unwillingness of the Secessionists to regard us as *freemen*, and look up to the flag of our country with trembling anxiety, knowing that the *franchise* alone can give us security for the future.

We speak with moderation and care, we lay no charges, but we fear that an ill-judged lenity to Rebels in this State will leave little to us and our children but the bare name of freedmen. We remember Louisiana! Better "smash the egg" than permit it to produce a viper.

We beg an early answer. Direct, simply, "Alfred Howe, Wilmington, North Carolina." Do not frank your letter: I send a stamp. For reference,

Jonathan C. Gibbs mentions the name of Rev. H. H. Garnett, a colored Presbyterian minister in Washington, and Hon. Judge Kelley, from Pennsylvania.

Alfred Howe, President.

| | |
|---|---|
| D. Sadgenar, | Owen Burney, |
| H. D. Sampson, | Henry Taylor, |
| Jonathan C. Gibbs, | Richard Reed. |

WASHINGTON, May 13, 1865.

GENTLEMEN,—I am glad that the colored citizens of North Carolina are ready to take part in the organization of government. It is unquestionably their right and duty.

I see little chance of peace or tranquillity in any Rebel State, unless the rights of all are recognized without distinction of color. On this foundation we must build.

The article on Reconstruction to which you call my attention proceeds on the idea, born of Slavery, that persons with a white skin are the only "citizens." This is a mistake.

As you do me the honor to ask me the proper stand for you to make, I have no hesitation in replying that you must insist on all the rights and privileges of a citizen. They belong to you. They are yours; and whoever undertakes to rob you of them is a usurper and impostor.

Of course you will take part in any primary meetings for political organization, open to citizens generally, and will not miss any opportunity to show your loyalty and fidelity.

Accept my best wishes, and believe me, Gentlemen,

Faithfully yours,

CHARLES SUMNER.

# ANDREW JOHNSON, "PROCLAMATION ESTABLISHING GOVERNMENT FOR NORTH CAROLINA"

## (May 29, 1865)

President Andrew Johnson launched his Reconstruction program on May 29, 1865, with two proclamations, one delineating his presidential pardon program and the other detailing the steps that former Confederate states needed to take to rejoin the Union. Johnson's North Carolina proclamation served as a model for his overall policy. He soon after issued similar documents for Mississippi, Georgia, Texas, Alabama, South Carolina, and Florida. In the North Carolina case, Johnson empowered Provisional Governor William W. Holden to reorganize county governments and summon a constitutional convention on the basis of white suffrage that declared slavery illegal, repudiated North Carolina's Confederate debt, and repealed the state's secession ordinance. White Southerners responded by forming conservative state legislatures, passing repressive Black Codes, and electing former Confederates to Congress. The scene thus became set for conflict between the legislative and executive branches of government over the president's Reconstruction project.

Whereas the 4th section of the 4th article of the Constitution of the United States declares that the United States shall guarantee to every State in the Union a republican form of government, and shall protect each of them against invasion and domestic violence; and whereas the President of the United States is, by the Constitution, made Commander-in-chief of the army and navy, as well as chief civil executive officer of the United States, and is bound by solemn oath faithfully to execute the office of President of the United States, and to take care that the laws be faithfully executed; and whereas the rebellion, which has been waged by a portion of the people of the United States against the properly constituted authorities of the government thereof, in the most violent and revolting form, but whose organized and armed forces have now been almost entirely overcome, has, in its revolutionary progress, deprived the people of the State of North Carolina of all civil government; and whereas it becomes necessary and proper to carry out and enforce the obligations of the United States to the people of North Carolina, in securing them in the enjoyment of a republican form of government:

Now, THEREFORE, in obedience to the high and solemn duties imposed upon me by the Constitution of the United States, and for the purpose of enabling the loyal people of said State to organize a State government, whereby justice may be established, domestic tranquillity insured, and loyal citizens protected in all their rights of life, liberty, and property, I, ANDREW JOHNSON, President of the United States, and commander-in-chief of the army and navy of the United States, do hereby appoint WILLIAM W. HOLDEN provisional governor of the State of North Carolina, whose duty it shall be, at the earliest practicable period, to prescribe such rules and regulations as may be necessary and proper for convening a convention, composed of delegates to be chosen by that portion of the people of said State who are loyal to the United States, and no others, for the purpose of altering or amending the constitution thereof; and with authority to exercise, within the limits of said State, all the powers necessary and proper to enable such loyal people of the State of North Carolina to restore said State to its constitutional relations to the Federal government, and to present such a republican form of State government as will entitle the State to the guarantee of the United States therefor, and its people to protection by the United States against invasion, insurrection, and domestic violence; *provided* that, in any election that may be hereafter held for choosing delegates to any State convention as aforesaid, no person shall be qualified as an elector, or shall be eligible as a member of such convention, unless he shall have previously taken and subscribed the oath of amnesty, as set forth in the President's proclamation of May 29, A.D. 1865, and is a voter qualified as prescribed by the constitution and laws of the State of North Carolina in force immediately before the 20th day of May, A.D. 1861, the date of the so-called ordinance of secession; and the said convention, when convened, or the legislature that may be thereafter assembled, will prescribe the qualification of electors, and the eligibility of persons to hold office under the constitution and laws of the State, a power the people of the several States composing the Federal Union have rightfully exercised from the origin of the government to the present time.

And I do hereby direct —

*First.* That the military commander of the department, and all officers and persons in the military and naval service, aid and assist the said Provisional Governor in carrying into effect this proclamation, and they are enjoined to abstain from, in any way, hindering, impeding, or discouraging the loyal people from the organization of a State government as herein authorized.

*Second.* That the Secretary of State proceed to put in force all laws of the United States, the administration whereof belongs to the State Department, applicable to the geographical limits aforesaid.

*Third.* That the Secretary of the Treasury proceed to nominate for appointment assessors of taxes, and collectors of customs and internal revenue, and such other officers of the Treasury Department as are authorized by law, and put in execution the revenue laws of the United States within the geographical limits aforesaid. In making appointments, the preference shall be given to qualified loyal persons residing within the districts where their respective duties are to be performed. But if suitable residents of the districts shall not be found, then persons residing in other States or districts shall be appointed.

*Fourth.* That the Postmaster General proceed to establish post offices and post routes, and put into execution the postal laws of the United States within the said State, giving to loyal residents the preference of appointment; but if suitable residents are not found, then to appoint agents, &c., from other States.

*Fifth.* That the district judge for the judicial district in which North Carolina is included proceed to hold courts within said State, in accordance with the provisions of the act of Congress. The Attorney General will instruct the proper officers to libel, and bring to judgment, confiscation, and sale, property subject to confiscation, and enforce the administration of justice within said State in all matters within the cognizance and jurisdiction of the Federal courts.

*Sixth.* That the Secretary of the Navy take possession of all public property belonging to the Navy Department within said geographical limits, and put in operation all acts of Congress in relation to naval affairs having application to the said State.

*Seventh.* That the Secretary of the Interior put in force the laws relating to the Interior Department applicable to the geographical limits aforesaid.

In testimony whereof, I have hereunto set my hand and caused the seal of the United States to be affixed.

Done at the city of Washington this twenty-ninth day of May, in the year of our Lord one thousand eight hundred and sixty-five, and of the Independence of the United States the eighty-ninth.

# Andrew Johnson,
## "Amnesty Proclamation"

### *(May 29, 1865)*

Johnson issued his Amnesty Proclamation on the same day that he announced his Presidential Reconstruction for North Carolina and the other former Confederate states. Following the spirit of Lincoln's December 1863 amnesty proclamation, Johnson proffered amnesty to all former Rebels willing to take the oath of allegiance to the U.S. Johnson exempted fourteen classes from amnesty, including those already enumerated by Lincoln, plus individuals who had violated previous loyalty oaths, commerce raiders, graduates of the U.S. Military and Naval academies, and those persons whose worth exceeded twenty thousand dollars. However, Johnson allowed persons in the exempted classes to make special applications and he granted numerous individual pardons.

Whereas the President of the United States, on the 8th day of December, A.D. eighteen hundred and sixty-three, and on the 26th day of March, A.D. eighteen hundred and sixty-four, did, with the object to suppress the existing rebellion, to induce all persons to return to their loyalty, and to restore the authority of the United States, issue proclamations offering amnesty and pardon to certain persons who had directly or by implication participated in the said rebellion; and whereas many persons who had so engaged in said rebellion have, since the issuance of said proclamations, failed or neglected to take the benefits offered thereby; and whereas many persons who have been justly deprived of all claim to amnesty and pardon thereunder, by reason of their participation directly or by implication in said rebellion, and continued hostility to the government of the United States since the date of said proclamation, now desire to apply for and obtain amnesty and pardon:

To the end, therefore, that the authority of the government of the United States may be restored, and that peace, order, and freedom may be established, I, ANDREW JOHNSON, President of the United States, do proclaim and declare that I hereby grant to all persons who have, directly or indirectly, participated in the existing rebellion, except as hereinafter excepted, amnesty and pardon, with restoration of all rights of property, except as to slaves, and except in cases where legal proceedings, under the laws of the United States providing for the confiscation of property of persons engaged in rebellion, have been instituted; but upon the condition, nevertheless, that every such person shall take and subscribe the following oath, (or affirmation,) and thenceforward keep and maintain said oath inviolate; and which oath shall be registered for permanent preservation, and shall be of the tenor and effect following, to wit:

> I, _____ _____, do solemnly swear, (or affirm,) in presence of Almighty God, that I will henceforth faithfully support, protect, and defend the Constitution of the United States, and the union of the States thereunder; and that I will, in like manner, abide by, and faithfully support all laws and proclamations which have been made during the existing rebellion with reference to the emancipation of slaves. So help me God.

The following classes of persons are excepted from the benefits of this proclamation: 1st, all who are or shall have been pretended civil or diplomatic officers or otherwise domestic or foreign agents of the pretended Confederate government; 2d, all who left judicial stations under the United States to aid the rebellion; 3d, all who shall have been military or naval officers of said pretended Confederate government above the rank of colonel in the army or lieutenant in the navy; 4th, all who left seats in the Congress of the United States to aid the rebellion; 5th, all who resigned or tendered resignations of their commissions in the army or navy of the United States to evade duty in resisting the rebellion; 6th, all who have engaged in any way in treating otherwise than lawfully as prisoners of war persons found in the United States service, as officers, soldiers, seamen, or in other capacities; 7th, all persons who have been, or are absentees from the United States for the purpose of aiding the rebellion; 8th, all military and naval officers in the rebel service, who were educated by the government in the Military Academy at West Point or the United States Naval Academy; 9th, all persons who held the pretended offices of governors of States in insurrection against the United States; 10th, all persons who left their homes within the jurisdiction and protection of the United States, and passed beyond the Federal military lines into the pretended Confederate States for the purpose of aiding the rebellion; 11th, all persons who have been engaged in the destruction of the commerce of the United States upon the high seas, and all persons who have made raids into the United States from Canada, or been engaged in destroying the commerce of the United States upon the lakes and rivers that separate the British Provinces from the United States; 12th, all persons who, at the time when they seek to obtain the benefits hereof by taking the oath herein prescribed, are in military, naval, or civil confinement, or custody, or under bonds of the civil, military, or naval authorities, or agents of the United States as prisoners of war, or persons detained for offences of any kind, either before or after conviction; 13th, all persons who have voluntarily participated in said rebellion, and the estimated value of whose taxable property is over twenty thousand dollars; 14th, all persons who have taken the oath of amnesty as prescribed in the President's proclamation of December 8th, A.D. 1863, or an oath of allegiance to the government of the United States since the date of said proclamation, and who have not thenceforward kept and maintained the same inviolate.

*Provided,* That special application may be made to the President for pardon by any person belonging to the excepted classes; and such clemency will be liberally extended as may be consistent with the facts of the case and the peace and dignity of the United States.

The Secretary of State will establish rules and regulations for administering and recording the said amnesty oath, so as to insure its benefit to the people, and guard the government against fraud.

In testimony whereof, I have hereunto set my hand, and caused the seal of the United States to be affixed.

# EMILY WATERS TO HER HUSBAND

## *(July 16, 1865)*

In the early months of Reconstruction, former masters and ex-slaves jockeyed for position, trying to establish working relationships in the new post-slavery world. At Louisiana's Roseland Plantation, former slave Emily Waters, whose husband was serving on occupation duty with the U.S. Colored Troops, found herself at the mercy of her former owner, John Humphries. Unable to pay what she considered unreasonable rent on her house, Emily feared that she and her children would become destitute. She pleaded with her husband to come home.

Roseland Plantation [*La.*] July 16th 1865

My Dear Husband I received a letter from you week before last and was glad to hear that you were well and happy.

This is the fifth letter I have written you and I have received only one— Please write as often as you can as I am always anxious to hear from you. I and the children are all well—but I am in a great deal of trouble as Master John Humphries has come home from the Rebel army and taken charge of the place and says he is going to turn us all out on the Levee unless we pay him (8.00) Eight Dollars a month for house rent— Now I have no money of any account and I am not able to get enough to pay so much rent, and I want you to get a furlough as soon as you can and come home and find a place for us to live in. and besides Amelia is very sick and wants you to come home and see her if possible she has been sick with the fever now over two weeks and is getting very low— Your mother and all the rest of your folks are well and all send their regards & want to see you as soon as you can manage to come— My mother sends her compliments & hopes to see you soon

My children are going to school, but I find it very hard to feed them all, and if you can not come I hope you will send me something to help me get along

I get all the work I can and am doing the best I can to get along, but if they turn me out I dont know what I shall do— However I will try & keep the children along until you come or send me some assistance

Thank God we are all well, and I hope we may always be so Give my regards to all the boys. Come home as soon as you can, and cherish me as ever Your Aff wife

Emily Waters

# THADDEUS STEVENS,
## "RECONSTRUCTION"

### *(September 6, 1865)*

Pennsylvania Representative Thaddeus Stevens
(1792–1868) stood unquestionably as the most
radical of Radical Republicans, the symbol of
equal rights and opportunity for the freedpeople
and of government extremism and misrule for
their former masters. Like Sumner, Stevens refused to compromise and held a special hatred for
the South's plantation leadership elite, which he
blamed for disunion. Determined to make the
Confederates pay for their treason, Stevens interpreted the former Rebel states as "conquered territory" and insisted that the Southern states
should not return to the Union until they guaranteed the freedmen full political and civil rights. He
favored various punishments for the ex-Confederates, including property confiscation and breaking up plantations into forty-acre plots for the
former slaves. Stevens's "Reconstruction" speech
to his Lancaster, Pennsylvania, constituents artic-
ulates clearly and forcefully his harsh Reconstruction program and why he and President Johnson
disagreed so forcefully on the question.

Fellow Citizens:

In compliance with your request, I have come to give my
views of the present condition of the Rebel States—of the
proper mode of reorganizing the Government, and the future prospects of the Republic. During the whole progress
of the war, I never for a moment felt doubt or despondency.
I knew that the loyal North would conquer the Rebel despots who sought to destroy freedom. But since that traitor-
ous confederation has been subdued, and we have entered
upon the work of "reconstruction" or "restoration," I can-

not deny that my heart has become sad at the gloomy prospects before us.

Four years of bloody and expensive war, waged against the United States by eleven States, under a government called the "Confederate States of America," to which they acknowledged allegiance, have overthrown all governments within those States which could be acknowledged as legitimate by the Union. The armies of the Confederate States having been conquered and subdued, and their territory possessed by the United States, it becomes necessary to establish governments therein, which shall be republican in form and principles, and form a more "perfect Union" with the parent Government. It is desirable that such a course should be pursued as to exclude from those governments every vestige of human bondage, and render the same forever impossible in this nation; and to take care that no principles of self-destruction shall be incorporated therein. In effecting this, it is to be hoped that no provision of the Constitution will be infringed, and no principle of the law of nations disregarded. Especially must we take care that in rebuking this unjust and treasonable war, the authorities of the Union shall indulge in no acts of usurpation which may tend to impair the stability and permanency of the nation. Within these limitations, we hold it to be the duty of the Government to inflict condign punishment on the rebel belligerents, and so weaken their hands that they can never again endanger the Union; and so reform their municipal institutions as to make them republican in spirit as well as in name.

We especially insist that the property of the chief rebels should be seized and appropriated to the payment of the National debt, caused by the unjust and wicked war which they instigated.

How can such punishments be inflicted and such forfeitures produced without doing violence to established principles?

Two positions have been suggested.

First—To treat those States as never having been out of the Union, because the Constitution forbids secession, and therefore, a fact forbidden by law could not exist.

Second—To accept the position to which they placed themselves as severed from the Union; an independent government *de facto,* and an alien enemy to be dealt with according to the laws of war.

It seems to me that while we do not aver that the United States are bound to treat them as an alien enemy, yet they have a right to elect so to do if it be for the interest of the Nation; and that the "Confederate States" are estopped from denying that position. South Carolina, the leader and embodiment of the rebellion, in the month of January, 1861, passed the following resolution by the unanimous vote of her Legislature:

"Resolved, That the separation of South Carolina from the Federal Union *is final,* and she has no further interests in the Constitution of the United States; and that the only appropriate negotiations between her and the Federal Government are as to their mutual relations as *foreign* States."

The convention that formed the Government of the Confederate States, and all the eleven states that composed it, adopted the same declaration, and pledged their lives and fortunes to support it. That government raised large armies and by its formidable power compelled the nations of the civilized world as well as our own Government to acknowledge them as an independent belligerent, entitled by the law of nations to be considered as engaged in a public war, and not merely in an insurrection. It is idle to deny that we treated them as a belligerent, entitled to all the rights, and subject to all the liabilities of an alien enemy. We blockaded their ports, which is an undoubted belligerent right; the extent of coast blockaded marked the acknowledged extent of their territory—a territory criminally acquired but *de facto* theirs. We acknowledged their sea-rovers as privateers and not as pirates, by ordering their captive crews to be treated as prisoners of war. We acknowledged that a commission from the Confederate Government was sufficient to screen Semmes and his associates from the fate of lawless buccaneers. Who but an acknowledged government *de jure* or *de facto,* could have power to issue such a commission? The invaders of the loyal States were not treated as out-laws, but as soldiers of war, because they were commanded by officers holding commissions from that Government. The Confederate States were for four years what they claimed to be, an alien enemy, in all their rights and liabilities. To say that they were States under the protection of that constitution which they were rending, and within the Union which they were assaulting with bloody defeats, simply because they became belligerents through crime, is making theory overrule fact to an absurd degree. It will, I suppose, at least be conceded that the United States, if not obliged so to do, have a right to treat them as an alien enemy now conquered, and subject to all the liabilities of a vanquished foe.

If we are also at liberty to treat them as never having been out of the Union, and that their declarations and acts were all void because they contravened the Constitution, and therefore they were never engaged in a public war, but were merely insurgents, let us inquire which position is best for the United States. If they have never been otherwise than States in the Union, and we desire to try certain of the leaders for treason, the Constitution requires that they should be indicted and tried *"by an impartial jury of the State and district wherein the crime shall have been committed, which district shall have been previously ascertained by law."*

The crime of treason can be committed only where the person is actually or potentially present. Jefferson Davis sitting in Richmond, counseling, or advising, or commanding an inroad into Pennsylvania, has committed no overt act in this State, and can be tried, if any where, only in the Richmond District. The doctrine of constructive presence, and constructive treason, will never, I hope, pollute our statutes, or judicial decisions. Select an *impartial* jury from Virginia, and it is obvious that no conviction could ever be had. Possibly a jury might be packed to convict, but that would not be an "impartial" jury. It would be judicial murder, and would rank in infamy with the trial of Lord Russell, except only that the one was the murder of an innocent man, the other of a traitor. The same difficulties would exist in attempting forfeitures, which can only follow conviction in States protected by the Constitution; and then it is said only for the life of the malefactor—Congress can pass no "bill of attainder."

Nor, under that theory, has Congress, much less the Executive, any power to interfere in remodelling those States upon reconstruction. What reconstruction is needed? Here are States which, they say, have never been out of the Union, and which are consequently now in it without asking leave of any one. They are competent to send Senators and members to Congress. The state of war has broken no constitutional ligaments, for it was only an insurrection of individuals, not a public war waged by States. Such is the reasoning, notwithstanding every State acted in its municipal capacity; and the court in the prize cases (2 Black 673) say: *"Hence in organizing this rebellion they have acted as States."* It is no loose unorganized rebellion, having no defined boundary or possession. It has a boundary, marked by lines of bayonets, and which can be crossed only by force— south of this line *is enemy's* territories, because it is claimed and held in possession by an ["]organized, hostile and belligerent power." What right has any one to direct a convention to be held in a sovereign State of this Union, to amend its constitution and prescribe the qualifications of voters? The sovereign power of the nation is lodged in Congress. Yet where is the warrant in the constitution for such sovereign power, much less the Executive, to intermeddle with the domestic institutions of a State, mould its laws, and regulate the elective franchise? It would be rank, dangerous and deplorable usurpation. In reconstruction, therefore, no reform can be effected in the Southern States if they have never left the Union. But reformation *must* be effected; the foundation of their institutions, both political, municipal and social, *must* be broken up and *relaid,* or all our blood and treasure have been spent in vain. This can only be done by treating and holding them as a conquered people. Then all things which we can desire to do, follow with logical and legitimate authority. As conquered territory, Congress would have full power to legislate for them; for the territories are not under the Constitution, except so far as the express power to govern them is given to Congress. They would be held in a territorial condition until they are fit to form State Constitutions, republican in fact, not in form only, and ask admission into the Union as new States. If Congress approve of their Constitutions, and think they have done works meet for repentance, they would be admitted as new States. If their Constitutions are not approved of, they would be sent back, until they have become wise enough so to purge their old laws as to eradicate every despotic and revolutionary principle—until they shall have learned to venerate the Declaration of Independence. I do not touch on the question of negro suffrage. If in the Union, the States have long ago regulated that, and for the Central Government to interfere with it would be mischievous impertinence. If they are to be admitted as new States they must form their own constitutions; and no enabling act could dictate its terms. Congress could prescribe the qualifications of voters while a Territory, or when proceeding to call a convention to form a State government. That is the extent of the power of Congress over the elective franchise, whether in a territorial or state condition. The President has not even this or any other power to meddle in the subject, except by advice to Congress—and they on territories. Congress, to be sure, has some sort of compulsory power by refusing the States admission until they shall have complied with its wishes over this subject. Whether those who have fought our battles should all be allowed to vote, or only those of a paler hue, I leave to be discussed in the future when Congress can take legitimate cognizance of it.

If capital punishments of the most guilty are deemed essential as examples, we have seen that, on the one theory, none of them can be convicted on fair trials—the complicity of the triers would defeat it. But, as a conquered enemy, they could not escape. Their trials would take place by courts-martial. I do not think they could thus be tried for treason; but they could be tried as belligerents, who had forfeited their lives, according to the laws of war. By the strict rights of war, as anciently practiced, the victor held the lives, the liberty and the property of the vanquished at his disposal. The taking of the life, or reduction to bondage of the captives, have long ceased to be practiced in case of ordinary wars; but the abstract right—the *summum jus*—is still recognized in exceptional cases where the cause of the war, or the character of the belligerent, or the safety of the victors justify its exercise. The same thing may be said of the seizure of property on land. Halleck (457) says some modern writers—Hautefeuille, for example—contends for the ancient rule, that private property on land may be subject to seizure. They are undoubtedly correct, with regard to the general abstract right, as deduced from ["]the law of nature and ancient practice." Vattel says: "When, therefore, he has subdued a hostile nation, he undeniably may, in the first place, do himself justice respecting the object which has given rise to the war, and *indemnify himself for the expenses and damages* which he has sustained by it." And at page 369: "A conqueror, who has taken up arms not only against the sovereign but against the nation herself, and whose intention it was to subdue a fierce and savage people, and once for all to reduce an obstinate enemy, such a conqueror may, with justice, lay burdens on the conquered nation, both as a compensation for the expenses of the war, and as a punishment."

I am happy to believe that the Government has come to this conclusion. I cannot otherwise see how Capt. Wirz can be tried by a Court Martial at Washington for acts done by him at Andersonville. He was in no way connected with our military organization, nor did he as a citizen connect himself with our Army so as to bring his case within any of the Acts of Congress. If he committed murder in Georgia, and Georgia was a State in the Union, then he should be tried according to her laws. The General Government has no jurisdiction over such crime, and the trial and execution of this wretch by a United States Military Court would be illegal. But if he was an officer of a belligerent enemy, making war as an independent people, now being conquered, it is a competent, holding them as a conquered foe, to try him for doing acts contrary to the laws of war, and if found guilty to execute or otherwise punish him. As I am sure the loyal man at the head of the Government will not involve the nation in illegal acts and thus set a precedent injurious to our national character, I am glad to believe that hereafter we shall treat the enemy as conquered, and remit their condition and reconstruction to the sovereign power of the nation.

In short, all writers agree that the victor may inflict punishment upon the vanquished enemy, even to the taking of his life, liberty, or the confiscation of all his property; but that this extreme right is never exercised except upon a cruel, barbarous, obstinate, or dangerous foe who has waged an unjust war.

Upon the character of the belligerent, and the justice of the war, and the manner of conducting it, depends our right to take the lives, liberty and property of the belligerent. This war had its origin in treason without one spark of justice. It was prosecuted before notice of it, by robbing our forts and armories, and our navy-yards; by stealing our money from the mints and depositories, and by surrendering our forts and navies by perjurers who had sworn to support the Constitution. In its progress our prisoners, by the authority of their government, were slaughtered in cold blood. Ask Fort Pillow and Fort Wagner. Sixty thousand of our prisoners have been deliberately starved to death because they would not enlist in the rebel armies. The graves at Andersonville have each an accusing tongue. The purpose and avowed object of the enemy "to found an empire whose corner-stone should be slavery," rendered its perpetuity or revival dangerous to human liberty.

Surely, these things are sufficient to justify the exercise of the extreme rights of war—"to execute, to imprison, to confiscate." How many captive enemies it would be proper to execute, as an example to nations, I leave others to judge. I am not fond of sanguinary punishments, but surely some victims must propitiate the manes of our starved, murdered, slaughtered martyrs. A court-martial could do justice according to law.

But we propose to confiscate all the estate of every rebel belligerent whose estate was worth $10,000, or whose land exceeded two hundred acres in quantity. Policy if not justice would require that the poor, the ignorant, and the coerced should be forgiven. They followed the example and teachings of their wealthy and intelligent neighbors. The rebellion would never have originated with them. Fortunately those who would thus escape form a large majority of the people, though possessing but a small portion of the wealth. The proportion of those exempt compared with the punished would be I believe about nine tenths.

There are about six millions of freedmen in the South. The number of acres of land is 465,000,000. Of this, those who own above two hundred acres each number about 70,000 persons, holding, in the aggregate, (together with the States,) about 394,000,000 acres, leaving for all the others below 200 each, about 71,000,000 of acres. By thus forfeiting the estates of the leading rebels, the government would have 394,000,000 of acres, beside their town property, and yet nine-tenths of the people would remain untouched. Divide this land into convenient farms. Give, if you please, forty acres to each adult male freedman. Suppose there are one million of them. That would require 40,000,000 of acres, which, deducted from 394,000,000, leaves three hundred and fifty-four millions of acres for sale. Divide it into suitable farms, and sell it to the highest bidders. I think it, including town property, would average at least ten dollars per acre. That would produce $3,540,000,000—three billions five hundred and forty millions of dollars.

Let that be applied as follows to wit:

1. Invest $300,000,000 in six per cent government bonds, and add the interest semi-annually to the pensions of those who have become entitled by this villainous war.

2. Appropriate $200,000,000 to pay the damages done to loyal men, North and South, by the rebellion.

3. Pay the residue, being $3,040,000,000 towards the payment of the National debt.

What loyal man can object to this? Look around you, and every where behold your neighbors, some with an arm, some with a leg, some with an eye, carried away by rebel bullets. Others horribly mutilated in every form. And yet numerous others wearing the weeds which mark the death of those on whom they leaned for support. Contemplate these monuments of rebel perfidy, and of patriotic suffering, and then say if too much is asked for our valiant soldiers.

Look again, and see loyal men reduced to poverty by the confiscations by the Confederate States, and by the Rebel States—see Union men robbed of their property, and their dwellings laid in ashes by rebel raiders, and say if too much is asked for them. But above all, let us inquire whether imperative duty to the present generation and to posterity, does not command us to compel the wicked enemy to pay the expenses of this unjust war. In ordinary transaction he who raises a false clamor, and prosecutes an unfounded suit, is adjudged to pay the costs on his defeat. We have seen, that, by the law of nations, the vanquished in an unjust war must pay the expense.

Our war debt is estimated at from three to four billions of dollars. In my judgment, when all is funded, and the pensions capitalized, it will reach more than four billions.

| | |
|---|---:|
| The interest at 6 per cent., only (now much more) | $240,000,000 |
| The ordinary expenses of our Government are | 120,000,000 |
| For some years the extraordinary expenses of our army and navy will be | 110,000,000 |
| Total | $470,000,000 |

Four hundred and seventy millions to be raised by taxation—our present heavy taxes will not, in ordinary years, produce but little more than half that sum. Can our people bear double their present taxation? He who unnecessarily causes it will be accursed from generation to generation. It is fashionable to belittle our public debt, lest the people should become alarmed, and political parties should suffer. I have never found it wise to deceive the people. They can always be trusted with the truth. Capitalists will not be affected, for they can not be deceived. Confide in the people, and you will avoid repudiation. Deceive them, and lead them into false measures, and you may produce it.

We pity the poor Englishmen whose national debt and burdensome taxation, we have heard deplored from our childhood. The debt of Great Britain is just about as much as ours, ($4,000,000,000) four billions. But in effect it is but half as large—it bears but three per cent. interest. The current year, the chancellor of the exchequer tells us, the interest was $131,806,990. Ours, when all shall be funded, will be nearly double.

The plan we have proposed would pay at least three-fourths of our debt. The balance could be managed with our present taxation. And yet to think that even that is to be perpetual is sickening. If it is to be doubled, as it must be, if "restoration" instead of "reconstruction" is to prevail, would to God the authors of it could see themselves as an execrating public and posterity will see them.

Our new Doctors of National law, who hold that the "Confederate States" were never out of the Union, but only insurgents and traitors, have become wiser than Grotius, and Puffendorf, and Rutherford, and Vattel, and all modern publicists down to Halleck and Phillimore. They all agree that such a state of things as has existed here for four years is *public war,* and constitutes the parties independent belligerents, subject to the same rules of war as the foreign nations engaged in open warfare.

The learned and able Professor at Law in the Cambridge University, Theophilus Parsons, lately said in a public speech—

"As we are victorious in war we have a right to impose upon the defeated party any terms necessary for our security. This right is perfect. It is not only in itself obvious, but it is asserted in every book on this subject, and is illustrated by all the wars of history. The rebels forced a war upon us; it was a long and costly and bloody war; and now that we have conquered them, we have all the rights which victory confers."

The only argument of the Restorationists is, that the States could not and did not go out of the Union because the Constitution forbids it. By the same reasoning you could prove that no crime ever existed. No man ever committed murder for the law forbids it! He is a shallow reasoner who could make theory overrule fact!

I prefer to believe the ancient and modern publicists, and the learned Professors of legal science, to the extemporized doctrines of modern Sciolists.

If "Restoration," as it is now properly christened, is to prevail over "Reconstruction," will some learned pundit of that school inform me in what condition Slavery and the Slave laws are? I assert that upon that theory not a Slave has been liberated, not a Slave law has been abrogated, but on the "Restoration" the whole Slave code is in legal force. Slavery was protected by our constitution in every State in the Union where it existed. While they remained under that protection no power in the Federal Government could abolish Slavery. If, however, the Confederate States were admitted to be what they claimed, an independent belligerent *de facto,* then the war broke all treaties, compacts and ties between the parties, and slavery was left to its rights under the law of nations. These rights were none; for the law declares that "Man can hold no property in man." (Phillimore, page 316.) Then the laws of war enabled us to declare every bondman free, so long as we held them in military possession. And the conqueror, through Congress, may declare them forever emancipated. But if the States are "States in the Union," then when war ceases they resume their positions with all their privileges untouched. There can be no "mutilated" restoration. That would be the work of Congress alone, and would be "Reconstruction."

While I hear it said everywhere that slavery is dead, I cannot learn who killed it. No thoughtful man has pretended that Lincoln's proclamation, so noble in sentiment, liberated a single slave. It expressly excluded from its operation all those within our lines. No slave within any part of the rebel States in our possession, or in Tennessee, but only those beyond our limits and beyond our power were declared free. So Gen. Smith conquered Canada by a proclamation! The President did not pretend to abrogate the Slave laws of any of the States. "Restoration," therefore, will leave the "Union as it was,["]—a hideous idea. I am aware that a very able and patriotic gentleman, and learned historian, Mr. [*George*] Bancroft, has attempted to place their freedom on different grounds. He says, what is undoubtedly true, that the proclamation of freedom did not free a slave. But he liberates them on feudal principles. Under the feudal system, when a king conquered his enemy, he parceled out his lands and conquered *subjects* among his chief retainers; the lands and serfs were held on condition of fealty and rendering military service when required. If the subordinate chief rebelled, he broke the condition on which he held them, and the lands and serfs became forfeited to the lord paramount. But it did not free the serfs. They, with the manors, were bestowed on other favorites. But the analogy fails in another important respect. The American slave-holder does not hold, by virtue of any grant from any Lord paramount—least of all by a grant from the General Government. Slavery exists by no law of the Union, but simply by local laws, by the laws of the States. Rebellion against the National authority is a breach of no condition of their tenure. It were more analogous to say that rebellion against a State under whose laws they held, might work a forfeiture. But rebellion against neither government would *per se* have any such effect. On whom would the Lord paramount again bestow the slaves? The theory is plausible, but has no solid foundation.

The President says to the rebel States: "Before you can participate in the government you must abolish Slavery and reform your election laws." *That* is the command of a conqueror. That is Reconstruction, not Restoration—

Reconstruction too by assuming the powers of Congress. This theory will lead to melancholy results. Nor can the constitutional amendment abolishing Slavery ever be ratified by three-fourths of the States, if *they* are States to be counted. Bogus Conventions of those States may vote for it. But no Convention honestly and fairly elected will ever do it. The frauds will not permanently avail. The cause of Liberty must rest on a firmer basis. Counterfeit governments, like the Virginia, Louisiana, Tennessee, Mississippi and Arkansas pretenses, will be disregarded by the sober sense of the people, by future law, and by the courts. "Restoration" is replanting the seeds of rebellion, which, within the next quarter of a century, will germinate and produce the same bloody strife which has just ended.

But, it is said, by those who have more sympathy with rebel wives and children than for the widows and orphans of loyal men, that this stripping the rebels of their estates and driving them to exile or to honest labor, would be harsh and severe upon innocent women and children. It may be so; but that is the result of the necessary laws of war. But it is revolutionary, say they. This plan would, no doubt, work a radical reorganization in Southern institutions, habits and manners. It is intended to revolutionize their principles and feelings. This may startle feeble minds and shake weak nerves. So do all great improvements in the political and moral world. It requires a heavy impetus to drive forward a sluggish people. When it was first proposed to free the slaves and arm the blacks, did not half the nation tremble? The prim conservatives, the snobs, and the male waiting-maids in Congress, were in hysterics.

The whole fabric of southern society *must* be changed, and never can it be done if this opportunity is lost. Without this, this Government can never be, as it never has been, a true republic. Heretofore, it had more the features of aristocracy than of democracy. The Southern States have been despotisms, not governments of the people. It is impossible that any practical equality of rights can exist where a few thousand men monopolize the whole landed property. The larger the number of small proprietors the more safe and stable the government. As the landed interest must govern, the more it is subdivided and held by independent owners, the better. What would be the condition of the State of

New York if it were not for her independent yeomanry? She would be overwhelmed and demoralized by the Jews, Milesians and vagabonds of licentious cities. How can republican institutions, free schools, free churches, free social intercourse, exist in a mingled community of nabobs and serfs; of the owners of twenty thousand acre manors with lordly palaces, and the occupants of narrow huts inhabited by "low white trash?" If the South is ever to be made a safe republic, let her lands be cultivated by the toil of the owners or the free labor of intelligent citizens. This must be done even though it drive her nobility into exile. If they go, all the better. It will be hard to persuade the owner of ten thousand acres of land, who drives a coach and four, that he is not degraded by sitting at the same table, or in the same pew, with the embrowned and hard-handed farmer who has himself cultivated his own thriving homestead of 150 acres. This subdivision of the lands will yield ten bales of cotton to one that is made now, and he who produced it will own it and *feel himself a man.*

It is far easier and more beneficial to exile 70,000 proud, bloated and defiant rebels, than to expatriate four millions of laborers, native to the soil and loyal to the Government. This latter scheme was a favorite plan of the Blairs, with which they had for awhile inoculated our late sainted President. But, a single experiment made him discard it and its advisers. Since I have mentioned the Blairs, I may say a word more of these persistent apologists of the South. For, when the virus of Slavery has once entered the veins of the slaveholder, no subsequent effort seems capable of wholly eradicating it. They are a family of considerable power, some merit, of admirable audacity and execrable selfishness. With impetuous alacrity they seize the White House, and hold possession of it, as in the late Administration, until shaken off by the overpowering force of public indignation. Their pernicious counsel had well nigh defeated the reelection of Abraham Lincoln; and if it should prevail with the present administration, pure and patriotic as President Johnson is admitted to be, it will render him the most unpopular Executive—save one—that ever occupied the Presidential chair. But there is no fear of that. He will soon say, as Mr. Lincoln did: "YOUR TIME HAS COME!"

This remodeling the institutions, and reforming the

rooted habits of a proud aristocracy, is undoubtedly a formidable task, requiring the broad mind of enlarged statesmanship, and the firm nerve of the hero. But will not this mighty occasion produce—will not the God of Liberty and order give us—such men? Will not a Romulus, a Lycurgus, a Charlemagne, a Washington arise, whose expansive views will found a free empire, to endure till time shall be no more?

This doctrine of Restoration shocks me. We have a duty to perform which our fathers were incapable of, which will be required at our hands by God and our Country. When our ancestors found a "more perfect Union" necessary, they found it impossible to agree upon a Constitution without tolerating, nay, guaranteeing, Slavery. They were obliged to acquiesce, trusting to time to work a speedy cure, in which they were disappointed. *They* had some excuse, some justification. But we can have none if we do not thoroughly eradicate Slavery and render it forever impossible in this republic. The Slave power made war upon the nation. They declared the "more perfect Union" dissolved—solemnly declared themselves a foreign nation, alien to this republic; for four years were in fact what they claimed to be. We accepted the war which they tendered and treated them as a government capable of making war. We have conquered them, and as a conquered enemy we can give them laws; can abolish all their municipal institutions and form new ones. If we do not make those institutions fit to last through generations of freemen, a heavy curse will be on us. Our glorious, but tainted republic has been born to new life through bloody, agonizing pains. But this frightful "Restoration" has thrown it into "cold obstruction, and to death." If the rebel States have never been out of the Union, any attempt to reform their State institutions, either by Congress or the President, is rank usurpation.

Is then all lost? Is this great conquest to be in vain? That will depend upon the virtue and intelligence of the next Congress. To Congress alone belongs the power of Reconstruction—of giving law to the vanquished. This is expressly declared by the Supreme Court of the United States in the Dorr case, 7th Howard, 42. The Court say, "Under this article of the Constitution (the 4th) it rests with Congress to decide what government is the established one in a State, for the United States guarantees to each a republican form of government," et cetera. But we know how difficult it will be for a majority of Congress to overcome preconceived opinions. Besides, before Congress meets, things will be so inaugurated—precipitated—it will be still more difficult to correct. If a majority of Congress can be found wise and firm enough to declare the Confederate States a conquered enemy, Reconstruction will be easy and legitimate; and the friends of freedom will long rule in the Councils of the Nation. If Restoration prevails the prospect is gloomy, and new "lords will make new laws." The Union party will be overwhelmed. The Copperhead party has become extinct with Secession. But with Secession it will revive. Under "Restoration" every rebel State will send rebels to Congress; and they, with their allies in the North, will control Congress, and occupy the White House. Then restoration of laws and ancient Constitutions will be sure to follow, our public debt will be repudiated, or the rebel National debt will be added to ours, and the people be crushed beneath heavy burdens.

Let us forget all parties, and build on the broad platform of "reconstructing" the government out of the conquered territory converted into new and free States, and admitted into the Union by the sovereign power of Congress, with another plank—"THE PROPERTY OF THE REBELS SHALL PAY OUR NATIONAL DEBT, *and indemnify freed-men and loyal sufferers*—and that under no circumstances will we suffer the National debt to be repudiated, or the interest scaled below the contract rates; nor permit any part of the rebel debt to be assumed by the nation."

Let all who approve of these principles rally with us. Let all others go with Copperheads and rebels. Those will be the opposing parties. Young men, this duty devolves on you. Would to God, if only for that, that I were still in the prime of life, that I might aid you to fight through this last and greatest battle of freedom!

# "A Freedmen's Bureau Officer Reports on Conditions in Mississippi"

## (September 1865)

In March 1865, Congress established the Bureau of Refugees, Freedmen, and Abandoned Lands (popularly known as the Freedmen's Bureau), a large-scale federal agency authorized to supervise and manage the substantial amount of war-torn abandoned territory and to assist refugees and freedpeople during the transition from war to peace and from slavery to freedom. Freedmen's Bureau agents in each state distributed food, helped establish schools, adjudicated legal cases, and assisted former slaves in negotiating labor contracts with their former masters, now their employers. In September 1865, this Freedmen's Bureau officer, stationed in Vicksburg, emphasized the unwillingness of whites to accept emancipation and their determination to keep the blacks as close to slaves as possible.

In the immediate vicinity of our Military Posts; and in locations that can readily be reached by the officers of this Bureau, the citizens are wary of abusing the blacks; they are so because this Bureau has arrested and punished people committing such offences, and the manner in which such cases have been dealt with, has shown people that abuse and imposition will not be tolerated; and that each offence are sure to be punished . . .

But in remote localities those that cannot well be reached by officers of the Bureau the blacks are as badly treated as ever. Colored people often report themselves to the Sub. Commissioners with bruised heads and lacerated backs and ask for redress.

In portions of the northern part of this Dist[rict] the colored people are kept in slavery still.

The white people tell them that they were free during the war but the war is now over and they must go to work again as before.

As to protection from the civil authorities there is no such thing outside of this city. There is not a justice of the peace or any other civil officer in the District, 8 counties of which I have charge that will listen to a complaint from a Negro.

And in the city since the adjudication of these cases has been turned over [to] the mayor the abuse of and impositions upon Negroes are increasing very visibly for the reason that very little if any attention is paid to any complaint of a negro against a white person. Negro testimony is admitted but judging from some of the decisions it would seem it carries very little weight.

In several cases black witnesses have been refused on the grounds that the testimony on the opposite side — white — could not be contravened and it was useless to bring in black witnesses against it . . .

# "FROM EDISTO ISLAND FREEDMEN TO ANDREW JOHNSON"

## (October 28, 1865)

In September 1865, President Johnson announced his policy of restoring land to pardoned former Confederates, overturning a previous policy of leasing forty-acre coastal plots to freedpeople. The following month, a three-man committee wrote on behalf of freedmen on Edisto Island, South Carolina, urging the president to reverse his policy. Freedmen's Bureau commissioner General O. O. Howard was forced to implement the president's policy.

## TO THE PRESIDENT OF THESE UNITED STATES

We the freedmen of Edisto Island South Carolina have learned from you through Major General O O Howard commissioner of the Freedmans Bureau, with deep sorrow and painful hearts of the possibility of government restoring these lands to the former owners. We are well aware of the many perplexing and trying questions that burden your mind and do therefore pray to god (the preserver of all and who has through our Late and beloved President (Lincoln) proclamation and the war made us A free people) that he may guide you in making your decisions and give you that wisdom that cometh from above to settle these great and Important questions for the best interests of the country and the Colored race. Here is where secession was born and nurtured. Here is w[h]ere we have toiled nearly all our lives as slaves and were treated like dumb Driven cattle. This is our home, we have made these lands what they are. We were the only true and Loyal people that were found in possession of these lands. We have been always ready to strike for liberty and humanity yea to fight if needs be to preserve this glorious union. Shall not we who are freedman and have been always true to this Union have the same rights as are enjoyed by others? Have we broken any Law of these United States? Have we forfeited our rights of property in Land? If not then! are not our rights as A free people and good citizens of these United States to be considered before the rights of those who were found in rebellion against this good and just Government (and now being conquered) come (as they seem) with penitent hearts and beg forgiveness for past offences and also ask if their lands cannot be restored to them? Are these rebellious spirits to be reinstated in their *possessions* and we who have been abused and oppressed for many long years not to be allowed the privilege of purchasing land But be subject to the will of these large Land owners? God forbid. Land monopoly is unjurious to the advancement of the course of freedom, and if Government does not make some provision by which we as freedmen can obtain A Homestead, we have not bettered our condition.

We have been encouraged by Government to take up these lands in small tracts, receiving certificates of the same. We have thus far taken sixteen thousand (16000) acres of Land here on this Island. We are ready to pay for this land when Government calls for it and now after what has been done will the good and just government take from us all this right and make us subject to the will of those who have cheated and oppressed us for many years? God Forbid!

We the freedmen of this Island and of the State of South Carolina—Do therefore petition to you as the President of these United States, that some provisions be made by which every colored man can purchase land, and hold it as his own. We wish to have A home if it be but A few acres. Without some provision is made our future is sad to look upon. Yes our situation is dangerous. We therefore look to you in this trying hour as A true friend of the poor and neglected race, for protection and Equal Rights, with the privilege of purchasing A Homestead—A Homestead right here in the heart of South Carolina.

We pray that God will direct your heart in making such provision for us as freedmen which will tend to unite these states together stronger than ever before. May God bless you in the administration of your duties as the President of these United States is the humble prayer of us all.

# ANDREW JOHNSON, "MESSAGE TO CONGRESS"

## (December 4, 1865)

In his first State of the Union message, President Johnson remarked that the Civil War's conclusion had confirmed that secession was null and void and affirmed that his goal was to assist the Southern states in returning to their normal position in the Union as quickly as possible. Johnson reported that he had appointed provisional governors in the former insurgent states and that the courts and postal system now functioned in the former Confederate states. The president noted that Southerners had elected representatives and senators and that it was Congress' prerogative to seat them. Regarding black suffrage, Johnson stated forthrightly that the U.S. Constitution mandated that the states, not the Executive or Legislative branches, determined voting qualifications.

### FELLOW-CITIZENS OF THE SENATE
### AND HOUSE OF REPRESENTATIVES

To express gratitude to God, in the name of the People, for the preservation of the United States, is my first duty in addressing you. Our thoughts next revert to the death of the late President by an act of parricidal treason. The grief of the nation is still fresh; it finds some solace in the consideration that he lived to enjoy the highest proof of its confidence by entering on the renewed term of the Chief Magistracy, to which he had been elected; that he brought the civil war substantially to a close; that his loss was deplored in all parts of the Union; and that foreign nations have rendered justice to his memory. His removal cast upon me a heavier weight of cares than ever devolved upon any one of his predecessors. To fulfill my trust I need the support and confidence of all who are associated with me in the various departments of Government, and the support and confidence of the people. There is but one way in which I can hope to gain their necessary aid; it is, to state with frankness the principles which guide my conduct, and their application to the present state of affairs, well aware that the efficiency of my labors will, in a great measure, depend on your and their undivided approbation.

The Union of the United States of America was intended by its authors to last as long as the States themselves shall last. "THE UNION SHALL BE PERPETUAL" are the words of the Confederation. "TO FORM A MORE PERFECT UNION," by an ordinance of the people of the United States, is the declared purpose of the Constitution. The hand of Divine Providence was never more plainly visible in the affairs of men than in the framing and the adopting of that instrument. It is, beyond comparison, the greatest event in American history; and indeed is it not, of all events in modern times, the most pregnant with consequences for every people of the earth? The members of the Convention which prepared it, brought to their work the experience of the Confederation, of their several States, and of other Republican Governments, old and new; but they needed and they obtained a wisdom superior to experience. And when for its validity it required the approval of a people that occupied a large part of a continent and acted separately in many distinct conventions, what is more wonderful than that, after earnest contention and long discussion, all feelings and all opinions were ultimately drawn in one way to its support?

The Constitution to which life was thus imparted contains within itself ample resources for its own preservation. It has power to enforce the laws, punish treason, and ensure domestic tranquillity. In case of the usurpation of the Government of a State by one man, or an oligarchy, it becomes a duty of the United States to make good the guarantee to that State of a republican form of government, and so to maintain the homogeneousness of all. Does the lapse of time reveal defects? A simple mode of amendment is provided in the Constitution itself, so that its conditions can always be made to conform to the requirements of advancing civilization. No room is allowed even for the thought of a possibility of its coming to an end. And these powers of self-preservation have always been asserted in their complete integrity by every patriotic Chief Magistrate—by Jefferson and Jackson, not less than by Washington and Madison. The parting advice of the Father of his Country, while yet President, to the people of the United States, was, that "the free Constitution, which was the work of their hands, might be sacredly maintained;" and the inaugural words of President Jefferson held up "the preservation of the General Government, in its constitutional vigor, as the sheet anchor of our peace at home and safety abroad." The Constitution is the work of "the People of the United States," and it should be as indestructible as the people.

It is not strange that the framers of the Constitution, which had no model in the past, should not have fully comprehended the excellence of their own work. Fresh from a struggle against arbitrary power, many patriots suffered from harassing fears of an absorption of the State Governments by the General Government, and many from a dread that the States would break away from their orbits. But the very greatness of our country should allay the apprehension of encroachments by the General Government. The subjects that come unquestionably within its jurisdiction are so numerous, that it must ever naturally refuse to be embarrassed by questions that lie beyond it. Were it otherwise, the Executive would sink beneath the burden; the channels of justice would be choked; legislation would be obstructed by excess; so that there is a greater temptation to exercise some of the functions of the General Government through the States than to trespass on their rightful sphere. "The absolute acquiescence in the decisions of the majority" was, at the beginning of the century, enforced by Jefferson "as the vital principle of republics," and the events of the last four years have established, we will hope forever, that there lies no appeal to force.

The maintenance of the Union brings with it "the support of the State Governments in all their rights;" but it is not one of the rights of any State Government to renounce its own place in the Union, or to nullify the laws of the Union. The largest liberty is to be maintained in the discussion of the acts of the Federal Government; but there is no appeal from its laws, except to the various branches of that

Government itself, or to the people, who grant to the members of the Legislative and of the Executive Departments no tenure but a limited one, and in that manner always retain the powers of redress.

"The sovereignty of the States" is the language of the Confederacy, and not the language of the Constitution. The latter contains the emphatic words: "The Constitution, and the laws of the United States which shall be made in pursuance thereof, and all treaties made or which shall be made under the authority of the United States, shall be the supreme law of the land; and the judges in every State shall be bound thereby, anything in the constitution or laws of any State to the contrary notwithstanding."

Certainly the Government of the United States is a limited government; and so is every State government a limited government. With us, this idea of limitation spreads through every form of administration, general, State, and municipal, and rests on the great distinguishing principle of the recognition of the rights of man. The ancient republics absorbed the individual in the State, prescribed his religion, and controlled his activity. The American system rests on the assertion of the equal right of every man to life, liberty, and the pursuit of happiness; to freedom of conscience, to the culture and exercise of all his faculties. As a consequence, the State Government is limited, as to the General Government in the interest of Union, as to the individual citizen in the interest of freedom.

States with proper limitations of power, are essential to the existence of the Constitution of the United States. At the very commencement, when we assumed a place among the Powers of the earth, the Declaration of Independence was adopted by States; so also were the Articles of Confederation; and when "the People of the United States" ordained and established the Constitution, it was the assent of the States, one by one, which gave it vitality. In the event, too, of any amendment to the Constitution, the proposition of Congress needs the confirmation of States. Without States, one great branch of the legislative government would be wanting. And, if we look beyond the letter of the Constitution to the character of our country, its capacity for comprehending within its jurisdiction a vast continental empire is due to the system of States. The best security for the perpetual existence of the States is the "supreme authority" of the Constitution of the United States. The perpetuity of the Constitution brings with it the perpetuity of the States; their mutual relation makes us what we are, and in our political system their connexion is indissoluble. The whole cannot exist without the parts, nor the parts without the whole. So long as the Constitution of the United States endures, the States will endure; the destruction of the one is the destruction of the other; the preservation of the one is the preservation of the other. . . .

I found the States suffering from the effects of a civil war. Resistance to the General Government appeared to have exhausted itself. The United States had recovered possession of their forts and arsenals; and their armies were in the occupation of every State which had attempted to secede. Whether the territory within the limits of those States should be held as conquered territory, under military authority emanating from the President as the head of the army, was the first question that presented itself for decision.

Now, military governments, established for an indefinite period, would have offered no security for the early suppression of discontent; would have divided the people into the vanquishers and the vanquished; and would have envenomed hatred, rather than have restored affection. Once established, no precise limit to their continuance was conceivable. They would have occasioned an incalculable and exhausting expense. Peaceful emigration to and from that portion of the country is one of the best means that can be thought of for the restoration of harmony; and that emigration would have been prevented; for what emigrant from abroad, what industrious citizen at home, would place himself willingly under military rule? The chief persons who would have followed in the train of the army would have been dependents on the General Government, or men who expected profit from the miseries of their erring fellow-citizens. The powers of patronage and rule which would have been exercised, under the President, over a vast, and populous, and naturally wealthy region, are greater than, unless under extreme necessity, I should be willing to entrust to any one man; they are such as, for myself, I could never, unless on occasions of great emergency, consent to exercise. The wilful use of such powers, if continued through a period of years, would have endangered the purity of the general administration and the liberties of the States which remained loyal.

Besides, the policy of military rule over a conquered territory would have implied that the States whose inhabitants may have taken part in the rebellion had, by the act of those inhabitants, ceased to exist. But the true theory is, that all pretended acts of secession were, from the beginning, null and void. The States cannot commit treason, nor screen the individual citizens who may have committed treason, any more than they can make valid treaties or engage in lawful commerce with any foreign Power. The States attempting to secede placed themselves in a condition where their vitality was impaired, but not extinguished—their functions suspended, but not destroyed.

But if any State neglects or refuses to perform its offices, there is the more need that the General Government should maintain all its authority, and, as soon as practicable, resume the exercise of all its functions. On this principle I have acted, and have gradually and quietly, and by almost imperceptible steps, sought to restore the rightful energy of the General Government and of the States. To that end, Provisional Governors have been appointed for the States, Conventions called, Governors elected, Legislatures assembled, and Senators and Representatives chosen to the Congress of the United States. At the same time, the Courts of the United States, as far as could be done, have been re-opened, so that the laws of the United States may be enforced through their agency. The blockade has been removed and the custom-houses re-established in ports of entry, so that the revenue of the United States may be collected. The Post Office Department renews its ceaseless activity, and the General Government is thereby enabled to communicate promptly with its officers and agents. The courts bring security to persons and property; the opening of the ports invites the restoration of industry and commerce; the post office renews the facilities of social intercourse and of business. And is it not happy for us all, that the restoration of each one of these functions of the General Government brings with it a blessing to the States over which they are extended? Is it not a sure promise of harmony and renewed attachment to the Union that, after all that has happened, the return of the General Government is known only as a beneficence?

I know very well that this policy is attended with some risk; that for its success it requires at least the acquiescence of the States which it concerns; that it implies an invitation to those States, by renewing their allegiance to the United States, to resume their functions as States of the Union. But it is a risk that must be taken; in the choice of difficulties, it is the smallest risk; and to diminish, and, if possible, to remove all danger, I have felt it incumbent on me to assert one other power of the General Government—the power of pardon. As no State can throw a defence over the crime of treason, the power of pardon is exclusively vested in the Executive Government of the United States. In exercising that power, I have taken every precaution to connect it with the clearest recognition of the binding force of the laws of the United States, and an unqualified acknowledgment of the great social change of condition in regard to slavery which has grown out of the war.

The next step which I have taken to restore the constitutional relations of the States, has been an invitation to them to participate in the high office of amending the Constitution. Every patriot must wish for a general amnesty at the earliest epoch consistent with public safety. For this great end there is need of a concurrence of all opinions, and the spirit of mutual conciliation. All parties in the late terrible conflict must work together in harmony. It is not too much to ask, in the name of the whole people, that, on the one side, the plan of restoration shall proceed in conformity with a willingness to cast the disorders of the past into oblivion; and that, on the other, the evidence of sincerity in the future maintenance of the Union shall be put beyond any doubt by the ratification of the proposed amendment to the Constitution, which provides for the abolition of slavery forever within the limits of our country. So long as the adoption of this amendment is delayed, so long will doubt, and jealousy, and uncertainty prevail. This is the measure which will efface the sad memory of the past; this is the measure which will most certainly call population, and capital, and security to those parts of the Union that need them most. Indeed, it is not too much to ask of the

States which are now resuming their places in the family of the Union to give this pledge of perpetual loyalty and peace. Until it is done, the past, however much we may desire it, will not be forgotten. The adoption of the amendment reunites us beyond all power of disruption. It heals the wound that is still imperfectly closed; it removes slavery, the element which has so long perplexed and divided the country; it makes of us once more a united people, renewed and strengthened, bound more than ever to mutual affection and support.

The amendment to the Constitution being adopted, it would remain for the States, whose powers have been so long in abeyance, to resume their places in the two branches of the National Legislature, and thereby complete the work of restoration. Here it is for you, fellow-citizens of the Senate, and for you, fellow-citizens of the House of Representatives, to judge, each of you for yourselves, of the elections, returns, and qualifications of your own members.

The full assertion of the powers of the General Government requires the holding of Circuit Courts of the United States within the districts where their authority has been interrupted. In the present posture of our public affairs, strong objections have been urged to holding those courts in any of the States where the rebellion has existed; and it was ascertained, by inquiry, that the Circuit Court of the United States would not be held within the District of Virginia during the autumn or early winter, nor until Congress should have "an opportunity to consider and act on the whole subject." To your deliberations the restoration of this branch of the civil authority of the United States is therefore necessarily referred, with the hope that early provision will be made for the resumption of all its functions. It is manifest that treason, most flagrant in character, has been committed. Persons who are charged with its commission should have fair and impartial trials in the highest civil tribunals of the country, in order that the Constitution and the laws may be fully vindicated; the truth clearly established and affirmed that treason is a crime, that traitors should be punished and the offence made infamous; and, at the same time, that the question may be judicially settled, finally and forever, that no State of its own will has the right to renounce its place in the Union.

The relations of the General Government towards the four millions of inhabitants whom the war has called into freedom, have engaged my most serious consideration. On the propriety of attempting to make the freedmen electors by the proclamation of the Executive, I took for my counsel the Constitution itself, the interpretations of that instrument by its authors and their contemporaries, and recent legislation by Congress. When, at the first movement towards independence, the Congress of the United States instructed the several States to institute governments of their own, they left each State to decide for itself the conditions for the enjoyment of the elective franchise. During the period of the Confederacy, there continued to exist a very great diversity in the qualifications of electors in the several States; and even within a State a distinction of qualifications prevailed with regard to the officers who were to be chosen. The Constitution of the United States recognises these diversities when it enjoins that, in the choice of members of the House of Representatives of the United States, "the electors in each State shall have the qualifications requisite for electors of the most numerous branch of the State Legislature." After the formation of the Constitution, it remained, as before, the uniform usage for each State to enlarge the body of its electors, according to its own judgment; and, under this system, one State after another has proceeded to increase the number of its electors, until now universal suffrage, or something very near it, is the general rule. So fixed was this reservation of power in the habits of the people, and so unquestioned has been the interpretation of the Constitution, that during the civil war the late President never harbored the purpose—certainly never avowed the purpose—of disregarding it; and in the acts of Congress, during that period, nothing can be found which, during the continuance of hostilities, much less after their close, would have sanctioned any departure by the Executive from a policy which has so uniformly obtained. Moreover, a concession of the elective franchise to the freedmen, by act of the President of the United States, must have been extended to all colored men, wherever found, and so must have established a change of suffrage in the Northern, Middle, and Western States, not less than in the Southern and Southwestern. Such an act would have created a new class of voters, and would have been an assumption of power by the President which nothing in the Constitution or laws of the United States would have warranted.

On the other hand, every danger of conflict is avoided when the settlement of the question is referred to the several States. They can, each for itself, decide on the measure, and whether it is to be adopted at once and absolutely, or introduced gradually and with conditions. In my judgment, the freedmen, if they show patience and manly virtues, will sooner obtain a participation in the elective franchise through the States than through the General Government, even if it had power to intervene. When the tumult of emotions that have been raised by the suddenness of the social change shall have subsided, it may prove that they will receive the kindliest usage from some of those on whom they have heretofore most closely depended.

But while I have no doubt that now, after the close of the war, it is not competent for the General Government to extend the elective franchise in the several States, it is equally clear that good faith requires the security of the freedmen in their liberty and their property, their right to labor, and their right to claim the just return of their labor. I cannot too strongly urge a dispassionate treatment of this subject, which should be carefully kept aloof from all party strife. We must equally avoid hasty assumptions of any natural impossibility for the two races to live side by side, in a state of mutual benefit and good will. The experiment involves us in no inconsistency; let us then, go on and make that experiment in good faith, and not be too easily disheartened. The country is in need of labor, and the freedmen are in need of employment, culture, and protection. While their right of voluntary migration and expatriation is not to be questioned, I would not advise their forced removal and colonization. Let us rather encourage them to honorable and useful industry, where it may be beneficial to themselves and to the country; and, instead of hasty anticipations of the certainty of failure, let there be nothing wanting to the fair trial of the experiment. The change in their condition is the substitution of labor by contract for the status of slavery. The freedman cannot fairly be accused of unwillingness to work, so long as a doubt remains about his freedom of choice in his pursuits, and the certainty of his recovering his stipulated wages. In this the interests of the employer and the employed coincide. The employer desires in his workmen spirit and alacrity, and these can be permanently secured in no other way. And if the one ought to be able to enforce the contract, so ought the other. The public interest will be best promoted, if the several States will provide adequate protection and remedies for the freedmen. Until this is in some way accomplished, there is no chance for the advantageous use of their labor; and the blame of ill-success will not rest on them.

I know that sincere philanthropy is earnest for the immediate realization of its remotest aims; but time is always an element in reform. It is one of the greatest acts on record to have brought four millions of people into freedom. The career of free industry must be fairly opened to them; and then their future prosperity and condition must, after all, rest mainly on themselves. If they fail, and so perish away, let us be careful that the failure shall not be attributable to any denial of justice. In all that relates to the destiny of the freedmen, we need not be too anxious to read the future; many incidents which, from a speculative point of view, might raise alarm, will quietly settle themselves.

Now that slavery is at an end or near its end, the greatness of its evil, in the point of view of public economy, becomes more and more apparent. Slavery was essentially a monopoly of labor, and as such locked the States where it prevailed against the incoming of free industry. Where labor was the property of the capitalist, the white man was excluded from employment, or had but the second best chance of finding it; and the foreign emigrant turned away from the region where his condition would be so precarious. With the destruction of the monopoly, free labor will hasten from all parts of the civilized world to assist in developing various and immeasurable resources which have hitherto lain dormant. The eight or nine States nearest the Gulf of Mexico have a soil of exuberant fertility, a climate friendly to long life, and can sustain a denser population than is found as yet in any part of our country. And the future influx of population to them will be mainly from the North, or from the most cultivated nations in Europe. From the sufferings that have attended them during our late struggle, let us look away to the future, which is sure to be laden for them with greater prosperity than has ever before been known. The removal of the monopoly of slave labor is a pledge that those regions will be peopled by a numerous and enterprising population, which will vie with any in the Union in compactness, inventive genius, wealth, and industry.

Our Government springs from and was made for the people—not the people for the Government. To them it owes allegiance; from them it must derive its courage, strength, and wisdom. But, while the Government is thus bound to defer to the people, from whom it derives its existence, it should, from the very consideration of its origin, be strong in its power of resistance to the establishment of inequalities. Monopolies, perpetuities, and class legislation, are contrary to the genius of free government, and ought not to be allowed. Here, there is no room for favored classes or monopolies[;] the principle of our Government is that of equal laws and freedom of industry. Wherever monopoly attains a foothold, it is sure to be a source of danger, discord, and trouble. We shall but fulfil our duties as legislators by according "equal and exact justice to all men," special privileges to none. The Government is subordinate to the people; but, as the agent and representative of the people, it must be held superior to monopolies, which, in themselves, ought never to be granted, and which, where they exist, must be subordinate and yield to the Government....

Our domestic contest, now happily ended, has left some traces in our relations with one at least of the great maritime Powers. The formal accordance of belligerent rights to the insurgent States was unprecedented, and has not been justified by the issue. But in the systems of neutrality pursued by the Powers which made that concession, there was a marked difference. The materials of war for the insurgent States were furnished, in a great measure, from the workshops of Great Britain; and British ships, manned by British subjects, and prepared for receiving British armaments, sallied from the ports of Great Britain to make war on American commerce, under the shelter of a commission from the insurgent States. These ships, having once escaped from British ports, ever afterwards entered them in every part of the world, to refit, and so to renew their depredations. The consequences of this conduct were most disastrous to the States then in rebellion, increasing their desolation and misery by the prolongation of our civil contest. It had, moreover, the effect, to a great extent, to drive the American flag from the sea, and to transfer much of our shipping and our commerce to the very Power whose subjects had created the necessity for such a change. These events took place before I was called to the administration of the Government. The sincere desire for peace by which I am animated led me to approve the proposal, already made, to submit the questions which had thus arisen between the countries to arbitration. These questions are of such moment that they must have commanded the attention of the great Powers, and are so interwoven with the peace and interests of every one of them as to have ensured an impartial decision. I regret to inform you that Great Britain declined the arbitration, but, on the other hand, invited us to the formation of a joint commission to settle mutual claims between the two countries, from which those for the depredations before mentioned should be excluded. The proposition, in that very unsatisfactory form, has been declined.

The United States did not present the subject as an impeachment of the good faith of a Power which was professing the most friendly dispositions, but as involving questions of public law, of which the settlement is essential to the peace of nations; and, though pecuniary reparation to their injured citizens would have followed incidentally on a decision against Great Britain, such compensation was not their primary object. They had a higher motive, and it was in the interests of peace and justice to establish important principles of international law. The correspondence will be placed before you. The ground on which the British Minister rests his justification is, substantially, that the municipal law of a nation, and the domestic interpretations of that law, are the measure of its duty as a neutral; and I feel bound to declare my opinion, before you and before the world, that that justification cannot be sustained before the tribunal of nations. At the same time I do not advise to any present attempt at redress by acts of legislation. For the future, friendship between the two countries must rest on the basis of mutual justice.

From the moment of the establishment of our free Constitution, the civilized world has been convulsed by revolutions in the interests of democracy or of monarchy; but through all those revolutions the United States have wisely and firmly refused to become propagandists of republicanism. It is the only government suited to our condition; but we have never sought to impose it on others; and we have consistently followed the advice of Washington to recommend it only by the careful preservation and prudent use of the blessing. During all the intervening period the policy of European Powers and of the United States has, on the whole, been harmonious. Twice, indeed, rumors of the invasion of some parts of America, in the interest of monarchy, have prevailed; twice my predecessors have had occasion to announce the views of this nation in respect to such interference. On both occasions the remonstrance of the United States was respected, from a deep conviction, on the part of European Governments, that the system of non-interference and mutual abstinence from propagandism was the true rule for the two hemispheres. Since those times we have advanced in wealth and power; but we retain the same purpose to leave the nations of Europe to choose their own dynasties and form their own systems of government. This consistent moderation may justly demand a corresponding moderation. We should regard it as a great calamity to ourselves, to the cause of good government, and to the peace of the world, should any European Power challenge the American people, as it were, to the defence of republicanism against foreign interference. We cannot foresee and are unwilling to consider what opportunities might present themselves, what combinations might offer to protect ourselves against designs inimical to our form of government. The United States desire to act in the future as they have ever acted heretofore; they never will be driven from that course but by the aggression of European Powers; and we rely on the wisdom and justice of those Powers to respect the system of non-interference which has so long been sanctioned by time, and which, by its good results, has approved itself to both continents.

The correspondence between the United States and France, in reference to questions which have become subjects of discussion between the two Governments, will, at a proper time, be laid before Congress.

When, on the organization of our Government, under the Constitution, the President of the United States delivered his inaugural address to the two Houses of Congress, he said to them, and through them to the country and to mankind, that "the preservation of the sacred fire of liberty and the destiny of the republican model of government are justly considered as deeply, perhaps as finally staked on the experiment intrusted to the American people." And the House of Representatives answered Washington by the voice of Madison: "We adore the invisible hand which has led the American people, through so many difficulties, to cherish a conscious responsibility for the destiny of republican liberty." More than seventy-six years have glided away since these words were spoken; the United States have passed through severer trials than were foreseen; and now, at this new epoch in our existence as one nation, with our Union purified by sorrows, and strengthened by conflict, and established by the virtue of the people, the greatness of the occasion invites us once more to repeat, with solemnity, the pledges of our fathers to hold ourselves answerable before our fellow-men for the success of the republican form of government. Experience has proved its sufficiency in peace and in war; it has vindicated its authority through dangers, and afflictions, and sudden and terrible emergencies, which would have crushed any system that had been less firmly fixed in the heart of the people. At the inauguration of Washington the foreign relations of the country were few, and its trade was repressed by hostile regulations; now all the civilized nations of the globe welcome our commerce, and their Governments profess towards us amity. Then our country felt its way hesitatingly along an untried path, with States so little bound together by rapid means of communication as to be hardly known to one another, and with historic traditions extending over very few years; now intercourse between the States is swift and intimate; the experience of centuries has been crowded into a few generations, and has created an intense, indestructible nationality. Then our jurisdiction did not reach beyond the inconvenient boundaries of the territory which had achieved independence; now, through cessions of lands, first colonized by Spain and France, the country has acquired a more complex character, and has for its natural limits the chain of

Lakes, the Gulf of Mexico, and on the east and the west the two great oceans. Other nations were wasted by civil wars for ages before they could establish for themselves the necessary degree of unity; the latent conviction that our form of government is the best ever known to the world, has enabled us to emerge from civil war within four years, with a complete vindication of the constitutional authority of the General Government, and with our local liberties and State institutions unimpaired. The throngs of emigrants that crowd to our shores are witnesses of the confidence of all peoples in our permanence. Here is the great land of free labor, where industry is blessed with unexampled rewards, and the bread of the workingman is sweetened by the consciousness that the cause of the country "is his own cause, his own safety, his own dignity." Here every one enjoys the free use of his faculties and the choice of activity as a natural right. Here, under the combined influence of a fruitful soil, genial climes, and happy institutions, population has increased fifteen-fold within a century. Here, through the easy development of boundless resources, wealth has increased with two-fold greater rapidity than numbers, so that we have become secure against the financial vicissitudes of other countries, and, alike in business and in opinion, are self-centered and truly independent. Here more and more care is given to provide education for every one born on our soil. Here religion, released from political connection with the civil government, refuses to subserve the craft of statesmen, and becomes, in its independence, the spiritual life of the people. Here toleration is extended to every opinion, in the quiet certainty that truth needs only a fair field to secure the victory. Here the human mind goes forth unshackled in the pursuit of science, to collect stores of knowledge and acquire an ever-increasing mastery over the forces of nature. Here the national domain is offered and held in millions of separate freeholds, so that our fellow-citizens, beyond the occupants of any other part of the earth, constitute in reality a people. Here exists the democratic form of government; and that form of government, by the confession of European statesmen, "gives a power of which no other form is capable, because it incorporates every man with the State, and arouses every thing that belongs to the soul."

Where, in past history, does a parallel exist to the public happiness which is within the reach of the people of the United States? Where, in any part of the globe, can institutions be found so suited to their habits or so entitled to their love as their own free Constitution? Every one of them, then, in whatever part of the land he has his home, must wish its perpetuity. Who of them will not now acknowledge, in the words of Washington, that "every step by which the people of the United States have advanced to the character of an independent nation, seems to have been distinguished by some token of Providential agency"? Who will not join with me in the prayer, that the invisible hand which has led us through the clouds that gloomed around our path, will so guide us onward to a perfect restoration of fraternal affection, that we of this day may be able to transmit our great inheritance, of State Governments in all their rights, of the General Government in its whole constitutional vigor, to our posterity, and they to theirs through countless generations?

# AMENDMENT 13

## *(Ratified December 6, 1865)*

Lincoln went to his grave hopeful that slavery finally would be abolished by Constitutional amendment. The amendment passed Congress on January 31, 1865, but the states had not ratified it when Johnson, who strongly favored it, assumed office in April. The new president used his influence with white Southerners to assent to the amendment, which was ratified on December 6, 1865. Significantly, eight of the Southern states that helped to ratify the amendment had not yet been restored to the Union, their delegations not yet represented in Congress.

*Section 1.* Neither slavery nor involuntary servitude, except as a punishment for crime whereof the party shall have been duly convicted, shall exist within the United States, or any place subject to their jurisdiction.

*Section 2.* Congress shall have power to enforce this article by appropriate legislation.

# "REPORT OF CARL SCHURZ ON THE STATES OF SOUTH CAROLINA, GEORGIA, ALABAMA, MISSISSIPPI, AND LOUISIANA"

## (December 19, 1865)

In July 1865, Carl Schurz (1829–1906) the influential German-American leader, general, and later Republican U.S. Senator and cabinet member, began an eleven-week tour of the South at President Johnson's behest. The president asked Schurz to report on conditions, especially in the Gulf States, hopeful that his observations would support Johnson's mild Reconstruction program. Instead, the lengthy and widely circulated report proved devastatingly critical of former Confederates, who, according to Schurz, remained disloyal and sought to retain the spirit if not the letter of slavery as an economic and social system. Though Johnson recruited other observers to write laudatory reports on Southern affairs, Schurz's account proved damaging. At every opportunity, Radical Republicans cited it against Johnson.

Sir: When you did me the honor of selecting me for a mission to the States lately in rebellion, for the purpose of inquiring into the existing condition of things, of laying before you whatever information of importance I might gather, and of suggesting to you such measures as my observations would lead me to believe advisable, I accepted the trust with a profound sense of the responsibility connected with the performance of the task. The views I entertained at the time, I had communicated to you in frequent letters and conversations. I would not have accepted the mission, had I not felt that whatever preconceived opinions

I might carry with me to the south, I should be ready to abandon or modify, as my perception of facts and circumstances might command their abandonment or modification. You informed me that your "policy of reconstruction" was merely experimental, and that you would change it if the experiment did not lead to satisfactory results. To aid you in forming your conclusions upon this point I understood to be the object of my mission, and this understanding was in perfect accordance with the written instructions I received through the Secretary of War.

These instructions confined my mission to the States of South Carolina, Georgia, Alabama, Mississippi, and the department of the Gulf. I informed you, before leaving the north, that I could not well devote more than three months to the duties imposed upon me, and that space of time proved sufficient for me to visit all the States above enumerated, except Texas. I landed at Hilton Head, South Carolina, on July 15, visited Beaufort, Charleston, Orangeburg, and Columbia, returned to Charleston and Hilton Head; thence I went to Savannah, traversed the State of Georgia, visiting Augusta, Atlanta, Macon, Milledgeville, and Columbus; went through Alabama, by way of Opelika, Montgomery, Selma, and Demopolis, and through Mississippi, by way of Meridian, Jackson, and Vicksburg; then descended the Mississippi to New Orleans, touching at Natchez; from New Orleans I visited Mobile, Alabama, and the Teche country, in Louisiana, and then spent again some days at Natchez and Vicksburg, on my way to the north. These are the outlines of my journey.

Before laying the results of my observations before you, it is proper that I should state the *modus operandi* by which I obtained information and formed my conclusions. Wherever I went I sought interviews with persons who might be presumed to represent the opinions, or to have influence upon the conduct, of their neighbors; I had thus frequent meetings with individuals belonging to the different classes of society from the highest to the lowest; in the cities as well as on the roads and steamboats I had many opportunities to converse not only with inhabitants of the adjacent country, but with persons coming from districts which I was not able to visit; and finally I compared the impressions thus received with the experience of the military and civil officers of the government stationed in that country, as well as of other reliable Union men to whom a longer residence on the spot and a more varied intercourse with the people had given better facilities of local observation than my circumstances permitted me to enjoy. When practicable I procured statements of their views and experience in writing as well as copies of official or private reports they had received from their subordinates or other persons. It was not expected of me that I should take formal testimony, and, indeed, such an operation would have required more time than I was able to devote to it.

My facilities for obtaining information were not equally extensive in the different States I visited. As they naturally depended somewhat upon the time the military had had to occupy and explore the country, as well as upon the progressive development of things generally, they improved from day to day as I went on, and were best in the States I visited last. It is owing to this circumstance that I cannot give as detailed an account of the condition of things in South Carolina and Georgia as I am able to give with regard to Louisiana and Mississippi.

Instead of describing the experiences of my journey in chronological order, which would lead to endless repetitions and a confused mingling of the different subjects under consideration, I propose to arrange my observations under different heads according to the subject matter. It is true, not all that can be said of the people of one State will apply with equal force to the people of another; but it will be easy to make the necessary distinctions when in the course of this report they become of any importance. I beg to be understood when using, for the sake of brevity, the term "the southern people," as meaning only the people of the States I have visited.

## CONDITION OF THINGS IMMEDIATELY AFTER THE CLOSE OF THE WAR.

In the development of the popular spirit in the south since the close of the war two well-marked periods can be distinguished. The first commences with the sudden collapse of

the confederacy and the dispersion of its armies, and the
second with the first proclamation indicating the "reconstruction policy" of the government. Of the first period I
can state the characteristic features only from the accounts
I received, partly from Unionists who were then living in
the south, partly from persons that had participated in the
rebellion. When the news of Lee's and Johnston's surren-
ders burst upon the southern country the general consternation was extreme. People held their breath, indulging in
the wildest apprehensions as to what was now to come.
Men who had occupied positions under the confederate
government, or were otherwise compromised in the rebellion, ran before the federal columns as they advanced and
spread out to occupy the country, from village to village,
from plantation to plantation, hardly knowing whether
they wanted to escape or not. Others remained at their
homes yielding themselves up to their fate. Prominent
Unionists told me that persons who for four years had
scorned to recognize them on the street approached them
with smiling faces and both hands extended. Men of standing in the political world expressed serious doubts as to
whether the rebel States would ever again occupy their position as States in the Union, or be governed as conquered
provinces. The public mind was so despondent that if readmission at some future time under whatever conditions had
been promised, it would then have been looked upon as a
favor. The most uncompromising rebels prepared for leaving the country. The masses remained in a state of fearful
expectancy.

This applies especially to those parts of the country
which were within immediate reach of our armies or had
previously been touched by the war. Where Union soldiers
had never been seen and none were near, people were at
first hardly aware of the magnitude of the catastrophe, and
strove to continue in their old ways of living.

Such was, according to the accounts I received, the character of that first period. The worst apprehensions were
gradually relieved as day after day went by without bringing the disasters and inflictions which had been vaguely
anticipated, until at last the appearance of the North Carolina proclamation substituted new hopes for them. The development of this second period I was called upon to

observe on the spot, and it forms the main subject of this report.

## RETURNING LOYALTY.

It is a well-known fact that in the States south of Tennessee and North Carolina the number of white Unionists who during the war actively aided the government, or at least openly professed their attachment to the cause of the Union, was very small. In none of those States were they strong enough to exercise any decisive influence upon the action of the people, not even in Louisiana, unless vigorously supported by the power of the general government. But the white people at large being, under certain conditions, charged with taking the preliminaries of "reconstruction" into their hands, the success of the experiment depends upon the spirit and attitude of those who either attached themselves to the secession cause from the beginning, or, entertaining originally opposite views, at least followed its fortunes from the time that their States had declared their separation from the Union.

The first southern men of this class with whom I came into contact immediately after my arrival in South Carolina expressed their sentiments almost literally in the following language: "We acknowledge ourselves beaten, and we are ready to submit to the results of the war. The war has practically decided that no State shall secede and that the slaves are emancipated. We cannot be expected at once to give up our principles and convictions of right, but we accept facts as they are, and desire to be reinstated as soon as possible in the enjoyment and exercise of our political rights." This declaration was repeated to me hundreds of times in every State I visited, with some variations of language, according to the different ways of thinking or the frankness or reserve of the different speakers. Some said nothing of adhering to their old principles and convictions of right; others still argued against the constitutionality of coercion and of the emancipation proclamation; others expressed their determination to become good citizens, in strong language, and urged with equal emphasis the necessity of their home institutions being at once left to their own control; others would go so far as to say they were glad that the war was ended, and they had never had any confidence in the confederacy; others protested that they had been opposed to secession until their States went out, and then yielded to the current of events; some would give me to understand that they had always been good Union men at heart, and rejoiced that the war had terminated in favor of the national cause, but in most cases such a sentiment was expressed only in a whisper; others again would grumblingly insist upon the restoration of their "rights," as if they had done no wrong, and indicated plainly that they would submit only to what they could not resist and as long as they could not resist it. Such were the definitions of "returning loyalty" I received from the mouths of a large number of individuals intelligent enough to appreciate the meaning of the expressions they used. I found a great many whose manner of speaking showed that they did not understand the circumstances under which they lived, and had no settled opinions at all except on matters immediately touching their nearest interests.

Upon the ground of these declarations, and other evidence gathered in the course of my observations, I may group the southern people into four classes, each of which exercises an influence upon the development of things in that section:

1. Those who, although having yielded submission to the national government only when obliged to do so, have a clear perception of the irreversible changes produced by the war, and honestly endeavor to accommodate themselves to the new order of things. Many of them are not free from traditional prejudice but open to conviction, and may be expected to act in good faith whatever they do. This class is composed, in its majority, of persons of mature age—planters, merchants, and professional men; some of them are active in the reconstruction movement, but boldness and energy are, with a few individual exceptions, not among their distinguishing qualities.

2. Those whose principal object is to have the States without delay restored to their position and influence in the Union and the people of the States to the absolute control of their home concerns. They are ready, in order to attain that object, to make any ostensible concession that will

not prevent them from arranging things to suit their taste as soon as that object is attained. This class comprises a considerable number, probably a large majority, of the professional politicians who are extremely active in the reconstruction movement. They are loud in their praise of the President's reconstruction policy, and clamorous for the withdrawal of the federal troops and the abolition of the Freedmen's Bureau.

3. The incorrigibles, who still indulge in the swagger which was so customary before and during the war, and still hope for a time when the southern confederacy will achieve its independence. This class consists mostly of young men, and comprises the loiterers of the towns and the idlers of the country. They persecute Union men and negroes whenever they can do so with impunity, insist clamorously upon their "rights," and are extremely impatient of the presence of the federal soldiers. A good many of them have taken the oaths of allegiance and amnesty, and associated themselves with the second class in their political operations. This element is by no means unimportant; it is strong in numbers, deals in brave talk, addresses itself directly and incessantly to the passions and prejudices of the masses, and commands the admiration of the women.

4. The multitude of people who have no definite ideas about the circumstances under which they live and about the course they have to follow; whose intellects are weak, but whose prejudices and impulses are strong, and who are apt to be carried along by those who know how to appeal to the latter.

Much depends upon the relative strength and influence of these classes. In the course of this report you will find statements of facts which may furnish a basis for an estimate. But whatever their differences may be, on one point they are agreed: further resistance to the power of the national government is useless, and submission to its authority a matter of necessity. It is true, the right of secession in theory is still believed in by most of those who formerly believed in it; some are still entertaining a vague hope of seeing it realized at some future time, but all give it up as a practical impossibility for the present. All movements in favor of separation from the Union have, therefore, been practically abandoned, and resistance to our military forces, on that score, has ceased. The demonstrations of hostility to the troops and other agents of the government, which are still occurring in some localities, and of which I shall speak hereafter, spring from another class of motives. This kind of loyalty, however, which is produced by the irresistible pressure of force, and consists merely in the non-commission of acts of rebellion, is of a negative character, and might, as such, hardly be considered independent of circumstances and contingencies.

## OATH-TAKING.

A demonstration of "returning loyalty" of a more positive character is the taking of the oaths of allegiance and amnesty prescribed by the general government. At first the number of persons who availed themselves of the opportunities offered for abjuring their adhesion to the cause of the rebellion was not very large, but it increased considerably when the obtaining of a pardon and the right of voting were made dependent upon the previous performance of that act. Persons falling under any of the exceptions of the amnesty proclamation made haste to avert the impending danger; and politicians used every means of persuasion to induce people to swell the number of voters by clearing themselves of all disabilities. The great argument that this was necessary to the end of reconstructing their State governments, and of regaining the control of their home affairs and their influence in the Union, was copiously enlarged upon in the letters and speeches of prominent individuals, which are before the country and need no further comment. In some cases the taking of the oath was publicly recommended in newspapers and addresses with sneering remarks, and I have listened to many private conversations in which it was treated with contempt and ridicule. While it was not generally looked upon in the State[s] I visited as a very serious matter, except as to the benefits and privileges it confers, I have no doubt that a great many persons took it fully conscious of the obligations it imposes, and honestly intending to fulfil them.

The aggregate number of those who thus had qualified themselves for voting previous to the election for the State conventions was not as large as might have been expected. The vote obtained at these elections was generally reported as very light—in some localities surprisingly so. It would, perhaps, be worth while for the government to order up reports about the number of oaths administered by the officers authorized to do so, previous to the elections for the State conventions; such reports would serve to indicate how large a proportion of the people participated in the reconstruction movement at that time, and to what extent the masses were represented in the conventions.

Of those who have not yet taken the oath of allegiance, most belong to the class of indifferent people who "do not care one way or the other." There are still some individuals who find the oath to be a confession of defeat and a declaration of submission too humiliating and too repugnant to their feelings. It is to be expected that the former will gradually overcome their apathy, and the latter their sensitiveness, and that, at a not remote day, all will have qualified themselves, in point of form, to resume the right of citizenship. On the whole, it may be said that the value of the oaths taken in the southern States is neither above nor below the value of the political oaths taken in other countries. A historical examination of the subject of political oaths will lead to the conclusion that they can be very serviceable in certain emergencies and for certain objects, but that they have never insured the stability of a government, and never improved the morals of a people.

## FEELING TOWARDS THE SOLDIERS AND THE PEOPLE OF THE NORTH.

A more substantial evidence of "returning loyalty" would be a favorable change of feeling with regard to the government's friends and agents, and the people of the loyal States generally. I mentioned above that all organized attacks upon our military forces stationed in the south have ceased; but there are still localities where it is unsafe for a man wearing the federal uniform or known as an officer of the government to be abroad outside of the immediate reach of our garrisons. The shooting of single soldiers and government couriers was not unfrequently reported while I was in the south, and even as late as the middle of September, Major Miller, assistant adjutant general of the commissioner of the Freedmen's Bureau in Alabama, while on an inspecting tour in the southern counties of that State, found it difficult to prevent a collision between the menacing populace and his escort. His wagon-master was brutally murdered while remaining but a short distance behind the command. The murders of agents of the Freedmen's Bureau have been noticed in the public papers. These, and similar occurrences, however, may be looked upon as isolated cases, and ought to be charged, perhaps, only to the account of the lawless persons who committed them.

But no instance has come to my notice in which the people of a city or a rural district cordially fraternized with the army. Here and there the soldiers were welcomed as protectors against apprehended dangers; but general exhibitions of cordiality on the part of the population I have not heard of. There are, indeed, honorable individual exceptions to this rule. Many persons, mostly belonging to the first of the four classes above enumerated, are honestly striving to soften down the bitter feelings and traditional antipathies of their neighbors; others, who are acting more upon motives of policy than inclination, maintain pleasant relations with the officers of the government. But, upon the whole, the soldier of the Union is still looked upon as a stranger, an intruder—as the "Yankee," "the enemy." It would be superfluous to enumerate instances of insult offered to our soldiers, and even to officers high in command; the existence and intensity of this aversion is too well known to those who have served or are now serving in the south to require proof. In this matter the exceptions were, when I was there, not numerous enough to affect the rule. In the documents accompanying this report you will find allusions confirming this statement. I would invite special attention to the letter of General Kirby Smith (accompanying document No. 9.)

This feeling of aversion and resentment with regard to our soldiers may, perhaps, be called natural. The animosities inflamed by a four years' war, and its distressing incidents, cannot be easily overcome. But they extend beyond the limits of the army, to the people of the north. I have read in southern papers bitter complaints about the unfriendly spirit exhibited by the northern people—complaints not unfrequently flavored with an admixture of vigorous vituperation. But, as far as my experience goes, the "unfriendly spirit" exhibited in the north is all mildness and affection compared with the popular temper which in the south vents itself in a variety of ways and on all possible occasions. No observing northern man can come into contact with the different classes composing southern society without noticing it. He may be received in social circles with great politeness, even with apparent cordiality; but soon he will become aware that, although he may be esteemed as a man, he is detested as a "Yankee," and, as the conversation becomes a little more confidential and throws off ordinary restraint, he is not unfrequently told so; the word "Yankee" still signifies to them those traits of character which the southern press has been so long in the habit of attributing to the northern people; and whenever they look around them upon the traces of the war, they see in them, not the consequences of their own folly, but the evidences of "Yankee wickedness." In making these general statements, I beg to be understood as always excluding the individual exceptions above mentioned.

It is by no means surprising that prejudices and resentments, which for years were so assiduously cultivated and so violently inflamed, should not have been turned into affection by a defeat; nor are they likely to disappear as long as the southern people continue to brood over their losses and misfortunes. They will gradually subside when those who entertain them cut resolutely loose from the past and embark in a career of new activity on a common field with those whom they have so long considered their enemies. Of this I shall say more in another part of this report. But while we are certainly inclined to put upon such things the most charitable construction, it remains nevertheless true, that as long as these feelings exist in their present strength, they will hinder the growth of that reliable kind of loyalty which springs from the heart and clings to the country in good and evil fortune. . . .

# What Has Been Accomplished.

While the generosity and toleration shown by the government to the people lately in rebellion has not met with a corresponding generosity shown by those people to the government's friends, it has brought forth some results which, if properly developed, will become of value. It has facilitated the re-establishment of the forms of civil government, and led many of those who had been active in the rebellion to take part in the act of bringing back the States to their constitutional relations; and if nothing else were necessary than the mere putting in operation of the mere machinery of government in point of form, and not also the acceptance of the results of the war and their development in point of spirit, these results, although as yet incomplete, might be called a satisfactory advance in the right direction. There is, at present, no danger of another insurrection against the authority of the United States on a large scale, and the people are willing to reconstruct their State governments, and to send their senators and representatives to Congress.

But as to the moral value of these results, we must not indulge in any delusions. There are two principal points to which I beg to call your attention. In the first place, the rapid return to power and influence of so many of those who but recently were engaged in a bitter war against the Union, has had one effect which was certainly not originally contemplated by the government. Treason does, under existing circumstances, not appear odious in the south. The people are not impressed with any sense of its criminality. And, secondly, there is, as yet, among the southern people an *utter absence of national feeling*. I made it a business, while in the south, to watch the symptoms of "returning loyalty" as they appeared not only in private conversation, but in the public press and in the speeches delivered and the resolutions passed at Union meetings. Hardly ever was there an expression of hearty attachment to the great republic, or an appeal to the impulses of patriotism; but whenever submission to the national authority was declared and advocated, it was almost uniformly placed upon two principal grounds: That, under present circumstances, the southern people could "do no better;" and then that submission was the only means by which they could rid themselves of the federal soldiers and obtain once more control of their own affairs. Some of the speakers may have been inspired by higher motives, but upon these two arguments they had principally to rely whenever they wanted to make an impression upon the popular mind. If any exception is to be made to this rule it is Louisiana, in whose metropolis a different spirit was cultivated for some time; but even there, the return in mass of those who followed the fortunes of the confederate flag during the war does not appear to have a favorable influence upon the growth of that sentiment. (See Gen. Canby's letter, accompanying document No. 8.) While admitting that, at present, we have perhaps no right to expect anything better than this submission—loyalty which springs from necessity and calculation—I do not consider it safe for the government to base expectations upon it, which the manner in which it manifests itself does not justify.

The reorganization of civil government is relieving the military, to a great extent, of its police duties and judicial functions; but at the time I left the south it was still very far from showing a satisfactory efficiency in the maintenance of order and security. In many districts robbing and plundering was going on with perfect impunity; the roads were infested by bands of highwaymen; numerous assaults occurred, and several stage lines were considered unsafe. The statements of Major General Woods, Brigadier General Kilby Smith and Colonel Gilchrist, (accompanying documents Nos. 11, 9 and 18,) give a terrible picture of the state of things in the localities they refer to. It is stated that civil officers are either unwilling or unable to enforce the laws; that one man does not dare to testify against another for fear of being murdered, and that the better elements of society are kept down by lawless characters under a system of terrorism. From my own observation I know that these things are not confined to the districts mentioned in the documents above referred to. Both the governors of Alabama and Mississippi complained of it in official proclamations. Cotton, horse and cattle stealing was going on in all the States I visited on an extensive scale. Such a state of demoralization would call for extraordinary measures in any country, and it is difficult to conceive how, in the face of the inefficiency of the civil authorities, the removal of the troops can be thought of. . . .

## THE NEGRO QUESTION—FIRST ASPECTS.

The principal cause of that want of national spirit which has existed in the south so long, and at last gave birth to the rebellion, was, that the southern people cherished, cultivated, idolized their peculiar interests and institutions in preference to those which they had in common with the rest of the American people. Hence the importance of the negro question as an integral part of the question of union in general, and the question of reconstruction in particular.

When the war came to a close, the labor system of the south was already much disturbed. During the progress of military operations large numbers of slaves had left their masters and followed the columns of our armies; others had taken refuge in our camps; many thousands had enlisted in the service of the national government. Extensive settlements of negroes had been formed along the seaboard and the banks of the Mississippi, under the supervision of army officers and treasury agents, and the government was feeding the colored refugees, who could not be advantageously employed, in the so-called contraband camps. Many slaves had also been removed by their masters, as our armies penetrated the country, either to Texas or to the interior of Georgia and Alabama. Thus a considerable portion of the laboring force had been withdrawn from its former employments. But a majority of the slaves remained on the plantations to which they belonged, especially in those parts of the country which were not touched by the war, and where, consequently, the emancipation proclamation was not enforced by the military power. Although not ignorant of the stake they had in the result of the contest, the patient bondmen waited quietly for the development of things. But as soon as the struggle was finally decided, and our forces were scattered about in detachments to occupy the country, the so far unmoved masses began to stir. The report went among them that their liberation was no longer a mere contingency, but a fixed fact. Large numbers of colored people left the plantations; many flocked to our

military posts and camps to obtain the certainty of their
freedom, and others walked away merely for the purpose
of leaving the places on which they had been held in slavery, and because they could now go with impunity. Still others, and their number was by no means inconsiderable,
remained with their former masters and continued their
work on the field, but under new and as yet unsettled conditions, and under the agitating influence of a feeling of
restlessness. In some localities, however, where our troops
had not yet penetrated and where no military post was
within reach, planters endeavored and partially succeeded
in maintaining between themselves and the negroes the relation of master and slave, partly by concealing from them
the great changes that had taken place, and partly by terrorizing them into submission to their behests. But aside
from these exceptions, the country found itself thrown into
that confusion which is naturally inseparable from a change
so great and so sudden. The white people were afraid of the
negroes, and the negroes did not trust the white people; the
military power of the national government stood there, and
was looked up to, as the protector of both.

Upon this power devolved the task to bring order into
that chaos. But the order to be introduced was a new order, of which neither the late masters nor the late slaves
had an adequate conception. All the elements of society
being afloat, the difficulties were immense. The military officers and agents of the Freedmen's Bureau, to whom the
negroes applied for advice and guidance, either procured
them such employment as could be found, or persuaded
them to return to their plantations and to continue in the
cultivation of the crops, promising them that their liberty,
rights, and interests should be protected. Upon the planters they urged the necessity of making fair and equitable
contracts with the freedmen, admonishing them to treat
their laborers as free men ought to be treated. These efforts met with such success as the difficulties surrounding
the problem permitted to expect. Large numbers of negroes went back to the fields, according to the advice they
had received, but considerable accumulations still remained in and around the towns and along the seaboard,
where there was no adequate amount of profitable employment for them. The making and approving of contracts pro-

gressed as rapidly as the small number of officers engaged in that line of duty made it possible, but not rapidly in proportion to the vast amount of work to be accomplished. The business experience of many of the officers was but limited; here and there experiments were tried which had to be given up. In numerous cases contracts were made and then broken, either by the employers or the laborers, and the officers in charge were overwhelmed with complaints from both sides. While many planters wanted to have the laborers who had left them back on their plantations, others drove those that had remained away, and thus increased the number of the unemployed. Moreover, the great change had burst upon the country in the midst of the agricultural labor season when the crops that were in the ground required steady work to make them produce a satisfactory yield, and the interruption of labor, which could not but be very extensive, caused considerable damage. In one word, the efforts made could not prevent or remedy, in so short a time, the serious disorders which are always connected with a period of precipitous transition, and which, although natural, are exceedingly embarrassing to those who have to deal with them.

The solution of the social problem in the south, if left to the free action of the southern people, will depend upon two things: 1, upon the ideas entertained by the whites, the "ruling class," of the problem, and the manner in which they act upon their ideas; and 2, upon the capacity and conduct of the colored people.

## OPINIONS OF THE WHITES.

That the result of the free labor experiment made under circumstances so extremely unfavorable should at once be a perfect success, no reasonable person would expect. Nevertheless, a large majority of the southern men with whom I came into contact announced their opinions with so positive an assurance as to produce the impression that their minds were fully made up. In at least nineteen cases of twenty the reply I received to my inquiry about their views on the new system was uniformly this : "You cannot make the negro work without physical compulsion." I heard this hundreds of times, heard it wherever I went, heard it in nearly the same words from so many different persons, that at last I came to the conclusion that this is the prevailing sentiment among the southern people. There are exceptions to this rule, but, as far as my information extends, far from enough to affect the rule. In the accompanying documents you will find an abundance of proof in support of this statement. There is hardly a paper relative to the negro question annexed to this report which does not, in some direct or indirect way, corroborate it.

Unfortunately the disorders necessarily growing out of the transition state continually furnished food for argument. I found but few people who were willing to make due allowance for the adverse influence of exceptional circumstances. By a large majority of those I came in contact with, and they mostly belonged to the more intelligent class, every irregularity that occurred was directly charged against the system of free labor. If negroes walked away from the plantations, it was conclusive proof of the incorrigible instability of the negro, and the impracticability of free negro labor. If some individual negroes violated the terms of their contract, it proved unanswerably that no negro had, or ever would have, a just conception of the binding force of a contract, and that this system of free negro labor was bound to be a failure. If some negroes shirked, or did not perform their task with sufficient alacrity, it was produced as irrefutable evidence to show that physical compulsion was actually indispensable to make the negro work. If negroes, idlers or refugees crawling about the towns, applied to the authorities for subsistence, it was quoted as incontestably establishing the point that the negro was too improvident to take care of himself, and must necessarily be consigned to the care of a master. I heard a Georgia planter argue most seriously that one of his negroes had shown himself certainly unfit for freedom because he impudently refused to submit to a whipping. I frequently went into an argument with those putting forth such general assertions, quoting instances in which negro laborers were working faithfully, and to the entire satisfaction of their employers, as the employers themselves had informed me. In a majority of cases the reply was that we northern people did not understand the negro, but that they (the southerners) did; that as to the particular instances I quoted I was probably mistaken; that I had not closely investigated the cases, or had been deceived by my informants; that they *knew* the negro would not work without compulsion, and that nobody could make them believe he would. Arguments like these naturally finished such discussions. It frequently struck me that persons who conversed about every other subject calmly and sensibly would lose their temper as soon as the negro question was touched.

## EFFECTS OF SUCH OPINIONS, AND GENERAL TREATMENT OF THE NEGRO.

A belief, conviction, or prejudice, or whatever you may call it, so widely spread and apparently so deeply rooted as this, that the negro will not work without physical compulsion, is certainly calculated to have a very serious influence upon the conduct of the people entertaining it. It naturally produced a desire to preserve slavery in its original form as much and as long as possible—and you may, perhaps, remember the admission made by one of the provisional governors, over two months after the close of the war, that the people of his State still indulged in a lingering hope slavery might yet be preserved—or to introduce into the new system that element of physical compulsion which would make the negro work. Efforts were, indeed, made to hold the negro in his old state of subjection, especially in such localities where our military forces had not yet penetrated, or where the country was not garrisoned in detail. Here and there planters succeeded for a limited period to keep their former slaves in ignorance, or at least doubt, about their new rights; but the main agency employed for that purpose was force and intimidation. In many instances negroes who walked away from the plantations, or were found upon the roads, were shot or otherwise severely punished, which was calculated to produce the impression among those remaining with their masters that an attempt to escape from slavery would result in certain destruction. A large proportion of the many acts of violence committed is undoubtedly attributable to this motive. The documents at-

tached to this report abound in testimony to this effect. For
the sake of illustration I will give some instances:

Brigadier General Fessenden reported to Major General
Gillmore from Winnsboro, South Carolina, July 19, as follows: "The spirit of the people, especially in those districts
not subject to the salutary influence of General Sherman's
army, is that of concealed and, in some instances, of open
hostility, though there are some who strive with honorable
good faith to promote a thorough reconciliation between
the government and their people. A spirit of bitterness and
persecution manifests itself towards the negroes. They are
shot and abused outside the immediate protection of our
forces *by men who announce their determination to take the
law into their own hands, in defiance of our authority.* To protect the negro and punish these still rebellious individuals it
will be necessary to have this country pretty thickly settled
with soldiers." I received similar verbal reports from other
parts of South Carolina. To show the hopes still indulged in
by some, I may mention that one of the sub-district commanders, as he himself informed me, knew planters within
the limits of his command who had made contracts with
their former slaves *avowedly* for the object of keeping them
together on their plantations, so that they might have them
near at hand, and thus more easily reduce them to their former condition, when, after the restoration of the civil power,
the "unconstitutional emancipation proclamation" would
be set aside.

Cases in which negroes were kept on the plantations, either by ruse or violence, were frequent enough in South
Carolina and Georgia to call forth from General Saxton a
circular threatening planters who persisted in this practice
with loss of their property, and from Major General Steed-
man, commander of the department of Georgia, an order
bearing upon the same subject. At Atlanta, Georgia, I had
an opportunity to examine some cases of the nature above
described myself. While I was there, 9th and 10th of August,
several negroes came into town with bullet and buckshot
wounds in their bodies. From their statements, which, however, were only corroborating information previously received, it appeared that the reckless and restless characters
of that region had combined to keep the negroes where
they belonged. Several freedmen were shot in the attempt

to escape; others succeeded in eluding the vigilance of their persecutors; large numbers, terrified by what they saw and heard, quietly remained under the restraint imposed upon them, waiting for better opportunities. The commander of the sub-district and post informed me that bands of guerillas were prowling about within a few miles of the city, making it dangerous for soldiers and freedmen to show themselves outside of the immediate reach of the garrison, and that but a few days previous to my arrival a small squad of men he had sent out to serve an order upon a planter, concerning the treatment of freedmen, had been driven back by an armed band of over twenty men, headed by an individual in the uniform of a rebel officer.

As our troops in Georgia were at that time mostly concentrated at a number of central points, and not scattered over the State in small detachments, but little information was obtained of what was going on in the interior of the country. A similar system was followed in Alabama, but enough has become known to indicate the condition of things in localities not immediately under the eye of the military. In that State the efforts made to hold the negro in a state of subjection appear to have been of a particularly atrocious nature. Rumors to that effect which reached me at Montgomery induced me to make inquiries at the post hospital. The records of that institution showed a number of rather startling cases which had occurred immediately after the close of the war, and some of a more recent date; all of which proved that negroes leaving the plantations, and found on the roads, were exposed to the savagest treatment. An extract from the records of the hospital is appended (accompanying document No. 20); also a statement signed by the provost marshal at Selma, Alabama, Major J. P. Houston (accompanying document No. 21). He says: "There have come to my notice officially twelve cases, in which I am morally certain the trials have not been had yet, that negroes were killed by whites. In a majority of cases the provocation consisted in the negroes' trying to come to town or to return to the plantation after having been sent away. The cases above enumerated, I am convinced, are but a small part of those that have actually been perpetrated." In a report to General Swayne, assistant commissioner of the Freedmen's Bureau, in Alabama, communicated to me by the general, Captain Poillon, agent of the bureau at Mobile, says of the condition of things in the southwestern part of the State, July 29: "There are regular patrols posted on the rivers, who board some of the boats; after the boats leave they hang, shoot, or drown the victims they may find on them, and all those found on the roads or coming down the rivers are almost invariably murdered. . . . The bewildered and terrified freedmen know not what to do—to leave is death; to remain is to suffer the increased burden imposed upon them by the cruel taskmaster, whose only interest is their labor, wrung from them by every device an inhuman ingenuity can devise; hence the lash and murder is resorted to to intimidate those whom fear of an awful death alone cause to remain, while patrols, negro dogs and spies, disguised as Yankees, keep constant guard over these unfortunate people." In a letter addressed to myself, September 9, Captain Poillon says: "Organized patrols, with negro hounds, keep guard over the thoroughfares; bands of lawless robbers traverse the country, and the unfortunate who attempts to escape, or he who returns for his wife or child, is waylaid or pursued with hounds, and shot or hung." (Accompanying document No. 22.)

In Mississippi I received information of a similar character. I would respectfully invite your attention to two letters—one by Colonel Hayne, 1st Texas cavalry, and one by Colonel Brinkerhoff—giving interesting descriptions of the condition of the freedmen, and the spirit of the whites shortly after the close of the war. (Accompanying documents Nos. 23 and 24.) Lieutenant Colonel P. J. Yorke, post commander at port Gibson, Mississippi, reported to General Davidson, on August 26, that a "county patrol" had been organized by citizens of his sub-district, which, for reasons given, he had been obliged to disband; one of these reasons was, in his own language, that: "The company was formed out of what they called picked men, *i.e.,* those only who had been actually engaged in the war, and were known as strong disunionists. The negroes in the sections of country these men controlled were kept in the most abject slavery, and treated in every way contrary to the requirements of General Orders No. 129, from the War Department." (Accompanying document No. 25.) As late as September

29, Captain J. H. Weber, agent of the Freedmen's Bureau, reported to Colonel Thomas, assistant commissioner of the bureau, in the State of Mississippi, as follows: "In many cases negroes who left their homes during the war, and have been within our military lines, and having provided homes here for their families, going back to get their wives and children, have been driven off, and told that they could not have them. In several cases guards have been sent to aid people in getting their families; in many others it has been impracticable, as the distance was too great. In portions of the northern part of this district the colored people are kept in slavery still. The white people tell them that they were free during the war, but the war is now over, and they must go to work again as before. The reports from sub-commissioners nearest that locality show that the blacks are in a much worse state than ever before, the able-bodied being kept at work under the lash, and the young and infirm driven off to care for themselves. As to protection from the civil authorities, there is no such thing outside of this city." (Accompanying document No. 26.)

The conviction, however, that slavery in the old form cannot be maintained has forced itself upon the minds of many of those who ardently desired its preservation. But while the necessity of a new system was recognized as far as the right of property in the individual negro is concerned, many attempts were made to introduce into that new system the element of physical compulsion, which, as above stated, is so generally considered indispensable. This was done by simply adhering, as to the treatment of the laborers, as much as possible to the traditions of the old system, even where the relations between employers and laborers had been fixed by contract. The practice of corporal punishment was still continued to a great extent, although, perhaps, not in so regular a manner as it was practiced in times gone by. It is hardly necessary to quote any documentary evidence on this point; the papers appended to this report are full of testimony corroborating the statement. The habit is so inveterate with a great many persons as to render, on the least provocation, the impulse to whip a negro almost irresistible. It will continue to be so until the southern people will have learned, so as never to forget it, that a black man has rights which a white man is bound to respect. . . .

## GENERAL IDEAS AND SCHEMES OF WHITES CONCERNING THE FREEDMEN.

Some of the planters with whom I had occasion to converse expressed their determination to adopt the course which best accords with the spirit of free labor, to make the negro work by offering him fair inducements, to stimulate his ambition, and to extend to him those means of intellectual and moral improvement which are best calculated to make him an intelligent, reliable and efficient free laborer and a good and useful citizen. Those who expressed such ideas were almost invariably professed Union men, and far above the average in point of mental ability and culture. I found a very few instances of original secessionists also manifesting a willingness to give the free-labor experiment a fair trial. I can represent the sentiments of this small class in no better way than by quoting the language used by an Alabama judge in a conversation with me. "I am one of the most thoroughly whipped men in the south," said he; "I am a genuine old secessionist, and I believe now, as I always did, we had the constitutional right to secede. But the war has settled that matter, and it is all over now. As to this thing of free negro labor, I do not believe in it, but I will give it a fair trial. I have a plantation and am going to make contracts with my hands, and then I want a real Yankee to run the machine for me; not one of your New Yorkers or Pennsylvanians, but the genuine article from Massachusetts or Vermont—one who can not only farm, but sing psalms and pray, and teach school—a real abolitionist, who believes in the thing just as I don't believe in it. If he does not succeed, I shall consider it proof conclusive that you are wrong and I am right."

I regret to say that views and intentions so reasonable I found confined to a small minority. Aside from the assumption that the negro will not work without physical compulsion, there appears to be another popular notion prevalent in the south, which stands as no less serious an obstacle in the way of a successful solution of the problem. It is that the negro exists for the special object of raising cotton, rice and sugar *for the whites,* and that it is illegitimate for him to indulge, like other people, in the pursuit of his own happiness in his own way. Although it is admitted that he has ceased to be the property of a master, it is not admitted that he has a right to become his own master. As Colonel Thomas, assistant commissioner of the Freedmen's Bureau in Mississippi, in a letter addressed to me, very pungently expresses it: "The whites esteem the blacks their property by natural right, and, however much they may admit that the relations of masters and slaves have been destroyed by the war and by the President's emancipation proclamation, they still have an ingrained feeling that the blacks at large belong to the whites at large, and whenever opportunity serves, they treat the colored people just as their profit, caprice or passion may dictate." (Accompanying document No. 27.) An ingrained feeling like this is apt to bring forth that sort of class legislation which produces laws to govern one class with no other view than to benefit another. This tendency can be distinctly traced in the various schemes for regulating labor which here and there see the light.

Immediately after the emancipation of the slaves, when the general confusion was most perplexing, the prevalent desire among the whites seemed to be, if they could not retain their negroes as slaves, to get rid of them entirely. Wild speculations were indulged in, how to remove the colored population at once and to import white laborers to fill its place; how to obtain a sufficient supply of coolies, &c., &c. Even at the present moment the removal of the freedmen is strongly advocated by those who have the traditional horror of a free negro, and in some sections, especially where the soil is more adapted to cultivation of cereals than the raising of the staples, planters appear to be inclined to drive the negroes away, at least from their plantations. I was informed by a prominent South Carolinian in July, that the planters in certain localities in the northwestern part of his State had been on the point of doing so, but better counsel had been made to prevail upon them; and Colonel Robinson, 97th United States Colored Infantry, who had been sent out to several counties in southern Alabama to administer the amnesty oath, reported a general disposition among the planters of that region to "set the colored people who had cultivated their crops during the summer, adrift as soon as the crops would be secured, and not to permit the negro to remain upon any footing of equality with the white man in that country." (Accompanying document No. 28.) The disposition to drive away all the negroes from the plantations was undoubtedly confined to a few districts; and as far as the scheme of wholesale deportation is concerned, practical men became aware, that if they wanted to have any labor done, it would have been bad policy to move away the laborers they now have before others were there to fill their places. All these devices promising at best only distant relief, and free negro labor being the only thing in immediate prospect, many ingenious heads set about to solve the problem, how to make free labor compulsory by permanent regulations. . . .

## The Freedman.

The first southern men with whom I came into contact after my arrival at Charleston designated the general conduct of the emancipated slaves as surprisingly good. Some went even so far as to call it admirable. The connexion in which they used these laudatory terms was this: A great many colored people while in slavery had undoubtedly suffered much hardship and submitted to great wrongs, partly inseparably connected with the condition of servitude, and partly aggravated by the individual wilfulness and cruelty of their masters and overseers. They were suddenly set free; and not only that: their masters but a short time ago almost omnipotent on their domains, found themselves, after their defeat in the war, all at once face to face with their former slaves as a conquered and powerless class. Never was the temptation to indulge in acts of vengeance for wrongs suffered more strongly presented than to the colored people of the south; but no instance of such individual revenge was then on record, nor have I since heard of any case of violence that could be traced to such motives. The transition of the southern negro from slavery to freedom was untarnished by any deeds of blood, and the apprehension so extensively entertained and so pathetically declaimed upon

by many, that the sudden and general emancipation of the
slaves would at once result in "all the horrors of St. Do-
mingo," proved utterly groundless. This was the first impression I received after my arrival in the south, and I
received it from the mouths of late slaveholders. Nor do I
think the praise was unjustly bestowed. In this respect the
emancipated slaves of the south can challenge comparison
with any race long held in servitude and suddenly set free.
As to the dangers of the future, I shall speak of them in
another connexion.

But at that point the unqualified praise stopped and the
complaints began: the negroes would not work; they left
their plantations and went wandering from place to place,
stealing by the way; they preferred a life of idleness and
vagrancy to that of honest and industrious labor; they either did not show any willingness to enter into contracts, or,
if they did, showed a stronger disposition to break them
than to keep them; they were becoming insubordinate and
insolent to their former owners; they indulged in extravagant ideas about their rights and relied upon the government to support them without work; in one word, they had
no conception of the rights freedom gave, and of the obligations freedom imposed upon them. These complaints I
heard repeated with endless variations wherever I went.
Nor were they made without some show of reason. I will
review them one after another.

*Unwillingness to work.* — That there are among the negroes a good many constitutionally lazy individuals is certainly true. The propensity to idleness seems to be rather
strongly developed in the south generally, without being
confined to any particular race. It is also true that the alacrity negroes put into their work depends in a majority of
cases upon certain combinations of circumstances. It is asserted that the negroes have a prejudice against working in
the cultivation of cotton, rice, and sugar. Although this
prejudice, probably arising from the fact that the cotton,
rice, and sugar fields remind the former slave of the worst
experiences of his past life, exists to some extent, it has not
made the freedmen now on the plantations unwilling to
cultivate such crops as the planters may have seen fit to
raise. A few cases of refusal may have occurred. But there
is another fact of which I have become satisfied in the

course of my observations, and which is of great significance: while most of the old slaveholders complain of the laziness and instability of their negro laborers, the northern men engaged in planting, with whom I have come into contact, almost uniformly speak of their negro laborers with satisfaction, and these northern men almost exclusively devote themselves to the cultivation of cotton. A good many southern planters, in view of the fact, expressed to me their intention to engage northern men for the management of their plantations. This circumstance would seem to prove that under certain conditions the negro may be expected to work well. There are two reasons by which it may be explained: first, that a northern man knows from actual experience what free labor is, and understands its management, which the late slaveholder, still clinging to the traditions of the old system, does not; and then, that the negro has more confidence in a northern man than in his former master. When a northern man discovers among his laboring force an individual that does not do his duty, his first impulse is to discharge him, and he acts accordingly. When a late slaveholder discovers such an individual among his laborers, his first impulse is to whip him, and he is very apt to suit the act to the impulse. Ill treatment is a doubtful encouragement for free laborers, and it proves more apt to drive those that are still at work away than to make the plantation attractive to others. But if the reasons above stated are sufficient to explain why the negroes work better for northern than for southern men, it will follow that a general improvement will take place as soon as the latter fulfil the same conditions — that is, as soon as southern men learn what free labor is and how to manage it in accordance with its principles, and as soon as they succeed in gaining the confidence of the colored people.

In the reports of officers of the Freedmen's Bureau, among the documents annexed to this, you will find frequent repetitions of the statement that the negro generally works well where he is decently treated and well compensated. Nor do the officers of the Freedmen's Bureau alone think and say so. Southern men, who were experimenting in the right direction, expressed to me their opinion to the same effect. Some of them told me that the negroes on their plantations worked "as well as ever," or even "far bet-

ter than they had expected." It is true the number of planters who made that admission was small, but it nearly
corresponded with the number of those who, according to
their own statements, gave free negro labor a perfectly fair
trial, while all those who prefaced everything they said with
the assertion that "the negro will not work without physical
compulsion" could find no end to their complaints. There
are undoubtedly negroes who will not do well under the
best circumstances, just as there are others who will do well
under the worst.

In another part of this report I have already set forth the
exceptional difficulties weighing upon the free-labor experiment in the south during this period of transition. The
sudden leap from slavery to freedom is an exciting event in
a man's life, and somewhat calculated to disturb his equa-
nimity for a moment. People are on such occasions disposed to indulge themselves a little. It would have shown
much more wisdom in the negroes if all of them had quietly
gone to work again the next day. But it is not reasonable to
expect the negroes to possess more wisdom than other
races would exhibit under the same circumstances. Besides,
the willingness to work depends, with whites as well as
blacks, somewhat upon the nature of the inducements held
out, and the unsatisfactory regulation of the matter of
wages has certainly something to do with the instability of
negro labor which is complained of. Northern men engaged
in planting almost uniformly pay wages in money, while
southern planters, almost uniformly, have contracted with
their laborers for a share in the crop. In many instances the
shares are allotted between employers and laborers with
great fairness; but in others the share promised to the laborers is so small as to leave them in the end very little or
nothing. Moreover, the crops in the south looked generally
very unpromising from the beginning, which naturally reduced the value falling to the lot of the laborer. I have
heard a good many freedmen complain that, taking all
things into consideration, they really did not know what
they were working for except food, which in many instances
was bad and scanty; and such complaints were frequently
well founded. In a large number of cases the planters were
not to blame for this; they had no available pecuniary means,
and in many localities found it difficult to procure provi-

sions. But these unfavorable circumstances, combined with
the want of confidence in southern men, were well calculated to have an influence upon the conduct of the negro as
a laborer.

I have heard it said that money is no inducement which
will make a negro work. It is certain that many of them, immediately after emancipation, had but a crude conception
of the value of money and the uses it can be put to. It may,
however, be stated as the general rule, that whenever they
are at liberty to choose between wages in money and a
share in the crop, they will choose the former and work better. Many cases of negroes engaged in little industrial pursuits came to my notice, in which they showed considerable
aptness not only for gaining money, but also for saving and
judiciously employing it. Some were even surprisingly successful. I visited some of the plantations divided up among
freedmen and cultivated by them independently without
the supervision of white men. In some instances I found
very good crops and indications of general thrift and good
management; in others the corn and cotton crops were in a
neglected and unpromising state. The excuse made was in
most cases that they had obtained possession of the ground
too late in the season, and that, until the regular crops could
be harvested, they were obliged to devote much of their
time to the raising and sale of vegetables, watermelons, &c.,
for the purpose of making a living in the meantime.

On the whole I feel warranted in making the following
statement: Many freedmen—not single individuals, but
whole "plantation gangs"—are working well; others do not.
The difference in their efficiency coincides in a great measure with a certain difference in the conditions under which
they live. The conclusion lies near, that if the conditions under which they work well become general, their efficiency
as free laborers will become general also, aside from individual exceptions. Certain it is, that by far the larger portion of the work done in the south is done by freedmen.

*Vagrancy.*—Large numbers of colored people left the
plantations as soon as they became aware that they could
do so with impunity. That they could so leave their former
masters was for them the first test of the reality of their
freedom. A great many flocked to the military posts and
towns to obtain from the "Yankees" reliable information as

to their new rights. Others were afraid lest by staying on the plantations where they had been held as slaves they might again endanger their freedom. Still others went to the cities, thinking that there the sweets of liberty could best be enjoyed. In some places they crowded together in large numbers, causing serious inconvenience. But a great many, probably a very large majority, remained on the plantations and made contracts with their former masters. The military authorities, and especially the agents of the Freedmen's Bureau, succeeded by continued exertions in returning most of those who were adrift to the plantations, or in finding other employment for them. After the first rush was over the number of vagrants grew visibly less. It may be said that where the Freedmen's Bureau is best organized there is least vagrancy among the negroes. Here and there they show considerable restlessness, partly owing to local, partly to general causes. Among the former, bad treatment is probably the most prominent; among the latter, a feeling of distrust, uneasiness, anxiety about their future, which arises from their present unsettled condition. It is true, some are going from place to place because they are fond of it. The statistics of the Freedmen's Bureau show that the whole number of colored people supported by the government since the close of the war was remarkably small and continually decreasing. This seems to show that the southern negro, when thrown out of his accustomed employment, possesses considerable ability to support himself. It is possible, however, that in consequence of short crops, the destitution of the country, and other disturbing influences, there may be more restlessness among the negroes next winter than there is at present. Where the results of this year's labor were very unsatisfactory, there will be a floating about of the population when the contracts of this year expire. It is to be expected, however, that the Freedmen's Bureau will be able to remedy evils of that kind. Other emancipatory movements, for instance the abolition of serfdom in Russia, have resulted in little or no vagrancy; but it must not be forgotten that the emancipated serfs were speedily endowed with the ownership of land, which gave them a permanent moral and material interest in the soil upon which they lived. A similar measure would do more to stop negro vagrancy in the south than the severest penal laws. In every country the number of vagrants stands in proportion to the number of people who have no permanent local interests, unless augmented by exceptional cases, such as war or famine.

*Contracts.*—Freedmen frequently show great disinclination to make contracts with their former masters. They are afraid lest in signing a paper they sign away their freedom, and in this respect they are distrustful of most southern men. It generally requires personal assurances from a United States officer to make them feel safe. But the advice of such an officer is almost uniformly followed. In this manner an immense number of contracts has been made, and it is daily increasing. A northern man has no difficulty in making contracts, and but little in enforcing them. The complaints of southern men that the contracts are not well observed by the freedmen are in many instances well founded. The same can be said of the complaints of freedmen with regard to the planters. The negro, fresh from slavery, has naturally but a crude idea of the binding force of a written agreement, and it is galling to many of the planters to stand in such relations as a contract establishes to those who formerly were their slaves. I was, however, informed by officers of the Freedmen's Bureau, and by planters also, that things were improving in that respect. Contracts will be more readily entered into and more strictly kept as soon as the intimate relations between labor and compensation are better understood and appreciated on both sides.

*Insolence and insubordination.*—The new spirit which emancipation has awakened in the colored people has undoubtedly developed itself in some individuals, especially young men, to an offensive degree. Hence cases of insolence on the part of freedmen occur. But such occurrences are comparatively rare. On the whole, the conduct of the colored people is far more submissive than anybody had a right to expect. The acts of violence perpetrated by freedmen against white persons do not stand in any proportion to those committed by whites against negroes. Every such occurrence is sure to be noticed in the southern papers, and we have heard of but very few.

When Southern people speak of the insolence of the negro, they generally mean something which persons who never lived under the system of slavery are not apt to appreciate. It is but very rarely what would be called insolence among equals. But, as an old planter said to me, "Our people cannot realize yet that the negro is free." A negro is called insolent whenever his conduct varies in any manner from what a southern man was accustomed to when slavery existed.

The complaints made about the insubordination of the negro laborers on plantations have to be taken with the same allowance. There have been, no doubt, many cases in which freedmen showed a refractory spirit, where orders were disobeyed, and instructions disregarded. There have been some instances of positive resistance. But when inquiring into particulars, I found not unfrequently that the employer had adhered too strictly to his old way of doing things. I hardly heard any such complaints from Northern men. I have heard planters complain very earnestly of the insubordinate spirit of their colored laborers because they remonstrated against the practice of corporeal punishment. This was looked upon as a symptom of an impending insurrection. A great many things are regarded in the old slave States as acts of insubordination on the part of the laborer which, in the free States, would be taken as perfectly natural and harmless. The fact is, a good many planters are at present more nervously jealous of their authority than before, while the freedmen are not always inclined to forget that they are free men.

*Extravagant notions.*—In many localities I found an impression prevailing among the negroes that some great change was going to take place about Christmas. Feeling uneasy in their present condition, they indulged in the expectation that government intended to make some further provision for their future welfare, especially by ordering distributions of land among them. To counteract this expectation, which had a tendency to interfere seriously with the making of contracts for the next season, it was considered necessary to send military officers, and especially agents of the Freedmen's Bureau, among them, who, by administering sound advice and spreading correct information, would induce them to suit their conduct to their actual circumstances. While in the south I heard of many instances in which this measure had the desired effect, and it is to be expected that the effect was uniformly good wherever judicious officers were so employed.

Impressions like the above are very apt to spread among the negroes, for the reason that they ardently desire to become freeholders. In the independent possession of landed property they see the consummation of their deliverance. However mistaken their notions may be in other respects, it must be admitted that this instinct is correct.

*Relations between the two races.* — There are whites in the south who profess great kindness for the negro. Many of them are, no doubt, sincere in what they say. But as to the feelings of the masses, it is hardly necessary to add anything to what I have already stated. I have heard it asserted that the negroes also cherish feelings of hostility to the whites. Taking this as a general assertion, I am satisfied that it is incorrect. The negroes do not trust their late masters because they do not feel their freedom sufficiently assured. Many of them may harbor feelings of resentment towards those who now ill-treat and persecute them, but as they practiced no revenge after their emancipation for wrongs suffered while in slavery, so their present resentments are likely to cease as soon as the persecution ceases. If the persecution and the denial of their rights as freemen continue, the resentments growing out of them will continue and spread. The negro is constitutionally docile and eminently good-natured. Instances of the most touching attachment of freedmen to their old masters and mistresses have come to my notice. To a white man whom they believe to be sincerely their friend they cling with greater affection even than to one of their own race. By some northern speculators their confidence has been sadly abused. Nevertheless, the trust they place in persons coming from the north, or in any way connected with the government, is most childlike and unbounded. There may be individual exceptions, but I am sure they are not numerous. Those who enjoy their confidence enjoy also their affection. Centuries of slavery have not been sufficient to make them the enemies of the white race. If in the future a feeling of mutual hostility should develop itself between the races, it will probably not be the fault of those who have shown such an inexhaustible patience under the most adverse and trying circumstances.

In some places that I visited I found apprehensions entertained by whites of impending negro insurrections. Whenever our military commanders found it expedient to subject the statements made to that effect by whites to close investigation, they uniformly found them unwarranted by fact. In many instances there were just reasons for supposing that such apprehensions were industriously spread for the purpose of serving as an excuse for further persecution. In the papers annexed to this report you will find testimony supporting this statement. The negro is easily led; he is always inclined to follow the advice of those he trusts. I do, therefore, not consider a negro insurrection probable as long as the freedmen are under the direct protection of the government, and may hope to see their grievances redressed without resorting to the extreme means of self-protection. There would, perhaps, be danger of insurrections if the government should withdraw its protection from them, and if, against an attempt on the part of the whites to reduce them to something like their former condition, they should find themselves thrown back upon their own resources. Of this contingency I shall speak below.

*Education.* — That the negroes should have come out of slavery as an ignorant class is not surprising when we consider that it was a penal offence to teach them while they were in slavery; but their eager desire to learn, and the alacrity and success with which they avail themselves of every facility offered to them in that respect, has become a matter of notoriety. The statistics of the Freedmen's Bureau show to what extent such facilities have been offered and what results have been attained. As far as my information goes, these results are most encouraging for the future.

## PROSPECTIVE — THE REACTIONARY TENDENCY.

I stated above that, in my opinion, the solution of the social problem in the south did not depend upon the capacity and conduct of the negro alone, but in the same measure upon the ideas and feelings entertained and acted upon by the whites. What their ideas and feelings were while under my observation, and how they affected the contact of the two races, I have already set forth. The question arises, what policy will be adopted by the "ruling class" when all restraint imposed upon them by the military power of the national government is withdrawn, and they are left free to regulate matters according to their own tastes? It would be presumptuous to speak of the future with absolute certainty; but it may safely be assumed that the same causes will always tend to produce the same effects. As long as a majority of the southern people believe that "the negro will not work without physical compulsion," and that "the blacks at large belong to the whites at large," that belief will tend to produce a system of coercion, the enforcement of which will be aided by the hostile feeling against the negro now prevailing among the whites, and by the general spirit of violence which in the south is fostered by the influence slavery exercised upon the popular character. It is, indeed, not probable that a general attempt will be made to restore slavery in its old form, on account of the barriers which such an attempt would find in its way; but there are systems intermediate between slavery as it formerly existed in the south, and free labor as it exists in the north, but more nearly related to the former than to the latter, *the introduction of which will be attempted.* I have already noticed some movements in that direction, which were made under the very eyes of our military authorities, and of which the Opelousas and St. Landry ordinances were the most significant. Other things of more recent date, such as the new negro code submitted by a committee to the legislature of South Carolina, are before the country. They have all the same tendency, because they all spring from the same cause.

It may be objected that evidence has been given of a contrary spirit by the State conventions which passed ordinances abolishing slavery in their States, and making it obligatory upon the legislatures to enact laws for the protection of the freedmen. While acknowledging the fact, I deem it dangerous to be led by it into any delusions. As to the motives upon which they acted when abolishing slavery, and their understanding of the bearings of such an act, we may safely accept the standard they have set up for themselves. When speaking of popular demonstrations in the south in favor of submission to the government, I stated that the principal and almost the only argument used was, that they found themselves in a situation in which "they could do no better." It was the same thing with regard to the abolition of slavery; wherever abolition was publicly advocated, whether in popular meetings or in State conventions, it was on the ground of necessity—not unfrequently with the significant addition that, as soon as they had once more control of their own State affairs, they could settle the labor question to suit themselves, whatever they might have to submit to for the present. Not only did I find this to be the common talk among the people, but the same sentiment was openly avowed by public men in speech and print. Some declarations of that kind, made by men of great prominence, have passed into the newspapers and are undoubtedly known to you. I append to this report a specimen, (accompanying document No. 40), not as something particularly remarkable, but in order to represent the current sentiment as expressed in the language of a candidate for a seat in the State convention of Mississippi. It is a card addressed to the voters of Wilkinson county, Mississippi, by General W. L. Brandon. The general complains of having been called "an unconditional, immediate emancipationist—an abolitionist." He indignantly repels the charge and avows himself a good pro-slavery man. "But, fellow-citizens," says he, "what I may in common with you have to submit to, is a very different thing. Slavery has been taken from us; the power that has already practically abolished it threatens totally and forever to abolish it. *But does it follow that I am in favor of this thing? By no means.* My honest conviction is, we must accept the situation as it is, *until we can get control once more of our own State affairs. We cannot do otherwise and get our place again in the Union, and occupy a position, exert an influence that will protect us against greater evils which threaten us.* I must, as any other man who votes or holds an office, submit *for the time* to evils I cannot remedy."

General Brandon was elected on that platform, and in the convention voted for the ordinance abolishing slavery, and imposing upon the legislature the duty to pass laws for the protection of the freedmen. And General Brandon is certainly looked upon in Mississippi as an honorable man, and an honest politician. What he will vote for when his people have got once more control of their own State affairs, and his State has regained its position and influence in the Union, it is needless to ask. I repeat, his case is not an isolated one. He has only put in print what, as my observations lead me to believe, a majority of the people say even in more emphatic language; and the deliberations of several legislatures in that part of the country show what it means. I deem it unnecessary to go into further particulars.

It is worthy of note that the convention of Mississippi—and the conventions of other States have followed its example—imposed upon subsequent legislatures the obligation not only to pass laws for the protection of the freedmen in person and property, but also *to guard against the dangers arising from sudden emancipation*. This language is not without significance; not the blessings of a full development of free labor, but only the dangers of emancipation are spoken of. It will be observed that this clause is so vaguely worded as to authorize the legislatures to place any restriction they may see fit upon the emancipated negro, in perfect consistency with the amended State constitutions; for it rests with them to define what the dangers of sudden emancipation consist in, and what measures may be required to guard against them. It is true, the clause does not authorize the legislatures to re-establish slavery in the old form; but they may pass whatever laws they see fit, stopping short only one step of what may strictly be defined as "slavery." Peonage of the Mexican pattern, or serfdom of some European pattern, may under that clause be considered admissible; and looking at the legislative attempts already made, especially the labor code now under consideration in the legislature of South Carolina, it appears not only possible, but eminently probable, that the laws which will be passed to guard against the dangers arising from emancipation will be directed against the spirit of emancipation itself.

A more tangible evidence of good intentions would seem to have been furnished by the admission of negro testimony in the courts of justice, which has been conceded in some of the southern States, at least in point of form. This being a matter of vital interest to the colored man, I inquired into the feelings of people concerning it with particular care. At first I found hardly any southern man that favored it. Even persons of some liberality of mind saw seemingly insurmountable objections. The appearance of a general order issued by General Swayne in Alabama, which made it optional for the civil authorities either to admit negro testimony in the State courts or to have all cases in which colored people were concerned tried by officers of the bureau or military commissions, seemed to be the signal for a change of position on the part of the politicians. A great many of them, seeing a chance for getting rid of the jurisdiction of the Freedmen's Bureau, dropped their opposition somewhat suddenly and endeavored to make the admission of negro testimony in the State courts palatable to the masses by assuring them that at all events it would rest with the judges and juries to determine in each case before them whether the testimony of negro witnesses was worth anything or not. One of the speeches delivered at Vicksburg, already referred to in another connexion, and a card published by a candidate for office (accompanying document No. 14), furnish specimens of that line of argument.

In my despatch from Montgomery, Alabama, I suggested to you that instructions be issued making it part of the duty of agents of the Freedmen's Bureau to appear in the State courts as the freedmen's next friend, and to forward reports of the proceedings had in the principal cases to the headquarters of the bureau. In this manner it would have been possible to ascertain to what extent the admission of negro testimony secured to the colored man justice in the State courts. As the plan does not seem to have been adopted, we must form our conclusions from evidence less complete. Among the annexed documents there are several statements concerning its results, made by gentlemen whose business it was to observe. I would invite your attention to the letters of Captain Poillon, agent of the Freedmen's Bureau at Mobile; Major Reynolds, assistant commissioner of the bureau at Natchez; and Colonel Thomas, assistant commissioner for the State of Mississippi. (Accompanying documents Nos. 41 and 27.) The opinions expressed in these papers are uniformly unfavorable. It is to be hoped that at other places better results have been attained. But I may state that even by prominent southern men, who were anxious to have the jurisdiction of the State courts extended over the freedmen, the admission was made to me that the testimony of a negro would have but little weight with a southern jury. I frequently asked the question, "Do you think a jury of your people would be apt to find a planter who has whipped one of his negro laborers guilty of assault and battery?" The answer almost invariably was, "You must make some allowance for the prejudices of our people."

It is probable that the laws excluding negro testimony from the courts will be repealed in all the States lately in rebellion if it is believed that a satisfactory arrangement of this matter may in any way facilitate the "readmission" of the States, but I apprehend such arrangements will hardly be sufficient to secure to the colored man impartial justice as long as the feelings of the whites are against him and they think that his rights are less entitled to respect than their own. More potent certainly than the laws of a country are the opinions of right and wrong entertained by its people. When the spirit of a law is in conflict with such opinions, there is but little prospect of its being faithfully put in execution, especially where those who hold such opinions are the same who have to administer the laws.

The facility with which southern politicians acquiesce in the admission of negro testimony is not surprising when we consider that the practical management of the matter will rest with their own people. I found them less accommodating with regard to "constitutional amendment." Nine-tenths of the intelligent men with whom I had any conversation upon that subject expressed their willingness to ratify the first section, abolishing slavery throughout the United States, but not the second section, empowering Congress "to enforce the foregoing by appropriate legislation." I feel warranted in saying that, while I was in the south, this was the prevailing sentiment. Nevertheless, I deem it probable that the "constitutional amendment" will be ratified by every State legislature, provided the government insists upon such ratification as a *conditio sine qua non* of readmission. It is instructive to observe how powerful and immediate an effect the announcement of such a condition by the government produces in southern conventions and legislatures. It would be idle to assume, however, that a telegraphic despatch, while it may beat down all parliamentary opposition to this or that measure, will at the same time obliterate the prejudices of the people; nor will it prevent those prejudices from making themselves seriously felt in the future. It will require measures of a more practical character to prevent the dangers which, as everybody that reads the signs of the times must see, are now impending. . . .

## NEGRO SUFFRAGE.

It would seem that the interference of the national authority in the home concerns of the southern States would be rendered less necessary, and the whole problem of political and social reconstruction be much simplified, if, while the masses lately arrayed against the government are permitted to vote, the large majority of those who were always loyal, and are naturally anxious to see the free labor problem successfully solved, were not excluded from all influence upon legislation. In all questions concerning the Union, the national debt, and the future social organization of the south, the feelings of the colored man are naturally in sympathy with the views and aims of the national government. While the southern white fought against the Union, the negro did all he could to aid it; while the southern white sees in the national government his conqueror, the negro sees in it his protector; while the white owes to the national debt his defeat, the negro owes to it his deliverance; while the white considers himself robbed and ruined by the emancipation of the slaves, the negro finds in it the assurance of future prosperity and happiness. In all the important issues the negro would be led by natural impulse to forward the ends of the government, and by making his influence, as part of the voting body, tell upon the legislation of the States, render the interference of the national authority less necessary.

As the most difficult of the pending questions are intimately connected with the status of the negro in southern society, it is obvious that a correct solution can be more easily obtained if he has a voice in the matter. In the right to vote he would find the best permanent protection against oppressive class-legislation, as well as against individual persecution. The relations between the white and black races, even if improved by the gradual wearing off of the present animosities, are likely to remain long under the troubling influence of prejudice. It is a notorious fact that the rights of a man of some political power are far less exposed to violation than those of one who is, in matters of public interest, completely subject to the will of others. A voter is a man of influence; small as that influence may be in the single individual, it becomes larger when that individual belongs to a numerous class of voters who are ready to make common cause with him for the protection of his rights. Such an individual is an object of interest to the political parties that desire to have the benefit of his ballot. It is true, the bringing face to face at the ballot-box of the white and black races may here and there lead to an outbreak of feeling, and the first trials ought certainly to be made while the national power is still there to prevent or repress disturbances; but the practice once successfully inaugurated under the protection of that power, it would probably be more apt than anything else to obliterate old antagonisms, especially if the colored people—which is probable, as soon as their own rights are sufficiently secured—divide their votes between the different political parties.

The effect of the extension of the franchise to the colored people upon the development of free labor and upon the security of human rights in the south being the principal object in view, the objections raised on the ground of the ignorance of the freedmen become unimportant. Practical liberty is a good school, and, besides, if any qualification can be found, applicable to both races, which does not interfere with the attainment of the main object, such qualification would in that respect be unobjectionable. But it is idle to say that it will be time to speak of negro suffrage when the whole colored race will be educated, for the ballot may be necessary to him to secure his education. It is also idle to say that ignorance is the principal ground upon which southern men object to negro suffrage, for if it were, that numerous class of colored people in Louisiana who are as highly educated, as intelligent, and as wealthy as any corresponding class of whites, would have been enfranchised long ago.

It has been asserted that the negro would be but a voting machine in the hand of his employer. On this point opinions seem to differ. I have heard it said in the south that the freedmen are more likely to be influenced by their schoolmasters and preachers. But even if we suppose the

employer to control to a certain extent the negro laborer's
vote, two things are to be taken into consideration: 1. The
class of employers, of landed proprietors, will in a few years
be very different from what it was heretofore in consequence of the general breaking up; a great many of the old
slaveholders will be obliged to give up their lands and new
men will step into their places; and 2. The employer will
hardly control the vote of the negro laborer so far as to
make him vote against his own liberty. The beneficial effect
of an extension of suffrage does not always depend upon
the intelligence with which the newly admitted voters exercise their right, but sometimes upon the circumstances in
which they are placed; and the circumstances in which the
freedmen of the south are placed are such that, when they
only vote for their own liberty and rights, they vote for the
rights of free labor, for the success of an immediate important reform, for the prosperity of the country, and for the
general interests of mankind. If, therefore, in order to control the colored vote, the employer, or whoever he may be,
is first obliged to concede to the freedman the great point
of his own rights as a man and a free laborer, the great social reform is completed, the most difficult problem is
solved, and all other questions it will be comparatively easy
to settle.

In discussing the matter of negro suffrage I deemed it
my duty to confine myself strictly to the practical aspects of
the subject. I have, therefore, not touched its moral merits
nor discussed the question whether the national government is competent to enlarge the elective franchise in the
States lately in rebellion by its own act; I deem it proper,
however, to offer a few remarks on the assertion frequently
put forth, that the franchise is likely to be extended to the
colored man by the voluntary action of the southern whites
themselves. My observation leads me to a contrary opinion.
Aside from a very few enlightened men, I found but one
class of people in favor of the enfranchisement of the
blacks: it was the class of Unionists who found themselves
politically ostracized and looked upon the enfranchisement of the loyal negroes as the salvation of the whole
loyal element. But their numbers and influence are sadly
insufficient to secure such a result. The masses are strongly
opposed to colored suffrage; anybody that dares to advo-

cate it is stigmatized as a dangerous fanatic; nor do I deem it probable that in the ordinary course of things prejudices will wear off to such an extent as to make it a popular measure. Outside of Louisiana only one gentleman who occupied a prominent political position in the south expressed to me an opinion favorable to it. He declared himself ready to vote for an amendment to the constitution of his State bestowing the right of suffrage upon all male citizens without distinction of color who could furnish evidence of their ability to read and write, without, however, disfranchising those who are now voters and are not able to fulfil that condition. This gentleman is now a member of one of the State conventions, but I presume he will not risk his political standing in the south by moving such an amendment in that body.

The only manner in which, in my opinion, the southern people can be induced to grant to the freedman some measure of self-protecting power in the form of suffrage, is to make it a condition precedent to "readmission.". . .

## CONCLUSION.

I may sum up all I have said in a few words. If nothing were necessary but to restore the machinery of government in the States lately in rebellion in point of form, the movements made to that end by the people of the south might be considered satisfactory. But if it is required that the southern people should also accommodate themselves to the results of the war in point of spirit, those movements fall far short of what must be insisted upon.

The loyalty of the masses and most of the leaders of the southern people, consists in submission to necessity. There is, except in individual instances, an entire absence of that national spirit which forms the basis of true loyalty and patriotism.

The emancipation of the slaves is submitted to only in so far as chattel slavery in the old form could not be kept up. But although the freedman is no longer considered the property of the individual master, he is considered the slave of society, and all independent State legislation will share the tendency to make him such. The ordinances abolishing slavery passed by the conventions under the pressure of circumstances, will not be looked upon as barring the establishment of a new form of servitude.

Practical attempts on the part of the southern people to deprive the negro of his rights as a freeman may result in bloody collisions, and will certainly plunge southern society into restless fluctuations and anarchical confusion. Such evils can be prevented only by continuing the control of the national government in the States lately in rebellion until free labor is fully developed and firmly established, and the advantages and blessings of the new order of things have disclosed themselves. This desirable result will be hastened by a firm declaration on the part of the government, that national control in the south will not cease until such results are secured. Only in this way can that security be established in the south which will render numerous immigration possible, and such immigration would materially aid a favorable development of things.

The solution of the problem would be very much facilitated by enabling all the loyal and free-labor elements in the south to exercise a healthy influence upon legislation. It will hardly be possible to secure the freedman against oppressive class legislation and private persecution, unless he be endowed with a certain measure of political power.

As to the future peace and harmony of the Union, it is of the highest importance that the people lately in rebellion be not permitted to build up another "peculiar institution" whose spirit is in conflict with the fundamental principles of our political system; for as long as they cherish interests peculiar to them in preference to those they have in common with the rest of the American people, their loyalty to the Union will always be uncertain.

I desire not to be understood as saying that there are no well-meaning men among those who were compromised in the rebellion. There are many, but neither their number nor their influence is strong enough to control the manifest tendency of the popular spirit. There are great reasons for hope that a determined policy on the part of the national government will produce innumerable and valuable conversions. This consideration counsels lenity as to persons, such as is demanded by the humane and enlightened spirit of our times, and vigor and firmness in the carrying out of principles, such as is demanded by the national sense of justice and the exigencies of our situation.

In submitting this report I desire to say that I have conscientiously endeavored to see things as they were, and to represent them as I saw them: I have been careful not to use stronger language than was warranted by the thoughts I intended to express. A comparison of the tenor of the annexed documents with that of my report, will convince you that I have studiously avoided overstatements. Certain legislative attempts at present made in the south, and especially in South Carolina, seem to be more than justifying the apprehensions I have expressed.

Conscious though I am of having used my best endeavors to draw, from what I saw and learned, correct general conclusions, yet I am far from placing too great a trust in my own judgment, when interests of such magnitude are at stake. I know that this report is incomplete, although as complete as an observation of a few months could enable me to make it. Additional facts might be elicited, calculated to throw new light upon the subject. Although I see no reason for believing that things have changed for the better since I left for the south, yet such may be the case. Admitting all these possibilities, I would entreat you to take no irretraceable step towards relieving the States lately in rebellion from all national control, until such favorable changes are clearly and unmistakably ascertained.

To that end, and by virtue of the permission you honored me with when sending me out to communicate to you freely and unreservedly my views as to measures of policy proper to be adopted, I would now respectfully suggest that you advise Congress to send one or more "investigating committees" into the southern States, to inquire for themselves into the actual condition of things, before final action is taken upon the readmission of such States to their representation in the legislative branch of the government, and the withdrawal of the national control from that section of the country.

I am, sir, very respectfully, your obedient servant,

CARL SCHURZ.

His Excellency ANDREW JOHNSON,
    *President of the United States.*

# LAWS OF THE STATE OF MISSISSIPPI

## *(1866)*

No sooner had the Civil War ended than whites in each of the former Confederate states passed special laws, the so-called Black Codes, designed to define the legal status and regulate the economic and social condition of the freedpeople. Whites reasoned that slavery's demise required new regulations setting forth the legal contours of race relations. Though the blacks gained rights formerly denied them as slaves (including the right to sue and be sued, the legalization of marriages and the offspring of such unions), the Black Codes circumscribed the freedmen and -women, keeping them tied to the land as agricultural laborers and under conditions as close to slavery as possible. Mississippi passed the first of these repressive ordinances, which served as models for other states. By early 1866, Freedmen's Bureau and U.S. Army officers nullified these laws. The codes exposed the unwillingness of white Southerners to accept the full meaning of emancipation, undermined Presidential Reconstruction, and fueled the rise of Radical Reconstruction.

## AN ACT to Confer Civil Rights on Freedmen, and for Other Purposes.

Section 1. *Be it enacted by the Legislature of the State of Mississippi,* That all freedmen, free negroes and mulattoes may sue and be sued, implead and be impleaded in all the courts of law and equity of this State, and may acquire personal property and choses in action, by descent or purchase, and may dispose of the same, in the same manner, and to the same extent that white persons may: Provided that the provisions of this section shall not be so construed as to allow any freedman, free negro or mulatto, to rent or lease any lands or tenements, except in incorporated towns or cities in which places the corporate authorities shall control the same.

SEC. 2. Be it further enacted, That all freedmen, free negroes and mulattoes may intermarry with each other, in the same manner and under the same regulations that are provided by law for white persons: Provided, that the clerk of probate shall keep separate records of the same.

SEC. 3. Be it further enacted, That all freedmen, free negroes and mulattoes, who do now and have heretofore lived and cohabited together as husband and wife shall be taken and held in law as legally married, and the issue shall be taken and held as legitimate for all purposes. That it shall not be lawful for any freedman, free negro or mulatto to intermarry with any white person; nor for any white person to intermarry with any freedman, free negro or mulatto; and any person who shall so intermarry shall be deemed guilty of felony, and on conviction thereof, shall be confined in the State Penitentiary for life; and those shall be deemed freedmen, free negroes and mulattoes who are of pure negro blood, and those descended from a negro to the third generation inclusive, though one ancestor of each generation may have been a white person.

SEC. 4. Be it further enacted, That in addition to cases in which freedmen, free negroes and mulattoes are now by law competent witnesses, freedmen, free negroes or mulattoes shall be competent in civil cases when a party or parties to the suit, either plaintiff or plaintiffs, defendant or defendants; also in cases where freedmen, free negroes and mulattoes is or are either plaintiff or plaintiffs, defendant or defendants, and a white person or white persons is or are the opposing party or parties, plaintiff or plaintiffs, defendant or defendants. They shall also be competent witnesses in all criminal prosecutions where the crime charged is alleged to have been committed by a white person upon or against the person or property of a freedman, free negro or mulatto: Provided that in all cases said witnesses shall be examined in open court on the stand, except however, they may be examined before the grand jury, and shall in all cases be subject to the rules and tests of the common law as to competency and credibility.

SEC. 5. Be it further enacted, That every freedman, free negro and mulatto, shall, on the second Monday of January, one thousand eight hundred and sixty-six, and annually thereafter, have a lawful home or employment, and shall have written evidence thereof, as follows, to wit: if living in any incorporated city, town or village, a license from the mayor thereof; and if living outside of any incorporated city, town or village, from the member of the board of police of his beat, authorizing him or her to do irregular and job work, or a written contract, as provided in section sixth of this act, which licenses may be revoked for cause, at anytime, by the authority granting the same.

SEC. 6. Be it further enacted, That all contracts for labor made with freedmen, free negroes and mulattoes, for a longer period than one month shall be in writing and in duplicate, attested and read to said freedman, free negro or mulatto, by a beat, city or county officer, or two disinterested white persons of the county in which the labor is to be performed, of which each party shall have one; and said contracts shall be taken and held as entire contracts, and if the laborer shall quit the service of the employer, before expiration of his term of service, without good cause, he shall forfeit his wages for that year, up to the time of quitting.

SEC. 7. Be it further enacted, That every civil officer shall, and every person may arrest and carry back to his or her legal employer any freedman, free negro or mulatto, who shall have quit the service of his or her employer before the expiration of his or her term of service without good cause, and said officer and person shall be entitled to receive for arresting and carrying back every deserting employee aforesaid, the sum of five dollars, and ten cents per mile from the place of arrest to the place of delivery, and the same shall be paid by the employer, and held as a set-off for so much against the wages of said deserting employee: Provided that said arrested party after being so returned may appeal to a justice of the peace or member of the board of police of the county, who on notice to the alledged employer, shall try summarily whether said appellant is legally

employed by the alleged employer and has good cause to
quit said employer; either party shall have the right of appeal to the county court, pending which the alleged deserter shall be remanded to the alleged employer, or
otherwise disposed of as shall be right and just, and the decision of the county court shall be final.

SEC. 8. Be it further enacted, That upon affidavit made
by the employer of any freedman, free negro or mulatto, or
other credible person, before any justice of the peace or
member of the board of police, that any freedman, free negro or mulatto, legally employed by said employer, has il-
legally deserted said employment, such justice of the peace
or member of the board of police, shall issue his warrant or
warrants, returnable before himself, or other such officer,
directed to any sheriff, constable or special deputy, commanding him to arrest said deserter and return him or her
to said employer, and the like proceedings shall be had as
provided in the preceding section; and it shall be lawful for
any officer to whom such warrant shall be directed, to execute said warrant in any county of this State, and that said
warrant may be transmitted without endorsement to any
like officer of another county, to be executed and returned
as aforesaid, and the said employer shall pay the cost of
said warrants and arrest and return, which shall be set off
for so much against the wages of said deserter.

SEC. 9. Be it further enacted, That if any person shall persuade or attempt to persuade, entice or cause any freedman, free negro or mulatto, to desert from the legal employment of any person, before the expiration of his or her
term of service, or shall knowingly employ any such deserting freedman, free negro or mulatto, or shall knowingly
give or sell to any such deserting freedman, free negro or
mulatto, any food, rayment or other thing, he or she shall be
guilty of a misdemeanor, and upon conviction, shall be
fined not less than twenty-five dollars and not more than
two hundred dollars and the costs, and if said fine and costs
shall not be immediately paid, the court shall sentence said
convict to not exceeding two months imprisonment in the
county jail, and he or she shall moreover be liable to the
party injured in damages: Provided, if any person shall, or
shall attempt to persuade, entice, or cause any freedman,
free negro or mulatto, to desert from any legal employment

of any person, with the view to employ said freedman, free negro or mulatto, without the limits of this State, such person, on conviction, shall be fined not less than fifty dollars and not more than five hundred dollars and costs, and if said fine and costs shall not be immediately paid, the court shall sentence said convict to not exceeding six months imprisonment in the county jail.

SEC. 10. Be it further enacted, That it shall be lawful for any freedman, free negro or mulatto to charge any white person, freedman, free negro or mulatto, by affidavit, with any criminal offence against his or her person or property and upon such affidavit the proper process shall be issued and executed as if said affidavit was made by a white person, and it shall be lawful for any freedman, free negro or mulatto, in any action, suit or controversy pending, or about to be instituted, in any court of law or equity of this State, to make all needful and lawful affidavits, as shall be necessary for the institution, prosecution or defence of such suit or controversy.

SEC. 11. Be it further enacted, That the penal laws of this State, in all cases not otherwise specially provided for, shall apply and extend to all freedmen, free negroes and mulattoes.

SEC. 12. Be it further enacted, That this act take effect and be in force from and after its passage.

Approved November 25, 1865.

# AN ACT TO BE ENTITLED "AN ACT TO REGULATE THE RELATION OF MASTER AND APPRENTICE, AS RELATES TO FREEDMEN, FREE NEGROES, AND MULATTOES."

SECTION 1. *Be it enacted by the Legislature of the State of Mississippi,* That it shall be the duty of all sheriffs, justices of the peace, and other civil officers of the several counties in this State, to report to the probate courts of their respective counties, semi-annually, at the January and July terms of said courts, all freedmen, free negroes and mulattoes, under the age of eighteen, within their respective counties, beats or districts, who are orphans, or whose parent or par-

ents have not the means, or who refuse to provide for and
support said minors, and thereupon it shall be the duty of
said probate court, to order the clerk of said court to apprentice said minors to some competent and suitable person, on such terms as the court may direct, having a
particular care to the interest of said minor: Provided, that
the former owner of said minors shall have the preference,
when in the opinion of the court, he or she shall be a suitable person for that purpose.

SEC. 2. Be it further enacted, That the said court shall be
fully satisfied that the person or persons to whom said minor shall be apprenticed, shall be a suitable person to have
the charge and care of said minor, and fully to protect the
interest of said minor. The said court shall require the said
master or mistress to execute bond and security, payable to
the State of Mississippi, conditioned that he or she shall
furnish said minor with sufficient food and clothing, to treat
said minor humanely, furnish medical attention in case of
sickness; teach or cause to be taught him or her to read and
write, if under fifteen years old, and will conform to any law
that may be hereafter passed for the regulation of the duties and relation of master and apprentice: Provided, that
said apprentice shall be bound by indenture, in case of
males until they are twenty-one years old, and in case of
females until they are eighteen, years old.

SEC. 3. Be it further enacted, That in the management
and control of said apprentices, said master or mistress
shall have power to inflict such moderate corporeal chas-
tisement as a father or guardian is allowed to inflict on his
or her child or ward at common law: Provided, that in no
case shall cruel or inhuman punishment be inflicted.

SEC. 4. Be it further enacted, That if any apprentice shall
leave the employment of his or her master or mistress,
without his or her consent, said master or mistress may pursue and recapture said apprentice, and bring him or her before any justice of the peace of the county whose duty it
shall be to remand said apprentice to the service of his or
her master or mistress; and in the event of a refusal on the
part of said apprentice so to return, then said justice shall
commit said apprentice to the jail of said county, on failure
to give bond, until the next term of the county court; and it
shall be the duty of said court, at the first term thereafter, to

investigate said case, and if the court shall be of opinion that said apprentice left the employment of his or her master or mistress without good cause, to order him or her to be punished, as provided for the punishment of hired freedmen, as may be from time to time provided for by law, for desertion, until he or she shall agree to return to his or her master or mistress: Provided, that the court may grant continuances, as in other cases; and provided, further, that if the court shall believe that said apprentice had good cause to quit his said master or mistress, the court shall discharge said apprentice from said indenture, and also enter a judgment against the master or mistress, for not more than one hundred dollars, for the use and benefit of said apprentice, to be collected on execution, as in other cases.

SEC. 5. Be it further enacted, That if any person entice away any apprentice from his or her master or mistress, or shall knowingly employ an apprentice, or furnish him or her food or clothing, without the written consent of his or her master or mistress, or shall sell or give said apprentice ardent spirits, without such consent, said person so offending shall be deemed guilty of a high misdemeanor, and shall, on conviction thereof before the county court, be punished as provided for the punishment of persons enticing from their employer hired freedmen, free negroes or mulattoes.

SEC. 6. Be it further enacted, That it shall be the duty of all civil officers of their respective counties to report any minors within their respective counties, to said probate court, who are subject to be apprenticed under the provisions of this act, from time to time, as the facts may come to their knowledge, and it shall be the duty of said court, from time to time, as said minors shall be reported to them or otherwise come to their knowledge, to apprentice said minors as hereinbefore provided.

SEC. 7. Be it further enacted, That in case the master or mistress of any apprentice shall desire, he or she shall have the privilege to summon his or her said apprentice, to the probate court, and thereupon, with the approval of the court, he or she shall be released from all liability as master of said apprentice, and his said bond shall be cancelled, and it shall be the duty of the court forthwith to re-apprentice said minor; and in the event any master of an apprentice shall die before the close of the term of service of said apprentice, it shall be the duty of the court to give the preference in re-apprenticing said minor to the widow, or other member of said master's family: Provided, that said widow, or other member of said family shall be a suitable person for that purpose.

SEC. 8. Be it further enacted, That in case any master or mistress of any apprentice, bound to him or her under this act, shall be about to remove, or shall have removed to any other State of the United States by the laws of which such apprentice may be an inhabitant thereof, the probate court of the proper county may authorize the removal of such apprentice to such State, upon the said master or mistress entering into bond, with security, in a penalty to be fixed by the judge, conditioned that said master or mistress will, upon such removal, comply with the laws of such State in such cases: Provided, that said master shall be cited to attend the court at which such order is proposed to be made, and shall have a right to resist the same by next friend, or otherwise.

SEC. 9. Be it further enacted, That it shall be lawful for any freedman, free negro or mulatto, having a minor child or children, to apprentice the said minor child or children as provided for by this act.

SEC. 10. Be it further enacted, That in all cases where the age of the freedman, free negro or mulatto, cannot be ascertained by record testimony, the judge of the county court shall fix the age.

SEC. 11. Be it further enacted, That this act take effect and be in force from and after its passage.

Approved November 22, 1865.


# AN ACT TO AMEND THE
# VAGRANT LAWS OF THE STATE.

SECTION 1. *Be it enacted by the Legislature of the State of Mississippi,* That all rogues and vagabonds, idle and dissipated persons, beggars, jugglers, or persons practicing unlawful games or plays, runaways, common drunkards, common night-walkers, pilferers, lewd, wanton, or lascivious persons, in speech or behavior, common railers and brawlers, persons who neglect their calling or employment, misspend what they earn, or do not provide for the support of themselves or their families, or dependants, and all other idle and disorderly persons, including all who neglect all lawful business, or habitually misspend their time by frequenting houses of ill-fame, gaming-houses or tippling shops, shall be deemed and considered vagrants under the provisions of this act, and on conviction thereof shall be fined not exceeding one hundred dollars, with all accruing costs, and be imprisoned at the discretion of the court not exceeding ten days.

Sec. 2. Be it further enacted, That all freedmen, free negroes and mulattoes in this State, over the age of eighteen years, found on the second Monday in January, 1866, or thereafter, with no lawful employment or business, or found unlawfully assembling themselves together either in the day or night time, and all white persons so assembling with freedmen, free negroes or mulattoes, or usually associating with freedmen, free negroes or mulattoes on terms of equality, or living in adultery or fornication with a freedwoman, free negro, or mulatto, shall be deemed vagrants, and on conviction thereof, shall be fined in the sum of not exceeding, in the case of a freedman, free negro or mulatto, fifty dollars, and a white man two hundred dollars, and imprisoned at the discretion of the court, the free negro not exceeding ten days, and the white man not exceeding six months.

Sec. 3. Be it further enacted, That all justices of the peace, mayors and aldermen of incorporated towns and cities of the several counties in this State, shall have jurisdiction to try all questions of vagrancy, in their respective towns, counties and cities, and it is hereby made their duty, whenever they shall ascertain that any person or persons, in their respective towns, counties and cities, are violating any of the provisions of this act, to have said party or parties arrested and brought before them, and immediately investigate said charge, and on conviction, punish said party or parties as provided for herein. And it is hereby made the duty of all sheriffs, constables, town constables, city marshals and all like officers, to report to some officer having jurisdiction, all violations of any of the provisions of this act, and it shall be the duty of the county courts to inquire if any officers have neglected any of the duties required by this act, and in case any officer shall fail or neglect any duty herein, it shall be the duty of the county court to fine said officer upon conviction, not exceeding one hundred dollars, to be paid into the county treasury for county purposes.

Sec. 4. Be it further enacted, That keepers of gaming houses, houses of prostitution, all prostitutes, public or private, and all persons who derive their chief support in employments that militate against good morals, or against law shall be deemed and held to be vagrants.

Sec. 5. Be it further enacted, That all fines and forfeitures collected under the provisions of this act shall be paid into the county treasury for general county purposes, and in case any freedman, free negro or mulatto, shall fail for five days after the imposition of any fine or forfeiture upon him or her for violation of any of the provisions of this act, to pay the same, that it shall be, and is hereby made the duty of the sheriff of the proper county to hire out said freedman, free negro or mulatto, to any person who will, for the shortest period of service, pay said fine or forfeiture and all costs: Provided, a preference shall be given to the employer, if there be one, in which case the employer shall be entitled to deduct and retain the amount so paid from the wages of such freedman, free negro or mulatto, then due or to become due; and in case such freedman, free negro or mulatto cannot be hired out he or she may be dealt with as a pauper.

Sec. 6. Be it further enacted, That the same duties and liabilities existing among white persons of this State shall attach to freedmen, free negroes and mulattoes, to support their indigent families, and all colored paupers; and that in order to secure a support for such indigent freedmen, free negroes and mulattoes, it shall be lawful, and it is hereby made the duty of the boards of county police of each county in this State, to levy a poll or capitation tax on each and every freedman, free negro or mulatto, between the ages of eighteen and sixty years, not to exceed the sum of one dollar annually, to each person so taxed, which tax, when collected, shall be paid into the county treasurer's hands, and constitute a fund to be called the Freedman's Pauper Fund, which shall be applied by the commissioners of the poor for the maintenance of the poor of the freedmen, free negroes and mulattoes of this State, under such regulations as may be established by the boards of county police, in the respective counties of this State.

SEC. 7. Be it further enacted, That if any freedman, free negro or mulatto shall fail, or refuse to pay any tax levied according to the provisions of the sixth section of this act, it shall be *prima facie* evidence of vagrancy, and it shall be the duty of the sheriff to arrest such freedman, free negro or mulatto, or such person refusing or neglecting to pay such tax, and proceed at once to hire, for the shortest time, such delinquent tax payer to any one who will pay the said tax, with accruing costs, giving preference to the employer, if there be one.

SEC. 8. Be it further enacted, That any person feeling himself or herself aggrieved by the judgment of any justice of the peace, mayor or alderman, in cases arising under this act, may, within five days, appeal to the next term of the county court of the proper county, upon giving bond and security in a sum not less than twenty-five, nor more than one hundred and fifty dollars, conditioned to appear and prosecute said appeal, and abide by the judgment of the county court, and said appeal shall be tried *de novo* in the county court, and the decision of said court shall be final.

SEC. 9. Be it further enacted, That this act be in force, and take effect from its passage.

Approved November 24, 1865.


# AN ACT TO PUNISH CERTAIN OFFENCES THEREIN NAMED, AND FOR OTHER PURPOSES.

SECTION 1. *Be it enacted by the Legislature of the State of Mississippi,* That no freedman, free negro or mulatto, not in the military service of the United States Government, and not licensed so to do by the board of police of his or her county, shall keep or carry fire-arms of any kind, or any ammunition, dirk or bowie knife, and on conviction thereof, in the county court, shall be punished by fine, not exceeding ten dollars, and pay the costs of such proceedings, and all such arms or ammunition shall be forfeited to the informer, and it shall be the duty of every civil and military officer to arrest any freedman, free negro or mulatto found with any such arms or ammunition, and cause him or her to be committed for trial in default of bail.

SEC. 2. Be it further enacted, That any freedman, free negro or mulatto, committing riots, routes, affrays, trespasses, malicious mischief, cruel treatment to animals, seditious speeches, insulting gestures, language or acts, or assaults on any person, disturbance of the peace, exercising the function of a minister of the Gospel, without a license from some regularly organized church, vending spirituous or intoxicating liquors, or committing any other misdemeanor, the punishment of which is not specifically provided for by law, shall, upon conviction thereof, in the county court, be fined, not less than ten dollars, and not more than one hundred dollars, and may be imprisoned, at the discretion of the court, not exceeding thirty days.

SEC. 3. Be it further enacted, That if any white person shall sell, lend or give to any freedman, free negro or mulatto, any fire-arms, dirk or bowie knife, or ammunition, or any spirituous or intoxicating liquors, such person or persons so offending, upon conviction thereof, in the county court of his or her county, shall be fined, not exceeding fifty dollars, and may be imprisoned, at the discretion of the court, not exceeding thirty days: Provided, that any master, mistress or employer of any freedman, free negro or mulatto, may give to any freedman, free negro or mulatto, apprenticed to or employed by such master, mistress or employer, spirituous or intoxicating liquors, but not in sufficient quantities to produce intoxication.

SEC. 4. Be it further enacted, That all the penal and criminal laws now in force in this State, defining offences and prescribing the mode of punishment for crimes and misdemeanors committed by slaves, free negroes or mulattoes, be and the same are hereby re-enacted, and declared to be in full force and effect, against freedmen, free negroes and mulattoes, except so far as the mode and manner of trial and punishment have been changed or altered by law.

SEC. 5. Be it further enacted, That if any freedman, free negro or mulatto, convicted of any of the misdemeanors provided against in this act, shall fail or refuse, for the space of five days after conviction, to pay the fine and costs imposed, such person shall be hired out by the sheriff or other officer, at public outcry, to any white person who will pay said fine and all costs, and take such convict for the shortest time.

SEC. 6. Be it further enacted, That this act shall be in force and take effect from and after its passage.

Approved November 29, 1865.

# JOSEPH S. FULLERTON TO ANDREW JOHNSON

## *(February 9, 1866)*

The Freedmen's Bureau Bill of March 1865 established the agency to operate for one year following the end of the Civil War. In February 1866,
when Republican congressmen sought to pass a
bill extending the life of the Bureau indefinitely
and expanding its jurisdiction and responsibilities, Johnson vetoed it. He maintained that the
agency was established as an exigency of war,
that peace rendered it unnecessary, and that its
judicial functions were unconstitutional. To gather
ammunition to eliminate the Bureau, Johnson so-
licited information from Colonel Joseph S. Fullerton (?–1897), General O. O. Howard's former Bureau
adjutant general, portions of whose report appear
here. Though Congress sustained Johnson's veto,
in July 1866 it passed another Freedmen's Bureau
Bill in spite of the president's veto.

## BUREAU OF REFUGEES, FREEDMEN AND ABANDONED LANDS

WASHINGTON, FEBRUARY 9TH 1866

. . . The Act provides for the relief of "Freedmen and Loyal
Refugees," which means that it provides for Freedmen only.
There is now no such class as "Loyal Refugees." These are
"catch" words which give to the Act the appearance of general legislation — Legislation for both the poor loyal whites
and the blacks of the South. Had the intention been to furnish relief to the loyal whites, it would have been easy to
insert the words "for relief of Freedmen & Loyal whites."
When the Act, approved March 3d. 1865, — originally estab-

lishing the bureau, was passed there were a large number of persons in the border States and within the lines of our Armies who on account of their loyalty to the government, had been driven or forced to fly from their homes in the South. These persons, generally being poor and without the necessities of life, were a charge upon the Government, and such were contemplated in the legislation for "Loyal Refugees." The war has ended; the country is at peace, and all of such persons have been provided for elsewhere, or have returned to their *former homes*, So that now there is no class known as "Loyal Refugees." After the surrender of the rebel armies, and until late in the following fall many refugees were furnished by the Commissioner of this Bureau with transportation to their homes, but none apply for such assistance now. Under the construction of this expression, the Agents of this Bureau have been instructed not to furnish supplies to the poor whites of the South, even to those who had been within the lines of our army and had returned to their homes, for they were not then "refugees." The Act then is to give relief only to "Freedmen." Commissary, Quarter master and Medical supplies are to be furnished to this class of persons; public lands are to be set apart and reserved especially for them; sites for schools and asylums, under certain conditions, are to be purchased, and special courts or tribunals are to be established for them by the Government. For the poor *loyal* whites of the South, even those who have served in our Army, there is nothing.

Aside from the fact of this being class legislation, it is such as will intensify, on the part of the poor whites of the South, the hatred that already exists between them and the blacks. This of course will be more or less disastrous to the latter class. When these poor whites realize that they have no special friends in the Bureau Agents sent south by the Government; that certain lands are not set apart for them; that Schools are not provided; that Government stores are not furnished; and that the freedman even has his special tribunals, backed by military power, where he can obtain very summary process, while they must wait for the slow and uncertain action of Civil Courts, then they will surely think that the Government intends to desert and discriminate against them, instead of raising them up from the political subjection in which they also have been held by the ruling class of the South.

As slavery has been "constitutionally" abolished the old State slave codes are now null and void, and the military force of the Government in the South, if necessary, can prevent their execution. Congress also has power under the Constitutional Amendment abolishing slavery, to enforce said amendment by appropriate legislation. Would it not be better then for Congress to pass an Act declaring all slave codes, or state laws that abridge the personal liberty of the freedmen, inoperative, and give the Agents of the government power to enforce such Act, rather than to set up an immense civil or semi-military government, within a civil government, to be placed in the hands of, in many cases, inexperienced or bad men—strangers to the people—for the protection of a certain class in the South?

The effect of establishing the Bureau upon the basis contemplated by this Act will be, I believe, to prevent the freedman, in a great measure, from acquiring that independence and self-reliance so necessary for his advancement. The Bureau as at present organized has been in existence for nearly ten months. During this time some damage and much good has been done by its agents. By some the freedman has been told that it is necessary for him, though free, to labor and work out his own salvation; by all he has been told that he is free. He knows now that he is free and with the tuition he has received he is now much better able to take care of himself, if let alone, than is generally supposed by his friends.

The bureau in its operations almost necessarily takes the place of a master. To it many of the freedmen look entirely for support, instruction and assistance. Even in those States where all civil rights have been conferred upon the freedman he does not go to the State Courts for a remedy, but to the bureau, for the process of civil law is too slow and the proceedings are not sufficiently convenient. The agents of the bureau decide for whom he shall work, for how much and when, and approve or disapprove all of his Contracts for labor. They have control in many places of his churches and schools, and some of them are endeavoring to control his finances. Special tribunals are to be organized in certain states for the trial of all cases where freedmen are concerned. Any system of Courts or Laws that look to the protection of a particular class must be objectionable and will be damaging in the end to such persons. It keeps them from endeavoring to gain admission to the state courts where they can obtain justice on the same footing as others. If we can judge from the past these courts will discriminate more against the white man than the State Courts can against the black. Some of these now in existence have been presided over by men inexperienced in law and evidence; men of strong prejudices in favor of the black men, who decide cases without reference to law, but the "right" as the right appears to them. Of course such justice is a farce, that pleases the black and exasperates the white. It is a bad plan by which to compel the people of the south to make just laws for the blacks: wholesome laws cannot be made under force. The longer these Courts remain in existence the harder it will be to give them up, and when given up the freedman, I fear, will be left in a worse condition than if they had not been established. The longer the offices of the bureau extend personal assistance to the freedman the less will he be prepared to take care of himself. Habitual dependence will prevent any class of people from making exertions for themselves. . . .

The freedmen can be better cared for, so far as the government should extend assistance, by the Military Authorities than in any other way: and this at a very small expense additional to the expense of supporting the troops in the south. If the head of the bureau, as at present, is in the War Department and issues orders and instructions from there, and then the officers and subalterns of the army are made ex-officio members of the bureau—or better, if it's made part of their military duty to have general supervision of the freedmen, as they have of other persons where civil law is inoperative, the system would be much simplified, a large expense would be saved, and great good could be done. These military agents would be obliged to carry out the orders of the head of the bureau, and they would have the power to do so. They would have no political, selfish, or pecuniary designs to carry out. They would have no desire to promote strife between the whites and blacks, and both of these classes having confidence in them would advance in their interests and become reconciled to the situation.

They will have no object to desire the continuance of the bureau longer than its existence is actually demanded in order that they may receive a support, for their offices would still continue.

The objection that some will offer to this proposition will be that the armies are being mustered out & there will not be material enough left for Agents of the bureau. But the Act in providing for a large number of Agents also provides, in Section 2., that the "President of the United States, through the War Department and the Commissioner, shall extend military jurisdiction and protection over all employees, agents and offices of this bureau in the exercise of the duties imposed or authorized by this act, or the act to which this is additional."

If there are enough officers & men in the Military service to extend such protection to the employees &c, surely there are enough to attend, as agents, to the requirements of the Bureau.

J. S. Fullerton  Bv. Brig. Genl. Vols.

# John Richard Dennett,
## "Vicksburg, Miss."

### (March 8, 1866)

Journalist John Richard Dennett's (1838–1874) eye-witness account of political and racial attitudes in Vicksburg, Mississippi, in 1866 suggests how "unreconstructed" many Southerners remained and how national questions—such as Johnson's veto of the Freedmen's Bureau Bill—preoccupied them. Dennett, a Harvard graduate and special correspondent for a newly launched magazine, *The Nation*, covered much the same landscape as Schurz and reached much the same discouraging conclusions. The recently defeated Confederates considered the North their "wanton oppressor."

The headquarters of the Freedmen's Bureau for Mississippi is at Vicksburg. It is chiefly busied with a general supervision of the affairs of the colored people, and occupies itself with details only when its interference is necessary. The examination and approval of contracts is not a part of its work, and the relations between employer and employed are controlled, in the first instance at least, by the civil authorities. Through its subordinate officials, its influence is extended to every part of the State, and, as might be expected, it is not a popular institution. Every sub-assistant commissioner, the Assistant Commissioner informs me, needs military force within call to sustain him. The freedmen are working very well, and are receiving good treatment; their labor being in great demand, it commands very good prices, and the planter finds it to his interest to use his laborers well. It is not from the oppressive acts of individuals, therefore, that the Negroes suffer most injustice, but from the spirit in which the civil authorities enforce the laws. Under the provisions of the vagrant law, for example, a white man as well as a Negro might be arrested; but in practice it is found that while honest and industrious Negroes are often arrested and punished, there is no arrest of notoriously idle and worthless white men. For this state of things the spirit of public opinion is responsible; and because this state of things exists the Bureau is a necessity. The hostility to schools for the Negroes is very general, and often very bitter and dangerous. In the middle of February a Dr. Lacy, an old man who had started a school in Okolona, was four times shot at as he walked in the street for no other reason than that he was a teacher of Negroes.

Such cases, whenever they occur, are reported by the officers of the Bureau to the military commander, General T. J. Woods. The case of Dr. Lacy has been reported. As yet nothing has been done in reference to it. In the town of Fayette the people will not permit schools to be maintained, and in Grenada they will not permit them to be opened.

In the face of such opposition, 5,240 children have been gathered into schools, and are receiving instruction from about 70 teachers, who are paid in small part by their pupils, but mainly by the Northern charitable associations. In the monthly reports returned by these teachers they are required, I notice, to give the number of pupils in their charge whose blood is mixed, and the number of those whose blood is purely African. Taking the returns of twelve schools which happened to be first set down in the consolidated report, I find it stated that, in the opinion of the teachers, the children of African blood number 287, and those of mixed blood number 777. A majority of the scholars live in the towns and cities.

In the office of the Assistant Commissioner, Colonel Thomas, I met several gentlemen attached to the Bureau, and resident in different parts of the State. They spoke of the condition of the Negroes as being generally prosperous, but there is much hostility, they say, on the part of the native white population to Northern men. The large landowners are anxious for immigration, but it is not so with the mass of the people. It is for their property rather than for their lives that the new-comers fear; but in respect to their lives they are by no means at ease. It would be easy to multiply instances, one gentleman told me; he would give me two. Not long since Colonel S——, of Hinds County, a Southerner, and a gentleman from the North were in treaty about going into cotton-planting together, and probably would have done so. But Colonel S——, after a little while, saw with regret that it would be necessary to break off the arrangements. He informed his prospective partner that he had reliable intelligence that more than a hundred men in the neighboring county of Holmes had bound themselves to prevent the settlement of Northern men among them, and had also determined that no discharged Negro soldier should be suffered to find employment in that section of country. My informant said it was beyond a doubt that Colonel S—— acted in perfect good faith.

Another case was that of Mr. A——, of Boston. He moved into Mississippi after the war, with the intention of becoming a planter, and at first was very much pleased with his prospects—so much pleased that when a little while ago he made a visit to Massachusetts, he wrote a letter to the Boston *Post* and praised his new neighbors highly. Soon he came back, and it was not long before he began to think himself mistaken. By-and-bye he became convinced that the people were too much opposed to Northern men for him to stay among them with safety. So he paid a considerable sum of money to the owner of the lands which he had intended to cultivate, was released from his bargain, and has left Mississippi.

On the last night of my stay in a Southern city I attended a political meeting, which had been called to endorse the President's recent veto message. It was held in the courthouse, and was composed of about two hundred persons, who were by no means enthusiastic. Resolutions were passed, and many speeches were made, in all of which the President was lavishly praised, and the Senate and House of Representatives spoken of with great disrespect. "The war being over," said one speaker, "we were looking for peace, but it seems that the rebellion has only changed hands; that treason has reached the halls of the Congress of the United States. But there is a man at the head who is able to cope with it. President Johnson has put down the rebellion at the South, and he is now prepared to put down the rebellion at the North."

Another speaker warned the Southern people to remember that there was a party at the North, the Radical party, who would never be content till the last silver spoon was taken from them and their lands divided; but there was also in the North a Democratic party which needed the active cooperation of the Southern people, and only needed that to hurl the Radicals from power.

The evening was not very far advanced when Colonel Joseph E. Davis, a brother of Jefferson Davis, was seen upon the floor and a committee was appointed to lead him to the platform. A speech from him was demanded, and he complied, speaking three or four minutes, when, as I think, at the suggestion of the chairman of the meeting he brought his remarks to an abrupt conclusion. The Vicksburg *Journal* says:

> He fully endorsed the action of President Johnson in vetoing that accursed measure to enlarge the powers of the Freedmen's Bureau. The bill, if passed, would have caused a revolution equal to, if not more dreadful than, the one through which we have just passed. We have a branch of the Freedmen's Bureau in our midst headed by officers of the most infamous character; who hold the offices for a given purpose; who gladly record the abuses and murders of Negroes, and forward such information, rather than assist our people without homes and means in obtaining the necessaries of life. You have these officers among you. I charge you to look out for them. Mr. Davis's feeble health would not admit of any extended remarks.

I might give many passages from the various speakers, but they would be wearisome. I give but one.

Mr. McKee, formerly a general in the Federal army, stepped forward and said that he approved of the veto message of the President and endorsed it fully. "But in that hall on that night he had heard language used by some of the speakers that made his blood run cold."

Though it seemed to me not very successful as a political gathering, the meeting revealed very plainly the feeling which prevails in all the Southern country. The speakers represented the South as being cruelly injured, insulted, and oppressed, and the North as her wanton oppressor.

# PART III

# RADICAL RECONSTRUCTION

Under the leadership of the Joint Committee on Reconstruction, in 1866 Congress asserted itself, taking control of Reconstruction by passing a series of acts designed to protect the freedpeople and to establish federal authority in the former Confederate states. In February 1866, Congress attempted to extend the existence of the Freedmen's Bureau (initially limited to one year after the conclusion of hostilities) indefinitely and to expand the agency's jurisdiction over cases tried in the former Confederate states that denied equal protection of the laws to African-Americans. Though Johnson vetoed the bill, a similar piece of legislation passed despite the president's veto in July.

In another bill, aimed directly at the Black Codes passed by the Southern states, Congress sought to enforce the equal rights of the freedpeople by federal legislation, defining as citizens all persons (with the exception of Indians not taxed) born in the United States and empowering the federal courts to protect citizens when any state or territory violated their civil rights. The Civil Rights Act of 1866 passed on April 9 over Johnson's veto. The president believed that the bill violated the prerogatives of the states, privileged blacks over whites, and undermined what he considered executive authority generally and his restoration program in particular. According to historian Hans L. Trefousse, the Civil Rights Act of 1866 "was the first major legislation ever to be passed over an executive veto, and it exacerbated the growing rift between the President and Congress."[30]

The 1866 Civil Rights Act raised essential constitutional questions, concerns that led the Joint Committee on Reconstruction to draft what became the landmark Fourteenth Amendment to the U.S. Constitution, passed by Congress on June 13, 1866 (but not ratified until July 9, 1868). Its intent was to protect the basic rights of black

Southerners. This amendment defined national citizenship and guaranteed certain civil rights to all citizens, including the right to due process and equal protection under the law. In a clear and powerful assertion of Congressional authority, the amendment empowered the legislative branch to enforce federal civil rights legislation by reducing congressional representation of states that abridged the suffrage of male voters. The amendment also disfranchised certain former Confederates and outlawed Confederate debt. Passing this amendment signified a bold move by Congress, one that President Johnson, as well as his Southern and conservative supporters, strongly rejected. These objections had little consequence when, after the fall 1866 elections, Radicals gained control of the Thirty-ninth Congress.

Radical supremacy in Congress set the scene for new, more stringent measures to regulate the former Rebel states. Thereafter ratification of the Fourteenth Amendment would become a prerequisite for the ex–Confederate states to reenter the Union. The legislation that the Radical-controlled Congress passed over President Johnson's repeated vetoes confirmed the supremacy of Congress over the executive branch and revolutionized the South. Led by old hard-line abolitionist politician-reformers Thaddeus Stevens of Pennsylvania, Charles Sumner of Massachusetts, and Benjamin F. Wade of Ohio, Congressional Radicals privileged slavery's overthrow and the protection of black civil rights over other political questions of the day. According to Eric Foner, these men and their supporters believed "the Civil War constituted a 'golden moment,' an opportunity for far-reaching change," and that the postwar United States would become a nation "whose citizens enjoyed equality of civil and political rights, secured by a powerful and beneficial national state."[31] Free labor backed by a strong national state became the Radicals' new economic ideal. They hoped that the South would come to share the North's competitive capitalism. The Radicals envisioned the freedpeople sharing the same opportunities for economic success as white Southerners.

During Presidential Reconstruction, moderate Republicans had focused on reunifying the nation and thus initially supported President Johnson. They hoped to amend the process to ensure greater Southern "loyalty" and guarantee a modicum of civil rights to the freedmen without infringing on states' rights. However, Johnson's intransigence, his antagonism toward blacks, his sympathy toward white Southerners, plus his vetoes of the Freedmen's Bureau Bill and the 1866 Civil Rights Act, drove moderates into the Radical camp. The Republicans had gained confidence and power in their landslide victories in the fall 1866 elections. In January 1867, Congress passed a bill enfranchising Washington, D.C., blacks, again over Johnson's veto, and Congress considered even more decisive political measures, including disfranchisement and martial law in the South and even Johnson's impeachment.[32]

In March 1867, following the refusal of the Southern states organized by Johnson to ratify the Fourteenth Amendment, Congress passed the first of a series of four Reconstruction Acts. Historians consider these acts the cornerstone of Radical Reconstruction, ushering in the new, Radical phase of thoroughly reconstructing the defeated Confederate states. Not surprisingly, Johnson vetoed each in succession. The Reconstruction Acts reflected the Radicals' determination to impose strict conditions on those states. White Southerners believed that the acts rendered their states conquered provinces.

The first act (March 2, 1867) divided the ten unreconstructed states (Tennessee, after ratifying the Fourteenth Amendment, had been readmitted to the Union in 1866) into five military districts and called for elections under universal manhood suffrage for constitutional conventions to frame basic laws. Congress required each state to ratify new constitutions that included black suffrage and the Fourteenth Amendment as preconditions for readmission to the Union. The act disfranchised some persons, prohibiting from voting those who had violated pre–Civil War loyalty oaths, had committed crimes, or who were disqualified from office by the Fourteenth Amendment.[33] Significantly, the act enfranchised African-American male voters in the former Rebel states, inaugurating their participation in politics. After the states had adopted these constitutions and ratified the Fourteenth Amendment, they could apply for readmission to the Union.

On March 23, when Southern state legislators failed to implement this process, Congress passed a second (supplemental) Reconstruction Act, authorizing the commanding generals of the military districts to supervise the election process, spelling out the oaths to be administered to registrars and voters, and providing for the ratification of the state constitutions by a majority of the states' registered voters. A third Reconstruction Act (July 19, 1867) subjected Johnson's state provisional governments to the military commanders, arming them with broad powers to remove state officials and to assess voter eligibility. Finally, the fourth Reconstruction Act (March 11, 1868) mandated that the ratification of the new Southern state constitutions required a majority of the actual number of voters, not a majority of those persons registered to vote in the ratification process.

Historian Hugh Davis underscores the importance of the new Southern state constitutions mandated by the Reconstruction Acts. Under close federal government scrutiny, the legislators totally revamped and modernized their basic laws. "These constitutions were quite innovative," Davis explains, "in that they laid the foundations of the Southern public school system, provided protection for all citizens' civil rights, funded railroad construction, and established the basis for a new system of free labor." Despite their best efforts, however, Republicans struggled to gain legitimacy for their party among white Southerners, "because it was imposed by a Northern Congress and relied largely on the support of the freedpeople."[34]

Foner correctly interprets the Reconstruction Acts, especially the implementation of black suffrage, as Congress' response to "the obstinacy of Johnson and the white South, and the determination of Radicals, blacks, and eventually Southern Unionists not to accept a Reconstruction program that stopped short of this demand." That said, he characterizes the Radical project as a "somewhat incongruous mixture of idealism and political expediency." At each step, moderate acts tempered radical elements. While the acts subjected the Southern states to temporary military rule to ensure order, they provided a means for them to gain readmission to the Union. The legislation "looked to a new political order for the South, but failed to place Southern Unionists in immediate control. It made no economic provisions for the freedmen. Even the commitment to black suffrage applied only to the defeated Confederacy, not the nation as a whole."[35]

Two events, the impeachment of Andrew Johnson in May 1868 and the election of Ulysses S. Grant in November of that year, signaled the end of Presidential Reconstruction. Johnson's stormy relationship with Congress harkened back to December 1865, when Congress refused to seat members elected by the Southern state provisional governments, and then worsened over disagreements over the Freedmen's Bureau and Civil Rights Bills. The president's vocal opposition to the Reconstruction Acts set him on a collision course with Congress, a situation exacerbated by Johnson's determination to reassign Radical-friendly commanding generals in the South and to remove Secretary of War Stanton from his cabinet, in direct violation of the Command of the Army Act and the Tenure of Office Act. As early as December 1867 some representatives sought to impeach Johnson, a move that finally came to pass on February 21, 1868, when the House of Representatives passed Pennsylvanian John Covode's resolution to impeach him for eleven articles of high crimes and misdemeanors. Johnson's trial lasted from March 29 until May 26, 1868, when the Senate acquitted him by one vote. Though he held office for the rest of his term, Johnson remained politically impotent.

During Presidential and Radical Reconstruction, Ulysses S. Grant, who became a hero as the commanding general of the Union armies, served as general-in-chief of the U.S. Army. Following his report on a Southern tour in December 1865, the general gradually came to support the Radical Republicans, though he served as Johnson's interim secretary of war (August 12, 1867, to January 14, 1868) following the president's ousting of Stanton from office.

The popular Grant captured the Republican presidential nomination in 1868, and defeated Democrat Horatio Seymour by 134 electoral votes. Despite scandals that marred his presidency, involving both members of his cabinet and close associates, Grant was reelected president in 1872, defeating Liberal Republican–Democratic candidate Horace Greeley by 220 electoral votes. As president, Grant witnessed ratification of the Fifteenth Amendment (adopted by Congress in 1869 and ratified by the states in

1870), guaranteeing that citizens' right to vote "shall not be abridged by the United States or any State on account of race, color, or previous condition of servitude." Under Grant the ten Southern states still under provisional governments regained their proper position in the Union. Alabama, Arkansas, Florida, Louisiana, North Carolina, and South Carolina met Congress' requirement in 1868. The remaining former Confederate states—Georgia, Mississippi, Texas, and Virginia—rejoined the Union in 1870.

As president, Grant also took steps to protect the freedpeople and Unionists from white paramilitary or vigilante groups such as the Ku Klux Klan. The Klan, established in May 1866 as a social club in Tennessee, marked an aggressive challenge to the newly empowered blacks and to the federal government's Reconstruction efforts. The terrorist organization quickly spread across the South, attacking and terrorizing blacks and white Republicans. Using violence as a political tool, the Klan sought to undo Reconstruction by undermining the Republican Party, destabilizing the Reconstruction governments, and reestablishing white supremacy through the forced subordination of people of color and their Union supporters.

Three Enforcement Acts (May 31, 1870; February 28, 1871; and April 20, 1871) imposed federal protection and supervision of voting in the South, outlawed terrorist conspiracies, and authorized the president to suspend the writ of habeas corpus in areas where lawlessness ruled. This legislation worked to some degree in preventing voter intimidation, fraud, and bribery, and in protecting the right under federal law of all citizens, black and white, to vote. Nonetheless, Klan violence became so severe that in 1871 Grant suspended the writ of habeas corpus in several South Carolina counties.

# Charles Sumner to the
# Duchess of Argyll

## *(April 3, 1866)*

Sumner's remarkable letter to his longtime friend
and correspondent, the British abolitionist Elizabeth, Georgiana Granville, Duchess of Argyll (1824–
1878), provides vivid insights into his fears
regarding the rights of the freedpeople, the state
of the country, and President Johnson's intransigence. Though Congress had passed the Civil
Rights Bill in order to offer Southern blacks legal
protection, the president quickly vetoed it. Only
granting the freedmen the vote, Sumner writes
with a degree of anguish, will "counterbalance the
rebels."

My dear Duchess,

. . . These are trying days for us. I am more anxious
now than during the war. The animal passions of the Nation aided the rally then. Now the appeal is to the intelligence, & to the moral & religious sentiments. How
strangely we are misrepresented in the *Times*. I read it
always, & find nothing true in its portraiture of our affairs.

Believe me, the people are with Congress. When it is
considered, that the Presdt has such an amazing part, it
is extraordinary to see how the conscience of the masses
has stood firm. Congress is misrepresented in England. I
speak of the Lower House now. In my opinion it is the
best that has ever been since the beginning of our govt.
It is full of talent & is governed by patriotic purpose.
There is no personal or party ambition, which prompts
its course. It is to save the country, that it takes its present responsibilities.

You say "Why not urge the Abolition of the Black
Codes"? This I have done from the beginning. There
are several speeches of mine, which you have never

seen, three years ago, against any exclusion of witnesses on account of color; also an elaborate report. A partial measure I carried. Since the cessation of hostilities this subject has occupied me constantly. In my speech at Worcester I dwelt on the Black Codes; then again in a speech early this session. At last we passed a Bill known as the Civil Rights Bill. It went through both Houses by unprecedented majorities. The Presdt. refuses to sign it. By our Constitution it requires a vote of 2/3ds to pass it over his Veto. It is still uncertain, if we can command this large vote. The division will be very close. The loss of this Bill will be a terrible calamity. It leaves the new crop of Black Laws in full force & gives to the old masters a new letter of license to do any thing with the freedman short of making him a chattel. A new serfdom may be substituted, & this is their cruel purpose.

But after most careful consideration I see no substantial protection for the freedman except in the franchise. He must have this (1) for his own protection (2) for the protection of the white Unionist & (3) for the peace of the country. We put the musket in his hands, because it was necessary. For the same reason we must give him the franchise. Unionists from the South tell me that unless this is done they will be defenceless. And here is the necessity for the universality of the suffrage. Every vote is needed to counterbalance the rebels.

It is very sad that we should be tried in this way. For our country it is an incalculable calamity. Nobody can yet see the end. Congress will not yield. The Presdt. is angry & brutal. Seward is the Marplot. In the cabinet, on the question of the last Veto, there were 4 against it to 3 for it; so even there among his immediate advisers the Presdt. is left in a minority. Stanton reviewed at length the Bill, section by section, in the cabinet & pronounced it an excellent & safe bill every way from beginning to end. But the Veto Message was already prepared & an hour later was sent to Congress.

You hear that I do not bear contradiction. Perhaps not. I try to bear every thing. But my conscience & feelings are sometimes moved, so that I may show impatience. It is hard to meet all these exigencies with calmness. I hope not to fail.

I despair of the Presdt. He is no Moses, but a Pharoah to the colored race, & they now regard him so. He has all the narrowness & ignorance of a certain class of whites, who have always looked upon the colored race as out of the pale of Humanity.

Ever Sincerely Yours,
Charles Sumner

# THE CIVIL RIGHTS ACT
## OF 1866

### *(April 9, 1866)*

On this date, Congress overrode Johnson's veto and the landmark Civil Rights Bill of 1866 became law. The measure, the first move to enforce the equal rights of the freedpeople by federal legislation (and a forerunner of the Fourteenth Amendment), defined citizenship for all persons born in the U.S. (excepting Indians not taxed) and guaranteed citizens the protection of the federal courts if states or federal territories deprived them of their civil rights. Republicans framed the bill in response to the notorious Black Codes passed in the Southern states in late 1865 and 1866. Johnson objected to the bill, arguing that it violated states' prerogatives and privileged people of color. The Congressional override was the first time the Legislative branch passed a major bill over an executive's objections.

## AN ACT TO PROTECT ALL PERSONS IN THE UNITED STATES IN THEIR CIVIL RIGHTS, AND FURNISH THE MEANS OF THEIR VINDICATION.

*Be it enacted by the Senate and House of Representatives of the United States of America in Congress assembled,* That all persons born in the United States and not subject to any foreign power, excluding Indians not taxed, are hereby declared to be citizens of the United States; and such citizens, of every race and color, without regard to any previous condition of slavery or involuntary servitude, except as a punishment for crime whereof the party shall have been duly convicted, shall have the same right, in every State and

186

Territory in the United States, to make and enforce contracts, to sue, be parties, and give evidence, to inherit, purchase, lease, sell, hold, and convey real and personal property, and to full and equal benefit of all laws and proceedings for the security of person and property, as is enjoyed by white citizens, and shall be subject to like punishment, pains, and penalties, and to none other, any law, statute, ordinance, regulation, or custom, to the contrary notwithstanding.

Sec. 2. *And be it further enacted,* That any person who, under color of any law, statute, ordinance, regulation, or custom, shall subject, or cause to be subjected, any inhabitant of any State or Territory to the deprivation of any right secured or protected by this act, or to different punishment, pains, or penalties on account of such person having at any time been held in a condition of slavery or involuntary servitude, except as a punishment for crime whereof the party shall have been duly convicted, or by reason of his color or race, than is prescribed for the punishment of white persons, shall be deemed guilty of a misdemeanor, and, on conviction, shall be punished by fine not exceeding one thousand dollars, or imprisonment not exceeding one year, or both, in the discretion of the court.

Sec. 3. *And be it further enacted,* That the district courts of the United States, within their respective districts, shall have, exclusively of the courts of the several States, cognizance of all crimes and offences committed against the provisions of this act, and also, concurrently with the circuit courts of the United States, of all causes, civil and criminal, affecting persons who are denied or cannot enforce in the courts or judicial tribunals of the State or locality where they may be any of the rights secured to them by the first section of this act; and if any suit or prosecution, civil or criminal, has been or shall be commenced in any State court, against any such person, for any cause whatsoever, or against any officer, civil or military, or other person, for any arrest or imprisonment, trespasses, or wrongs done or committed by virtue or under color of authority derived from this act or the act establishing a Bureau for the relief of Freedmen and Refugees, and all acts amendatory thereof, or for refusing to do any act upon the ground that it would be inconsistent with this act, such defendant shall have the right to remove such cause for trial to the proper district or circuit court in the manner prescribed by the "Act relating to habeas corpus and regulating judicial proceedings in certain cases," approved March three, eighteen hundred and sixty-three, and all acts amendatory thereof. The jurisdiction in civil and criminal matters hereby conferred on the district and circuit courts of the United States shall be exercised and enforced in conformity with the laws of the United States, so far as such laws are suitable to carry the same into effect; but in all cases where such laws are not adapted to the object, or are deficient in the provisions necessary to furnish suitable remedies and punish offences against law, the common law, as modified and changed by the constitution and statutes of the State wherein the court having jurisdiction of the cause, civil or criminal, is held, so far as the same is not inconsistent with the Constitution and laws of the United States, shall be extended to and govern said courts in the trial and disposition of such cause, and, if of a criminal nature, in the infliction of punishment on the party found guilty.

Sec. 4. *And be it further enacted,* That the district attorneys, marshals, and deputy marshals of the United States, the commissioners appointed by the circuit and territorial courts of the United States, with powers of arresting, imprisoning, or bailing offenders against the laws of the United States, the officers and agents of the Freedmen's Bureau, and every other officer who may be specially empowered by the President of the United States, shall be, and they are hereby, specially authorized and required, at the expense of the United States, to institute proceedings against all and every person who shall violate the provisions of this act, and cause him or them to be arrested and imprisoned, or bailed, as the case may be, for trial before such court of the United States or territorial court as by this act has cognizance of the offence. And with a view to affording reasonable protection to all persons in their constitutional rights of equality before the law, without distinction of race or color, or previous condition of slavery or involuntary servitude, except as a punishment for crime, whereof the party shall have been duly convicted, and to the prompt discharge of the duties of this act, it shall be the duty of the circuit courts of the United States and the superior courts of the Territories of the United States, from time to time, to increase the number of commissioners, so as to afford a speedy and convenient means for the arrest and examination of persons charged with a violation of this act; and such commissioners are hereby authorized and required to exercise and discharge all the powers and duties conferred on them by this act, and the same duties with regard to offences created by this act, as they are authorized by law to exercise with regard to other offences against the laws of the United States.

Sec. 5. *And be it further enacted,* That it shall be the duty of all marshals and deputy marshals to obey and execute all warrants and precepts issued under the provisions of this act, when to them directed; and should any marshal or deputy marshal refuse to receive such warrant or other process when tendered, or to use all proper means diligently to execute the same, he shall, on conviction thereof, be fined in the sum of one thousand dollars, to the use of the person upon whom the accused is alleged to have committed the offense. And the better to enable the said commissioners to execute their duties faithfully and efficiently, in conformity with the Constitution of the United States and the requirements of this act, they are hereby authorized and empowered, within their counties respectively, to appoint, in writing, under their hands, any one or more suitable persons, from time to time, to execute all such warrants and other process as may be issued by them in the lawful performance of their respective duties; and the persons so appointed to execute any warrant or process as aforesaid shall have authority to summon and call to their aid the bystanders or posse comitatus of the proper county, or such portion of the land or naval forces of the United States, or of the militia, as may be necessary to the performance of the duty with which they are charged, and to insure a faithful observance of the clause of the Constitution which prohibits slavery, in conformity with the provisions of this act; and said warrants shall run and be executed by said officers anywhere in the State or Territory within which they are issued.

Sec. 6. *And be it further enacted,* That any person who shall knowingly and willfully obstruct, hinder, or prevent any officer, or other person charged with the execution of any warrant or process issued under the provisions of this act, or any person or persons lawfully assisting him or them, from arresting any person for whose apprehension such warrant or process may have been issued, or shall rescue or attempt to rescue such person from the custody of the officer, other person or persons, or those lawfully assisting as aforesaid, when so arrested pursuant to the authority herein given and declared, or shall aid, abet, or assist any person so arrested as aforesaid, directly or indirectly, to escape from the custody of the officer or other person legally authorized as aforesaid, or shall harbor or conceal any person for whose arrest a warrant or process shall have been issued as aforesaid, so as to prevent his discovery and arrest after notice or knowledge of the fact that a warrant has been issued for the apprehension of such person, shall, for either of said offences, be subject to a fine not exceeding one thousand dollars, and imprisonment not exceeding six months, by indictment and conviction before the district court of the United States for the district in which said offense may have been committed, or before the proper court of criminal jurisdiction, if committed within any one of the organized Territories of the United States.

Sec. 7. *And be it further enacted,* That the district attorneys, the marshals, their deputies, and the clerks of the said district and territorial courts shall be paid for their services the like fees as may be allowed to them for similar services in other cases; and in all cases where the proceedings are before a commissioner, he shall be entitled to a fee of ten dollars in full for his services in each case, inclusive of all services incident to such arrest and examination. The person or persons authorized to execute the process to be issued by such commissioners for the arrest of offenders against the provisions of this act shall be entitled to a fee of five dollars for each person he or they may arrest and take before any such commissioner as aforesaid, with such other fees as may be deemed reasonable by such commissioner for such other additional services as may be necessarily performed by him or them, such as attending at the examination, keeping the prisoner in custody, and providing him with food and lodging during his detention, and until the final determination of such commissioner, and in general for performing such other duties as may be required in the premises; such fees to be made up in conformity with the fees usually charged by the officers of the courts of justice within the proper district or county, as near as may be practicable, and paid out of the Treasury of the United States on the certificate of the judge of the district within which the arrest is made, and to be recoverable from the defendant as part of the judgment in case of conviction.

Sec. 8. *And be it further enacted,* That whenever the President of the United States shall have reason to believe that offences have been or are likely to be committed against the provisions of this act within any judicial district, it shall be lawful for him, in his discretion, to direct the judge, marshal, and district attorney of such district to attend at such place within the district, and for such time as he may designate, for the purpose of the more speedy arrest and trial of persons charged with a violation of this act; and it shall be the duty of every judge or other officer, when any such requisition shall be received by him, to attend at the place and for the time therein designated.

Sec. 9. *And be it further enacted,* That it shall be lawful for the President of the United States, or such person as he may empower for that purpose, to employ such part of the land or naval forces of the United States, or of the militia, as shall be necessary to prevent the violation and enforce the due execution of this act.

Sec. 10. *And be it further enacted,* That upon all questions of law arising in any cause under the provisions of this act a final appeal may be taken to the Supreme Court of the United States.

# BENJAMIN C. TRUMAN, "RELATIVE TO THE CONDITION OF THE SOUTHERN PEOPLE AND THE STATES IN WHICH THE REBELLION EXISTED"

## *(April 9, 1866)*

In the immediate aftermath of the debates over the Civil Rights Bill, Johnson submitted to the Senate a glowing report on conditions in the South by his friend and former aide, the journalist Benjamin C. Truman (1835–1916). In early September 1865, Truman began recording his impressions in what became an eight-month-long tour of eight of the eleven former Confederate states. In contrast to the indictments of Schurz and Dennett, Truman found much to praise generally about the former Rebels and, particularly, about race relations and the progress of Reconstruction under Johnson's program. "It is the former slave-owners who are the best friends the negro has in the south," Truman concluded.

I will speak first of the sentiments of the white people, touching their relations with the general government and the people of the north.

I distinguish between *loyalty* and *patriotism;* and I believe the distinction not ill-grounded. That glorious spontaneous burst of popular enthusiasm with which the north responded as one man to the echoing thunders of Sumter was the most sublime exhibition of *patriotism* the world has yet witnessed; the quietness, and even cheerfulness, with which the same people once yielded obedience to the rule of James Buchanan, whose administration they hated and despised, was an instance of *loyalty,* such as only American citizens could have furnished.

The north never rebelled against James Buchanan, nor seriously proposed to; but I assert without hesitation, that, now the war has swept over the south, there is no more disposition in that section of the country to rebel against the national government than there was in the north at the time above referred to.

If any general assertion can be made that will apply to the masses of the people of the south, it is that they are at the present time *indifferent* toward the general government. For four years of eventful life as a nation, they were accustomed to speak of and regard "our government" as the one which had its seat in Richmond; and thousands who at first looked upon that government with great suspicion and distrust, gradually, from the mere lapse of time and the force of example, came to admit it into their ideas as *their* government. The great body of the people in any country always move slowly; the transfer of allegiance from one *de facto* government to another is not effected in a day, whatever oaths of loyalty may be taken; and I have witnessed many amusing instances of mistakes on the part of those of whose attachment to the government there could be no question. Ignorance and prejudice always lag furthest behind any radical change, and no person can forget that the violent changes of the past few years have left the ideas of the populace greatly unsettled and increased their indifference. Fully one-half of the southern people never cherished an educated and active attachment to any government that was over them, and the war has left them very much as it found them.

The rank and file of the disbanded southern army — those who remained in it to the end — are the backbone and sinew of the south. Long before the surrender, corps, divisions, brigades, and regiments had been thoroughly purged of the worthless class — the skulkers — those of whom the south, as well as any other country, would be best rid; and these it is that are now prolonging past bitternesses. These are they, in great part, as I abundantly learned by personal observation, that are now editing reckless newspapers, and that put forth those pernicious utterances that so little represent the thinking, substantial people, and are so eagerly seized out and paraded by certain northern journalists, who themselves as little represent the great north. To the disbanded regiments of the rebel army, both officers and men, I look with great confidence as the best and altogether most hopeful element of the south, the real basis of reconstruction and the material of worthy citizenship. On a thousand battle-fields they have tested the invincible power of that government they vainly sought to overthrow, and along a thousand picket lines, and under the friendly flag of truce, they have learned that the soldiers of the Union bore them no hatred, and shared with them the common attributes of humanity. Around the returned soldier of the south gathers the same circle of admiring friends that we see around the millions of hearth-stones in our own section, and from him they are slowly learning the lesson of charity and of brotherhood. I know of very few more potent influences at work in promoting real and lasting reconciliation and reconstruction than the influence of the returned southern soldier.

The question above all others that our people are anxious to ask is, In case of a war with a foreign nation, what would be the action of the south? Of course, all answers to this must be founded chiefly on speculation, since a great deal would depend upon the character of the nation with whom we were at war, and much upon the action of the government between now and any such event. I need hardly say that, whatever might be their sympathies, in case of a war with England, not a regiment of men could be recruited in the south in her support, even if it were freely permitted. In other cases it would be different. There is a certain loose floating population in the south, as everywhere, and largely disproportionate to that of the north, in consequence of the more complete disruption caused by the war, that would be eager to enlist in any army, whether for or against the United States. It would be necessary, then, as things are at present, to keep a strict surveillance over the harbors of the principal ports to prevent them from sailing to join the common enemy, if such an object was desired, though I am far from certain that the class spoken of would not be well rid of in foreign camps. They would consist almost entirely of that class of persons who are preparing to emigrate to Mexico and Brazil; men whose reputations in the rebel army were greatly overdone, or men who never did any service at the front, but who were valorous with words alone. If a large foreign army were to invade the south, and march uninterruptedly through the country—a very improbable contingency— without doubt it would receive many recruits. In Texas it would probably get eight thousand recruits—discontented, roving men, who are not engaged in any profitable employment, and are adding nothing to the State's productive capacity. I estimate that there are five thousand men in that State—deserters, principally, and rebel refugees from Arkansas and Missouri—that are to-day depending entirely upon robbery and murder for a precarious subsistence. These would, of course, rejoice at such an opportunity. In other States the proportion would be very much less. But if no invasion were accomplished, the substantial assistance that a foreign enemy would receive at the hands of the late insurgents would be quite insignificant; and the fears that many otherwise well-informed persons entertain in this regard are highly absurd. Naturally, the American people, as a nation, are devoted to the arts of peace. The soldiers of the late rebel army are, if possible, infinitely more wearied and disgusted with war and all its works than those of our army, and long for nothing so much as quiet. The best proof of this is the fact that our noble volunteers, though crowned with the honors of almost limitless success and victory, are clamorous and even mutinous to be discharged from military duty. Therefore, I am constrained to believe that, with few exceptions, the great masses of those who have been in the rebel army will never again seek to enter the lists. If there is anything that I certainly learned in the south, it was that its people are tired of war and are anxious to establish and perpetuate peace. . . .

It is my belief that the south—the great, substantial, and prevailing element—is more loyal now than it was at the end of the war—more loyal to-day than yesterday, and that it will be more loyal to-morrow than to-day. It would be impossible to present the numerous and scattered evidences upon which I base this belief; but I entertain it in all sincerity, and believe it to be consonant with the facts. "No revolution ever goes backward" is a convenient but shallow truism; or, rather, expressive of no truth whatever, since every revolution has its ultimate revulsion, partially at least; and just as certainly as for four years the mass of popular sentiment in the south was slowly solidifying and strengthening in favor of the bogus confederacy, just so certain it is that from the date of its downfall that opinion has been slowly returning to its old attachments. For many years the dream of independence had been increasingly cherished and nurtured in the breasts of thousands; for four years that dream was a living fact, penetrating the consciousness of all, and receiving the sympathies of scarcely less than all; and then came the sudden and appalling crash—the awakening from this dream to the unwelcome but inexorable truth that the pleasing vision had vanished. As weeks, months, and years steadily accumulate, and the remembrances of that brief happiness vanish in the distance, the yearning for it will grow weak and inconstant. That dream will never be revived, in my opinion—never; and if I am satisfied of anything in relation to the south, it is that the great majority of its leading men have forever renounced all expectations of a separate nationality.

If I were asked to reconcile the above statements with the grossly palpable appearances that argue to the contrary, especially as seen in some of the late constitutional conventions, I would simply answer that this apparent contradiction is an inevitable product of human inconsistency; or, rather, the "consistency of politicians." For four years they found themselves required—most of them by preference, all of them by circumstances which they could not, if they would, control—to argue in favor of the right of secession and independent government. It is strange how soon and how inevitably defence leads to conviction. I cannot say that, when the confederacy went down, there was not in all its borders a citizen who did not yield it so much of allegiance as he ever gave to any government; but I do not hesitate to declare that there were not five prominent politicians *still remaining within it* who could truly and conscientiously declare that they had not given it, first or last, their sympathy. It has furnished me an interesting branch of historical study to look up the antecedents of those men who, when our troops made their appearance, were forward in their professions of unwavering Unionism. Alas for political human nature! Scarcely one of them but had either accepted an office under the confederacy, or signified his willingness to do so.

There comes now a sudden and imperious necessity that they cannot blink, to declare, by their acts at least, that they were wrong in all this; but who could expect politicians and editors, before they had been reduced to a condition of absolute vassalage, to reverse their "records" *ab initio,* and declare freely and without hesitation that all their utterances of the past four years had been mistaken? But this unwillingness does not necessarily involve a corresponding sluggishness of belief. I record it as my profound conviction, gathered from hundreds of intimate and friendly conversations with leading men in the south, that there are not fifty respectable politicians who still believe in the "constitutional right of secession," though they are exceedingly slow to acknowledge it in public speeches or published articles. Our conversations generally ended with the confession—which to me was entirely satisfactory, as meaning much more than was intended—"Whatever may be said about the *right* of secession, the thing itself may as well be laid aside, for it is certainly *not practicable,* and probably *never will be. . . .*"

I will now proceed to the second great topic, to wit: "The freedmen and their affairs."

Almost the only key that furnishes a satisfactory solution to the southern question in its relations to the negro, that gives a reasonable explanation to the treatment which he receives and the estimation in which he is held, is found in the fact—too often forgotten in considering this matter—that the people from their earliest days have regarded slavery as his proper estate, and emancipation as a bane to his happiness. That a vast majority of the southern people honestly entertain this opinion no one who travels among them for eight months can doubt.

To one who looks out from this stand-point of theory, and can see no other that is rational, the question presents itself in a different aspect. Every one who conscientiously seeks to know the whole truth should not ignore their beliefs while he censures the resulting practices. Holding that the negro occupies a middle ground between the human race and the animal, they regard it as a real misfortune to him that he should be stripped of a protector, and that the immortal proclamation of President Lincoln was wicked, or at least mistaken, and a scourge to society. The persis-

tency and honesty with which many, even of the greatest
men of the south, hold to this opinion, is almost unaccount-
able to a northern man, and is an element of such magnitude that it cannot well be omitted from the consideration.

Resulting as a proper corollary from these premises, we
have seen various laws passed in some of the States, but
more particularly in Mississippi—which State, I am bound
to say, has displayed the most illiberal spirit toward the
freedmen of all the south—imposing heavy taxes on negroes engaged in the various trades, amounting to a virtual
prohibition. Petty, unjust, and discriminating licenses are
levied in this State upon mechanics, storekeepers, and various artisans. Following the same absurd train of argument
that one will hear in the north in regard to the "proper
sphere of women," their legislature and their common
councils contend that in these pursuits the negro is out of
his place; that he is not adapted to such labors, but only to
the ruder tasks of the field. What are known as the "poor
whites" sustain, in fact originate, this legislation, upon the
insane dread they share in common with certain skilled laborers at the north, of competition and an overcrowding of
the supply. This folly and injustice on the part of the lawmakers is being corrected in many sections. The negro,
however, has not been discouraged, even in Mississippi; his
industry and his thrift are overleaping all obstacles, and in
Jackson there are at least two colored craftsmen of most
kinds to one of the whites.

From the surrender of the rebel armies up to the Christmas holidays, and more especially for a few weeks preceding the latter, there was a nervousness exhibited throughout
the south, in relation to their late slaves, that was little consonant to their former professions of trust in them. There
were vague and terrible fears of a servile insurrection—a
thing which the simple-minded negroes scarcely dreamed
of. In consequence of this there were extensive seizures of
arms and ammunition, which the negroes had foolishly collected, and strict precautions were taken to avoid any outbreak. Pistols, old muskets, and shotguns were taken away
from them as such weapons would be wrested from the
hands of lunatics. Since the holidays, however, there has
been a great improvement in this matter; many of the
whites appear to be ashamed of their former distrust, and

the negroes are seldom molested now in carrying the fire-
arms of which they make such a vain display. In one way or
another they have procured great numbers of old army
muskets and revolvers, particularly in Texas, and I have, in
a few instances, been amused at the vigor and audacity with
which they have employed them to protect themselves
against the robbers and murderers that infest that State.

Another result of the above-mentioned settled belief in
the negro's inferiority, and in the necessity that he should
not be left to himself without a guardian, is that in some
sections he is discouraged from leaving his old master. I
have known of planters who considered it an offence
against neighborhood courtesy for another to hire their old
hands, and in two instances that were reported the dispu-
tants came to blows over the breach of etiquette. It is only,
however, in the most remote regions, where our troops
have seldom or never penetrated, that the negroes have not
perfect liberty to rove where they choose. Even when the
attempt is made to restrain them by a system of passes from
their employers, or from police patrols, it is of little avail;
for the negroes, in their ignorance and darkness of understanding, are penetrated with a singularly strong conviction
that they "are not free so long as they stay at the old place;"
and all last summer and fall they pretty thoroughly demonstrated their freedom by changing their places of residence.
Such a thorough chaos and commingling of population has
seldom been seen since the great barbarian invasion of the
Roman empire. In this general upheaval thousands of long-
scattered families were joyously reunited. It is a strange
fact, however, and one which I have abundantly established
by the testimony of hundreds of the negroes themselves,
that a large majority of them have finally returned voluntarily and settled down in the old cabins of their former
quarters. The negro clings to old associations—it was only a
temporary impulse of their new-found freedom to wander
away from them; and at last they returned, generally wearied, hungry, and forlorn. In most cases, or at least in many
cases, it was not so much from any affection toward their
former masters as it was from a mere instinctive attachment to the homes of their youth—the familiar scenes in
the midst of which they were born and reared. When I was
in Selma, Alabama, last fall, a constant stream of them, of

all ages and conditions, were pouring through that city on their way, as they always told me, to Mississippi or Tennessee. Many were transported free by our government, while many were on foot, trudging hopefully but painfully forward toward their old homes, from which they had been taken to escape our armies.

I believe that in some of the most interior districts, especially in Texas, the substance of slavery still remains, in the form of the bondage of custom, of fear, and of inferiority; but nowhere are there any negroes so ignorant of the great change that has taken place as to submit to the lash. In no place did I hear the slightest allusion to any punishment of this sort having been inflicted since the rebellion ended. In every case it was violent stabbing or shooting, resulting from a personal encounter. The negro was aware of his rights, and was defending them. His friends need never fear his re-enslavement; it never can, never will take place. His head is filled with the idea of freedom, and anything but the most insidious and blandishing encroachments upon his freedom he will perceive and resist. The planters everywhere complain of his "demoralization" in this respect.

As to the personal treatment received by the negro at the hands of the southern people there is wide-spread misapprehension. It is not his former master, as a general thing, that is his worst enemy, but quite the contrary. I have talked earnestly with hundreds of old slave-owners, and seen them move among their former "chattels," and I am not mistaken. The feeling with which a very large majority of them regard the negro is one of genuine commiseration, although it is not a sentiment much elevated above that with which they would look upon a suffering animal for which they had formed an attachment. Last summer the negroes, exulting in their new-found freedom, as was to have been expected, were gay, thoughtless, and improvident; and, as a consequence, when the winter came hundreds of them felt the pinchings of want, and many perished. The old planters have often pointed out to me numerous instances of calamity that had come under their own observation in the case of their former slaves and others.

It was one of the most pernicious effects of slavery that it confined the attention of the owner entirely to the present bodily condition of his slaves, and ignored all calculations upon his future mental or moral growth; it gave him that mean opinion of the negroes' capacity that he still retains. The planter reasoned only from the actual facts, and never from possibilities. Inheriting his slaves, and finding them always brutish, stupid, and slow of understanding, he committed the logical inaccuracy of preventing them from ever becoming anything else, and proceeded to argue that they never could become so. To a certain extent it is true, as has been forcibly said, that "those who have seen most of the negro know least of him," though the assertion should be reduced to this—that they know far less of him as a human being than we of the north, but much more respecting his mere animal characteristics. Notwithstanding all this, I insist that there was in most cases a real attachment between master and slave, and still is, especially between the family and house servants.

It is the former slave-owners who are the best friends the negro has in the south—those who, heretofore, have provided for his mere physical comfort, generally with sufficient means, though entirely neglecting his better nature, while it is the "poor whites" that are his enemies. It is from these he suffers most. In a state of slavery they hated him; and, now that he is free, there is no striking abatement of this sentiment, and the former master no longer feels called by the instincts of interest to extend that protection that he once did. On the streets, by the roadside, in his wretched hut, in the field of labor—everywhere, the inoffensive negro is exposed to their petty and contemptible persecutions; while, on the other hand, I have known instances where the respectable, substantial people of a community have united together to keep guard over a house in which the negroes were taking their amusement, and from which, a few nights before, they had been rudely driven by white vagabonds, who found pleasure in their fright and suffering. I reiterate, that the former owners, as a class, are the negroes' best friends in the south, although many of this class diligently strive to discourage the freedmen from any earnest efforts to promote their higher welfare. When one believes that a certain race of beings are incapable of advancement, he is very prone to withhold the means of that advancement. And it is in this form that a species of slavery will longest be perpetuated—it is in these strongholds that it will last die out. I am pretty sure that there is not a single negro in the whole south who is not receiving pay for his labor according to his own contract; but, as a general thing, the freedmen are encouraged to collect about the old mansion in their little quarters, labor for their former master for set terms, receiving, besides their pay, food, quarters, and medical attendance, and thus continuing on in their former state of dependence. The cruelties of slavery, and all of its outward forms, have entirely passed away; but, as might have been expected, glimmerings of its vassalage, its subserviency, and its helplessness, linger.

# Carl Schurz, "The Logical Results of the War"

## (September 8, 1866)

In early September, in advance of the midterm elections of 1866, Schurz delivered this fiery political speech at National Hall in Philadelphia. In it, he condemned the president's Reconstruction program as reactionary. Comparing Johnson unfavorably with his predecessor, Schurz alleged that the martyred Lincoln never would have allowed Southern Unionists or the freedpeople to suffer at the mercy of the unrepentant Rebels. Schurz supported a proposed new Constitutional amendment that would provide due process and would disfranchise persons who denied citizens their rights. Anticipating the Radical Republicans' own Reconstruction program, Schurz proclaimed that the battle lines with Johnson were drawn.

I declare here before the American people, and I call to witness every honest man on the face of the globe, if, after having taken the money of the National creditor, upon the distinct promise that his interest should be fairly secured; if, after having called upon the Southern loyalist for coöperation, upon the distinct promise that his rights should be protected; if, after having summoned the negro to the battlefield, upon the distinct and solemn promise that his race should be forever and truly free; if, after having done all this, the Government of this Republic restores the rebel States to the full enjoyment of their rights and the full exercise of their power in the Union, without previously exacting such irreversible stipulations and guarantees as will fully, and beyond peradventure, secure the National creditor, the Southern Union man and the emancipated negro against those encroachments upon their rights which the reaction now going on is bringing with it, it will be the most unnatural, the most treacherous, the most dastardly act ever committed by any nation in the history of the world. It will be such an act as will render every man who participates in it unfit forever to sit in the company of gentlemen.

You remember the scorn and contempt with which the rebels spoke about the "mean-spirited Yankee." Do this, betray those who stood by you in the hour of need, and at that moment you will deserve it all. Do this, and your bitterest enemy in the South will have a right to ask the negro, "Did we not tell you the Yankees would cheat you?" And the negro will have to reply, "You did; and you were right." Not because they hated you, but because they despised you, the people of the South ventured upon the rebellion. Do this, betray your friends into the hands of their enemies, and they will despise you more than ever before, and you will have to say to yourselves that you deserve it.

And yet a policy like this I have heard designated as the "Lincoln and Johnson policy." In the name of common decency, in the name of the respect we owe to the memory of our martyred President, I solemnly protest against this insidious coupling of names. The Lincoln policy! I knew Abraham Lincoln well; and at times when many earnest and true men were dissatisfied with his ways, and when I myself could not resist an impulse of impatience, yet I never lost my faith in him, because I knew him well. The workings of his mind were slow; but the pure and noble sympathies of his heart, true as the magnet needle, always guided them to the polar star of universal justice. He was not one of those bold reformers who will go far ahead of the particular requirements of the hour; he laboriously endeavored to comprehend what the situation demanded, and when he once clearly understood it, at once he planted his foot, and no living man ever saw Abraham Lincoln make a step backward. His march was ahead, and each dawning day found him a warmer advocate of the progressive ideas of our great age.

I have heard it said, and it is one of the staple arguments of Mr. Johnson's friends, that Abraham Lincoln would never have imposed upon the rebel States a condition precedent to restoration because it was not in the Baltimore platform. If Mr. Lincoln had been assassinated in the year 1862, they might, with equal justice, have said, because emancipation was not in the Chicago platform of 1860, he would never have been in favor of emancipation. I undertake to say he would have been as firm an advocate of impartial suffrage to-day as he was of emancipation, had he lived to see how necessary the one is to secure and complete the other. True, he never ranted about the hanging and impoverishing of traitors, but in his soul slept the sublime ideal of merciful justice and just mercy. He would not have thought of taking bloody revenge on the Union's enemies, but he would never have ceased to think of being just to the Union's friends. Abraham Lincoln and this "policy"! He would rather have suffered himself to be burnt at the stake than to break or endanger the pledge he had given to the Southern Union man when he called upon him for assistance, and to the negro soldier, when he summoned him to the field of battle; and if he could rise from the dead and walk among us to-day, we would see him imploring mercy upon the accursed souls of his assassins. But even his large heart, with its inexhaustible mine of human kindness, would have no prayer for those who strive to undo, or culpably suffer to be undone, the great work which was the crowning glory of his life.

Let Andrew Johnson's friends look for arguments wherever they choose, but let the grave of the great martyr of liberty be safe against their defiling touch. In the name of the National heart I protest against the infamous trick of associating Abraham Lincoln with a policy which drove into exile the truest men of the South, and culminated in the butchery of New Orleans. If Andrew Johnson has chosen his pillory, let him stand there alone, enveloped in the incense of bought flattery, adored by every villain in the land, and loaded down with the maledictions of the downtrodden and degraded.

Americans, the lines are drawn, and the issues of the contests are clearly made up.

You want the Union fully restored. We offer it to you—a Union based upon universal liberty, impartial justice and equal rights, upon sacred pledges faithfully fulfilled, upon the faith of the Nation nobly vindicated; a Union without a slave and without a tyrant; a Union of truly democratic States; a Union capable of ripening to full maturity all that is great and hopeful in the mind and heart of the American people; a Union on every square foot of which free thought may shine out in free utterance; a Union between the most promising elements of progress, between the most loyal impulses in every section of this vast Republic; in one word, a Union between the true men of the North and the true men of the South.

The reactionists, with their champion, Andrew Johnson, also offer you a Union—a Union based upon deception unscrupulously practiced, upon great promises treacherously violated, upon the National faith scandalously broken; a Union whose entrails are once more to be lacerated by the irrepressible struggle between slavery and liberty; a Union in a part of which the rules of speech will be prescribed by the terrorism of the mob, and free thought silenced by the policeman's club and the knife of the assassin; a Union tainted with the blood of its truest friends and covered with the curses of its betrayed children; a Union between the fighting traitors of the South and the scheming traitors of the North; a Union between the New York rioters of 1863 and the Memphis and New Orleans rioters of 1866.

You want magnanimity to a beaten foe. We offer it to you. We demand no blood, no persecution, no revenge. We only insist that when the Republic distributes the charitable gift of pardon and grace, the safety and rights of her faithful children are entitled to the first consideration. We are ready to grasp the hand of the South. We only want first to ascertain whether the blood of our slaughtered friends is already dried on it. Peace and good-will to all men is the fondest wish of our heart and we are anxious to give and secure it even to the bitterest of our enemies as soon as they show an honest willingness to grant it to all of our friends.

The reactionists, with their champion, Andrew Johnson, speak, too, of magnanimity. Magnanimity! What magnanimity is this which consists in forgiveness to the Union's enemies and forgetfulness to the Union's friends? which puts the dagger into the hands of the former with which to strike at the lives of the latter? Magnanimity, indeed! It is mercy in the prostituting embrace of treason; it is persecution and murder in the garb of grace.

Are the American people sunk so deeply—can they be so completely lost to all sense of decency and honor—that such an insult to their common sense, and to the generous impulses of their hearts, should be offered to them with impunity? Or is it possible that those who but yesterday would have defied the world in arms, should to-day, with craven pusillanimity, recoil before the difficulties which the revived hopes of defeated traitors oppose to their onward march? I appeal to your understandings. Let the clear, practical eye of the American be turned upon the task immediately before us, and see how simple it is. You have but to speak and the dangers which surround you will vanish. Let the National will rise up from the ballot-boxes of November with a strength which laughs at resistance, and with a clearness of utterance which admits of no doubt, and the reaction which now surges against you like a sea of angry waves will play around your feet like the harmless rivulet set running by an April shower. Even Andrew Johnson's damaged intellect will quickly perceive that, although he may succeed in buying up a few forlorn wretches, it is a hopeless enterprise to debauch the great heart of the American people. He will learn in season that it would indeed be highly imprudent for him to think of dictatorship, and that if he ventured too far in his treacherous course, the American people are not incapable of remembering what he has so strenuously impressed upon their minds, that "treason must be made odious," and that "traitors must be punished." The late rebels will soon understand that those who defeated them in the field still live; and that it will be a wise thing for the South to lose no time in accommodating themselves to a necessity from which there is no escape. Nay, even to our friend, Henry Ward Beecher, it may finally become clear that by boldly and unflinchingly insisting upon what is right, the Union can just as quickly, and far more firmly, be restored than by accepting with fidgety impatience that which is wrong. But above all, our loyal friends in the South, white and black, whose cry for help is to-day thrilling the heart of every just man in the land, will raise their heads with proud confidence, feeling that they do not stand alone among their enemies, but that as they, in the gloomiest hours of danger, were true to the Republic, the Republic, so help her, God, will be true to them.

Yes, let the National will once more make itself understood to friend and foe, and the dangers which are now hanging over us like a black cloud will quickly clear away.

Before its thunder tones the armed legions of the rebellion could not stand; before it the iniquitous designs of the reaction will soon vanish in utter hopelessness. Andrew Johnson's wretched brigade will be dispersed as by a whirlwind; the arm of the daring demagogue, which is now so defiantly lifted against the popular conscience, will fall palsied by his side, and the truly loyal men of America will quickly, justly and firmly restore the shaken fabric of the Union.

We have passed through gloomy days of late; days of grievous disappointment, of deep humiliation, of sorrowful anxiety. But when the other night I stood upon the balcony of the Union League House and saw the countless multitude surging below, a multitude greater in number than the hosts which marched with Sherman to the sea, or the Army of the Potomac when it swept over the ramparts of Richmond, and that multitude, as once our battalions were summoned to the battlefield by the paternal voice of Abraham Lincoln, now following the solemn call of the same voice issuing from the grave; and when I saw from that ocean of human faces radiating forth the electric light of intelligence and love of liberty; and when I thought that the volcanic bursts of enthusiasm there were but one throb of the patriotic emotions which are to-day again swelling the great heart of the loyal North, then my soul felt itself lifted out of the gloom of dark apprehensions and I ceased to fear for the future of the Republic. Then it became certain again to my mind, that the great people of the New World, who fought a four years' battle of conscience, have not forgotten their exalted mission on earth, and that the very gates of hell cannot shake their mighty determination to wield, with a firm hand, the National power, until justice is done to all, and until, with safety to all, the Republic can be set afloat upon the broadest channel of self-government.

We have already heard the triumphant morning gun of Vermont, booming with increased volume. Far-off San Francisco has merrily responded; old Maine in the North stands ready to send us a cheering echo, and all over the land our hosts are mustering with the inspiring confidence that to march on is to conquer.

Our time has come. Forward into line, Republicans! This is to be the final battle of the war. Let it be the greatest victory of right and justice.

# STATEMENT OF
# RHODA ANN CHILDS

## (September 25, 1866)

Georgia freedwoman Rhoda Ann Childs's chilling testimony before a Freedmen's Bureau agent documents the brutal racial and sexual violence of Reconstruction. With her husband, a former soldier in the U.S. Colored Troops, absent, Rhoda stood vulnerable to the abuse of eight white men. This horrific episode suggests not only the gratuitous violence of the period, but also the legacy of sectional and race hatred following Confederate defeat.

Rhoda Ann Childs came into this office and made the following statement:

"Myself and husband were under contract with Mrs. Amelia Childs of Henry County, and worked from Jan. 1, 1866, until the crops were laid by, or in other words until the main work of the year was done, without difficulty. Then, (the fashion being prevalent among the planters) we were called upon one night, and my husband was demanded; I Said he was not there. They then asked where he was. I Said he was gone to the water mellon patch. They then Seized me and took me Some distance from the house, where they 'bucked' me down across a log, Stripped my clothes over my head, one of the men Standing astride my neck, and beat me across my posterior, two men holding my legs. In this manner I was beaten until they were tired. Then they turned me parallel with the log, laying my neck on a limb which projected from the log, and one man placing his foot upon my neck, beat me again on my hip and thigh. Then I was thrown upon the ground on my back, one of the men Stood upon my breast, while two others took hold of my feet and stretched My limbs as far apart as they could, while the man Standing upon my breast applied the Strap to my private parts until fatigued into stopping, and I was more dead than alive. Then a man, Supposed to be an ex-confederate Soldier, as he was on crutches, fell upon me and ravished me. During the whipping one of the men ran his pistol into me, and Said he had a hell of a mind to pull the trigger, and Swore they ought to Shoot me, as my husband had been in the 'God damned Yankee Army,' and Swore they meant to kill every black Son-of-a-bitch they could find that had ever fought against them. They then went back to the house, Seized my two daughters and beat them, demanding their father's pistol, and upon failure to get that, they entered the house and took Such articles of clothing as Suited their fancy, and decamped. There were concerned in this affair eight men, none of which could be recognized for certain.

her
Roda Ann  X  Childs
mark

# George Fitzhugh, "Camp Lee and the Freedman's [*sic*] Bureau"

## *(October 1866)*

Virginian George Fitzhugh (1806–1881) ranked as one of the Old South's foremost intellectuals, justifying slavery, racial hierarchies, and the plantation system by comparing them favorably to free labor and the North's emerging bourgeois capitalist marketplace. In *Sociology for the South* (1854) and *Cannibals All* (1859), he criticized ideas of freedom and equality, noting that they bred cutthroat competition and internecine class warfare, rendering citizens "cannibals all." Following the Civil War, Fitzhugh served as a Freedmen's Bureau agent, adjudicating court cases involving freedmen and -women. Writing in 1866 in *De Bow's Review*, Fitzhugh expressed sympathy toward people of color but remained convinced that blacks would forever require white supervision, preferably that of their former masters.

Camp Lee, about a mile from Richmond, is but a branch or appendage of the Freedman's Bureau in that city. For this reason, and because we ourselves live at Camp Lee, and until recently held our court in Richmond, we have thought it would be appropriate to treat of the two in connection. Admitted behind the curtains, were we curious, prying, or observant, we might have collected materials for an article at once rich, racy and instructive; but we are, unfortunately, abstracted, and see or hear very little that is going on around us. What we have seen and heard, so far as we deem it interesting, we will relate, without breach of confidence, because nothing has been told us in confidence, and we have seen or heard nothing at all discreditable to any officer of the Bureau.

The institution has a very pretty name, but unlike the

rose, "would not smell as sweet by any other name." In truth, it is simply and merely a negro nursery; a fact which would have been obvious even to the blind, if led into our little court-room, where the stove was in full blast, and about a hundred cushites were in attendance, as suitors, witnesses or idle lookers-on. You may be sure, Mr. Editor, we smoked desperately and continuously. As this habit of ours, of smoking whilst sitting on the Bench, has been made the subject of remark in some of the Northern papers, we deem this explanation due to our contemporaries and to posterity; for as part, parcel, or appurtenance of the Negro Nursery, we shall certainly descend to posterity. Indeed, a good many of our Federal friends will be obliged to us for this explanation, for our soldiers smoked terribly in Richmond, quite as terribly as Uncle Toby's soldiers swore in Flanders.

This Negro Nursery is an admirable idea of the Federals, which, however, they stole from us. For we always told them the darkeys were but grown-up children that needed guardians, like all other children. They saw this very soon, and therefore established the Freedmen's Bureau; at first for a year, thinking that a year's tuition under Yankee school ma'ams and Federal Provost Marshals would amply fit them for self-support, liberty and equality, and the exercise of the right of suffrage. They have now added two years more to the duration of the Bureau, because they now see that the necessity for nursing the negroes is twice as urgent as they thought it at first. At the end of that time, they will discover that their pupils are irreclaimable *"mauvais sujets,"* and will be ready to throw up "in divine disgust" the whole negro-nursing and negro-teaching business, and to turn the affair over to the State authorities.

The American people, by that time, must become satisfied that they have expended enough, aye, and far too much, of blood and treasure in the hopeless attempt to make citizens of negroes. They must first be made men, and the Bureau is a practical admission and assertion that they are not men, and will not be for two years hence. By that time they think the Ethiopian will change his skin. We are sure he will not. Negro he is, negro he always has been, and negro he always will be. Never has he been, and never will he be a man, physically, morally, or intellectually, in the European or American sense of the term. None are so thoroughly aware that the term "negro" is, in its ordinary acceptation, the negation of manhood, as the abolitionists and the negroes themselves. They are no longer negroes, but "colored people." Those who call them other than negroes, are acting falsely and hypocritically, for they thereby as good as assert that these blacks have changed their natures, moral and intellectual, and risen to an equality with the whites.

They are our fellow-beings, children, not men, and therefore to be compassionated and taken care of.

The Bureau has occasioned much irritation, and in some instances, no doubt, been guilty of wrong and injustice to our people; but it has saved the South a world of money and of trouble, and expended a great deal of money among us, at a time when we could spare neither men nor money to keep order among the negroes, or to support the helpless ones. We can bear it for two years longer, but after that time we must have negro-nurseries of our own; that is, like the Federals, we must institute a distinct and separate government for the negroes. A majority of those living in the country will subside, if they have not already subsided, into the *"statu quo ante bellum."* The crowds of paupers, beggars, rogues, and vagabonds, infesting our cities and their suburbs, must be summarily dealt with by State bureaux located in each considerable town. No bureaux or bureau officers will be needed in the country, or in villages—nor are they even now needed.

We have resided at Camp Lee for more than a year. During that whole time there have been from three to five hundred negroes here, furnished with houses by the Federal authorities, part of which were built by the Confederates during the war for military purposes, and part by the State Agricultural Society. The grounds are still owned by that Society. The brick house, however, in which we reside was originally erected by Colonel John Mayo, deceased, father-in-law of General Winfield Scott. The dwelling-house, called the Hermitage, was burned down many years ago. The Society added a story to these brick buildings, and erected two-storied porticos in front and at the sides of them. They now make quite an imposing appearance, with a portico of a hundred and fifty feet in front, and wings of about eighty on the lower floor, and one of equal extent on the upper floor. We are, just now, the sole occupant of the lower floor, and a French lady the sole occasional occupant of the upper floor.

Most of this building, until a few weeks since, was occupied by Mrs. Gibbons, her daughter and Miss Ellison. Whilst they were here, Camp Lee was tolerable, and often very agreeable, even to us, separated as we are from our family. We hope, and have reason to expect, that they will return during this fall. In front of this building, we have a market-garden of two acres, which so far, owing to the drought, has been a great failure, but which Daniel Coleman (Freedman), our gardener, assures us will do wonderfully well as a fall garden. But we are quite incredulous. We are great at theory, and hence generally fail in practice.

Just beside our vegetable-garden stands Mrs. Gibbons' zoological-garden. Here she would sometimes have as many as a hundred and twenty negro orphans, of both sexes, and various ages. The buildings for them were ample and commodious. Mrs. G.'s attention and kindness to her wards was assiduous, untiring, and very successful. When she first took these infants in charge, some time last fall, the mortality among them was fearful; but after about two months, by frequent ablutions, close shaving of their heads, abundance of warm and clean clothing, and plenty of good and various food, they were rendered remarkably healthy, and so continued until their removal to Philadelphia. Mrs. G. removed, in all, about two hundred to that city. We presume they have not been so healthful there, for we learn, indirectly, that the Board of Health of that city has advised, or required, their removal. Poor things! Camp Lee was a Paradise to them. Immorality and crime in every form, want and disease, will fill up the balance of their existence. They will be feeble, hated, persecuted and despised. They lost nothing in losing their parents; but lost all in losing their masters. They will meet with no more kind Mrs. Gibbons in this cold, harsh, cruel world.

Mrs. Gibbons is a member of the Society of Friends, deputed by an association of ladies, of Philadelphia, belonging to that society, to superintend the negro orphan asylum at this place. The Bureau furnishes the ordinary rations to these infants, and the association abundance of whatever else that is needed for their comfortable subsistence. When Mrs. Gibbons left, she had on hand some fifty-five new comers, not yet prepared to be sent North. These were sent over to Howard Grove, another branch of the Negro Nursery at Richmond. We believe most of the sick, aged and infirm negroes are sent there. It was a Confederate hospital during the war, and is now a negro nursery and hospital. We have never visited it since the war. Near it is Chimborazo Hospital, now Nursery, and this also was a Confederate hospital. There were a great many negroes there last winter, but we believe the Bureau has succeeded in getting rid of all but the infants and infirm. We learn there are nine ladies there, teaching literary or industrial schools.

Miss Ellison was the teacher at this place. This teaching, however, is, we fear, but a cruel farce, that but incites to insubordination, and will induce the negroes to run a muck against the whites, in which Cuffee will come off second best. These negro orphans have lost their parents, but we feel quite positive that in three instances out of four their parents are not both dead. Negroes possess much amiableness of feeling but not the least steady, permanent affection. "Out of sight, out of mind," is true of them all. They never grieve twenty-four hours for the death of parents, wives, husbands, or children. Some of the negroes at this place informed us, many months ago, that many of Mrs. Gibbons' orphans had parents in Richmond. About four weeks since, a very interesting little negro child, about two years old, was deserted by its mother, picked up in the streets of Richmond, and brought to Mrs. Gibbons. Not ten days since, just at the approach of a terrific storm, a negro mother left her little daughter, of about five years old, exposed in the field, within a few hundred yards of this place. It was picked up by some kind-hearted negro, and is now in the keeping of the French lady. It is clever, and extremely emaciate. It has been starved. But we do not blame the poor mother. She, too, deprived of a master, was no doubt starving, and the best she could possibly do was thus to expose her child, with the hope that some humane person able to provide for it might find it and take it in charge. . . .

The negroes in the country are contented, and valuable laborers. Having no rent to pay, abundance of food and fuel, and money enough at all times to buy plain necessary clothing, they are never punished by absolute want, never become restless or insubordinate. Besides, they dwell too far apart to combine for any mischievous purposes. But the excessive numbers of negroes about our towns, for want of employment, are continually in a state bordering on actual starvation, and all starving men are desperate and dangerous. We know from daily and careful observation that the Bureau in Richmond has and still is exerting itself to the utmost of its very limited powers to abate this nuisance, by refusing rations, and advising and persuading the negroes to remove into the country, where they can all find employment. Force, not "moral suasion," governs all men, whether white or black. If the Bureau had the power to take these idle negroes up, and hire them out to the highest bidder, or put them out to the lowest, and were about to exercise the power, the negroes would at once squander, and find masters in the country. But the Radicals are afraid that if negroes are treated no better than poor white people, it will be said that they are re-enslaved, and subjected to a worse form of slavery than that from which they have just escaped. The result of all this must be, that a very large standing army must be kept up in the South by the Federal Government; portions of it stationed at every town south of the Ohio and Mason and Dixon's line; or the Constitution must be amended so as to authorize the several States to maintain standing armies. But even after all this is done, there will be frequent bloody collisions between the races in all of our Southern towns. Negroes, so useful in the country, are an abominable nuisance in town. Mobs at the South, after a time, will drive them out, as mobs have often done at the North. The Radicals hold the wolf by the ears. They have not tamed him, and instead of letting him go, are trying to mend their hold. This wolf is the opposing races in our towns and cities. In conquering the South and freeing the negroes, they but bought the elephant—and now they know not what to do with him. But he is *their* elephant, not ours, and we are of opinion should be left with them to be nursed and cared for. In two more years they will grow heartily tired of nursing this elephant and holding the wolf by the ears. Standing armies and Freedmen's Bureaus are rather more expensive cages than the country can now afford. These negro nurseries will be broken up, and their in-

mates, probably, be turned over to us at the South, to try
our hands at nursing. If the North, after turning them over
to us, will not intermeddle in their management, we will at
once tame them, and make them useful, and instead of
costing the nation some thirty millions a year, they will
yield a neat annual profit to it of some two hundred millions. Then you will hear no more of idle, discontented,
starving negroes. All will be well provided for, and all happy
and contented.

We have the highest respect for all the offices of the Bureau in Richmond, from the commanding general down.
They have even treated us with great courtesy and kindness; and we are witness to the fact that they discharge their
duties with zeal, industry and integrity. Therefore, in calling
the Bureau a negro nursery or a congeries of negro nurseries, we intend no disrespect—but only wish to convey to the
public a full, accurate and comprehensive idea of the true
character of the institution. Besides, we have been one of
the nurses ourselves, and would not bring discredit on our
own calling. . . .

# FREDERICK DOUGLASS, "RECONSTRUCTION"

## (December 1866)

During the Civil War Douglass, America's foremost black abolitionist, repeatedly pushed Lincoln to free the slaves, arm African-Americans as soldiers, and empower people of color with full civil rights. As Reconstruction unfolded, Douglass condemned the Black Codes and pressed for black suffrage. Along with other Republicans, during the midterm 1866 elections, he worked to undo President Johnson and, in a series of articles in *Atlantic Monthly*, he assessed the meaning of the overwhelming Republican victories (Republicans in the House of Representatives gained a two-thirds majority and therefore could override any future presidential vetoes). According to Douglass, the recent elections signified a people's mandate for a new Reconstruction program, one that would protect the rights of all people, regardless of color or class. He urged the new Thirty-ninth Congress to remove every vestige of slavery from American life and to enfranchise the freedmen. Only political action, Douglass averred, would protect their hard-won new freedoms.

The assembling of the Second Session of the Thirty-ninth Congress may very properly be made the occasion of a few earnest words on the already much-worn topic of reconstruction.

Seldom has any legislative body been the subject of a solicitude more intense, or of aspirations more sincere and ardent. There are the best of reasons for this profound interest. Questions of vast moment, left undecided by the last session of Congress, must be manfully grappled with by this. No political skirmishing will avail. The occasion demands statesmanship.

Whether the tremendous war so heroically fought and so victoriously ended shall pass into history a miserable failure, barren of permanent results,—a scandalous and shocking waste of blood and treasure,—a strife for empire, as Earl Russell characterized it, of no value to liberty or civilization,—an attempt to re-establish a Union by force, which must be the merest mockery of a Union,—an effort to bring under Federal authority States into which no loyal man from the North may safely enter, and to bring men into the national councils who deliberate with daggers and vote with revolvers, and who do not even conceal their deadly hate of the country that conquered them; or whether, on the other hand, we shall, as the rightful reward of victory over treason, have a solid nation, entirely delivered from all contradictions and social antagonisms, based upon loyalty, liberty, and equality, must be determined one way or the other by the present session of Congress. The last session really did nothing which can be considered final as to these questions. The Civil Rights Bill and the Freedmen's Bureau Bill and the proposed constitutional amendments, with the amendment already adopted and recognized as the law of the land, do not reach the difficulty, and cannot, unless the whole structure of the government is changed from a government by States to something like a despotic central government, with power to control even the municipal regulations of States, and to make them conform to its own despotic will. While there remains such an idea as the right of each State to control its own local affairs,—an idea, by the way, more deeply rooted in the minds of men of all sections of the country than perhaps any one other political idea,—no general assertion of human rights can be of any practical value. To change the character of the government at this point is neither possible nor desirable. All that is necessary to be done is to make the government consistent with itself, and render the rights of the States compatible with the sacred rights of human nature.

The arm of the Federal government is long, but it is far too short to protect the rights of individuals in the interior of distant States. They must have the power to protect themselves, or they will go unprotected, spite of all the laws the Federal government can put upon the national statute-book.

Slavery, like all other great systems of wrong, founded in the depths of human selfishness, and existing for ages, has not neglected its own conservation. It has steadily exerted an influence upon all around it favorable to its own continuance. And to-day it is so strong that it could exist, not only without law, but even against law. Custom, manners, morals, religion, are all on its side everywhere in the South; and when you add the ignorance and servility of the ex-slave to the intelligence and accustomed authority of the master, you have the conditions, not out of which slavery will again grow, but under which it is impossible for the Federal government to wholly destroy it, unless the Federal government be armed with despotic power, to blot out State authority, and to station a Federal officer at every crossroad. This, of course, cannot be done, and ought not even if it could. The true way and the easiest way is to make our government entirely consistent with itself, and give to every loyal citizen the elective franchise,—a right and power which will be ever present, and will form a wall of fire for his protection.

One of the invaluable compensations of the late Rebellion is the highly instructive disclosure it made of the true source of danger to republican government. Whatever may be tolerated in monarchical and despotic governments, no republic is safe that tolerates a privileged class, or denies to any of its citizens equal rights and equal means to maintain them. What was theory before the war has been made fact by the war.

There is cause to be thankful even for rebellion. It is an impressive teacher, though a stern and terrible one. In both characters it has come to us, and it was perhaps needed in both. It is an instructor never a day before its time, for it comes only when all other means of progress and enlightenment have failed. Whether the oppressed and despairing bondman, no longer able to repress his deep yearnings for manhood, or the tyrant, in his pride and impatience, takes the initiative, and strikes the blow for a firmer hold and a longer lease of oppression, the result is the same,—society is instructed, or may be.

Such are the limitations of the common mind, and so thoroughly engrossing are the cares of common life, that only the few among men can discern through the glitter and dazzle of present prosperity the dark outlines of approaching disasters, even though they may have come up to our very gates, and are already within striking distance. The yawning seam and corroded bolt conceal their defects from the mariner until the storm calls all hands to the pumps. Prophets, indeed, were abundant before the war; but who cares for prophets while their predictions remain unfulfilled, and the calamities of which they tell are masked behind a blinding blaze of national prosperity?

It is asked, said Henry Clay, on a memorable occasion, Will slavery never come to an end? That question, said he, was asked fifty years ago, and it has been answered by fifty years of unprecedented prosperity. Spite of the eloquence of the earnest Abolitionists,—poured out against slavery during thirty years,—even they must confess, that, in all the probabilities of the case, that system of barbarism would have continued its horrors far beyond the limits of the nineteenth century but for the Rebellion, and perhaps only have disappeared at last in a fiery conflict, even more fierce and bloody than that which has now been suppressed.

It is no disparagement to truth, that it can only prevail where reason prevails. War begins where reason ends. The thing worse than rebellion is the thing that causes rebellion. What that thing is, we have been taught to our cost. It remains now to be seen whether we have the needed courage to have that cause entirely removed from the Republic. At any rate, to this grand work of national regeneration and entire purification Congress must now address itself, with full purpose that the work shall this time be thoroughly done. The deadly upas, root and branch, leaf and fibre, body and sap, must be utterly destroyed. The country is evidently not in a condition to listen patiently to pleas for postponement, however plausible, nor will it permit the responsibility to be shifted to other shoulders. Authority and power are here commensurate with the duty imposed. There are no cloud-flung shadows to obscure the way. Truth shines with brighter light and intenser heat at every moment, and a country torn and rent and bleeding implores relief from its distress and agony.

If time was at first needed, Congress has now had time. All the requisite materials from which to form an intelligent judgment are now before it. Whether its members look at the origin, the progress, the termination of the war, or at the mockery of a peace now existing, they will find only one unbroken chain of argument in favor of a radical policy of reconstruction. For the omissions of the last session, some excuses may be allowed. A treacherous President stood in the way; and it can be easily seen how reluctant good men might be to admit an apostasy which involved so much of baseness and ingratitude. It was natural that they should seek to save him by bending to him even when he leaned to the side of error. But all is changed now. Congress knows now that it must go on without his aid, and even against his machinations. The advantage of the present session over the last is immense. Where that investigated, this has the facts. Where that walked by faith, this may walk by sight. Where that halted, this must go forward, and where that failed, this must succeed, giving the country whole measures where that gave us half-measures, merely as a means of saving the elections in a few doubtful districts. That Congress saw what was right, but distrusted the enlightenment of the loyal masses; but what was forborne in distrust of the people must now be done with a full knowledge that the people expect and require it. The members go to Washington fresh from the inspiring presence of the people. In every considerable public meeting, and in almost every conceivable way, whether at court-house, school-house, or cross-roads, in doors and out, the subject has been discussed, and the people have emphatically pronounced in favor of a radical policy. Listening to the doctrines of expediency and compromise with pity, impatience, and disgust, they have everywhere broken into demonstrations of the wildest enthusiasm when a brave word has been spoken in favor of equal rights and impartial suffrage. Radicalism, so far from being odious, is not the popular passport to power. The men most bitterly charged with it go to Congress with the largest majorities, while the timid and doubtful are sent by lean majorities, or else left at home. The strange controversy between the President and the Congress, at one time so threatening, is disposed of by the people. The high reconstructive powers which he so confidently, ostentatiously, and haughtily claimed, have been disallowed, denounced, and utterly repudiated; while those claimed by Congress have been confirmed.

# "PRESIDENT JOHNSON'S MESSAGE"

## (December 3, 1866)

Despite his party's serious losses in the 1866 mid-term elections, Johnson nevertheless believed that he retained the support of the American people; he believed that they would sustain his Reconstruction policies over those of the Radical Republicans, including the Fourteenth Amendment, which passed Congress on June 13, 1866. In his second annual message, Johnson listed what he considered his successes in restoring the Union and insisted that he would continue in accord with the Founding Fathers' intentions. The president urged Congress to admit to the Senate and House of Representatives persons elected from the former Confederate states. As 1867 dawned, Johnson remained confident, defiant, and unyielding to his increasingly vocal critics.

In my message of the 4th of December, 1865, Congress was informed of the measures which had been instituted by the Executive with a view to the gradual restoration of the States in which the insurrection occurred to their relations with the General Government. Provisional Governors had been appointed, conventions called, Governors elected, Legislatures assembled, and Senators and Representatives chosen to the Congress of the United States. Courts had been opened for the enforcement of laws long in abeyance. The blockade had been removed, customhouses re-established, and the internal revenue laws put in force, in order that the people might contribute to the national income. Postal operations had been renewed, and efforts were being made to restore them to their former condition of efficiency. The States themselves had been asked to take part in the high function of amending the Constitution, and of thus sanctioning the extinction of

African slavery as one of the legitimate results of our internecine struggle.

Having progressed thus far, the executive department found that it had accomplished nearly all that was within the scope of its constitutional authority. One thing, however, yet remained to be done before the work of restoration could be completed, and that was the admission to Congress of loyal Senators and Representatives from the States whose people had rebelled against the lawful authority of the General Government. This question devolved upon the respective Houses, which, by the Constitution, are made the judges of the elections, returns, and qualifications of their own members; and its consideration at once engaged the attention of Congress.

In the mean time, the executive department—no other plan having been proposed by Congress—continued its efforts to perfect, as far as was practicable, the restoration of the proper relations between the citizens of the respective States, the States, and the Federal Government, extending, from time to time, as the public interests seemed to require, the judicial, revenue, and postal systems of the country. With the advice and consent of the Senate, the necessary officers were appointed, and appropriations made by Congress for the payment of their salaries. The proposition to amend the Federal Constitution so as to prevent the existence of slavery within the United States or any place subject to their jurisdiction, was ratified by the requisite number of States, and, on the 18th day of December, 1865, it was officially declared to have become valid as a part of the Constitution of the United States. All of the States in which the insurrection had existed promptly amended their constitutions so as to make them conform to the great change thus effected in the organic law of the land; declared null and void all ordinances and laws of secession; repudiated all pretended debts and obligations created for the revolutionary purposes of the insurrection; and proceeded, in good faith, to the enactment of measures for the protection and amelioration of the condition of the colored race. Congress, however, yet hesitated to admit any of these States to representation; and it was not until towards the close of the eighth month of the session that an exception was made in favor of Tennessee by the admission of her Senators and Representatives.

I deem it a subject of profound regret that Congress has thus far failed to admit to seats loyal Senators and Representatives from the other States whose inhabitants, with those of Tennessee, had engaged in the rebellion. Ten States—more than one-fourth of the whole number—remain without representation! The seats of fifty members in the House of Representatives and of twenty members in the Senate are yet vacant—not by their own consent, not by a failure of election, but by the refusal of Congress to accept their credentials. Their admission, it is believed, would have accomplished much towards the renewal and strengthening of our relations as one people, and removed serious cause for discontent on the part of the inhabitants of those States. It would have accorded with the great principle enunciated in the Declaration of American Independence, that no people ought to bear the burden of taxation and yet be denied the right of representation. It would have been in consonance with the express provisions of the Constitution, that "each State shall have at least one Representative," and "that no State, without its consent, shall be deprived of its equal suffrage in the Senate." These provisions were intended to secure to every State, and to the people of every State, the right of representation in each House of Congress; and so important was it deemed by the framers of the Constitution that the equality of the States in the Senate should be preserved, that not even by an amendment of the Constitution can any State, without its consent, be denied a voice in that branch of the national Legislature.

It is true, it has been assumed that the existence of the States was terminated by the rebellious acts of their inhabitants, and that the insurrection having been suppressed, they were thenceforward to be considered merely as conquered territories. The legislative, executive, and judicial departments of the Government have, however, with great distinctness and uniform consistency, refused to sanction an assumption so incompatible with the nature of our republican system and with the professed objects of the war. Throughout the recent legislation of Congress, the undeniable fact makes itself apparent, that these ten political communities are nothing less than States of this Union. At the very commencement of the rebellion each House declared, with a unanimity as remarkable as it was significant, that the war was not "waged, upon our part, in any spirit of oppression, nor for any purpose of conquest or subjugation, nor purpose of overthrowing or interfering with the rights or established institutions of those States, but to defend and maintain the supremacy of the Constitution and all laws made in pursuance thereof, and to preserve the Union with all the dignity, equality and rights of the several States unimpaired; and that as soon as these objects" were "accomplished the war ought to cease." In some instances Senators were permitted to continue their legislative functions, while in other instances Representatives were elected and admitted to seats after their States had formally declared their right to withdraw from the Union, and were endeavoring to maintain that right by force of arms. All of the States whose people were in insurrection, as States, were included in the apportionment of the direct tax of $20,000,000 annually, laid upon the United States by the act approved 5th August, 1861. Congress, by the act of March 4, 1862, and by the apportionment of representation thereunder, also recognized their presence as States in the Union; and they have, for judicial purposes, been divided into districts, as States alone can be divided. The same recognition appears in the recent legislation in reference to Tennessee, which evidently rests upon the fact that the functions of the State were not destroyed by the rebellion, but merely suspended; and that principle is of course applicable to those States which, like Tennessee, attempted to renounce their place in the Union.

The action of the executive department of the Government upon this subject has been equally definite and uniform, and the purpose of the war was specifically stated in the proclamation issued by my predecessor on the 22d day of September, 1862. It was then solemnly proclaimed and declared that "hereafter, as heretofore, the war will be prosecuted for the object of practically restoring the constitutional relation between the United States and each of the States and the people thereof, to which States that relation is or may be suspended or disturbed."

The recognition of the States by the judicial department of the Government has also been clear and conclusive in all proceedings affecting them as States, had in the Supreme, Circuit, and District Courts.

In the admission of Senators and Representatives from any and all of the States, there can be no just ground of apprehension that persons who are disloyal will be clothed with the powers of legislation; for this could not happen when the Constitution and the laws are enforced by a vigilant and faithful Congress. Each House is made the "judge of the elections, returns, and qualifications of its own members," and may, "with the concurrence of two-thirds, expel a member." When a Senator or Representative presents his certificate of election, he may at once be admitted or rejected; or, should there be any question as to his eligibility, his credentials may be referred for investigation to the appropriate committee. If admitted to a seat, it must be upon evidence satisfactory to the House of which he thus becomes a member that he possesses the requisite constitutional and legal qualifications. If refused admission as a member, for want of due allegiance to the Government, and returned to his constituents, they are admonished that none but persons loyal to the United States will be allowed a voice in the legislative councils of the nation, and the political power and moral influence of Congress are thus effectively exerted in the interests of loyalty to the Government and fidelity to the Union. Upon this question, so vitally affecting the restoration of the Union and the permanency of our present form of government, my convictions, heretofore expressed, have undergone no change; but, on the contrary, their correctness has been confirmed by reflection and time. If the admission of loyal members to seats in the respective Houses of Congress was wise and expedient a year ago, it is no less wise and expedient now. If this anomalous condition is right now—if, in the exact condition of these States at the present time, it is lawful to exclude them from representation, I do not see that the question will be changed by the efflux of time. Ten years hence, if these States remain as they are, the right of representation will be no stronger, the right of exclusion will be no weaker.

The Constitution of the United States makes it the duty of the President to recommend to the consideration of

Congress "such measures as he shall judge necessary or expedient." I know of no measure more imperatively demanded by every consideration of national interest, sound policy, and equal justice, than the admission of loyal members from the now unrepresented States. This would consummate the work of restoration, and exert a most salutary influence in the re-establishment of peace, harmony, and fraternal feeling. It would tend greatly to renew the confidence of the American people in the vigor and stability of their institutions. It would bind us more closely together as a nation, and enable us to show to the world the inherent and recuperative power of a Government founded upon the will of the people, and established upon the principles of liberty, justice, and intelligence. Our increased strength and enhanced prosperity would irrefragably demonstrate the fallacy of the arguments against free institutions drawn from our recent national disorders by the enemies of republican government. The admission of loyal members from the States now excluded from Congress, by allaying doubt and apprehension, would turn capital, now awaiting an opportunity for investment, into the channels of trade and industry. It would alleviate the present troubled condition of those States, and, by inducing emigration, aid in the settlement of fertile regions now uncultivated, and lead to an increased production of those staples which have added so greatly to the wealth of the nation and the commerce of the world. New fields of enterprise would be opened to our progressive people, and soon the devastations of war would be repaired, and all traces of our domestic differences effaced from the minds of our countrymen.

# EXCERPTS FROM CLAUDE
## AUGUST CROMMELIN, *A*
## *YOUNG DUTCHMAN VIEWS*
## *POST—CIVIL WAR AMERICA*

### *(December 1866)*

Soon after Appomattox, Claude August Crommelin (1840–1874), an elite Dutchman, embarked on
a tour of the U.S., visiting New England, the Middle Atlantic States, the Upper Mississippi Valley,
and the war-ravaged South. Drawing upon family
connections, Crommelin met important Americans and recorded keen insights into the mood
and manners of those he observed. Crommelin
noted in particular the social and economic conditions in late 1866 in Charleston, South Carolina,
and the opinions of white Southerners toward
freedpeople, Yankees generally, and Radical Republicans in particular.

Saturday 8 December 1866

Departed for Charleston on board the *Saratoga*. Rain and
fog at the time of departure, and we were obliged to anchor
in the Narrows until the fog lifted.

. . . Some of his figures may be noted here: wages of Negroes, field hands $10 to 15 per month, domestic servants
$12 to 15, everything including board. Most owners—not
planters, about planters he didn't say anything—are glad to
be rid of their slaves and value today's system much higher
than the old one. During the war the price of gold skyrock-
eted to 5000 percent, meaning $1 in gold for $50 currency.
But he had also knowledge of a barrel of flour worth $10 in
gold being sold for $1,200 currency. It is clear that this was
the cause for much speculation, and the bribery to be declared officially unfit for army service must have been un-
believable. Later desertion grew to enormous proportions.

He claimed that the planters didn't want a return to the slave trade as they maintained that this would have depreciated the value of their old slaves, making the growing of cotton before the war already highly unprofitable. This could never have been a reason to go to war, as he said. He told me that field hands were worth only $500 before the war. He disregarded all stories about the punishing of those men who taught the Negroes, but he did say that for helping slaves to flee to the North the death penalty could still be imposed, although never really enforced. At the occasion of testamentary manumission the testator also had to provide funds to make the freed slave leave the state, this being the cause that there are hardly any freedmen in South Carolina. He also claims that the president against the Congress can count on the regular army and 300,000 men from the South. He calls all Northerners "the most vile, lying, cheating, hypocritical set of people on earth."

One of the waiters amused me by ventilating the same opinion regarding the North, because his father, a shoemaker of about 60 years of age, was suspected there because of his age of not being able to make shoes anymore, something one would have gladly entrusted him with in the South. One other of his complaints was that in school the rich boys got preferential treatment over poor boys. But as this seemed to have happened in North or South Carolina as well, this statement against the North was not very convincing in my opinion.

Regarding Reconstruction, the 'burden' of his argument was this: we don't care, let them do what they want to do in the North, we are just as happy outside the Union as in it again.

Wednesday 12 December 1866

At first sight Charleston made a very dismal impression. One still can see the craters, only just filled in, made by the bombs during the bombardment of eighteen months, day and night. Furthermore a whole section of the town burned down in the first year of the war, although this fire had nothing to do with the bombardment. The ruins have not yet been cleared away; everything is as it was the day after the fire. The multitude of Negroes, the colorful scarves that the women use as headgear, the market surrounded by tame turkey vultures, the many mules, the gentlemen on horseback, everything combines to provide a real Southern spectacle. But the almost complete absence of carriages, the ruinous exterior of the houses, and other particulars clearly show the sad situation of the inhabitants. Nowhere are houses being built, and the vacant lots in the 'Burnt District' are evidence that everything is dead. Charleston's credit is so low that a plan to give away city bonds to the lot owners in exchange for a mortgage on their lots fell through. . . .

In the evening visited with Governor Aiken, who has suffered a lot during the war, just as all Lowndeses, Hugers, and others. All planters, whose wealth consisted almost uniquely in slaves, are ruined. They have given everything, and because of the emancipation they have lost the last they had. Only their land is left, but with the labor problem and the scarcity of capital, that land cannot be made profitable. Some have borrowed northern capital at outrageous rates of interest, and generally they have not been able to pay off their debt, partly because of the unfavorable season for almost all crops, and also because of the insufficient number of hands available and consequent lack of care. Of course, Governor Aiken claims that the Negroes are lazy and will never be willing to work. He estimates the cotton crop at 1,000,000 bales, while in New York the same crop is estimated at 2,300,000, but mostly from Texas. He asserts that the Mexican War and the annexation of Texas were not provoked by the South. He did concede that the position of the South in the slavery question in Missouri, Kansas, and Nebraska had been an attempt to maintain the majority. In his opinion this was foolish, as slave labor was not suitable for Kansas or Nebraska. If they had kept quietly within the framework of the old slave laws and not sought any extension of the system, the question would never have come to a head. The slaveholders possibly would have emancipated their slaves of their own free will, partly because that kind of labor would become unprofitable in the long run, as had already happened in Virginia and Tennessee. But when he pointed out that under the old regime a crop of 10 million bales would have been possible, his solution of the problem became very doubtful in my opinion. He takes a gloomy view of the future and hopes that the importation of coolies will solve the labor problem. He maintains that 2,000,000 Negroes have run away, and the available labor decreased with that number.

Aiken, just as Mr. Wilkinson—whom I visited later and where Mrs. Wilkinson and Lou and Ella made me a hearty welcome as an old friend—expect that the Negro will fall back into barbarism instead of improve. Everyone is depressed and concedes that all are ruined completely, and that the wealth of the country in horses and mules has decreased. Reconstruction will take a long time, especially as long as northern capital will remain wary because of the political instability.

Naturally all are angry at Congress, and the general expectation is that the Radical party will carry everything before it. They see themselves reduced to the status of territories, which wouldn't even make much of a difference, as the state legislatures cannot do anything without the consent of the military commanders, who don't even hesitate to reverse arrests of the courts. Small wonder that deep despondency and indifference are widespread. Many are really devastated.

The usual Southern gaiety has not greatly suffered, however, which I witnessed at a party at two Misses Mackay's, where Lou and Ella Wilkinson took me. Dress was very simple, most so with the gentlemen who came in their sports coats, but the dancing wasn't less enthusiastic. I liked the girls, but they could not hide their hatred of the Yankees, that goes so far that they refuse to greet an U.S. officer, whom they had known before, on the street. . . .

In the evening visited with Mrs. Hayne, where Mr. Buvard Hayne, her son, whom I had met at the Cotonnets, had invited me. Mr. Hayne's brother was the well known 'nullificator' of 1832. Eldest daughter was the lovely Mrs. Barnwell, Miss Hayne, Mr. Theodore Hayne. The most typical Southern family I have met until now. The mother is a most pleasant woman, with all the special characteristics. All were extremely well-bred, with a measure of French polish and lightheartedness, but without any real warmth and depth. For one evening most pleasant and charming, but in the long run by far not what those damned Yankees are.

Here I witnessed the real Yankee hatred to perfection.

They are made out—but always half laughing—as the original, perfect villains. Most lamented seems to be the loss of all personal comforts: no servants, no carriages, no money is the continuing refrain, and this seems to weigh heavier than anything else. Real serious, deeply felt anger I haven't seen anywhere. Although half laughingly, I here heard the theory of the 'divine institution' too, and I believe it was more seriously meant than it seemed at first sight. They did acknowledge the existence of a law against the education of Negroes, but keep telling me that it was a dead letter. They did concede that Negroes were maltreated sometimes, and admired their behavior at present. . . .

### Saturday 15 December 1866

Bad weather, cold and rainy. A couple of visits; cotton gin and rice mill. In the afternoon a visit with Mrs. Wilkinson and Mrs. Gibbes. Mrs. Gibbes is an archetypical Southern woman, a bit like Mary St. Clair. 'Lolling in her rocking chair,' she talked incessantly in an indifferent and nonchalant tone. Her stories all boil down to the same topic, but are not very consistent in regard of the Negroes. She said that if only the Yankees and the Freedmen's Bureau would be gone, everything would adjust itself, the Negroes would fall back into their old habits and go to work as usual, and everything would be fine again. Everybody keeps telling himself that only if one would leave us to ourselves, we would manage quite well. But will the North do that in view of the still prevailing atmosphere?

I have no doubts that the treatment of the Negroes has generally been good. Mrs. Wilkinson confirmed to me that whoever maltreated his slaves was ostracized from society, and others pointed out the interest masters had in good treatment of their slaves. Slaves cost between \$1,200 and 1,500 for a field hand, \$1,500–2,000 for a house servant, sometimes as high as \$2,500. Undoubtedly of course, there were exceptions, especially in the backwoods and among the smaller slaveholders.

Fiercest against the Yankees are the ladies. Lou Wilkinson said to me this very evening, "I wish I could have a rope around all their necks and hang them all," and when her mother objected—on my behalf—she said "Oh, but I wouldn't like to see all the corpses dangling in the air, but I do wish they were all hanged." Later, when she talked about the possibility of being a Yankee herself, "Oh, I would put a rope round my own neck and hang myself first, and I would take it nobly, not like those mean Yankees." The hatred against the flag is general: "that ugly gridiron flag," said Mrs. Hayne. The men are indifferent and only think of recovering their material prosperity. In general this is a frivolous people, without any depth and seriousness, and it is mostly this that they cannot bear to see in the Yankees.

More and more people confirm that the reason behind the war has been the idea that the North intended to abolish slavery and by doing so infringe on their rights. After the election of Lincoln, an abolitionist in their opinion, the question came to a head, and the South felt constrained to dust off their favorite doctrine of 'states' rights.' They were convinced that they had the right to leave the Union, and the responsibility to take this step rests squarely with their leaders, and especially with those under oath to maintain the Union. In my opinion they saw the near future as too dark. In itself the breaking up of such a Union, when a part of the people is clearly unhappy with it, does not seem to be such a crime, at least as far as I can see. One cannot bind people for eternity, and whenever one has really valid reasons, most insurrections are justifiable. On the other hand, it is undeniable that the other party had the right to maintain the existing government and Union. Both parties fought for opposite principles, both defensible in their own right.

One of the standing claims is that the people of the South are so much more 'gentlemanlike, generous, magnanimous' and what not than those 'mean, sneaking, hypocritical Yankees.' Mrs. Wilkinson once answered an officer, who had said to her—most impolitely—"We'll soon put down all that aristocracy and make tinkers and tailors of you all," "Then Sir, Southern gentlemen will make a profession of those trades." And when another said, "Well, the Union flag is waving over you again," she retorted, "Yes, the stars are there and those that love them may take the stripes with them (on their back)." Boasting of the good society, of the fine carriages, the many servants, the style they had, is the order of the day, and the chief complaint is that the Yankees have taken all that away.

In regard of the sale of domestic slaves, Mrs. Wilkinson told me that most of them were quite indifferent about this as they ended up with good masters anyhow. Only those who had served a lifetime in the same family and had absorbed the family pride would have found it very hard. A Negro coachman, who drove me yesterday, claimed that the Negroes did appreciate their new freedom, and although he too maintained that most had been well treated, he said that some of them still bore the scars of beatings thick as hail on their backs.

# HENRY LATHAM, *BLACK AND WHITE: A JOURNAL OF A THREE MONTHS' TOUR IN THE UNITED STATES*

## *(1867)*

The conservative British barrister Henry Latham (1828?–1871) also traveled to the U.S. during Reconstruction, observing people and places from New York to New Orleans, with stops in Richmond, Petersburg, Norfolk, Charleston, Augusta, Atlanta, and Mobile. A detailed and insightful narrator, Latham toured the Southern states at the very moment that the Radical Republicans were about to assume control of Reconstruction. In addition to printing the journals of his American tour, Latham appended a separate chapter on "The Negro." It was his opinion that before the Civil War, slavery proved more harmful to relations between white Southerners and Northerners than to blacks. He doubted whether blacks and whites could live together harmoniously, explaining: "It is difficult to find in history an instance of two distinct races with equal rights living peaceably together as one nation."

## THE NEGRO.

At the time the war broke out, it is estimated that there were, roughly speaking, 4,000,000 slaves in the Southern States. Their former masters state, and I believe with truth, that the slaves as a rule were neither over-worked nor treated with cruelty. It is absurd to suppose the contrary. That which is valuable and cannot be easily replaced is always taken care of. It is where there are no restrictions upon the importation, and the supply is abundant, as in the Chinese coolie trade, that you find the temptation to cruelty not over-ridden by self-interest. It is difficult also, I believe, to gainsay the position, that nowhere where the negro is left to himself in Africa has he reached any higher stage of civilization than he possessed as a Southern slave. His hours of labour were shorter and his diet more plentiful, than those of the English agricultural labourer. He had such clothing and shelter as the climate required. The slaves of the planter were in the same position as the cattle of the English farmer; and the interest that the farmer has in seeing his beasts well cared for operated in favour of the negro slave as strongly as it does in favour of all other chattels. It was the interest of the planter that, as long as his slaves were fit for work, they should be kept in working order; that as children they should be so reared as to make them strong and healthy; and when they were past work, that kindly feeling which a man always has towards everything which he calls his own, was sufficiently strong to ensure them a sustenance in old age. No doubt there were sometimes wicked cases of wanton cruelty, which were not common, and were exceptional as the cases are in this country which are brought into court by the Society for the Prevention of Cruelty to Animals. I am willing to accept the Southerners' statement that as regards health, happiness, education, and morality, the negro-slaves were as well off as any other 4,000,000 of their race. That the slaves were not greatly discontented with their lot seems clear from the fact that the traveller can with difficulty find in the South an able-bodied white man who did not bear arms in the Confederate army. When the masters went to the war, they in fact left their wives, their children, and their goods in the keeping of their slaves. The plantations were left in charge of the old men, the women and children; yet, during the war, the crops were sown and harvested as when the masters were at home; and there were no outrages or insurrections on the plantations, except when the Northern armies passed by.

The position taken by the ablest apologists for the slave-owner would affirm that the treatment of the slaves was nearly as good as the fact of their slavery admitted; that the institution was not created by the present generation, but by their forefathers. 'They had not originated, but inherited it, and had to make the best of it. It was in no way peculiar to the Southern States of America; it had existed over the whole world. It was a condition of society recognised by the Old Testament as the natural state of things, and when mentioned in the New Testament, not reprobated. It had been abolished by some nations, it was still retained by others. It was retained by the Southern States, because they had no other labour to substitute for it, and if the negro was emancipated it would not be possible to rely upon his labour. The civilization of the white race is the result of more than a thousand years of trial and training. The negro race was in the first stage of this probation; they had not yet completed their first century of slavery. Those among them who possessed industry and steadiness of character could earn enough to purchase their emancipation. None of them were fitted to receive the franchise.'

It is hardly worthwhile to consider how far it is true that slavery is a probation for the first steps in civilization, an education for future self-government. It may, I think, be taken as a fact that, before the war, such speculations as to the future of the negro race did not occupy the minds of Southern planters more than the British stockbreeder is at present influenced by Dr. Darwin's theories.

Nor is it worth while to consider how far it was probable, if the North had never interfered with the strong hand, that a gradual emancipation would have taken place in time. The only existing safety-valve through which the slave could escape into freedom was by purchase, and on that safety-valve was this weight—the more industrious the man the more valuable the slave. The living surrounded by slave-labour had so affected the Southern character that it was not easy for them to appreciate the benefits which a gradual emancipation would have brought about. They laughed at the doctrine of the dignity of labour. Hard hands and the sweat of the brow were the portion of the slave, servile. With the lower class of white men who owned no slaves, emancipation was disliked because it would raise the servile race to an equality with themselves. The slave-owners saw clearly that, however gradually brought about, emancipation would result in loss to them; for free labour, however competitive, can never be as profitable to the master as slave-labour has been—capital would have to give up a larger share of profits to the workman. The hearts of the white race were hardened, and it may be doubted whether they would ever have seen that the time had come when the bondmen ought to be let go. They saw only that the slaves were not discontented with their lot, and that all things were prosperous.

The institution of slavery broke down in the Southern States of America, not by reason of any injustice to the negroes, but in consequence of the effect produced by slavery upon the character and temper of the white race. It rendered them incapable of maintaining a friendly intercourse with the Northern States.

The Northern half of the same nation were leading under a colder sky an entirely antagonistic life. They were successful in commerce, they toiled in factories, and reaped with their own hands great harvests of wheat. They were continually increased in numbers by emigrants whose chief fortune was the labour of their hands; while many of the families in the South traced their descent to emigrants who had landed with their retainers from vessels fitted out at their own cost. Except the great bond of the Federal Government, which was tied when neither were strong enough to stand alone, the Northern and Southern States had few ideas in common. When they met in council they disagreed upon the most indifferent matters. They did not so much quarrel about slavery, as because slavery had rendered them at heart hateful to one another. . . .

If the negro dies out, there is an end of him and all the troubles he has caused, at least as far as America is concerned. If he survives, what is to be his future? At the present time there can be no doubt that the black race is inferior to the white. That it is inferior in mental vigour is proved by the fact of its former contented servitude; that it is inferior in bodily stamina is proved by the statistics of mortality in the Northern armies, according to which under the same conditions, the number of deaths in hospital among the black troops was double the mortality among the white men.

Will he become blended with the white race, and be gradually absorbed by intermarriage, as the German and the Irish element do, losing their nationality in the next generation, and becoming fused into one homogeneous mass? There does not appear to be any probability of it. No white man ever marries a black woman, and the instances of a white woman marrying a black man are rare and exceptional. There has been at present no intercourse between the races except such as takes place between an inferior and a superior race. The mixed race is the result of the intercourse between the white man and the negress, and this will not effect the absorption of the whole black race.

Suppose the half-breeds to increase largely in numbers, will they form a link between the black man and the white, and promote friendship between the two? In Mexico the greatest of the many causes of anarchy has been the existence of the large class of half-bloods, now more numerous than the Indians. They are so numerous as to possess practically a casting vote, and having neither principle nor stability, side first with the Spaniard and then with the Indian, according as their interest suggests.

Will the negroes gather themselves together in communities, and occupy the low hot fertile rice lands in the South, where the white men cannot live; and so play a useful part, utilizing valuable lands which without them must henceforth lie waste? It is to be hoped that the Government will take measures to prevent it. The moment the pressure of the white race is removed from them they would relapse into savage life. To attain to better things and a higher cultivation, they must be mingled with the whites, and have industry and education forced on them. The more they are separated, the more debased and antagonistic will they become. The most serious symptoms of negro outbreaks which have occurred have been in the Sea Islands where the negroes have collected together in consequence of a proclamation of General Sherman's. A black prophet and a religious revival might lead to any amount of bloodshed. The natural home of the negro in Africa is supposed to be on the alluvial plains near the great rivers; but it is a curious fact that in similar places in the Southern States they did not multiply. They were most prolific in Virginia. It was where the white man lived and cared for them and their offspring that the greatest number of slaves were reared. If they continue to exist in America, the negro must live as a distinct race among a people superior to himself. It is difficult to find in history an instance of two distinct races with equal rights living peaceably together as one nation.

The Americans have done already things which other nations have found impossible. It may be that they will succeed in this also; and there is no race so pliant, so docile, and free from offence, as the negro. The danger will be from the unscrupulousness of politicians. When once the negro vote in the South has become organized, like the Irish vote in the North, it will be as great a nuisance to the nation. If the freedmen, as they increase in intelligence, become factious and impracticable, they will find themselves moving towards Liberia faster than the Mormons went to Utah. That which cannot be assimilated must be cast out.

Their wisest advisers will be those who urge them to keep quiet and avail themselves of the means of education now open to them: not to separate from their white neighbours, but to make themselves first useful to them, and then indispensable: not to think too much of Freedmen's Conventions at Washington, or negro candidates for the Vice-Presidency; but to be as little conspicuous in politics as possible, and to bear in mind that if education does not precede an extension of the suffrage, it must follow it.

There are at the present moment two gentlemen of colour sitting as members of the State Legislature in the State of Massachusetts, and the story of their election is very curious as the largest wholesale practical joke since the English traveller wrote to the 'Times' to describe the series of murders perpetrated in an American railway train. The republican party, to gratify those among their supporters who were suffering from what is commonly called 'Nigger on the brain,' nominated two coloured candidates, not in the least intending them to get in, but merely with a view to make political capital out of their nomination. The democrats, their opponents, saw the mistake in a moment, the wires were pulled and the word passed, and the democrats plumped for the coloured gentlemen, who were elected by triumphant majorities, to the dismay and discomfiture of their proposers.

A practical joke once in a way is all very well; but it is to be hoped that the white race in the South will before long accept the situation, and resume their political duties: for it would be a poor joke for them if possibilities were to be realized, and Congress were found after the next election to consist one half of Northern republicans and the other half of Southern negroes.

# "AN ACT TO PROVIDE FOR MORE EFFICIENT GOVERNMENT OF THE REBEL STATES"

## *(March 2, 1867)*

After the Southern states organized under Johnson's Reconstruction program failed to ratify the Fourteenth Amendment (passed by Congress June 13, 1866), Congress put in place the first of four Reconstruction Acts, asserting control over the Southern states and instituting what historians term Congressional or Radical Reconstruction. Congress, having refused to seat the Southern states' Senators and Representatives, declared that the governments organized by Johnson were still provisional. The first Reconstruction Act, passed over the president's veto, placed the ten still unreconstructed states (Tennessee had been readmitted to the Union in July 1866) under military rule. The act required that each state conduct elections based on universal manhood suffrage (excluding those disfranchised for various reasons, including disloyalty, crimes, or by the Fourteenth Amendment) for constitutional conventions that would then frame basic laws, including universal suffrage, for each state. Upon adopting the new constitutions and ratifying the Fourteenth Amendment, the states could be readmitted to the Union. Passage of this act essentially took control of the Reconstruction process away from the president and ushered in a more radical second phase of Reconstruction.

Whereas no legal State governments or adequate protection for life or property now exists in the rebel States of Virginia, North Carolina, South Carolina, Georgia, Mississippi, Alabama, Louisiana, Florida, Texas, and Arkansas;

and whereas it is necessary that peace and good order should be enforced in said States until loyal and republican State governments can be legally established: Therefore,

*Be it enacted by the Senate and House of Representatives of the United States of America in Congress assembled,* That said rebel States shall be divided into military districts and made subject to the military authority of the United States as hereinafter prescribed, and for that purpose Virginia shall constitute the first district; North Carolina and South Carolina the second district; Georgia, Alabama, and Florida the third district; Mississippi and Arkansas the fourth district; and Louisiana and Texas the fifth district.

Sec. 2. *And be it further enacted,* That it shall be the duty of the President to assign to the command of each of said districts an officer of the army, not below the rank of brigadier-general, and to detail a sufficient military force to enable such officer to perform his duties and enforce his authority within the district to which he is assigned.

Sec. 3. *And be it further enacted,* That it shall be the duty of each officer assigned as aforesaid, to protect all persons in their rights of person and property, to suppress insurrection, disorder, and violence, and to punish, or cause to be punished, all disturbers of the public peace and criminals; and to this end he may allow local civil tribunals to take jurisdiction of and to try offenders, or, when in his judgment it may be necessary for the trial of offenders, he shall have power to organize military commissions or tribunals for that purpose, and all interference under color of State authority with the exercise of military authority under this act, shall be null and void.

Sec. 4. *And be it further enacted,* That all persons put under military arrest by virtue of this act shall be tried without unnecessary delay, and no cruel or unusual punishment shall be inflicted, and no sentence of any military commission or tribunal hereby authorized, affecting the life or liberty of any person, shall be executed until it is approved by the officer in command of the district, and the laws and regulations for the government of the army shall not be affected by this act, except in so far as they conflict with its provisions: *Provided,* That no sentence of death under the provisions of this act shall be carried into effect without the approval of the President.

Sec. 5. *And be it further enacted,* That when the people

of any one of said rebel States shall have formed a constitution of government in conformity with the Constitution of the United States in all respects, framed by a convention of delegates elected by the male citizens of said State, twenty-one years old and upward, of whatever race, color, or previous condition, who have been resident in said State for one year previous to the day of such election, except such as may be disfranchised for participation in the rebellion or for felony at common law, and when such constitution shall provide that the elective franchise shall be enjoyed by all such persons as have the qualifications herein stated for electors of delegates, and when such constitution shall be ratified by a majority of the persons voting on the question of ratification who are qualified as electors for delegates, and when such constitution shall have been submitted to Congress for examination and approval, and Congress shall have approved the same, and when said State, by a vote of its legislature elected under said constitution, shall have adopted the amendment to the Constitution of the United States, proposed by the Thirty-ninth Congress, and known as article fourteen, and when said article shall have become a part of the Constitution of the United States, said State shall be declared entitled to representation in Congress, and senators and representatives shall be admitted therefrom on their taking the oath prescribed by law, and then and thereafter the preceding sections of this act shall be inoperative in said State: *Provided,* That no person excluded from the privilege of holding office by said proposed amendment to the Constitution of the United States, shall be eligible to election as a member of the convention to frame a constitution for any of said rebel States, nor shall any such person vote for members of such convention.

SEC. 6. *And be it further enacted,* That, until the people of said rebel States shall be by law admitted to representation in the Congress of the United States, any civil governments which may exist therein shall be deemed provisional only, and in all respects subject to the paramount authority of the United States at any time to abolish, modify, control, or supersede the same; and in all elections to any office under such provisional governments all persons shall be entitled to vote, and none others, who are entitled to vote, under the provisions of the fifth section of this act; and no person shall be eligible to any office under any such provisional governments who would be disqualified from holding office under the provisions of the third *article* of said constitutional amendment.

SCHUYLER COLFAX,
*Speaker of the House of Representatives.*
LA FAYETTE S. FOSTER,
*President of the Senate, pro tempore.*

———

IN THE HOUSE OF REPRESENTATIVES,
March 2, 1867.

The President of the United States having returned to the House of Representatives, in which it originated, the bill entitled "An act to provide for the more efficient government of the rebel States," with his objections thereto, the House of Representatives proceeded, in pursuance of the Constitution, to reconsider the same; and

*Resolved,* That the said bill do pass, two thirds of the House of Representatives agreeing to pass the same.

Attest:                          EDWD. McPHERSON,
                                        *Clerk of H. R. U. S.*

# EDITORIAL IN THE *CHARLOTTESVILLE CHRONICLE* ON RADICAL RECONSTRUCTION

## *(March 6, 1867)*

Responding to the Reconstruction Act, the *Charlottesville Chronicle* encouraged Virginians to comply with Congress' demands as quickly as possible in order to prevent Radical control of their state. Though the newspaper considered the terms of the legislation "cruel and merciless," the editor nonetheless argued that immediately calling a state convention and reentering the Union with black suffrage would prove less odious and degrading than enduring the perceived multiple evils of martial law, black suffrage, the proscription of the state's leading whites, and, possibly, land confiscation. The journalist reasoned that because Virginia had a numerical majority of whites over blacks, once readmitted to the Union whites could regain control of the state and revise their constitution again, this time disfranchising blacks.

There are three courses for the Legislature to take: the first is to fight. The second is to fold arms and do nothing. The third is to call a State convention.

There would be a unanimous voice in favor of the first, if we had any power to make a decent resistance.

The question is between the second and third. The third leads to an acceptance of the cruel and merciless terms imposed upon us. The second leads to the same thing—and to much more.

The question now is, Who shall get the control of the

State under the new dispensation of universal suffrage—
the whites or the blacks?

The provisional government, with universal black and
qualified white suffrage, is already upon us. The court-
house bells in all the counties will soon summon white and
black alike to the polls. In addition to this, while the provisional government lasts, we shall have martial law in
Virginia—the liberty of every man in the hands of federal
officers.

It has been said that we had better have military law
than submit to such degradation as implied in the acceptance of the terms. This is true ten times over.

But military law is not the alternative. It is military law
and negro suffrage and the proscription of our leading
men. These three things come upon us without our lifting a
finger.

This is not all; *there will be a convention* to ratify the
terms proposed. . . . [The Radicals] will have a convention
and they will put the state back in the Union, and they will
give us a State constitution. That constitution will be like
the constitution of Tennessee; it will perpetuate the power
in their hands.

There are 600,000 whites in Virginia. We can control
the State: we can guide, if we cannot arrest, the storm.
And the more rapid our movements the more complete
will be our masterships of the situation. Wait—and wait—
and wait, and the Radicals will organize the negroes
against us.

A state convention can be framed in literal compliance
with the act of Congress, which will take all minor elections
from the people—leaving only the Governor, the members
of the General Assembly, and members of Congress to be
elected by the popular vote. And it may be that a property
and educational qualification can be secured as a condition
of holding office of any kind.

We are, therefore, for a convention—at once. It is not
worth while to resist the deluge; the man who trusts in God
will build the ark that shall float upon the tempestuous waters.

We are very far from despair, black as the prospect is.
The immediate aim of our State should be to get back in

the Union as quickly as possible. There we shall be measurably at least shielded from the Radical storm. If we stay our course much longer, we shall have confiscation added to negro suffrage. There we have at least reached a *resting place;* there we can get control of our State affairs; there we can *make another State constitution.*

# "THE PROSPECT OF RECONSTRUCTION"

## (March 14, 1867)

The editors of *The Nation,* which was founded in 1865 by abolitionists, prided themselves on supporting equality before the law and equal economic opportunity. Following passage of the Reconstruction Act, the magazine's editors underscored the broad benefits to the nation of an immediate and compulsory Reconstruction irrespective of the opinions or wishes of former Confederates. Critical of Southerners for rejecting the Fourteenth Amendment, the editor hoped nevertheless that Southern leaders would grasp "the wisdom of submitting for a time to a limited disability rather than to keep their States out of all participation in the Government." *The Nation* predicted optimistically that the former Confederate states would comply with Congress' demand that Southern whites would not control their former slaves' ballots, and that Reconstruction would be complete within twelve to eighteen months.

The eyes of the country are just now turned more to the South than to Congress. The latter having passed a law providing a definite method by which the Southern States may regain their old footing in the Union, yet having left something to their option, the chief questions of political interest are whether those States will conform to the terms of the offer, and if so, what will be the result of their action.

The so-called legislatures of two States have already acted decisively, and in opposite directions. The Legislature of Virginia (we cannot well avoid the use of phrases that seem to admit a legality which we wholly deny) has passed a bill providing for the election of a convention in May, with liberty to colored men to vote. The Legislature of Louisiana, on the contrary, has passed resolutions declaring the acts of Congress void, and has summoned a convention, to be elected by white men only. Governor Wells has met this action by a proclamation announcing the law of Congress to be in force, and declaring all elections not held conformably thereto to be void. The Legislature of North Carolina has adjourned without taking any action.

In several States there are decided indications of a rising agitation, the sentiments of the white population being divided as to the expediency of reorganizing in accordance with the law, or of remaining inactive. Ex-Gov. Brown leads the movement in favor of reorganization in Georgia, where he is opposed by Col. Gartrell (formerly a member of Congress) and others. The only prominent Mississippian who has recommended such action is Gen. Chalmers, but he will soon be supported by others, although Gov. Humphreys is understood to be opposed to doing anything under the law. In North Carolina, the minority of the Legislature, comprising all who heartily welcomed the restoration of the Union in 1865, have taken steps toward the summoning of a convention in an informal manner. We have not heard of anything definite from the other States.

Upon the whole, we judge that, if the law is faithfully enforced by the President and his subordinates, the whole South will speedily conform to the terms of Congress. The amendment enacted at the instance of Mr. Shellabarger deprives the Southern whites of the option between military government and universal suffrage, which Mr. Sherman's proposition left to them; so that, whether they elect conventions or not, they must admit colored men to vote at all their current elections, while their only chance of escaping from military *surveillance* is by adopting constitutions recognizing the political equality of all men. The disfranchising clause affects only a very limited class, not including a single man under twenty-seven years of age; and it is improbable that the mass of people not excluded by law from political action will long continue to exclude themselves out of mere sympathy for the old race of politicians who are shut out. Even among the disfranchised class there are many sensible enough to comprehend the wisdom of submitting for a time to a limited disability rather than to keep their States out of all participation in the Government. Congress has deprived the stubborn of their favorite argument, that it was better to control the States, without seats in Congress, than to gain a place in Congress by sharing power with the colored race; for they are no longer to be left in supreme control of their States, and they can now see clearly the necessity of being represented in Congress.

It cannot be denied, however, that the soundest reasoning may fail to afford a basis for predicting the action of the Southern people. After the elections last fall it certainly seemed as if none but idiots would, in the situation of the Southern whites, refuse to accept the constitutional amendment as a basis of reconstruction. Yet they did so with comparative unanimity. And we presume that if they had a similar option under the Sherman statute they would reject it, even if they knew that worse terms would be imposed. But the new law gives them only the option between involuntary universal suffrage with military rule, and voluntary universal suffrage without military rule. This is, of course, upon the assumption that Mr. Johnson will execute the law in good faith. If he orders it to be set aside upon the first decision of a petty court against its validity, or if he repeats the let-alone policy adopted at the Alexandria election, the law will effect no good. But we think that he has too much sense of his own danger to make any such rash experiments on the forbearance of Congress.

Measures have been initiated in both Houses of Congress for the purpose of putting the machinery of reorganization in motion, under the direct supervision of the national authorities; and some measure of the kind will doubtless be enacted forthwith. This is clearly the proper method; and the only wonder is that so able a body as the late Committee of Fifteen should have so utterly failed in its duty as not to have reported such a bill at the last session. We rejoice, for the sake of all sections, North and South, that Congress has finally adopted the doctrine which we have steadily advocated, even when its success seemed hopeless, viz., that reconstruction should be *immediate* and *compulsory*, and not left to the choice of the insurrectionary population, either as to time or mode. Nothing could be more opposed to the theory of the Constitution than the let-alone policy which, while denying the validity of the *de facto* governments at the South, provided no means for the creation of legitimate governments. This false position, the result of timidity and distrust of the people, has been all along the weak point of the Radical policy. Its abandonment will give general satisfaction.

Under all the circumstances, there can be no doubt that nearly or quite all of the Southern States will be properly organized and reinstated in the Union within twelve or eighteen months from this time. The only question concerning our subject that really remains for solution in the future is as to the practical working of the new governments, and especially of universal suffrage.

It has been confidently asserted—and we have ourselves shared the apprehension—that the negroes, being confessedly ignorant, poor, and unorganized, would be surely controlled by their old masters when they came to vote. Of course there is much to be said upon that side; and, had universal suffrage been conceded in 1865, we think that such must have been the result in districts not fully garrisoned by national troops. But for nearly two years past urgent efforts have been made to introduce light among the colored people; and Northern men and women have steadily gained influence over them, while their Southern masters have, to a very large extent, thrown away whatever influence they may have had by their oppressive laws and obstinate resistance to the elevation of the colored race. Of this latter fact, the immense emigration of negroes from South Carolina and Georgia, and the loud complaints of planters in Louisiana and Texas, afford conclusive proof. The colored people have, moreover, organized themselves in every large town of the South, if not even more widely, during the last two years; and, with such assistance as their white allies will be prompt to give, they will be fully able to inform their brethren on plantations of the issues and the candidates. We therefore believe that the last hope of the disloyal will fail them, and that the colored voters will generally sustain candidates acceptable to the North.

No one can doubt that the complete restoration of the Southern States, freed from all their old inequalities and oppressions, will materially benefit the whole country. An impartial administration of justice will give new energy to the laborer; for who that has ever worked while in doubt of being paid (whether at mechanical or mental labor) has not felt the impossibility of putting forth all his energy and skill? Labor in the South has been performed for two centuries with a certainty of *not* being paid, and for the last two years in a total uncertainty upon that point. The lash, which formerly supplied a motive for drudging effort, has been latterly withdrawn, or at least has not come as promptly and surely as it was wont. What wonder is it that, with the accustomed terror removed, and no certain hope supplied, the labor system of the South has failed to produce the old results? But this defect will be thoroughly cured by a sound reconstruction, which will assure to all classes their rights. It will also remove from the white people the fear of confiscation and punishment, which now hampers the efforts of some of the most effective men at the South. It will take away the last element of uncertainty from our political future, and leave us free to enter upon plans of business without fear of political disturbances. On every ground, moral, political, and financial, we welcome the near approach of a perfect reunion of the States.

# "IMPEACHMENT FROM A LEGAL POINT OF VIEW"

## *(March 14, 1867)*

Prior to 1867, some Radical Republicans, convinced that the president's constant obstructionism would prohibit reconstructing the nation, sought to impeach Johnson. Most congressmen, however, favored other means of controlling him, requiring Johnson to send military orders through General Ulysses S. Grant, the general-in-chief, and passing on March 2, 1867 (over Johnson's veto), the Tenure of Office Act, a bill that restricted the executive's patronage power. Later that month, *The Nation* summarized research on the history of impeachment by Columbia College law professor Theodore William Dwight (1822–1892). The magazine's editor wrote that understanding the legal precedents of impeachment mattered to anyone who "dreads as we dread the conversion of a legal process into a weapon of party warfare." Nine months later, the House of Representatives failed in its first attempt to impeach Johnson.

Professor Dwight, of Columbia College, has recently made a very thorough examination of the nature of impeachment, of the crimes for which this mode of prosecution may be resorted to, and of the method of procedure, and the conclusions he has reached have been published in *The American Law Register*, and subsequently in a pamphlet which now lies before us. As he is the first lawyer of any prominence, so far as we know, who has undertaken to discuss impeachment as a legal question simply, and as he is removed both by position and habits from the arena of party strife, what he says on this subject is worthy the attention of everybody to whom the forms of law, as they are to us, are of deep and paramount importance, and who dreads as we dread the conversion of a legal process into a weapon of party warfare.

Mr. Dwight has made a very full and minute examination of the precedents from which the founders of this Government derived all their notions of what impeachment was, and from which, in fact, the word impeachment derives all its meaning, and he finds that impeachment and indictment are but two different modes of attaining the same end, but both are legal processes and governed in their course by legal principles. A man can only be impeached in England in cases in which he might be indicted. He is impeached on the presentment of the House of Commons; he is indicted on the presentment of a grand jury. But neither impeachment nor indictment means anything more than that there is sufficient reason to believe the defendant guilty of the offences laid to his charge to warrant his being put on his trial before the proper court, and pending the trial he is to be subjected to no greater inconvenience or restraint or deprivation than may be deemed necessary to secure his attendance from day to day. Says Mr. Dwight:

"It may be asked why, then, is the cumbrous process of impeachment ever resorted to? The answer is, that there were often found in England persons who could not readily be tried by the common law courts, either owing to an influence which overshadowed the ordinary tribunals, or because technical rules of practice made the usual remedies scarcely worth pursuing. Moreover, impeachment was often adopted as an instrument of faction, and was especially active when society was disturbed by party contests or was in the throes of a revolution. In fact, through this process, Parliament ultimately triumphed over the executive, and Parliamentary government, with ministers responsible to the Commons for executive acts, was formed.

"When the United States Constitution was framed, trial by impeachment was fully developed. It was not, however, adopted in that instrument as a regular mode of criminal procedure, to be employed in lieu of an indictment. It was made a means of trial of a crime so far as it had a political bearing. It is used as a means of depriving officers of their offices and of disqualifying them from holding such positions in the future. Still, it is requisite that a *crime* should be committed as a basis for the accusation. The Constitution provides, in substance, that the offence, so far as it has a purely criminal aspect, shall be tried in the ordinary courts;

while so far as it affects the official character, it shall be the subject of impeachment. Though the English theory and procedure still substantially continue, impeachment in our law has a comparatively narrow scope. The House of Representatives, in analogy to the English House of Commons, has the exclusive power of impeachment, and the judicial power is vested in the Senate, in analogy to its deposit in the House of Lords."

# "Congress and the Constitution"

## (March 28, 1867)

Following passage of the Reconstruction Act, *The Nation* raised fundamental questions about which side in the Reconstruction debate, Congressional Radicals or President Johnson, properly interpreted the U.S. Constitution. Johnson, the editor explained, assumed that civil government essentially had been restored in the former Confederate states, and thus opposed Congress authorizing martial law in the South and regulating voting rights. Advocating that the nation's leaders adhere strictly to the Constitution but not construct it in a strict manner, *The Nation* sided with the Radicals.

. . . Some journals—the New York *Times* for one—which, during the war, unhesitatingly justified the suspension of the *habeas corpus* without the authority of Congress, the establishment of military commissions in loyal States, and various other measures the unconstitutionality of which is no longer in doubt, if it ever was—are now amazed and afflicted at what they assume to be the unquestioned disregard of Congress for the Constitution. In this lamentation they are of course joined by that larger number of journals which denounced the unconstitutional acts of Mr. Lincoln, but applauded to the skies the more unconstitutional (because less necessary) acts of Mr. Johnson. . . .

The next objection is to the suspension of the *habeas corpus* by act of Congress, a measure for which we have no special affection, but as to which we must here consider only the question of legitimate *power*, and not the question of expediency. It is said that the rebellion is over, and therefore that the power to suspend this writ has expired. It is true that all organized war is over; but is it to be imagined that the suspension of the writ must cease upon the instant that the last rebel army lays down its arms? Do all the rights of war cease at that moment? If so, no prisoner of war could have been lawfully detained after that time, and all the precautions and machinery incident to a state of war must then have been instantly abandoned. We all know that there is no such rule. Mr. Johnson certainly never acted upon it. No government or military commander ever did. The state of war lasts until society is restored to its natural and normal condition. If the war is between distinct nations, it lasts until a treaty is signed, even though months elapse, during which the vanquished nation has not a man under arms. If the war is a civil one, it lasts until civil government is fully restored by legitimate authority. This has not been done in the Southern States. Mr. Johnson thinks it has, and utterly ignores all contrary opinions. His veto messages have been carefully framed not to controvert the arguments by which Congress justified its action, but to give the impression to the world at large that no such arguments were thought of by any one. There is something ingenious, but not ingenuous, in this mode of carrying on a public controversy; and the fact that ten men read the veto messages to one who reads the speeches or other arguments in confutation of them, gave Mr. Johnson an immense advantage. Such tricks of argument are common among unscrupulous lawyers, and it is by some such persons, we surmise, that the Presidential messages have been written.

Of the same class is the objection to the recent law regulating the elective franchise in the rebel States. Mr. Johnson suggests, with an air of mild surprise, that it has never before been deemed within the power of Congress to regulate that subject within any of the States. The fact that these States had become so utterly disorganized as to make the interference of the national Government necessary, in pursuance of an express provision of the Constitution, and the further fact that he had himself acted upon this theory, regulating the right of suffrage in these same States according to his own will, he entirely keeps out of sight.

This poor example of an unworthy Executive is religiously followed by all his supporters and apologists. They gladly quote every hasty expression of impatience with constitutional restraint which they can find in the speeches of Congressmen opposed to the President's doctrine; but they never allow their readers to suspect that the Congressional policy is believed by any one to be warranted by the Constitution. The establishment of martial law in the rebel States is probably the most doubtful of any of the measures of Congress; yet its validity, assuming the continuance of the war, has been expressly affirmed by four judges of the Supreme Court, one of them being a Georgia Democrat. Nor did the opinion of the majority of the court in the Milligan case at all affect this question, unless by inference it conceded the power to Congress. Mr. Johnson certainly claimed this power for himself, maintaining and administering martial law until civil government in *his* opinion was regularly organized. Congress simply proposes to do the same thing until in *its* opinion civil government is regularly organized. Its power to do so is far more clear than was Mr. Johnson's, while its jurisdiction to determine the validity of the governments set up at the South is indisputable.

In conclusion, we expect always to advocate a strict adherence to the Constitution, but not a strict construction of it. Such a construction has been vehemently advocated, but never maintained. Jefferson, who was its ablest advocate among our earliest statesmen, was compelled to violate it; and Calhoun himself would have done so had he been President in a time of emergency. No human wisdom could frame a detailed plan of government that would not at some period suffocate the nation if strictly construed. We do not believe that the framers of the Constitution ever contemplated the possibility of such a war as we have just witnessed, and we therefore do not believe that all its restrictions were designed to be severely applied to such a case. A very wide scope must be allowed to legislative action under such difficulties, and a liberal interpretation should be given to the general words of the Constitution. But we do not imagine that Congress is absolved by these difficulties from obedience to the fundamental law, nor have we seen any evidence that Congress supposes itself to be so. It has preferred some other dictionary to Johnson's, and this is the origin of all the trouble.

# "THE PROSPECT AT THE SOUTH"

## (March 28, 1867)

As the former Confederate states mobilized to meet the requirements of the Reconstruction Act (and the three supplementary measures that followed it), for the first time in their history, white Southerners found themselves engaging with black voters and soliciting blacks' votes. *The Nation* raised the question of which entitlement—education for the freedpeople or their enfranchisement—mattered most. The editor concluded that suffrage was the foundation upon which all other liberties would build.

The addresses of Messrs. Wade Hampton, Arthur, Talley, and others to the colored men the other day in Charleston, S. C., prove pretty clearly that those were right who maintained that negro suffrage, if it did nothing else, would at least secure decent treatment for the negroes from their white neighbors. If we had not witnessed so many wonderful things during the last six years, we should find it exceedingly difficult to believe that the white orators who spoke on this occasion were really men of the same breed as those who supplied South Carolina with its law, morals, theology, and political philosophy before the war. If there was anything fixed in Southern notions of the arrangement of the universe, it was that the negro was utterly incapable of taking care of himself, that he would only work under the lash, that education would simply develop his powers of mischief, and that civilization could only be preserved in communities in which negroes abounded by the rigid domination of the whites. When, therefore, one hears Mr. Wade Hampton informing a crowd of colored men that they are fellow-citizens, and that the prosperity of the State will depend on their cordial co-operation with the whites in industry and politics; and Mr. Arthur informing them "that education would go far to make them mentally and morally the equals of the whites;" and Mr. Talley inviting them "to work shoulder to shoulder with the whites" for the regeneration of the South, and to trust to their "old friends," their white neighbors, rather than to Northerners, those who refused to believe that the franchise could do the negro any good may well rub their eyes. Luckily, too, the character of this meeting has been such as to make all arguments based on what occurred at it *à fortiori* arguments. It took place in the chief city of the State in which most of the extreme Southern theories of politics and religion were hatched and preached; in which the negroes bear the largest proportion to the white population, and in which, therefore, their admission to political equality may be expected, on the old Southern theory of their character and capacity, to work the greatest mischief; and, though last not least, the white speakers were drawn from the class which has always been foremost in its hostility not only to negro emancipation but to free society, or to any form of society in which the laborer is not owned. When Wade Hampton comes out and avows his submission to the new order of things and his hopefulness about it, the weaker brethren of his political church may well take courage and be of good cheer.

We have always feared that if the work of educating the Southern negroes were allowed to flag when the franchise was bestowed on them, if they were not, as fast as possible, brought into contact with Northern opinion by the diffusion amongst them of the arts of reading and writing, they might so use their political power as to do serious injury both to themselves and the country. That this is no chimera we know from what we see happening amongst the Irish wherever they are congregated in large masses, as they are now in some of our large cities and in the coal districts of Pennsylvania. And we have feared that if the provision of means of popular education were left optional with the States, the whites might be so opposed to it and the negroes so indifferent about it that schools might never be established in sufficient numbers to cope with the dense and almost heathen ignorance with which the South is overshadowed. We feared, too, that if the provision of security for life and property at the South were left, as a

great many good people a year ago wanted it to be left, to
"the laws of political economy," Northern philanthropy
would, once the troops were withdrawn, be allowed but
scant opportunities for its work. And we confess we have
not got over these fears. It is true there is manifested
amongst the negroes a very remarkable and, we believe, an
increasing thirst for knowledge, and that the best class of
whites do see clearly the extent to which Southern prosperity must depend on the intelligence of its inhabitants of all
races. But, on the other hand, we have not yet seen the normal working of the new state of things. The whites are bus-
ily engaged at present in getting rid of the Yankees. They
have tried one way and failed; they are now trying another,
and how they will behave when the Yankees are gone we
believe nobody knows. We say, therefore, that there is no
certainty as to the course Southerners will take in the matter of education once the hand of the North has been taken
off them, and the data we have for the formation of a judgment as to the extent to which the negroes will be able or
ready to provide it for themselves are still too slight to warrant anybody in speaking confidently about it.

But one thing is clear, that the ballot will provide for
the negro, what we have always predicted it would provide,
the first essential of civilization, and that is security from
violence. This comes before education and before everything else; without it civilization is not possible, and the
Federal Government could not have effectually provided
it. But with the ballot every negro has the means of pun-
ishing any officer of the Government for inattention to
any claim for lawful redress. Every politician now knows
that to succeed at the South he must address colored people in a civil and respectful manner, and the habit once
formed amongst politicians, it will rapidly diffuse itself
amongst all other classes. Whenever we have to co-operate
with men in any field, we must be polite to them, must at
least pretend to respect them; and, exaggerated as the assertion may seem, there is nothing which raises a degraded
race more rapidly than respectful treatment at the hands
of those whom they have been accustomed to look up to.
No men or women of ordinary mould can long respect
themselves if nobody else seems to respect them, and although self-respect is not the first of the virtues, it lies at

the root of nearly all the others. In reforming people who have for any cause fallen very low, half the work is done when we have given them a proper sense of their own dignity and value. This, too, we fully believe the suffrage will give the freedmen, and from this we confidently expect all other things to flow.

# "LAND FOR THE LANDLESS"

## *(May 16, 1867)*

No subject during the debates over Reconstruction elicited more vitriol, north and south, than the confiscation of Southern farms and plantations and the redistribution of property to the freedpeople. Whereas some Radicals, most notably Senator Charles Sumner and Representative Thaddeus Stevens, spoke freely and loosely of redistributing "forty acres" of land to the freedmen, the editor of *The Nation* forcefully opposed this proposal. The magazine noted that not only was land redistribution impractical, but that it would discourage white Southerners from forming new governments, distract the freedmen from imbibing free labor ideals, and, most grievously, corrupt local politics.

Mr. Sumner gave expression in the Senate, two months ago or more, to the opinion that the grant of "a piece of land" to each colored head of a family "was necessary to conclude the glorious work of emancipation." In answer to enquiries as to where "the piece of land" was to come from, he said it might come from land sold for taxes, and might *have* come out of the property of applicants for pardon as a condition of the pardon. The exact size of "the piece of land" was not settled by Mr. Sumner. This important detail, as well as we can make out, was left to Mr. Phillips, who has decided that the superficial area of the farm which each negro head of a family ought to have, in order to complete the work of emancipation, is forty acres. Mr. Phillips, as might be expected, is not troubled with Mr. Sumner's doubts about where the land ought to be got. He has determined offhand, and with a confidence which makes the difficulty that has been found in governing the world perfectly incomprehensible, that the required number of forty-acre farms ought to be secured by wholesale confiscation of rebel property. But even Mr. Phillips does not seem to have given the subject all the attention it merits; for there was not a word said about it at the last meeting of the Anti-Slavery Association until, towards the close, Colonel Higginson delivered himself of his views upon it, which seems to have wakened Mr. Phillips up to a sense of his neglect, for he drew a confiscation resolution on the spot, and it was passed, of course, without a moment's delay. Whether Mr. Sumner originated the idea or not, it is certain that it has made considerable progress, and, as might be expected, finds great favor amongst the Southern Radicals, and is now a topic at loyalist meetings. At the Hunnicutt convention, a few weeks ago, it was received with enthusiasm; and if the great body of the freedmen throughout the South are not greatly taken by it when it is urged upon their attention, it will show that they surpass in wisdom and self-restraint and honesty any landless class that has ever yet appeared in history. The Southern whites already begin to be considerably alarmed by it, especially in the States in which the blacks are in the majority, and Governor Perry uses it freely, and we may be sure others will do the same, to dissuade the white population from voting for a convention under the Reconstruction act. The amount of mischief which the agitation of the scheme may do, either in postponing reconstruction or preventing the great body of the late rebels from taking part in it, is, we think, incalculable. The argument of the advocates of the confiscation scheme is substantially this: Land is necessary to complete the glorious work of emancipation—forty acres, or thereabouts, for each head of a family; in most States the whites take every pains to prevent negroes acquiring land, and will not sell it even to those who are able to purchase it; the Government does not own any land in the rebel States, or not enough; it is, therefore, right and expedient to seize the land of persons who have taken part in the rebellion or aided it—that is, of the entire landholding class—and divide it amongst the poor, both black and white.

Now, we totally deny the assumption that the distribution of other people's land to the negroes is necessary to complete the work of emancipation. We admit that farmers make the best citizens of a republic, and that the possession of land does exercise a conservative and elevating influence on character, but so does the possession of railroad stock or Government bonds or good clothes. But there is no mysterious virtue in land which makes the manner in which it is acquired of no consequence; like everything else, whether it will prove a blessing or a curse to the holder depends on how he gets it. . . . Farms taken from the rightful owners by the strong hand of power as a piece of political vengeance wreaked without the intervention of courts of justice, in defiance of the forms of law and to the ruin of the innocent and helpless, have never, we are glad to say, brought anything to the takers but political and moral blight and damnation. No community built up in this way ever enjoyed its booty, or ever held it without being depraved by it. This mode of political propagandism has been tried by the English in Ireland, by the Turks in Turkey, by the Spaniards in America, and it has in every case debauched those who tried it. At the South the white has for two hundred years robbed the black, and he is atoning for it to-day in sackcloth and ashes; if we now set the black to rob the white, we may be sure that like retribution will speedily follow. The negro is just entering on free life, and if he is fit to vote, as we believe he is if evil-minded demagogues will let him alone, he is also fit to win a farm for himself as a poor white man has to win it. If it be deemed desirable that he should have land without waiting to earn it, it ought to be given him out of Government lands, and it would be better for the nation to spend five hundred millions in settling him on them rather than allow or encourage him to use his ballot for the purpose of helping himself to his neighbor's goods.

Nor does the proposal to allow the poor whites to share with him in the fruits of confiscation deprive the scheme of one particle of its repulsiveness. Equality is a good thing, but there are certain transactions which it cannot redeem. A division of rich men's land amongst the landless, as the result of a triumph at the polls, would give a shock to our whole social and political system from which it would hardly recover without the loss of liberty. Every election would thenceforward threaten property, and men of property, we may be sure, would find, as they have found under similar circumstances in all countries, the means of protecting themselves—but not through constitutional government.

What the negroes want is education. Let us vote millions for schools, tens of millions for books and papers, but not one cent for gifts or largesses. No man in America has any right to anything which he has not honestly earned, or which the lawful owner has not thought proper to give him. We do not want to see reproduced, in the middle of the nineteenth century and in a Christian republic, the depraved and worthless mob who, in the declining days of Rome, purchased with their votes the privilege of living in idleness on the spoil of the public enemy. We are thus earnest in calling attention to this matter because there are a hundred indications that the talk of confiscation is already unsettling the minds of the negroes, turning their steps away from the paths of peaceful industry, and teaching them to look for comfort and independence in the wilds of political intrigue.

# THE RECONSTRUCTION ACT:
## PRO AND CON
### (June 27 and 28, 1867)

In June 1867, two Alabama newspapers, the *Mobile Advertiser and Register* and the *Montgomery Daily Advertiser,* jousted over whether Alabamians should comply with the Reconstruction Act. Opposing the bill on Constitutional grounds was John Forsyth, editor of the *Advertiser and Register,* the state's leading conservative Democratic newspaper (he referred to it as the "S.S.S. bills," for Sherman-Shellabarger Senate Bill). Responding to Forsyth, editor W. W. Screws of the *Daily Advertiser* argued that boycotting a state convention would empower the Radicals and their black supporters to disfranchise whites and "reconstruct the State by the vote of the negroes alone."

### JOHN FORSYTH:
### "THE ARGUMENT OF NUMBERS"
*Mobile (Ala.) Advertiser and Register, June 27, 1867*

The Montgomery Advertiser publishes a list of the Alabama papers that stand with itself in favor of the Congressional plan of reconstruction, pure and simple. The argument of numbers is the poorest of arguments. In seasons of passion, majorities are almost certain to be wrong. . . .

Those who go for the S.S.S. bills in their totality, simply submit to be radicalized by Radicalism. No amount of pretty talk, warm professions, or plausible excuses, serve to veneer the stubborn fact of abandonment of the Constitution of the Nation, and the hopes of liberty in the future to the pressure of Radical threats and Radical force.

If we know ourselves, we think only of the good of the

country. But we do confess to a strong and mastering personal ambition to keep our own record clear and to do no act in these times of trial that will bring the blush of shame to our cheeks or to those who bear our name. We will not, therefore, ratify and endorse and pronounce good a system of legislation expressly framed to degrade the South and dethrone constitutional liberty in our whole country, and thereby give rule and power to the open enemies of free government. Others may bend the knee to expediency and abandon principle, submit to tyranny in the blind hope that humility will purchase liberty in the end, but as for us and our house we will serve only the constitution of our country, in our hearts and in our deeds.

## W. W. SCREWS: "WHY OPPOSE A CONVENTION?"

*Montgomery (Ala.) Daily Advertiser, June 28, 1867*

A few men in this state oppose the holding of a Convention. Why, it is hard to tell. If they believe that negro suffrage can be prevented by it they are very credulous. Let's see. There is to be an election soon as to whether or not the people want a Convention. Every negro that is registered will vote. At the same time there will be an election for delegates to the Convention who will assemble in this city in case the vote is in favor of a Convention. Every registered negro will vote. The constitution adopted by that Convention, will be submitted to all the voters, black and white. Suppose the majority of voters is against a Convention or elect members that will reject the terms offered. What next? The term of the present Congress lasts until December year and if the present offer is rejected it will disfranchise the great body of [unreadable] whites, and reconstruct the State by the vote of the negroes alone. Its temper has been sufficiently shown already to convince any one that it will not take a step backward.

# "The Freedmen"

## (July 1867)

During Reconstruction, religious sects like the Philadelphia-based African Methodist Episcopal (A.M.E.) Church and the interdenominational American Missionary Association (A.M.A.) of New York made considerable inroads proselytizing and teaching among the freedpeople. Numerous Northern denominations and philanthropic groups sent teachers and preachers to the South and, with Freedmen's Bureau support, established churches and schools for the former slaves. Sarah Louise "Sallie" Daffin (c. 1838–?) held a strong commitment to uplifting the freedpeople. Descended from a free black Philadelphia middle-class family, and a graduate of Philadelphia's Institute for Colored Youth, during the Civil War and afterward Daffin taught at several freedmen's schools in Virginia, North Carolina, Maryland, and Tennessee. In her 1867 article, Daffin, then working at an A.M.A. school in Arlington, Virginia, implored Northern black congregations to send teachers with "high moral and religious reputations" to educate the freedpeople.

The continually increasing educational demands of the Freedmen upon us, necessitates immediate action on the part of every Church, Association and individual.

Numbers of white churches and benevolent associations of the North have been unsparing in their efforts and means in carrying on a work among our people South, whose vastness can claim no limitation.

At this time we can perceive indications of the importance of the colored people themselves taking hold of the work, and endeavoring to assist in removing the great stumbling block of ignorance out of the way, that Christianity and Education may be firmly rooted on a soil where once slavery and its accompanying legions of crime and woe held precedence.

Our colored churches should be aroused to a proper sense of their duty, and send forth their own teachers into the fields of the South. *The great need is colored teachers.* Not those who can only boast of education—but we want those whose moral and religious reputations will bear any test that will be likely to meet them at every point.

Let care be exercised by our Bishops in sending ministers and missionaries to the Freedmen. Let them be men of ability and influence—men who are the true representatives of our race, and of whom we will not be ashamed.

# THADDEUS STEVENS, "RECONSTRUCTION"

## (July 9, 1867)

Stevens, who on March 2, 1867, had introduced both the Reconstruction Act and the Tenure of Office Act, labored tirelessly to implement Congressional Reconstruction and to rein in the president. On July 8, he presented a bill in the House that added detail and clarified both the first Reconstruction Act and the second Reconstruction Act (enacted March 23, 1867). In this speech the following day, Stevens cogently stated his belief that by seceding and waging a war for independence, the Confederates had forfeited their Constitutional rights as Americans. Castigating Johnson for overstepping his presidential powers, Stevens underscored his opinion that Congress, and only that body, could reconstruct the former Confederate states. "They are our property; their citizens are our subjects."

Mr. Stevens, of Pennsylvania. I trust that in that time I shall be able to state the position which I hold to be the correct one with regard to this bill, without attempting to answer the various remarks which have been made by gentlemen on the other side.

I confess, sir, that a small portion of the blame with reference to the acts of the President since we adjourned, may be attributed to Congress, in that it used improper language in the acts heretofore passed. And this, it appears to me, was owing to an indistinct conception of the condition of the territory for which we were legislating. If we had then all agreed, as we have since, that the States that were lately in rebellion were conquered territory and as such subject to the power of this nation, and had treated them accordingly, we should have had very little trouble in reconstructing government in the South upon the principle of the admission of new States. But, sir, we were not all perfectly agreed in our understanding of the laws of nations as applicable to this question; nor is it wonderful that we should thus have differed, when even some of the judges of the Supreme Court have differed in their opinions upon this subject. I will state what I suppose to have been our real position.

The nation was afflicted with a civil war which for a time was an insurrection. Some twelve million of the inhabitants of the country claimed that they no longer belonged to this nation. They set up an independent government. They established all the machinery of government, both of a national government and of States under that national government. They raised large armies to defend their pretensions. We, at the period when we declared against them a blockade, admitted them to be, not an independent nation, but an independent belligerent, rising above the rank of insurrectionists, and entitled to all the privileges and subject to all the liabilities of an independent belligerent. The nations of Europe so treated them. We so treated them in our dealings with prisoners of war. In short, there could be no doubt of the fact.

We were, then, at war as two independent nations; and it depended upon the will of the conqueror whether the defeated party should be treated merely as a vanquished nation, or whether we should, in addition, punish them as individuals for the violation of the sovereign rights of the nation. We conquered. What did we conquer? We conquered the confederate government. We conquered all the States forming the confederate government. We conquered a government that had been erected and maintained by those who declared that they owed no allegiance to the Government of the United States. For these conquered rebels to pretend that they had any rights under a Constitution which they had thus repudiated and attempted to destroy, and that the States which had been arrayed in hostility to the nation were still states within this Union, as asserted to-day by the gentleman from Wisconsin, [Mr. ELDRIDGE,] seems to me a bold absurdity. Yet that was the doctrine of the President. That is the doctrine which some gentlemen maintain here.

Under military law we treated them as conquered provinces. What is the law with regard to provinces conquered from a foreign independent belligerent? When you conquer territory from a foreign nation or an independent belligerent, the territory thus conquered is governed by military power, by the Commander-in-Chief of the Army, being in this case the President, until the legislative power of the nation shall have spoken and directed what laws shall govern. But the moment the legislative power of the nation interposes the military authority ceases to have sway, and the Commander-in-Chief has no more to say in regard to this matter than a corporal of militia. He is to do just what the legislative power orders him to do, and he can do nothing else.

A great deal is said about the President acting as Commander-in-Chief of the Army. Until he was superseded in his authority by Congress I have no fault to find with his maintaining military rule in the South. But he assumed to exercise legislative powers; he assumed to establish governments; he assumed to appoint civil officers; he assumed that these conquered provinces should come back at once to the enjoyment of all the rights of loyal States under the Constitution, and be entitled to all the privileges which they had possessed prior to their rebellion. Now, sir, as I said before, nothing of this kind came within the power of the Commander-in-Chief. What is the duty of the Commander-in-Chief? If Congress sends an army to quell the Indian war in Nebraska, what is the Commander-in-Chief to do? Congress orders that army to go there. It raises and equips the army. What do the officers do? They pass no act of legislation; they go there and order the troops when to charge and when to retreat; they drill them; they put them through military exercises. But they can do no act that looks like regulating the object of the war or the object with which the army is sent there. Why, sir, the Constitution of the United States makes express reservation of all such power to Congress. It expressly declares that Congress shall have power "to make rules for the government and regulation of the land and naval forces." The Executive has nothing to do with it; the judiciary have nothing to do with it. Congress is the only and the controlling power. Congress has enacted the rules and articles of war. Could the President of the United States interfere with those? Could he add new articles, new rules, new regulations? Certainly not.

The military officers that were sent as commanders in the States were simply appointed as agents of Congress. To be sure, the original bill provided a military supervision simply, and we had intended to follow it up with a law putting reconstruction into the hands of civilians. That is what I should have been disposed to do now, (and I had prepared a bill with that view,) using the military simply as a police and appointing civilians to reconstruct. But if Congress chooses to take officers of the Army and assign them to this duty, they then become the agents of Congress, and neither the President nor any officer under him has any right to interfere or do anything but execute what Congress commands.

Now, sir, it being reduced, I think, to a plain proposition that Congress is the only power that can reconstruct and reclaim these outlying States, the President had no right to call upon the Attorney General or any other officer of the Government to interfere in any manner in such reconstruction. There is but one appeal, and that is either to the agents appointed by Congress or to Congress. It has been well decided in Dorr's case that all power on this subject is vested in Congress. But, sir, we need not look to any such decision. It ought to be known before this time by the President of the United States—it is known, I trust, by the scholars in every colored school in this District—that the Constitution of the United States does not apply to any Territory. The States are parties to the Constitution; they are the contracting powers; they are the substantive body. Territory, however, acquired by purchase or conquest or by inheritance is the property only of that substantive power, of that power bound up by the Constitution; and that power alone is governed by the Constitution, but does not extend for any purpose into any Territory or conquered province. Why, then, talk about the Constitution regulating the action of Congress in a province, in a Territory, in a conquered State, whether conquered from a legitimate State or an illegitimate State?

I may be asked how we would treat the confederate States of America. Just as Congress chooses. They are our property; their citizens are our subjects. Their lives, their liberties are subject to the supreme will of this body, always controlled by the laws of nations, the laws of war, and the laws of humanity. There is no other power on earth; there is no branch of the Government; there is no power in the Government, except what I have mentioned, that has any right to interfere or to say one word on the subject. If you wish to punish the malefactors for violated majesty, that is another matter. Possibly you might do so through your courts of justice. At least you might attempt it, but I do not suppose you can do it. But there is one thing clear: that territory not being yet declared by Congress to be in a state of peace or restoration is under the military authority of the Government, and any tribunal constituted by the military authority, any military tribunal, any court-martial can try any one of those who belonged to the belligerent forces. Jefferson Davis, or any man of the army of the confederacy conquered by us, is this day liable to trial by military tribunal and to sentence. Mr. Speaker, while I would not be bloody-minded, yet if I had my way I would long ago have organized a military tribunal under military power, and I would have put Jefferson Davis and all the members of his cabinet on trial for the murders at Andersonville, the murders at Salisbury, the shooting down our prisoners of war in cold blood. Every man of them is responsible for those crimes.

# "The Negro's Claim to Office"

## (August 1, 1867)

This editorial in *The Nation* employed the rhetorical question of electing an African-American to the vice presidency as a means of explaining the meaning and power of "race" and in combating racial and ethnic discrimination. Appearing at the moment when freedmen were registering to vote for the first time in the Southern states, but were excluded from voting in most Northern states, the editor put the responsibility for overcoming racism and proscription on the blacks themselves. Once they had proven themselves worthy of opportunity and privilege, they would receive the political opportunities they had earned.

Men who say a great deal and are fond of startling effects must needs sometimes say things that it is not very easy to make good in calm discussion. Mr. Wade and Mr. Phillips have of late both got into difficulty owing to their having, in their eagerness to be in the advance ground of radicalism, taken up positions which it was easier to occupy than defend. Mr. Wade startled the world a few weeks ago by some rather confused talk about the duty of the Government toward the laboring classes, and as his discoveries were not favorably received by the public, detachments of newspaper correspondents had to be sent to his rescue to disengage him from the unbelievers. Mr. Phillips also having secured all the objects for which he labored for thirty years, began to find himself rather hard pressed for congenial occupation, and has accordingly begun to agitate for the election of a colored man to the Vice-Presidency. The public having received his arguments on this subject with irreverence, not to say with hilarity, and there being some indications that he has advanced too far, detachments of his friends are also coming to his rescue. *Harper's Weekly,* accordingly, undertakes to show, last week, that it is by no means "absurd" to claim the Vice-Presidency for the colored people, and that the election of a colored man to office will be the only sure sign that the caste feeling has died out with regard to negroes, and that therefore "we should labor for their election to office both as a sign and as a help." That is to say, by electing negroes to office, we shall help to destroy the prejudice against them, and at the same time furnish proof that the prejudice has ceased to exist.

This view of the case is, it seems to us, based on a false impression of the cause of the prejudice against colored people, as well as of the principle which should regulate the bestowal of public offices. This prejudice is not confined to the United States; it exists in a greater or less degree all over the Western World. It exists in almost as great a degree in aristocratic circles in England as in Southern circles in this country; it is nowhere stronger than in white circles in Jamaica, where the negroes have been free for nearly forty years, and have filled almost all public offices, and figured at the governor's levees, and dined at his table, though we admit it rages nowhere with such virulence as amongst the Anglo-Saxon race. Nor is the African race the only object of it. Hindoos and Chinese are exposed to it in almost the same degree. The contempt with which the average Englishman regards the Hindoo can hardly be surpassed by anything which the negro has in this country to undergo from the most besotted Democrat; and yet the Englishman has seen the Hindoo in all the pomp and pride and circumstance of royalty, and of every other great office; he has seen him serve gallantly in war, and knows him to be acute, refined, and descended from ancestors who, if their glory differed from European glory, were, nevertheless, glorious. Hindoos now are admitted to every department of the government service, sit on the bench, practice in the courts, and yet nobody will say that their official dignities have done much to raise them in the estimation of Englishmen. What they have done is to raise England and Englishmen in the estimation of Hindoos.

The dislike of Englishmen and Americans to colored people, and their unwillingness to admit their equality, is not due simply to difference of feature, or color, or race, but to difference of feature, color, and race combined with apparent want of mental, moral, and physical vigor. People whom an Anglo-Saxon can "lick" easily he never respects, and cannot readily be got to respect. The Indian is as repulsive in appearance as the negro, and less capable of civilization, and yet, during all the earlier period of American history, an admixture of Indian blood in one's veins was considered as something to be proud of; and it will be observed that this feeling has declined, and the Indian has fallen into the contempt which at present surrounds him, in the ratio of the decline of his powers of mischief. When he was capable of putting the scalps of a whole colony in danger nobody greatly objected to having a squaw for a grandmother, but since he lost his power of taking scalps at all, nobody likes to acknowledge relationship with him. Taking scalps, to be sure, may not *per se* be a remarkable indication of anything but ferocity and cunning; but the power of combining and carrying on a destructive war does indicate considerable power both of mind and body. Now the disability of the negro in the eyes of American society is due to the fact that he has never done anything which was an evidence of great capacity. He has never achieved wealth, which, in an Anglo-Saxon community, is the greatest evidence of power, and he has achieved neither literary, nor scientific, nor *military* distinction. That he has never had a chance to do so it may be easy to show; but society, in judging people, does not take opportunities or want of opportunities into account. Its decisions are shaped simply by accomplished results. When a man talks to it of what he might do if he had a chance, it laughs and leaves him. The only field in which the friends of the negro have been as yet able to produce strong indications of capacity superior to that of white men, is that of art; but it is only very recently that Americans and Englishmen have begun to look on painters or musicians or actors as anything better than vagabond adventurers of whom the community would be well rid.

We hold, therefore, as we have once before said when discussing this same subject, that the removal of the white prejudice against the negro depends almost entirely on the negro himself. You can work sufficiently on the religious and moral feelings of the white community to secure for him justice and political equality, and a fair chance in the race of life; but as long as the great mass of negroes—in fact, the whole colored population *as a class*—are in a lower state of civilization than the rest of the population, less learned, less wealthy, less cultivated, less refined, less progressive, have, in short, achieved less in every walk of life, it is chimerical to ask the white majority to bestow on negroes, as a class, special marks of honor by selecting a colored man for the Vice-Presidency or other high office, simply *because of his color*; and yet, as we understand them, this is what Mr. Phillips and *Harper's Weekly* ask us to do.

The right of negroes, *as negroes*, to seats in the State legislatures and in Congress we do not question; nay, we assert it, because in the existing state of society in this country negroes can only be fairly represented by negroes. The admission of colored men to the representative body, as long as a sixth of the population are colored, and are separated in feeling and antecedents and condition by a wide gulf from their white neighbors, is not the bestowal of an honor, it is an act of justice. But the election, by the whole Union, to a high Federal office, of a colored man for the sole reason that the fraction of the community to which he belonged was poor and mean and despised, would, in our opinion, be a degradation and perversion of the office, and would not help the colored population, because it would outrage the sense of justice and sense of propriety of the best portion of the whites. There is something very amusing in the simplicity with which Mr. Phillips tries to persuade himself and persuade others, that as soon as people saw a negro foisted into the Vice-Presidency by political manoeuvering, the whites would begin to respect the colored population more than they had previously done. He might as well talk of regulating the temperature by forcing the mercury up and down in a thermometrical tube. Election to office is, and always has been, and we trust always will be, the result of the popular estimate of a man's character, not the cause of it. Therefore, whenever we see a negro in the Vice-Presidency, it will, we admit, be a *sign* that negroes, as a class, have risen in popular estimation. But to raise them in popular estimation, we must go about exhorting them to do the things and lead the life which win popular esteem, instead of exhorting the whites to bestow highest honors or their gifts on the class which has done least to deserve them, or to bestow the most important political trusts on the class which has done least to prove its fitness for them.

The offices of government, as we understand government, are established for the service of the whole community, and not for the consolation of the unfortunate or unsuccessful, and if there be one political abuse from which, more than any other, the country has in these latter days suffered, it is the practice of bestowing nominations and appointments with reference not to the candidate's fitness or to the public needs, but with reference to such arbitrary and senseless considerations as "the claims" of particular sections or localities or interests. It is to this abuse of its power by the convention that we owe our present valuable ruler, Andrew Johnson, and it is to this abuse of their power by the President and Senate that we have owed and do still owe most of our worst diplomatic officers, and many of the worst in other branches of the public service. It is to the idea, too, out of which this abuse springs—that offices are "spoils" or prizes and not trusts—that we owe much of the jobbing which marks the election of United States senators. Many a valuable man is lost to the Senate because some one section of a State has "claims" involving the choice of somebody else. To this abuse Mr. Phillips wants to give an immense extension.

It is said that the arguments now used for the election of negroes to high office are such as have been and are constantly used in favor of the election or appointment of persons belonging to other despised or unfortunate classes, or interests. We deny it *in toto*. During the long contest in England which preceded the admission of Jews to the House of Commons, nobody ever thought of claiming seats for them as a means of raising Jews in the popular estimation. This work the advocates of their claims well knew the Jews must do for themselves. What was demanded in the case of the Jews, as well as of the Irish Catholics, was the removal as an act of justice of all legal barriers to their holding office. The moral and social barriers they were left to remove themselves by the ordinary means—that is, by industry, learning, energy, activity, eloquence, and public spirit. Baron Rothschild got his seat in the House of Commons not as a means of elevating his race, but because his race was elevated; because it had shown itself in every country in Europe foremost in the work of civilization; because its members were the first in the ranks of commerce, literature, arts, and arms, and because, in short, it had become ridiculous and absurd to exclude a Jew, as Jew, from post of honor. The mere social prejudice against Jews is still strong in every Christian country—stronger with many people than the prejudice against negroes—but as long as Jews are amongst the wealthiest merchants and bankers, the ablest lawyers and scientific men in the world, no prejudice can shut them out from more than their share, calculated on numbers, of political honors.

The foreign population in this country is more numerous than the negro population, and has contributed far more to its wealth and strength and fame and prosperity. Foreigners are found in the most distinguished places in all walks of life, but how many foreigners are there in Congress? What foreigner has yet been nominated for the governorship of a State or the Vice-Presidency? Two or three have filled second-rate embassies; but, so far as we know, no high official position has yet been conferred by the popular vote on a man of foreign birth, and we have yet to meet with a foreigner who is fool enough to complain of this as a grievance or as an indication that foreigners are treated as "political outcasts." The exclusion is a natural one, and because natural perfectly just. As long as native Americans do most of the brain work of the country, have most to do with the supply of its ideas and the direction of its industry, the high political positions will fall to their lot. If the day should ever come when high political positions shall be distributed, as treasury clerkships and custom-house places now are, as a mode of relieving or encouraging the helpless or friendless or destitute or incompetent, a serious blow will assuredly be struck at the stability of the government, and we, for our part, hope that nothing of the kind will ever be submitted to by the people either for the sake of the negroes or any other race or tribe, because we know that when negroes have contributed their fair share to the work of civilization and good government, no prejudice can, in a free Christian country, prevent them from receiving their fair share of the prizes.

# "SAMSON AGONISTES AT WASHINGTON"

## *(August 24, 1867)*

On March 2, 1867, Congress passed the Tenure of Office Act over Johnson's veto, restricting the president's patronage powers. It required the approval of the Senate in dismissing officers appointed with congressional consent. Legislators intended the bill, along with the Reconstruction Act, to assume control of the Reconstruction process and to limit Johnson's power. Accordingly, on August 12, 1867, the president removed the popular secretary of war, Edwin M. Stanton, a supporter of the Radicals' Reconstruction program, and, five days later, transferred General Philip H. Sheridan, who had zealously implemented the Reconstruction Act, from the Fifth Military District (Texas and Louisiana) to the Department of the Missouri. This cartoon, published in *Harper's Weekly* on August 24, 1867, depicted Johnson pulling down two massive columns (representing Stanton and Sheridan), causing Reconstruction to collapse on his head. Like Samson in the Bible and later John Milton's tragedy *Samson Agonistes* (1671), Johnson destroys himself.

SAMSON AGONISTES AT WASHINGTON.

# George Fitzhugh, "Cui Bono?—The Negro Vote"

## (September 17, 1867)

White conservative Southerners like Fitzhugh feared not only black voters, but what they correctly perceived was the national Republicans' determination to establish their party in the former Confederate states led by the newly enfranchised blacks and white Unionists. Overstating black voters' numbers, their intentions, their militancy, and their eventual impact, Fitzhugh predicted a black revolution, whereby the freedmen would take political control from white Republicans and enslave their former masters. "They are all armed and ready; all burning for a fight." Fitzhugh urged Radicals to reverse themselves on the question of black suffrage. Otherwise the South would ignite in race war.

Messrs. Editors—The Radicals have overreached themselves. The negroes throughout the South are determined not to become their allies and supple tools, but to set up a party of their own, and to vote for none but negro candidates for office. They naturally reject with scorn and contempt the Radical proposition that henceforth there shall be no distinctions of color or race, but that all men shall stand on their own merits. They see, that under a thin disguise, this is a proposition that the negroes shall do the voting, and the Radicals fill all the offices. Four millions of negroes in the South, they insist, by virtue of their numbers and their loyalty, are entitled to fill most of the Federal and State offices at the South, and not to become mere hewers of wood and drawers of water for a handful of false, hypocritical, newly-converted white Unionists. Thrown upon their individual merit regardless of color or race, and they know that no negroes would be elected or appointed to office, for more capable white men are everywhere to be found. Obliterate all distinctions of race, and the negroes at the South, like those at the North, would become outcasts, pariahs, paupers and criminals. They would be confined to the most loathsome and least lucrative employments, and spend half their time in prisons, work-houses and poor-houses. They know that mere political equality would at once condemn them to social slavery—and they see at the North, that this social slavery, or slavery to skill and capital, of an inferior to a superior race, is the worst possible condition in which human beings can be placed. You, and your readers, must see that the negroes will not be satisfied with a nominal, but deceptive equality, but are everywhere determined to become masters of those who lately owned them as slaves. We admire their pluck. They are all armed and ready; all burning for a fight. They are impatient at the tedious process of reconstruction, and lavish much more abuse upon the Federal soldiers, the Freedman's Bureau and the Radicals, than upon the Secessionists. So soon as invested with the voting franchise, they will be full masters of the situation, for they constitute a majority on every acre of good land (except a little about the mountains) from Maryland to Florida, from the Atlantic to the Mississippi, and from the Rio Grande to Memphis. By mere voting, and selecting none but negroes as county, state and federal officers, in the favored regions where they constitute the majority, in two or three years they might expel the whites from all the fertile sections of the South, and turn those sections into hunting, ranging, fowling and fishing grounds, just as they were held, or infested by the Indians. Nature seems to have intended all the fertile portions of the South for mere roaming grounds for savages, for no where else on the globe would bountiful Nature enable savages to live with so little labor. It would be far easier for negro savages to live without labor on the sea, gulf and river coasts in the South, than in any parts of Africa. Wild fruits are ten-times as abundant in these favored sections of the South as in any parts of Africa; and so are fish, oysters, water fowl, and forest game. Give the negroes the right of suffrage, and at once they become masters of the situation throughout every acre of good land in the South, except about the mountains. They would only have to elect negro judges, sheriffs, justices of the peace, constables, jurors, etc., in order to expel the whole white population, except here and there a few old, infirm, silly, infatuated landholders. Our mechanics have nothing to do, and are rapidly emigrating. White common laborers or hirelings have all disappeared. We have not seen a single one since the war. There is nothing for our educated, enterprising young men to do here, and they are all removing. We have no industrial pursuits, except farming, and that is carelessly, lazily and languidly pursued by a few white landowners, and by troops of freedmen, who work occasionally, in a desultory way—say, on the average, three days in the week. The negro tenants, next year, will claim half of our lands, and negro judges, jurors, justices, etc., will sustain their claims—that is, provided, negro suffrage turns over the South to negro rule. It is a monstrous absurdity, cruelty and attempted deception, to invite white men from the North to settle in the South, subject themselves to negro rule, and probably, ere long, to be massacred by negroes. No! Let the whites at the North first expel the Radicals from power, deny to the negro the rights of citizenship, make him a subordinate, or mere coarse, common laborer, as God and Nature designed he should be, and these white men from the North will find the South a delightful residence. Now, no sane man would live here longer than he could make arrangements to quit but for the hope and expectation that Radical rule is nearly ended, and that the Northern Democrats, soon to come into power, will do justice to the whites of the South, and the whites of the North, by putting the negro to work, and leaving voting, legislating, and governing, to the whites.

We have said that the negroes, so soon as they become invested with the right of suffrage, will become masters of the situation, and may seize on and hold all of the property of the whites, without redress on their parts; for negro jurors, justices and judges, taught by Northern Abolition emissaries that they (the negroes) are the rightful owners of all Southern lands and other property, would be sure to profit by the lessons they have thus learned. But they are impatient. This is too slow a process for them. We assure you, and your readers, and the entire North, that the freedmen (with very few exceptions) are anxious, impatient, burning with desire to begin the fight—the war of races—at once. They hold incendiary meetings, caucuses and conven-

tions every day. They are all around; they are continually
drilling in defiance of law. They have every where secret
military organizations; they daily defy and insult the Federal troops and the Freedman's Bureau. They are ready and
anxious to fight all the whites both North and South. They
believe themselves far better soldiers than the whites, and
are ready to attempt the expulsion or extermination of the
whites. Unless the elections at the North, this fall, show a
decided Democratic gain, the war of the races will begin
ere the commencement of another year. And what will be
the consequences? Why, a few hundreds or thousands,
whites, men, women and children, will be massacred by the
negroes; and then, in retaliation, hundreds of thousands of negroes will be exterminated by the infuriated whites. This
war of races will brutalize whites as well as blacks. Yet,
knowingly, willfully, premeditatedly and advisedly, the
Radical leaders are bringing about this inhuman and
bloody result. And for why? Not to make allies of the negroes, for the negroes hate and despise them, and are everywhere busy in building up a negro party and in nominating
negro candidates for office. They are equally the enemies of
radical measures and radical men. In all their meetings in
the cotton states, they denounce the direct tax on cotton,
and will be sure to oppose the protective tariff; or indirect
tax on cotton and other necessaries of life; for such taxes
fall most heavily on the laboring classes. They will, for like
reasons, be sure to advocate the repudiation of the National debt; whilst white representatives from the South
would vote for its payment to the uttermost cent; for such
payment would obviously be part of the terms of Reconstruction, which no honest Southron would attempt to violate. Besides, this war of races would involve the North also
in war, increase the National debt, greatly increase Federal
taxation, destroy altogether the Northern market for her
merchandise and manufactures at the South; put a stop to
the production of cotton, rice, sugar and tobacco; render
reconstruction equally hopeless and undesirable; divide,
probably, the Union into a half dozen separate nations, and
involve the whole country, without distinction of race or
section, in one common, irremediable ruin. But we hope
and believe that Northern men begin to see that the continuance of radical rule is rapidly bringing about these di-

sastrous results, and that they will soon hurl these cruel, dishonest and disorganizing rulers from the seats of power, do justice to the South, restore the Union on constitutional terms, and renew amicable and profitable relations between the lately hostile sections.

# "The Virginia Election"

## (October 31, 1867)

George Fitzhugh was not alone in overreacting to
the prospect of black voters in the Reconstruction
era South. The editor of *The Nation,* while pleased
to report that Virginians had taken steps toward
complying with the Reconstruction Acts, alleged
that black voters in the state had come under the
political control of an extreme Radical, Unionist
editor the Reverend James W. Hunnicutt (1814–
1880), author of *The Conspiracy Unveiled* (1863),
a work that condemned secession as a slaveholders' plot. *The Nation* prophesied that Reconstruction would fail if the Republicans pitted whites
against blacks.

Virginia is the first State in which a full vote of both races
has been polled under the Reconstruction Act. Although
there is a considerable preponderance of white voters in
the State, there seems to be no doubt that the call for a
convention is sustained by a large majority, and that the
convention will be Radical in politics. So far, this is a very
acceptable result. But it is attended with some drawbacks
which deserve attention, especially as they proceed from
causes which may find a larger field of operation and produce very serious results.

We have on several occasions alluded to the dangerous
effects which might be produced among the freedmen of
the South by the current talk about confiscation, and the
suggestions of politicians that the negro might properly use
his ballot as a means of personal advantage. It is evident
that our warnings were only too much needed and our
fears too well founded. The fear, once common at the
North, that the votes of the negroes would be controlled by
their masters, has been entirely dispelled. The fear, common among a different class, that the negroes would use
their power brutally, long since passed away. But while it is
clear both that the negroes will vote in a mass for a Repub-

lican ticket, and that they will be in the main a law-abiding class, it is also plain that they are in danger of falling into the hands of demagogues who will use them without scruple for purposes which will finally prove disastrous to the race.

Mr. Hunnicutt, of Richmond, is the foremost example of this class. Originally, no doubt, a well-meaning man, zealous for liberty and loyalty, he has been perverted by the prospect of power which his great influence among the colored people opened to him, and embittered by the hatred of his white neighbors. His public language has sometimes had an affectation of liberality, but it is manifest that his actions have all been governed by a narrow desire to keep the Republican party of the State under his own control. He has persuaded the colored people to distrust every white man outside his own little clique; and has urged them to a course of political action which has excluded every respectable white man from their alliance, although thousands were willing and even anxious to co-operate with them upon honorable terms. The natural result of such bigotry was shown in the recent vote of Richmond, where there are hundreds of white Republicans fully as radical as Mr. Greeley or Senator Wilson, yet who were driven to support a Conservative ticket; so that Mr. Hunnicutt and his associates received less than fifty white votes in the whole city. It is true that Mr. Hunnicutt secured his election, which was all that he cared about; but at the cost of consolidating the whole white race in opposition. We rejoice to believe that this event, in view of the narrow escape which Mr. Hunnicutt had from entire defeat, will prove fatal to his higher aspirations. But there are more important interests at stake than the fortunes of a single demagogue. The Republican party puts its existence in peril by tolerating such a policy as has been adopted in Richmond. The national leaders of the party must find some means of liberalizing the party managers at the South, or the whole plan of reconstruction will fail, dragging the party to ruin with it.

We say it deliberately, *no scheme of reconstruction can succeed with the white race at the South unanimously opposed to it.* It can succeed though every rebel, in States where all the whites are rebels, oppose it. It can succeed against the will of nine-tenths of the whole white population of the South. But if it is so managed as to disgust the whole white race as a race, irrespective of birthplace, politics, associations, and interest, it must inevitably fail.

# "WHAT SHALL WE DO WITH THE INDIANS?"

## *(October 31, 1867)*

Though generally forgotten in the history and historical memory of the Civil War and Reconstruction era, the government's Indian policy nevertheless attracted considerable attention from contemporaries. When a Sioux rebellion erupted in Minnesota in August 1862, a military commission sentenced 303 warriors to death for "murders and outrages" against whites. President Lincoln later pardoned all but thirty-eight of the Indians. Lincoln, following conventional wisdom of his day, considered Indians a separate "race" and advocated reform of the nation's policy toward them. Native peoples should become wards of the state, abandon their nomadic ways, live on reservations, and grow crops. In other words, one historian quipped, "They should surrender most of their land and cease to be Indians." *The Nation's* solution to the Indian problem was simple: offer them the same legal protection and hold them accountable to the same responsibilities as whites. "The truth is," the editor concluded, "the Indians have always been more ready than we. Our work has been one of continual repression."

It is plain that something must be done with the Indians, and that it must be something different from anything yet done. We must have peace by some means. The frontiers must rest in security and the highways to the Pacific must be unobstructed. But peace involves one of two things—either the extermination of the Indian or his subjection to law and habits of industry. Extermination is a word easily said; but to put it in execution will cost untold millions of money and a life for a life. Let it be remembered that the Indians number nearly 300,000, and it has cost $70,000 per head to kill those we have put out of the way. To many minds the work of their regeneration is an equally desperate and hopeless undertaking; but those who are more intimately acquainted with the question are able to prove the contrary. The civilization of the Indian is the easiest and cheapest as well as only honorable way of securing peace.

But if we expect to civilize the Indian, it must be attempted by more rational methods than we have heretofore used. Is it reasonable to expect recovery from disease, or a healthy growth, unless the causes of the disease are removed and the conditions of life supplied? Now, the prime conditions of true social order and personal wellbeing are wanting in Indian society. The first condition is LAW to protect person and property, to restrain crime, encourage industry, and favor such prosperity as will give the Indian more interest in peace than in war. No community can develop material prosperity, social order, or individual character without the protection of life and the fruits of labor. Indians are no exception to this rule, or they would be our superiors. It is a well-known fact that the Indians have no government worthy the name. What they have is not sufficient to secure justice between man and man, nor does it even attempt it. The tribes of the Indian Territory are a partial exception. Nor is this state of anarchy altogether the fault of the Indians; it has been perpetuated and made worse by the action of our own Government. In many respects the relations of our Government to them have made their advance in civilization harder instead of easier. What wonder that they have not made greater progress? Something has been done by private citizens for their advancement, and it has been successful enough to prove that better things may be expected under better conditions. But this is not a work for private citizens alone. The United States Government can only supply social order by law, and until this is done benevolent efforts are as water poured out on the sand.

What the Indians most need is the extension of our laws over them. We are responsible for not having done it before. And the law must be brought home to each individual. It must surround every man for his personal protection and restraint. It may seem needless to say this, but all our talk and action in the past has only regarded general justice and has amounted to nothing. We have gone no further than to try and control the international intercourse of Indians and whites, and this in a most general way. We have not thought of controlling, or allowing any control of, Indians among themselves. But there can be no prosperity where each man is not defended against his neighbor, nor can the law have any restraining power unless it at the same time creates an interest in itself by the protection it affords.

There is no great difficulty in carrying this plan into effect. We only need to treat Indians like men, treat them as we do ourselves, putting on them the same responsibilities, letting them sue and be sued, and taxing them as fast as they settle down and have anything to tax. The times are ripe for this movement. Experience has convinced us that the *theory* on which our Indian affairs have been administered is wrong. We have conceded a tribal sovereignty to them which has had no existence in fact, and which, had it originally existed, was of late years impossible, in view of the sovereignty of the United States. On this ground we have treaties with them as foreign nations. And much of our inconsistent and seemingly treacherous dealing with them has been more the necessary result of this vicious theory than of wilful wickedness. Not that the latter has been wanting, however. Again, our Government is itself purified of the false idea of State sovereignty, which has doubtless countenanced the same error in regard to the Indian tribal governments. There is now a consciousness of sovereignty in the nation which is ready to assert its power in behalf of the general welfare; and the progress of the nation in regard to the recognition of human rights, the exaltation of manhood for its own sake, irrespective of race, color, or position, opens the way to this work, while the methods and agencies developed by the necessities of the freedmen solve the question of ways and means.

But are the Indians ready for it? Will they submit to the government of our laws? Is it possible to get the wild Comanches or the terrible Sioux to come under the control of law, assume the habits and occupations of civilized life, and appeal for redress of injuries to a court of justice instead of to the war-club? We think it is. The Indians are now, in large numbers, ready and anxious for the protection and order which our laws would bring; and those who are now wildest and most intractable are not beyond reach. They will be ready as soon as we. In proof of this, look at the Sioux nation; it is the most numerous body of Indians on the Continent, and covers all lands, we may say, between the Pacific Railroad and the British line, and from the western border of Iowa and Minnesota to the Rocky Mountains. It has many different tribes, going under all sorts of names; some of them the fiercest and most dreaded Indians of the plains, and others as peaceable and tractable as the very best. What makes the difference? Simply this: some of these tribes or bands have for fifty or sixty years been planting, more or less, and have been greatly affected by their semi-agricultural life; the others are of the same stock, but their life is more roving and in consequence wilder. But this change has all been produced in little more than half a century, and the same cause has been working change of late years among the Indians of the plains, driven by scarcity of game to depend more on the fruits of the farm. Its results may as yet be imperceptible to the distant observer, but careful study of the facts proves that none of these Indians are unchangeable as to habits of life or even personal characteristics. The Comanches are often mentioned as the eminent types of incorrigible wildness; but it is a fact that previous to the war of the rebellion a large number of them had settled down on a reservation. When we look at the poor inducements they had to do so, we wonder they did it; but if they did it then, will they not do the same when protection, order, prosperity, and life shall be their inducement—in fact and not in words?

The truth is the Indians have always been more ready than we. Our work has been one of continual repression. When the State constitution of Minnesota was adopted in 1857, it was expected from its wording that educated Indians able to read and write their own language and having a knowledge of the constitution of the State would be admitted to citizenship and the ballot. At least they believed it, and the prospect gave a wonderful impulse to their labors in the schoolroom and in the field. They were preparing to live like men. But such a thing could not be thought of by their white brethren; and in the act of denying citizenship to the Indians in 1857–8 the State of Minnesota threw away the opportunity of preventing the terrible massacres of

1862. Had law been permitted to reign among the Sioux in 1858, when they were anxious for it, the massacres of 1862 would have been impossible. This very summer the Indians in North-eastern Nebraska and Dakota have been restrained by the United States agents by force from going forth into the harvest-fields around, where their labor was wanted and where they might have earned bread for their families. It takes the strong hand of government to push them back into barbarism. Who is it that is not ready for civilization?

# Andrew Johnson, "Third Annual Message"

## (December 3, 1867)

In his December 1867 annual message, President
Johnson reflected on a trying year. Congress had
successfully taken the Reconstruction process
away from him, limiting both his patronage and
his powers as commander-in-chief. And in that
month, an unsuccessful move surfaced in the
House of Representatives to impeach him. With
characteristic boldness, in his address Johnson
admitted his major point of contention with the
Radicals in Congress: his belief that the former
Confederate states had never left the Union and
thus could not be treated Constitutionally as "conquered territory." Going on the offensive, Johnson
branded many of the Republicans' actions unconstitutional usurpations of federal power, vindictive
and politically motivated, and prone "to Africanize
the half of our country."

### FELLOW-CITIZENS OF THE SENATE
### AND HOUSE OF REPRESENTATIVES

When a civil war has been brought to a close, it is manifestly the first interest and duty of the state to repair the
injuries which the war has inflicted, and to secure the benefit of the lessons it teaches as fully and as speedily as possible. This duty was, upon the termination of the rebellion,
promptly accepted, not only by the executive department,
but by the insurrectionary States themselves, and restoration in the first moment of peace was believed to be as easy
and certain as it was indispensable. The expectations, however, then so reasonably and confidently entertained were
disappointed by legislation from which I felt constrained
by my obligations to the Constitution to withhold my assent.

It is therefore a source of profound regret that in complying with the obligation imposed upon the President by the Constitution to give to Congress from time to time information of the state of the Union I am unable to communicate any definitive adjustment, satisfactory to the American people, of the questions which since the close of the rebellion have agitated the public mind. On the contrary, candor compels me to declare that at this time there is no Union as our fathers understood the term, and as they meant it to be understood by us. The Union which they established can exist only where all the States are represented in both Houses of Congress; where one State is as free as another to regulate its internal concerns according to its own will, and where the laws of the central Government, strictly confined to matters of national jurisdiction, apply with equal force to all the people of every section. That such is not the present "state of the Union" is a melancholy fact, and we must all acknowledge that the restoration of the States to their proper legal relations with the Federal Government and with one another, according to the terms of the original compact, would be the greatest temporal blessing which God, in His kindest providence, could bestow upon this nation. It becomes our imperative duty to consider whether or not it is impossible to effect this most desirable consummation.

The Union and the Constitution are inseparable. As long as one is obeyed by all parties, the other will be preserved; and if one is destroyed, both must perish together. The destruction of the Constitution will be followed by other and still greater calamities. It was ordained not only to form a more perfect union between the States, but to "establish justice, insure domestic tranquillity, provide for the common defense, promote the general welfare, and secure the blessings of liberty to ourselves and our posterity." Nothing but implicit obedience to its requirements in all parts of the country will accomplish these great ends. Without that obedience we can look forward only to continual outrages upon individual rights, incessant breaches of the public peace, national weakness, financial dishonor, the total loss of our prosperity, the general corruption of morals, and the final extinction of popular freedom. To save our country from evils so appalling as these, we should renew our efforts again and again.

To me the process of restoration seems perfectly plain and simple. It consists merely in a faithful application of the Constitution and laws. The execution of the laws is not now obstructed or opposed by physical force. There is no military or other necessity, real or pretended, which can prevent obedience to the Constitution, either North or South. All the rights and all the obligations of States and individuals can be protected and enforced by means perfectly consistent with the fundamental law. The courts may be everywhere open, and if open their process would be unimpeded. Crimes against the United States can be prevented or punished by the proper judicial authorities in a manner entirely practicable and legal. There is therefore no reason why the Constitution should not be obeyed, unless those who exercise its powers have determined that it shall be disregarded and violated. The mere naked will of this Government, or of some one or more of its branches, is the only obstacle that can exist to a perfect union of all the States.

On this momentous question and some of the measures growing out of it I have had the misfortune to differ from Congress, and have expressed my convictions without reserve, though with becoming deference to the opinion of the legislative department. Those convictions are not only unchanged, but strengthened by subsequent events and further reflection. The transcendent importance of the subject will be a sufficient excuse for calling your attention to some of the reasons which have so strongly influenced my own judgment. The hope that we may all finally concur in a mode of settlement consistent at once with our true interests and with our sworn duties to the Constitution is too natural and too just to be easily relinquished.

It is clear to my apprehension that the States lately in rebellion are still members of the National Union. When did they cease to be so? The "ordinances of secession" adopted by a portion (in most of them a very small portion) of their citizens were mere nullities. If we admit now that they were valid and effectual for the purpose intended by their authors, we sweep from under our feet the whole ground upon which we justified the war. Were those States afterwards expelled from the Union by the war? The direct contrary was averred by this Government to be its purpose, and was so understood by all those who gave their blood and treasure to aid in its prosecution. It can not be that a successful war, waged for the preservation of the Union, had the legal effect of dissolving it. The victory of the nation's arms was not the disgrace of her policy; the defeat of secession on the battlefield was not the triumph of its lawless principle. Nor could Congress, with or without the consent of the Executive, do anything which would have the effect, directly or indirectly, of separating the States from each other. To dissolve the Union is to repeal the Constitution which holds it together, and that is a power which does not belong to any department of this Government, or to all of them united. . . .

The acts of Congress in question are not only objectionable for their assumption of ungranted power, but many of their provisions are in conflict with the direct prohibitions of the Constitution. The Constitution commands that a republican form of government shall be guaranteed to all the States; that no person shall be deprived of life, liberty, or property without due process of law, arrested without a judicial warrant, or punished without a fair trial before an impartial jury; that the privilege of habeas corpus shall not be denied in time of peace, and that no bill of attainder shall be passed even against a single individual. Yet the system of measures established by these acts of Congress does totally subvert and destroy the form as well as the substance of republican government in the ten States to which they apply. It binds them hand and foot in absolute slavery, and subjects them to a strange and hostile power, more unlimited and more likely to be abused than any other now known among civilized men. It tramples down all those rights in which the essence of liberty consists, and which a free government is always most careful to protect. It denies the habeas corpus and the trial by jury. Personal freedom, property, and life, if assailed by the passion, the prejudice, or the rapacity of the ruler, have no security whatever. It has the effect of a bill of attainder or bill of pains and penalties, not upon a few individuals, but upon whole masses, including the millions who inhabit the subject States, and even their unborn children. These wrongs, being expressly forbidden, can not be constitutionally inflicted upon any portion of our people, no matter how they may have come within our jurisdiction, and no matter whether they live in States, Territories, or districts.

I have no desire to save from the proper and just consequences of their great crime those who engaged in rebellion against the Government, but as a mode of punishment the measures under consideration are the most unreasonable that could be invented. Many of those people are perfectly innocent; many kept their fidelity to the Union untainted to the last; many were incapable of any legal offense; a large proportion even of the persons able to bear arms were forced into rebellion against their will, and of those who are guilty with their own consent the degrees of guilt are as various as the shades of their character and temper. But these acts of Congress confound them all together in one common doom. Indiscriminate vengeance upon classes, sects, and parties, or upon whole communities, for offenses committed by a portion of them against the governments to which they owed obedience was common in the barbarous ages of the world; but Christianity and civilization have made such progress that recourse to a punishment so cruel and unjust would meet with the condemnation of all unprejudiced and right-minded men. The punitive justice of this age, and especially of this country, does not consist in stripping whole States of their liberties and reducing all their people, without distinction, to the condition of slavery. It deals separately with each individual, confines itself to the forms of law, and vindicates its own purity by an impartial examination of every case before a competent judicial tribunal. If this does not satisfy all our desires with regard to Southern rebels, let us console ourselves by reflecting that a free Constitution, triumphant in war and unbroken in peace, is worth far more to us and our children than the gratification of any present feeling.

I am aware it is assumed that this system of government for the Southern States is not to be perpetual. It is true this military government is to be only provisional, but it is through this temporary evil that a greater evil is to be made perpetual. If the guaranties of the Constitution can be broken provisionally to serve a temporary purpose, and in a part only of the country, we can destroy them everywhere and for all time. Arbitrary measures often change, but they generally change for the worse. It is the curse of despotism that it has no halting place. The intermitted exercise of its power brings no sense of security to its subjects, for they can never know what more they will be called to endure when its red right hand is armed to plague them again. Nor is it possible to conjecture how or where power, unrestrained by law, may seek its next victims. The States that are still free may be enslaved at any moment; for if the Constitution does not protect all, it protects none.

It is manifestly and avowedly the object of these laws to confer upon negroes the privilege of voting and to disfranchise such a number of white citizens as will give the former a clear majority at all elections in the Southern States. This, to the minds of some persons, is so important that a violation of the Constitution is justified as a means of bringing it about. The morality is always false which excuses a wrong because it proposes to accomplish a desirable end. We are not permitted to do evil that good may come. But in this case the end itself is evil, as well as the means. The subjugation of the States to negro domination would be worse than the military despotism under which they are now suffering. It was believed beforehand that the people would endure any amount of military oppression for any length of time rather than degrade themselves by subjection to the negro race. Therefore they have been left without a choice. Negro suffrage was established by act of Congress, and the military officers were commanded to superintend the process of clothing the negro race with the political privileges torn from white men.

The blacks in the South are entitled to be well and humanely governed, and to have the protection of just laws for all their rights of person and property. If it were practicable at this time to give them a Government exclusively their own, under which they might manage their own affairs in their own way, it would become a grave question whether we ought to do so, or whether common humanity would not require us to save them from themselves. But under the circumstances this is only a speculative point. It is not proposed merely that they shall govern themselves, but that they shall rule the white race, make and administer State laws, elect Presidents and members of Congress, and shape to a greater or less extent the future destiny of the whole country. Would such a trust and power be safe in such hands? . . .

I repeat the expression of my willingness to join in any plan within the scope of our constitutional authority which promises to better the condition of the negroes in the South, by encouraging them in industry, enlightening their minds, improving their morals, and giving protection to all their just rights as freedmen. But the transfer of our political inheritance to them would, in my opinion, be an abandonment of a duty which we owe alike to the memory of our fathers and the rights of our children.

The plan of putting the Southern States wholly and the General Government partially into the hands of negroes is proposed at a time peculiarly unpropitious. The foundations of society have been broken up by civil war. Industry must be reorganized, justice reestablished, public credit maintained, and order brought out of confusion. To accomplish these ends would require all the wisdom and virtue of the great men who formed our institutions originally. I confidently believe that their descendants will be equal to the arduous task before them, but it is worse than madness to expect that negroes will perform it for us. Certainly we ought not to ask their assistance till we despair of our own competency.

The great difference between the two races in physical, mental, and moral characteristics will prevent an amalgamation or fusion of them together in one homogeneous mass. If the inferior obtains the ascendency over the other, it will govern with reference only to its own interests—for it will recognize no common interest—and create such a tyranny as this continent has never yet witnessed. Already the negroes are influenced by promises of confiscation and plunder. They are taught to regard as an enemy every white man who has any respect for the rights of his own race. If this continues it must become worse and worse, until all order will be subverted, all industry cease, and the fertile fields of the South grow up into a wilderness. Of all the dangers which our nation has yet encountered, none are equal to those which must result from the success of the effort now making to Africanize the half of our country. . . .

The great interests of the country require immediate relief from these enactments. Business in the South is paralyzed by a sense of general insecurity, by the terror of confiscation, and the dread of negro supremacy. The Southern trade, from which the North would have derived so great a profit under a government of law, still languishes, and can never be revived until it ceases to be fettered by the arbitrary power which makes all its operations unsafe. That rich country—the richest in natural resources the world ever saw—is worse than lost if it be not soon placed under the protection of a free constitution. Instead of being, as it ought to be, a source of wealth and power, it will become an intolerable burden upon the rest of the nation.

Another reason for retracing our steps will doubtless be seen by Congress in the late manifestations of public opinion upon this subject. We live in a country where the popular will always enforces obedience to itself, sooner or later. It is vain to think of opposing it with anything short of legal authority backed by overwhelming force. It can not have escaped your attention that from the day on which Congress fairly and formally presented the proposition to govern the Southern States by military force, with a view to the ultimate establishment of negro supremacy, every expression of the general sentiment has been more or less adverse to it. The affections of this generation can not be detached from the institutions of their ancestors. Their determination to preserve the inheritance of free government in their own hands and transmit it undivided and unimpaired to their own posterity is too strong to be successfully opposed. Every weaker passion will disappear before that love of liberty and law for which the American people are distinguished above all others in the world.

How far the duty of the President "to preserve, protect, and defend the Constitution" requires him to go in opposing an unconstitutional act of Congress is a very serious and important question, on which I have deliberated much and felt extremely anxious to reach a proper conclusion. Where an act has been passed according to the forms of the Constitution by the supreme legislative authority, and is regularly enrolled among the public statutes of the country, Executive resistance to it, especially in times of high party excitement, would be likely to produce violent collision between the respective adherents of the two branches of the Government. This would be simply civil war, and civil war must be resorted to only as the last remedy for the worst of evils. Whatever might tend to provoke it should be most carefully avoided. A faithful and conscientious magistrate will concede very much to honest error, and something even to perverse malice, before he will endanger the public peace; and he will not adopt forcible measures, or such as might lead to force, as long as those which are peaceable remain open to him or to his constituents. It is true that cases may occur in which the Executive would be compelled to stand on its rights, and maintain them regardless of all consequences. If Congress should pass an act which is not only in palpable conflict with the Constitution, but will certainly, if carried out, produce immediate and irreparable injury to the organic structure of the Government, and if there be neither judicial remedy for the wrongs it inflicts nor power in the people to protect themselves without the official aid of their elected defender—if, for instance, the legislative department should pass an act even through all the forms of law to abolish a coordinate department of the Government—in such a case the President must take the high responsibilities of his office and save the life of the nation at all hazards. The so-called reconstruction acts, though as plainly unconstitutional as any that can be imagined, were not believed to be within the class last mentioned. The people were not wholly disarmed of the power of self-defense. In all the Northern States they still held in their hands the sacred right of the ballot, and it was safe to believe that in due time they would come to the rescue of their own institutions. It gives me pleasure to add that the appeal to our common constituents was not taken in vain, and that my confidence in their wisdom and virtue seems not to have been misplaced.

# J. T. TROWBRIDGE, *A PICTURE OF THE DESOLATED STATES; AND THE WORK OF RESTORATION, 1865–1868* (1868)

The popular Northern writer John Townsend Trowbridge (1827–1916), author of the antislavery novel *Neighbor Jackwood* (1857), visited eight Southern states in mid-1865 and early 1866, recording his observations of places and conversations with a broad range of whites and blacks. He first summarized his findings in *The South: A Tour of Its Battlefields and Ruined Cities, a Journey Through the Desolated States, and Talks with the People* (1866) and two years later brought the story up-to-date in *A Picture of the Desolated States; and the Work of Restoration*. Trowbridge likened the condition of the South to "a man recovering from a dangerous malady: the crisis is past, appetite is boundless, and only sustenance and purifying air are needed to bring health and life in fresh waves." Much like *The Nation*'s proposal for solving the Indian problem, Trowbridge urged simply that justice be accorded all men. He predicted that Southern whites ultimately would accept black suffrage. Like social change across time and place, it too would take time.

. . . It now only remains for me to sum up briefly my answers to certain questions which are constantly put to me, regarding Southern emigration, the loyalty of the people, and the future of the country.

The South is in the condition of a man recovering from a dangerous malady: the crisis is past, appetite is boundless, and only sustenance and purifying air are needed to bring health and life in fresh waves. The exhausted country calls for supplies. It has been drained of its wealth, and of its young men. Capital is eagerly welcomed and absorbed. Labor is also needed. There is much shallow talk about getting rid of the negroes, and of filling their places with foreigners. But war and disease have already removed more of the colored race than can be well spared; and I am confident that, for the next five or ten years, leaving the blacks where they are, the strongest tide of emigration that can be poured into the country will be insufficient to meet the increasing demand for labor.

Northern enterprise, emancipation, improved modes of culture, and the high prices of cotton, rice, sugar, and tobacco, cannot fail to bring about this result. The cotton crop, if no accident happens to it, will this year reach, I am well satisfied, not less than two million bales, and bring something like two hundred and fifty million dollars, — as much as the five million bales of 1859 produced. Next year it will approximate to its old average standard in bulk, and greatly exceed it in value; and the year after we shall have the largest cotton crop ever known. Meanwhile the culture of rice and sugar will have fully revived, and become enormously profitable. Nor will planting alone flourish. Burned cities and plantation-buildings must be restored, new towns and villages will spring up, old losses must be repaired, and a thousand new wants supplied. Trade, manufactures, the mechanic arts, all are invited to share in this teeming activity.

Particular location the emigrant must select for himself, according to his own judgment, tastes, and means. Just now I should not advise Northern men to settle far back from the main routes of travel, unless they go in communities, purchasing and dividing large plantations, and forming societies independent of any hostile sentiment that may be shown by the native inhabitants. But I trust that in a year or two all danger of discomfort or disturbance arising from this source will have mostly passed by.

The loyalty of the people is generally of a negative sort: it is simply disloyalty subdued. They submit to the power which has mastered them, but they do not love it; nor is it reasonable to expect that they should. Many of them lately in rebellion, are, I think, honestly convinced that secession was a great mistake, and that the preservation of the Union, even with the loss of slavery, is better for them than any such separate government as that of which they had a bitter taste. Yet they do not feel much affection for the hand which corrected their error. They acquiesce quietly in what cannot be helped, and sincerely desire to make the best of their altered circumstances. . . .

Of another armed rebellion not the least apprehension need be entertained. The South has had enough of war for a long time to come; it has supped full of horrors. The habiliments of mourning, which one sees everywhere in its towns and cities, will cast their dark shadow upon any future attempt at secession, long after they have been put away in the silent wardrobes of the past. Only in the case of a foreign war might we expect to see a party of malignant malcontents go over to the side of the enemy. They would doubtless endeavor to drag their States with them, but they would not succeed. Fortunately those who are still so anxious to see the old issue fought out are not themselves fighting men, and are dangerous only with their tongues.

Of *unarmed* rebellion, of continued sectional strife, stirred up by Southern politicians, there exists very great danger. Their aims are distinct, and they command the sympathy of the Southern people. To obtain the exclusive control of the freedmen, and to make such laws for them as shall embody the prejudices of a late slave-holding society; to govern not only their own States, but to regain their forfeited leadership in the affairs of the nation; to effect the repudiation of the national debt, or to get the Confederate debt and the Rebel State debts assumed by the whole country; to secure payment for their slaves, and for all injuries and losses occasioned by the war; these are among the chief designs of a class who will pursue them with what recklessness and persistency we know.

How to prevent them from agitating the nation in the future as in the past, and from destroying its prosperity, is become the most serious of questions. If you succeed in capturing an antagonist who has made a murderous assault upon you, common sense, and a regard for your own safety and the peace of society, require at least that his weapons, or the power of using them, should be taken from him. These perilous schemes are the present weapons of the nation's conquered enemy; and does not prudent statesmanship demand that they should be laid forever at rest before he walks again at large in the pride of his power?

All that just and good men can ask, is this security. Vindictiveness, or a wish to hold the rebellious States under an iron rule, should have no place in our hearts. But if the blood of our brothers was shed in a righteous cause,—if for four years we poured out lives and treasures to purchase a reality, and no mere mockery and shadow,—let us honor our brothers and the cause by seeing that reality established. If treason is a crime surely it can receive no more fitting or merciful punishment than to be deprived of its power to do more mischief. Let peace, founded upon true principles, be the only retribution we demand. Let justice be our vengeance.

It was my original intention to speak of the various schemes of reconstruction claiming the consideration of the country. But they have become too numerous, and are generally too well known, to be detailed here. The Southern plan is simple; it is this: that the States, lately so eager to destroy the Union, are now entitled to all their former rights and privileges in that Union. Their haste to withdraw their representatives from Congress, is more than equalled by their anxiety to get them back in their seats. They consider it hard that, at the end of the most stupendous rebellion and the bloodiest civil war that ever shook the planet, they cannot quietly slip back in their places, and, the sword having failed, take up once more the sceptre of political power they so rashly flung down. Often, in conversation with candid Southern men, impatient for this result, I was able to convince them that it was hardly to be expected that the government, emerging victorious from the dust of such a struggle, and finding its foot on that sceptre, should take it off with very great alacrity. And they were forced to acknowledge that, had the South proved victorious, its enemies would not have escaped so easily.

This plan does not tolerate the impediment of any Congressional test oath. When I said to my Southern friends that I should be glad to see those representatives, who could take the test oath, admitted to Congress, this was the usual reply:—

"We would not vote for such men. We had rather have no representatives at all. We want representatives to *represent* us, and no man *represents* us who can take your test oath. We are Rebels, if you choose to call us so, and only a good Rebel can properly represent us."

This is the strongest argument I have heard against the admission of loyal Southern members to Congress. And if the white masses of the lately rebellious States are alone, and indiscriminately, to be recognized as the people of those States, it is certainly a valid argument.

"It is enough," they maintained, "that a representative in Congress takes the ordinary oath to support the government; *that* is a sufficient test of his loyalty;"—forgetting that, at the outbreak of the rebellion, this proved no test at all.

Such is the Southern plan of reconstruction. Opposed to it is the plan on which I believe a majority of the people of the loyal States are agreed, namely, that certain guaranties of future national tranquillity should be required of those who have caused so great a national convulsion. But as to what those guaranties should be, opinions are divided, and a hundred conflicting measures are proposed for the settlement of the difficulty.

For my own part, I see but one plain rule by which our troubles can be finally and satisfactorily adjusted; and that is, the enactment of simple justice for all men. Anything that falls short of this falls short of the solution of the problem.

The "Civil Rights Bill,"—enacted since the greater portion of these pages were written,—is a step in the direction in which this country is inevitably moving. The principles of the Declaration of Independence, supposed to be our starting-point in history, are in reality the goal towards which we are tending. Far in advance of our actual civilization, the pioneers of the Republic set up those shining pillars. Not until all men are equal before the law, and none is hindered from rising or from sinking by any impediment which does not exist in his own constitution and private circumstances, will that goal be reached.

Soon or late the next step is surely coming. That step is universal suffrage. It may be wise to make some moral or intellectual qualification a test of a man's fitness for the franchise; but anything which does not apply alike to all classes, and which all are not invited to attain, is inconsistent with the spirit of American nationality.

But will the Southern people ever submit to negro suffrage? They will submit to it quite as willingly as they submitted to negro emancipation. They fought against that as long as any power of resistance was in them; then they accepted it; they are now becoming reconciled to it; and soon they will rejoice over it. Such is always the history of progressive ideas. The first advance is opposed with all the might of the world until its triumph is achieved; then the world says, "Very well," and employs all its arts and energies to defeat the next movement, which triumphs and is finally welcomed in its turn.

At the close of the war, the South was ready to accept any terms which the victorious government might have seen fit to enforce. The ground was thoroughly broken; it was fresh from the harrow; and then was the time for the sowing of the new seed, before delay had given encouragement and opportunity to the old rank weeds. The States had practically dissolved their relations to the general government. Their chief men were traitors, their governors and legislators were entitled to no recognition, and a new class of free citizens, composing near half the population, had been created. If, in these changed circumstances, all the people of those States had been called upon to unite in restoring their respective governments, and their relations to the general government, we should have had a simple and easy solution of the main question at issue. Our allies on the battle-field would have become our allies at the ballot-box, and by doing justice to them we should have gained security for ourselves.

But are the lately emancipated blacks prepared for the franchise? They are, by all moral and intellectual qualifications, as well prepared for it as the mass of poor whites in the South. Although ignorant, they possess, as has been said, a strong instinct which stands them in the place of actual knowledge. That instinct inspires them with loyalty to the government, and it will never permit them to vote so unwisely and mischievously as the white people of the South voted in the days of secession. Moreover, there are among them men of fine intelligence and leading influence, by whom, and not by their old masters, as has been claimed, they will be instructed in their duty at the polls. And this fact is most certain,—that they are far better prepared to have a hand in making the laws by which they are to be governed, than the whites are to make those laws for them.

How this step is now to be brought about is not easy to

determine; and it may not be brought about for some time to come. In the mean while it is neither wise nor just to allow the representation of the Southern States in Congress to be increased by the emancipation of a race that has no voice in that representation; and some constitutional remedy against this evil is required. And in the mean while the protection of the government must be continued to the race to which its faith is pledged. Let us hope not long.

The present high price of cotton, and the extraordinary demand for labor, seem providential circumstances, designed to teach both races a great lesson. The freedmen are fast learning the responsibilities of their new situation, and gaining a position from which they cannot easily be displaced. Their eagerness to acquire knowledge is a bright sign of hope for their future. By degrees the dominant class must learn to respect those who, as chattels, could only be despised. Respect for labor rises with the condition of the laborer. The whites of the South are not by choice ignorant or unjust, but circumstances have made them so. Teach them that the laborer is a man, and that labor is manly,—a truth that is now dawning upon them,—and the necessity of mediation between the two races will no longer exist.

Then the institutions of the South will spontaneously assimilate to our own. Then we shall have a Union of States, not in form only, but in spirit also. Then shall we see established the reality of the cause that has cost so many priceless lives and such lavish outpouring of treasure. Then will disloyalty die of inanition, and its deeds live only in legend and in story. Then breaks upon America the morning glory of that future which shall behold it the Home of Man, and the Lawgiver among the nations.

# CORNELIA HANCOCK TO PHILADELPHIA FRIENDS ASSOCIATION FOR THE AID AND ELEVATION OF THE FREEDMEN

## (January 1868)

Cornelia Hancock (1840–1927), a New Jersey Quaker, first distinguished herself as a young Civil War nurse after the battle of Gettysburg. She then assisted displaced African-Americans at Washington, D.C.'s Contraband Hospital and worked as a nurse at City Point Hospital, Virginia. Following Appomattox, Hancock moved to South Carolina to care for the freedpeople, establishing, with support from the Freedmen's Bureau and donations from the Philadelphia Yearly Meeting of the Society of Friends, the Laing School for Negroes in Mount Pleasant, near Charleston. Writing in early 1868 to Philadelphia Friends, Hancock summarized the challenges and opportunities presented by teaching former slaves. Like many other reformers who worked in the South, she regretted that the freedpeople had not received land of their own to cultivate. Hancock considered education the key to uplifting the freedpeople—"the only systematic agency for permanent good."

Mount Pleasant, S. C., January 1868
Philadelphia Friends Association for the Aid and
Elevation of the Freedmen

Dear Friends

Thinking there may be some among you who still feel an interest in this far-off school, I will note what of interest has transpired since our return.

The school was opened the First of Eleventh month, and continued until the Holidays. New Year's, or "Emancipation Day," was selected for our anniversary. This seems to me a more fitting time and a more important anniversary than Christmas. Our new school-house was found exceedingly convenient for the occasion, as we could have the grown people too. They repeated the 23rd Psalm and sung two hymns, when the work of distributing was commenced, the generosity of individuals supplying the materials. (It may be well once more to remark that the funds of the Association are never encroached on for these celebrations.) They choose their presents according to their standing in their classes, which we ascertain by keeping a record of marks.

As such anniversaries come round, I always try to note the progress of civilization among these children. In raising any community from the depths of degradation that slavery produces, we cannot expect them to abandon all their old habits, and adopt the customs of cultivated people in a day; so I try to look for changes to take place in years.

And surely great changes have taken place with these children. No one ought to feel discouraged in looking forward to their future, although they have yet no elevating or educating *home* influences, which will, of course, operate much against them in this generation. They have the lessons of extreme poverty and much oppression yet to suffer. The depressed state of business in the South makes it very hard for them to get employment at remunerative rates; and the dense ignorance existing in the grown people's minds makes it extremely difficult for them to settle upon any business that requires forethought or calculation. This affects their interest very much in settling upon land.

Their chief anxiety is to get possession of land; and a very common contract here is to give them possession of land for *two years*, for the sake of clearing. This they accept, and it invariably proves a good bargain for the planter, and a poor one for the colored man. You cannot reason with them, as you could were they possessed of educated intelligence; for anything that is to occur in two years is almost beyond their reckoning. The care the planter extended to them in slavery developed this improvidence for the future, and the present is a much more important time for them than any other. How I wish the Government had apportioned them some confiscated land at the close of the war. Had that been done, by this time thrifty little farms would have been the result; but now they live two years in a place until the land becomes productive, when the planter takes possession again, and another two years' labor must be commenced that will end the same. I hope yet for some liberal legislation, either through General or State Governments; but let what will be done now, —much time has been lost.

I consider the *schools* have been the only systematic agency for permanent good, and I hope every contributor to their support may have the feeling that the money has not been wasted. An *education bill* is being passed in this State, that, during another year, may get into working order, so as to relieve our friends from the support of this school; but I hope *this school year* may be continued under their auspices, so as to make no break in the continuous training of these children. Some of our best scholars have left this place to live in Charleston, and they have been sufficiently advanced to enter the best classes of the schools in that city. So our school must have kept pace with theirs. We re-opened the schools at the beginning of the new year, and the cotton season being past, they were large, and have continued with a good average. Our unfinished building is being gradually brought nearer to completion. Friends at Kennett Square, through Dr. Mendenhall and H. Darlington, have furnished Mary P. Jacobs with funds to put a good ceiling upon the large room up stairs, and Fanny E. Gauze, with the aid of relatives and friends, has much improved the condition of hers. My contributions have put our classroom in complete school order with black-boards all round the room, etc.; so I feel quite contented with its present appearance, although we still need books. Your school at Rickersville, which Isabella Lenair teaches, has been prosperous, and has given great satisfaction to that neighborhood. The *Sewing School* is of great interest to me still; it is now open every afternoon, and the children are improving rapidly. Several girls have determined to make dresses. We have tried to make the school pay something, by taking in sewing; and some weeks our dividends have gone up as high as *seventeen cents each*. That may not sound large in the *North*, but seventeen cents cash is hard to earn here.

In closing, I desire that *Friends* will support this school *this year out*. Then, if the caterpillars do not attack their crops another year, we will try to get along without their aid, though retaining grateful hearts to them for their help in times of great need, and believing that *they* must feel a consciousness of having done a great work for this community. Personally thanking all who have facilitated my labors here,

I am sincerely their friend,
Cornelia Hancock

# Francis L. Cardozo, "Break Up the Plantation System"

## (January 14, 1868)

The freeborn, biracial son of a prominent white Charlestonian and a free black woman, Francis Louis Cardozo (1837–1903) ranked as one of South Carolina's most distinguished and influential black leaders during Reconstruction. Educated in Glasgow and London, upon returning to the U.S., he worked as a minister, educator, and politician, also serving as South Carolina's secretary of state (1868–1872) and state treasurer (1872–1877). He was South Carolina's first African-American to hold government office. Elected as a delegate to the state's 1868 constitutional convention, Cardozo proposed the sale and partition of large, debt-ridden plantations in order to provide family farms for poor people broadly defined, both black and white.

In discussing this measure, I would say to the gentleman who preceded me, and those who will follow, that they will accomplish their object much sooner and with much more satisfaction by not impugning the motives of those with whom they differ. The gentleman who spoke last made gratuitous assumptions and ascribed mercenary motives that, were it not for personal friendship, might be retorted upon him with perhaps worse effect than he made them. He asserted that the gentlemen who opposed him opposed his race. I intend to show that his race is not at all connected with the matter. In giving my view of the measure, I shall not resort to mere declamations or appeals to passion or prejudice. In the first place, I doubt its legality. It is true, it is said the Convention does not propose to legislate, but I contend that a request from this body carries a certain moral influence. It shows what it would do if it had the power. It is virtually legislation. I regard any stay law as unjust and unconstitutional. It is unjust to the creditors. Let every man who contracts a debt, pay it. If he is an honest man he will pay his debts at any sacrifice. In our country it is unfortunate, as Americans, that we have a character by no means enviable as repudiators. Look at the attempt to repudiate the national debt. As an American, I protest against any further repudiation whatever, either in the form of a stay law or illegal legislation. I deem it inappropriate for us to touch the matter at all. We are sent here to form a Constitution. To travel outside of our proper province will probably be to incur odium, displeasure and dissatisfaction. I wish to confine the action of this Convention to its proper sphere. The first question that arises is, what claim have these debtors on our sympathies more than creditors? Are the debtors greater in number than creditors? If we legislate in favor of any, will it be doing the greatest good to the greatest number? I maintain it will not. It is a class measure. This will be but the beginning. We will be burdened with applications, and the burden will be upon those who introduced this measure, not upon those who refused to legislate for other special favorite classes. I ask not only what are the claims of the debtors, but also what are the nature of these sales? Was it the transfer of real estate? I think everyone here will say no. Nine tenths of the debts were contracted for the sale of slaves. I do not wish we should go one inch out of the way to legislate either for the buyer or seller. They dealt in that kind of property, they knew its precarious tenure, and therefore let them suffer. When the war commenced every rebel sold his property to give money to a common cause. And their slaves were sold for the same object, to maintain a war waged for the purpose of perpetually enslaving a people. That was the object. The ladies of the South stripped themselves of their jewels, and the men sold their lands and their slaves for that object. Now, let them suffer for it. As the gentleman from Charleston very ably said, "they have cast the die, let them take the chances."

There is also another reason, and one of the strongest, why the Convention should not take any action on the subject, but postpone it indefinitely. One of the greatest bulwarks of slavery was the infernal plantation system, one man owning his thousand, another his twenty, and another fifty thousand acres of land. This is the only way by which we will break up that system, and I maintain that our freedom will be of no effect if we allow it to continue. What is the main cause of the prosperity of the North? It is because every man has his own farm and is free and independent. Let the lands of the South be similarly divided. I would not say for one moment they should be confiscated, but if sold to maintain the war, now that slavery is destroyed, let the plantation system go with it. We will never have true freedom until we abolish the system of agriculture which existed in the Southern states. It is useless to have any schools while we maintain this stronghold of slavery as the agricultural system of the country. The gentleman has said that if these plantations were sold now, they would pass into the hands of a few mercenary speculators. I deny it and challenge a single proof to sustain the assertion. On the contrary I challenge proof to show that if the plantations are not sold, the old plantation masters will part with them. If they are sold, though a few mercenary speculators may purchase some, the chances are that the colored man and the poor man would be the purchasers. I will prove this, not by mere assertion, but by facts. About one hundred poor colored men of Charleston met together and formed themselves into a Charleston Land Company. They subscribed for a number of shares at $10 per share, one dollar payable monthly. They have been meeting for a year. Yesterday they purchased six hundred acres of land for $6,600 that would have sold for $25,000 or $50,000 in better times. They would not have been able to buy it had not the owner through necessity been compelled to sell. This is only one instance of thousands of others that have occurred in this city and state. I look upon it, therefore, as the natural result of the war that this system of large plantations, of no service to the owner or anybody else, should be abolished.

I think Providence has not only smiled upon every effort for abolishing this hideous form of slavery, but that since the war it has given unmistakable signs of disapprobation wherever continued, by blasting the cotton crops in that part of the country. Men are now beginning not to plant cotton but grain for food, and in doing so they are establishing a system of small farms, by which not only my race, but the poor whites and ninety-nine hundredths of the other thousands will be benefited. The real benefit from this legislation would inhere to not more than thirty thousand landholders against the seven hundred thousand poor people of the State. If we are to legislate in favor of a class at all, any honest man, any man who has the interest of the people at heart will legislate in favor of the greater number. In speaking against the landholders, and in taking this position I do not cherish one feeling of enmity against them as a class or individuals. But this question takes a larger range and is one in which the whole country is involved. I can never sacrifice the interests of nine or ten millions to the interests of three hundred thousand, more especially when the three hundred thousand initiated the war and were the very ones who established an infernal Negro code and want to keep their·lands until better times. They do not want that a nigger or a Yankee shall ever own a foot of their land. Now is the time to take the advantage. Give them an opportunity, breathing time, and they will reorganize the same old system they had before the war. I say then, just as General Grant said when he had Lee hemmed in around Petersburg, now is the time to strike, and in doing so we will strike for our people and posterity, and the truest interest of our country.

# "THE IMPEACHMENT," NEW
# YORK TIMES

## (February 24, 1868)

Though steps to impeach President Johnson failed
in December 1867, efforts in the House of Representatives to remove him from office resumed in
February when he again defied the Tenure of Office Act by dismissing Secretary of War Edwin M.
Stanton (1814–1869). Johnson appointed General
Lorenzo Thomas (1804–1875), adjutant general
of the army, Secretary of War ad interim. The *New
York Times* concurred with House Republicans
that Johnson had defiantly violated the law but
pointed out that he had done so intentionally to
test its constitutionality. The U.S. Supreme Court,
the newspaper maintained, not the U.S. Senate,
was the appropriate venue to determine whether
Johnson had acted unconstitutionally.

The Republican Party in Congress seems at last to be unanimous in favor of impeachment. Those who have hitherto
been most conservative in this matter seem now most zealous and demonstrative on the other side. There can be very
little doubt that the President will be impeached by the
House and sent before the Senate for trial—the specific
misdemeanor for which he is arraigned being the violation
of the Tenure of Office Law, in the removal of Secretary
STANTON and the appointment of Gen. [Lorenzo]
THOMAS in his place ad interim.

There can be no doubt, we presume, that the President's
action is in violation of the law. The first section declares
that "every person holding any civil office to which he has
been appointed by and with the advice and consent of the
Senate, is and shall be entitled to hold such office until a
successor shall have been *in like manner* appointed and
duly qualified." This clause deprives the President of the
power to remove any such officer without the consent of
the Senate. The second section gives him the power to sus-

pend officers "during the recess of the Senate" until its next meeting and for one month thereafter, under certain specified circumstances, and to fill vacancies in the same way and upon the same conditions. . . .

The President's removal of Mr. STANTON and his appointment of Gen. THOMAS were in distinct and unmistakable defiance of these provisions of that law. It is also clear that this violation of the law has been *intentional* on the President's part—not with a view, as the heated zealots of Congress assume, of usurping power and overthrowing the institutions of the country, but for the purpose of *testing the constitutionality of the law,* and of procuring a judicial definition of the limits and prerogatives of the Executive Department of the Government under the Constitution of the United States. . . .

He is not only entitled to such a decision, but the whole country is interested in having it given. Under our form of government, as under every form of government which has been or can be devised, doubts will arrive as to the proper distribution of authority and power. We have, unlike Governments of a different form, a written Constitution by which the limits of official authority are defined, and the powers and prerogatives of the several departments of the Government are described and conferred; and, consequently, the only controversies that can arise out of attempts on the part of one department to encroach on the jurisdiction of another, become questions of construction. . . .

There can be no doubt, we presume, in any one's mind, that the Supreme Court is the proper tribunal for the decision of the question involved in this particular conflict between the President and Congress. . . .

The impeachment of the President, if pushed to trial in advance of such a decision by the Supreme Court, is in violation of this principle.

# S. A. ATKINSON, "THE SUPREME HOUR HAS COME"

## *(March 13, 1868)*

In 1868 the Southern states held elections to approve the new state constitutions mandated by the Reconstruction Act. Georgia's delegates drafted a new document enfranchising the freedmen, establishing a free public school system, and instituting a system of debt relief. Responding to the state's proposed new basic law, editor S. A. Atkinson of the pro-Democratic weekly *Athens Southern Banner* urged Georgians to defeat the constitution in the April referendum because, in his opinion, it would surrender control of the state to "a negro oligarchy." Georgians ultimately ratified the constitution and the Fourteenth Amendment, and in July 1868, Congress readmitted the state to the Union. In December 1869, however, when the General Assembly expelled its black legislators and refused to enforce the Fourteenth Amendment, Congress remanded Georgia to military rule. Not until July 1870, after its African-American legislators took their seats and the state ratified the Fifteenth Amendment (passed February 26, 1869), did Congress finally restore Georgia to the Union.

Radicalism has so far advanced in its infamous work as to call for the full exercise of every energy that can be enlisted in its defeat. The purpose of that abandoned and shameless organization to control the political destinies of the state by an alliance with negroes and Northern adventurers is too manifest not to be seen and scorned by every just right-minded citizen. . . .

Every white man should gird on the armor for a good fight with the hydra-headed monster which assails civil liberty. If the Constitution framed by the Radical Convention is adopted we do sincerely believe that the State will be controlled by the negroes as certainly as though every whiteman [*sic*] in the State were disfranchised. One hundred thousand men, voting as a unit, cannot fail to attract to their embrace a large element of abandoned wretches, like many of those in the Convention, who could never make a sign among decent white men. We believe also, that the adoption of this hell-born conspiracy against the white race, must result in violence and strife, if not in the extermination of either the white or black race from the State. Two races, so nearly equal in numbers, never have lived in a free government on terms of peaceful equality. We value the well being of the black race too much to willingly see them deluded into a conflict which cannot fail to be fatal to them, as well as, fearful for the whites. We value the peace of society too much to be silent when a heaving earth quake is about to belch forth its horrid fires upon us. We shall therefore enter upon the great canvas with every energy enlisted—every impulse aroused, and we hope to have the active aid of every white man, and every prudent and sensible black man in this portion of the State. We have no object to observe but the good of society.

Already the Radical papers are being circulated in every neighborhood, full of ingenious appeals in support of the monstrous frauds embraced in the new constitution. Let the county committees see to it that Democratic papers are sent to counteract the poison instilled by these Convention organs. Let those who need relief be shown that the method proposed is a cheat and a swindle, and cannot stand. Let it be shown that with 100,000 negroes at the ballot box, the white men of Upper Georgia forever lose the control of the State which their numbers have long commanded; and that this populous section becomes but a province, an appendage, of a negro oligarchy.

We appeal to our readers to wake up to the magnitude of the struggle before us. It is no common issue—or ordinary campaign, involving only a choice of individuals. It is the crisis of liberty. Let us meet it like the sons of the fathers of freedom—like honest men, who value honor, integrity, and justice, beyond the glitterized bribe of political power, or the tempting chances of pecuniary advantage.

# "Karinus," Letter to the Editor—"Equal Suffrage in Michigan"

## (March 17, 1868)

Racial proscription during the era of the Civil War and Reconstruction was not limited to the Southern states, a fact emphasized by Southern and Northern critics of Radical Reconstruction. Repeatedly referendums in Northern states on enfranchising their relatively small African-American male populations failed to pass. In this letter to the editor of a Michigan newspaper, "Karinus" noted the hypocrisy of Northerners, especially Republicans, who riveted universal suffrage on the South but refused to accept black enfranchisement in their own states.

Occasionally we hear an avowed Republican proclaim his aversion to the clause in our new constitution granting the elective franchise to the colored freedmen of the State. Of these we would simply ask, are they Republicans from principle? Are they, in pursuance of that principle, supporters of the reconstruction policy of the Government? If they are supporters of the policies of the government, which is but the principle of justice, upon what principle do they justify their opposition to Equal Suffrage in Michigan? It is much more difficult for a professed Republican to assign a cogent reason for such a position than for the "Democracy. . . ." But because of the patriotic tendencies of the negro, in late years, the democracy regard him as a "degenerated son of noble ancestry," and refuse him fraternal fellowship. None of these causes, however, should control the sentiment of Republicans. The Republican and the negro, when Democracy inaugurates treason and rebellion, fight a common battle for a common cause. . . . Shall Michigan, then, who has so nobly stood by the policies of the government, contradict and stultify herself by refusing to do in her own dominion what she has commanded Congress to do for the whole domain? Shall they contravene every vote given by our Senators and Representatives in Congress, who were elected by the same people to represent the same principle in Congress that they are called upon to enforce in their own State next Spring? . . . We are at a loss to account for this sudden retrogration from the magnanimous standard of the fathers of the republic, which is meant to be the rule and guide of modern Republicanism. All the State constitutions adopted after the declaration of Independence up to 1792, except South Carolina, extended the right of franchise to legal voters irrespective of color. None of the alarming consequences grew out of that prerogative in those days which are predicted as being the result of a like prerogative at this time. . . . In view of these antecedents it is very difficult to account for the seemingly unhappy instinct which move men of late to curse a nigger. Whatever may have been the modernly progressive tendency of things in reference to art and science, it seems to have been terribly retrogressive in regard to prejudices among races. . . . It is reduced simply to the fact that the negro, as a general thing, will vote the Republican ticket. Shall it be then, that for this offence the Democracy shall deprive the freedman of his vote, by the aid of renegade, unreliable Republicans? We shall see.

# "This Little Boy Would Persist in Handling Books Above His Capacity"

### (March 21, 1868)

This two-panel wood engraving appeared in *Harper's Weekly* eight days before Andrew Johnson's impeachment trial opened. The cartoon depicts Johnson atop a stepladder reaching for the U.S. Constitution, only to be flattened by the weight of the heavy tome. Though the House of Representatives impeached Johnson on eleven articles, the Senate vote dashed the cartoonist's wishful thinking. It acquitted Johnson by one vote on May 16.

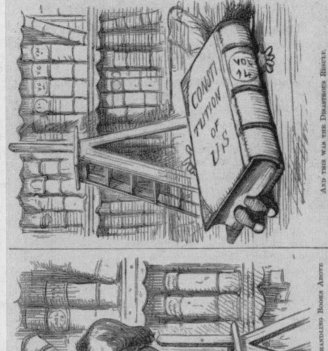

THIS LITTLE BOY WOULD PERSIST IN HANDLING BOOKS ABOVE HIS CAPACITY.

AND THIS WAS THE DISASTROUS RESULT.

# THADDEUS STEVENS, "SPEECH ON IMPEACHMENT TRIAL OF ANDREW JOHNSON"

## *(April 27, 1868)*

As an author of both the Reconstruction and Tenure of Office Acts, and as Johnson's most acerbic and vocal critic, Stevens, not surprisingly, led the move to impeach the president for alleged high crimes and misdemeanors. He wrote one of the articles of impeachment, reported the charges of impeachment to the Senate, and served on the board of managers that prosecuted the case. In his April 27, 1868, speech Stevens charged Johnson with repeatedly violating the Constitution by exceeding his prerogatives, breaking various laws and, at a crucial period in the nation's history, overturning the workings of the government.

. . . When Andrew Johnson took upon himself the duties of his high office he swore to obey the Constitution and take care that the laws be faithfully executed. That, indeed, is and has always been the chief duty of the President of the United States. The duties of legislation and adjudicating the laws of his country fall in no way to his lot. To obey the commands of the sovereign power of the nation, and to see that others should obey them, was his whole duty—a duty which he could not escape, and any attempt to do so would be in direct violation of his official oath; in other words, a *misprision of perjury*.

I accuse him, in the name of the House of Representatives, of having perpetrated that foul offense against the laws and interests of his country.

On the 2d day of March, 1867, Congress passed a law, over the veto of the President, entitled "An act to regulate the tenure of certain civil offices," the first section of which is as follows:

"*Be it enacted by the Senate and House of Representatives of the United States of America in Congress assembled*, That every person holding any civil office to which he has been appointed by and with the advice and consent of the Senate, and every person who may hereafter be appointed to any such office and shall become duly qualified to act therein, is and shall be entitled to hold such office until a successor shall have been in like manner appointed and duly qualified, except as herein otherwise provided: *Provided*, That the Secretaries of State, of the Treasury, of War, of the Navy, and of the Interior, the Postmaster General, and the Attorney General, shall hold their offices respectively for and during the term of the President by whom they may have been appointed, and for one month thereafter, subject to removal by and with the advice and consent of the Senate."

The second section provides that when the Senate is not in session, if the President shall deem the officer guilty of acts which require his removal or suspension, he may be suspended until the next meeting of the Senate; and that within twenty days after the meeting of the Senate the reasons for such suspension shall be reported to that body; and, if the Senate shall deem such reasons sufficient for such suspension or removal, the officer shall be considered removed from his office; but if the Senate shall not deem the reasons sufficient for such suspension or removal, the officer shall forthwith resume the functions of his office, and the person appointed in his place shall cease to discharge such duties.

On the 12th day of August, 1867, the Senate then not being in session, the President suspended Edwin M. Stanton, Secretary of the Department of War, and appointed U. S. Grant, General, Secretary of War *ad interim*. On the 12th day of December, 1867, the Senate being then in session, he reported, according to the requirements of the act, the causes of such suspension to the Senate, which duly took the same into consideration. Before the Senate had concluded its examination of the question of the sufficiency of such reasons he attempted to enter into arrangements by which he might obstruct the due execution of the law, and thus prevent Edwin M. Stanton from forthwith resuming the functions of his office as Secretary of War, according to the provisions of the act, even if the Senate should decide in his favor.

And in furtherance of said attempt, on the 21st day of February, 1868, he appointed one Lorenzo Thomas, by letter of authority or commission, Secretary of War *ad interim,* without the advice and consent of the Senate, although the same was then in session, and ordered him (the said Thomas) to take possession of the Department of War and the public property appertaining thereto, and to discharge the duties thereof.

We charge that, in defiance of frequent warnings, he has since repeatedly attempted to carry those orders into execution, and to prevent Edwin M. Stanton from executing the laws appertaining to the Department of War and from discharging the duties of the office. . . .

In impeachments, more than in indictments, the averring of the fact charged carries with it all that it is necessary to say about intent. In indictments you charge that the defendant, "instigated by the devil," and so on; and you might as well call on the prosecution to prove the presence, shape, and color of his majesty, as to call upon the managers in impeachment to prove intention. I go further than some, and contend—that no corrupt or wicked motive need instigate the acts for which impeachment is brought. It is enough that they were official violations of law. The counsel have placed great stress upon the necessity of proving that they were wilfully done. If by that he means that they were voluntarily done I agree with him. A mere accidental trespass would not be sufficient to convict. But that which is *voluntarily* done is *wilfully* done, according to every honest definition; and whatever malfeasance is willingly perpetrated by an office-holder is a misdemeanor in office, whatever he may allege was his intention.

The President justifies himself by asserting that all previous Presidents had exercised the same right of removing officers, for cause to be judged of by the President alone. Had there been no law to prohibit it when Mr. Stanton was removed the cases would have been parallel, and the one might be adduced as an argument in favor of the other. But, since the action of any of the Presidents to which he refers, a law had been passed by Congress, after a stubborn controversy with the Executive, denying that right and prohibiting it in future, and imposing a severe penalty upon any executive officer who should exercise it; and that, too, after the President had himself made issue on its constitutionality and been defeated. No pretext, therefore, any longer existed that such right was vested in the President by virtue of his office. Hence the attempt to shield himself under such practice is a most lame evasion of the question at issue. Did he "take care that this law should be faithfully" executed? He answers that acts that would have violated the law, had it existed, were practiced by his predecessors. How does that justify his own malfeasance?

The President says that he removed Mr. Stanton simply to test the constitutionality of the tenure-of-office law by a judicial decision. He has already seen it tested and decided by the votes, twice given, of two-thirds of the Senators and of the House of Representatives. It stood as a law upon the statute-books. No case had arisen under that law, or is referred to by the President, which required any judicial interposition. If there had been, or should be, the courts were open to any one who felt aggrieved by the action of Mr. Stanton. But instead of enforcing that law he takes advantage of the name and the funds of the United States to resist it, and to induce others to resist it. Instead of attempting, as the Executive of the United States, to see that that law was faithfully executed, he took great pains and perpetrated the acts alleged in this article, not only to resist it himself, but to seduce others to do the same. He sought to induce the General-in-Chief of the Army to aid him in an open, avowed obstruction of the law as it stood unrepealed upon the statute-book. He could find no one to unite with him in perpetrating such an act until he sunk down upon the unfortunate individual bearing the title of Adjutant General of the Army. Is this taking care that the laws shall be faithfully executed? Is this attempting to carry them into effect, by upholding their validity, according to his oath? On the other hand, was it not a high and bold attempt to obstruct the laws and take care that they should not be executed? He must not excuse himself by saying that he had doubts of its constitutionality and wished to test it. What right had he to be hunting up excuses for others, as well as himself, to violate this law? Is not this confession a misdemeanor in itself?

The President asserts that he did not remove Stanton under the tenure-of-office law. This is a direct contradiction of his own letter to the Secretary of the Treasury [*Hugh McCulloch*], in which, as he was bound by law, he communicated to that officer the fact of the removal. This portion of the answer may, therefore, be considered as disposed of by the non-existence of the fact, as well as by his subsequent report to the Senate.

The following is the letter just alluded to, dated August 14, 1867:

> SIR: In compliance with the requirements of the act entitled "An act to regulate the tenure of certain civil offices," you are hereby notified that on the 12th instant Hon. Edwin M. Stanton was suspended from his office as Secretary of War, and General U. S. Grant authorized and empowered to act as Secretary *ad interim*.
>
> Hon. Secretary of the Treasury.

Wretched man! A direct contradiction of his solemn answer! How necessary that a man should have a good conscience or a good memory! Both would not be out of place. How lovely to contemplate what was so assiduously inculcated by a celebrated pagan into the mind of his son: "Virtue is truth, and truth is virtue." And still more, virtue of every kind charms us, yet that virtue is strongest which is effected by justice and generosity. Good deeds will never be done, wise acts will never be executed, except by the virtuous and the conscientious.

May the good people of this Republic remember this good old doctrine when they next meet to select their rulers, and may they select only the brave and the virtuous.

Has it been proved, as charged in this article, that Andrew Johnson in vacation suspended from office Edwin M. Stanton, who had been duly appointed and was then executing the duties of Secretary of the Department of War, without the advice and consent of the Senate; did he report the reasons for such suspension to the Senate within twenty days from the meeting of the Senate; and did the Senate proceed to consider the sufficiency of such reasons? Did the Senate declare such reasons insufficient, whereby the said Edwin M. Stanton became authorized to forthwith resume and exercise the functions of Secretary of War, and displace the Secretary *ad interim*, whose duties were then to cease and terminate; did the said Andrew Johnson, in his official character of President of the United States, attempt to obstruct the return of the said Edwin M. Stanton and his resumption forthwith of the functions of his office as Secretary of the Department of War; and has he continued to attempt to prevent the discharge of the duties of said office by said Edwin M. Stanton, Secretary of War, notwithstanding the Senate decided in his favor? If he has, then the acts in violation of law, charged in this article, are full and complete. . . .

That charge is, that the President did attempt to prevent the due execution of the tenure-of-office law by entangling the General in the arrangement; and unless both the President and the General have lost their memory and mistaken the truth with regard to the promises with each other, then this charge is made out. In short, if either of these gentlemen has correctly stated these facts of attempting the obstruction of the law the President has been guilty of violating the law and of *misprision of official perjury*.

But, again, the President alleges his right to violate the act regulating the tenure of certain civil offices, because, he says, the same was inoperative and void as being in violation of the Constitution of the United States. Does it lie in his mouth to interpose this plea? He had acted under that law and issued letters of authority, both for the long and short term, to several persons under it, and it would hardly lie in his mouth after that to deny its validity unless he confessed himself guilty of law-breaking by issuing such commissions.

Let us here look at Andrew Johnson accepting the oath "to take care that the laws be faithfully executed."

On the 2d of March, 1867, he returned to the Senate the "tenure-of-office bill"—where it originated and had passed by a majority of more than two thirds—with reasons elaborately given why it should not pass finally. Among these was the allegation of its unconstitutionality. It passed by a vote of 35 yeas to 11 nays. In the House of Representatives it passed by more than two-thirds majority; and when the vote was announced the Speaker, as was his custom, proclaimed the vote, and declared in the language of the Constitution, "that two-thirds of each house having voted for it, notwithstanding the objections of the President, it has become a law."

I am supposing that Andrew Johnson was at this moment waiting to take the oath of office, as President of the United States, "that he would obey the Constitution and take care that the laws be faithfully executed." Having been sworn on the Holy Evangels to obey the Constitution, and being about to depart, he turns to the person administering the oath and says, "Stop; I have a further oath. I do solemnly swear that I will not allow the act entitled 'An act regulating the tenure of certain civil offices,' just passed by Congress over the presidential veto, to be executed; but I will prevent its execution by virtue of my own constitutional power."

How shocked Congress would have been—what would the country have said to a scene equaled only by the unparalleled action of this same official, when sworn into office on that fatal 5th day of March which made him the successor of Abraham Lincoln! Certainly he would not have been permitted to be inaugurated as Vice-President or President. Yet such in effect has been his conduct, if not under oath at least with less excuse, since the fatal day which inflicted him upon the people of the United States. Can the President hope to escape if the fact of his violating that law be proved or confessed by him, as has been done? Can he expect a sufficient number of his triers to pronounce that law unconstitutional and void—those same triers having passed upon its validity upon several occasions? . . .

I have now discussed but one of the numerous articles, all of which I believe to be fully sustained, and few of the almost innumerable offenses charged to this wayward, unhappy official. I have alluded to two or three others which I could have wished to have had time to present and discuss, not for the sake of punishment, but for the benefit of the country. One of these was an article charging the President with usurping the legislative power of the nation, and attempting still his usurpations.

With regard to usurpation, one single word will explain my meaning. A civil war of gigantic proportions, covering sufficient territory to constitute many States and nations, broke out, and embraced more than ten millions of men, who formed an independent government, called the Confederate States of America. They rose to the dignity of an independent belligerent, and were so acknowledged by all civilized nations, as well as by ourselves. After expensive and bloody strife we conquered them, and they submitted to our arms. By the law of nations, well understood and undisputed, the conquerors in this unjust war had the right to deal with the vanquished as to them might seem good, subject only to the laws of humanity. They had a right to confiscate their property to the extent of indemnifying themselves and their citizens; to annex them to the victorious nation, and pass just such laws for their government as they might think proper.

This doctrine is as old as Grotius and as fresh as the Dorr rebellion. Neither the President nor the judiciary had any right to interfere, to dictate any terms, or to aid in reconstruction further than they were directed by the sovereign power. That sovereign power in this republic is the Congress of the United States. Whoever, besides Congress, undertakes to create new States or to rebuild old ones, and fix the condition of their citizenship and union, usurps powers which do not belong to him, and is dangerous or not dangerous, according to the extent of his power and his pretensions. Andrew Johnson did usurp the legislative power of the nation by building new States, and reconstructing, as far as in him lay, this empire. He directed the defunct States to come forth and live by virtue of his breathing into their nostrils the breath of life. He directed them what constitutions to form, and fixed the qualifications of electors and of office-holders. He directed them to send forward members to each branch of Congress, and to aid him in representing the nation. When Congress passed a law declaring all these doings unconstitutional and fixed a mode for the admission of this new territory into the nation he proclaimed it unconstitutional, and advised the people not to submit to it nor to obey the commands of Congress. I have not time to enumerate the particular acts which constitute his high-handed usurpations. Suffice it to say that he seized all the powers of the government within these States, and, had he been permitted, would have become their absolute ruler. This he persevered in attempting notwithstanding Congress declared more than once all the governments which he thus created to be void and of none effect.

But I promised to be brief, and must abide by the promise, although I should like the judgment of the Senate upon this, to me, seeming vital phase and real purpose of all his misdemeanors. To me this seems a sublime spectacle. A nation, not free, but as nearly approaching it as human institutions will permit of, consisting of thirty millions of people, had fallen into conflict, which among other people always ends in anarchy or despotism, and had laid down their arms, the mutineers submitting to the conquerors. The laws were about to regain their accustomed sway, and again to govern the nation by the punishment of treason and the reward of virtue. Her old institutions were about to be reinstated so far as they were applicable, according to the judgment of the conquerors. Then one of their inferior servants, instigated by unholy ambition, sought to seize a portion of the territory according to the fashion of neighboring anarchies, and to convert a land of freedom into a land of slaves. This people spurned the traitors, and have put the chief of them upon his trial, and demand judgment upon his misconduct. He will be condemned, and his sentence inflicted without turmoil, tumult, or bloodshed, and the nation will continue its accustomed course of freedom and prosperity without the shedding any further of human blood and with a milder punishment than the world has been accustomed to see, or perhaps than ought now to be inflicted.

Now, even if the pretext of the President were true and not a mere subterfuge to justify the chief act of violation with which he stands charged, still that would be such an abuse of the patronage of the Government as would demand his impeachment for a high misdemeanor. Let us again for a moment examine into some of the circumstances of that act. Mr. Stanton was appointed Secretary of War by Mr. Lincoln in 1862, and continued to hold under Mr. Johnson, which, by all usage, is considered a reappointment. Was he a faithful officer, or was he removed for corrupt purposes? After the death of Mr. Lincoln, Andrew Johnson had changed his whole code of politics and policy, and instead of obeying the will of those who put him into power he determined to create a party for himself to carry out his own ambitious purposes. For every honest purpose of Government, and for every honest purpose for which Mr. Stanton was appointed by Mr. Lincoln, where could a better man be found? None ever organized an army of a million of men and provided for its subsistence and efficient action more rapidly than Mr. Stanton and his predecessor [*Simon Cameron*].

It might, with more propriety, be said of this officer than of the celebrated Frenchman, that he "organized victory." He raised and by his requisitions distributed more than a billion dollars annually, without ever having been charged or suspected with the malappropriation of a single dollar; and when victory crowned his efforts he disbanded that immense Army as quietly and peacefully as if it had been a summer parade. He would not, I suppose, adopt the personal views of the President; and for this he was suspended until restored by the emphatic verdict of the Senate. Now, if we are right in our narrative of the conduct of these parties and the motives of the President, the very effort at removal was a high-handed usurpation as well as a corrupt misdemeanor for which of itself he ought to be impeached and thrown from the place he was abusing. But he says that he did not remove Mr. Stanton for the purpose of defeating the tenure-of-office law. Then he forgot the truth in his controversy with the General of the Army. And because the General did not aid him, and finally admit that he had agreed to aid him in resisting that law, he railed upon him like a very drab.

The counsel for the respondent allege that no removal of Mr. Stanton ever took place, and that therefore the sixth section of the act was not violated. They admit that there was an order of removal and a rescission of his commission; but as he did not obey it, they say it was no removal. That suggests the old saying that it used to be thought that "when the brains were out the man was dead." That idea is proved by learned counsel to be absolutely fallacious. The brain of Mr. Stanton's commission was taken out by the order of removal—the rescission of his commission—and his head was absolutely cut off by that gallant soldier, General Thomas, the night after the masquerade. And yet, according to the learned and delicate counsel, until the mortal remains, everything which could putrefy, was shovelled out and hauled into the muck-yard there was no removal. But it is said that this took place merely as an experiment to make a judicial case. Now, suppose there is anybody who, with the facts before him, can believe that this was not an afterthought, let us see if that palliates the offense.

The President is sworn to take care that the laws be faithfully executed. In what part of the Constitution or laws does he find it to be his duty to search out for defective laws that stand recorded upon the statutes in order that he may advise their infraction? Who was aggrieved by the tenure-of-office bill that he was authorized to use the name and the funds of the government to relieve? Will he be so good as to tell us by what authority he became the obstructor of an unrepealed law instead of its executor, especially a law whose constitutionality he had twice tested? If there were nothing else than his own statement he deserves the contempt of the American people, and the punishment of its highest tribunal. If he were not willing to execute the laws passed by the American Congress and unrepealed, let him resign the office which was thrown upon him by a horrible convulsion and retire to his village obscurity. Let him not be so swollen by pride and arrogance, which sprang from the deep misfortune of his country, as to attempt an entire revolution of its internal machinery, and the disgrace of the trusted servants of his lamented predecessor.

# "THE RESULT OF THE TRIAL"

## (May 21, 1868)

Johnson's impeachment trial lasted until May 26, 1868. On May 16, the Senate voted on article number eleven (written by Stevens), acquitting the president by one vote. Voting again ten days later on the second and third articles, the senators reached the same verdict. Following the first vote, *The Nation* commented that despite Johnson's acquittal, the House had been justified in initiating impeachment proceedings. The editor predicted that regardless of the Senate's failure to convict Johnson, his impeachment and the fact that thirty-five of fifty-four senators considered him guilty would leave Johnson discredited and powerless for the remainder of his presidency.

The vote on the verdict, even if it has not resulted in conviction, has abundantly justified the House in impeaching the President. When thirty-five out of fifty-four senators pronounce him guilty, it would be absurd as well as unjust to say that there was not "probable cause" for instituting the prosecution, and one may take this view of the matter even after making some allowance for the influence of party feeling and political excitement. The trial of a President by the Senate for offences committed in the course of a long quarrel with Congress touching the limits of his power under the Constitution cannot be a fair one in the sense in which we speak of a fair trial before an ordinary tribunal, where the accused and the judge have never previously had any relations whatever. The Senate, being a branch of the legislature, must have many imperfections as a court of justice; to expect that it will not, is to expect that senators will prove themselves more than men. All the public can ask of them is that they will make all possible efforts to rid their minds during the trial of pride, prejudice, and passion, and govern themselves to the best of their ability by the law and the evidence. That in the present instance they have done so we have never seen good reason to question, and we therefore think their action a sufficient vindication of the action of the House in preferring the charges. One may still doubt the policy of its course, but one cannot accuse it of mere vindictiveness, or mere subservience to party spirit in pursuing it.

The failure to convict is to be regretted for several reasons, but that it leaves Mr. Johnson in the Presidential chair we no longer include amongst the number. In the first place, it is not unlikely that during the remainder of his term he will behave well; in the second, even if he should desire to do mischief, his powers of mischief now, as we have already pointed out, are almost *nil*; and in the third, if he should commit fresh follies and extravagances, although the scandal will be great, it will be more than compensated for by the fact that they will help the Republican party during the coming campaign. His last follies helped it materially in 1866. Moreover, after the exhibition we have had during the last week or two of the taste and temper of the men who would in case of his deposition have had charge of the Government, it is difficult to believe that the country would have gained by the change, and it is quite certain that the party would have lost by it, for it would have had to bear the burden of their indiscretions.

But the acquittal, although the largeness of the vote for conviction may justify the House morally, is not likely to strengthen the confidence of the country in the judgment of the majority. Moreover, it has some tendency to create a certain amount of confidence in the President's judgment. It leaves him less hopelessly in the wrong than he seemed six months ago, and it leaves him in possession of the honors of the field. His escape, to be sure, has been very narrow, but in politics, as in war, an inch of a miss is as good as a mile. He was, before the trial, in the position of a man whom Congress might crush, but would not; now, he is in the position of a man whom Congress tried to crush, but could not. It is certainly not Congress that has gained by this change.

# REPUBLICAN NATIONAL
# PLATFORM OF 1868

## *(May 21, 1868)*

Soon after Johnson's acquittal, the Republicans met in Chicago to hammer out the party's platform for the November 1868 presidential campaign. While strongly supporting black suffrage in the South, party leaders continued to favor the policy of allowing Northern voters to decide on universal suffrage on a state-by-state basis. The Republicans denounced debt repudiation as a "national crime" and pledged to honor the bounties and pensions due soldiers and sailors who fought for the Union. Widows and orphans also would receive support—"a sacred legacy bequeathed to the nation's protecting care."

The National Republican party of the United States, assembled in National Convention in the city of Chicago, on the 21st day of May, 1868, make the following declaration of principles:

1. We congratulate the country on the assured success of the reconstruction policy of Congress, as evinced by the adoption, in the majority of the States lately in rebellion, of constitutions securing equal civil and political rights to all; and it is the duty of the Government to sustain those institutions and to prevent the people of such States from being remitted to a state of anarchy.

2. The guaranty by Congress of equal suffrage to all loyal men at the South was demanded by every consideration of public safety, of gratitude, and of justice, and must be maintained; while the question of suffrage in all the loyal States properly belongs to the people of those States.

3. We denounce all forms of repudiation as a national crime; and the national honor requires the payment of the public indebtedness in the uttermost good faith to all cred-

itors at home and abroad, not only according to the letter, but the spirit of the laws under which it was contracted.

4. It is due to the labor of the nation that taxation should be equalized, and reduced as rapidly as the national faith will permit.

5. The national debt, contracted as it has been for the preservation of the Union for all time to come, should be extended over a fair period for redemption; and it is the duty of Congress to reduce the rate of interest thereon, whenever it can be honestly done.

6. That the best policy to diminish our burden of debt is to so improve our credit that capitalists will seek to loan us money at lower rates of interest than we now pay, and must continue to pay so long as repudiation, partial or total, open or covert, is threatened or suspected.

7. The Government of the United States should be administered with the strictest economy; and the corruptions which have been so shamefully nursed and fostered by Andrew Johnson call loudly for radical reform.

8. We profoundly deplore the untimely and tragic death of Abraham Lincoln, and regret the accession to the Presidency of Andrew Johnson, who has acted treacherously to the people who elected him and the cause he was pledged to support; who has usurped high legislative and judicial functions; who has refused to execute the laws; who has used his high office to induce other officers to ignore and violate the laws; who has employed his executive powers to render insecure the property, the peace, liberty and life, of the citizen; who has abused the pardoning power; who has denounced the national legislature as unconstitutional: who has persistently and corruptly resisted, by every means in his power, every proper attempt at the reconstruction of the States lately in rebellion; who has perverted the public patronage into an engine of wholesale corruption; and who has been justly impeached for high crimes and misdemeanors, and properly pronounced guilty thereof by the vote of thirty-five Senators.

9. The doctrine of Great Britain and other European powers, that because a man is once a subject he is always so, must be resisted at every hazard by the United States, as a relic of feudal times, not authorized by the laws of nations, and at war with our national honor and independence. Nat-

uralized citizens are entitled to protection in all their rights of citizenship, as though they were native-born; and no citizen of the United States, native or naturalized, must be liable to arrest and imprisonment by any foreign power for acts done or words spoken in this country; and, if so arrested and imprisoned, it is the duty of the Government to interfere in his behalf.

10. Of all who were faithful in the trials of the late war, there were none entitled to more especial honor than the brave soldiers and seamen who endured the hardships of campaign and cruise, and imperilled their lives in the service of the country; the bounties and pensions provided by the laws for these brave defenders of the nation are obligations never to be forgotten; the widows and orphans of the gallant dead are the wards of the people—a sacred legacy bequeathed to the nation's protecting care.

11. Foreign immigration, which in the past has added so much to the wealth, development, and resources, and increase of power to this republic, the asylum of the oppressed of all nations, should be fostered and encouraged by a liberal and just policy.

12. This convention declares itself in sympathy with all oppressed peoples struggling for their rights.

13. That we highly commend the spirit of magnanimity and forbearance with which men who have served in the rebellion, but who now frankly and honestly coöperate with us in restoring the peace of the country and reconstructing the southern State governments upon the basis of impartial justice and equal rights, are received back into the communion of the loyal people; and we favor the removal of the disqualifications and restrictions imposed upon the late rebels in the same measure as the spirit of disloyalty will die out, and as may be consistent with the safety of the loyal people.

14. That we recognize the great principles laid down in the immortal Declaration of Independence, as the true foundation of democratic government; and we hail with gladness every effort toward making these principles a living reality on every inch of American soil.

# CAREY STYLES, "NOT OUR 'BROTHER'"

## *(June 24, 1868)*

In the summer of 1868, white Southerners hotly debated the pros and cons of ratifying their revised state constitutions and the Fourteenth Amendment. That year, Carey Wentworth Styles (1825–1897), a native South Carolinian and later a Georgia state senator, assumed editorship of the *Atlanta Constitution*. He vehemently opposed Georgia rejoining the Union if readmission required that whites accept blacks as equal members in the brotherhood of man. The vast majority of whites of his day shared Styles's stereotypical view of people of color. Despite Styles's racist rhetoric, Georgians ratified the constitution and the amendment, and Congress readmitted their state to the Union in July 1868, only to return it to military rule in December 1869 for violating the Fourteenth Amendment.

The advocates of negro suffrage do not base his claim on any natural or acquired right. In a state of nature he is without law or government. As a slave, he has taken no step in civilization. We do not trace to him any of the achievements in the art, science and literature, which mark the progressive developments of mankind. The ancient Egyptian and the modern Congo negro were as widely different as any two species of our race. In this country, unlike the Indian, the negro had no normal right. His slavery was the penance of sin or the cupidity of African slave-dealers. He had no natural right to the soil, he has acquired none. . . . He was ignorant by his own incapacity. Today, as then, he is unfit to rule the State. In contact with the white man he has advanced some—the nearer the approach the higher the development. The Democratic party is opposed to giving him this prerogative. It does not believe him capable of wielding it for the good of the country. It regards him as inferior by nature to the white race—as even below the Indian, and with less claim than the latter to the franchise right. Should he in time prove his capacity for self-government, the Democratic party will concede it to him. The Democratic party accepts the negro as "a man"—not as "a brother." The latter it will never concede. It is his friend. It will protect him in every civil right. It is unwilling, however, to make him Congressman, Governor, and Judge. It will not consent to degrade its own race by elevating an inferior above it. It is unwilling that the foreigner, when he emigrates to this country, shall go through years of privilege before he shall vote, when the negro, but recently from the barbarism of Africa, shall exercise that right without restraint. . . .

We are willing to treat the negro as "a man;" to encourage him in his industrial pursuits and in the elevation of his moral and mental being, but not to accept him as a "brother." As such we have no affinity for him. He is farther from our ideas of brotherhood than the Indian or the Chinaman. . . . We simply claim that the Caucasian race has ever stood and will continue to stand in the foreground on the drama of the world. . . .

# AMENDMENT 14

## *(Ratified July 9, 1868)*

Historians generally consider the deeply conten-
tious Fourteenth Amendment to be the most important of the so-called Reconstruction Amendments.
The bill resulted from what Radical Republicans
considered the urgency of protecting the freedpeople and Southern Unionists during Presidential Reconstruction. The amendment consisted of
four parts and an enforcement clause. First, it defined citizenship and protected citizens from
states abridging the privileges and immunities of
citizenship without due process of law. Second,
the amendment empowered Congress to lower
the representation of states that abridged voting
rights. Third, it disfranchised certain former Confederate officials. Fourth, the amendment guaranteed the federal but repudiated the Confederate
debt incurred during the Civil War. Though Congress passed the Fourteenth Amendment in June
1866, its ratification, requiring affirmative votes
of three-fourths of the states, took over two years.
It took effect in July 1868. Opposition to the
amendment and debates over its implications and
meaning dominated much of Congressional Reconstruction. It remains a central text in American
civil and human rights campaigns.

*Section 1.* All persons born or naturalized in the United
States, and subject to the jurisdiction thereof, are citizens of
the United States and of the State wherein they reside. No
State shall make or enforce any law which shall abridge the
privileges or immunities of citizens of the United States;
nor shall any State deprive any person of life, liberty, or
property, without due process of law; nor deny to any person within its jurisdiction the equal protection of the laws.

*Section 2.* Representatives shall be apportioned among

the several States according to their respective numbers, counting the whole number of persons in each State, excluding Indians not taxed. But when the right to vote at any election for the choice of electors for President and Vice President of the United States, Representatives in Congress, the Executive and Judicial officers of a State, or the members of the Legislature thereof, is denied to any of the male inhabitants of such State, being twenty-one years of age, and citizens of the United States, or in any way abridged, except for participation in rebellion, or other crime, the basis of representation therein shall be reduced in the proportion which the number of such male citizens shall bear to the whole number of male citizens twenty-one years of age in such State.

*Section 3.* No person shall be a Senator or Representative in Congress, or elector of President and Vice President, or hold any office, civil or military, under the United States, or under any State, who, having previously taken an oath, as a member of Congress, or as an officer of the United States, or as a member of any State legislature, or as an executive or judicial officer of any State, to support the Constitution of the United States, shall have engaged in insurrection or rebellion against the same, or given aid or comfort to the enemies thereof. But Congress may by a vote of two-thirds of each House, remove such disability.

*Section 4.* The validity of the public debt of the United States, authorized by law, including debts incurred for payment of pensions and bounties for services in suppressing insurrection or rebellion, shall not be questioned. But neither the United States nor any State shall assume or pay any debt or obligation incurred in aid of insurrection or rebellion against the United States, or any claim for the loss or emancipation of any slave; but all such debts, obligations and claims shall be held illegal and void.

*Section 5.* The Congress shall have power to enforce, by appropriate legislation, the provisions of this article.

# Henry McNeal Turner, "I Claim the Rights of a Man"

## (September 3, 1868)

Henry McNeal Turner (1834–1915), born a free person of color in South Carolina, was an ordained A.M.E. minister, a black community leader in Baltimore and Washington, D.C., and then chaplain of the 1st U.S. Colored Troops. Following the Civil War, he worked as a Freedmen's Bureau agent and then as presiding elder for A.M.E. missions in Georgia. Turner entered state politics in 1867, first as a delegate to Georgia's constitutional convention, and then, in 1868, he was elected to the first of two terms in the state legislature. He proved most successful in organizing black Republicans in the state. In his fiery response to the September 1868 expulsion of blacks (himself included) from the Georgia legislature, Turner admonished his fellow blacks, "Never lift a finger nor raise a hand in defense of Georgia, until Georgia acknowledges that you are men and invests you with the rights pertaining to manhood." In later years, Turner became a bishop of the A.M.E. Church and championed the self-repatriation of American blacks to Africa.

Mr. Speaker: Before proceeding to argue this question upon its intrinsic merits, I wish the members of this House to understand the position that I take. I hold that I am a member of this body. Therefore, sir, I shall neither fawn nor cringe before any party, nor stoop to beg them for my rights. Some of my colored fellow members, in the course of their remarks, took occasion to appeal to the sympathies of members on the opposite side, and to eulogize their character for magnanimity. It reminds me very much, sir, of slaves begging under the lash. I am here to demand my rights and to hurl thunderbolts at the men who would dare to cross the threshold of my manhood. There is an old aphorism which says, "fight the devil with fire," and if I should observe the rule in this instance, I wish gentlemen to understand that it is but fighting them with their own weapon.

The scene presented in this House, today, is one unparalleled in the history of the world. From this day, back to the day when God breathed the breath of life into Adam, no analogy for it can be found. Never, in the history of the world, has a man been arraigned before a body clothed with legislative, judicial or executive functions, charged with the offense of being a darker hue than his fellow men. I know that questions have been before the courts of this country, and of other countries, involving topics not altogether dissimilar to that which is being discussed here today. But, sir, never in the history of the great nations of this world—never before—has a man been arraigned, charged with an offense committed by the God of Heaven Himself. Cases may be found where men have been deprived of their rights for crimes and misdemeanors; but it has remained for the state of Georgia, in the very heart of the nineteenth century, to call a man before the bar, and there charge him with an act for which he is no more responsible than for the head which he carries upon his shoulders. The Anglo-Saxon race, sir, is a most surprising one. No man has ever been more deceived in that race than I have been for the last three weeks. I was not aware that there was in the character of that race so much cowardice or so much pusillanimity. The treachery which has been exhibited in it by gentlemen belonging to that race has shaken my confidence in it more than anything that has come under my observation from the day of my birth.

What is the question at issue? Why, sir, this Assembly, today, is discussing and deliberating on a judgment; there is not a Cherub that sits around God's eternal throne today that would not tremble—even were an order issued by the Supreme God Himself—to come down here and sit in judgment on my manhood. Gentlemen may look at this question in whatever light they choose, and with just as much indifference as they may think proper to assume, but I tell you, sir, that this is a question which will not die today. This event shall be remembered by posterity for ages yet to come, and while the sun shall continue to climb the hills of heaven.

Whose legislature is this? Is it a white man's legislature, or is it a black man's legislature? Who voted for a constitutional convention, in obedience to the mandate of the Congress of the United States? Who first rallied around the standard of Reconstruction? Who set the ball of loyalty rolling in the state of Georgia? And whose voice was heard on the hills and in the valleys of this state? It was the voice of the brawny-armed Negro, with the few humanitarian-hearted white men who came to our assistance. I claim the honor, sir, of having been the instrument of convincing hundreds—yea, thousands—of white men, that to reconstruct under the measures of the United States Congress was the safest and the best course for the interest of the state.

Let us look at some facts in connection with this matter. Did half the white men of Georgia vote for this legislature? Did not the great bulk of them fight, with all their strength, the Constitution under which we are acting? And did they not fight against the organization of this legislature? And further, sir, did they not vote against it? Yes, sir! And there are persons in this legislature today who are ready to spit their poison in my face, while they themselves opposed, with all their power, the ratification of this Constitution. They question my right to a seat in this body, to represent the people whose legal votes elected me. This objection, sir, is an unheard-of monopoly of power. No analogy can be found for it, except it be the case of a man who should go into my house, take possession of my wife and children, and then tell me to walk out. I stand very much in the position of a criminal before your bar, because I dare to be the exponent of the views of those who sent me here. Or, in other words, we are told that if black men want to speak, they must speak through white trumpets; if black men want their sentiments expressed, they must be adulterated and sent through white messengers, who will quibble and equivocate and evade as rapidly as the pendulum of a clock. If this be not done, then the black men have committed an outrage, and their representatives must be denied the right to represent their constituents.

The great question, sir, is this: Am I a man? If I am such,

I claim the rights of a man. Am I not a man because I happen to be of a darker hue than honorable gentlemen around me? Let me see whether I am or not. I want to convince the House today that I am entitled to my seat here. A certain gentleman has argued that the Negro was a mere development similar to the orangoutang or chimpanzee, but it so happens that, when a Negro is examined, physiologically, phrenologically and anatomically, and I may say, physiognomically, he is found to be the same as persons of different color. I would like to ask any gentleman on this floor, where is the analogy? Do you find me a quadruped, or do you find me a man? Do you find three bones less in my back than in that of the white man? Do you find fewer organs in the brain? If you know nothing of this, I do; for I have helped to dissect fifty men, black and white, and I assert that by the time you take off the mucous pigment—the color of the skin—you cannot, to save your life, distinguish between the black man and the white. Am I a man? Have I a soul to save, as you have? Am I susceptible of eternal development, as you are? Can I learn all the arts and sciences that you can? Has it ever been demonstrated in the history of the world? Have black men ever exhibited bravery as white men have done? Have they ever been in the professions? Have they not as good articulative organs as you? Some people argue that there is a very close similarity between the larynx of the Negro and that of the orangoutang. Why, sir, there is not so much similarity between them as there is between the larynx of the man and that of the dog, and this fact I dare any member of this House to dispute. God saw fit to vary everything in nature. There are no two men alike—no two voices alike—no two trees alike. God has weaved and tissued variety and versatility throughout the boundless space of His creation. Because God saw fit to make some red, and some white, and some black, and some brown, are we to sit here in judgment upon what God has seen fit to do? As well might one play with the thunderbolts of heaven as with that creature that bears God's image—God's photograph. . . .

The honorable gentleman from Whitfield (Mr. Shumate), when arguing this question, a day or two ago, put forth the proposition that to be a representative was not to be an officer—"it was a privilege that citizens had a right to enjoy." These are his words. It was not an office; it was a "privilege." Every gentleman here knows that he denied that to be a representative was to be an officer. Now, he is recognized as a leader of the Democratic party in this House, and generally cooks victuals for them to eat; makes that remarkable declaration, and how are you, gentlemen on the other side of the House, because I am an officer, when one of your great lights says that I am *not* an officer? If you deny my right—the right of my constituents to have representation here—because it is a "privilege," then, sir, I will show you that I have as many privileges as the whitest man on this floor. If I am not permitted to occupy a seat here, for the purpose of representing my constituents, I want to know how white men can be permitted to do so. How can a white man represent a colored constituency, if a colored man cannot do it? The great argument is: "Oh, we have inherited" this, that and the other. Now, I want gentlemen to come down to cool, common sense. Is the created greater than the Creator? Is man greater than God? It is very strange, if a white man can occupy on this floor *a seat created by colored votes*, and a black man cannot do it. Why, gentlemen, it is the most shortsighted reasoning in the world. A man can see better than that with half an eye; and even if he had no eye at all, he could forge one, as the Cyclops did, or punch one with his finger, which would enable him to see through that.

It is said that Congress never gave us the right to hold office. I want to know, sir, if the Reconstruction measures did not base their action on the ground that no distinction should be made on account of race, color or previous condition. Was not that the grand fulcrum on which they rested? And did not every reconstructed state have to reconstruct on the idea that no discrimination, in any sense of the term, should be made? There is not a man here who will dare say No. If Congress has simply given me merely sufficient civil and political rights to make me a mere political slave for Democrats, or anybody else—giving them the opportunity of jumping on my back in order to leap into political power—I do not thank Congress for it. Never, so help me God, shall I be a political slave. I am not now speaking for those colored men who sit with me in this House, nor do I say that they endorse my sentiments [cries from the colored members, "We Do!"], but assisting Mr. Lincoln to take me out of servile slavery did not intend to put me and my race into *political* slavery. If they did, let them take away my ballot—I do not want it, and shall not have it. [Several colored members: "Nor we!"] I don't want to be a mere tool of that sort. I have been a slave long enough already.

I tell you what I would be willing to do: I am willing that the question should be submitted to Congress for an explanation as to what was meant in the passage of their Reconstruction measures, and of the Constitutional Amendment. Let the Democratic party in this House pass a resolution giving this subject that direction, and I shall be content. I dare you, gentlemen, to do it. Come up to the question openly, whether it meant that the Negro might hold office, or whether it meant that he should merely have the right to vote. If you are honest men, you will do it. If, however, you will not do that, I would make another proposition: Call together, again, the convention that framed the constitution under which we are acting; let them take a vote upon the subject, and I am willing to abide by their decision. . . .

These colored men, who are unable to express themselves with all the clearness and dignity and force of rhetorical eloquence, are laughed at in derision by the Democracy of the country. It reminds me very much of the man who looked at himself in a mirror and, imagining that he was addressing another person, exclaimed: "My God, how ugly you are!" These gentlemen do not consider for a moment the dreadful hardships which these people have endured, and especially those who in any way endeavored to acquire an education. For myself, sir, I was raised in the cotton field of South Carolina, and in order to prepare myself for usefulness, as well to myself as to my race, I determined to devote my spare hours to study. When the overseer retired at night to his comfortable couch, I sat and read and thought and studied, until I heard him blow his horn in the morning. He frequently told me, with an oath, that if he discovered me attempting to learn, that he would whip me to death; and I have no doubt he would have done so, if he had found an opportunity. I prayed to Almighty God to assist me, and He did, and I thank Him with my whole heart and soul. . . .

So far as I am personally concerned, no man in Georgia has been more conservative than I. "Anything to please the white folks" has been my motto; and so closely have I adhered to that course, that many among my own party have classed me as a Democrat. One of the leaders of the Republican party in Georgia has not been at all favorable to me for some time back, because he believed that I was too "conservative" for a Republican. I can assure you, however, Mr. Speaker, that I have had quite enough, and to spare, of such "conservatism." . . .

But, Mr. Speaker, I do not regard this movement as a thrust at me. It is a thrust at the Bible—a thrust at the God of the Universe, for making a man and not finishing him; it is simply calling the Great Jehovah a fool. Why, sir, though we are not white, we have accomplished much. We have pioneered civilization here; we have built up your country; we have worked in your fields and garnered your harvests for two hundred and fifty years! And what do we ask of you in return? Do we ask you for compensation for the sweat our fathers bore for you—for the tears you have caused, and the hearts you have broken, and the lives you have curtailed, and the blood you have spilled? Do we ask retaliation? We ask it not. We are willing to let the dead past bury its dead; but we ask you now for our *rights*. You have all the elements of superiority upon your side; you have our money and your own; you have our education and your own; and you have our land and your own too. We, who number hundreds of thousands in Georgia, including our wives and families, with not a foot of land to call our own—strangers in the land of our birth; without money, without education, without aid, without a roof to cover us while we live, nor sufficient clay to cover us when we die! It is extraordinary that a race such as yours, professing gallantry and chivalry and education and superiority, living in a land where ringing chimes call child and sire to the church of God—a land where Bibles are read and Gospel truths are spoken, and where courts of justice are presumed to exist; it is extraordinary that, with all these advantages on your side, you can make war upon the poor defenseless black man. You know we have no money, no railroads, no telegraphs, no advantages of any sort, and yet all manner of injustice is placed upon us. You know that the black people of this country acknowledge you as their superiors, by virtue of your education and advantages. . . .

You may expel us, gentlemen, but I firmly believe that you will some day repent it. The black man cannot protect a country, if the country doesn't protect him; and if, tomorrow, a war should arise, I would not raise a musket to defend a country where my manhood is denied. The fashionable way in Georgia, when hard work is to be done, is for the white man to sit at his ease while the black man does the work; but, sir, I will say this much to the colored men of Georgia, as, if I should be killed in this campaign, I may have no opportunity of telling them at any other time: Never lift a finger nor raise a hand in defense of Georgia, until Georgia acknowledges that you are men and invests you with the rights pertaining to manhood. Pay your taxes, however, obey all orders from your employers, take good counsel from friends, work faithfully, earn an honest living, and show, by your conduct, that you can be good citizens.

Go on with your oppressions. Babylon fell. Where is Greece? Where is Nineveh? And where is Rome, the Mistress Empire of the world? Why is it that she stands, today, in broken fragments throughout Europe? Because oppression killed her. Every act that we commit is like a bounding ball. If you curse a man, that curse rebounds upon you; and when you bless a man, the blessing returns to you; and when you oppress a man, the oppression also will rebound. Where have you ever heard of four millions of freemen being governed by laws, and yet have no hand in their making? Search the records of the world, and you will find no example. "Governments derive their just powers from the consent of the governed." How dare you to make laws by which to try me and my wife and children, and deny me a voice in the making of these laws? I know you can establish a monarchy, an autocracy, an oligarchy, or any other kind of *ocracy* that you please; and that you can declare whom you please to be sovereign; but tell me, sir, how you can clothe me with more power than another, where all are sovereigns alike? How can you say you have a republican form of government, when you make such distinction and enact such proscriptive laws?

Gentlemen talk a good deal about the Negroes "building no monuments." I can tell the gentlemen one thing: that is, that we could have built monuments of fire while the war was in progress. We could have fired your woods, your barns and fences, and called you home. Did we do it? No, sir! And God grant that the Negro may never do it, or do anything else that would destroy the good opinion of his friends. No epithet is sufficiently opprobrious for us now. I saw, sir, that we have built a monument of docility, of obedience, of respect, and of self-control, that will endure longer than the Pyramids of Egypt.

We are a persecuted people. Luther was persecuted; Galileo was persecuted; good men in all nations have been persecuted; but the persecutors have been handed down to posterity with shame and ignominy. If you pass this bill, you will never get Congress to pardon or enfranchise another rebel in your lives. You are going to fix an everlasting disfranchisement upon Mr. Toombs and the other leading men of Georgia. You may think you are doing yourselves honor by expelling us from this House; but when we go, we will do as Wickliffe and as Latimer did. We will light a torch of truth that will never be extinguished—the impression that will run through the country, as people picture in their mind's eye these poor black men, in all parts of this Southern country, pleading for their rights. When you expel us, you make us forever your political foes, and you will never find a black man to vote a Democratic ticket again; for, so help me God, I will go through all the length and breadth of the land, where a man of my race is to be found, and advise him to beware of the Democratic party. Justice is the great doctrine taught in the Bible. God's Eternal Justice is founded upon Truth, and the man who steps from Justice steps from Truth, and cannot make his principles to prevail.

# "REMARKS OF WILLIAM E. MAT[T]HEWS"

## (January 1869)

On Sunday, October 25, 1868, William E. Matthews, an agent of the A.M.E. Church responsible for missionary work in the South, spoke before the Reverend Henry Ward Beecher's famous Plymouth Church in Brooklyn, New York. Matthews noted that during Reconstruction his denomination had organized five hundred congregations and erected three hundred church buildings in the former Confederate states. As slaves, Matthews added, the people reveled in ignorance and superstition. As freedpeople and as members of the A.M.E. Church, they radiated "praise and prayer from every hill-top and plain from Virginia to the Gulf of Mexico." Beecher informed his congregation that the experiences of the freedpeople since emancipation reaffirmed "the duty of the strong to bear with the weak."

Christian Friends: I thank you, as I have no word to express, for this manifestation of practical Christianity in giving me an opportunity to present to your sympathy and support the cause I represent. I am not insensible to the fact—I am almost overwhelmed by it—of standing on the platform of Plymouth Church, face to face with this people, and in presence of the man who has done so much for the millions of my brethren. For the battle you have fought, and for the words of cheer and hope spoken when all around them was dark with despair, I can only say—I thank you.

I come from Baltimore, where I was born and reared, and I come bearing letters of recommendation from the Hon. Hugh L. Bond, the Rev. Edwin Johnson, Rev. John F. W. Ware, Rev. Dr. Sutherland, of Washington, Major-General Howard, and other noble men in that section of the country, who know me and the cause I represent.

I am here as the representative of the missionary work now being performed at the South by the African Methodist Episcopal Church—a church organized and governed entirely by colored men.

This African Methodist Church was organized fifty-two years ago, in 1816; so you see that I do not come with some new-born experiment, but for an organization which has been tested, and which, under God, has been instrumental in presenting to American Christianity the largest body of Christianized Africans to be found the world over.

I will as briefly as possible give the history of its rise and progress, what it has achieved and what it still desires to perform. Prior to the year 1816, there were a great many colored people in the State of Pennsylvania who were members of the great Methodist Church of this country. All the rights and Christian courtesies which others enjoyed were accorded to them; but about this time you know how the great spirit of caste overleaped the plantations of the South and entered your Northern homes—how it even entered the sacred temple of worship, and ignoring that great truth proclaimed by Paul on Mars' Hill, that "God of a truth had made of one blood all men, to dwell on all the face of the earth," the ministers of this church plainly told the colored portion of the membership that such was the condition of public opinion that they could no longer remain with them, and the sooner they took themselves away the better it would be for all concerned. A few of the more intelligent of the colored men—Richard Allen, David Coaker, and six others—feeling the great wrong done them, resolved to form a church of their own, where they could worship God under their own vine and fig-tree, with none to molest or make afraid. These men, poor in pocket but rich in heart, rented a loft over a blacksmith's shop, and in the month of April, 1816, they there formed this African Methodist Episcopal Church. From that small commencement of eight men for a congregation, and a loft for a sanctuary, this communion has increased, east, west, north, south, until, as I before stated, we possess the largest body of black Christians to be found the world over.

We now number a membership of two hundred and twenty-five thousand. We have some eight hundred church edifices scattered throughout the country; one college,

(Wilberforce,) near Xenia, Ohio; a training-school for ministers in South-Carolina; and a newspaper, the *Christian
Recorder,* of Philadelphia, with a circulation of from eight
to ten thousand; and all this the work *of colored men.* All
the money required, all the power of head and heart needed
in propelling so great a work, has come from black men.

But you must know that, prior to the rebellion, no organization could exist at the South that had not at its head a
white man; and as this was a church governed entirely by
colored men, our church had no existence in the South, the
only exceptions to this rule being the States of Maryland,
Kentucky, and the District of Columbia. In these States we
have a large membership and fine church property; but
whenever we attempted to plant our church in Virginia, the
Carolinas, or Georgia, or any of the States where our people mostly lived, the law would interpose. In some instances,
a *posse* of police would enter, arrest the minister and as
many of the congregation as they could manage. This was
done to the Rev. John M. Brown, now Bishop Brown, in the
city of New-Orleans, not many years since.

When the war of the rebellion broke forth, and when
our government (for, thank God! I can now say *our* government) had been educated up to the idea of accepting
black men to help fight its battles, the ministers of this
church were among the first to offer their services. Indeed,
our churches in Washington, Baltimore, Philadelphia, and
this city were turned into recruiting rendezvous, where
mass meetings were held, and our leading ministers came
before the people and told them to forget the past, and to
buckle on their armor and go forth to vindicate the country's honor and preserve the nation's flag; and they did go
forth, and Rev. H. M. Turner, then the pastor of one of our
churches in Washington, but now engaged in organizing
churches in Georgia, and one of the men recently expelled
from the legislature of that State on account of color, was
the first colored man to receive a commission from the
United States—that as chaplain of the First U. S Colored
troops, which he raised almost by himself, by the power of
his own influence. When Turner and others of our ministers
went into the Southern States and saw the deplorable spiritual condition of the blacks, their utter ignorance of the
elements which are required for a fully developed Chris-

tian character, they determined that our church must be planted there in order that the Gospel might be preached to them in all the richness of its promise and all its breadth and depth. For you must know that these millions had never been permitted to listen to a "whole gospel." In many of the Southern States, they had no church privileges at all. In others they were permitted to occupy the loft in the white churches, and at the close of the minister's regular discourse he would address a few words to his black hearers. No matter what text his sermon had been based upon, the text from which he spoke to the colored people would always be, *"Servants, obey your masters,"* telling them that, if they would only obey the superior will of some one else, *no matter what that will was,* they might possibly get into some corner of heaven; but even of this there was no absolute certainty. They were taught nothing about the importance of Christian character or the meaning and force of that little word *integrity*.

Now, this African Church is endeavoring to supply this need. They are sending into the South men of broad, comprehensive views, men who know the needs of the people, and who are endeavoring to hedge them about by such influences as will enable them to emerge from their transition state healthier, stronger, and wiser, so that they may be a blessing to themselves, their country, and their age. We have already succeeded in organizing some five hundred congregations and erecting some three hundred church buildings south of the Potomac. Indeed, we have already succeeded in making that South-land, which a few years ago was black with its ignorance and superstitions, resound with praise and prayer from every hill-top and plain from Virginia to the Gulf of Mexico.

In all the large cities our churches are in a healthy condition—not only self-supporting, but giving a surplus for more destitute regions; but in Texas, Arkansas, Georgia, and other portions of the South where labor is disorganized, the people are unable to raise money enough to meet the common necessities of life. They, therefore, have no money to give to the men whom we send them. The consequence is, that we have some eighty men who are either wholly or partly dependent upon our Missionary Society for their support; and it is for this purpose, Christian friends, that I invoke your sympathy, and, I trust, your material help.

Time will not permit me to go more fully into the details of this work. My appeal is before you, and in those beautiful words of Bishop Heber I would ask you,

> *Shall you whose minds are lighted*
> *With wisdom from on high,*
> *Shall you to men benighted*
> *The lamp of life deny?*
>
> *Salvation! O salvation!*
> *The joyful sound proclaim,*
> *Till earth's remotest nation*
> *Has learnt Messiah's name.*

Help us to help these woe-smitten children up to manhood and to God, and you shall receive that benediction sweeter than any joy the world can give. It will be the voice of the Master, "Inasmuch as ye have done it to these my little ones, ye have done it unto me."

# Ulysses S. Grant, "Inaugural Address"

## (March 4, 1869)

Grant, the Union's great war hero, stayed as neutral as possible in the bitter quarrel between Johnson and the Radicals. Victorious over New York Democrat Horatio Seymour in the presidential election of 1868 (winning 214 electoral votes to 80), Grant promised in his first inaugural address to work harmoniously with Congress and, even when he disagreed with legislators, to execute the laws faithfully. Grant obviously had paid close attention to Johnson's travails. In his speech, Grant pledged to try to heal sectional wounds and expressed confidence that the Fifteenth Amendment (passed by Congress on February 26, 1869) would be ratified during his presidency. Indeed, ratification of the amendment and the restoration of all of the Southern states to their congressional privileges were among the major accomplishments of Grant's White House years.

## CITIZENS OF THE UNITED STATES

Your suffrages having elected me to the office of President of the United States, I have, in conformity to the Constitution of our country, taken the oath of office prescribed therein. I have taken this oath without mental reservation, and with the determination to do to the best of my ability all that it requires of me. The responsibilities of the position I feel, but accept them without fear. The office has come to me unsought; I commence its duties untrammelled. I bring to it a conscious desire and determination to fill it to the best of my ability to the satisfaction of the people.

On all leading questions agitating the public mind I will always express my views to Congress, and urge them according to my judgment; and when I think it advisable, will exercise the constitutional privilege of interposing a veto to defeat measures which I oppose. But all laws will be faithfully executed whether they meet my approval or not.

I shall on all subjects have a policy to recommend, but none to enforce against the will of the people. Laws are to govern all alike, those opposed as well as those who favor them. I know no method to secure the repeal of bad or obnoxious laws so effective as their stringent execution.

The country having just emerged from a great rebellion, many questions will come before it for settlement in the next four years which preceding Administrations have never had to deal with. In meeting these it is desirable that they should be approached calmly, without prejudice, hate or sectional pride, remembering that the greatest good to the greatest number is the object to be attained.

This requires security of person, property, and free religious and political opinion in every part of our common country, without regard to local prejudice. All laws to secure these ends will receive my best efforts for their enforcement.

A great debt has been contracted in securing to us and our posterity the Union. The payment of this, principal and interest, as well as the return to a specie basis, as soon as it can be accomplished without material detriment to the debtor class or to the country at large, must be provided for. To protect the national honor every dollar of government indebtedness should be paid in gold, unless otherwise expressly stipulated in the contract. Let it be understood that no repudiator of one farthing of our public debt will be trusted in public place, and it will go far towards strengthening a credit which ought to be the best in the world, and will ultimately enable us to replace the debt with bonds bearing less interest than we now pay. To this should be added a faithful collection of the revenue, a strict accountability to the treasury for every dollar collected, and the greatest practicable retrenchment in expenditure in every department of government.

When we compare the paying capacity of the country now—with the ten States in poverty from the effects of war, but soon to emerge, I trust, into greater prosperity than ever before—with its paying capacity twenty-five years ago, and calculate what it probably will be twenty-five years hence, who can doubt the feasibility of paying every dollar then with more ease than we now pay for useless luxuries? Why, it looks as though Providence had bestowed upon us a strong box in the precious metals locked up in the sterile mountains of the far west, and which we are now forging the key to unlock, to meet the very contingency that is now upon us.

Ultimately it may be necessary to insure the facilities to reach these riches, and it may be necessary also that the general government should give its aid to secure this access. But that should only be when a dollar of obligation to pay secures precisely the same sort of dollar to use now, and not before. Whilst the question of specie payments is in abeyance, the prudent business man is careful about contracting debts payable in the distant future. The nation should follow the same rule. A prostrate commerce is to be rebuilt and all industries encouraged.

The young men of the country, those who from their age must be its rulers twenty-five years hence, have a peculiar interest in maintaining the national honor. A moment's reflection as to what will be our commanding influence among the nations of the earth in their day, if they are only true to themselves, should inspire them with national pride. All divisions, geographical, political, and religious, can join in this common sentiment. How the public debt is to be paid, or specie payments resumed, is not so important as that a plan should be adopted and acquiesced in.

A united determination to do is worth more than divided counsels upon the method of doing. Legislation upon this subject may not be necessary now, nor even advisable, but it will be when the civil law is more fully restored in all parts of the country, and trade resumes its wonted channels.

It will be my endeavor to execute all laws in good faith, to collect all revenues assessed, and to have them properly accounted for and economically disbursed. I will, to the best of my ability, appoint to office those only who will carry out this design.

In regard to foreign policy, I would deal with nations as equitable law requires individuals to deal with each other, and I would protect the law-abiding citizen, whether of native or foreign birth, wherever his rights are jeopardized or the flag of our country floats. I would respect the rights of all nations, demanding equal respect for our own. If others depart from this rule in their dealings with us, we may be compelled to follow their precedent.

The proper treatment of the original occupants of this land, the Indians, is one deserving of careful study. I will favor any course toward them which tends to their civilization and ultimate citizenship.

The question of suffrage is one which is likely to agitate the public so long as a portion of the citizens of the nation are excluded from its privileges in any State. It seems to me very desirable that this question should be settled now, and I entertain the hope and express the desire that it may be by the ratification of the fifteenth article of amendment to the Constitution.

In conclusion, I ask patient forbearance one toward another throughout the land, and a determined effort on the part of every citizen to do his share toward cementing a happy Union, and I ask the prayers of the nation to Almighty God in behalf of this consummation.

# Lydia Maria Child, "Homesteads"

## (March 28, 1869)

Child (1802–1880) was one of nineteenth-century America's best-known women—a literary innovator, social reformer, and progressive. She cut a wide publishing swath, including novels, short stories, children's literature, journalistic sketches, domestic advice books, antislavery fiction, and works on aging. A fervent critic of racism and slavery, Child used her pen to chronicle the horrors of the "peculiar institution" and to champion a nation reconstructed on a basis of racial equality. In 1869, she published an appeal to President Grant and Congress to redress Johnson's failure to institute land reform and provide homesteads for the freedpeople, "by confiscation, fines, or sale for taxes."

In the March number of the *American Missionary* is a very interesting account of Moses Fisher. Taking advantage of the confusion of wartime, he absconded from his master's premises, and started with his family for the United States camp. They travelled forty miles through the deepest recesses of the woods, careful to keep in solitary places, lest they should be seized and dragged back into slavery. The parents carried on their heads their little stock of rags, dishes, and kettles, and the children trudged after, leading their blind old grandmother. How many such groups the stars looked down upon, while the armies of the North were fighting for one idea and slowly finding another! At last, the weary fugitives came in sight of the United States flag, and under cover of the night crept into the camp. There they poured forth their grateful hearts in thanks to God for the freedom they had gained, and there they remained to render willing and faithful service for the protection they received. A Bible was wrapped up in the rags they "toted" on their heads. None of them could read a word of it; but Moses felt assured he had a treasure shut up there, that some time or other would be unlocked for him. All through the war, he guarded it carefully, sleeping with it under his head, and hiding it in safe places in time of danger.

When the war was over, Moses, with thousands of his brothers, were left without resources, to wander among a people who hated them for their loyalty to the United States. There were thousands of acres of wild land in the South, but none for the homeless freedmen. A timid Congress "dawdled" away its opportunities, and the President busied himself with restoring plantations to rebel masters. They were all too much occupied with conciliating the Democratic Party, to think of providing the black soldiers and servants of the United States army with a patch of ground whereon to raise food for their families.

But no discouragements could dishearten Moses Fisher. He had nothing but his wife and children, his rags and kettles. But he made a bargain with a white man to clear up an almost impenetrable swamp, for the privilege of cultivating for three years such land as he could subdue. There the whole family toiled at ditching and grubbing the soil, with such rude implements as they could contrive. In summer, the mother and children picked berries and carried them to market; at other times, they made up bundles of light-wood, which they carried on their backs in search of purchasers. In one season, the mother and her little girl picked and sold forty-three dollars worth of berries; and the father and his little boy tapped and dipped two hundred and sixty dollars worth of turpentine; but of this sum he was obliged to give half to the owner of the soil. Undismayed by the formidable obstacles they had to contend with, this brave family toiled on, month after month, cutting away thick underbrush, grubbing up tangled roots, and planting corn and potatoes. With the logs they hewed they made themselves a comfortable shelter, and a few rude articles of furniture. Before their harvest was ripe, a log-barn was erected wherein to store it. In a shattered box brought from the army was stored the precious Bible, which as yet none of them could read. But at last some of the noble army of Northern teachers penetrated into that region. The nearest school was five miles off. But for two years the little boy

and girl trudged thither in the morning and back again in
the afternoon, scarcely ever missing a day. From their little
tongues the patient and trusting father at last heard the
contents of the Bible he had treasured so long. One day the
Northern teacher walked home with these bright, industrious children, and was warmly welcomed by the grateful
parents. They showed with great satisfaction the hundred
bushels of corn which they had stored in their little barn.
The Bible was brought from its box and its history related.
"All the while I was toting it about," said Moses, "I knowed
there was a heap o' good inside of it, and I had faith that
some time or other it would come out of it to me; and now
my little children are teaching me the heavenly message."

This simple story of persevering faith and patience affected me deeply; and it made it harder than ever to forgive
Congress for not having provided these poor outcasts of
slavery with small homesteads of their own, at moderate
prices. Poor Moses, after wearing out his muscles with incessant toil for three years, will not own one rood of the
land he has cleared. He will still be landless and homeless,
and compelled for daily food to submit to the hard terms of
grasping, unpitying masters, who are accustomed to consider his race fore-ordained to toil without wages. If it had
been made easy for the freedmen to become owners of
land, how much their industry would have been stimulated
and the wealth of the nation increased! Nothing improves
the characters of human beings like having a home of their
own; and a country has no element of prosperity so certain
as that of laborers who own the soil they cultivate. . . .

I never for one moment wished that any class or condition of men at the South should be without homesteads
and the means of obtaining an independent living by their
own industry and enterprise. To the "poor whites" who
fought against us in the blindness of their ignorance, I
would offer every facility for obtaining as much land as
they would cultivate, and I would try to raise them up to the
idea that honest labor is honorable above all things. And
though my sympathies do not flow out so readily to the
slaveholders as to their victims, white and black, I do not
forget that they also were the victims of a bad institution,
and that we, if we had been brought up under the influences of slavery, should have formed the same bad habits

and the same false principles. Their sons will mature into truer manhood, under a better order of things. And I should be sorry to see the generation that is passing away deprived of homesteads and a sufficiency of land. Incurably violent and arrogant as they are, I would not impoverish them if I could. But I *would* so manage affairs, by confiscation, fines, or sale for taxes, that one rebel master should not hold in his exclusive possession from one thousand to twenty thousand acres, while his loyal laborers cannot own ground enough for a potato patch. In some way or other, this great evil *can* be remedied, and the good of all classes in the country requires that it *should* be remedied, as soon as possible.

# AMENDMENT 15

## *(Ratified February 3, 1870)*

The Fifteenth Amendment (passed by Congress on February 26, 1869, and ratified by the states on February 3, 1870) was the last of the three Reconstruction Amendments and the final measure framed by Congress with hopes of paving the way to true equality. The amendment specified that suffrage for citizens "shall not be denied or abridged by the United States or by any State on account of race, color, or previous condition of servitude," and included an enforcement provision. Significantly, while the Reconstruction Acts riveted black enfranchisement on the former Confederate states, this amendment forced universal suffrage on the Northern states, which had stubbornly resisted enfranchising black men, even after emancipation. As its critics have pointed out, for all its promise the Fifteenth Amendment failed to address restrictions on office holding, disfranchisement by legal subterfuge, and the general disfranchisement of women, white and black.

*Section 1.* The right of citizens of the United States to vote shall not be denied or abridged by the United States or by any State on account of race, color, or previous condition of servitude.

*Section 2.* The Congress shall have power to enforce this article by appropriate legislation.

# Frederick Douglass, "At Last, At Last, the Black Man Has a Future"

## *(April 22, 1870)*

On April 22, 1870, Douglass came to Albany, New York, to participate in that city's celebration of the ratification of the Fifteenth Amendment. His evening speech, just one of many talks he delivered to commemorate the amendment, electrified the overflow audience in Tweddle Hall. According to Douglass, the long-awaited suffrage amendment ushered in a new day for black men, finally giving them a future in America. It signified "progress, civilization, knowledge, manhood" and presented blacks not only with exhilarating new opportunities but grave new responsibilities. The black leader prophesied that the Fifteenth Amendment would bind Americans together and contribute to a stronger Union.

. . . You did not expect to see it; I did not expect to see it; no man living did expect to live to see this day. In our moments of unusual mental elevation and heart-longings, some of us may have caught glimpses of it afar off; we saw it only by the strong, clear, earnest eye of faith, but none dared even to hope to stand upon the earth at its coming. Yet here it is. Our eyes behold it; our ears hear it, our hearts feel it, and there is no doubt or illusion about it. The black man is free, the black man is a citizen, the black man is enfranchised, and this by the organic law of the land. No more a slave, no more a fugitive slave, no more a despised and hated creature, but a man, and, what is more, a man among men.

Henceforth we live in a new world. The sun does not rise nor set for us as formerly. "Old things have passed away and all things have become new."

I once went abroad among men with all my quills erect. There was cause for it. I always looked for insult and buffetings, and was seldom disappointed in finding them. Now civility is the rule, and insult the exception.

At last, at last, the black man has a future. Heretofore all was dark, mysterious, chaotic. We were chained to all the unutterable horrors of never ending fixedness. Others might improve and make progress, but for us there was nothing but the unending monotony of stagnation, of moral, mental and social death. The curtain is now lifted. The dismal death-cloud of slavery has passed away. Today we are free American citizens. We have ourselves, we have a country, and we have a future in common with other men.

One of the most remarkable features of this grand revolution is its thoroughness. Never was revolution more complete. Nothing has been left for time. No probation has been imposed. The Hebrews tarried in the wilderness forty years before they reached the land of promise. The West India slaves had their season of apprenticeship. Feudal slavery died a lingering death in Europe. Hayti rose to freedom only by degrees and by limited concessions. Religious liberty as now enjoyed came only in slow installments; but our liberty has come all at once, full and complete. The most exacting could not ask more than we have got; the most urgent could not have demanded it more promptly. We have all we asked, and more than we expected.

Even William Lloyd Garrison (I speak it not reproachfully) halted when the advance to suffrage was sounded; and he was not alone. It seemed too much to ask, that a people so long accustomed to the restraints of slavery should be all at once lifted into the complete freedom of citizenship. It was too fast and too far. For once, the clear-eyed preacher, pioneer and prophet failed to discern the signs of the times. While the midnight darkness of slavery lasted, none more clearly than he saw the true course, or more steadily pursued it; but the first streak of daylight confused his vision, and he halted; while at halt, a part of the hosts he had led moved on. While we can never fully pay the debt of gratitude we owe to William Lloyd Garrison for his long and powerful advocacy of our emancipation from chattel slavery, other names loom up for grateful mention when equal suffrage is under consideration.

We cannot be too grateful to the brave and good men through whose exertions our enfranchisement has been accomplished. It would, of course, be impossible to do justice to all who have participated in this noble work. We have no scales by which to weigh and measure the value of our individual benefactors. This must be left to other times and other men. Impartial history will bring many who are obscure for a moment into future notice, and will shower upon their memories all merited honors. In this hour of joy and gratitude we can do no more than view the grand army as a whole, and bow our heads in warmest admiration and gratitude to all. . . .

But what does this Fifteenth amendment mean to us? I will tell you. It means that the colored people are now and will be held to be, by the whole nation, responsible for their own existence and their well or ill being. It means that we are placed upon an equal footing with all other men, and that the glory or shame of our future is to be wholly our own. For one, I accept this new situation gladly. I do so for myself and I do so for you; and I do so in the full belief that the future will show that we are equal to the responsibility which this great measure has imposed upon us.

What does this measure mean? I will tell you. It means progress, civilization, knowledge, manhood. It means that you and I and all of us shall leave the narrow places in which we now breathe, and live in the same comfort and independence enjoyed by other men. It means industry, application to business, economy in the use of our earnings, and the building up of a solid character—one which will deserve and command the respect of our fellow citizens of all races. It means that color is no longer to be a calamity; that race is to be no longer a crime; and that liberty is to be the right of all.

The black man has no longer an apology for lagging behind in the race of civilization. If he rises the glory is to be his, if he falls the shame will be his. He is to be the architect of his own fortunes. If we are despised, it is because we make ourselves despicable, if we are honored it is because we exhibit qualities deserving of honor. Character, not color, is to be the criterion. A great many of the American people are disturbed about the present state of things. They like a strong government. Carlyle says we are rushing to ruin with cataract speed. Others are croakers in the mournful style of Poe's raven—we shall never again see such days as were the earlier days of our republic, say they—never such statesmen as Clay, Calhoun, Webster, and others. The two races cannot work well together. However, he would let the croakers croak on. He never felt more hopeful than now, and the croakers do not disturb him. We had them during the war, and we shall continue to have them. During the dark hours of the war, when we needed strong words to hold us up, there were croakers. They said we never would put down rebellion, or abolish slavery, or reconstruct the South, and we have accomplished all. South Carolina has adopted all the amendments.

He compassionated his Democratic brethren. They are in a state of honest alarm, and we ought to say some word of comfort to them. He would tell his Democratic friends, that Jefferson wrote the Fourteenth Amendment. That amendment is but the carrying out of Democratic doctrine—that all men are created equal, and have the inalienable right to life, liberty and the pursuit of happiness. We gave the credit to Garrison, Lundy, and others. When God told the children of Israel to go free, the great truth had its origin.

We are a great nation—not we colored people particularly, but all of us. We are all together now. We are fellow-citizens of a common country. What a country—fortunate in its institutions, in its Fifteenth amendment, in its future. We are made up of a variety of nations—Chinese, Jews, Africans, Europeans, and all sorts. These different races give the Government a powerful arm to defend it. They will vie with each other in hardship and peril, and will be united in defending it from all its enemies, whether from within or without.

# CARL SCHURZ,
## "ENFORCEMENT OF THE FIFTEENTH AMENDMENT"
### *(May 19, 1870)*

Within three months of the ratification of the Fifteenth Amendment, Congress found it necessary to pass a series of Enforcement Acts to protect freedmen, Southern Unionists, and Republicans from violent acts by formal and informal paramilitary terrorist groups, including the Ku Klux Klan. Congress had heated debates over passage of each Enforcement Act, with Democrats and conservatives arguing that they signified a dangerous move toward centralization and denial of states' rights. In 1870, Carl Schurz, then a senator from Missouri, defended the first Enforcement Act as necessary to protect the rights of the newly enfranchised and to suppress fraud, intimidation, and violence then rampant in the South.

The May 31, 1870, act empowered the federal courts and the president (by mobilizing the army) to punish persons who interfered with voting rights. The February 28, 1871, act authorized federal supervision of congressional elections. The third act (April 20, 1871) outlawed groups like the Klan and authorized the president to suspend the writ of habeas corpus if necessary.

... Does this bill really take away from the States the power to legislate on the subject? Look at it closely. Does it? Not at all, sir. It leaves the States just as free as they ever were to legislate for the prompt and vigorous enforcement of protection of the right of every voter to the free exercise of the suffrage. Does it not? In that respect it does not impose the least restriction on the power of the States. In that direction the States may go just as far as they please. But the bill does provide that a State shall no longer have the power to swindle any of its citizens out of their rights.

A State shall have full power to do that which is right in its own way; but it is prohibited from doing that which is wrong in any way. It is this, I suppose, that Democrats will insist upon calling an arbitrary limitation of State rights. Or is it true, what is asserted also, that this legislation does not find anything analogous in the Constitution of the United States? In the Constitution, sir, we find one clause which ordains that no State shall have the power to grant titles of nobility. What does that mean? It means that no State shall elevate, by the grant of privileges, one class of its citizens above the rest. And what is contemplated by the fifteenth amendment and by the law designed to enforce it? That no State shall have the power to degrade, by the withholding of rights, any portion of its citizens below the rest. Is not the correspondence here evident? But here suddenly the indignation of our Democratic friends is aroused, and in the prohibition to degrade men they find an intolerable encroachment on State-rights and local self-government. And just there, I apprehend, is the rub. It is not so much the technicalities of the bill; it is the spirit, the purpose of the bill they oppose. It is as the Senator from Maryland has just openly and boldly proclaimed, that if the bill were ever so perfect, he would vote against it on general principles. He nods his assent; and I am sure I cannot mistake him; and the same thing we have been given to understand by every Democratic Senator who has addressed the Senate on this question.

Let us see what their complaints are, then. Strip them of all the verbiage of technical points, sift them to the bottom, and you will find there a residue of the old proslavery logic still. As they once asserted that true liberty implied the right of one man to hold another man as his slave, they will tell you now that they are no longer true freemen in their States because under the authority of the States they can no longer deprive other men of their rights. As they once asserted that true self-government consisted in the power of a State to exclude a large portion of its citizens from self-government, so they will say now that we strike a blow at self-government because we insist upon legislation securing every citizen of the States in the enjoyment of self-government. Is it not so?

Destruction of self-government! What a prodigious discovery our Democratic associates have made! Sir, it is not because this bill lays its hands upon self-government to destroy it, but because by the fifteenth amendment, and the legislation made in pursuance thereof, the general sway of self-government is to be for the first time established all over this country, that I am in favor of the principles of this act. What is true self-government? What does it consist in? True self-government consists in a political organization of society which secures to the generality of its members, that is to say, to the whole people, and not to a part of them only, the right and the means to coöperate in the management of their common affairs, either directly, or, where direct action is impossible, by a voluntary delegation of power. It ceases to be true self-government as soon as the powers of government are conferred as an exclusive privilege on one portion of the people and are withheld from the rest. And how is self-government exercised? By the right of suffrage. The representative system knows no other instrumentality. Suffrage is the means by which it lives and breathes.

To make self-government true, general and secure, therefore, the right of suffrage must be made secure to the generality of the citizens. You limit the right of suffrage by arbitrary exclusions, and just in that measure and to that extent will you impair the integrity of self-government. Protect every citizen in the free exercise of the right of suffrage and you do the thing best calculated to make self-government a general and living reality. I do not express any opinion here of the policy of restricting suffrage by an educational test, for it will not affect the principle.

And now the Democrats accuse us of destroying self-government by the very means which are instrumental in securing it in all the subdivisions of the Republic. I repeat, there never was a more preposterous charge. Sir, in a very large portion of this Republic that which could justly be called self-government of the people never existed. Now, at last, we are establishing it there by placing the right of suffrage on the broadest democratic basis, thus making the people of all the States, in the true sense of the term, self-governing bodies. And it is for this that we are denounced by our Democratic friends here as the sworn enemies of self-government and State-rights. Sir, I apprehend it is not for self-government and State-rights that our Democratic associates are standing up; but, drawing logical conclusions from the reasoning they have been indulging in, it is for State wrongs they contend. It is not for the liberty of all, but it is for the liberty of one to restrict and impair the liberty of another. It is not for true self-government of the people, but it is for the government of one part of the people over another part.

The time is past, sir, when the cry of State-rights will serve as a guise for such pretensions. I, too, am a friend and earnest advocate of State-rights, as far as State-rights are the embodiment of true local self-government. True, I do not cling to those traditional notions which an historical period now passed by and absolved has brought down to us. I do not cherish that sentimental—I might almost say that superstitious—reverence for individual States, which attributes to them as historical persons a sort of transcendental sanctity; but I do believe that their value can hardly be overestimated as compact political sub-organizations, through which and in which the self-government of the people is exercised, and within which it finds its most appropriate and efficient organs. I am therefore in favor of leaving to the States as large a scope of independent action as may be consistent with the safety of the Republic and the rights of the citizens.

In fact, sir, in my opinion, true local self-government is the great fountain from which the popular mind draws its healthiest and most invigorating inspirations. It is not only a machinery of political action, but it is one of the most efficient educational agencies of our social system. There is nothing better calculated to make a man understand and protect his interests, nothing more inspiring and instructive to the heart and mind of man than the independent management of his own affairs, upon his own responsibility; and there is nothing more inspiring and invigorating to a community of men, than free cooperation for common ends on a common responsibility in which the interest of each individual is involved.

That, sir, is what puts men upon their own feet. When they have accustomed themselves to depend on their own wisdom or energy for success, and to blame themselves and not others for failure and mishap in individual and com-

mon concerns, then they will become truly independent beings, such as the citizens of a democratic republic ought to
be. Therefore, it is of high importance that as many responsibilities as possible should be laid at the door of every citizen by local self-government.

We are apt to grow eloquent in the praise of the educational systems established in many of our States. They are,
indeed, praiseworthy: and yet they are as such by no means
superior to the educational systems enjoyed in some other
countries.

It may be said that in some German States the system is
even better developed than in the most advanced States of
New England; and yet we perceive here a higher average of
popular intelligence. We find that the American is generally
quicker of perception, readier in the comprehension of the
practical problems of life, more vigorous and energetic in
action, than people formed by a better school system elsewhere. Why is this so? Not because our babies are born
smarter here; not because our boys and girls learn to read,
write and cipher better in our schools; not because their
instruction in geography and natural science is more thorough; but the reason is, that as soon as the young American
issues from the hands of his schoolmaster and enters the
arena of practical life, he finds in the rights and duties and
responsibilities of self-government a more powerful incen-
tive and a larger field for the exercise of all his faculties and
for the immediate application of all his acquirements. Thus
self-government and popular education aid, inspire and
complement one another; and hence the great results we
observe.

And now let me impress upon our Democratic friends
that for this very reason nothing is more important, nay,
more necessary, for the harmonious development of the social forces of this Republic, as they now stand side by side
and have to work together, than that all, even the lowliest
classes of the people, should be drawn within the circle of
this beneficent combination of educational influences, and
that they should be carefully protected in their complete
enjoyment. And if you study our social problems without
prejudice you will find that just this is one of the most valuable results of that Constitutional revolution which so
sorely distresses the Democratic mind.

But for the precise reason which I have just indicated the revolution which is to protect all American citizens in the exercise of self-government ought not to be carried so far as to encroach upon its legitimate scope. I am, therefore, strenuously opposed to all unnecessary accumulation of powers in the hands of the General Government, and especially to any undue centralization of administrative functions. In my opinion, and I say this to my party friends, it would be well for us to bridle that tendency which we have so frequently had occasion to observe, to thrust the hand of the National Government into local affairs on every possible occasion, and even to disregard and throw aside the most fundamental safeguards of popular rights for the correction of passing abuses.

I know it is fashionable to call that radicalism; but I apprehend it is false radicalism in the highest degree. We ought not to accustom ourselves, nor those who are to follow us in these seats, to the employment of arbitrary powers, and still less ought we to accustom the people to look always to the National Government for redress whenever anything goes wrong in their home concerns. Destroy their habit of holding themselves responsible for the management of their home affairs, deprive them of the great lesson of failure to be corrected by themselves, and they will soon cease to study and understand the nature of the evils under which they labor, as well as the remedies to be applied. Thus the educating power of our institutions will be fatally impaired.

There can be nothing more preposterous, in my opinion, than the system prevailing in some foreign countries, where the people are permitted to vote upon the greatest and most complicated questions of general policy while they are not permitted to manage upon their own responsibility their home affairs at their own doors; the great popular school of political knowledge and experience, which consists in self-government, being thus closed to them. Certainly, it is not to be wondered at if in such countries universal suffrage becomes a mere instrument in the hands of despotism; an instrument which, indeed, may serve from time to time to subvert one form of despotism, but only to substitute for it another.

Therefore I am for State-rights as the embodiment of

true and general self-government, and I am convinced that this is the prevailing sentiment among the American people. It would be a sad day for this Republic if it should cease to be so. It is true the exigencies of the civil war have quite naturally developed a tendency to accumulate and centralize power in the hands of the National Government, and while that accumulation was necessary to save the existence of the Republic, the people of the United States willingly and patriotically and cheerfully acquiesced in it; but as soon as the pressure of necessity ceases, as soon as it becomes apparent that the great problems for the solution of which we are struggling may be solved just as well by the simple operations of local self-government as by the interference of the National power, then the tide will just as certainly set in the opposite direction. I am sure the people of the United States will never countenance an accumulation of power merely for power's sake, and the Republican party will do well to consider whether it is not better for their usefulness and ascendancy to direct than to resist that tide.

For this reason I earnestly deprecate those hazardous interpretations which have been applied to that clause of the Constitution which makes it the duty of the United States to guarantee to every State a republican form of government. I certainly recognize that duty as a great, solemn and sacred one; but I deny that it confers upon the National Government the power to do all within the range of the human imagination. I deny that it authorizes or enables us to use the arm of the National authority for the purpose of realizing by force what conception each of us may entertain of the "ideal republic."

In whatever way political philosophers may define the term "a republican form of government," it seems to me that the Constitution of the United States in its amended, or, as our Democratic friends would have it, in its revolutionized state, has provisions which give a fair index of the powers conferred upon Congress by the guaranty clause. There we read that Congress shall see to it that no State establishes or maintains slavery or involuntary servitude; there we read that Congress shall see to it that every man born upon this soil or naturalized, and therefore a citizen of the United States, shall be protected in all the rights, privileges and immunities of citizens in every State of this Union; there we read that Congress shall see to it that every citizen of the United States shall be protected in his right to the ballot, irrespective of race or color.

But the Constitutional revolution has enlarged the powers of Congress for the purpose of establishing and securing true and general self-government in all of these States, not for the purpose of circumscribing its scope and functions within narrower limits. It has, indeed, overthrown what I call State wrongs; but it was not designed to abolish what I would call the legitimate sphere of State-rights. And I venture to say—and I cannot repeat this warning too often—the party which would attempt to carry that revolution much farther in the direction of an undue centralization of power would run against a popular instinct far stronger than party allegiance has ever proved to be.

But, sir, on the other hand, the party that would refuse to recognize and acquiesce in the great results of this beneficent revolution; the party that would attempt to subvert the institution of general self-government under National protection, as now established in the Constitution; the party that would strive to overthrow this new order of things, such a party certainly cannot fail to encounter the condemnation of the people and to meet disgrace and destruction, for such a party openly, by its own confession, constitutes itself the enemy of the peace and glory of this Republic. And I would say to my friend from New Jersey that I did not come to this country, where I hope to enjoy the blessings of liberty and self-government, to aid any party in designs like these.

Now, sir, permit me to address a few words to the leaders of the Democratic organization on this floor; and they know I speak to them as men whose character and ability I esteem, and whose personal friendship I value. You, gentlemen, tell us that you are in favor of true self-government. If you really are, look around you and see how much you can do to contribute to its success and security. In your party are the men who threaten and endanger it by the most iniquitous attempts to deprive certain classes of people of their political rights by fraud, intimidation and violence; thus to subvert the new order of things, throwing the country into chaos again. Your voices are potent with them; not ours. If you really are true friends to self-government, then let your voices be heard in condemnation of the disastrous course so many of your friends are still following. Let them be loudly heard in favor of the great principle of equal rights, the only basis upon which the political future of this Republic can develop itself.

You, gentlemen, tell us that you are opposed to an undue assumption and exercise of power on the part of the General Government. If you are, see how powerfully you can aid in preventing it by removing all those reasons and causes and pretexts which may bring it on. What are those reasons and causes? Do they not consist in those disorders which are troubling the people of the South as to the safety of the Unionists and the rights of the newly-enfranchised, disorders invariably excited by men who profess to belong to your party? And do you not know as well as I that as soon as the people of the United States once apprehend that a serious reaction, with only an apparent chance of success, is set on foot against the great results of the war, the tide of public sentiment will just as surely and promptly set back in favor of a more extended and vigorous exertion of the National power, and you will be impotent to arrest it? For there are certain things in regard to which the American people will not permit themselves to be trifled with; and foremost among those things stand the great results which we have so laboriously evolved out of the civil war now behind us. There is the danger; and he who is no enemy to self-government, he who is no friend to a dangerous accumulation of power, will certainly use every endeavor to avert it. For our part we would much rather reason down the disturbers of the peace in the South than strike them down; but to our voices they will not listen; to yours they will. They are within the reach of your persuasion. There is the field where you can prove your devotion to self-government and your dislike of centralized power.

You tell us also, gentlemen, that legislation like this is odious to you. Look around you and see how much you can do to make it superfluous. We, too, should be glad never to be under the necessity of resorting to it. If you want to avoid it the means is simple. Prevail upon your friends never to threaten or trouble any class of voters in the free exercise of their rights, have those rights secured and protected by appropriate State legislation, and that State legislation respected by your friends, and such measures as this will never be practically applied. Nay, more than that, if you are really in earnest, then I would advise you to accept this measure as a gage of good faith instead of opposing it. It would be far better than your attempts to throw doubt upon the legality of the Constitutional amendments, your studious efforts to hold out to your partisans the prospect of their overthrow, and of the subversion of all that has been accomplished for the final settlement of our controversies and the peace of the country.

Yes, make up your minds, gentlemen, to the fact that your old doctrines are exploded forever and cannot be revived. Give up your useless and disturbing agitation against accomplished results. Go to your Southern friends and counsel them not to ruin themselves by vainly resisting the inevitable. Thus you will do more for the cause of self-government, more to prevent a dangerous centralization of power, you will render a far higher service to this generation and to posterity, than by indulging in those lugubrious wails and lamentations to which you have accustomed us on the floor of the Senate—the lamentation that we are governed by an atrocious despotism because one man shall no longer have the right to deprive another man of his rights; that self-government has received its death-blow because nobody shall henceforth be excluded from its exercise, and that liberty has fled forever from these shores because at last the Republic has thrown her protecting shield over the rights of all, even the lowliest of her children.

Mr. President, I do not stand here to plead the cause of my party only. If I did so, if there were nothing nearer and dearer to my heart than partisan success and partisan power, I should hold very different language. I would then say to my Democratic friends, "By all means go on with your opposition against the results of the war; go on with your mischievous warfare against the new order of things; go on with vain and disturbing agitation to restore what has ceased to be and can never again be;" for if they do, they will only prove that they are still living in a past which this Nation has long outgrown; that they are still bent upon sacrificing the interests of the living generation to idols which are dead; that they are still bound to keep open the wounds of the past, and to defeat those hopes of peace and good understanding which the country so fondly cherishes, and the realization of which depends entirely upon a final settlement of the controversies which the war has left to us. And thus exhibiting their unwillingness to understand and appreciate the exigencies of the present, they will demonstrate even to the dullest mind their incapacity to control our future; and then the people of the United States, sagacious and prudent as they are, will appreciate the fact and treat them accordingly. Acting thus, our opponents will only condemn themselves to continued impotency.

If, therefore, I pleaded for nothing but the interest of my party I would encourage them to persevere in their course. But I plead for the cause of our country—for its peace, its prosperity, its happiness and its good name; and I cannot permit myself to forget that the people will not be secure in the enjoyment of those blessings as long as there is a large and influential party insidiously striving to undermine the foundation upon which alone they can grow, and to plunge the country again into the confusion of endless and bitter struggles. It is for this reason that I entreat our Democratic friends to desist from their disturbing and most mischievous agitation.

Some time ago my friend from New Jersey closed his speech on the admission of the Senator from Mississippi [Mr. REVELS], who is the first representative of the colored race on this floor, with a most eloquent and touching appeal in favor of peace, harmony and good understanding; so eloquent, indeed, as to cause the usual decorum of the Senate to be broken by demonstrations of applause. I take that Senator at his word. Yes, let there be peace and harmony and good understanding, and let us all unite in doing the one thing needful to bring it about. The Senator must instinctively feel what that one thing needful is. He cannot conceal from his own eyes that there is but one settlement of our present controversy possible; that only one can be final, permanent and conclusive; and that is, the settlement which we advocate. He must see that the black man, being once admitted to the polls, the decree cannot be reversed. He must see that those broad hints, so frequently thrown out by Democratic Senators in the course of this very debate, that the fifteenth amendment is invalid and may still at some future time be overthrown, can only serve to encourage the false hopes of the rebel element in the South, can only serve to excite the worst impulses in an unthinking multitude in the North and can result in nothing but mischief, the most wanton, the most cruel mischief.

If the honorable Senator from New Jersey is really so ardent a friend of peace, harmony and fraternal feeling, let him go among his associates and tell them,

Enough of this; it is better to be right by the light of today than to be consistent with the errors of yesterday. If there lingers in your hearts a doubt as to the legality of the ratification of these Constitutional amendments, in the name of all that is good and great, waive that doubt; waive it for the peace of the country; waive it for the sake of those great interests which we are all called upon to serve. Do not insist upon exciting the evil passions which with so much trouble we have at last succeeded in quieting; do not tear open the wounds of the past again; do not torment the country with new struggles about those fearful questions which have kept the people so long in restless agitation, and are now at last on the point of final settlement, if we only permit them to be settled.

In uniting his party upon such a platform, the platform of such noble and conciliatory sentiments, my friend from New Jersey, who addressed me so eloquently yesterday, would do an act worthy of himself; he would render an inestimable service to our common country; and he might then at last even stagger my conviction, a conviction I have been compelled to entertain so far, that the blessings of liberty and self-government which I came to enjoy in this country, would be very unsafe if unfortunately the party of which he is a member should again obtain possession of the powers of the National Government.

But, sir, if the leaders of the Democratic party will not listen to language like this, then I think we shall be safe in taking an appeal to the masses. The people of the United States will see, if the Democratic leaders do not, that of all the policies thought of for the settlement of pending controversies, that proposed by the Republican party, the settlement of equal rights and general self-government, is the only one which by any possibility can be final and conclusive, for it is the only one in full accordance with the genius of republican institutions. The people will see, if the Democratic leaders do not, that the highest interests of the country demand that settlement to be made promptly and without cavil; for without it we shall not obtain that peace which is necessary to enable us to devote our whole attention to those moral and material problems of the present and future which so loudly call for solution. The people will, if the Democratic leaders do not, appreciate the greatness and beneficence of the idea upon which the new order of things, the settlement we propose, rests—true and general self-government exercised in and through the States; States whose power moves independently in its appropriate sphere; potent in doing that which is right; impotent to abridge the rights of even the meanest of their people; and the protecting shield of the National authority thrown over all.

The transcendent greatness of this consummation the American people will appreciate and I trust they will take good care not to put the National power into the hands of any men or of any organization of men who still speak of overthrowing the great Constitutional amendments, the price of so much blood and anxiety and struggle, the only safe foundation for the future peace and glory of this Republic.

# "An Act to Enforce the Right of Citizens of the United States to Vote in the Several States of This Union, and for Other Purposes"

## (May 31, 1870)

The first Enforcement Act signaled a shift away from legislative to judicial and executive authority in protecting constitutional rights. It specified stiff financial penalties for those persons who wrongfully prevented qualified persons from voting. The act made it a felony for groups such as the Klan to conspire against, harass, or deny persons the franchise.

*Be it enacted by the Senate and House of Representatives of the United States of America in Congress assembled,* That all citizens of the United States who are or shall be otherwise qualified by law to vote at any election by the people in any State, Territory, district, county, city, parish, township, school district, municipality, or other territorial subdivision, shall be entitled and allowed to vote at all such elections, without distinction of race, color, or previous condition of servitude; any constitution, law, custom, usage, or regulation of any State or Territory, or by or under its authority, to the contrary notwithstanding.

SEC. 2. *And be it further enacted,* That if by or under the authority of the constitution or laws of any State, or the laws of any Territory, any act is or shall be required to be done as a prerequisite or qualification for voting, and by such constitution or laws persons or officers are or shall be charged with the performance of duties in furnishing to citizens an opportunity to perform such prerequisite, or to become qualified to vote, it shall be the duty of every such person and officer to give to all citizens of the United States the same and equal opportunity to perform such prerequisite, and to become qualified to vote without distinction of race, color, or previous condition of servitude; and if any such person or officer shall refuse or knowingly omit to give full effect to this section, he shall, for every such offence, forfeit and pay the sum of five hundred dollars to the person aggrieved thereby, to be recovered by an action on the case, with full costs, and such allowance for counsel fees as the court shall deem just, and shall also, for every such offence, be deemed guilty of a misdemeanor, and shall, on conviction thereof, be fined not less than five hundred dollars, or be imprisoned not less than one month and not more than one year, or both, at the discretion of the court. . . .

SEC. 4. *And be it further enacted,* That if any person, by force, bribery, threats, intimidation, or other unlawful means, shall hinder, delay, prevent, or obstruct, or shall combine and confederate with others to hinder, delay, prevent, or obstruct, any citizen from doing any act required to be done to qualify him to vote or from voting at any election as aforesaid, such person shall for every such offence forfeit and pay the sum of five hundred dollars to the person aggrieved thereby, to be recovered by an action on the case, with full costs, and such allowance for counsel fees as the court shall deem just, and shall also for every such offence be guilty of a misdemeanor, and shall, on conviction thereof, be fined not less than five hundred dollars, or be imprisoned not less than one month and not more than one year, or both, at the discretion of the court.

SEC. 5. *And be it further enacted,* That if any person shall prevent, hinder, control, or intimidate, or shall attempt to prevent, hinder, control, or intimidate, any person from exercising or in exercising the right of suffrage, to whom the right of suffrage is secured or guaranteed by the fifteenth amendment to the Constitution of the United States, by means of bribery, threats, or threats of depriving such person of employment or occupation, or of ejecting such person from rented house, lands, or other property, or by threats of refusing to renew leases or contracts for labor, or by threats of violence to himself or family, such person so offending shall be deemed guilty of a misdemeanor, and shall, on conviction thereof, be fined not less than five hundred dollars, or be imprisoned not less than one month and not more than one year, or both, at the discretion of the court. . . .

SEC. 9. *And be it further enacted*, That the district attorneys, marshals, and deputy marshals of the United States, the commissioners appointed by the circuit and territorial courts of the United States, with powers of arresting, imprisoning, or bailing offenders against the laws of the United States, and every other officer who may be specially empowered by the President of the United States, shall be, and they are hereby, specially authorized and required, at the expense of the United States, to institute proceedings against all and every person who shall violate the provisions of this act, and cause him or them to be arrested and imprisoned, or bailed, as the case may be, for trial before such court of the United States or territorial court as has cognizance of the offence. And with a view to afford reasonable protection to all persons in their constitutional right to vote without distinction of race, color, or previous condition of servitude, and to the prompt discharge of the duties of this act, it shall be the duty of the circuit courts of the United States, and the superior courts of the Territories of the United States, from time to time, to increase the number of commissioners, so as to afford a speedy and convenient means for the arrest and examination of persons charged with a violation of this act; and such commissioners are hereby authorized and required to exercise and discharge all the powers and duties conferred on them by this act, and the same duties with regard to offences created by this act as they are authorized by law to exercise with regard to other offences against the laws of the United States.

# PROCEEDINGS OF THE KU KLUX TRIALS AT COLUMBIA, S.C., IN THE UNITED STATES CIRCUIT COURT, NOVEMBER TERM, 1871

## (1872)

The Ku Klux Klan was the best known of various white secret terrorist groups across the South during Reconstruction. Its members intimidated the freedpeople and their white supporters by threats and by violent actions to prevent them from voting, from organizing politically, from establishing churches and schools, and from engaging in behavior that white conservatives deemed inappropriate. The Klan originated in Tennessee in 1866 as a fraternal club among ex-Confederates but quickly took on a political agenda, terrorizing those who opposed Southern Democrats. Night-riding Klansmen whipped, raped, and murdered those whom they sought to control, not only freedpeople and white Republicans, but also preachers, teachers, state legislators, and federal law enforcement officers. Klan activity contributed to the fall of Radical governments in several states, most notably in Georgia and Mississippi. The third Enforcement Act (often termed the Ku Klux Act) authorized the president to suspend the writ of habeas corpus in counties threatened by Klan violence. This came to pass in October 1871 when President Grant declared nine upcountry South Carolina counties in a "condition of lawlessness." In some cases, he dispatched troops to suppress Klan violence. In 1871, the U.S. Circuit Court convened in Columbia, South Carolina, and recorded extensive and detailed testimony about Klan activities in the state.

## Testimony of Amzi Rainey.

Amzi Rainey, a witness for the prosecution, being duly sworn, testified as follows:

Q. Where do you live?
A. On Mr. Gill's place.
Q. In York County?
A. Yes; in York County.
Q. How long have you lived in York County?
A. I have been born and raised there.
Q. How old are you?
A. About twenty-eight years old.
Q. Have you been a voter in York County?
A. Yes, sir.
Q. Have you voted?
A. Yes, sir.
Q. Nobody has ever questioned your right to vote there, have they?
A. No, sir.
Q. Did you vote at the last election?
A. Yes, sir.
Q. Vote for A. S. Wallace?
A. Yes, sir.
Q. Vote the rest of the Republican ticket?
A. Yes, sir.
Q. Now, will you tell the jury whether the Ku Klux raided on you, and what they said and what they did to you? Tell us all about it?
A. Well, on a Saturday night, about ten o'clock—
Q. When was that?
A. It was about the last of March, as near as I can recollect. I was laying down—I laid down at the first dark—and was laying down by the fire. The rest done been abed, and, about ten o'clock, my little daughter called me, and said: "Pappy, it is time we are going to bed; get up;" and just as I got up, and turned around, I looked out of the window, and I see some four or five disguised men coming up, and I ran up in the loft, and they came on; come to the door; and when they come to the door, they commenced beating and knocking. "God damn you, open the door! open the door!

open the door!" and commenced beating at each side—
there is two doors—and they commenced beating both
doors, and my wife run to one of the doors, and they
knocked the top hinges off of the first, and she run across
the house to the other, and again that time they got the two
hinges knocked off the other door, and the bolt held the
door from falling, and she got it open—that is, she pulled
the bolt back and throwed it down, and when they come in,
they struck her four or five licks before they said a word—

Mr. Johnson. We object to all this, may it please your
Honors.

The Court. Let him go on.

A. They asked her who lived here. She said, "Rainey—
Amzi Rainey." "What Amzi Rainey? What Amzi Rainey?"
And she said, "Amzi Rainey," and he struck her another
lick, and says: "Where is he? God damn him, where is he?"
And she says: "I don't know." And one said: "O, I smell him,
God damn him; he has gone up in the loft." He says: "We'll
kill him, too," and they come up then. This Sam Good, they
made him light a light—

Q. Who is Sam Good?

A. It is a black man, that lives on the same place.

Q. You say he had come on with them?

A. Yes, sir. And he lit a light, and they made him and my
wife go up before, and he followed them up there, and I was
in a box, and they said: "Oh, he is in this box, God damn
him, I smell him; we'll kill him!" and the other says: "Don't
kill him yet;" and they took me down. This man that struck
my wife first, ran back to her and says: "God damn her, I
will kill her now; I will kill her out;" and the one that went
after me, he says: "Don't kill her;" and he commenced beating her then; struck her some four or five more licks, and
then run back and struck me; he run back to her then, and
drawed his pistol, and says: "Now, I am going to blow your
damn brains out;" and the one by me threw the pistol up,
and says: "Don't kill her." He aimed to strike me over the
head, and struck me over the back, and sunk me right down.
Then, after he had done that, my little daughter—she was
back in the room with the other little children—he says: "I
am going to kill him;" and she run out of the room, and
says: "Don't kill my pappy; please don't kill my pappy!" He

shoved her back, and says: "You go back in the room, you God damned little bitch; I will blow your brains out!" and fired and shot her, sure enough—

Q. Did he hit her?

A. Yes, sir; he hit her; and after he had done that, she went back into the room, and they commenced shooting over me—two shots over me, and two shots over my wife; they shot about fifteen shots; and I had a sleeve jacket on; it was woolen, and they set fire to it—just in a light blaze of fire—and after that was done, they hollered to me: "Put out that fire, I would burn up, and damned if I wouldn't go to hell." Then my little daughter had catched her hand full of blood, got to the door, and just throwed it out; and they looked around and see that, and see her; and then they took me—

Q. Where did they hit your daughter?

A. Hit her on the forehead; the ball glanced off from her head. Then they took me right off.

Q. Off where?

A. Off up the road, about a hundred and fifty yards; and they wanted to kill me up there, and one said, "No, don't kill him, let's talk a little to him first." Then, he asked me which way did I vote. I told him I voted the Radical ticket. "Well," he says, "now you raise your hand and swear that you will never vote another Radical ticket, and I will not let them kill you." And he made me stand and raise my hand before him and my God, that I never would vote another Radical ticket, against my principle.

Q. Did you swear so?

A. I did raise my hand and swear. Then he took me out among the rest of them, and wouldn't let them shoot me, and told me to go back home.

Q. Did they make anybody else swear right there that they wouldn't vote the Radical ticket? Was Sam Good there?

A. Yes, sir.

Q. What did they do to him?

A. They asked him which way he voted. He says the Radical ticket, and they asked if he would ever vote any Radical ticket, and Sam told them "No, sir." And that was all that I heard passed 'twixt them and Sam.

Q. What did they do when you went home?

A. After I went back, my wife, she hobbled out—

Q. When you left them, what did they do to you?

A. Told me to run; and throwed two big rocks after me, about the size of my fist.

Q. Did they hit you?

A. No, sir; one went one side into a wood pile, and the other struck the chimney.

Q. How many of the Ku Klux were there?

A. It looked to me like there was about twenty-five.

Q. How were they dressed?

A. Had on—some of them had on white gowns, and some of them had on red ones, and had on false faces and something over their heads.

Q. Did you know any of them?

A. No, sir.

Q. Didn't know any of them?

A. Didn't know any of them.

Q. What time in the night was this?

A. About ten o'clock—'twixt ten and eleven o'clock.

Q. Do you know what they did to your daughter in the other room?

A. Yes, sir.

Q. Did you see it yourself?

A. I didn't see it; have only her word for it.

Q. I won't ask you that then.?

A. I didn't see that.

Mr. Corbin. You may have the witness.

Mr. Johnson. We have no questions, may it please your Honors. . . .

## TESTIMONY OF DICK WILSON.

Dick Wilson, a witness for the prosecution, being duly sworn, testified as follows:

## DIRECT EXAMINATION BY MR. CORBIN.

Q. Where do you live?

A. I live in York District, sir.

Q. On whose place, in York County?

A. Dr. Lowry's.

Q. Did you vote at the last election?

A. Yes, sir.

Q. Which ticket did you vote?

A. I voted the Republican ticket.

Q. Did you vote for Mr. Wallace?

A. Yes, sir.

Q. Have you voted there before?

A. Yes, sir.

Q. Nobody questioned your right to vote when you did vote?

A. Not particularly, at the ballot box.

Q. Now tell us whether the Ku Klux visited you, and where?

A. Well, they visited me on the 11th April, about two hours before—well, about, 'twixt two and three o'clock in the morning. I had been up till it was light, and laid down and got into a sleep, and I woke up, and these men were in the yard; two of the men came to the house, and the other four went to my son's house.

Q. What is his name?

A. Richard. These men came to my house. First words I noticed them saying was, "Open the door." Next word was, "Make up a light; make up a light." I immediately then jumped up and drew on my pants, and by that time the door fell in the middle of the floor. They commenced firing under the door and around the house. I stood still then. They stopped then for a minute, and asked me to make up a light again. I jumped to the fire and made up a light. The next question, "Who lives here?" Says I, "Dick Wilson." "Is this old Dick?" I told them, "Yes, sir." "Where is your son?" "I don't know, sir, where he is." "You are a dam'd liar, sir; walk out here; I have a word with you, sir." "Very well, I will come out." "Come out; come out right now; come out." I walked out. "Go on down here before me, sir, to the other house." And there was four men in there; a big light in the house; a good knot of pine on the fire, and they went searching cupboards and trunks, and looking everywhere. I could see them as plain as I can see you right now. Well, they searched the house all over, and they could not find him. They said, "Look under the floor." Well, they tried to get up the floor, but the floor was so well nailed they didn't get it

up. One of the men, in the middle of the house, turned
around and says, "What G—d damned rascal you've got
there?" Some man says, "That is old Dick Wilson." "What
are you going to do with that damned old son-of-a-bitch?"
"Well, we haint determined on what we'll do with him."
They still searched on, and couldn't find him.

Q. Couldn't find what?

A. Couldn't find my son, and they came out. After they
came out, then the question is put me, "Where is your son?"
Says I, "Gentlemen, I don't know." "Your son; don't you call
me any gentleman; we are just from hell fire; we haven't
been in this country since Manassas; we come to take Scott
and his ring; you damned niggers are ruining the country,
voting for men who are breaking the treasury; where is
your son, I say?" "I don't know, sir, where he is." "You are a
damned liar, sir; and I will make you tell where he is. Don't
you rather the men of this country would rule it, sir, as
these men as is ruling it?" Says I, "I didn't know there was
any other men ruling but the men of this country." "Is Scott
a man of this country, sir?" Says I, "I don't know; I never
seen him." "Then, why is it you don't go to some good old
citizen in the country who would tell you how to vote?"
Says I, "I went to men who I thought knowed and ought to
know." "Who were they?" "Well," I says, "that was Mr. Wallace." "Yes; just as damned a rascal as you are." "I went to
Mr. Wallace, and I went to several other gentlemen that I
did name out." "Well, what about the League?" I told him
that I did belong to the League.

Q. What—the Union league?

A. Yes, sir. "I suppose, then, you are a good old Radical?" Says I, "I don't know whether I have been; I have
tried to be." "Yes, and damn you, we'll make a Democrat of
you to-night." That was the next word. Another little one
jumped up there, with some horns on his head, and says:
"We'll take the damned rascal off and remind him of what
we have told him before this; we have told him this long
ago, and we want to be obeyed; now we will take satisfaction; walk on here, sir; take the road before me." I walked
on. "Drop your breeches, God damn you." I just ran out of
them. "Stretch out; we want to make a Democrat out of you
to-night." I stretched out full length, just as long as I could
get; I would have got a little longer if I could.

Q. Did you drop your pants?

A. Dropped them down—just fell out, full length.

Q. And then what?

A. One went that side and two on this side. Well, they commenced whipping me; I commenced begging them so powerful. "Don't beg, God damn you; if you beg I'll kill you." One of them said, "Stop this whipping right off. One of you gentlemen take that pistol and go to his head, and t'other to his feet, and if he hollows or moves I will blow his brains out." Then they commenced whipping me; they just ruined me; they cut me all to pieces; they did do it, and I wouldn't mind it so much if they had scattered the licks, but they whipped all in one place; that is what they done; they stopped on me then for a while. "Will you vote the Democratic ticket next time?" "Yes, I will vote any way you want me to vote; I don't care how you want me to vote, master, I will vote." Says he, "there now, put it to him; God damn him he has not told us yet where his son is; we have got that much, and we will get the balance." They commenced whipping me again. I told them at last I did not know where he was, and I didn't know where he was. After they got done whipping me, they ordered me to get up as quick as I could; I couldn't get up very fast; quick as I got up, I drawed up my pants; couldn't button them nohow. Had them in my hands. "Now let's see how fast you can run." Well, I was going to strain every leader that was in me, because I was hurt so that I could hardly move; but I intended to do my best. The other says, "I have a word or two to speak to him. I will give you ten days—you and your son both—to go and put a card in Grist's office, and show it; and let it come out in the papers in ten days from now, to show that you are done with the Republican party, Scott, and his damned Ring; and if you don't do it, I will come back for you both again; and if I can't get you at night, I will take you in daylight. Go off in the house, and shut the door." I went off in the house sure enough. I shut the door. I was lying down on the floor. I wasn't able to go to bed. I got worse after I got to the house.

Q. How bad were you whipped?

A. I was whipped badly. I had on me a pair of pants too large; and next day I had to tie a string on them so they would meet.

Q. Your back was all whipped to pieces?

A. Just all hove up. It was not cut up so, but was bruised.

Q. What did they whip you with?

A. With ramrods.

Q. Take them out of their guns?

A. Took them out and twisted them up.

Q. What were they—iron ramrods?

A. I don't know. There was one felt very much like it. I can't say positive that they was iron ramrods. They had this brass put on them where they rammed the powder and stuff down in the guns. These was there next morning—white oak ramrods.

Q. Did you find them?

A. Yes, sir.

Q. How much did you find of the ramrod?

A. I found two pieces right at the house, and betwixt my house and the creek I found the other.

Q. There were three broken?

A. Yes, sir; both of them.

Q. How big were they?

A. About the size of my finger.

Q. Did you go and put a card in the paper as they told you to?

A. No, sir; I did not; I did not do anything.

Q. Did you stay at home nights after that?

A. Yes, sir; I stayed at home; they told me to stay at home, and I done it.

Q. How long before you were able to work after that?

A. I went and knocked about, but I wasn't able to do a piece of work under a week; and to do a good day's work, I wasn't able to do it in two weeks; because I couldn't walk. I couldn't sit down; and when I lay down, I would have to lay right flat down on my stomach.

Q. How many were they there?

A. I didn't see but six.

Q. All have disguises on?

A. Yes, sir.

## CROSS-EXAMINATION BY MR. STANBERY.

Q. Did you know any of them in their disguise?

A. Well, sir, I did.

Q. You did know?

A. I did know.

Q. How could you tell, if they were disguised?

A. I saw the men's hands, shoes, clothing, everything they had on.

Q. Did you know the men?

A. One was Dr. Parker.

Q. Who was the other?

A. Was Mr. John James Miller.

Q. The other?

A. John Lytle.

Q. Who was the other?

A. The other one was Mr. Bill Lowrey.

Q. Who was the other?

A. Now the other man—I believe there were more—but will not swear to that man. I believe they were there.

Q. I only ask who you knew were there?

A. I won't be positive that these men were there; and that was Mr. Bishop Sandifer and Mr. Thomasson; but the other men, I did not say I knew them two men, but these other four, I know them; there were six altogether.

Q. And you told four of the six, notwithstanding they were disguised?

A. I knew four of them out of the six.

Q. How were they disguised?

A. Well, they had a little cloth over the head that came down and fastened back of the head. They had on common coats. This one had on a calico dress, the other one had on a red dress opened down before; the other had on looked like black overcoats, came way down here [indicating below the knee.]

Q. Had they false faces?

A. Well, they first had simply a false face, made to cover over the head, eyes and nose, and all the mouth was out, just a place where they could see, you know.

Q. It was cloth?

A. Yes, sir.

Q. All the head, and the eyes, and the nose, everything,

and the face was concealed, but the mouth; but you told four of them because you saw their underclothing?

A. Yes, sir.

Q. You told it from their shoes, and saw their underclothing?

A. I knew their hands, and I knew the men by their conversation. I got a full understanding of their voices.

Q. How far did they live from you?

A. Mr. Miller lived about three mile and a half, or four mile, I will say, at the outside.

Q. How far did either of the others live from you?

A. Dr. Parker lived about three miles from me, or a little better.

Q. How far did the other live?

A. Mr. Lytle lived about a mile and a half from me.

Q. How far did the fourth live?

A. Mr. Lowrey lived on the same plantation, about two miles.

Q. Now you told them by their hands, as well as by their underclothing?

A. Yes, sir.

Q. How can you be so familiar with their hands?

A. I know Mr. Lowrey by his hands; I've been working with him; he had been with me the day before.

Q. What sort of a hand has he?

A. He has a white hand, but has a finger that stands crooked; and he had sores on his hands, and that is the way I knew him.

Q. Did each of the other three have fingers of that sort, and sores on their hands?

A. No, sir.

Q. How did you know their hands?

A. I knew the men by their discourse; I knew them by their hands and by their discourse; I didn't say I knew them all by their hands; by their hands I knew two of them.

Q. You knew one by his hands?

A. Yes, sir, I went into this thing when they came to my house; they said they had risen from the dead; I wanted to see what sort of men they was; I went a purpose to see who they was; whether they were spirits, or whether they were human; but when I came to find out, they was men like me. . . .

## Testimony of Kirkland L. Gunn.

Kirkland L. Gunn, a witness for the prosecution, being duly sworn, testified as follows:

Q. (by Mr. Corbin). Where do you reside?

A. York County.

Q. How long have you resided there?

A. I was born and raised there.

Q. In what portion of the County?

A. My father lives in the south portion of the County.

Q. What is your age?

A. Twenty-one years.

Q. What is your profession and business?

A. I am a photographer.

Q. Have you carried on that business in York County?

A. I have, sir.

Q. State whether you have been initiated a member of the Ku Klux Klan?

A. I was initiated in January, 1871, and became a member of the Ku Klux Klan.

Q. Where?

A. At Wesley Smith's, near his house.

Q. Did you take the oath?

A. I did.

Q. Was the oath read to you?

A. The constitution and by-laws were read to me.

Q. Do you remember the oath?

A. Yes, sir.

Q. What was the oath, in substance?

A. It was, not to reveal the secrets of the Klan; that the purpose of the Klan was to put down Radicalism, and rule the negro suffrage. [A paper was here handed the witness.]

Q. State if that is substantially what was read to you on that occasion?

A. Yes, sir; the obligation is the same, (the witness was here requested to read the paper through,) it is the same that was read to me. The constitution and by-laws of the Ku Klux Klan were here read by the Attorney General in open Court.

Q. State the general purpose and object of the order as you understood them?

A. I heard them stated to me. It was to put down the Radical party and rule negro suffrage.

Q. How were those purposes to be carried out?

A. It was told to me by members of the Klan that it was to be by whipping negroes and intimidating them and keeping them from voting, and to kill all such white men as took Radical offices, and who then occupied offices.

Q. How was the organization armed?

A. Some were armed with pistols and some with shot guns, and some with muskets—just whatever was convenient.

Q. What was the Ku Klux gown?

A. A long gown made of some dark colored stuff. I never saw one in daylight.

Q. Was that worn on all occasions while on duty?

A. This was my understanding; that it was to be worn on all occasions.

Q. Were these operations to be carried on in the daylight or dark?

A. All this was in the night. Whenever the Klan was on duty, they were known and designated by number.

Q. How were they numbered?

A. Each man was to be numbered. Sometimes they would begin with No. 1, and sometimes they would begin with five hundred; they would begin with any number they chose, and then run on.

Q. What was the object of that?

A. To keep from calling names.

Q. Was it to assist in their concealment?

A. Yes, sir.

Q,. Who was the highest officer who commanded whenever a meeting was called or when they went on a raid?

A. I didn't know the highest officer; the Chief was the highest I knew.

Q. What did they call this business of going after colored men and whipping them?

A. Raiding.

Q. Did you ever go on any raiding?

A. I never was on one; was called to go on two raids.

Q. By whom?

A. By order of the Chief. I was told so by the person who

brought the message. John Wallace was the person who brought me the first message.

Q. Who was the Chief?

A. John Mitchell.

Q. Is this the man here? [pointing to the defendant, J. W. Mitchell.]

A. Yes, sir.

Q. Was he Chief of the Klan?

A. Yes, sir.

Q. What was the name of the Klan?

A. It was called Mitchell's Klan.

Q. Have you frequently seen this person?

A. I have met him several times, and met him once in the capacity of Chief.

Q. State the circumstances of the meeting?

A. I was told by Wallace, there was to be a meeting held at Barkley's Mill, for the purpose of raiding Bill Kell, and to kill him for being President of the Union League. Those were the words Wallace stated to me.

Q. What was Wallace's position in the Klan?

A. He was known as a Night Hawk.

Q. How long did you receive this order before the time of the meeting?

A. I think it was two days before the meeting.

Q. Pursuant to that notice did you meet the Klan?

A. I did.

Q. State who you met there?

A. I met there that person, J. W. Mitchell, Whiley, Ed. Leech, Arney Neil, Chas. W. Foster, Wesley Smith, Joe Smith, Thomas McAllen, and a good many others I knew, but I cannot remember their names now.

Q. How many persons were present at that meeting?

A. I should say from thirty to thirty-five persons.

Q. Were they mounted or on foot?

A. They were all mounted.

Q. Were they disguised or not?

A. Some were disguised and some were not.

Q. Did you go on that raid?

A. No, sir.

Q. Why?

A. Because Mr. Hugh Kell was there. It was thought he

was sent there for the purpose of letting it be known if Kell was killed—that he might be a witness.

Q. Was Hugh Kell a member of the Klan?

A. I don't know whether he was or not.

Q. Who brought the disguises there, and who took them away?

A. Mr. Mitchell did.

Q. What did he bring the disguise in?

A. He brought it in a sack.

Q. What did he carry them in?

A. In a sack.

Q. Did you see him put them in?

A. I saw him put one disguise in a sack.

Q. Was there any talk of killing Hugh Kell?

A. I heard someone say he was to be killed, but I heard no one say they wanted to kill him.

Q. What did they do finally?

A. There were some rough words between Mitchell and Kell. I don't know what they were, but they were rough, from what I heard others say of them. Mr. Mitchell ordered the Klan to go home and wait till he ordered them out again.

Q. Did you know Bill Kell—the man they proposed to kill?

A. No, sir.

Q. What other raid do you know of?

A. I was ordered to go on one raid on Jenny Good.

Q. Did you go upon that raid?

A. No, sir.

Q. Why not?

A. I had no saddle to ride.

Q. From whom did you receive the order to go there?

A. I don't remember now who told me they were going to have a raid.

Q. Who did he say he gave orders to for that raid?

A. Charles Byers.

Q. Was that Klan located near you?

A. About two miles from where I was.

Q. Who were the two Chiefs of the Klan residing there?

A. Byers and Mitchell.

Q. Did they order out the members of the other Klan?

A. They would invite the members of the other Klan to go with them—not order them.

Q. Were you invited to go on that raid?

A. Yes, sir.

Q. How many members were there in Mitchell's Klan?

A. I don't know.

Q. Have you any means of knowing from those you saw?

A. I don't know; there might have been members of other Klans.

Q. How many men were there in Charley Byers' Klan?

A. I think sixteen or seventeen; I don't remember the number.

Q. Do you know of any other Klan in that vicinity?

A. I do not, but have heard of others.

Q. Did you ever recognize a person by the name of Squire Sam Brown as a Ku Klux?

A. I have, sir.

Q. Where?

A. At Wiley's store.

Q. How did you recognize him?

A. By a sign.

Q. What sign did you give him?

A. Passing the hand over the right ear; he answered by passing his hand over his left ear.

Q. What conversation, if any, did you hear there from Samuel Brown?

A. He and Wesley Smith were standing, and they had been engaged in conversation. Smith stood up, and Brown gave him that sign; then he turned to Smith and asked, respecting me, "is this man all right?" Then he said "you know I would not have such business, without having men that were all right." Then, after some further conversation, I heard him say, "I can go and take my Klan, and whip more damn niggers than any other Klan in York County."

Q. Where does Squire Sam Brown live?

A. I don't know. I think it is west of Yorkville.

Q. Do you see that gentleman in Court here?

A. Yes, sir; there he sits (pointing.)

Q. State what were the signs and passwords of the order, and how they use them on occasion?

A. One was passing the right hand over the right ear;

this was answered by passing the left hand over the left ear; the next sign was putting the right hand in the pocket of the pants, leaving the thumb to be seen; if you wished to find out if a person belonged to the organization he returned it with his left hand in the same way; the next sign was putting the heel of the right foot in the hollow of the left; this was answered by putting the left heel in the hollow of the right foot.

Q. What were the passwords?

A. If you met a man or a party you would say, "S-a-y, who are you?" This was answered by, "N-o-t-h-i-n-g," without pronouncing the word.

Q. Have you frequently met and recognized members of the order by these words?

A. I have met them by signs, but not by words.

Q. Had they a grip; if so, explain it?

A. In grasping the hand the little finger would go between the fourth and little finger of the hand you grasped, and the forefinger would stretch up and touch the wrist.

Q. Have you frequently exchanged that grip?

A. Very often, sir.

## CROSS-EXAMINATION BY MR. WILSON.

Q. Have you any knowledge of Dr. Thomas Whitesides being a member of this order?

A. I do not know that he is a member.

Q. Have you not reason for knowing that he is not?

A. I have given him signs and he did not return them.

Q. You tried, then, by giving him the signs and he did not answer?

A. Yes, sir; I gave him signs and he did not respond.

Q. What sign did you give him?

A. Passing the right hand over the right ear.

Q. Have you any other reason for knowing he is not a member?

A. I heard him say it was the most damnable thing in the country?

Q. (by Mr. C. D. Melton.) What are the relations between you and Mr. Mitchell; are they those of friendship or otherwise?

A. As to my feelings, they have always been those of friendship.

Q. There was some cause of misunderstanding, was there not?

A. Not on my part. I had my photographic instrument in the church that he had something to do with, and he told me to take it out, but it caused no hard feeling on my part.

Q. Had you any conversation on the subject with Mr. McKeow?

A. I have no recollection of it.

Q. You say you never used any harsh language?

A. No, sir; none.

Q. And never had any unkind feelings towards Mr. Mitchell?

A. No, sir; I had none.

Q. (by Mr. Corbin.) When do you say it was that you recognized Mr. Whitesides was not a member of the order?

A. I think it was last March.

Q. Had you any special conversation about the Ku Klux order?

A. Yes, sir; he said something about the Ku Klux; he had some negroes that they visited, and he and his brother went to try to pacify them; he said it was the most damnable curse, or the most damnable affair in the country; I then gave him the sign, but he did not respond. . . .

## TESTIMONY OF HENRY LATHAM.

Henry Latham, colored, was the next witness called for the prosecution. He was duly sworn and testified as follows:

## DIRECT EXAMINATION BY MR. CORBIN.

Q. Where do you live?

A. At Mr. William Shearer's plantation I was living.

Q. In York County?

A. Yes, sir.

Q. Did the Ku Klux Klan ever visit you?

A. Yes, sir.

Q. When was it?

A. It was before cold weather got done—before we planted corn.

Q. Some time last winter?

A. Some time in the winter.

Q. Tell the jury all about it?

A. I heard them before they found me, down at Mr. Ramsay's, and I tried to see if I could escape them; they was shooting down there, and I thought I would try to dodge them. I couldn't get up well, on account of the rheumatism; but they seed me; they was too smart for me. I went out and watched by a hickory tree; and when I got tired of watching, I mashed up some old wood and took it in, and they coming on me.

Q. Who came on you?

A. Mr. Shearer.

Q. Who else?

A. There was all the Shearers came in; Mr. Riggings, I don't think that he came in; but his horse was there when they sot down with me.

Q. How many were there?

A. Seven in the crowd.

Q. All come in.

A. No, sir; they didn't; but—

Q. Tell us what they did to you?

A. They came in; they cussed me.

Q. Tell us what they said?

A. They said: "God damn you, who are you?" I says: "Henry Latham, sir." "Who is he?" I says: "Henry Latham, sir;" then I looked at one at the window, and saw his red eye, and he jobbed his pistol in my face, and says: "Who are you?" and I told him "Henry Latham, sir," and acted as well as I could to keep them from killing me. Robert Riggings told me he was going to make me a good old Democrat; that was the first of it. Mr. Riggings said he was going to make me a good old Democrat. I says: "You can't do it." He says: "Well, you'll see." I says: "How will you do it?" He says: "I am going to fetch a crowd and shoot in your house, and make you a good old Democrat." I says: "No; don't do that, Mr. Riggings." He says: "I will do it some other way." I says: "How?" "Never mind, you'll see."

That was along in the middle of the week, before they whipped me.

Q. When was it that they came to see you?

A. Saturday night; and when I heard them, I knowed I would catch it. I wasn't able to run, and I went and got behind a tree. Well, it was too cold; I couldn't lay out at night, and I thought I would dodge back into the house and be easy, and sit down and mash up the old wood and put it on, and just as I put the last stick on, he jobbed me with his pistol, and says: "Who are you? God damn you, who are you?" I says: "Henry Latham, sir." "God damn you, come out of there." "Yes, sir," and I followed him up and got to the fence, and before I got to the fence, he said "he would cut my God damn throat." I thought now if I prayed a little bit, I wouldn't be uneasy. When I throwed my leg up to get over the fence, the pain hurt me so I hollered. "What ails you, God damn you?" I told him that it was the rheumatism. "Well," he says, "God damn you, come over here, I will take that out of you," and kicked me and turned my bone wrong in here [indicating the spine].

Q. How many times did they kick you?

A. I cannot tell. They kicked me and told me to run; well, I tried to run all I could, but a man full of pains can't run much; I wouldn't speak of them, no way, out of the way; I just grunted when they kicked me.

Q. What did they do with you up the road?

A. They beat me with poles about that thick [pointing to his wrist]. They had long ones, and hit me in the same place where they kicked me.

Q. How many times did they strike you?

A. I don't reckon more than six or seven times apiece; five of them hit me, but there was seven in the crowd; they didn't give me but, I don't think, more than six or seven apiece; they asked me if I would ever vote another Radical ticket, and I told them no, sir, if that was the way they did, I wouldn't ever no more; they asked me if I was a League man; "Well show me a League sign, God damn you;" I catched myself right here (the left lapel of the coat.) Mr. Kell, he was a Radical man; he put us all into the League; and they said, "God damn you, what did you join it for?" I said I didn't know there was any harm in it. "Well, God damn him, give him hell;" and then they begun.

Q. After they got done whipping you how did you feel?

A. I felt very bad.

Q. What injury did they do to your spine?

A. They turned the bones wrong side out; well, I never got over it; I don't know as I ever will; they kicked the bones wrong and injured the bone; they told me to run when I started back, and I went to get my coat, and they kicked me in the same place again, and I catched my coat in my fingers and hung on to it and run with it, and while I was running they run the horses up to keep me from knowing the horses; Dock Shearer's horse, Bob Rigging's horse—I knowed the horses; I had plowed Bob Rigging's horse.

Q. Did you go home?

A. Yes, sir; they told me, "God damn you, go to the house." When I started to pick up my coat, they said run, and while I was running, they run the horses.

The defense waived cross examination. . . .


## Testimony of Harriet Simril.

Harriet Simril (colored) was called as a witness for the prosecution, and, being duly sworn, testified as follows:

Q. Who is your husband?

A. Sam Simmons.

Q. Where do you live?

A. At Clay Hill, in York County.

Q. How long have you lived there?

A. A good many years.

Q. Has your husband lived there a good many years?

A. Yes, sir.

Q. Did he vote at the last election?

A. Yes, sir.

Q. Do you know what politics he is?

A. He is a Radical.

Q. Did the Ku Klux ever visit your house?

A. Yes, sir; I think along in the spring.

Q. About what time in the spring?

A. I cannot tell you exactly.

Q. Have they been there more than once?

A. Yes, sir; they came on him three times.

Q. Now tell the jury what they did each time?

A. The first time they came my old man was at home; they hollered out, "Open the door," and he got up and opened the door; they asked him what he had in his hand; he told them the door-pin; they told him to come out, and he came out; these two men that came in, they came in, and wanted me to make up a light; the light wasn't made up very good, and they stuck matches to a pine stick, and looked about to see if they could see anything; they never said anything, and these young men walked up, and they took my old man out after so long, and they wanted him to join this Democratic ticket; and, after that, they went a piece above the house, and hit him about five cuts with the cowhide.

Q. Do you know whether he promised to be a Democrat or not?

A. He told them he would rather quit all politics, if that was the way they was going to do him.

Q. What did they do to you?

A. That is the second time they came. They came back, after the first time, on Sunday night, after my old man again, and this second time the crowd was bigger.

Q. Did they call for your old man?

A. Yes, sir; they called for him, and I told them he wasn't here; then they argued me down, and told me he was here; I told them no, sir, he wasn't here; they asked me where was my old man; I told them I couldn't tell; when he went away he didn't tell me where he was going; they searched about in the house a long time, and staid with me an hour that time; searched about a long time, and made me make up a light; and after I got the light made up, then they began to search again, and question me again about the old man, and I told them I didn't know where my old man had gone.

Q. What did they do to you?

A. Well, they were spitting in my face, and throwing dirt in my eyes; and, when they made me blind, they bursted open my cupboard; I had five pies in my cupboard, and they eat all my pies up, and then took two pieces of meat; then they made me blow up the light again, cursing me; and after awhile they took me out of doors, and told me all they wanted was my old man to join the Democratic ticket; if he joined the Democratic ticket, they would have no more to do with him; and after they had got me out of doors, they dragged me into the big road, and they ravished me out there.

Q. How many of them?

A. There was three?

Q. One right after the other?

A. Yes, sir.

Q. Threw you down on the ground?

A. Yes, sir; they throwed me down.

Q. Do you know who the men were who ravished you?

A. Yes, sir; can tell who the men were; there were Ches. McCollum, Tom McCollum and this big Jim Harper.

Q. Who ravished you first?

A. Tom McCollum grabbed me, first, by the arm.

Q. What next?

A. All nasty talk they put out of their mouths. [Witness here detailed the conversation on the part of her tormentors, but it was of too obscene a nature to permit of publication.]

Q. What was your condition when they left you? How did you feel?

A. After they got done with me I had no sense for a long time. I laid there—I don't know how long.

Q. Did you get up that night?

A. Yes, sir; and walked back to the house again.

Q. Have the Ku Klux ever come to you again?

A. No, sir; they never came back no more after that; they came back, too, but I was never inside the house.

Q. Did your husband lay out at night?

A. Yes, sir; and I did, too—took my children, and when it rained thunder and lightning.

Q. When they came back, what did they do?

A. When they came back, I wasn't there; I went there the next morning, and there was a burnt chunk down in the corner.

Q. Did it burn the house any?

A. No, sir; it didn't burn it—they done that to scare my old man; and after that my old man and me drowned our fire out every night, and went away.

Q. Did they come there any more?

A. They didn't come any more, at all; the house was burned the next morning when I went to it.

Q. Did they burn your house down?

A. Yes, sir; I don't know who burnt it down, but the next morning when I went to my house it was in ashes.

Q. Why did you lay out?

A. We laid out in the woods.

The Court. Why did you lay out?

A. We went away up towards the river.

Q. To get out of the way of the Ku Klux?

A. Yes, sir; I got out of the way of them.

Q. That is what you went for?

A. Yes, sir.

Q. How long did you and your old man lay out?

A. I think we laid out for four nights. Yes; we lay out four nights; I cannot tell, exactly, how many nights, but he lay out a long time before I lay out.

Q. Did those Ku Klux have on masks and gowns?

A. Yes, sir; they had on gowns, and they had on false caps on their faces.

The defense waived cross-examination.

# Hiram R. Revels, "Abolish
# Separate Schools"

## *(1871)*

Mississippian Hiram Rhodes Revels (1827?–1901),
the first African-American to be seated in the U.S.
Senate, served in that body from February 23,
1870, to March 3, 1871. A free black native of
North Carolina, Revels attended a Quaker semi-
nary in Indiana, graduated from Knox College in
Illinois, and was ordained an A.M.E. minister. During the Civil War, he recruited black troops and
reportedly served as chaplain in a regiment of the
U.S. Colored Troops. Relocating to Mississippi
during Reconstruction, Revels worked for the
Freedmen's Bureau and held local and state political offices. Once Congress reinstated the Magno-
lia State to the Union, he was elected to fill
Jefferson Davis's unexpired senatorial seat. An eloquent spokesman for black civil and political
rights and fairness for members of both races,
Revels argued in 1871 in the Senate against segregation in District of Columbia schools, on public conveyances, and in all avenues of American
life. In his opinion, racism came from segregation, not from the behavior or character of people
of color.

Mr. President, I rise to express a few thoughts on this subject. It is not often that I ask the attention of the Senate on
any subject, but this is one on which I feel it is my duty to
make a few brief remarks.

In regard to the wishes of the colored people of this city,
I will simply say that the trustees of colored schools and
some of the most intelligent colored men of this place have
said to me that they would have before asked for a bill
abolishing the separate colored schools and putting all children on an equality in the common schools if they had

thought they could obtain it. They feared they could not; and this is the only reason why they did not ask for it before.

I find that the prejudice in this country to color is very great, and I sometimes fear that it is on the increase. For example, let me remark that it matters not how colored people act, it matters not how they behave themselves, how well they deport themselves, how intelligent they may be, how refined they may be—for there are some colored persons who are persons of refinement; this must be admitted—the prejudice against them is equally as great as it is against the most low and degraded colored man you can find in the streets of this city or in any other place.

This, Mr. President, I do seriously regret. And is this prejudice right? Have the colored people done anything to justify the prejudice against them that does exist in the hearts of so many white persons, and generally of one great political party in this country? Have they done anything to justify it? No, sir. Can any reason be given why this prejudice should be fostered in so many hearts against them simply because they are not white? I make these remarks in all kindness, and from no bitterness of feeling at all.

Mr. President, if this prejudice has no cause to justify it, then we must admit that it is wicked, we must admit that it is wrong; we must admit that it has not the approval of Heaven. Therefore I hold it to be the duty of this nation to discourage it, simply because it is wicked, because it is wrong, because it is not approved of by Heaven. If the nation should take a step for the encouragement of this prejudice against the colored race, can they have any ground upon which to predicate a hope that Heaven will smile upon them and prosper them? It is evident that it is the belief of Christian people in this country and in all other enlightened portions of the world that as a nation we have passed through a severe ordeal, that severe judgments have been poured upon us on account of the manner in which a poor, oppressed race was treated in this country.

Sir, this prejudice should be resisted. Steps should be taken by which to discourage it. Shall we do so by taking a step in this direction, if the amendment now proposed to the bill before us is adopted? Not at all. That step will rather encourage, will rather increase this prejudice; and this is one reason why I am opposed to the adoption of the amendment.

Mr. President, let me here remark that if this amendment is rejected, so that the schools will be left open for all children to be entered into them, irrespective of race, color, previous condition, I do not believe the colored people will act imprudently. I know that in one or two of the late insurrectionary states the legislatures passed laws establishing mixed schools, and the colored people did not hurriedly shove their children into those schools; they were very slow about it. In some localities where there was but little prejudice or opposition to it they entered them immediately; in others they did not do so. I do not believe that it is in the colored people to act rashly and unwisely in a manner of this kind.

But, sir, let me say that it is the wish of the colored people of this District, and of the colored people over this land, that this Congress shall not do anything which will increase that prejudice which is now fearfully great against them. If this amendment be adopted you will encourage that prejudice; you will increase that prejudice; and, perhaps, after the encouragement thus given, the next step may be to ask Congress to prevent them from riding in the streetcars, or something like that. I repeat, let no encouragement be given to a prejudice against those who have done nothing to justify it, who are poor and perfectly innocent, as innocent as infants. Let nothing be done to encourage that prejudice. I say the adoption of this amendment will do so.

Mr. President, I desire to say here that the white race has no better friend than I. The Southern people know this. It is known over the length and breadth of this land. I am true to my own race. I wish to see all done that can be done for their encouragement, to assist them in acquiring property, in becoming intelligent, enlightened, useful, valuable citizens. I wish to see this much done for them, and I believe God makes it the duty of this nation to do this much for them; but at the same time, I would not have anything done which would harm the white race.

Sir, during the canvass in the state of Mississippi I traveled into different parts of that state, and this is the doctrine that I everywhere uttered: That while I was in favor of building up the colored race I was not in favor of tearing down the white race. Sir, the white race need not be harmed in order to build up the colored race. The colored race can be built up and assisted, as I before remarked, in acquiring property, in becoming intelligent, valuable, useful citizens, without one hair upon the head of any white man being harmed.

Let me ask, will establishing such schools as I am now advocating in this District harm our white friends? Let us consider this question for a few minutes. By some it is contended that if we establish mixed schools here a great insult will be given to the white citizens, and that the white schools will be seriously damaged. All that I ask those who assume this position to do is to go with me to Massachusetts, to go with me to some other New England states where they have mixed schools, and there they will find schools in as prosperous and flourishing a condition as any to be found in any part of the world. They will find such schools there; and they will find between the white and colored citizens friendship, peace and harmony.

When I was on a lecturing tour in the state of Ohio, I went to a town, the name of which I forget. The question whether it would be proper or not to establish mixed schools had been raised there. One of the leading gentlemen connected with the schools in that town came to see me and conversed with me on the subject. He asked me, "Have you been to New England, where they have mixed schools?" I replied, "I have, sir." "Well," said he, "please tell me this: does not social equality result from mixed schools?" "No, sir; very far from it," I responded. "Why," said he, "how can it be otherwise?" I replied, "I will tell you how it can be otherwise, and how it is otherwise. Go to the schools and you see there white children and colored children seated side by side, studying their lessons, standing side by side and reciting their lessons, and perhaps in walking to school they may walk together; but that is the last of it. The white children go to their homes; the colored children go to theirs; and on the Lord's day you will see those colored children in colored churches, and the white children in white churches; and if an entertainment is given by a white family, you will see the white children there, and the colored children at entertainments given by persons of their color." I aver, sir, that mixed schools are very far from bringing about social equality.

Then, Mr. President, I hold that establishing mixed schools will not harm the white race. I am their friend. I said in Mississippi, and I say here, and I say everywhere, that I would abandon the Republican party if it went into any measures of legislation really damaging to any portion of the white race; but it is not in the Republican party to do that.

In the next place, I desire to say that school boards and school trustees and railroad companies and steamboat companies are to blame for the prejudice that exists against the colored race, or to their disadvantage in those respects. Go to the depot here, now, and what will you see? A well-dressed colored lady with her little children by her side, whom she has brought up intelligently and with refinement, as much so as white children, comes to the cars; and where is she shown to? Into the smoking car, where men are cursing, swearing, spitting on the floor; where she is miserable, and where her little children have to listen to language not fitting for children who are brought up as she has endeavored to bring them up to listen to.

Now, sir, let me ask, why is this? It is because the white passengers in a decent, respectable car are unwilling for her to be seated there? No, sir; not as a general thing. It is a rule that the company has established, that she shall not go there.

Let me give you a proof of this. Some years ago I was in the state of Kansas and wanted to go on a train of cars that ran from the town where I lived to St. Louis, and this rule prevailed there, that colored people should go into the smoking car. I had my wife and children with me and was trying to bring up my children properly, and I did not wish to take them into the smoking car. So I went to see the superintendent who lived in that town, and I addressed him thus: "Sir, I propose to start for St. Louis tomorrow on your road, and wish to take my family along; and I do not desire to go into the smoking car. It is all that I can do to stand it myself, and I do not wish my wife and children to go there and listen to such language as is uttered there by men talking, smoking, spitting, and rendering the car very foul; and I want to ask you now if I cannot obtain permission to take my family into a first-class car, as I have a first-class ticket?" Said he: "Sir, you can do so; I will see the conductor and instruct him to admit you." And he did admit me, and not a white passenger objected to it, not a white passenger gave any evidence of being displeased because I and my family were there.

Let me give you another instance. In New Orleans, and also in Baltimore, cities that I love and whose citizens I love, some trouble was raised some time ago because colored people were not allowed to ride in the streetcars. The question was taken to the courts; and what was the decision? That the companies should make provision for colored passengers to go inside of the cars. At first they had a car with a certain mark, signifying that colored people should enter. I think the words were, in Baltimore, "Colored people admitted into this car"; and in New Orleans they had a star upon the car. They commenced running. There would be a number of white ladies and white gentlemen who wanted to go in the direction that this car was going, and did not want to wait for another; and notwithstanding there was a number of colored persons in the car, they went in and seated themselves just as if there had not been a colored person there. The other day in Baltimore, I saw one of these cars passing along with the words, "Colored persons admitted into this car." The car stopped, and I saw a number of white ladies and gentlemen getting in, and not one colored person there. It was the same way in New Orleans. Let me tell you how it worked in New Orleans. The company finally came to the conclusion that if white persons were willing to ride with them without a word of complaint, they could not consistently complain of colored persons going into cars that were intended for white persons; and so they replaced their rule and opened the cars for all to enter. And ever since that time all have been riding together in New Orleans, and there has not been a word of complaint. So it will be I believe in regard to the school. Let lawmakers cease to make the difference, let school trustees and school boards cease to make the difference, and the people will soon forget it.

Mr. President, I have nothing more to say. What I have said I have said in kindness; and I hope it will be received in that spirit.

# ROBERT BROWN ELLIOTT,
## "THE AMNESTY BILL"

### *(March 14, 1871)*

Born and educated in Liverpool, England, Robert
Brown Elliott (1842–1884) migrated to Boston in
1867 and then moved to South Carolina as Congressional Reconstruction began. He edited the
*South Carolina Leader*, an African-American newspaper that espoused Republican principles. He
later read law and was admitted to the South Carolina bar. Though probably not an American citizen,
Elliott nonetheless was elected a delegate to South
Carolina's 1868 constitutional convention, where
he championed compulsory education for children
ages six to sixteen and universal manhood suffrage, and opposed a poll tax. Elected to the state
House of Representatives, Elliott next was appointed the state's assistant adjutant general. In
that capacity, he established South Carolina's Black
Militia, which tried unsuccessfully to suppress
Klan violence in the state's uplands. Elected to the
House of Representatives in 1870, in March 1871,
Elliott forcefully opposed an amnesty bill designed
to remove political disabilities against former Confederates.

The House now has under consideration a bill of vast importance to the people of the section that I have the honor
in part to represent. It is a proposition to remove the political disabilities of persons lately engaged in rebellion
against the sovereignty of the Government of the United
States. I believe that I have been noted in the State from
which I come as one entertaining liberal views upon this
very question; but, at a time like this, when I turn my eyes
to the South and see the loyal men of that section of the
country suffering at the hands of the very men whom it is
proposed today by this Forty-Second Congress of the

United States to relieve them of their political disabilities, I must here and now enter my solemn protest against any such proposition.

It is nothing but an attempt to pay a premium for disloyalty and treason at the expense of loyalty. I am not surprised that the gentleman from Kentucky should introduce such a proposition here. It was due to the class of men that it is proposed to relieve that such a proposition should come from the gentleman from Kentucky [George Madison Adams] and gentlemen upon that side of the House. I can appreciate the feeling of sympathy that the gentleman from Kentucky entertains for these men in the South who are today prohibited from holding Federal offices. They are his allies. They are his compatriots. They are today disfranchised simply because they rushed madly into rebellion against this, the best Government that exists under heaven, at their own instances, with the advice, and with the consent of such gentlemen as the gentleman from Kentucky. But when I hear gentlemen like the gentleman from Illinois [John Franklin Farnsworth], who spoke upon this question on Friday last, advance views and opinions such as that gentleman then advanced I must be allowed to express my surprise, ay, sir, my regret, that at this time such words should fall from the lips of a man whom I have been taught long to regard as one of those who are unflinching in their devotion to the cause of liberty and the preservation and maintenance of this great Government.

The gentleman from Illinois [Mr. Farnsworth] took occasion, in his argument on Friday last, to compare the condition of the man who is today disfranchised and the man who is allowed to hold office in the South. He drew a parallel between the disfranchised old man and his servant, or slave, who today holds office or may do so. He tells you that you should take into consideration the condition of this poor old man who, because he simply happened to join the rebellion after having taken an oath to support the Constitution of the Government of the United States, is prohibited from holding office, while his slave is allowed to hold office under the State and the United States governments. Ay, sir, the reason of this difference between the political status of the two is simply this: that while this old man, with whom the gentleman from Illinois sympathizes in his heart, was rebellious against the Government which had fostered and sustained and protected him, his slave was loyal to that Government, loyal to its Army, and loved its flag, which the man who had been reared under it, had learned only to despise. The difference is this: that while that "poor old man," of whom the gentleman speaks so sympathetically, would only curse the Government, would only ill-treat and murder its loyal adherents, the slave was the friend of that Government, and the protector and defender of those who were endeavoring to uphold it.

In discussing this question, and as a reason why this bill should pass, the gentleman from Illinois [Mr. Farnsworth] stated that the removal of disabilities would do good, and that to maintain those disabilities could effect no good purpose. Sir, I say that this removal would be injurious, not only to the loyal men of the South, but also to the Government itself. To relieve those men of their disabilities at this time would be regarded by the loyal men of the South as an evidence of the weakness of this great Government, and of an intention on the part of this Congress to foster the men who today are outraging the good and loyal people of the South. It would be further taken as evidence of the fact that this Congress desires to hand over the loyal men of the South to the tender mercies of the rebels who today are murdering and scourging the southern States.

The gentleman from Illinois, in his argument, was pleased to ask this question, which he proposed to answer himself: are these men who are disfranchised and prohibited from holding offices the men who commit the murders and outrages of which complaint is made? And his answer to that question was that they are not. But permit me to say to that gentleman that those men are responsible for every murder, responsible for every species of outrage that is committed in the South. They are men who, by their evil example, by their denunciations of Congress, by their abuse of the President of the United States, and of all connected with this Government, have encouraged, aided, and abetted the men who commit these deeds. They contribute to this state of things by their social influence, by their money and the money sent from the northern States—money furnished by Tammany Hall for the purpose of keeping up these outrages in order to insure a Democratic triumph in the South in 1872.

And I am here today to tell you, in the name of the loyal men of the South, that it is the fact that money is sent to the South by the Democratic party of the North to aid these men in keeping up this state of lawlessness for the purpose of over-awing the loyal people there and preventing them from expressing their preferences at the ballot box; that the number of arms shipped to the southern States, and which are brought there upon every New York steamer that arrives, is an evidence of the fact that these men who have the means, who have the influence, are responsible for these outrages, and not the poor, miserable tools who are their instruments in carrying them out. I ask this House, I ask gentlemen on this side especially, whether they are willing to join hands with those who propose today to relieve these men of their disabilities? Are they willing to tell the loyal men of the South, whose only offense is that they have been true to the Government, that they have sustained Congress in its just and lawful acts, that they have maintained the authority of Congress; are gentlemen willing to tell these loyal men that Congress is not disposed to protect them, but, on the contrary, is willing at their expense to pay a premium for disloyalty?

I speak not today in behalf of the colored loyalists of the South alone. I wish it to be distinctly understood that I represent here a constituency composed of men whose complexions are like those of gentlemen around me as well as men whose complexions are similar to my own. I represent a constituency as loyal as the constituency of any other gentleman upon this floor. Those men appeal to you today to do justice to them. They ask you to protect them by legislation, instead of placing them under the heel of those men who have ruled in the South with an iron hand since the Reconstruction Acts were passed. I come here backed up by a majority as large probably as that of any gentleman on this floor; I come here representing a Republican district; but unless this Congress will aid those loyal men of the South, unless, instead of passing propositions of this kind, it will turn its attention, and that speedily, to the protection of property and life in the South, the Republican party in this House cannot expect the support of those whom I represent.

# "An Act to Enforce the Provisions of the Fourteenth Amendment to the Constitution of the United States, and for Other Purposes"

## *(April 20, 1871)*

The third Enforcement Act, often termed the Ku Klux Act, declared terrorist groups like the Klan illegal and empowered the president to suspend the writ of habeas corpus in areas under Klan influence. The most sweeping of the Enforcement Acts, this legislation enumerated crimes, including conspiracies to deprive citizens of suffrage, holding office, serving on juries, and enjoying equal protection of the law as punishable under federal law if state law failed to do so. Significantly, this act made private criminal acts the province of the federal courts. According to one historian, the act "pushed Republicans to the outer limits of constitutional change."

*Be it enacted by the Senate and House of Representatives of the United States of America in Congress assembled,* That any person who, under color of any law, statute, ordinance, regulation, custom, or usage of any State, shall subject, or cause to be subjected, any person within the jurisdiction of the United States to the deprivation of any rights, privileges, or immunities secured by the Constitution of the United States, shall, any such law, statute, ordinance, regulation, custom, or usage of the State to the contrary notwithstanding, be liable to the party injured in any action at law, suit in equity, or other proper proceeding for redress; such proceeding to be prosecuted in the several district or circuit courts of the United States, with and subject to the

427

same rights of appeal, review upon error, and other remedies provided in like cases in such courts, under the provisions of the act of the ninth of April, eighteen hundred and sixty-six, entitled "An act to protect all persons in the United States in their civil rights, and to furnish the means of their vindication"; and the other remedial laws of the United States which are in their nature applicable in such cases.

SEC. 2. That if two or more persons within any State or Territory of the United States shall conspire together to overthrow, or to put down, or to destroy by force the government of the United States, or to levy war against the United States, or to oppose by force the authority of the government of the United States, or by force, intimidation, or threat to prevent, hinder, or delay the execution of any law of the United States, or by force to seize, take, or possess any property of the United States contrary to the authority thereof, or by force, intimidation, or threat to prevent any person from accepting or holding any office or trust or place of confidence under the United States, or from discharging the duties thereof, or by force, intimidation, or threat to induce any officer of the United States to leave any State, district, or place where his duties as such officer might lawfully be performed, or to injure him in his person or property on account of his lawful discharge of the duties of his office, or to injure his person while engaged in the lawful discharge of the duties of his office, or to injure his property so as to molest, interrupt, hinder, or impede him in the discharge of his official duty, or by force, intimidation, or threat to deter any party or witness in any court of the United States from attending such court, or from testifying in any matter pending in such court fully, freely, and truthfully, or to injure any such party or witness in his person or property on account of his having so attended or testified, or by force, intimidation, or threat to influence the verdict, presentment, or indictment, of any juror or grand juror in any court of the United States, or to injure such juror in his person or property on account of any verdict, presentment, or indictment lawfully assented to by him, or on account of his being or having been such juror, or shall conspire together, or go in disguise upon the public highway or upon the premises of another for the purpose, either directly or indirectly, of depriving any person or any class of persons of the equal protection of the laws, or of equal privileges or immunities under the laws, or for the purpose of preventing or hindering the constituted authorities of any State from giving or securing to all persons within such State the equal protection of the laws, or shall conspire together for the purpose of in any manner impeding, hindering, obstructing, or defeating the due course of justice in any State or Territory, with intent to deny to any citizen of the United States the due and equal protection of the laws, or to injure any person in his person or his property for lawfully enforcing the right of any person or class of persons to the equal protection of the laws, or by force, intimidation, or threat to prevent any citizen of the United States lawfully entitled to vote from giving his support or advocacy in a lawful manner towards or in favor of the election of any lawfully qualified person as an elector of President or Vice-President of the United States, or as a member of the Congress of the United States, or to injure any such citizen in his person or property on account of such support or advocacy, each and every person so offending shall be deemed guilty of a high crime, and, upon conviction thereof in any district or circuit court of the United States or district or supreme court of any Territory of the United States having jurisdiction of similar offences, shall be punished by a fine not less than five hundred nor more than five thousand dollars, or by imprisonment, with or without hard labor, as the court may determine, for a period of not less than six months nor more than six years, as the court may determine, or by both such fine and imprisonment as the court shall determine. And if any one or more persons engaged in any such conspiracy shall do, or cause to be done, any act in furtherance of the object of such conspiracy, whereby any person shall be injured in his person or property, or deprived of having and exercising any right or privilege of a citizen of the United States, the person so injured or deprived of such rights and privileges may have and maintain an action for the recovery of damages occasioned by such injury or deprivation of rights and privileges against any one or more of the persons engaged in such conspiracy, such action to be prosecuted in the proper district or circuit court of the United States, with and subject to the same rights of appeal, review upon error, and other remedies provided in like cases in such courts under the provisions of the act of April ninth, eighteen hundred and sixty-six, entitled "An act to protect all persons in the United States in their civil rights, and to furnish the means of their vindication."

SEC. 3. That in all cases where insurrection, domestic violence, unlawful combinations, or conspiracies in any State shall so obstruct or hinder the execution of the laws thereof, and of the United States, as to deprive any portion or class of the people of such State of any of the rights, privileges, or immunities, or protection, named in the Constitution and secured by this act, and the constituted authorities of such State shall either be unable to protect, or shall, from any cause, fail in or refuse protection of the people in such rights, such facts shall be deemed a denial by such State of the equal protection of the laws to which they are entitled under the Constitution of the United States; and in all such cases, or whenever any such insurrection, violence, unlawful combination, or conspiracy shall oppose or obstruct the laws of the United States or the due execution thereof, or impede or obstruct the due course of justice under the same, it shall be lawful for the President, and it shall be his duty to take such measures, by the employment of the militia or the land and naval forces of the United States, or of either, or by other means, as he may deem necessary for the suppression of such insurrection, domestic violence, or combinations; and any person who shall be arrested under the provisions of this and the preceding section shall be delivered to the marshal of the proper district, to be dealt with according to law.

SEC. 4. That whenever in any State or part of a State the unlawful combinations named in the preceding section of this act shall be organized and armed, and so numerous and powerful as to be able, by violence, to either overthrow or set at defiance the constituted authorities of such State, and of the United States within such State, or when the constituted authorities are in complicity with, or shall connive at the unlawful purposes of, such powerful and armed combinations; and whenever, by reason of either or all of the causes aforesaid, the conviction of such offenders and the preservation of the public safety shall become in such district impracticable, in every such case such combinations shall be deemed a rebellion against the government of the United States, and during the continuance of such rebellion, and within the limits of the district which shall be so under the sway thereof, such limits to be prescribed by proclamation, it shall be lawful for the President of the United States, when in his judgment the public safety shall require it, to suspend the privileges of the writ of habeas corpus, to the end that such rebellion may be overthrown: *Provided,* That all the provisions of the second section of an act entitled "An act relating to habeas corpus, and regulating judicial proceedings in certain cases," approved March third, eighteen hundred and sixty-three, which relate to the discharge of prisoners other than prisoners of war, and to the penalty for refusing to obey the order of the court, shall be in full force so far as the same are applicable to the provisions of this section: *Provided further,* That the President shall first have made proclamation, as now provided by law, commanding such insurgents to disperse: *And provided also,* That the provisions of this section shall not be in force after the end of the next regular session of Congress.

SEC. 5. That no person shall be a grand or petit juror in any court of the United States upon any inquiry, hearing, or trial of any suit, proceeding, or prosecution based upon or arising under the provisions of this act who shall, in the judgment of the court, be in complicity with any such combination or conspiracy; and every such juror shall, before entering upon any such inquiry, hearing, or trial, take and subscribe an oath in open court that he has never, directly or indirectly, counselled, advised, or voluntarily aided any such combination or conspiracy; and each and every person who shall take this oath, and shall therein swear falsely, shall be guilty of perjury, and shall be subject to the pains and penalties declared against that crime, and the first section of the act entitled "An act defining additional causes of challenge and prescribing an additional oath for grand and petit jurors in the United States courts," approved June seventeenth, eighteen hundred and sixty-two, be, and the same is hereby, repealed.

SEC. 6. That any person or persons, having knowledge that any of the wrongs conspired to be done and mentioned in the second section of this act are about to be committed, and having power to prevent or aid in preventing the same, shall neglect or refuse so to do, and such wrongful act shall be committed, such person or persons shall be liable to the person injured, or his legal representatives, for all damages caused by any such wrongful act which such first-named person or persons by reasonable diligence could have prevented; and such damages may be recovered in an action on the case in the proper circuit court of the United States, and any number of persons guilty of such wrongful neglect or refusal may be joined as defendants in such action: *Provided,* That such action shall be commenced within one year after such cause of action shall have accrued; and if the death of any person shall be caused by any such wrongful act and neglect, the legal representatives of such deceased person shall have such action therefor, and may recover not exceeding five thousand dollars damages therein, for the benefit of the widow of such deceased person, if any there be, or if there be no widow, for the benefit of the next of kin of such deceased person.

SEC. 7. That nothing herein contained shall be construed to supersede or repeal any former act or law except so far as the same may be repugnant thereto; and any offences heretofore committed against the tenor of any former act shall be prosecuted, and any proceeding already commenced for the prosecution thereof shall be continued and completed, the same as if this act had not been passed, except so far as the provisions of this act may go to sustain and validate such proceedings.

# PART IV

## RECONSTRUCTION'S END AND LEGACY

Historians usually identify 1877, the year when the last federal troops left the South, as the official end of Reconstruction. However, interest in Reconstruction, especially concern for and a commitment to black freedom, began to wane for most Northerners even before the mid-1870s. Journalist Nicholas Lemann states correctly that even though the Reconstruction Acts of 1867 had made ratification of the Fourteenth Amendment a precondition for readmission to the Union, "it required the presence of the U.S. Army in the South to give the Fourteenth Amendment the force of law. As soon as the federal government stopped using troops as enforcers, in the mid-eighteen-seventies, the Southern states ignored the Fourteenth Amendment, and continued to do so for nearly a century."[36]

In May 1872, Congress passed the General Amnesty Act, removing political disabilities imposed by section 3 of the Fourteenth Amendment. A month later, it abolished the Freedmen's Bureau. In July 1874, the Freedman's Savings Bank, established to provide the freedpeople with basic banking facilities and to promote saving money, shut its doors. The Panic of 1873 and local concerns, not the rights of African-American Southerners, preoccupied most Northerners. To a significant degree, by the early 1870s, Americans had lost interest in Reconstruction. They tried to put the Civil War behind them and look forward.

The burning embers of sectionalism and race hatred, however, remained dimly lit during Reconstruction. Racial violence ran through the Reconstruction era like a leitmotif, peaking during the 1870s when race riots at Meridian, Mississippi (1871), Colfax, Louisiana (1873), Vicksburg, Mississippi (1874), New Orleans and Coushatta, Louisiana (1874), Yazoo City and Clinton, Mississippi (1875), and Hamburg and Ellenton, South Carolina (1876), marred the Southern landscape. The Enforcement Acts had proven insufficient to protect the freedpeople from whites determined to retain racial control over them.

For years Radical Republican senator Charles Sumner had attempted to push through Congress a federal statute protecting the civil rights of blacks, specifically the granting of equal access to public facilities to persons of all races. Following Sumner's death in March 1874, his bill found champions in Senator Frederick T. Frelinghuysen of New Jersey and Massachusetts representative Benjamin F. Butler. The Civil Rights Act of 1875 finally came to pass in February of that year. This last major piece of Reconstruction era legislation aimed to protect the freedpeople in public venues. It mandated nondiscriminatory accommodations in inns, public conveyances, and theaters, prohibited jury discrimination based on race, and declared all racial discrimination cases the purview of the federal courts. The bill was one of the most controversial Congressional bills of its day because, its critics asserted, it legislated social equality. After less than a decade, in 1883, the U.S. Supreme Court declared the equal-accommodations sections of the 1875 Civil Rights Act unconstitutional. In its decision in the *Civil Rights Cases* (1883), the court held that the Thirteenth and Fourteenth Amendments regulated state, not private, actions and further denied that discrimination in public settings stemmed from slavery. Congress, the court insisted, held power to correct instances of state discrimination after they had occurred, but had no mandate to prevent such actions from occurring. In his famous lone dissent, Justice John Marshall Harlan (1833–1911) argued that the freedpeople continued to suffer from the "badges of slavery and servitude" and that Congress had fashioned the Thirteenth and Fourteenth Amendments to eradicate discrimination in private and public contexts.

With all branches of the federal government increasingly uninterested in the plight of the freedpeople, white Southerners in the 1870s and afterward looked for ways to construct an economic modus operandi with Northern capitalists, all the while retaining racial control at home. Though blacks acquired capital, formed communities, continued to vote, and held seats in state and local governments until late in the century, whites contrived to fashion new forms of controlling them.[37] These included, according

to Foner, "exclusion from juries, severe punishment for trifling crimes, the continued apprenticeship of their children
against parental wishes, and a general inability to obtain justice."[38] In spite of the Fifteenth Amendment, white Southerners found ways to discourage blacks from voting by
implementing residency requirements, discriminatory poll
taxes, literacy tests, and so-called Grandfather clauses. When
these tactics fell short, whites employed brute force.

The economic collapse of 1873, the loss of Republican
interest in and support for remaking the South, the continued racial violence in the South, the systematic overthrow
of Radical governments in the South after 1869, and the
landslide victory of Democrats in the 1874 Congressional
elections ("the greatest reversal of partisan alignments in
the entire nineteenth century," Foner writes) marked the
beginning of the end for America's Reconstruction experiment.[39] By the summer of 1876, only three states—Florida,
Louisiana, and South Carolina—remained under Radical
control. The results of the controversial presidential election of 1876 signaled Reconstruction's end.

That famous campaign, pitting the Ohio Republican
Rutherford B. Hayes against the New York Democrat Samuel J. Tilden, ended inconclusively with Hayes twenty electoral votes shy of the 185 necessary for election and election
returns in four states contested between the two parties. To
resolve the dilemma, Congress appointed a bipartisan Electoral Commission that declared Hayes the victor. An informal arrangement between Southern Democrats and Hayes's
supporters resolved the deadlock. The so-called Compromise of 1877 smoothed the way for Hayes to assume the
presidency in exchange for economic and political concessions to the South, including the removal of the remaining
federal troops from the region, the appointment of a Southerner to Hayes's cabinet, and the general awarding of "Home
Rule" to the former Confederate states. White Southerners'
much-anticipated period of "Redemption" had arrived. Reconstruction was over, a circumstance, according to historian
Steven Hahn, that "ushered in a new era of state-organized
violence in defense of private property and respectable
property holders at all levels of government."[40]

Unquestionably, Reconstruction marked one of the
great turning points in American history. "Never as radical

as has been charged," explains historian Hans L. Trefousse, "it nevertheless represented a real effort to enforce equal rights by federal legislation."[41] Over a century ago, another historian, William Garrott Brown, wrote that the withdrawal of federal troops from the South in 1877 occasioned "a turning of the current of affairs into a new channel, as clearly marked as any to be found in our history since the revolution." Whereas General Robert E. Lee's surrender at Appomattox had signified the Confederacy's death and slavery's end, in 1877 the nation "reached the end of the entire prior period during which American political history was mainly an affair of North and South."[42] As Trefousse observed, Reconstruction's demise also signaled a shift from the diminution of power of the Executive branch in the years following Lincoln's assassination to the assertion of the power of the presidency in the early twentieth century.[43]

The saga of Reconstruction included many causes won and lost. Had Lincoln's quest for "a just, and a lasting peace" been attained? Absolutely not. The South's post-1870s "Redemption" by so-called Bourbon Democrats led to the era of Jim Crow, what Hahn terms "a post-emancipation regime of domination and subordination."[44] Recently historian Stephen Kantrowitz observed that among Reconstruction's "most important political developments were the virtual revolution in Southern life, the consolidation of national citizenship, and the forces that arose to limit those projects."[45] To be sure, by 1877, the nation had reunited, but serious questions pertaining to free labor, civil and states' rights, and racial inequality remained unanswered. These became Reconstruction's complex legacy. Issues of liberty and equal rights continued to plague the U.S. until the Second Reconstruction of the 1960s.

# CHARLES STEARNS, THE
# BLACK MAN OF THE SOUTH,
# AND THE REBELS; OR, THE
# CHARACTERISTICS OF THE
# FORMER, AND THE RECENT
# OUTRAGES OF THE LATTER

## (1872)

Before the Civil War, the Massachusetts-born abolitionist and journalist Charles B. Stearns (1818–1899) served as a reporter for two antislavery newspapers, the *Liberator* and the *National Anti-Slavery Standard*. Stearns was committed to nonresistance prior to the mid-1850s, but his experiences in "Bleeding Kansas" changed him. "When I deal with men made in God's image, I will never shoot them," he explained, "but these pro-slavery Missourians are demons from the bottomless pit and may be shot with impunity." During Reconstruction, Stearns settled on a fifteen-hundred-acre Georgia plantation, intending both to uplift the freedpeople and to share his profits with his African-American employees. In *The Black Man of the South, and the Rebels*, Stearns blamed slavery for what he considered the exasperating backwardness and immorality of the ex-slaves, but he made clear his outrage with the atrocities committed against blacks by native whites. As a result, Stearns welcomed President Grant's use of the army against Klansmen who understood "no power on earth except the military power of the United States."

While this dark cloud was overhanging my own abode, events were transpiring in other places foreboding still more evil to all the friends of the Union in the state of

Georgia. I allude to the expulsion from our House of Representatives of twenty-five "persons of color" simply on account of their being "guilty of a skin not colored like our own"; and the admission of an equal number of democrats to fill their places, thus lessening the republican majority by fifty votes. Of course all legislation after this was carried on in the interests of the democratic party, as the republican majority at the outset had been quite small, the republican candidate for speaker having been elected by a majority of only one vote. But the majority in the Senate was greater, so that on joint ballot the republicans had a respectable majority.

It was some draw back to the nefarious schemes of these insane disorganizers, that none of their corrupt legislation could receive the sanction of the governor, as he remained true to the party that had elected him, amid this, and all the other changes that came over the "body politic," in our state. If it had not been for this well known fact, our situation would have been fearful indeed. The protection of the military had been withdrawn, and our representatives had been admitted to Congress, thus creating the impression that Georgia was a loyal state in the Union. But the triumph of these wretched men was short, for by the action of Congress, the entire admission of Georgia was delayed, and the seats of its senators declared vacated, until the rights of these ejected ones could be fully ascertained.

Far be it from me to criticise in a captious manner the action of Congress in this respect, but I cannot help feeling that it did wrong in afterwards admitting to their seats, the senators elected before the proper organization of the Legislature; in accordance with the provisions of the Reconstruction act, under which they were elected. This act declared that no "person prohibited from holding office under the United States, or under any state, by section third of the proposed amendment to the Constitution of the United States, known as article fourteen, shall be deemed eligible to any office in either of said states, unless relieved from disability, as provided by said amendment." This section is as follows:

> No person shall be a senator or representative in Congress, or elector of President or Vice President, or hold any office, civil or military, under the

United States, or under any state, who having previously taken an oath, as a member of Congress or as an officer of the United States, or as a member of any State Legislature, or as an executive or judicial officer of any State to support the Constitution of the United States, shall have engaged in insurrection or rebellion against the same, or given aid and comfort to the enemies thereof. But Congress may by a vote of two thirds of each House remove such disability.

A supplementary act passed by Congress July 19, 1867, declared that "the words executive or judicial office in any State, shall be construed to include all civil offices created by law, for the administration of any general law, or the administration of justice."

In accordance with these provisions, and with his duty as military commander of the district, four days after the organization of the Legislature, General Meade sent a letter to Governor Bullock, calling his attention to the matter, and declaring that he could not recognize the Legislature, until satisfied that these Reconstruction acts had been complied with. Gov. Bullock forwarded these documents to the Legislature, endorsing the position of Gen. Meade, and recommending to the Legislature an appointment of a committee, to ascertain the eligibility of its members. This committee was duly appointed, after various propositions to modify its powers, and an attempt on the part of Mr. Tumlin, of Randolph, to defy the power of Congress in reference to the matter, by introducing a resolution declaring that Congress had no right to "define the terms upon which the members of the Legislature might hold their office." The names of the committee appointed were as follows: "O'Neal, of Lowndes, Shumate, of Whitfield, Harper, of Tirrell, Lee, of Newton, and Bryant, of Richmond," three of whom were republicans, and two democrats.

The chairman of the committee reported that two of the members were ineligible, a minority of republicans reported that one person was ineligible, and a minority of democrats that none were ineligible. The house by a vote of 95 to 53, adopted the minority report of the democrats, and declared that all the members were eligible.

But behind all this, legislative scenes were enacted, which, to say the least, failed to do credit to the logical acumen or straightforward character of those concerned in this examination. It was a matter of common notoriety, that quite a large number of the members of the Legislature had participated in the rebellion, and by the wording of the Reconstruction acts, which asserted the ineligibility of *all* engaged in the rebellion, after having sworn to support the Const. of the United States, they were not entitled to their seats. Doubtless the members of Congress who voted for the Reconstruction acts, were aware of the omission of the word voluntary, in reference to those who rendered "aid and comfort" to the rebellion. But even if they did not intend to omit that word, the strict letter of the law must be complied with; and it was not proper for the Georgia Legislature to apply an interpretation of its own, to these acts, unless the language was susceptible of a variety of interpretations.

In this case, the language is so plain, that "he who runneth may read." "No person who has supported the rebellion, after having sworn to support the Constitution of the United States, shall be eligible to office."

But honesty and common sense were eschewed; darker counsels prevailed, and the whole committee, and a large majority of the House, endorsed the character of nearly all of the members, and the direst consequences ensued. About two months afterwards, according to the prophecy of those who opposed this unwise conduct, all the colored members of the Legislature, numbering some twenty-eight or thirty, I think, were excluded from their seats, and their places filled by good democrats.

It is very much to the discredit of the colored members of the Legislature, as far as perspicuity of vision is concerned, that they favored the reception of those ineligible members—except the three declared so by the committee. But it is accounted for, on the score of the known magnanimity of the colored race, towards their former oppressors; and should, therefore, be looked upon with leniency; especially as prominent republicans, and those to whom they had been accustomed to look for political guidance, urged them to this course.

What shall be said of such measures, on the part of

sworn friends of the Union cause, and of the colored race? A more unfortunate movement could hardly have been made. By it, the balance of power was thrown into the hands of the vanquished party; and the fruits of our hotly contested election, were partially lost. It is true, that these mistaken men, solemnly assert their honesty and conscientiousness, in this matter; that, believing the Reconstruction act meant to say, "voluntary aid," when it did not, and being satisfied that none of these men had rendered "voluntary aid," they were bound by their consciences, to support them as entitled to their seats.

But honesty and conscientiousness, do not always prove safe guides, in political, any more than in moral matters. The result of all this conscientiousness, was as disastrous to the cause of freedom, as if there had been no "conscience" in the matter. When men's minds are made up to pursue a particular course, it is not always easy to detach firmness from conscientiousness. Doubtless the Puritan fathers imagined they were conscientious, in the hanging of Quaker women; but it is difficult for us to believe, to-day, that no other than conscientious feelings, influenced them in such cruel acts. Conscientiousness includes the exercise of our judgement, as to the facts in the case, and diligent attention to all the means of light, in the case under consideration. I cannot but believe, that if those republicans, who decided that these members were eligible, under the Reconstruction acts, had exercised their common sense a little more fully, they would have come to a far different conclusion.

And I am the more inclined to this opinion, from the fact that the judgement of the great body of the republican party of the State, outside of the Legislature, led them to deny the eligibility of these members, and the report of the committee was received with astonishment, by many of the members of the Legislature itself. I am free to confess, however, that some of those who favored the retention of these ineligible democrats, sincerely believed, with their great New York compeers, that amnesty and kind measures were better adapted to pacifying the lion of rebellion, than the severity and awe, usually practiced by professional lion-tamers. Patting a mad dog on the head, may ward off the danger of hydrophobia from his bite, but it requires considerable faith in a mad dog's divinity, to adopt such precautionary measures, and no others.

But notwithstanding the unfavorable aspect of the case at this time, "the wise were caught in their own craftiness," for this action of the Legislature, led to the exclusion of Georgia from the Union, for nearly two years, until the country had become ready for the adoption of other measures of protection, and Andrew Johnson had been shorn of his power to do harm, by the inauguration of his successor. . . .

One day "Aunt Suky," a colored woman seventy-five years old, and bent nearly double from weakness and hard usage, called upon me, and after looking around cautiously to see if any other white person was present, told me she had been beaten on her head by her employer, with a large hickory stick, until she was covered with blood, because she did not bring him some salt, immediately, when he called for it. Her head was then bound up from the effect of the blows, and she came to ask me, if there was no redress for her; but said, I must not tell any one she had been to see me, as they had threatened her life if she informed on them. I was obliged to tell her there was no remedy in her case.

In March, 1869, I learned of the killing of a colored man named Israel, not far from Apling, by a white man, who also cut Israel's father badly. The cause was, that the colored man had informed of a theft of cotton, committed by the white man. As usual, no notice was taken of the event. About the same time, Sam Buck, a colored man, was killed by a white man, not far from here, cause unknown, but no notice was taken of the occurrence.

In the same spring, a colored woman, sixty years old, named Sally, was brutally beaten on her head with a pair of tongs by her mistress, for refusing to leave her child and take care of a white woman's child. She lay for a long time in a very dangerous condition.

About the same time, some colored men stopped at my house, and reported the recent killing of three of their comrades by the Ku-Klux, in Lincoln county, adjoining ours.

The summer before, a colored man was attacked in the woods, by a party of white men, against whom he defended himself, and killed one of his assailants in so doing. He was immediately taken and hung by the remainder of the party.

About the same time, J. D., a colored man, living a few miles from here, was met in the road by three men, a horseback, one of whom dismounted, and went up to him, and stabbed him terribly in different parts of his body. I am well acquainted with the assailant and with the colored man, and received from the lips of the colored man, the particulars of the case.

In 1867, three white men in front of my house, boasted of the crimes they had committed against the colored people; one of them laughing heartily while he described the appearance of the woman whom he had beaten; saying, "she was the bloodiest looking beast you ever saw." Another of them said, he made it a point to whip one or more negroes soundly every year, as an example to the others. Another owned that he had fired at a negro for disobeying an order, and "should have shot him, but he dodged behind a tree." Neither of these men were rowdies in the common acceptation of the term, but *well-to-do* farmers, living very near my place, and I do not suppose they imagined they had done wrong.

The first year of my residence here, a white and black man had some altercation on a plantation a few miles from here. The next day, a gang of armed white men rode up to the place, seized the black man's wife, and threatened to kill her, unless she would point out the hiding place of her husband. Overhearing this threat, with true connubial affection, he sprang from his concealment, when he was immediately fired upon by the whole crowd, as if he had been a dog or stray hog, and his body was literally riddled with bullets. Several of the white men were arrested for the cold-blooded murder, but of course were soon discharged.

Previous to this a white man undertook to do violence to the person of a negro girl *at a public place*. She was defended by her brother, when the white man took his revolver and shot him dead instantly. In this case the white man left the county, fearing the rage of the negroes, and also the interference of the Freedmen's Bureau, which was then in operation. Quite a number of colored persons have been taken from the officers of justice in this county, by a mob of white men and *put to death*. In two cases they were taken from the jail in Apling, and in one while on their way to the prison. I learned the particulars of one of these cases from the jailer himself, who was called out of his house at midnight, and forced to deliver up the keys of the jail to the mob, who took the prisoner, and hung him from a bridge near the town. This was the same Apling where the author came so near sharing the same fate.

I give the particulars of the other case, as given me by Aunt Rinah Hill, who has lived on my place several years, and is a woman of veracity. She says, that in the summer of 1869, a little child belonging to R. R., ten or twelve miles from here, bit off the finger of a colored child on the place, whose mother was named Minty. She ran after the white child, without reflecting upon the criminality of a black person pursuing a white one, and meant as she said, "merely to slap it on its ear." The child's father, seeing the black woman pursuing his child, rushed upon her and beat her tremendously with a large white oak stick. This of course roused the ire of Berry, the colored woman's husband, and he attempted to interfere, when the oppressed victim of "imperialism" and "centralization," exercised his "natural right" to shoot a black man, and fired at Berry, wounding him in the thigh. Berry fled to Augusta, and on his way passed by our place, and Aunt Rinah gave him a drink of water. The next day he returned guarded by two men in a buggy before him, and the same behind him, and with another at his side a horseback. The next news from this party was, that Berry and his wife, after having been lodged in jail at Apling, were taken out by *a mob and hung*; and it was reported that the heart of the man was cut out and given to the dogs. So great is the horror of the colored people of Apling jail, that some of them declare they never will be taken there alive, and one of them not long since, when on his way for an alleged theft, undertook to escape from the constable, who shot him through his body, without the least compunction.

I cannot begin to recall the instances, of maimed and wounded men, who have come to me with the story of their wrongs. Some with great gashes cut in their heads, some with wounds in their bodies, and others with mangled and shattered arms; to all of which, I have been under the sad necessity of saying, "I can do nothing for you, except to call upon the United States government to protect you;" which seemed to them, almost a mockery of their woes.

It is not for me to say who is to blame, for this failure of the government to protect its citizens. It is, perhaps, inherent in the nature of the government itself, and can only be remedied by a radical change in our governmental theory. No true man can cry out against "centralization," when without it, there never *can* be, any safety for "the black man of the South," from "the outrages of the rebels." We have entreated long and loud for protection; petitions have been forwarded to Congress, entreating its interference; and Gov. Bullock has exerted himself nobly, in behalf of his colored constituents; but Congress has chosen to hear the cries of the enemies of the Union, rather than those of its defenders. Some of the blame rests upon those betrayers of our cause, who, in connection with rebel democrats, have visited Washington, and poured into the ears of Congress, and of the President, such misstatements of our condition, as have led them to doubt the necessity of their interference. In the meantime, the craven, false-hearted cry of "universal amnesty," has uttered its fearful notes, all over the land; sounding in the ears of the terror-stricken Southern Unionist, as dismally as the yells of rejoicing, that went up from ten thousand rebel throats, when McDowell's panic-stricken squadrons, fled from the furious hosts precipitated upon them, at the unfortunate Bull Run rout. While we have been surrounded by implacable foes, thirsting for the blood of all true Union men, and have imploringly cast our eyes Northward for assistance, as the dying soldier on the battle-field, lifts his head occasionally, to see if no friendly hand can be found to wet his parched lips; those to whom we fondly looked as the embodiment of all our hopes, have sternly covered their eyes, and looked away from our imploring gaze, being dazzled by visions of future political glory; and instead of responding, "You shall be protected," have uttered honeyed words, in dulcimer strains, that have electrified the hearts of our enemies; but have sent a mournful sound, like that of retreating squadrons, into our ears, filling us with blank dismay, and awaking in our pierced hearts, the most melancholy forebodings for the future.

But to return to my narrative of rebel atrocities. Lincoln county, adjoining this county, is emphatically, "the valley of the shadow of death," for the poor colored man. Ever since I commenced residing here, have terrific stories of his abuse, in that county, reached my ears. Among the many tales of violence perpetrated there, I will simply give publicity to the following, as it is in every one's mouth. In the summer of 1868, when political excitement ran high, there were two colored men, father and son, named Roundtrees, and another colored man named Billy Tully, who were quite prominent republicans, and it therefore became necessary to sacrifice them. Accordingly, one night they were aroused from their slumbers, taken from their beds, and carried to a neighboring mill-dam. They were then offered their choice, to join the democratic club, or to walk out on that mill-dam and *be shot*. With true Spartan courage, they chose the latter fate, when they were immediately placed on the mill-dam, and given the poor privilege of jumping into the water, to escape the rebel bullets, as the Indians often allow a prisoner a chance to run for his life, while they are firing at him. They all three jumped into the water, at a given signal from these "well-disposed" and "repentant" rebel democrats, to deprive whom of political power is considered so very oppressive, and for whom we are so constantly exhorted to "kill the fatted calf." One of the Roundtrees and Tully were shot dead, the other managed to escape by dodging in and out of the water, amid the shower of rebel bullets aimed at his devoted head. He was severely wounded, but fled to Augusta, and was for some time cared for at the "Freedmen's hospital" in that city. . . .

Imagine how it would be in New England, even, if there was no punishment for assault and battery, and then consider the extreme excitability of the southern character, and also they having been accustomed to nothing but deference from the blacks; and the enigma of their acts is easily solved. It is not because the Southern people, in their every day intercourse with the world, are any worse than other people, but it is the peculiar circumstances in which they are placed, that leads them to act so savagely. I make these remarks, because those who have seen the Southerners when not excited, cannot believe that such urbane gentlemen can conduct themselves so unseemly towards the blacks. The reader must never forget, that while many outrages are committed at the North, their perpetrators are almost always punished by law, but here this is seldom the case; and this fact constitutes the great difference between

Southern and Northern society on this point. What the friends of the blacks are laboring for, is the establishment of law for their protection.

Let the broad ægis of law be lifted up in behalf of the colored man, and the ample folds of the mantle of justice be thrown around the white man, and these evils will nearly cease. When it cannot be done by our civil law, we ask for the establishment of military authority, as absolutely necessary to protect both black and white.

# THOMAS NAST, "THE MAN WITH THE (CARPET) BAGS"

## (November 9, 1872)

The renowned cartoonist Thomas Nast's wood engraving in *Harper's Weekly* appears to be a caricature of a carpetbagger, a Northerner going south to avail himself of economic and political opportunities in the defeated former Confederate states. But, no, Nast's cartoon ridiculed Missouri senator Carl Schurz, the German-American leader who had bolted the Republicans, charging Grant with political corruption and dissenting from the president's Southern policy. Schurz was a leader of the Liberal Republican party that nominated Horace Greeley in the presidential campaign against Grant in 1872. The cartoon's caption reads: "The Man with the (Carpet) Bags. The Bag in front of him, filled with others' faults, he always sees. The one behind him, filled with his own faults, he never sees." Grant easily defeated Greeley 286 to 66 electoral votes and by a popular majority of 763,000 votes.

# JAMES S. PIKE, THE
# PROSTRATE STATE

## (1874)

Like Stearns, James Shepherd Pike (1811–1882) was a Northern newspaperman, a vocal abolitionist, and a Republican who came south during Reconstruction. He served as President Lincoln's minister to the Netherlands during the Civil War. Unlike Stearns, however, Pike opposed slavery because of his extreme antipathy toward blacks and, accordingly, condemned the role of African-Americans in Reconstruction. His *The Prostrate State* summarized Pike's observations of blacks and Republican government in South Carolina, where, during Radical Reconstruction, blacks held a majority of the elected federal and state offices. Underscoring what he considered blacks' incapacity for self-government, Pike described blacks in the crudest stereotypes of his day and warned of the Palmetto State's "Africanization."

. . . One of the things that first strike a casual observer in this negro assembly is the fluency of debate, if the endless chatter that goes on there can be dignified with this term. The leading topics of discussion are all well understood by the members, as they are of a practical character, and appeal directly to the personal interests of every legislator, as well as to those of his constituents. When an appropriation bill is up to raise money to catch and punish the Ku-klux, they know exactly what it means. They feel it in their bones. So, too, with educational measures. The free school comes right home to them; then the business of arming and drilling the black militia. They are eager on this point. Sambo can talk on these topics and those of a kindred character, and their endless ramifications, day in and day out. There is no end to his gush and babble. The intellectual level is that of a bevy of fresh converts at a negro camp-meeting. Of course this kind of talk can be extended indefinitely. It is the doggerel of debate, and not beyond the reach of the lowest parts. Then the negro is imitative in the extreme. He can copy like a parrot or a monkey, and he is always ready for a trial of his skill. He believes he can do any thing, and never loses a chance to try, and is just as ready to be laughed at for his failure as applauded for his success. He is more vivacious than the white, and, being more volatile and good-natured, he is correspondingly more irrepressible. His misuse of language in his imitations is at times ludicrous beyond measure. He notoriously loves a joke or an anecdote, and will burst into a broad guffaw on the smallest provocation. He breaks out into an incoherent harangue on the floor just as easily, and being without practice, discipline, or experience, and wholly oblivious of Lindley Murray, or any other restraint on composition, he will go on repeating himself, dancing as it were to the music of his own voice, forever. He will speak half a dozen times on one question, and every time say the same things without knowing it. He answers completely to the description of a stupid speaker in Parliament, given by Lord Derby on one occasion. It was said of him that he did not know what he was going to say when he got up; he did not know what he was saying while he was speaking, and he did not know what he had said when he sat down.

But the old stagers admit that the colored brethren have a wonderful aptness at legislative proceedings. They are "quick as lightning" at detecting points of order, and they certainly make incessant and extraordinary use of their knowledge. No one is allowed to talk five minutes without interruption, and one interruption is the signal for another and another, until the original speaker is smothered under an avalanche of them. Forty questions of privilege will be raised in a day. At times, nothing goes on but alternating questions of order and of privilege. The inefficient colored friend who sits in the Speaker's chair cannot suppress this extraordinary element of the debate. Some of the blackest members exhibit a pertinacity of intrusion in raising these points of order and questions of privilege that few white men can equal. Their struggles to get the floor, their bellowings and physical contortions, baffle description. The Speaker's hammer plays a perpetual tattoo all to no pur-

pose. The talking and the interruptions from all quarters go
on with the utmost license. Every one esteems himself as
good as his neighbor, and puts in his oar, apparently as often for love of riot and confusion as for any thing else. It is
easy to imagine what are his ideas of propriety and dignity
among a crowd of his own color, and these are illustrated
without reserve. The Speaker orders a member whom he
has discovered to be particularly unruly to take his seat.
The member obeys, and with the same motion that he sits
down, throws his feet on to his desk, hiding himself from
the Speaker by the soles of his boots. In an instant he appears again on the floor. After a few experiences of this
sort, the Speaker threatens, in a laugh, to call "the gemman"
to order. This is considered a capital joke, and a guffaw follows. The laugh goes round, and then the peanuts are
cracked and munched faster than ever; one hand being employed in fortifying the inner man with this nutriment of
universal use, while the other enforces the views of the ora-
tor. This laughing propensity of the sable crowd is a great
cause of disorder. They laugh as hens cackle—one begins
and all follow.

But underneath all this shocking burlesque upon legislative proceedings, we must not forget that there is something very real to this uncouth and untutored multitude. It
is not all sham, nor all burlesque. They have a genuine interest and a genuine earnestness in the business of the assembly which we are bound to recognize and respect,
unless we would be accounted shallow critics. They have an
earnest purpose, born of a conviction that their position
and condition are not fully assured, which lends a sort of
dignity to their proceedings. The barbarous, animated jar-
gon in which they so often indulge is on occasion seen to be
so transparently sincere and weighty in their own minds
that sympathy supplants disgust. The whole thing is a wonderful novelty to them as well as to observers. Seven years
ago these men were raising corn and cotton under the whip
of the overseer. To-day they are raising points of order and
questions of privilege. They find they can raise one as well
as the other. They prefer the latter. It is easier, and better
paid. Then, it is the evidence of an accomplished result. It
means escape and defense from old oppressors. It means
liberty. It means the destruction of prison-walls only too

real to them. It is the sunshine of their lives. It is their day of jubilee. It is their long-promised vision of the Lord God Almighty.

Shall we, then, be too critical over the spectacle? Perhaps we might more wisely wonder that they can do so well in so short a time. The barbarians overran Rome. The dark ages followed. But then the day finally broke, and civilization followed. The days were long and weary; but they came to an end at last. Now we have the printing-press, the railroad, the telegraph; and these denote an utter revolution in the affairs of mankind. Years may now accomplish what it formerly took ages to achieve. Under the new lights and influences shall not the black man speedily emerge? Who knows? We may fear, but we may hope. Nothing in our day is impossible. Take the contested supposition that South Carolina is to be Africanized. We have a Federal Union of great and growing States. It is incontestably white at the centre. We know it to possess vital powers. It is well abreast of all modern progress in ideas and improvements. Its influence is all-pervading. How can a State of the Union escape it? South Carolina alone, if left to herself, might fall into midnight darkness. Can she do it while she remains an integral part of the nation?

But will South Carolina be Africanized? That depends. Let us hear the judgment of an intelligent foreigner who has long lived in the South, and who was here when the war began. He does not believe it. White people from abroad are drifting in, bad as things are. Under freedom the blacks do not multiply as in slavery. The pickaninnies die off from want of care. Some blacks are coming in from North Carolina and Virginia, but others are going off farther South. The white young men who were growing into manhood did not seem inclined to leave their homes and migrate to foreign parts. There was an exodus after the war, but it has stopped, and many have come back. The old slave-holders still hold their lands. The negroes were poor and unable to buy, even if the land-owners would sell. This was a powerful impediment to the development of the negro into a controlling force in the State. His whole power was in his numbers. The present disproportion of four blacks to three whites in the State he believed was already decreasing. The whites seemed likely to more than hold their own, while the blacks would fall off. Cumulative voting would encourage the growth and add to the political power of the whites in the Legislature, where they were at present overslaughed.

Then the manufacturing industry was growing in magnitude and vitality. This spread various new employments over the State, and every one became a centre to invite white immigration. This influence was already felt. Trade was increased in the towns, and this meant increase of white population. High taxes were a detriment and a drag. But the trader put them on to his goods, and the manufacturer on to his products, and made the consumer pay.

But this important question cannot be dismissed in a paragraph. It requires further treatment. It involves the fortunes of the State far too deeply, and the duties of the white people and the interests of the property holder, are too intimately connected with a just decision of it, to excuse a hasty or shallow judgment. We must defer its further consideration to another occasion. It is the question which is all in all to South Carolina.

# Robert Brown Elliott, "The Civil Rights Bill"

## (January 6, 1874)

Elliott, the African-American congressman from South Carolina, was a tireless advocate of black rights during Congressional Reconstruction. In 1871, he forcefully promoted the Ku Klux Act and, following his reelection in 1872, supported Senator Charles Sumner's longstanding efforts to pass civil rights legislation mandating equal access to public facilities—including railroads, theaters, hotels, schools, cemeteries, churches, and juries—for persons of all races. In January 1874, Elliott delivered a moving speech endorsing Sumner's bill, dismissing states' rights arguments propounded by Southern Democrats and grounding his advocacy of Sumner's proposed legislation in the Fourteenth Amendment's equal-protection clause.

. . . Are we then, sir, with the amendments to our Constitution staring us in the face; with these grand truths of history before our eyes; with innumerable wrongs daily inflicted upon five million citizens demanding redress, to commit this question to the diversity of legislation? In the words of Hamilton, "Is it the interest of the government to sacrifice individual rights to the preservation of the rights of an artificial being called the states? There can be no truer principle than this, that every individual of the community at large has an equal right to the protection of government. Can this be a free government if partial distinctions are tolerated or maintained?"

The rights contended for in this bill are among "the sacred rights of mankind, which are not to be rummaged for among old parchments or musty records; they are written as with a sunbeam in the whole volume of human nature, by the hand of the divinity itself, and can never be erased or obscured by mortal power."

But the Slaughterhouse cases!—The Slaughterhouse cases!

The honorable gentleman from Kentucky, always swift to sustain the failing and dishonored cause of proscription, rushes forward and flaunts in our faces the decision of the Supreme Court of the United States in the Slaughterhouse cases, and in that act he has been willingly aided by the gentleman from Georgia. Hitherto, in the contests which have marked the progress of the cause of equal civil rights, our opponents have appealed sometimes to custom, sometimes to prejudice, more often to pride of race, but they have never sought to shield themselves behind the Supreme Court. But now, for the first time, we are told that we are barred by a decision of that court, from which there is no appeal. If this be true we must stay our hands. The cause of equal civil rights must pause at the command of a power whose edicts must be obeyed till the fundamental law of our country is changed.

Has the honorable gentleman from Kentucky considered well the claim he now advances? If it were not disrespectful I would ask, has he ever read the decision which he now tells us is an insuperable barrier to the adoption of this great measure of justice?

In the consideration of this subject, has not the judgment of the gentleman from Georgia been warped by the ghost of the dead doctrines of states' rights? Has he been altogether free from prejudices engendered by long training in that school of politics that well-nigh destroyed this government?

Mr. Speaker, I venture to say here in the presence of the gentleman from Kentucky and the gentleman from Georgia, and in the presence of the whole country, that there is not a line or word, not a thought or dictum even, in the decision of the Supreme Court in the great Slaughterhouse cases, which casts a shadow of doubt on the right of Congress to pass the pending bill, or to adopt such other legislation as it may judge proper and necessary to secure perfect equality before the law to every citizen of the Republic. Sir, I protest against the dishonor now cast upon our Supreme Court by both the gentleman from Kentucky and the gentleman from Georgia. In other days, when the whole country was bowing beneath the yoke of slavery, when press, pulpit, platform, Congress and courts felt the fatal power of the slave oligarchy, I remember a decision of that court which no American now reads without shame and humiliation. But those days are past; the Supreme Court of today is a tribunal as true to freedom as any department of this government, and I am honored with the opportunity of repelling a deep disgrace which the gentleman from Kentucky, backed and sustained as he is by the gentleman from Georgia, seeks to put upon it.

What were these Slaughterhouse cases? The gentleman should be aware that a decision of any court should be examined in the light of the exact question which is brought before it for decision. That is all that gives authority to any decision.

The State of Louisiana, by act of her Legislature, had conferred on certain persons the exclusive right to maintain stock-landings and slaughterhouses within the city of New Orleans, or the parishes of Orleans, Jefferson, and Saint Bernard, in that State. The corporation which was thereby chartered were invested with the sole and exclusive privilege of conducting and carrying on the live-stock, landing, and slaughter-house business within the limits designated.

The supreme court of Louisiana sustained the validity of the act conferring these exclusive privileges, and the plaintiffs in error brought the case before the Supreme Court of the United States for review. The plaintiffs in error contended that the act in question was void, because, first, it established a monopoly which was in derogation of common right and in contravention of the common law; and, second, that the grant of such exclusive privileges was in violation of the thirteenth and fourteenth amendments of the constitution of the United States.

It thus appears from a simple statement of the case that the question which was before the court was not whether a State law which denied to a particular portion of her citizens the rights conferred on her citizens generally, on account of race, color, or previous condition of servitude, was unconstitutional because in conflict with the recent amendments, but whether an act which conferred on certain citizens exclusive privileges for police purposes was in conflict therewith, because imposing an involuntary servitude forbidden by the thirteenth amendment, or abridging the rights and immunities of citizens of the United States, or denying the equal protection of the laws, prohibited by the fourteenth amendment.

On the part of the defendants in error it was maintained that the act was the exercise of the ordinary and unquestionable power of the State to make regulation for the health and comfort of society—the exercise of the police power of the State, defined by Chancellor Kent to be "the right to interdict unwholesome trades, slaughter-houses, operations offensive to the senses, the deposit of powder, the application of steam-power to propel cars, the building with combustible materials, and the burial of the dead in the midst of dense masses of population, on the general and rational principle that every person ought so to use his own property as not to injure his neighbors, and that private interests must be made subservient to the general interests of the community."

The decision of the Supreme Court is to be found in the 16th volume of Wallace's Reports, and was delivered by Associate Justice Miller. The court hold, first, that the act in question is a legitimate and warrantable exercise of the police power of the State in regulating the business of stock-landing and slaughtering in the city of New Orleans and the territory immediately contiguous. Having held this, the court proceeds to discuss the question whether the conferring of exclusive privileges, such as those conferred by the act in question, is the imposing of an involuntary servitude, the abridging of the rights and immunities of citizens of the United States, or the denial to any person within the jurisdiction of the State of the equal protection of the laws.

That the act is not the imposition of an involuntary servitude the court hold to be clear, and they next proceed to examine the remaining questions arising under the fourteenth amendment. Upon this question the court hold that the leading and comprehensive purpose of the thirteenth, fourteenth, and fifteenth amendments was to secure the complete freedom of the race, which, by the events of the war, had been wrested from the unwilling grasp of their owners. I know no finer or more just picture, albeit painted in the neutral tints of true judicial impartiality, of the motives and events which led to these amendments. Has the gentleman from Kentucky read these passages which I now quote? Or has the gentleman from Georgia considered well the force of the language therein used? Says the court on page 70:

> The process of restoring to their proper relations with the Federal Government and with the other States those which had sided with the rebellion, undertaken under the proclamation of President Johnson in 1865, and before the assembling of Congress, developed the fact that, notwithstanding the formal recognition by those States of the abolition of slavery, the condition of the slave race would, without further protection of the Federal Government, be almost as bad as it was before. Among the first acts of legislation adopted by several of the States in the legislative bodies which claimed to be in their normal relations with the Federal Government, were laws which imposed upon the colored race onerous disabilities and burdens, and curtailed their rights in the pursuit of life, liberty, and property to such an extent that their freedom was of little value, while they had lost the protection which they had received from their former owners from motives both of interest and humanity.

They were in some States forbidden to appear in the towns in any other character than menial servants. They were required to reside on and cultivate the soil, without the right to purchase or own it. They were excluded from any occupations of gain, and were not permitted to give testimony in the courts in any case where a white man was a party. It was said that their lives were at the mercy of bad men, either because the laws for their protection were insufficient or were not enforced.

These circumstances, whatever of falsehood or misconception may have been mingled with their presentation, forced upon the statesmen who had conducted the Federal Government in safety through the crisis of the rebellion, and who supposed that by the thirteenth article of amendment they had secured the result of their labors, the conviction that something more was necessary in the way of constitutional protection to the unfortunate race who had suffered so much. They accordingly passed through Congress the proposition for the fourteenth amendment, and they declined to treat as restored to their full participation in the Government of the Union the States which had been in insurrection until they ratified that article by a formal vote of their legislative bodies.

Before we proceed to examine more critically the provisions of this amendment, on which the plaintiffs in error rely, let us complete and discuss the history of the recent amendments, as that history related to the general purpose which pervades them all. A few years' experience satisfied the thoughtful men who had been the authors of the other two amendments that, notwithstanding the restraints of those articles on the States and the laws passed under the additional powers granted to Congress, these were inadequate for the protection of life, liberty, and property, without which freedom to the slave was no boon. They were in all those States denied the right of suffrage. The laws were administered by the white man alone. It was urged that a race of men distinctively marked as was the negro, living in the midst of another and dominant race, could never be fully secured in their person and their property without the right of suffrage.

Hence the fifteenth amendment, which declares that "the right of a citizen of the United States to vote shall not be denied or abridged by any State on account of race, color, or previous condition of servitude." The negro having, by the fourteenth amendment, been declared to be a citizen of the United States, is thus made a voter in every State of the Union.

We repeat, then, in the light of this recapitulation of events almost too recent to be called history, but which are familiar to us all, and on the most casual examination of the language of these amendments, no one can fail to be impressed with the one pervading purpose found in them all, lying at the foundation of each, and without which none of them would have been even suggested: we mean, the freedom of the slave race, the security and firm establishment of that freedom, and the protection of the newly-made freeman and citizen from the oppressions of those who had formerly exercised unlimited dominion over him. It is true that only the fifteenth amendment in terms mentions the negro by speaking of his color and his slavery. But it is just as true that each of the other articles was addressed to the grievances of that race, and designed to remedy them, as the fifteenth.

These amendments, one and all, are thus declared to have as their all-pervading design and ends the security of the recently enslaved race, not only their nominal freedom, but their complete protection from those who had formerly exercised unlimited dominion over them. It is in this broad light that all these amendments must be read, the purpose to secure the perfect equality before the law of all citizens of the United States. What you give to one class you must give to all, what you deny to one class you shall deny to all, unless in the exercise of the common and universal police power of the state, you find it needful to confer exclusive privileges on certain citizens, to be held and exercised still for the common good of all.

Such are the doctrines of the Slaughterhouse cases—doctrines worthy of the Republic, worthy of the age, worthy of the great tribunal which thus loftily and impressively enunciates them. Do they—I put it to any man, be he lawyer or not; I put it to the gentleman from Georgia—do they give color even to the claim that this Congress may not now legislate against a plain discrimination made by state laws or state customs against that very race for whose complete freedom and protection these great amendments were elaborated and adopted? Is it pretended, I ask the honorable gentleman from Kentucky or the honorable gentleman from Georgia—is it pretended anywhere that the evils of which we complain, our exclusion from the public inn, from the saloon and table of the steamboat, from the sleeping coach on the railway, from the right of sepulture in the public burial ground, are an exercise of the police power of the state? Is such oppression and injustice nothing but the exercise by the state of the right to make regulations for the health, comfort and security of all her citizens? Is it merely enacting that one man shall so use his own as not to injure another's? Is the colored race to be assimilated to an unwholesome trade or to combustible materials, to be interdicted, to be shut up within prescribed limits? Let the gentleman from Kentucky or the gentleman from Georgia answer. Let the country know to what extent even the audacious prejudice of the gentleman from Kentucky will drive him, and how far even the gentleman from Georgia will permit himself to be led captive by the unrighteous teachings of a false political faith.

If we are to be likened in legal view to "unwholesome trades," to "large and offensive collections of animals," to "noxious slaughterhouses," to "the offal and stench which attend on certain manufactures," let it be avowed. If that is still the doctrine of the political party, to which the gentlemen belong, let it be put upon record. If state laws which deny us the common rights and privileges of other citizens, upon no possible or conceivable ground save one of prejudice, or of "taste" as the gentleman from Texas termed it, and as I suppose the gentlemen will prefer to call it, are to be placed under the protection of a decision which affirms the right of a state to regulate the police power of her great cities, then the decision is in conflict with the bill before us. No man will dare maintain such a doctrine. It is as shocking to the legal mind as it is offensive to the heart and conscience of all who love justice or respect manhood. I am astonished that the gentleman from Kentucky or the gentleman from Georgia should have been so grossly misled as to rise here and assert that the decision of the Supreme Court in these cases was a denial to Congress of the power to legislate against discriminations on account of race, color or previous conditions of servitude because that Court has decided that exclusive privileges conferred for the common protection of the lives and health of the whole community are not in violation of the recent amendments. The only ground upon which the grant of exclusive privileges to a portion of the community is ever defended is that the substantial good of all is promoted; that in truth it is for the welfare of the whole community that certain persons should alone pursue certain occupations. It is not the special benefit conferred on the few that moves the legislature, but the ultimate and real benefit of all, even of those who are denied the right to pursue those specified occupations. Does the gentleman from Kentucky say that my good is promoted when I am excluded from the public inn? Is the health or safety of the community promoted? Doubtless his prejudice is gratified. Doubtless his democratic instincts are pleased; but will he or his able coadjutor say that such exclusion is a lawful exercise of the police power of the state, or that it is not a denial to me of the equal protection of the laws? They will not so say.

But each of these gentlemen quote at some length from the decision of the court to show that the court recognizes a difference between citizenship of the United States and citizenship of the states. That is true and no man here who supports this bill questions or overlooks the difference. There are privileges and immunities which belong to me as a citizen of the United States, and there are other privileges and immunities which belong to me as a citizen of my state. The former are under the protection of the Constitution and laws of the United States, and the latter are under the protection of the constitution and laws of my state. But what of that? Are the rights which I now claim—the right to enjoy the common public conveniences of travel on public highways, of rest and refreshment at public inns, of education in public schools, of burial in public cemeteries—rights which I hold as a citizen of the United States or of my state? Or, to state the question more exactly, is not the denial of such privileges to me a denial to me of the equal protection of the laws? For it is under this clause of the Fourteenth Amendment that we place the present bill, no state shall "deny to any person within its jurisdiction the equal protection of the laws." No matter, therefore, whether his rights are held under the United States or under his particular state, he is equally protected by this amendment. He is always and everywhere entitled to the equal protection of the laws. All discrimination is forbidden; and while the rights of citizens of a state as such are not defined or conferred by the Constitution of the United States, yet all discrimination, all denial of equality before the law, all denial of equal protection of the laws whether state or national laws, is forbidden.

The distinction between the two kinds of citizenship is clear, and the Supreme Court has clearly pointed out this distinction, but it has nowhere written a word or line which denies to Congress the power to prevent a denial of equality of rights whether those rights exist by virtue of citizenship of the United States or of a state. Let honorable members mark well this distinction. There are rights which are conferred on us by the United States. There are other rights conferred on us by the states of which we are individually the citizens. The Fourteenth Amendment does not forbid a state to deny to all its citizens any of those rights which the state itself has conferred with certain exceptions which are pointed out in the decision which we are examining. What it does forbid is inequality, is discrimination or, to use the words of the amendment itself, is the denial "to any person within its jurisdiction, the equal protection of the laws." If a state denies to me rights which are common to all her other citizens, she violates this amendment, unless she can show, as was shown in the Slaughterhouse cases, that she does it in the legitimate exercise of her police power. If she abridges the rights of all her citizens equally, unless those rights are specifically guarded by the Constitution of the United States, she does not violate this amendment. This is not to put the rights which I hold by virtue of my citizenship of South Carolina under the protection of the national government; it is not to blot out or overlook in the slightest particular the distinction between rights held under the United States and rights held under the states; but it seeks to secure equality to prevent discrimination, to confer as complete and ample protection on the humblest as on the highest.

The gentleman from Kentucky, in the course of the speech to which I am now replying, made a reference to the state of Massachusetts which betrays again the confusion which exists in his mind on this precise point. He tells us that Massachusetts excludes from the ballot box all who cannot read and write, and points to that fact as the exercise of a right which this bill would abridge or impair. The honorable gentleman from Massachusetts (Mr. Dawes) answered him truly and well, but I submit that he did not make the best reply; why did he not ask the gentleman from Kentucky if Massachusetts had ever discriminated against any of her citizens on account of color or race or previous condition of servitude? When did Massachusetts sully her proud record by placing on her statute book any law which admitted to the ballot the white man and shut out the black man? She has never done it; she will not do it; she cannot do it so long as we have a Supreme Court which reads the constitution of our country with the eyes of justice; nor can Massachusetts or Kentucky deny to any man on account of his race, color or previous condition of servitude, that perfect equality of protection under the laws so long as Congress shall exercise the power to enforce by appropriate legislation the great and unquestionable securities embodied in the Fourteenth Amendment to the Constitution. . . .

Now, sir, recurring to the venerable and distinguished gentleman from Georgia (Mr. Stephens) who has added his remonstrance against the passage of this bill, permit me to say that I share in the feeling of high personal regard for that gentleman which pervades this House. His years, his ability, and his long experience in public affairs entitle him to the measure of consideration which has been accorded to him on this floor. But in this discussion I cannot and will not forget that the welfare and rights of my whole race in this country are involved. When, therefore, the honorable gentleman from Georgia lends his voice and influence to defeat this measure, I do not shrink from saying that it is not from him that the American House of Representatives should take lessons in matters touching human rights or the joint relations of the state and national governments. While the honorable gentleman contented himself with harmless speculations in his study, or in the columns of a newspaper, we might well smile at the impotence of his efforts to turn back the advancing tide of opinion and progress, but, when he comes again upon this national arena, and throws himself with all his power and influence across the path which leads to the full enfranchisement of my race, I meet him only as an adversary; nor shall age or any other consideration restrain me from saying that he now offers this government, which he has done his utmost to destroy, a very poor return for its magnanimous treatment, to come here and seek to continue, by the assertion of doctrines obnoxious to the true principles of our government, the burdens and oppressions which rest upon five millions of his countrymen who never failed to lift their earnest prayers for the success of this government when the gentleman was seeking to break up the union of these states and to blot the American Republic from the galaxy of nations. [Loud applause.]

Sir, it is scarcely twelve years since that gentleman shocked the civilized world by announcing the birth of a government which rested on human slavery as its cornerstone. The progress of events has swept away that pseudo government which rested on greed, pride and tyranny; and the race whom he then ruthlessly spurned and trampled on is here to meet him in debate, and to demand that the rights which are enjoyed by its former oppressors—who vainly sought to overthrow a government which they could not prostitute to the base uses of slavery—shall be accorded to those who even in the darkness of slavery kept their allegiance true to freedom and the Union. Sir, the gentleman from Georgia has learned much since 1861; but he is still a laggard. Let him put away entirely the false and fatal theories which have so greatly marred an otherwise enviable record. Let him accept, in its fullness and beneficence, the great doctrine that American citizenship carries with it every civil and political right which manhood can confer. Let him lend his influence with all his masterly ability, to complete the proud structure of legislation which makes this nation worthy of the great declaration which heralded its birth, and he will have done that which will most nearly redeem his reputation in the eyes of the world and best vindicate the wisdom of that policy which has permitted him to regain his seat upon this floor.

To the diatribe of the gentleman from Virginia (Mr. Harris) who spoke on yesterday, and who so far transcended the limits of decency and propriety as to announce upon this floor that his remarks were addressed to white men alone, I shall have no word of reply. Let him feel that a Negro was not only too magnanimous to smite him in his weakness, but was even charitable enough to grant him the mercy of his silence. I shall, sir, leave to others less charitable the unenviable and fatiguing task of sifting out of that mass of chaff the few grains of sense that may, perchance, deserve notice. Assuring the gentleman that the Negro in this country aims at a higher degree of intellect than that exhibited by him in this debate, I cheerfully commend him to the commiseration of all intelligent men the world over—black men as well as white men.

Sir, equality before the law is now the broad, universal, glorious rule and mandate of the Republic. No state can violate that. Kentucky and Georgia may crowd their statute books with retrograde and barbarous legislation; they may rejoice in the odious eminence of their consistent hostility to all the great steps of human progress which have marked our national history since slavery tore down the Stars and Stripes on Fort Sumter; but, if Congress shall do its duty, if Congress shall enforce the great guarantees which the Supreme Court has declared to be the one pervading purpose of all the recent amendments, then their unwise and unenlightened conduct will fall with the same weight upon the gentlemen from those states who now lend their influence to defeat this bill, as upon the poorest slave who once had no rights which the honorable gentlemen were bound to respect.

But, sir, not only does the decision in the Slaughterhouse cases contain nothing which suggests a doubt of the power of Congress to pass the pending bill, but it contains an express recognition and affirmance of such power. I quote from page 81 of the volume:

> "Nor shall any State deny to any person within its jurisdiction the equal protection of the laws:"
>
> In the light of the history of these amendments and the pervading purpose of them which we have already discussed, it is not difficult to give a meaning to this clause. The existence of laws in the states where the newly emancipated Negroes resided, which discriminated with gross injustice and hardship against them as a class, was the evil to be remedied by this clause, and by it such laws are forbidden.
>
> If, however, the states did not conform their views to its requirements, then, by the fifth section of the article of amendment, Congress was authorized to enforce it by suitable legislation. We doubt very much whether any action of a state not directed by way of discrimination against the Negroes as a class, or on account of their race, will ever be held to come within the purview of this provision. It is so clearly a provision for that race and that emergency, that a strong case would be necessary for its application to any other. But as it is a state that is to be dealt with, and not alone the

validity of its laws, we may safely leave that matter until Congress shall have exercised its power, or some case of state oppression, by denial of equal justice in its courts, shall have claimed a decision at our hands.

No language could convey a more complete assertion of the power of Congress over the subject embraced in the present bill than is here expressed. If the states do not conform to the requirements of this clause, if they continue to deny to any person within their jurisdiction the equal protection of the laws or, as the Supreme Court had said, "deny equal justice in its Courts" then Congress is here said to have power to enforce the Constitutional guarantee by appropriate legislation. That is the power which this bill now seeks to put in exercise. It proposes to enforce the Constitutional guarantee against inequality and discrimination by appropriate legislation. It does not seek to confer new rights, nor to place rights conferred by state citizenship under the protection of the United States, but simply to prevent and forbid inequality and discrimination on account of race, color or previous condition of servitude. Never was there a bill more completely within the constitutional power of Congress. Never was there a bill which appealed for support more strongly to that sense of justice and fair play which has been said, and in the main with justice, to be a characteristic of the Anglo-Saxon race. The Constitution warrants it; the Supreme Court sanctions it; justice demands it.

Sir, I have replied to the extent of my ability to the arguments which have been presented by the opponents of this measure. I have replied also to some of the legal propositions advanced by gentlemen on the other side; and now that I am about to conclude, I am deeply sensible of the imperfect manner in which I have performed the task. Technically, this bill is to decide upon the civil status of the colored American citizen; a point disputed at the very formation of our present form of government, when by a short-sighted policy repugnant to true republican government, one Negro counted as three fifths of a man. The logical result of this mistake of the framers of the Constitution strengthened the cancer of slavery, which finally spread its poisonous tentacles over the Southern portion of the body politic. To arrest its growth and save the nation we have passed through the harrowing operation of intestine war, dreaded at all times, resorted to at the last extremity, like the surgeon's knife, but absolutely necessary to extirpate the disease which threatened with the life of the nation the overthrow of civil and political liberty on this continent. In that dire extremity the members of the race which I have the honor in part to represent—the race which pleads for justice at your hands to-day—forgetful of their inhuman and brutalizing servitude at the South, their degradation and ostracism at the North, flew willingly and gallantly to the support of the national government. Their sufferings, assistance, privations and trials in the swamps and in the rice fields, their valor on the land and on the sea, form a part of the ever-glorious record which makes up the history of a nation preserved, and might, should I urge the claim, incline you to respect and guarantee their rights and privileges as citizens of our common Republic. But I remember that valor, devotion and loyalty are not always rewarded according to their just deserts, and that after the battle some who have borne the brunt of the fray may, through neglect or contempt, be assigned to a subordinate place, while the enemies in war may be preferred to the sufferers.

The results of the war, as seen in reconstruction, have settled forever the political status of my race. The passage of this bill will determine the civil status, not only of the Negro, but of any other class of citizens who may feel themselves discriminated against. It will form the capstone of that temple of liberty, begun on this continent under discouraging circumstances, carried on in spite of the sneers of monarchists and the cavils of pretended friends of freedom, until at last it stands, in all its beautiful symmetry and proportions, a building the grandest which the world has ever seen, realizing the most sanguine expectations and the highest hopes of those who, in the name of equal, impartial and universal liberty, laid the foundation stone. . . .

# JOHN MERCER LANGSTON, "EQUALITY BEFORE THE LAW"

## (May 17, 1874)

Like Elliott, other African-American leaders also lobbied for Sumner's civil rights bill, especially following the senator's death on March 11, 1874. In May of that year, John Mercer Langston (1829–1897) presented a lecture on equal rights and citizenship at Oberlin College, from which he had graduated in 1849. Born a slave in Virginia, Langston was freed after the death of his slaveholding father, went to Ohio to study, and eventually became a lawyer. During the Civil War, he was a leading recruiter for the U.S. Colored Troops. During much of Reconstruction, he served as dean of Howard University's law department. In his Oberlin address, Langston argued that the Reconstruction amendments were meaningless if some citizens were denied civil or political privileges that others enjoyed.

... It is no more interesting to the patriot than to the philanthropist to trace the changes which have been made during the last decade in our legislation and law. Nor is there anything in these changes to cause regret or fear to the wise and sagacious lawyer or statesman. This is particularly true since, in the changes made, we essay no novel experiments in legislation and law, but such as are justified by principles drawn from the fountains of our jurisprudence, the Roman civil and the common law. It has been truthfully stated that the common law has made no distinction on account of race or color. None is now made in England or in any other Christian country of Europe. Nor is there any such distinction made, to my knowledge, in the whole body of the Roman civil law.

Among the changes that have been wrought in the law

472

of our country, in the order of importance and dignity, I would mention, first, that slavery abolished, not by State but national enactment, can never again in the history of our country be justified or defended on the ground that it is a municipal institution, the creature of State law. Henceforth, as our emancipation has been decreed by national declaration, our freedom is shielded and protected by the strong arm of national law. Go where we may, now, like the atmosphere about us, law protects us in our locomotion, our utterance, and our pursuit of happiness. And to this leading and fundamental fact of the law the people and the various States of the Union are adjusting themselves with grace and wisdom. It would be difficult to find a sane man in our country who would seriously advocate the abrogation of the 13th amendment to the Constitution.

In our emancipation it is fixed by law that the place where we are born is *ipso facto* our country; and this gives us a domicile, a home. As in slavery we had no self ownership, nor interest in anything external to ourselves, so we were without country and legal settlement. While slavery existed, even the free colored American was in no better condition; and hence exhortations, prompted in many instances by considerations of philanthropy and good-will, were not infrequently made to him to leave his native land, to seek residence and home elsewhere, in distant and inhospitable regions. These exhortations did not always pass unheeded; for eventually a national organization was formed, having for its sole purpose the transportation to Africa of such colored men as might desire to leave the land of their birth to find settlement in that country. And through the influence of the African Colonization Society not a few, even, of our most energetic, enterprising, industrious and able colored men, not to mention thousands of the humbler class, have been carried abroad.

It may be that, in the providence of God, these persons, self-expatriated, may have been instrumental in building up a respectable and promising government in Liberia, and that those who have supported the Colonization Society have been philanthropically disposed, both as regards the class transported and the native African. It is still true, however, that the emancipated American has hitherto been driven or compelled to consent to expatriation because denied legal home and settlement in the land of his nativity. Expatriation is no longer thus compelled; for it is now settled in the law, with respect to the colored, as well as all other native-born Americans, that the country of his birth, even this beautiful and goodly land, is his country. Nothing, therefore, appertaining to it, its rich and inexhaustible resources, its industry and commerce, its education and religion, its law and Government, the glory and perpetuity of its free institutions and Union, can be without lively and permanent interest to him, as to all others who, either by birth or adoption, legitimately claim it as their country.

With emancipation, then, comes also that which is dearer to the true patriot than life itself: country and home. And this doctrine of the law, in the broad and comprehensive application explained, is now accepted without serious objection by leading jurists and statesmen.

The law has also forever determined, and to our advantage, that nativity, without any regard to nationality or complexion, settles, absolutely, the question of citizenship. One can hardly understand how citizenship, predicated upon birth, could have ever found place among the vexed questions of the law; certainly American law. We have only to read, however, the official opinions given by leading and representative American lawyers, in slaveholding times, to gain full knowledge to the existence of this fact. According to these opinions our color, race and degradation, all or either, rendered the colored American incapable of being or becoming a citizen of the United States. . . .

With freedom decreed by law, citizenship sanctioned and sustained thereby, the duty of allegiance on the one part, and the right of protection on the other recognized and enforced, even if considerations of political necessity had not intervened, the gift of the ballot to the colored American could not have long been delayed. The 15th amendment is the logical and legal consequences of the 13th and 14th amendments of the Constitution. Considerations of political necessity, as indicated, no doubt hastened the adoption of this amendment. But in the progress of legal development in our country, consequent upon the triumph of the abolition movement, its coming was inevitable. And, therefore, as its legal necessity, as well as political, is recognized and admitted, opposition to it has well-nigh disappeared. Indeed, so far from there being anything like general and organized opposition to the exercise of political powers by the enfranchised American, the people accept it as a fit and natural fact.

Great as the change has been with regard to the legal status of the colored American, in his freedom, his enfranchisement, and the exercise of political powers, he is not yet given the full exercise and enjoyment of all the rights which appertain by law to American citizenship. Such as are still denied him are withheld on the plea that their recognition would result in social equality, and his demand for them is met by considerations derived from individual and domestic opposition. Such reasoning is no more destitute of logic than law. While I hold that opinion sound which does not accept mere prejudice and caprice instead of the promptings of nature, guided by cultivated taste and wise judgment as the true basis of social recognition; and believing, too, that in a Christian community, social recognition may justly be pronounced a duty, I would not deal in this discussion with matters of society. I would justify the claim of the colored American to complete equality of rights and privileges upon well considered and accepted principles of law.

As showing the condition and treatment of the colored citizens of this country, anterior to the introduction of the Civil Rights Bill, so called, into the United States Senate, by the late Hon. Charles Sumner, I ask your attention to the following words from a letter written by him:

"I wish a bill carefully drawn, supplementary to the existing Civil Rights Law, by which all citizens shall be protected in equal rights:—

"1. On railroads, steamboats and public conveyances, being public carriers.
"2. At all houses in the nature of 'inns.'
"3. All licensed houses of public amusement.
"4. At all common schools.

"Can you do this? I would follow as much as possible the language of the existing Civil Rights Law, and make the new bill supplementary."

It will be seen from this very clear and definite statement of the Senator, that in his judgment, in spite of and contrary to common law rules applied in the case, certainly of all others, and recognized as fully settled, the colored citizen was denied those accommodations, facilities, advantages and privileges, furnished ordinarily by common carriers, innkeepers, at public places of amusement and common schools; and which are so indispensable to rational and useful enjoyment of life, that without them citizenship itself loses much of its value, and liberty seems little more than a name.

The judicial axiom, *"omnes homines oequales sunt,"* is said to have been given the world by the jurisconsults of the Antonine era. From the Roman, the French people inherited this legal sentiment; and, through the learning, the wisdom and patriotism of Thomas Jefferson and his Revolutionary compatriots, it was made the chief corner-stone of jurisprudence and politics. In considering the injustice done the colored American in denying him common school advantages, on general and equal terms with all others, impartial treatment in the conveyances of common carriers, by sea and land, and the enjoyment of the usual accommodations afforded travelers at public inns, and in vindicating his claim to the same, it is well to bear in mind this fundamental and immutable principle upon which the fathers built, and in the light of which our law ought to be construed and enforced. This observation has especial significance as regards the obligations and liabilities of common carriers and inn-keepers; for from the civil law we have borrowed those principles largely which have controlling force in respect to these subjects. It is manifest, in view of this statement, that the law with regard to these topics is neither novel nor unsettled; and when the colored American asks its due enforcement in his behalf, he makes no unnatural and strange demand.

Denied, generally, equal school advantages, the colored citizen demands them in the name of that equality of rights and privileges which is the vital element of American law. Equal in freedom, sustained by law; equal in citizenship, defined and supported by the law; equal in the exercise of political powers, regulated and sanctioned by law; by what refinement of reasoning, or tenet of law, can the denial of common school and other educational advantages be justified? To answer, that so readeth the statute, is only to drive us back of the letter to the reasonableness, the soul of the law, in the name of which we would, as we do, demand the repeal of that enactment which is not only not law, but contrary to its simplest requirements. It may be true that that which ought to be law is not always so written; but, in this matter, that only ought to remain upon the statute book, to be enforced as to citizens and voters, which is law in the truest and best sense.

Without dwelling upon the advantages of a thorough common school education, I will content myself by offering several considerations against the proscriptive, and in favor of the common school. A common school should be one to which all citizens may send their children, not by favor, but by right. It is established and supported by the Government; its criterion is a public foundation; and one citizen has as rightful claim upon its privileges and advantages as any other. The money set apart to its organization and support, whatever the sources whence it is drawn, whether from taxation or appropriation, having been dedicated to the public use, belongs as much to one as to another citizen; and no principle of law can be adduced to justify any arbitrary classification which excludes the child of any citizen or class of citizens from equal enjoyment of the advantages purchased by such fund, it being the common property of every citizen equally, by reason of its public dedication.

Schools which tend to separate the children of the country in their feelings, aspirations and purposes, which foster and perpetuate sentiments of caste, hatred, and ill-will, which breed a sense of degradation on the one part and of superiority on the other, which beget clannish notions rather than teach and impress an omnipresent and living principle and faith that we are all Americans, in no wise realize our ideal of common schools, while they are contrary to the spirit of our laws and institutions.

Two separate school systems, tolerating discriminations in favor of one class against another, inflating on the one part, degrading on the other; two separate school systems, I say, tolerating such state of feeling and sentiment on the part of the classes instructed respectively in accordance therewith, cannot educate these classes to live harmoniously together, meeting the responsibilities and discharging the duties imposed by a common government in the interest of a common country.

The object of the common school is two-fold. In the first place it should bring to every child, especially the poor child, a reasonable degree of elementary education. In the second place it should furnish a common education, one similar and equal to all pupils attending it. Thus furnished, our sons enter upon business or professional walks with an equal start in life. Such education the Government owes to all classes of the people.

The obligations and liabilities of the common carrier of passengers can, in no sense, be made dependent upon the nationality or color of those with whom he deals. He may not, according to law, answer his engagements to one class and justify non-performance or neglect as to another by considerations drawn from race. His contract is originally and fundamentally with the entire community, and with all its members he is held to equal and impartial obligation. On this subject the rules of law are definite, clear, and satisfactory. These rules may be stated concisely as follows: It is the duty of the common carrier of passengers to receive all persons applying and who do not refuse to obey any reasonable regulations imposed, who are not guilty of gross and vulgar habits of conduct, whose characters are not doubtful, dissolute or suspicious or unequivocally bad, and whose object in seeking conveyance is not to interfere with the interests or patronage of the carrier so as to make his business less lucrative.

And, in the second place, common carriers may not impose upon passengers oppressive and grossly unreasonable orders and regulations. Were there doubt in regard to the obligation of common carriers as indicated, the authorities are abundant and might be quoted at large. Here, however, I need not make quotations. The only question which can arise as between myself and any intelligent lawyer, is as to whether the regulation made by common carriers of passengers generally in this country, by which passengers and colored ones are separated on steamboats, railroad cars, and stage coaches, greatly to the disadvantage, inconvenience, and dissatisfaction of the latter class, is reasonable. As to this question, I leave such lawyer to the books and his own conscience. We have advanced so far on this subject, in thought, feeling, and purpose, that the day cannot be distant when there will be found among us no one to justify such regulations by common carriers, and when they will be made to adjust themselves, in their orders and regulations with regard thereto to the rules of the common law. The grievance of the citizen in this particular is neither imaginary nor sentimental. His experience of sadness and pain attests its reality, and the awakening sense of the people generally, as discovered in their expressions, the decisions of several of our courts, and the recent legislation of a few States, shows that this particular discrimination, inequitable as it is illegal, cannot long be tolerated in any section of our country.

The law with regard to inn-keepers is not less explicit and rigid. They are not allowed to accommodate or refuse to accommodate wayfaring persons according to their own foolish prejudices or the senseless and cruel hatred of their guests.

Their duties are defined in the following language, the very words of the law:

> "Inns were allowed for the benefit of travelers, who have certain privileges whilst they are in their journeys, and are in a more peculiar manner protected by law.
>
> "If one who keeps a common inn refuses to receive a traveler as a guest into his house, or to find him victuals or lodging upon his tendering a reasonable price for the same, the inn-keeper is liable to render damages in an action at the suit of the party grieved, and may also be indicted and fined at the suit of the King.
>
> "An inn-keeper is not, if he has suitable room, at liberty to refuse to receive a guest who is ready and able to pay him a suitable compensation. On the contrary, he is bound to receive him, and if, upon false pretenses, he refuses, he is liable to an action."

These are doctrines as old as the common law itself; indeed, older, for they come down to us from Gaius and Papinian. All discriminations made, therefore, by the keepers of public houses in the nature of inns, to the disadvantage of the colored citizen, and contrary to the usual treatment accorded travelers, is not only wrong morally, but utterly illegal. To this judgment the public mind must soon come.

Had I the time, and were it not too great a trespass upon your patience, I should be glad to speak of the injustice and illegality, as well as inhumanity, of our exclusion, in some localities, from jury, public places of learning and amusement, the church and the cemetery. I will only say, however, (and in this statement I claim the instincts, not less than the well-formed judgment of mankind, in our behalf,) that such exclusion at least seems remarkable, and is difficult of defense upon any considerations of humanity, law, or Christianity. Such exclusion is the more remarkable and indefensible since we are fellow-citizens, wielding like political powers, eligible to the same high official positions, responsible to the same degree and in the same manner for the discharge of the duties they impose; interested in the progress and civilization of a common country, and anxious, like all others, that its destiny be glorious and matchless. It is strange, indeed, that the colored American may find place in the Senate, but it is denied access and welcome to the public place of learning, the theatre, the church and the graveyard, upon terms accorded to all others.

But, Mr. President and friends, it ill becomes us to complain; we may not tarry to find fault. The change in public sentiment, the reform in our national legislation and jurisprudence, which we this day commemorate, transcendent and admirable, augurs and guarantees to all American citizens complete equality before the law, in the protection and enjoyment of all those rights and privileges which pertain to manhood, enfranchised and dignified. To us the 13th amendment of our Constitution, abolishing slavery and perpetuating freedom; the 14th amendment establishing citizenship and prohibiting the enactment of any law which shall abridge the privileges or immunities of citizens of the United States, or which shall deny the equal protection of the laws to all American citizens; and the 15th amendment, which declares that the RIGHT of citizens of the United States to vote shall not be denied or abridged by the United States or by any State, on account of race, color, or previous condition of servitude, are national utterances which not only recognize, but sustain and perpetuate our freedom and rights.

To the colored American, more than to all others, the language of these amendments is not vain. To use the language of the late Hon. Charles Sumner, "within the sphere of their influence no person can be *created*, no person can be *born*, with civil or political privileges not enjoyed equally by all his fellow-citizens; nor can any institution be established recognizing distinction of birth. Here is the great charter of every human being, drawing vital breath upon this soil, whatever may be his condition and whoever may be his parents. He may be poor, weak, humble or black; he may be of Caucasian, Jewish, Indian or Ethiopian race; he may be of French, German, English or Irish extraction; but before the Constitution all these distinctions disappear. He is not poor, weak, humble or black; nor is he Caucasian, Jew, Indian or Ethiopian; nor is he French, German, English or Irish—he is a *man*, the equal of all his fellow-men. He is one of the children of the State, which like an impartial parent, regards all its offspring with an equal care. To some it may justly allot higher duties according to higher capacities; but it welcomes all to its equal hospitable board. The State, imitating the Divine Justice, is no respecter of persons."

With freedom established in our own country, and equality before the law promised in early Federal, if not State legislation, we may well consider our duty with regard to the abolition of slavery, the establishment of freedom and free institutions upon the American continent, especially in the island of the seas, where slavery is maintained by despotic Spanish rule, and where the people declaring slavery abolished, and appealing to the civilized world for sympathy and justification of their course, have staked all upon "the dread arbitrament of war." There can be no peace on our continent, there can be no harmony among its people till slavery is everywhere abolished and freedom established and protected by law; the people themselves, making for themselves, and supporting their own government. Every nation, whether its home be an island or upon a continent, if oppressed, ought to have, like our own, a "new birth of freedom," and its "government of the people, by the people, and for the people," shall prove at once its strength and support.

# James T. Rapier,
## "Civil Rights"

### (June 9, 1874)

Descended from Alabama free blacks, James Thomas Rapier (1837–1883) received an education in Canada and returned to Alabama after the Civil War to establish himself as a successful cotton planter. Entering politics, in 1867 he served as a delegate to Alabama's state constitutional convention and in 1871 was appointed an assessor of internal revenue. After establishing a Republican newspaper in 1872, Rapier was elected to Congress, where he worked to obtain federal support for Southern schools and final passage of Sumner's civil rights bill. Addressing Congress in June 1874, Rapier passionately argued that until the African-American received the same civil rights as the white American he would be denied the "full measure of rights as a man."

. . . I must confess it is somewhat embarrassing for a colored man to urge the passage of this bill, because if he exhibit an earnestness in the matter and express a desire for its immediate passage, straightway he is charged with a desire for social equality, as explained by the demagogue and understood by the ignorant white man. But then it is just as embarrassing for him not to do so, for, if he remain silent while the struggle is being carried on around, and for him, he is liable to be charged with a want of interest in a matter that concerns him more than any one else, which is enough to make his friends desert his cause. So in steering away from Scylla I may run upon Charybdis. But the anomalous, and I may add the supremely ridiculous, position of the negro at this time, in this country, compel me to say something. Here his condition is without a comparison, parallel alone to itself. Just think that the law recognizes my right upon this floor as a law-maker, but that there is no law to secure to me any accommodations whatever while traveling here to discharge my duties as a Representative of a large and wealthy constituency. Here I am the peer of the proudest, but on a steamboat or car I am not equal to the most degraded. Is not this most anomalous and ridiculous? . . .

I submit that I am degraded as long as I am denied the public privileges common to other men, and that the members of this House are correspondingly degraded by recognizing my political equality while I occupy such a humiliating position. What a singular attitude for law-makers of this great nation to assume, rather come down to me than allow me to go up to them. Sir, did you ever reflect that this is the only Christian country where poor, finite man is held responsible for the crimes of the infinite God whom you profess to worship? But it is; I am held to answer for the crime of color, when I was not consulted in the matter. Had I been consulted, and my future fully described, I think I should have objected to being born in this gospel land. The excuse offered for all this inhuman treatment is that they consider the negro inferior to the white man, intellectually and morally. This reason might have been offered and probably accepted as truth some years ago, but no one now believes him incapable of a high order of culture, except some one who is himself below the average of mankind in natural endowments. This is not the reason as I shall show before I have done.

Sir, there is a cowardly propensity in the human heart that delights in oppressing somebody else, and in the gratification of this base desire we always select a victim that can be outraged with safety. As a general thing the Jew has been the subject in most parts of the world; but here the negro is the most available for this purpose; for this reason in part he was seized upon, and not because he is naturally inferior to any one else. Instead of his enemies believing him to be incapable of a high order of mental culture, they have shown that they believe the reverse to be true, by taking the most elaborate pains to prevent his development. And the smaller the caliber of the white man the more frantically has he fought to prevent the intellectual and moral progress of the negro, for the simple but good reason that he has most to fear from such a result. He does not wish to see the negro approach the high moral standard of a man and gentleman.

Let me call your attention to a case in point. Some time since a well-dressed colored man was traveling from Augusta to Montgomery. The train on which he was stopped at a dinner-house. The crowd around the depot seeing him well dressed, fine-looking, and polite, concluded he must be a gentleman, (which was more than their righteous souls could stand,) and straightway they commenced to abuse him. And, sir, he had to go into the baggage-car, open his trunks, show his cards, faro-bank, dice, &c., before they would give him any peace: or, in other words, he was forced to give satisfactory evidence that he was not a man who was working to elevate the moral and intellectual standard of the negro before they would respect him. I have always found more prejudice existing in the breasts of men who have feeble minds and are conscious of it, than in the breasts of those who have towering intellects and are aware of it. Henry Ward Beecher reflected the feelings of the latter class when on a certain occasion he said: "Turn the negro loose; I am not afraid to run the race of life with him." He could afford to say this, all white men cannot; but what does the other class say? "Build a Chinese wall between the negro and the school-house, discourage in him pride of character and honest ambition, cut him off from every avenue that leads to the higher grounds of intelligence and usefulness, and then challenge him to a contest upon the highway of life to decide the question of superiority of race." By their acts, not by their words, the civilized world can and will judge how honest my opponents are in their declarations that I am naturally inferior to them. No one is surprised that this class opposes the passage of the civil-rights bill, for if the negro were allowed the same opportunities, the same rights of locomotion, the same rights to comfort in travel, how could they prove themselves better than the negro. . . .

The professed belief and practice are sadly at variance, and must be intelligently harmonized before I can be made to believe that they are willing to acknowledge that I have any rights under the Constitution or elsewhere. He boasts of the magnanimity of Kentucky in allowing the negro to vote without qualification, while, to enjoy the same privilege in Massachusetts he is required to read the constitution of that State. He was very unhappy in this comparison.

Why, sir, his State does not allow the negro to vote at all. When was the constitution of Kentucky amended so as to grant him the elective franchise? They vote there by virtue of the fifteenth amendment alone, independent of the laws and constitution of that Commonwealth; and they would to-day disfranchise him if it could be done without affecting her white population. The Old Bay State waited for no "act of Congress" to force her to do justice to all of her citizens, but in *ante bellum* days provided in her constitution that all male persons who could read and write should be entitled to suffrage. That was a case of equality before the law, and who had a right to complain? There is nothing now in the amended Federal Constitution to prevent Kentucky from adopting the same kind of clause in in her constitution; when the convention meets to revise the organic law of that State, I venture the assertion that you will never hear a word about it; but it will not be out of any regard for her colored citizens, but the respect for that army of fifty-thousand ignorant white men she has within her borders, many of whom I see every time I pass through that State, standing around the several depots continually harping on the stereotyped phrase, "The damned negro won't work."

I would not be surprised though if she should do better in the future. I remember when a foreigner was just as unpopular in Kentucky as the negro is now; when the majority of the people of that State were opposed to according the foreigner the same rights they claimed for themselves; when that class of people were mobbed in the streets of her principal cities on account of their political faith, just as they have done the negro for the last seven years. But what do you see to-day? One of that then proscribed class is Kentucky's chief Representative upon this floor. Is not this an evidence of a returning sense of justice? If so, would it not be reasonable to predict that she will in the near future send one of her now proscribed class to aid him in representing her interests upon this floor?

Mr. Speaker, there is another member of this body who has opposed the passage of this bill very earnestly, whose position in the country and peculiar relations to the Government compel me to refer to him before I conclude. I allude to the gentleman from Georgia, [Mr. STEPHENS.] He returns to this House after an absence of many years with the same old ideas respecting State-rights that he carried away with him. He has not advanced a step; but unfortunately for him the American people have, and no longer consider him a fit expounder of our organic law. Following to its legitimate conclusion the doctrine of State-rights, (which of itself is secession,) he deserted the flag of his country, followed his State out of the Union, and a long and bloody war followed. With its results most men are acquainted and recognize; but he, Bourbon-like, comes back saying the very same things he used to say, and swearing by the same gods he swore by in other days. He seems not to know that the ideas which he so ably advanced for so many years were by the war swept away, along with that system of slavery which he intended should be the chief cornerstone, precious and elect, of the transitory kingdom over which he was second ruler.

Sir, the most of us have seen the play of Rip Van Winkle, who was said to have slept twenty years in the Katskill Mountains. On his return he found that the small trees had grown up to be large ones; the village of Falling Waters had improved beyond his recollection; the little children that used to play around his knees and ride into the village upon his back had grown up to be men and women and assumed the responsibilities of life; most of his friends, including Nick Vedder, had gone to that bourn whence no traveler returns; but, saddest of all, his child, "Mene," could not remember him. No one can see him in his efforts to recall the scenes of other days without being moved almost to tears. This, however, is fiction. The life and actions of the gentleman from Georgia most happily illustrate this character. This is a case where truth is stranger than fiction; and when he comes into these Halls advocating the same old ideas after an absence of so many years, during which time we have had a conflict of arms such as the world never saw, that revolutionized the entire body-politic, he stamps himself a living "Rip Van Winkle."

I reiterate, that the principles of "State-rights," for the recognition of which, he now contends, are the ones that were in controversy during our late civil strife. The arguments *pro* and *con* were heard in the roar of battle, amid the shrieks of the wounded, and the groans of the dying; and the decision was rendered amid shouts of victory by the Union soldiers. With it all appear to be familiar except him, and for his information I will state that upon this question an appeal was taken from the forum to the sword, the highest tribunal known to man, that it was then and there decided that National rights are paramount to State-rights, and that liberty and equality before the law should be coextensive with the jurisdiction of the Stars and Stripes. And I will further inform him that the bill now pending is simply to give practical effect to that decision.

I sympathize with him in his inability to understand this great change. When he left here the negro was a chattel, exposed for sale in the market places within a stone's throw of the Capitol; so near that the shadow of the Goddess of Liberty reflected by the rising sun would fall within the slave-pen as a forcible reminder that there was no hopeful day, nothing bright in the future, for the poor slave. Then no negro was allowed to enter these Halls and hear discussions on subjects that most interested him. The words of lofty cheer that fell from the lips of Wade, Giddings, Julian, and others were not allowed to fall upon his ear. Then, not more than three negroes were allowed to assemble at any place in the capital of the nation without special permission from the city authorities. But on his return he finds that the slave-pens have been torn down, and upon their ruins temples of learning have been erected; he finds that the Goddess of Liberty is no longer compelled to cover her radiant face while she weeps for our national shame, but looks with pride and satisfaction upon a free and regenerated land; he finds that the laws and regulations respecting the assembling of negroes are no longer in force, but on the contrary he can see on any public holiday the Butler Zouaves, a fine-looking company of colored men, on parade.

Imagine, if you can, what would have been the effect of such a sight in this city twelve years ago. Then one negro soldier would have caused utter consternation. Congress would have adjourned; the Cabinet would have sought protection elsewhere; the President would have declared martial law; troops and marines would have been ordered out; and I cannot tell all that would have happened; but now such a sight does not excite a ripple on the current of affairs; but over all, and worse to him than all, he finds the negro here, not only a listener but a participant in debate.

While I sympathize with him in his inability to comprehend this marvelous change, I must say in all earnestness that one who cannot understand and adjust himself to the new order of things is poorly qualified to teach this nation the meaning of our amended Constitution. The tenacity with which he sticks to his purpose through all the vicissitudes of life is commendable, though his views be objectionable.

While the chief of the late confederacy is away in Europe fleeing the wrath to come in the shape of Joe Johnston's history of the war, his lieutenant, with a boldness that must challenge the admiration of the most impudent, comes into these Halls and seeks to commit the nation through Congress to the doctrine of State-rights, and thus save it from the general wreck that followed the collapse of the rebellion. He had no other business here. Read his speech on the pending bill; his argument was cunning, far more ingenious than ingenuous. He does not deny the need or justness of the measure, but claims that the several States have exclusive jurisdiction of the same. I am not so willing as some others to believe in the sincerity of his assertions concerning the rights of the colored man. If he were honest in this matter, why is it he never recommended such a measure to the Georgia Legislature? If the several States had secured to all classes within their borders the rights contemplated in this bill, we would have had no need to come here; but they having failed to do their duty, after having had ample opportunity, the General Government is called upon to exercise its right in the matter.

Mr. Speaker, time will not allow me to review the history of the American negro, but I must pause here long enough to say that he has not been properly treated by this nation; he has purchased and paid for all, and for more, than he has yet received. Whatever liberty he enjoys has been paid for over and over again by more than two hundred years of forced toil; and for such citizenship as is allowed him he paid the full measure of blood, the dearest price required at the hands of any citizen. In every contest, from the beginning of the revolutionary struggle down to the war between the States, has he been prominent. But we all remember in our late war when the Government was so hard pressed for troops to sustain the cause of the Union, when it was so difficult to fill up the ranks that had been so fearfully decimated by disease and the bullet; when every train that carried to the front a number of fresh soldiers brought back a corresponding number of wounded and sick ones; when grave doubts as to the success of the Union arms had seized upon the minds of some of the most sanguine friends of the Government; when strong men took counsel of their fears; when those who had all their lives received the fostering care of the nation were hesitating as to their duty in that trying hour, and others questioning if it were not better to allow the star of this Republic to go down and thus be blotted out from the great map of nations than to continue the bloodshed; when gloom and despair were wide-spread; when the last ray of hope had nearly sunk below our political horizon, how the negro then came forward and offered himself as a sacrifice in the place of the nation, made bare his breast to the steel, and in it received the thrusts of the bayonet that were aimed at the life of the nation by the soldiers of that government in which the gentleman from Georgia figured as second officer.

Sir, the valor of the colored soldier was tested on many a battlefield, and to-day his bones lie bleaching beside every hill and in every valley from the Potomac to the Gulf; whose mute eloquence in behalf of equal rights for all before the law, is and ought to be far more persuasive than any poor language I can command.

Mr. Speaker, nothing short of a complete acknowledgment of my manhood will satisfy me. I have no compromises to make, and shall unwillingly accept any. If I were to say that I would be content with less than any other member upon this floor I would forfeit whatever respect any one here might entertain for me, and would thereby furnish the best possible evidence that I do not and cannot appreciate the rights of a freeman. Just what I am charged with by my political enemies. I cannot willingly accept anything less than my full measure of rights as a man, because I am unwilling to present myself as a candidate for the brand of inferiority, which will be as plain and lasting as the mark of Cain. If I am to be thus branded, the country must do it against my solemn protest.

Sir, in order that I might know something of the feelings of a freeman, a privilege denied me in the land of my birth, I left home last year and traveled six months in foreign lands, and the moment I put my foot upon the deck of a ship that unfurled a foreign flag from its mast-head, distinctions on account of my color ceased. I am not aware that my presence on board the steamer put her off her course. I believe we made the trip in the usual time. It was in other countries than my own that I was not a stranger, that I could approach a hotel without the fear that the door would be slammed in my face. Sir, I feel this humiliation very keenly; it dwarfs my manhood, and certainly it impairs my usefulness as a citizen.

The other day when the centennial bill was under discussion I would have been glad to say a word in its favor, but how could I? How would I appear at the centennial celebration of our national freedom, with my own galling chains of slavery hanging about me? I could no more rejoice on that occasion in my present condition than the Jews could sing in their wonted style as they sat as captives beside the Babylonish streams; but I look forward to the day when I shall be in the full enjoyment of the rights of a freeman, with the same hope they indulged, that they would again return to their native land. I can no more forget my manhood, than they could forget Jerusalem.

# "An Act to Protect All Citizens in Their Civil and Legal Rights"

## *(March 1, 1875)*

On his deathbed, Sumner pleaded with a friend, "You must take care of the Civil Rights Bill, my bill," which, thanks to Senator Frederick T. Frelinghuysen and Representative Benjamin F Butler, finally went into effect on March 1, 1875. Though earlier versions of the bill had included equal accommodations for both races in cemeteries and schools, the final legislation applied only to inns, public conveyances, and theaters, but also prohibited discrimination in the selection of juries. Federal courts held jurisdiction in both civil and criminal cases resulting from violations of the bill. Despite its supporters' hopes and dreams, the 1875 bill, according to an authority, "was more a broad assertion of principle than a blueprint for further coercive action by the federal government." In practice, few people of color challenged discriminatory acts and the much-contested Civil Rights Act of 1875 became virtually "a dead letter."

Whereas, it is essential to just government we recognize the equality of all men before the law, and hold that it is the duty of government in its dealings with the people to mete out equal and exact justice to all, of whatever nativity, race, color, or persuasion, religious or political; and it being the appropriate object of legislation to enact great fundamental principles into law: Therefore,

*Be it enacted by the Senate and House of Representatives of the United States of America in Congress assembled,* That all persons within the jurisdiction of the United States shall be entitled to the full and equal enjoyment of the accommodations, advantages, facilities, and privileges of inns, public conveyances on land or water, theaters, and other places of public amusement; subject only to the conditions and limitations established by law, and applicable alike to citizens of every race and color, regardless of any previous condition of servitude.

SEC. 2. That any person who shall violate the foregoing section by denying to any citizen, except for reasons by law applicable to citizens of every race and color, and regardless of any previous condition of servitude, the full enjoyment of any of the accommodations, advantages, facilities, or privileges in said section enumerated, or by aiding or inciting such denial, shall, for every such offense, forfeit and pay the sum of five hundred dollars to the person aggrieved thereby, to be recovered in an action of debt with full costs; and shall also, for every such offense, be deemed guilty of a misdemeanor, and, upon conviction thereof, shall be fined not less than five hundred nor more than one thousand dollars, or shall be imprisoned not less than thirty days nor more than one year: *Provided,* That all persons may elect to sue for the penalty aforesaid or to proceed under their rights at common law and by State statutes; and having so elected to proceed in the one mode or the other, their right to proceed in the other jurisdiction shall be barred. But this proviso shall not apply to criminal proceedings, either under this act or the criminal law of any State: *And provided further,* That a judgment for the penalty in favor of the party aggrieved, or a judgment upon an indictment, shall be a bar to either prosecution respectively.

SEC. 3. That the district and circuit courts of the United States shall have, exclusively of the courts of the several States, cognizance of all crimes and offenses against, and violations of, the provisions of this act; and actions for the penalty given by the preceding section may be prosecuted in the territorial, district, or circuit courts of the United States wherever the defendant may be found, without regard to the other party; and the district attorneys, marshals, and deputy marshals of the United States, and commissioners appointed by the circuit and territorial courts of the United States, with powers of arresting and imprisoning or bailing offenders against the laws of the United States, are hereby specially authorized and required to institute proceedings against every person who shall violate the provisions of this act, and cause him to be arrested and imprisoned or bailed, as the case may be, for trial before such court of the United States, or territorial court, as by law has cognizance of the offense, except in respect of the right of action accruing to the person aggrieved; and such district attorneys shall cause such proceedings to be prosecuted to their termination as in other cases: *Provided,* That nothing contained in this section shall be construed to deny or defeat any right of civil action accruing to any person, whether by reason of this act or otherwise; and any district attorney who shall willfully fail to institute and prosecute the proceedings herein required, shall, for every such offense, forfeit and pay the sum of five hundred dollars to the person aggrieved thereby, to be recovered by an action of debt, with full costs, and shall, on conviction thereof, be deemed guilty of a misdemeanor, and be fined not less than one thousand nor more than five thousand dollars: *And provided further,* That a judgment for the penalty in favor of the party aggrieved against any such district attorney, or a judgment upon an indictment against any such district attorney, shall be a bar to either prosecution respectively.

Sec. 4. That no citizen possessing all other qualifications which are or may be prescribed by law shall be disqualified for service as grand or petit juror in any court of the United States, or of any State, on account of race, color, or previous condition of servitude; and any officer or other person charged with any duty in the selection or summoning of jurors who shall exclude or fail to summon any citizen for the cause aforesaid shall, on conviction thereof, be deemed guilty of a misdemeanor, and be fined not more than five thousand dollars.

Sec. 5. That all cases arising under the provisions of this act in the courts of the United States shall be reviewable by the Supreme Court of the United States, without regard to the sum in controversy, under the same provisions and regulations as are now provided by law for the review of other causes in said court.

# "The Negro Spirit"

## *(July 21, 1876)*

On July 4, 1876, a seemingly minor breach of racial etiquette in the tiny village of Hamburg, South Carolina, sparked a race riot with national overtones. The melee resulted when an all-black militia company marching down the town's main street refused to give way to two white men in a carriage. When the militia commander proved unwilling to apologize or appear in court, members of local white rifle clubs assembled, demanding that the black militiamen surrender their weapons. When they refused, fighting began, and about forty militiamen retreated to their armory. Soon hundreds of whites, including many from nearby Augusta, Georgia, armed with a cannon, laid siege to the building. Whites captured twenty-five militiamen, murdering five, and then ransacked black homes and shops in the town. Though federal troops restored order in Hamburg, the whites who murdered the blacks were acquitted and, as the *New York Times* reported, the "Hamburg Massacre" outraged blacks and suggested their inability to receive racial justice.

The colored indignation meeting at Market Hall last night attracted about one thousand colored men and about five hundred whites. The former crowded in the street in front of the hall, while the latter lined the sidewalk on the west side of Meeting street, and listened to the speeches, without taking any part in the meeting. The American flags, two kerosene reflectors and three candles afforded the illumination and decoration for the occasion. About 8:30 o'clock two drums and a fife, followed by about fifteen negro boys, marched up to the meeting, and in a few moments the proceedings were begun by a negro named J. L. Graves, who read the following list of officers, whose names are worth remembering:

President, W. H. Thompson; Vice Presidents, F. J. Pew, W. H. Pinckney, William Vanderhorst, Richard Nesbitt, W. J. Broddie, Thomas Aiken, B. H. Smalls, Aaron McCov, C. S. Miller, J. J. Grant, G. E. Johnson, Mathias Smith, A. Finlay, J. H. Hall, James Green, Isaac Sawyer, H. M . Pinckney, William Richardson, P. M. Gregorie, J. J. Young; Secretaries, J. L. Graves, A. T. Stevens, Christopher Smalls, E. G. Logan, J. B. Howard.

Thompson, the Chairman, having taken possession of the meeting, announced that the proceedings would be opened with prayer by Rev. Joseph E. Haynes. After the prayer, Thompson opened the meeting, saying that the colored troops had arrived at the time when "this thing must cease." If the whites intended to continue it, they couldn't do it without trouble. [Cheers.] He wanted the white people in South Carolina to know that the negroes protected their wives and children while they were fighting against the Union, and they must remember this. If this was the first act of the sort, they could stand still and await the action of the Governor. The Chairman then introduced Rev. R. H. Cain, better and more familiarly known as Daddy Cain. Considering the business in which Daddy Cain has been recently engaged, he made a very temperate speech. There was no reason, he said, why the colored people might not join peaceably together in the condemnation of so heinous a crime as the murder of the offensive citizens of Hamburg. [Cheers.] It is true that they blocked up the streets on the 4th of July; but did not the white soldiers break up the streets of Charleston on the 28th of June? For this offense the colored Militia had been ordered to give up their arms. He wondered if the noble Anglo-Saxon would submit to have their arms taken from them. No! they would not; they knew their rights, and the negroes were learning from them rapidly. ["Dat's so."] He desired to be understood as saying that this thing must stop. Every wrong done in this State injures its prosperity, injures its commerce, its agriculture, and its business, and drives away those people who could best help to build up the common prosperity. The colored people (he said) expected to be law-abiding citizens of the State, but they wanted every man who violated the laws of the State to be brought to justice and to punishment. This meeting had no political coloring. They met as citizens to express in a peaceable way their opinion of a great outrage. The colored men wanted peace; they wanted the right to go where they pleased and to do what they pleased, so long as they did no wrong. Suppose the colored men should organize bands in Charleston and Co-moahee to kill the white men and burn up the houses, would there be peace? ["No, no," from the crowd.] It remains, therefore, for us to unite in denouncing this outrage, and to demand that Gov. Chamberlain shall bring these men to justice and the perpetrators to punishment.

Rev. E. J. Adams, who was the next speaker, had no words to express his indignation in reference to the Hamburg outrage. He was not here for war. The colored men wanted peace and would have it if they had to fight for it. [Cheers.] They knew they were not equal to the task of waging war, but they were men enough to show pluck. They had been warned by the *News and Courier* not to attend this meeting because, perchance, the bread might be taken out of their mouths; but it should be remembered that somebody else's mouth might be without bread. They should demand of Gov. Chamberlain that these men be brought to justice and be dealt with in the spirit of the law. . . .

In the meantime, the colored Secretary of the meeting had started to read an address and a series of resolutions, which were scarcely heard by the crowd, but which were vociferously applauded whenever the leaders on the steps would give the signal. The address and resolutions are exceedingly violent in tone, as will be seen by the subjoined extracts:

"Now, against these outrages we have here, and in the name of humanity, in the name of civilization, in the name of outraged law, in the name of good government, and the peace and welfare of this nation, we enter our unqualified condemnation of these crimes and outrages. We protest against these men, and their aiders and abettors, and, in the name of the majesty of law and order, we demand that Gov. Chamberlain shall at once invoke all the powers of this State to bring M. C. Butler and his clan to justice, and that no means or treasure be spared to punish these criminals. And we invoke the consideration of this whole nation, and the powers of the Federal Government, to see to it that the great principals of equal justice before the law, and equal protection under this Government, be maintained throughout this nation, so that safety to life and property, and the right to vote as conscience shall dictate to every citizen, shall be forever secured to all throughout this broad land.

"We tell you that it will not do to go too far in this thing. Remember there are 80,000 black men in this State who can bear Winchester rifles, and know how to use them, and that there are 200,000 women who can light a torch and use the knife, and that there are 100,000 boys and girls who have not known the lash of the white master; who have tasted freedom once and forever, and that there is a deep determination never, so help their God, to submit to be shot down by lawless regulators for no crimes committed against society and law. There is a point at which forbearance ceases to be a virtue; cowards driven to desperation often destroy those who corner them. The negro in this country will not always be docile, he will not always be restrained by this law-abiding character. The rising generation are as brave and daring as are white men. Already that spirit is taking deep root in the minds of thousands who have nothing to lose in the contest, and who would rejoice in an opportunity to sacrifice their lives for their liberty.

"*Whereas,* We have exercised becoming fortitude and patience in expectation of government intolerance by and legal redress through those whom our suffrages have placed in authority, and whose constitutional duties it is to see that the laws be executed in mercy, yet we have been so often grievously disappointed that our hopes are blasted, for, while colored men are for every crime (and many fancied ones) punished in the farthest extent of the law, the white, after the commission of the most brutish crimes against us which is known to the laws of the land, invariably escapes with impunity; and,

"*Whereas,* These crimes being unworthy of barbarous heathens, much less a people boasting of their advanced civilization, we are not only pained but stung to indignation, and in view of the brutal murder of a number of our people in the "Massacre of Hamburg, S. C.," by the whites of South Carolina and Georgia, we are goaded to exasperation, for our wonted forbearance now ceases to be a virtue, and self-preservation demands that, while calling upon the

proper authorities for redress of these grievances and a reform of existing abuses, a vigorous and impartial execution
of the law, we must immediately take counsel for defense.
Therefore, be it

"*Resolved,* That the massacre of colored citizens at
Hamburg, S. C., is unworthy of any civilization community,
and deserves the censure and condemnation of the civilized world, and that we entertain the deepest sympathy for
the grief-stricken families of those victims, (of hate,) and
will do all in our power for the relief of the widows and
orphans, as well as for those who have been despoiled of
their household goods.

"*Resolved,* That we call upon the Governor of South
Carolina to see that the laws of the land be faithfully executed upon all perpetrators of the bloody deed at Hamburg; and be it further

"*Resolved,* That in case this one legal demand be not
granted, and the protection of our lives, liberty, and property be not to our satisfaction guaranteed and secured in
the future by the State Government, then self-preservation,
predicated upon the barbarous attitude assumed and being
maintained by the whites, warns the colored citizens to
peaceably assemble and petition the national Government,
through legal channels, 'for redress of grievances.' "

# CARL SCHURZ, "HAYES
# VERSUS TILDEN"

## *(August 31, 1876)*

The November 1876 presidential election was a
turning point in U.S. history. Americans of both
North and South generally favored an end to Reconstruction's political, racial, and sectional ten-
sions. By the mid-1870s white Southerners, the
so-called Bourbon Democrats, already had "re-
deemed" much of their section. In summer 1876,
only three Southern state governments remained
under Radical Republican control. For their part,
white Northerners found the Reconstruction era
squabbles over states' rights and the "Negro question" increasingly unappealing. The Republican
presidential candidate, Ohio governor Rutherford
B. Hayes (1822–1893), was a man of unquestioned
honesty and a champion of emancipation and
black education. His Democratic rival, New York
governor Samuel Jones Tilden (1814–1884), had
been indifferent to emancipation and supported
Andrew Johnson's conservative restoration policies. He earned a national reputation by bringing
down New York's corrupt Tweed and Canal "Rings."
Though, as Carl Schurz observed in his August
1876 Cincinnati speech, both Hayes and Tilden
promoted themselves as reformers, Schurz considered the Ohioan more committed to needed
civil service reform and the New Yorker more
prone to distributing spoils. In the election, Tilden received a popular vote majority of 250,000
votes, but Hayes's supporters successfully challenged sufficient electoral votes in Florida, Louisiana, and South Carolina to garner him a 185 to
184 electoral majority and the presidency. Inter-
estingly, following his election, Hayes appointed
Schurz his Secretary of the Interior, enabling Schurz

himself to advance the cause of civil service reform.

The platforms, as well as the candidates of each, promise what they call "reform." I will confess at once that I have lost my faith in the professions and promises made in party platforms. They have at last become, on either side, one of the cheapest articles of manufacture in this country, and that industry continues to flourish even without a protective tariff and in spite of the general depression of business. But civil service reform is not produced in that way. If we desire to ascertain by the success of which party that reform is most likely to be promoted, we must look to the character and principles of the candidates as well as to the component elements and general tendencies of the parties behind them. I am firmly convinced that one part of the necessary change, the driving from the public service of the corrupt officials who now pollute it, will be amply secured by the election of either of the two candidates for the Presidency. Governor Tilden has won his reputation as a reformer mainly by the prosecution of the canal ring in the State of New York. I will not follow others in questioning his motives, but readily admit that prosecution to have been an enterprise requiring considerable courage, circumspection and perseverance, for which he should have full credit. Should he be elected President, he will undoubtedly eject from their places, and, if possible, otherwise punish, all the dishonest officers now in the service; making a "clean sweep," he will eject them, together with the good ones. Nor have we any reason to expect, with regard to the cleaning process, less from Governor Hayes, should he be elected to the Presidency. It is well known that Governor Hayes was not my favorite candidate for the Presidential nomination, and I am not in the least inclined to extol him with extravagant praise. What I shall say of him will be simple justice to his character and record. You, citizens of Ohio, have had the best opportunity to form your judgment of him, from a near observation of his official and private conduct, and as far as I know, that judgment, whether expressed by friend or foe, is absolutely unanimous. Three times he has been elected Governor of your State, against the strongest candidates of the opposition. True, he has had no occasion to break up canal rings, or other extensive and powerful corrupt combinations, for the simple reason that in Ohio they did not exist. But it is universally recognized not only that Governor Hayes is a man whose personal integrity stands above the reach of suspicion, a man of a high sense of honor, but that his administrations were singularly pure, irreproachable and efficient in every respect. If he had no existing corruption to fight, he certainly did not permit any to grow up. Nobody suspects him of being capable of tolerating a thief within the reach of his power, much less to protect one by favor or even by negligence. It is also well known that, while a party man, he always surrounded himself with the best and most high-toned elements of the organization, and kept doubtful characters at a distance. He is esteemed as a man of a very strong and high sense of duty and that quiet energy which does not rest until the whole duty is faithfully performed. The endeavor to purify the Government and to keep it pure will, therefore, with him not be a matter of artificial policy, but of instinctive desire, one of the necessities of his nature. He is honest and enforces honesty around him simply because he cannot be and do otherwise. In saying this I have only given the verdict of his opponents, and when here and there the assertion is put forth that Governor Hayes's Administration of the National Government would only be a continuance of the present way of doing things, it is one of those empty and contemptible partisan flings which prove only to what ridiculous extremities those are reduced who are bent upon inventing some charge against a man of unblemished character and a most honorable and pure record of public service.

The first cleaning-out process, then, seems well enough assured in any event. But the more important question occurs, in what manner that cleaning-out process is to be accomplished, and what is to follow. Where have we to look for that greater and lasting reform which is to insure an honest and efficient public service and a higher moral tone in our political life for the future? On this point both candidates have spoken in their letters of acceptance, and their utterances are entitled to far greater consideration than the party platforms. Look at the letter of Governor Hayes first. It is explicit, and remarkable for the clearness and straightforwardness of its expressions. Here are his words:

More than forty years ago a system of making appointments to office grew up, based upon the maxim "to the victors belong the spoils." The old rule, the true rule, that honesty, capacity and fidelity constitute the only real qualifications for office, and that there is no other claim, gave place to the idea that party services were to be chiefly considered. All parties in practice have adopted this system. It has been essentially modified since its first introduction. It has not, however, been improved. At first the President, either directly or through the heads of Department, made all the appointments, but gradually the appointing power, in many cases, passed into the control of Members of Congress. The offices in these cases have become not merely the rewards for party services, but rewards for services to party leaders. The system destroys the independence of the separate departments of the Government. It tends directly to extravagance and official incapacity. It is a temptation to dishonesty; it hinders and impairs that careful supervision and strict accountability by which alone faithful and efficient public service can be secured; it obstructs the prompt removal and sure punishment of the unworthy; in every way it degrades the civil service and the character of the Government. It is felt, I am confident, by a large majority of the Members of Congress to be an intolerable burden and an unwarrantable hindrance to the proper discharge of their legitimate duties. It ought to be abolished. The reform should be thorough, radical and complete. We should return to the principles and practices of the founders of the Government—supplying by legislation, when needed, that which was formerly the established custom. They neither expected nor desired from the public officers any partisan service. They meant that public officers should give their whole service to the Government and to the people. They meant that the officer should be secure in his tenure as long as his personal character remained untarnished, and the performance of his duties satisfactory. If elected, I shall conduct the administration of the Government upon these principles, and all Constitutional

powers vested in the Executive will be employed
to establish this reform.

Then he pledges himself to the "speedy, thorough and
unsparing prosecution and punishment of all public officers who betray official trusts." And finally, "believing that
the restoration of the civil service to the system established
by Washington and followed by the early Presidents can be
best accomplished by an Executive who is under no temptation to use the patronage of his office to promote his own
reëlection," he "performs what he regards as a duty in stating his inflexible purpose, if elected, not to be a candidate
for election to a second term."

This is the clearest and completest program of civil service reform ever put forth by a public man in this Republic.
Not a single essential point is forgotten,—and what is more,
there is in it no vagueness or equivocation of statement or
promise. No back door is left for escape. Each point is distinct, precise, specific and unmistakable. It covers the whole
ground with well-defined propositions. If this program is
carried out, the reform of the civil service will be thorough
and genuine; and if the reform is permanently established,
the main source of the corruption and demoralization of
our political concerns, the spoils system, will be effectually
stopped. It will be the organization of the service on business principles. Even the opponents of Governor Hayes
will be compelled to admit this. Some of them have indeed
attempted to find fault with one or the other of his propositions, but their objections are easily disposed of. A few
Democratic papers argue that if officers are kept in their
places as long as their personal character remains untarnished and the performance of their duties satisfactory, the
result will be "a permanent aristocracy of officeholders." Is
this so? Look back into the history of the Republic and you
will find that under the early Administrations down to John
Quincy Adams, public officers were kept in place as long as
their character remained untarnished and the performance
of their duty satisfactory. Where was the "aristocracy of officeholders" during that period? The officers of the Government were then a set of quiet, industrious, modest and
unobtrusive gentlemen who did not try to control party
politics, and did not steal, but did, as a general rule, studi-

ously endeavor, by strict attention to their official business, to win the approval of the Government which employed them, and an honorable name for themselves. But no sooner was the good old custom supplanted by the system which transformed the offices of the Government into the spoils of party warfare, and made appointments and removals depend not upon the question of integrity and competence, but upon party service and claims to party reward, than a remarkable change occurred in the character as well as the pretensions of the officeholding class. No longer did they remain the quiet, unobtrusive and dutiful public servants they had been before, but they gradually attempted to control party politics in the different States, and transformed themselves into a regularly organized force of political prætorians employed by ambitious leaders to override the public opinion of the country. If there ever was anything that might be called an officeholding aristocracy in the worst sense of the term, it did not exist under the early Administrations when good official conduct was considered a valid title to continuance in place, but it was created by the spoils system which stripped the officer of his simple character of a servant of the Government, and made him a party agent, or in case of those of higher grade, a party satrap, obsequious to those above him and insolent to the people, over whom they thenceforth considered themselves appointed to exercise power and influence. If the civil service reform proposed by Governor Hayes reduces them to their proper level as servants of the people again, it will not be the creation, it will be the destruction of that odious sort of an officeholding aristocracy. Besides, the idea that a letter-carrier, or a customhouse officer, or a revenue agent, or a Department clerk, will become a member of an aristocracy, if left in office as long as he behaves himself well, has something so intensely ludicrous that it need scarcely be discussed. We might as well speak of an aristocracy of railroad conductors or hotel waiters.

Another very curious objection to Governor Hayes's reform plan is put forth by my esteemed friend Mr. Godwin in his recently published letter in favor of Governor Tilden, which has deservedly attracted much attention. He thinks that if officers are to be secure in their tenure as long as their character remains untarnished and the performance of their duties satisfactory, this principle will "give *all* the present incumbents an indefinite tenure, perpetuate their hold of the trusts they have so many of them abused" and be "in its practical operation an act of indemnity for all the felons and rogues who now infest and pollute the public offices." The critics of Governor Hayes's letter of acceptance seem indeed to be in terrible stress for an objection. When the principle is laid down that the tenure of an officer shall be secure as long "as his character remains untarnished and the performance of his duties satisfactory"—can that be interpreted as meaning that the tenure of an officer shall also be secure, when he has become a bad fellow, so that his character is tarnished and the performance of his duties unsatisfactory? When Governor Hayes pledges himself to a "speedy, thorough and unsparing prosecution and punishment of all public officers who betray public trusts," does that mean that those who have betrayed official trusts shall go unprosecuted and unpunished? Is that an act of indemnity to all felons and rogues who now infest and pollute the public service? Oh, Mr. Godwin, lifelong friendship for Governor Tilden may carry even a man of ability and great attainments beyond the point of safety in criticizing his opponents. The most charitable explanation of Mr. Godwin's objection is, perhaps, that he never read Governor Hayes's letter of acceptance. He can now, even after his criticism, read it with profit as a study on true civil service reform. No, the plan put forth by Governor Hayes is nothing more, and nothing less, than the revival of the principle and practice which prevailed under the early Administrations, whose elevated tone and purity are still the pride of American history; the principles and practice of the men whose wisdom and virtues we have exalted in the Centennial year with glowing eulogies; the men who, could they now appear among us, would say: "If you want truly to honor our names, do it a little less by praising our virtues, and a little more by following our example."

Now, let us see what promise of civil service reform the Democratic candidate, Governor Tilden, holds out to us. In order to be perfectly fair to him I will quote the whole text of that part of his letter which refers to that subject:

The Convention justly affirms that reform is necessary in the civil service, necessary to its purification, necessary to its economy and efficiency, necessary in order that the ordinary employment of the public business may not be "a prize fought for at the ballot-box, a brief reward of party zeal, instead of posts of honor assigned for proven competency, and held for fidelity in the public employ." The Convention wisely added that "reform is necessary even more in the higher grades of the public service. President, Vice-President, Judges, Senators, Representatives, Cabinet officers, these and all others in authority are the people's servants. Their offices are not a private perquisite; they are a public trust." Two evils infest the official service of the Federal Government: One is the prevalent and demoralizing notion that the public service exists not for the business and benefit of the whole people, but for the interest of the officeholders, who are in truth but the servants of the people. Under the influence of this pernicious error public employments have been multiplied; the numbers of those gathered into the ranks of officeholders have been steadily increased beyond any possible requirement of the public business, while inefficiency, peculation, fraud and malversation of the public funds, from the high places of power to the lowest, have overspread the whole service like a leprosy. The other evil is the organization of the official class into a body of political mercenaries, governing the caucuses and dictating the nominations of their own party, and attempting to carry the elections of the people by undue influence, and by immense corruption-funds systematically collected from the salaries or fees of officeholders. The official class in other countries, sometimes by its own weight and sometimes in alliance with the army, has been able to rule the unorganized masses even under universal suffrage. Here it has already grown into a gigantic power capable of stifling the inspirations of a sound public opinion, and of resisting an easy change of Administration, until misgovernment becomes intolerable and public spirit has been stung to the pitch of a civic revolution. The first step in reform is the elevation of the standard by which the appointing power selects agents to execute official trusts. Next in importance is a conscientious fidelity in the exercise of the authority to hold to account and displace untrustworthy or incapable subordinates. The public interest in an honest, skilful performance of official trust must not be sacrificed to the usufruct of the incumbents. After these immediate steps, which will insure the exhibition of better examples, we may wisely go on to the abolition of unnecessary offices, and, finally, to the patient, careful organization of a better civil service system, under the tests, wherever practicable, of proved competency and fidelity.

When you have read this somewhat elaborate paragraph and pondered over it a while, you still ask yourselves: How far does he mean to go and where does he mean to stop? There is plenty of well-expressed criticism; but what is the tangible, specific thing he means to do? The difference between these utterances and those contained in Governor Hayes's letter is striking and significant. There are none of the precise, clean-cut, sharply-defined propositions put forth by Governor Hayes, indicating how the spoils system with its demoralizing influences is to be eradicated and what is to be put in its place.

When we try to evolve from this mountain of words the practical things which Governor Tilden promises to do, we find that they consist simply in the appointment of new men, according to an "elevated standard," whatever that may be, and in holding officers to account for their doings, of course. When the offices are filled with new men superfluous offices are "wisely" to be cut off, and finally the "patient and careful organization of a better civil service system" is to be proceeded with "under the tests, whenever practicable, of proved competency and fidelity." It seems, then, when we boil it all down and I think I am doing Governor Tilden's language no violence in saying so that, first, the offices are to be filled with good Democrats in the way of a "clean sweep" and a "new deal of the spoils," and that afterwards it shall be "patiently and carefully" considered how and where "tests of proven competency and fidelity" can be established, so as to fill the offices with good men. But, first of all things, "the offices for the Democrats, the spoils for the victors." Does any candid man pretend that it means anything else? Governor Tilden is a profuse writer, having an infinite assortment of words at his command. If he meant anything else, would he not have been able to say so in a precise form of expression? For the short allusion to subsequent systematic reform, to be "patiently and carefully" approached, is even more studiously vague and shadowy than the many paragraphs in party platforms, with the valuelessness of which we have in the course of time become so justly disgusted.

Or is there any sensible man in the land, even among Governor Tilden's independent friends, who expects anything else than simply a new distribution of the spoils? If there is, let him read the Democratic newspapers, let him look round among the leaders as well as the rank and file, and he will soon become aware of his mistake. Who does not know that the principle, "To the victors belong the spoils," was first inaugurated by the Democratic party; that the spoils system of the civil service was developed by that party in all its characteristic features; that for the last forty years it has been its traditional and constant policy and practice, and at this moment their struggle for success is in a great measure inspired by the hope of an opportunity to precipitate themselves upon the public plunder? Is Governor Tilden the man, in case of his election, to constitute himself a breakwater against the universal tendency, the unanimous, impatient will of his party? Or is there, I ask you candidly, and especially those of my independent friends who, although animated with the desire of genuine reform, are inclined to aid the Democrats, is there in the Democratic party any influential element that would urge a Democratic President to advance thorough measures of civil service reform in a non-partisan sense, or that would earnestly support him if he did? If there exists such an influential element, where is it? Is it in the rich men's Manhattan Club, or in Tammany Hall or anti-Tammany in New York, among the "swallow-tails" or the "short-hairs"? Or is it among the old State-rights Democrats, East and West? Or among the Confederates in the South? Or among the Irish population or the Roman Catholic Democrats generally? If there is in any section of the Democratic party any desire for a genuine reform of the civil service, anything but a demand for a new deal of the spoils, show it to me. I shall certainly be the last man to deny that there are many good, honest, patriotic, well-meaning and able citizens in the Democratic organization and among its leaders. I count among them not a few valued and trusted personal friends. But where are the advocates of genuine civil service reform among them? As far as I know, we have heard only the solitary voice of Senator Gordon, who submitted in the last session of Congress a commendable proposition for the reform of the revenue service; but the commendation it received in the organs of public opinion came almost exclusively from the Republican or independent side. And now will Governor Tilden, if elected, without support in his own party, at the risk of his popularity with his own friends, brace himself up against the furious onset of hungry patriots, and say: "The interests of the service, the cause of reform, demand that the offices of the Government be no longer looked upon as the spoils of party victory; I shall, therefore, keep in office all faithful and efficient officers no matter whether they are Republicans, and turn out only the unworthy ones; go home, my Democratic friends, that I may judiciously discriminate at leisure"? Or will he tell Democratic Congressmen: "The principles on which the civil service is to be reformed demand that I should not permit any Congressional interference with the responsibilities of the appointing power; therefore put your recommendations of your friends in your pockets and let me alone, my good fellow-Democrats"?

What man in his five senses expects Governor Tilden to do this? Has he ever promised anything of the kind? Certainly he has not. Is he not too inveterate a Democrat and too closely wedded to the traditions of his party to think of it?

Well, then, what sort of reform will be brought about by a Democratic victory? I assume even that Governor Tilden and the men he may put into his Cabinet will sincerely desire to put only the best available Democrats into office, and will employ every honest effort to that end. But what will be the result? The accession of the Democrats to power will be signalized by the most furious rush for office ever witnessed in the history of this Republic. For years and years hundreds of thousands have been lying in wait, eagerly watching for the opportunity. You find them not only in the North, East and West, but still more in the South. The Southern people have many good qualities, but it is a notorious fact that among them the number of men thinking themselves peculiarly entitled to public place has always been conspicuously numerous. Now they have been on short fare for many years, and long waiting has sharpened their appetite. They will also be quick to remember that Democratic success could be brought about only by a united Southern vote, and that above all others they have claims to reward. Our brave Confederate friends have won renown by many a gallant charge during the war, but all their warlike feats will be left in the shade by the tremendous momentum of the charge they will execute upon the offices of the Government. It will be a rush of such eagerness, turbulence and confusion that men of this generation will in vain seek for a parallel. And now amidst all this, urged on by a universal cry of impatience from all sections of the Democratic party that every radical must be driven from place at once, do you think it for a moment possible that the President and the members of the Cabinet will breast that storm and sit down with cool deliberation, to gather evidence about the character and qualifications of every applicant for the seventy or eighty thousand places to be filled, so as to keep improper men out of office? Is it not absolutely certain that the offices will be filled helter-skelter, as so often before, and that of the applicants those, as a rule, will be the most successful who are the most intrusive and persistent in elbowing their way to the front? Can it in the nature of things be otherwise? And what will become of the cause of reform? . . .

I, therefore, declare this to be my honest conviction, not only that Governor Hayes, as a man of patriotism and integrity, will, if elected to the Presidency, be true to his word, in using all the Constitutional powers of his office to carry out to the letter the program put forth by himself, but that, powerful as the opposition he will have to encounter may be, the chances will be strongly in favor of the success and lasting establishment of the reformed system, sustained as it will be by the best elements of the Republican party and a patriotic public opinion.

Indeed, when examining the relative positions taken by the two candidates for the Presidency, and the prospects they open to us, the opponents of Governor Hayes seem to be utterly at a loss to discover a flaw in the systematic reform he proposes to establish. They find themselves forced back upon the small expedient of discrediting his intentions. "Governor Hayes," they say, "cannot be in earnest with this plan, for if he were believed to be in earnest there would be a multitude of Republican politicians who would rather see their candidate defeated than such a reform succeed." There may be such Republican politicians. But Governor Hayes's own word, publicly spoken, warrants me in telling you that he is in earnest, and uncompromisingly in earnest. If there were Republicans who would try to defeat him for that reason, I am confident it would not change his position. Governor Hayes will ever be proud to have stood up for so good a cause, and would rather be defeated as its faithful champion, than succeed by betraying it. But now I ask you, my independent friends, if that cause is so good that the spoils politician would fear its success more even than the failure of his party, is not there, for you, as sincere friends of reform, every reason to desire and work for its triumph? Considering with candor every circumstance surrounding us, carefully weighing every probability and feeling the necessity of thorough and lasting reform, is it possible that you should hesitate in your choice? Can you fail to see that here is a battlefield worthy of your efforts, here the line of advance towards the objects which, as true reformers, you must hold highest? A change! is your cry. Yes, a change! is mine. But do you not, with me, insist upon a change that opens the prospect of lasting improvement? Is a change of parties all you want, whatever the consequence? If you are in earnest, you will want more; you will want a change in the very being, in the nature of parties.

That is the great thing needful. But in the success of Hayes, not that of Tilden, will you find it. Can you doubt, then, that a change to Hayes will be a greater and much more wholesome change than that to Tilden? What is a change to Tilden? A change from Republican to Democratic spoils in politics. What is a change to Hayes? A change from the spoils system to a true reform of the civil service and the overthrow of machine politics. That is the prediction I make, and with confidence I look into the future to see it verified. Can the duty of sincere friends of reform be doubtful? I at least see mine as clearly as ever, and to the last will I perform it.

# THOMAS WENTWORTH HIGGINSON, "SOME WAR SCENES REVISITED"

## *(July 1878)*

In 1877, the year Hayes assumed the presidency, Thomas Wentworth Higginson (1823–1911) left Rhode Island for the South, making a sentimental tour of the scenes of his Civil War military experiences in Virginia, South Carolina, and Florida. Americans remember Higginson, the Harvard-trained Unitarian minister, as a fervent abolitionist, freedom fighter in "Bleeding Kansas," supporter of John Brown, and colonel of the First South Carolina Volunteers, the earliest regiment of emancipated slaves mustered into the U.S. Army. Higginson's accurate and detailed *Army Life in a Black Regiment* (1870), originally published as essays in *Atlantic Monthly*, was an important Reconstruction era text celebrating black equality and manhood. It remains a literary masterpiece. Higginson's 1878 "Some War Scenes Revisited" provides a clear-eyed Northerner's view of Southern conditions as Reconstruction faded into memory. The blacks he encountered exhibited "much more manhood than they once did," the "results from the changed feeling created toward a race of freedmen and voters."

Nothing in actual life can come so near the experience of Rip Van Winkle as to revisit war scenes after a dozen years of peace. Alice's adventures in Wonderland, when she finds herself dwarfed after eating the clover leaf, do not surpass the sense of insignificance that comes over any one who once wore uniform when he enters, as a temporary carpet-bagger, some city which he formerly ruled or helped to rule with absolute sway. An ex-commander of colored troops has this advantage, that the hackmen and longshore-men may remember him if nobody else does; and he at once possesses that immense practical convenience which comes only from a personal acquaintance with what are called the humbler classes. In a strange place, if one can establish relations with a black waiter or a newspaper correspondent, all doors fly open. The patronage of the great is powerless in comparison.

When I had last left Jacksonville, Florida, in March, 1864, the town was in flames: the streets were full of tongues of fire creeping from house to house; the air was dense with lurid smoke. Our steamers dropped rapidly down the river, laden to the gunwale with the goods of escaping inhabitants. The black soldiers, guiltless of all share in the flames, were yet excited by the occasion, recalled their favorite imagery of the Judgment Day, and sang and shouted without ceasing. I never saw a wilder scene. Fourteen years after, the steamboat came up to the same wharf, and I stepped quietly ashore into what seemed a summer watering-place: the roses were in bloom, the hotel verandas were full of guests, there were gay shops in the street, the wharves were covered with merchandise and with people. The delicious air was the same, the trees were the same; all else was changed. The earthworks we had built were leveled and overgrown; there was a bridge at the ford we used to picket; the church in whose steeple we built a lookout was still there, but it had a new tower, planned for peaceful purposes only. The very railroad along which we skirmished almost daily was now torn up, and a new track entered the town at a different point. I could not find even the wall which one of our men clambered over, loading and firing, with a captured goose between his legs. Only the blue sky and the soft air, the lovely atmosphere of Florida, remained; the distant line of woods had the same outlook, and when the noon guns began to be fired for Washington's birthday I could hardly convince myself that the roar was not that of our gunboats, still shelling the woods as they had done so many years before. Then the guns ceased; the past withdrew into yet deeper remoteness. It seemed as if I were the only man left on earth to recall it. An hour later, the warm grasp of some of my old soldiers dispelled the dream of oblivion.

I had a less vivid sense of change at Beaufort, South

Carolina, so familiar to many during the war. The large white houses still look peacefully down the placid river, but there are repairs and paint everywhere, and many new houses or cabins have been built. There is a new village, called Port Royal, at the railroad terminus, about a mile from my first camp at Old Fort plantation; and there is also a station near Beaufort itself, approached by a fine shell-road. The fortifications on the old shell-road have almost disappeared; the freedmen's village near them, named after the present writer, blew away one day in a tornado, and returned no more. A great national cemetery is established near its site. There are changes enough, and yet the general effect of the town is unaltered; there is Northern energy there, and the discovery of valuable phosphates has opened a new branch of industry; but after all it is the same pleasant old sleepy Beaufort, and no military Rip Van Winkle need feel himself too rudely aroused.

However, I went South not to see places, but people. On the way from Washington I lingered for a day or two to visit some near kinsfolk in Virginia, formerly secessionists to a man, or, to be more emphatic, to a woman. Then I spent a Sunday in Richmond, traversed rapidly part of North Carolina and Georgia, spent a day and two nights in Charleston, two days at Beaufort, and visited various points in Florida, going as far as St. Augustine. I had not set foot in the Southern States for nearly fourteen years, but I remembered them vividly across that gap of time, and also recalled very distinctly a winter visit to Virginia during college days. With these memories ever present, it was to me a matter of great interest to observe the apparent influence of freedom on the colored people, and the relation between them and the whites.

And first, as to the material condition of the former slaves. Sydney Smith, revisiting Edinburgh in 1821, after ten years' absence, was struck with the "wonderful increase of shoes and stockings, streets and houses." The change as to the first item, in South Carolina, tells the story of social progress since emancipation. The very first of my old acquaintances whom I met in that region was the robust wife of one of my soldiers. I found her hoeing in a field, close beside our old camp-ground, I had seen that woman hoeing in the same field fifteen years before. The same sky was above her, the same soil beneath her feet; but the war was over, slavery was gone. The soil that had been her master's was now her own by purchase; and the substantial limbs that trod it were no longer bare and visibly black, but incased in red-striped stockings of the most conspicuous design. "Think of it!" I said to a clever Massachusetts damsel in Washington, "the whole world so changed, and yet that woman still hoes." "In hose," quoth the lively maiden; and I preserve for posterity the condensed epigram.

Besides the striped stockings, which are really so conspicuous that the St. Augustine light-house is painted to match them, one sees a marked, though moderate progress in all the comforts of life. Formerly the colored people of the sea islands, even in their first days of freedom, slept very generally on the floor; and when our regimental hospital was first fitted up, the surgeon found with dismay that the patients had regarded the beds as merely beautiful ornaments, and had unanimously laid themselves down in the intervening spaces. Now I noticed bedstead and bedding in every cabin I visited in South Carolina and Florida. Formerly the cabins often had no tables, and families rarely ate together, each taking food as was convenient; but now they seemed to have family meals, a step toward decent living. This progress they themselves recognized. Moreover, I often saw pictures from the illustrated papers on the wall, and the children's school-books on the shelf. I rarely met an ex-soldier who did not own his house and ground, the inclosures varying from five to two hundred acres; and I found one man on the St. John's who had been offered $3000 for his real estate. In many cases these homesteads had been bought within a few years, showing a steady progress in self-elevation.

I do not think the world could show a finer sample of self-respecting peasant life than a colored woman, with whom I came down the St. John's River to Jacksonville, from one of the little settlements along that magnificent stream. She was a freed slave, the wife of a former soldier, and was going to market, basket in hand, with her little boy by her side. She had the tall erect figure, clear black skin, thin features, fine teeth, and intelligent bearing that marked so many of my Florida soldiers. She was dressed very plainly, but with scrupulous cleanliness: a rather faded gingham dress, well-worn tweed sack, shoes and stockings, straw hat with plain black ribbon, and neat white collar and cuffs. She told me that she and her husband owned one hundred and sixty acres of land, bought and paid for by their own earnings, at $1.25 per acre; they had a log-house, and were going to build a frame-house; they raised for themselves all the food they needed, except meat and flour, which they bought in Jacksonville. They had a church within reach (Baptist); a school-house of forty pupils, taught by a colored teacher; her husband belonged to the Good Templars, as did all the men in their neighborhood. For miles along the St. John's, a little back from the river, such settlements are scattered; the men cultivating their own plots of ground, or working on the steam-boats, or fishing, or lumbering. What more could be expected of any race, after fifteen years of freedom? Are the Irish voters of New York their superiors in condition, or the factory operatives of Fall River?

I met perhaps a hundred men, in different places, who had been under my command, and whose statements I could trust. Only one of these complained of poverty; and he, as I found, earned good wages, had neither wife nor child to support, and was given to whisky. There were some singular instances of prosperity among these men. I was told in Jacksonville that I should find Corporal McGill "de most populous man in Beaufort." When I got there, I found him the proprietor of a livery stable populous with horses at any rate; he was worth $3000 or $4000, and was cordial and hospitable to the last degree. At parting, he drove me to the station with his best carriage and horses; and I regret to add that while he was refusing all compensation his young steeds ran away, and as the train whirled off I saw my "populous" corporal double-quick down the shell-road, to recapture his equipage. I found Sergeant Hodges a master carpenter at Jacksonville; Corporal Hicks was a preacher there, highly respected; and I heard of Corporal Sutton as a traveling minister farther up the river. Sergeant Shemeltella, a fine-looking half-Spaniard from St. Augustine, now patrols, with gun in hand, the woods which we once picketed at Port Royal Ferry, and supplies game to the markets of Charleston and Savannah. And without extending the list I may add that some of these men, before attaining prosperity, had to secure, by the severest experience, the necessary judgment in business affairs. It will hardly be believed that the men of my regiment alone sunk $30,000 in an impracticable building association, and in the purchase of a steamboat which was lost uninsured. One of the shrewdest among them, after taking his share of this, resolved to be prudent, put $750 in the Freedmen's Bank, and lost that too. Their present prosperity must be judged in the light of such formidable calamities as these.

I did not hear a single charge of laziness made against the freed colored people in the States I visited. In Virginia it was admitted that they would work wherever they were paid, but that many were idle for want of employment. Rev. Dr. Pinckney, in a recent address before the Charleston Historical Society, declares that the negroes "do not refuse to work; all are planting;" and he only complains that they work unskillfully. A rice-planter in Georgia told me that he got his work done more efficiently than under the slave system. Men and women worked well for seventy-five cents a day; many worked under contract, which at first they did not understand or like. On the other hand, he admitted, the planters did not at once learn how to manage them as freedmen, but had acquired the knowledge by degrees; so that even the strikes at harvest-time, which had at first embarrassed them, were now avoided. Another Georgia planter spoke with much interest of an effort now making by the colored people in Augusta to establish a cotton factory of their own, in emulation of the white factories which have there been so successful. He said that this proposed factory was to have a capital of fifty thousand dollars in fifty dollar shares, and that twenty-eight thousand dollars of it were already raised. The white business agent of one of the existing factories was employed, he said, as the adviser of those organizing this. He spoke of it with interest as a proper outlet for the industry of the better class of colored people, who were educated rather above field labor. He also spoke with pride of the normal school for colored people at Atlanta.

The chief of police in Beaufort, South Carolina, a colored man, told me that the colored population there required but little public assistance, though two thousand of them had removed from the upper parts of the State within a year and a half, thinking they could find better wages at Beaufort. This removal struck me as being of itself a favorable indication, showing that they were now willing to migrate, whereas they were once hopelessly fixed to the soil, and therefore too much in the power of the land owners. The new industry of digging phosphates for exportation to England employs a good many in Beaufort County, and they earn by this from seventy-five cents to a dollar a day. Others are employed in loading vessels at the new settlement of Port Royal; but the work is precarious and insufficient, and I was told that if they made two dollars a week they did well. But it must be remembered that they have mostly little patches of land of their own, and can raise for themselves the corn and vegetables on which they chiefly live. I asked an old man if he could supply his family from his own piece of ground. "Oh, yes, mars'r," he said (the younger men do not say "mars'r," but "boss"), and then he went on, with a curious accumulation of emphasis: "I raise plenty too, much more dan I destroy,"—meaning simply "very much more."

The price of cotton is now very low, and the sea-island cotton has lost forever, perhaps, its place in the English market. Yet Rev. Dr. Pinckney, in the address just quoted, while lamenting the ravages of war in the sea islands, admits that nearly half as much cotton was raised in them in 1875 as in 1860, and more than half as much corn, the population being about the same, and the area cultivated less than one third. To adopt his figures, the population in 1860 was 40,053; acres under cultivation, 274,015; corn, 618,959 bushels; cotton, 19,121 bales. In 1875 the population was 43,060; acres under cultivation, 86,449; corn, 314,271 bushels; cotton, 8199 bales.

When we consider the immense waste of war, the destruction of capital, the abandonment of estates by those who yet refuse to sell them, and the partial introduction of industry other than agricultural, this seems to me a promising exhibit. And when we observe how much more equitable than formerly is now the distribution of the products between capitalist and laborer, the case is still better. Dr. Pinckney's utmost complaint in regard to South Carolina is that the result of the war "has been injurious to the whites, and not beneficial to the blacks." Even he, a former slaveholder, does not claim that it has injured the blacks; and this, from his point of view, is quite a concession. Twenty years hence he may admit that whatever the result of war may have been, that of peace will be beneficial to both races.

In observing a lately emancipated race, it is always harder to judge as to the condition of the women than of the men, especially where the men alone have been enfranchised. My friend the judge, in Virginia, declared that the colored men and women were there so unlike that they seemed like different races: the men had behaved "admirably," he said; the women were almost hopelessly degraded. On the other hand, my white friends of both sexes at Beaufort took just the opposite view, and thought the women there quite superior to the men, especially in respect to whisky. Perhaps the influences of the two regions may have made the difference, as the sea islands have had the presence, ever since the beginning of the war, of self-devoted and well-educated teachers, mostly women, while such teachers have been much rarer in Virginia. They have also been rare in Florida; but then the Florida negroes are a superior class.

Certainly it was pleasant to me to hear favorable accounts of this and that particular colored woman of whom I had known something in war times. Almost the first old acquaintance named to me on the sea islands, for instance, was one Venus, whose marriage to a soldier of my regiment I chronicled in war times. "Now, cunnel," said that soldier in confidence, "I want for get me one good lady." And when I asked one of his friends about the success of the effort, he said triumphantly, "John's gwine for marry Venus." Now the record of Venus as a good lady was so very questionable in her earlier incarnations that the name was not encouraging; but I was delighted to hear of the goddess, fifteen years later, as a most virtuous wife and a very efficient teacher of sewing in Miss Botume's school. Her other sewing-teacher, by the way, is Juno.

I went into schools, here and there; the colored people seemed to value them very much, and to count upon their own votes as a means of securing these advantages, instead of depending, as formerly, on Northern aid. The schools I visited did not seem to me so good as those kept by Northern ladies during the war, at Port Royal; but the present schools form a part of a public system, and are in that respect better, while enough of the Northern teachers still remain to exert a beneficial influence, at least on the sea islands. I was sorry to be in Charleston only on Saturday, when the Shaw Memorial School was not in session. This is a large wooden building, erected on land bought with part of a fund collected in the colored regiments for a monument to Colonel Shaw. This school has an average attendance of five hundred and twenty, with twelve teachers, white and black. The Morris Street School for colored children, in Charleston, has fourteen hundred pupils. These two schools occupy nearly half of the four columns given by the Charleston News and Courier of April 12, 1878, to the annual exhibition of public schools. The full programme of exercises is given, with the names of the pupils receiving prizes and honors; and it seems almost incredible that the children whose successes are thus proudly recorded can be the sons and daughters of freed slaves. And I hold it utterly ungenerous, in view of such facts, to declare that the white people of the South have learned nothing by experience, and are "incapable of change."

Public officials at Beaufort told me that in that place most of the men could now sign their names, — certainly a great proof of progress since war times. I found some of my friends anxious lest school should unfit the young people for the hard work of the field; but I saw no real proof of this, nor did the parents confirm it. Miss Botume, however, said that the younger women now thought that, after marriage, they ought to be excused from field labor, if they took care of their homes and children; a proposal so directly in the line of advancing civilization that one can hardly object to it. The great solicitude of some of the teachers in that region relates to the passage of some congressional bill which shall set aside the tax sales under which much real estate is now held; but others think that there is no fear of this, even under a democratic administration.

This leads naturally to the question, What is to be the relation between the two races in those Southern States of which I speak? I remember that Corporal Simon Crier, one of the oddities of my regiment, used to declare that when the war was over, he should go to "Libery;" and, when

pressed for a reason, used to say, "Dese yer secesh will ne-
ber be cibilized in my time." Yet Simon Crier's time is not
ended, for I heard of him as peacefully dwelling near
Charleston, and taking no part in that insignificant colonization movement of which we hear so much more at the
North than at the South. Taking civilization in his sense,—a
fair enough sense,—we shall find Virginia, South Carolina,
and Florida holding an intermediate position; being probably behind North Carolina, West Virginia, and the border
States, but decidedly in advance of Georgia, Alabama, and
Mississippi.

It is certain that there is, in the States I visited, a condition of outward peace and no conspicuous outrages; and
that this has now been the case for many months. All will
admit that this state of things must be a blessing, unless
there lies beneath it some covert plan for crushing or
reënslaving the colored race. I know that a few good men at
the North honestly believe in the existence of some such
plan; I can only say that I thoroughly disbelieve in it. Taking
the nature of the Southern whites as these very men describe it,—impulsive and ungoverned,—it is utterly incon-
ceivable that such a plan, if formed, should not show itself
in some personal ill usage of the blacks, in the withdrawal
of privileges, in legislation endangering their rights. I can
assert that, carrying with me the eyes of a tolerably suspicious abolitionist, I saw none of these indications. During
the war, I could hardly go anywhere within the Union lines
for twenty-four hours without being annoyed by some sign
of race hostility, or being obliged to interfere for the protection of some abused man or woman. During this trip, I
had absolutely no occasion for any such attitude. The
change certainly has not resulted from any cringing de-
meanor on the part of the blacks, for they show much more
manhood than they once did. I am satisfied that it results
from the changed feeling created towards a race of freedmen and voters. How can we ask more of the States formerly in rebellion than that they should be abreast of New
England in granting rights and privileges to the colored
race? Yet this is now the case in the three States I name; or
at least if they fall behind at some points, they lead at some
points. Let us look at a few instances.

The republican legislature of Connecticut has just refused to incorporate a colored military company; but the colored militia regiment of Charleston was reviewed by General Hampton and his staff just before my visit. One of the colored officers told me that there was absolutely no difference in the treatment accorded this regiment and that shown toward the white militia, who were reviewed the day before; and Messrs. Whipper and Jones, the only dissatisfied republican leaders whom I saw, admitted that there was no opposition whatever to this arming of the blacks. I may add that while I was in Virginia a bill was reported favorably in the legislature for the creation of a colored militia company, called the State Guard, under control of their own officers, and reporting directly to the adjutant-general.

I do not know a Northern city which enrolls colored citizens in its police, though this may here and there have happened. I saw colored policemen in Charleston, Beaufort, and Jacksonville, though the former city is under democratic control; and I was told by a leading colored man that the number had lately been increased in Charleston, and that one lieutenant of police was of that race. The republican legislature of Rhode Island has just refused once more to repeal the bill prohibiting intermarriages, while the legislature of South Carolina has refused to pass such a bill. I can remember when Frederick Douglas was ejected from the railway cars in Massachusetts, because of his complexion; and it is not many years since one of the most cultivated and ladylike colored teachers in the nation was ejected from a street car in Philadelphia, her birthplace, for the same reason. But I rode with colored people in first-class cars throughout Virginia and South Carolina, and in street cars in Richmond and Charleston. I am told that this last is the case also in Savannah and New Orleans, but can testify only to what I have seen. In Georgia, I was told, the colored people were not allowed in first-class cars; but they had always a decent second-class car, opening from the smoking-car, with the door usually closed between.

All these things may be true, and still a great deal may remain to be done; but it is idle to declare that the sun has not risen because we do not yet see it in the zenith. Even the most extreme Southern newspapers constantly contain paragraphs that amaze us, not only in contrast to slavery times, but in contrast to the times immediately following the war. While I was in South Carolina the Charleston News and Courier published, with commendation, the report of a bill, passed by the Maryland legislature, admitting colored lawyers to practice, after the court of appeals had excluded them; and it copied with implied approval the remark of the Baltimore Gazette: "Raise the educational test, the rigidity of the examinations for admission, or the moral test as high as you please, but let us have done with the color test."

It is certain that every republican politician whom I saw in South Carolina, black or white, spoke well of Governor Hampton, with two exceptions,—Mr. W. J. Whipper, whom Governor Chamberlain refused to commission as judge, and Mr. Jones, who was clerk of the house of delegates through its most corrupt period. I give their dissent for what it is worth, but the opinion of others was as I have said. "We have no complaint to make of Governor Hampton; he has kept his pledges," was the general remark. For instance, a bill passed both houses by a party vote, requiring able-bodied male prisoners, under sentence in county jails, to work on the public roads and streets. The colored people remonstrated strongly, regarding it as aimed at them. Governor Hampton vetoed the bill, and the house, on reflection, sustained the veto by a vote of one hundred and two to ten. But he is not always so strong in influence: there is a minority of "fire-eaters" who resist him; he is denounced by the "upcountry people" as an aristocrat; and I was told that he might yet need the colored vote to sustain him against his own party. Grant that this assumes him to be governed by self-interest; that strengthens the value of this evidence. We do not expect that saints will have the monopoly of government at South or North; what we need is to know that the colored vote in South Carolina makes itself felt as a power, and secures its rightful ends.

The facts here stated are plain and unquestionable. When we come to consider the political condition of the former slaves, we find greater difficulties in taking in the precise position. First, it must be remembered that even at the North the practical antagonism towards colored voters lasted long after their actual enfranchisement, and has worn out only by degrees. Samuel Breck, in his very entertaining reminiscences, tells us that in Philadelphia, in the early part of this century, the colored voters seldom dared to come to the polls, for fear of ill usage. Then we must remember that in South Carolina, the State which has been most under discussion in this essay, the colored voters were practically massed, for years, under the banner of spoliation, and the antagonism created was hardly less intense than that created by the Tweed dynasty in New York. As far as I can judge, neither the "carpet-bag" frauds nor the "Ku-Klux" persecutions have been exaggerated, and they certainly kept each other alive, and have, at least temporarily, ceased together. No doubt the atrocities committed by the whites were the worst, inasmuch as murder is worse than robbery, but few in South Carolina will now deny that the provocation was simply enormous.

And it is moreover true that this state of things left bad blood behind it, which will long last. It has left jealousies which confound the innocent with the guilty. Judging the future by the past, the white South Carolinian finds it almost impossible to believe that a republican state administration can be decently honest. This is a feeling quite apart from any national attitude, and quite consistent with a fair degree of loyalty. Nor does it take the form of resistance to colored voters as such. The Southern whites accept them precisely as Northern men in cities accept the ignorant Irish vote,—not cheerfully, but with acquiescence in the inevitable; and when the strict color-line is once broken they are just as ready to conciliate the negro as the Northern politician to flatter the Irishman. Any powerful body of voters may be cajoled to-day and intimidated to-morrow and hated always, but it can never be left out of sight. At the South, politics are an absorbing interest: people are impetuous; they divide and subdivide on all local issues, and each faction needs votes. Two men are up for mayor or sheriff, or what not: each conciliates every voter he can reach, and each finds it for his interest to stand by those who help him. This has been long predicted by shrewd observers, and is beginning to happen all over the South. I heard of a dozen instances of it. Indeed, the vote of thanks passed by the Mississippi legislature to its colored senator, Mr. Bruce, for his vote on the silver bill was only the same thing on a larger scale. To praise him was to censure Mr. Lamar.

It may be said, "Ah, but the real test is, Will the black voters be allowed to vote for the republican party?" To assert this crowning right will undoubtedly demand a good deal of these voters; it will require courage, organization, intelligence, honesty, and leaders. Without these, any party, in any State, will sooner or later go to the wall. As to South Carolina, I can only say that one of the ablest republican lawyers in the State, a white man, unsuspected of corruption, said to me, "This is a republican State, and to prove it such we need only to bring out our voters. For this we do not need troops, but that half a dozen well-known Northern republicans should canvass the State, just as if it were a Northern State. The colored voters need to know that the party at the North has not, as they have been told, deserted them. With this and a perfectly clean list of nominees, we can carry the legislature, making no nominations against Hampton." "But," I asked, "would not these meetings be broken up?" "Not one of them," he said. "They will break up our local meetings, but not those held by speakers from other States. It would ruin them with the nation." And this remark was afterwards indorsed by others, white and black. When I asked one of the few educated colored leaders in the State, "Do you regret the withdrawal of the troops by President Hayes?" "No," he said; "the only misfortune was that they were not withdrawn two years earlier. That would have put us on our good behavior, obliged us to command respect, and made it easier to save the republican party. But it can still be saved."

There is no teacher so wholesome as personal necessity. In South Carolina a few men and many women cling absolutely to the past, learning nothing, forgetting nothing. But the bulk of thinking men see that the old Southern society is as absolutely annihilated as the feudal system, and that there is no other form of society now possible except such as prevails at the North and West. "The purse-proud Southerner," said Rev. Dr. Pinckney, in his address at Charleston, "is an institution which no longer exists. The race has passed away as completely as the Saurian tribes, whose bones we are now digging from the fossil beds of the Ashley." "The Yankees ought to be satisfied," said one gentleman to me: "every live man at the South is trying with all his might to be a Yankee." Business, money, financial prosperity,—these now form the absorbing Southern question. At the Exchange Hotel in Richmond, where I spent a Sunday, the members of the Assembly were talking all day about the debt,—how to escape bankruptcy. I did not overhear the slightest allusion to the negro or the North. It is likely enough that this may lead to claims on the national treasury, but it tends to nothing worse. The dream of reënslaving the negro, if it ever existed, is like the negro's dream, if he ever had it, of five acres and a mule from the government. Both races have long since come down to the stern reality of self-support. No sane Southerner would now take back as slaves, were they offered, a race of men who have been for a dozen years freemen and voters.

Every secessionist risked his all upon secession, and has received as the penalty of defeat only poverty. It is the mildest punishment ever inflicted after an unsuccessful civil war, and it proves in this case a blessing in disguise. Among Southern young men it has made energy and industry fashionable. Formerly, if a Southern planter wished to travel, he borrowed money on his coming crop, or sold a slave or two. Now he must learn what John Randolph, of Roanoke, once announced as the philosopher's stone, to "pay as you go." The Northern traveler asks himself, Where are the white people of the South? You meet few in public conveyances; you see no crowd in the streets. In the hotels of Washington you rarely hear the Southern accent, and, indeed, my Virginia friends declared that some of its more marked intonations were growing unfashionable. Out of one hundred and three Southern representatives in Congress, only twenty-three have their families with them. On one of the few day trains from Washington to Richmond, there was but one first-class car, and there were not twenty passengers, mostly from the Northern States. Among some fifty people on the steamboat from Savannah to Jacksonville, there were not six Southerners. Everywhere you hear immigration desired and emigration recognized as a fact. My friend the judge talked to me eloquently about the need of more Northern settlers, and the willingness of all to receive them; the plantations would readily be broken up to accommodate any purchaser who had money. But within an hour, his son, a young law student, told me that as soon as he was admitted to the bar he should go West.

The first essential to social progress at the South is that each State should possess local self-government. The States have been readmitted as States, and can no more be treated as Territories than you can replace a bird in the egg. They must now work out their own salvation, just as much as Connecticut and New Jersey. If any abuses exist, the remedy is not to be found in federal interference, except in case of actual insurrection, but in the voting power of the blacks, so far as they have strength or skill to assert it; and where that fails, in their power of locomotion. They must leave those counties or States which ill-use them for others which treat them better. If a man is dissatisfied with the laws of Massachusetts, and cannot get them mended, he can at least remove into Rhode Island or Connecticut, and the loss of valuable citizens will soon make itself felt.

This is the precise remedy possessed by the colored people at the South, with the great advantage that they have the monopoly of all the leading industries, and do not need the whites more, on the whole, than the whites need them. They have reached the point where civilized methods begin to prevail. When they have once enlisted the laws of political economy on their side, this silent ally will be worth more than an army with banners.

# D. H. CHAMBERLAIN, "RECONSTRUCTION AND THE NEGRO"

## (February 1879)

Daniel Henry Chamberlain (1835–1907) was a Massachusetts native who, after studying at Yale and Harvard, served with an all-black cavalry troop in the Civil War and then after the war settled in South Carolina. Elected a delegate to the state's constitutional convention, Chamberlain rose quickly in South Carolina's Republican party, serving as attorney general under Governor Robert K. Scott (1868–72) and then as governor (1874–76). In condemning the Hamburg Massacre as "a barbarity which could only move a civilized person to shame and disgust," Chamberlain drove away Democratic supporters, and he lost his bid for reelection in South Carolina's contested 1876 election. Following his departure from South Carolina, Chamberlain practiced law and became increasingly conservative in his historical memory of Reconstruction. In 1879, however, when reflecting on Reconstruction, especially the role of African-Americans in its stormy history, Chamberlain gave the freedpeople high marks. "No people or race," he explained, had overcome so much to earn "the very highest title to exercise the rights and assume the duties of self-government."

The condition of the colored race of the South has been, for at least forty years, the leading question in our politics. For the most part it has been an unwelcome question, forcing itself into prominence and compelling attention against the choice and interest of most of our political leaders and their followers. The two forces which would otherwise have shaped our political ends—commerce and empire—have feared and hated this issue. The business interests of the country have constantly deprecated its agitation; the pride of empire, the sentiment of nationality, has always deplored its existence and struggled to banish it from the political field. The statesmen who from 1835 to 1860 held the foremost places of political honor and influence were engaged in a continuous effort to settle it by superficial compromises. Their successors at the North, with comparatively few exceptions, refused practically to recognize its essential and controlling power except under the final stress of unavoidable necessity. The same influences were strongly felt at the close of the war. Not a few of the leaders of the party which had pushed the conflict of arms to a successful close resumed the old temper of compromise in dealing with the new phases which this question then presented. Business and the desire for a formal national unity loudly demanded the restoration of the South without further changes than such as the war had actually accomplished.

Throughout this long conflict, the history of which is too fresh to need fuller statement, the nature of the issue touched and enlisted the deepest forces that affect human society. It was primarily an ethical question, a strict question of moral right and wrong. No economical or political tests could alone decide it. Conscience and the moral sense claimed jurisdiction of the question whether the colored race should be treated as men or as brutes, as brethren or as aliens and outcasts from the human family. The moral convictions of the North would permit no settlement which did not recognize the complete manhood of this race. The stubborn and fanatic bigotry of the South would consent to no settlement which did not leave the political power of the States exclusively in the hands of the white race. Under these influences and circumstances the question, by what methods conformable to our system of government the civil rights belonging generally to other citizens might be practically secured to the colored race, became, in the judgment of a majority of the people, the most serious political problem growing out of the war. The result was the enactment by Congress, over the President's veto, of the reconstruction act of March 2, 1867, making it the condition of the restoration of the seceding States that new constitutions should be adopted, framed by "delegates elected by the male citizens, twenty-one years old and upward, of whatever race, color, or previous condition," and securing to all such persons the elective franchise. Under the provisions of this act all the seceding States were finally restored to their practical relations to the Union.

In the light of present results, the policy of universal suffrage thus enforced at the South is condemned not only by those who originally opposed it, but by many who were hitherto its advocates. It becomes, therefore, an appropriate inquiry, whether universal suffrage at the South, or especially what is commonly called negro suffrage, was a mistake. Such an inquiry should be made, if possible, without reference to partisan opinions or interests. The present condition of the colored race of the South can not be viewed with toleration by any right-minded man who is acquainted with the facts. It is certain, too, from the nature of the question itself, as well as its close relations to all our public interests, that it will remain, as heretofore, an issue which can not be avoided. Settlements may be attempted which shall again leave this race to its fate, to an unaided and friendless struggle with the hostile forces which surround it; but such settlements will settle nothing. In the mean time it is well to consider whether whatever degree of failure may be fairly said to characterize the present results of the plan of Southern reconstruction is due either to the principle applied in the general enfranchisement of the colored race, or to the incapacity of that race to properly exercise the rights conferred.

In determining the correctness of the principle adopted in the enfranchisement of the colored race, it is essential to recall the chief features of the situation when that measure was adopted. A war of four years, with its enormous sacrifices of life and property, had just ended. The cause of the war was the existence under the Government of the republic of the system of chattel slavery. Aside from this system the Government was essentially republican. All other leading influences had, for more than three quarters of a century, tended toward its harmonious growth, development, and consolidation. Territory and population had increased beyond precedent. A commanding position had been reached among the nations. All the elements of national prosperity and greatness had been developed to a high degree. Slavery, the one anti-republican influence, had put at

hazard all this growth and glory. It had struck at the life of
the nation. The struggle had agonized the land. The plain
and inevitable lesson of this experience was, that our Government, to be safe, must be self-consistent; that, in Mr.
Lincoln's words, "this Government cannot endure permanently half slave and half free"; that no anti-republican element can be safely suffered to remain in the fabric of our
Government.

This lesson was strongly enforced by the influence of the
great principles which inspired the founders of our Government, and still constituted the professed faith of the republic. By those principles the nation was "dedicated to the
proposition that all men are created equal." Except in the
slave States the suffrage had been the sign and safeguard of
that civil equality contemplated by the fathers. The extension of the suffrage had kept even pace with the progress of
our most prosperous and enlightened communities. The
enjoyment by all citizens of the right of suffrage was therefore regarded as the true corner-stone of our Government
as well as the best if not the only guarantee of individual
freedom. In fixing the political conditions of the seceding
States, the traditions and principles of our Government
united in pointing to universal suffrage as the true defense
of public welfare and personal rights.

But, at the time of which we speak, disloyalty to the national Government characterized the whole white population of the South. The weapons of armed rebellion had but
just been wrenched from their hands. To permit the political power of the restored States to be wielded exclusively
by this class, was to invite the recurrence of the dangers so
lately experienced. A basis of loyalty must be found on
which to build the new governments. The colored race
alone furnished this indispensable condition of reconstruction. Their loyalty to the Union was undoubted. It was deep,
passionate, unfaltering. If, then, the conquered communities
of the South were to be restored to political life and to resume their position as States, the logic of republican principles, the principles of the Declaration of Independence, and
the logic of events and surrounding circumstances, alike
pointed to the immediate enfranchisement of the colored
race as the chief feature in a wise plan of reconstruction.
Gradual enfranchisement could not meet the conditions

then existing. Tests of property or education, if ever wise or admissible, under our theory of Government, were clearly inadmissible here. The application of these tests would exclude those whose influence and participation could alone insure a republican basis for the new governments and the political predominance of those who were loyal to the General Government.

Other considerations led to the same conclusions. It was believed, as the result of our political experience as a whole, that the best method of dealing with the so-called "dangerous classes"—those who have, for the most part, neither property nor education—was to admit them to the full privileges of citizenship. Such, with slight exceptions hardly requiring mention, had been the policy adopted in all the remaining States. It was believed, upon the same authority, that the exercise of the rights of free citizens was the best school for the education of the citizen in the proper discharge of the duties imposed by his rights. These beliefs were the results of experience. They were not theories merely. They were the practical, working rules by which our most successful political communities had carried on the business of government. Those who shaped the plan of reconstruction were convinced that the civil rights and future welfare of the colored race demanded that the ballot should be placed in its hands. They felt that the national Government was charged with the duty of recognizing and securing, so far as legislation could go, the complete civil and political equality of the colored race with the other races under our Government. This was especially due to that race by reason of its whole previous history in this country, as well as its peculiar position at the close of the war. But it was not sentiment alone that guided to this result. All other policies were open to insuperable objections. Direct military supervision of the South, the continuance of the abnormal condition existing from 1865 to 1867, or the return to power of those who had previously exercised exclusive political control, were the only remaining policies. Neither of these policies could be justified by reason or experience. That temporary evils would arise from the immediate enfranchisement of the colored race no man doubted, but the men who supported the measure believed, with Macaulay, that "there is only one cure for the evils which newly-acquired freedom produces—and that cure is *freedom*. When a prisoner leaves his cell, he cannot bear the light of day; he is unable to discriminate colors or recognize faces. But the remedy is not to remand him into his dungeon, but to accustom him to the rays of the sun. . . . Many politicians of our time are in the habit of laying it down as a self-evident proposition that no people ought to be free till they are fit to use their freedom. The maxim is worthy of the fool in the old story, who resolved not to go into the water till he had learned to swim! If men are to wait for liberty till they become wise and good in slavery, they may indeed wait for ever." They believed, with Mackintosh, that "justice is the permanent interest of all men, and of all commonwealths," and that "the love of liberty is the only source and guard of the tranquillity and greatness of America." They believed, with Abraham Lincoln, "All honor to Jefferson; to a man who, in the concrete pressure of a struggle for national independence by a single people, had the coolness, forecast, and capacity to introduce into a merely revolutionary document an abstract truth, applicable to all men and all times, and so to embalm it there, that to-day and in all coming days it shall be a rebuke and a stumbling-block to the harbingers of reappearing tyranny and oppression." To men of real faith in the principles of our government, to men who loved and practiced justice, who held that governments exist for the good of all the people, the immediate and unconditional enfranchisement of the colored race of the South was an act and policy supported by the highest sanctions of political justice and civil prudence.

The charges now brought with most frequency and apparent effect against this policy are, first, that it was unjust and cruel to the white people of the South thus to subject them to negro rule; and, second, that the enfranchisement of the colored race was a deliberate giving over of society to the control of ignorance, a reversal of the order of Nature and Providence which demands that society shall rest on intelligence and capacity, not on ignorance and inexperience.

To the first charge the reply is that colored suffrage was not the subjection of the white race to negro rule. The white race retained its suffrage, with all its immense advantages of property and education. Colored suffrage was simply placing the two races on the same plane of civil and political rights. It was the giving of a fair field and an equal chance to the members of both races. It was the removing of all legal or artificial hindrances from the path of the one race, without diminishing a single right or adding a single burden to the other race. Nor was this true only of the legal situation and relations of the two races. No restriction or hindrance in fact existed, under this policy, to the freest and most effective use and influence of all the advantages which property, education, and political experience necessarily gave to the white race as a whole. No such obstacle existed either as a proper consequence of the policy of colored suffrage, or of the temper of that race toward the other race. That policy had no elements but justice and civil equality; that temper was friendly and generous. The sole cause of the political supremacy of the colored race at the South was the willful and deliberate refusal of the white race to contribute its proper and natural influence to the practical work of government. They chose to yield to the embittering influences of defeat and race-hatred, rather than to act the part of faithful citizens in guiding and controlling those whose ignorance and inexperience most imperatively required their aid. The necessary results of such conduct on the part of a class occupying such relations to any community, under our form of government, are obvious and uniform. It was as if to-day the greater part of the tax-paying and educated class in New England and New York should cease from all influence or aid in the work of government, and sullenly leave public affairs to the control of such as might be left to take it. Or, more exactly, it was as if that class, not content with refusing all aid in the conduct of public affairs, should seek, in a spirit of bitter and vengeful hostility, to deride, dishonor, and embitter those into whose hands they had surrendered the political power. It is certain that no state or community could suffer such a separation and antagonism of its elements without plunging, more or less rapidly, into temporary misrule.

But with what patience would just and reasonable men listen to the charge, especially when coming from those who had forsworn their political duties, that this result was due to the false and cruel policy which had established universal suffrage? The indignant reply would be: "Your sufferings are self-inflicted, the just penalties of your own folly and crime; you have sown the wind, and you reap the whirlwind." The best success of self-government anywhere presupposes a fair degree of coöperation between all classes in carrying on the work of government. If such coöperation is refused by the class representing property and education, that recusant class, not the policy or principle of self-government, is chargeable with the results, whatever they may be. "I do not admit," said Governor Dix, in vetoing the proposed city charter of New York in 1872, "that misgovernment in this city is proof of the failure of republican government. When the Legislature gives to New York municipal government in conformity with the general idea of American institutions, it performs its whole duty. All further responsibility is on the people of New York City themselves. If they culpably neglect their own affairs, if they will not give to their own political affairs the same attention which the rest of the people, in their several localities, are in the habit of giving, they must suffer the consequences."

The second main charge brought against the policy of universal suffrage in our reconstruction, is perhaps sufficiently answered already. Instead of violating or disregarding any natural or moral law, or law of human nature or society, it was the dictate and expression of the highest morality applied to the affairs of government, the recognition and protection of the natural and inalienable right of all men—the opportunity, without artificial shackles or hindrances, to run the race of life. It is safe to say that there is no political community of considerable importance, either State, city, or large town, in our country, in which the voluntary and complete withdrawal of the greater part of the educated and property-owning class from all participation in public affairs would not speedily produce the state of things which has been denounced, when seen at the South, as the forcible and artificial elevation of the ignorant and irresponsible over the educated and responsible. The cause of such results wherever seen, under our Government, is the same. It is the violation of moral duty and natural law by those who are endowed with the chief power of securing and upholding good government. To raise an outcry against universal suffrage because of results traceable directly to the neglect of their unquestionable duties as citizens, by the educated and tax-paying classes, is a conscious mockery or a pitiable mistake. No better words have been spoken of late on this point than these of Goldwin Smith: "There is yet another class *dangerous* in its way—the class of political seceders. Malcontents from this country are always telling their sympathizing friends in Europe that the best men here stand aloof from politics. The answer is, that those who in a free country stand aloof from politics *can not be the best men*. A man is not bound to seek the prizes of public life; he will perhaps exercise more influence for good if he does not; he is not bound to become the slave of party; he is not bound to sit in any conclave of political iniquity. But he is bound to do his utmost, in such ways as are morally open to him, to get the best men elected, and to make the right principles prevail. If he can not do much, he is still bound to do what he can. Striking pictures have been drawn of men with high foreheads and intellectual countenances condemned to sit in council beside low brows and stolid faces. But would the matter be mended if the low brows and stolid faces had the council to themselves?"

And if, it may be further asked, the "low brows and stolid faces" do have the council to themselves, is it the fault of universal suffrage? Does it suggest the remedy of the restriction of the suffrage until the "high foreheads and intellectual countenances," without effort on their part, shall have the council to themselves? Not till we abandon all pretense of faith in the cardinal doctrines of republican government as understood and practiced hitherto in the United States, will it be admitted that it is the province or aim of government to secure to "high foreheads and intellectual countenances" anything more than it secures to "low brows and stolid faces," namely, a fair chance to exercise their own faculties, follow their own ends, and influence the course of public affairs according to their abilities and the dictates of their own judgments, subject only and equally to such impartial legal restraints as may be necessary to prevent crime and preserve public order. It is not claimed that there is anything sacred about the right to vote, except as it is believed and proved to be the best means of securing those other rights which *are* sacred and inalienable—"life, liberty, and the pursuit of happiness."

The ballot is no more than a means of securing the best government, and the best government is that under which all the people rise to the highest plane of intellectual and moral development. The American idea is that, by giving and securing to all the right to vote, the result in the large will always be, at least in any American community, that the various classes will have, each its appropriate influence; that good government being the general interest will be the general aim; and that in the process of reaching this end the whole community will be educated and elevated to a degree never resulting from other methods. And further, it is a part of this idea of government, that if for a time evils arise and prevail, the remedy will be constantly in the hands of those who suffer, and that, whenever such evils arrest the public attention or threaten the public welfare, the general interest will compel their correction and removal. If, then, under this system and in this country, the "low brows and stolid faces" anywhere or at any time have the council to themselves, it is because the "high foreheads and intellectual countenances" have failed to use their proper influence. No single instance can probably be pointed out in our history, where it is not certain that the evils of bad government could have been promptly corrected by the earnest and faithful efforts of the educated and property-owning classes. The Southern States under colored suffrage were not exceptions to this rule. No class ever had greater advantages for securing a proper share of influence in public affairs than the white race of the South in 1867; no class were ever more open or responsive to the influences of property and education than the colored race of the South. The plan of reconstruction did not set the colored race to rule over the white; it did not place ignorance above education. Such results, if they have ever existed, were due to causes which would produce in New England evils similar to those which have prevailed in South Carolina and Louisiana.

If we turn now to an examination of the conduct and capacity of the colored race as shown during the period of its free exercise of the suffrage, it will appear that that race exhibited qualities entitling it to all the political privileges conferred by the reconstruction measures. It is necessary here to shut out the partisan clamor and misrepresentation of the day, and attend only to the authentic facts as the ground of judgment. First, then, it may be said that the colored race gave to the Southern States wise, liberal, and just constitutions. Under influences which elsewhere had led to punitory and proscriptive measures toward those who had supported slavery and rebellion, the organic law of the ten States embraced in the reconstruction act of 1867 shows no instance of a purpose or effort to exclude any classes or individuals from an equal share in all political privileges. The demands of public education were fully recognized and provided for. The methods and principles of taxation were just and enlightened. The modes of selecting judicial officers were such as prevail in the most prosperous States of the North. In a word, the constitutions of the reconstructed States would to-day command the almost unqualified approval of all competent and impartial judges and critics. And the same conclusion will follow from an examination of the general legislation in these States during the same period. It was, with few exceptions, dictated by the public wants and suited to the public needs.

In the ordinary conduct of the practical affairs of government, much must be said in approval of the spirit and methods which then prevailed. Elections were free, fair, and honest. Political canvasses were conducted by the colored race without violence, or disorder, or excessive rancor. The power which they held they put fairly at hazard with each recurring election. They neither cheated nor intimidated nor sought to intimidate their opponents. Their popular assemblages listened with respect and attention to the arguments of their bitterest political foes on those rare occasions when their foes condescended to address them with argument. Public order was maintained. Crime was detected and punished. Life and property were as safe as in most of the States.

There was a period of official corruption and profligacy in the States in which the colored vote predominated, extending generally from 1869 to 1874. It arose from causes already explained. It was confined to official life; it was produced and inspired by a few leaders who had, for purposes of plunder, made their way to public places. As in the similar condition of affairs which prevailed in the city of New York from 1866 to 1873, official corruption at the South for a time baffled investigation and defied public sentiment. In

its worst stages it did not equal this description, given by
the "Committee of Seventy," of corruption in New York: "It
has bought Legislatures, controlled Governors, corrupted
newspapers, defiled courts of justice, violated the ballot-
box, threatened all forms of civil and religious liberty, awed
the timid rich, bribed the toiling masses, and cajoled respectable citizens, and has finally grown so strong and reckless as to openly defy the intelligence and virtue which is
believed to be inert, voiceless, and powerless to stay its ag-
gressions, or to assert the supremacy of honesty and justice." Southern corruption assumed more grotesque, and
perhaps more offensive forms, than were displayed elsewhere; but it was never so powerful, daring, or pervasive as
in other sections of the country. It never polluted the
sources of political power; it never violated the ballot-box;
it never bribed the "toiling masses." It may be said with
perfect truth that the colored voters of the South never sustained public men whom they believed to be corrupt. They
adhered with rare fidelity to those who had once gained
their confidence. But, whenever a public man was shown to
be corrupt, the colored voters rejected him with as much
certainty and promptness as the voters of the North have
shown. It is not true—with whatever frequency or confidence the assertion may have been made—that the colored
race of the South deliberately or consciously sustained
leaders or public officers who were found guilty of dishonest conduct or corrupt practices. Such leaders and officers
were deprived of office and power. From 1873 till 1876,
when political power was violently wrested from them, it is
the truth of history that there was at the South a steady
progress toward good government, purity of administration, reform of abuses, and the choice of capable and honest public officers, in those States in which the colored race
had most complete control. There were here, as there are in
all communities, sham reformers. At periods of special excitement, or under peculiar influences and circumstances,
the reform movement was checked, and corrupt and dishonored leaders seemed for a time to regain power. But
such reverses were overcome, and in 1876 those who had
most conspicuously shown their ability and courage in the
work of reform were in substantial control of the political
power of the colored race. In South Carolina, where per-

haps official corruption had been greatest, the progress of reform had been such as to compel the acknowledgment, by those who had most violently denounced colored suffrage, that the best assurance of good government in the future lay in the continuance of the power of those who were then successfully working out, through the political party supported by the colored vote, the correction of public abuses.

This condition of affairs, it is to be remembered, was the result solely of the movement for reform within the political party which owed its power mainly to the colored race. The reforms accomplished were demanded and supported by the colored voters. The reform leaders were chosen and sustained in their work by the sympathy and approval of a vast majority of that class of voters. If, as was the fact in the crusade against corruption in New York, party lines could have been disregarded; if the white minority had looked only to securing the best means for reform and good government, the reform movement would have advanced to complete success without serious hindrance or delay. Such coöperation would have been welcomed by the colored race. A better agency for peaceful and permanent reform was never presented. The colored race by nature and habit were mild, peaceful, order-loving, teachable, patient, and religious. Taught by such influences and methods as are made use of in other States, this race would have yielded to the sway of reason and justice in their political conduct, far more readily than did the masses through which for a time corrupt leaders and public officers maintained their power in New York. The work of maintaining good government without the aid and with the hostility of the greater part of the class possessing property and education must always be extremely difficult. No people or race that has shown itself able, under such conditions, to establish wise and liberal constitutions and laws, to set in successful operation the great agencies which produce and uphold our best civilization, and, when attacked and wellnigh overcome by official corruption and profligacy, to defeat and destroy this enemy, and to restore the rule of public integrity and honor, is without the very highest title to exercise the rights and assume the duties of self-government. This title the colored race earned by their conduct from 1868 to 1876.

The fact of the present suppression and overthrow of colored suffrage at the South is now made the ground of the argument that the race was not equal to the duties of self-government. It is said that every people worthy of freedom and self-government will have freedom and self-government. It is said that the inability of a people to cope, in physical and material resources, with its enemies, is proof that such a people is not entitled to retain its political power. Such conclusions are as illogical as they are immoral. Under the principles of our Government and of all just government, rights are not dependent on numbers or physical strength or material resources. The right to vote, and to have that vote honestly counted—the right to hold and exercise the political power conferred by a majority of the votes when honestly counted—these are rights, under our Government, totally independent of the power or wealth or education of the voters. If at any time or in any place these rights are denied or defeated, there the most characteristic principle of our political system is dishonored. Nor is it an answer to this to say—even if the statement were true in any sense—that better government has been secured by the defeat of the will of a majority of the voters. In the first place, there can be no legitimate State government, good or bad, under our system, which does not derive its title from the actual legal result of the votes cast. A government otherwise derived is tainted by an original and incurable vice. In the next place, no government, however wise and pure in administration, is worth the price of a violation of the first principles upon which all governments, under our system, must rest. To hold otherwise is to make government dependent for its sanction, not on the consent of the governed nor on the will of the majority, but on the consent and will of any number or combination of persons who may chance to possess the preponderance of physical strength and resources.

The present political supremacy of the white race in at least five of the Southern States is the result of the violent exclusion or fraudulent suppression of the colored vote. No honest and well-informed man will question this. In South Carolina, Mississippi, and Louisiana, the result has been reached by a system of deliberate, organized violence in all its forms, supplemented and crowned by the most daring and stupendous election frauds. It is an intolerable affront to every sentiment of humanity or dictate of justice, to argue that any results secured by such means are less detestable than the atrocities and crimes by which they were wrought. Whoever prevents any lawful voter from casting his vote, or constrains him to cast it contrary to his will, or deprives it, when cast, of its equal share in determining the result of the election, is guilty of a palpable and vulgar fraud. The defense of such fraud, by a reference to any results which may follow, is a specimen of degrading Jesuitism.

What morality and reason thus affirm, experience confirms. The only serious menace to the prosperity, unity, and life of the nation has proceeded directly from a departure from the doctrine of equal civil and political rights—the claim and exercise of exclusive political control by a few over the many. The South from 1789 to 1860 was the complete type and embodiment of communities in which political power is held exclusively by property and education. By a law as sure and uniform in its results as the operations of Nature, these communities became oligarchies in the most odious sense of the term, hostile in spirit and action to all republican ideas. In seventy years from the foundation of the Government "ordained to establish justice and secure the blessings of liberty," the wealth, education, and piety of the South stood ready, sword in hand, to destroy that Government, and to maintain in its place a government proclaimed by its founders to rest on the corner-stone of human slavery. And to-day again, as in 1860, the same oligarchical power, crushing the colored race under its feet, seeks with bloody and rapacious hands to grasp the national power as the agency through which it may extend and perpetuate its own spirit and practice of caste and oppression.

# THE *CIVIL RIGHTS CASES*
# AND JUSTICE HARLAN'S
# DISSENT
## *(1883)*

Historians generally regard the 1883 *Civil Rights Cases* as the end point of Reconstruction. In considering five discrimination cases, the U.S. Supreme Court judged the equal-accommodations sections of the Civil Rights Act of 1875 to be unconstitutional. The government contended that the Thirteenth and Fourteenth Amendments outlawed private cases of discrimination, but the court disagreed.

Writing for the majority, Associate Justice Joseph P. Bradley (1813–1892) argued that the Fourteenth Amendment concerned state acts, not acts of private individuals, and that the amendment empowered Congress only to correct, not to prevent, discrimination once it had occurred. Bradley went on to maintain that discriminatory practices in public facilities and accommodations, such as inns, theaters, and trains, were not the result of slavery and hence were not outlawed by the Thirteenth Amendment. Private conduct, he averred, was not amenable to legislation. Bradley also commented pointedly on shifting attitudes towards the ex-slaves by Northerners. The associate justice noted that the time had finally come for the freedman "when he takes the rank of a mere citizen, and ceases to be the special favorite of the laws, and when his rights, as a citizen or a man, are to be protected in the ordinary modes by which other men's rights are protected."

In his famous and powerful lone dissent, Associate Justice John Marshall Harlan argued "the substance and spirit of the recent Amendments of the

Constitution have been sacrificed by a subtle and ingenious verbal criticism." He wrote that because amusements, hotels, and public conveyances, though owned privately, provided public services, their owners could not practice discrimination and therefore were under government regulation. Harlan also argued that certain discriminatory acts constituted "badges of slavery and servitude" and, accordingly, the Thirteenth Amendment empowered Congress to remove them by legislative action. He concluded by warning, "Today, it is the colored race which is denied, by corporations and individuals wielding public authority, rights fundamental in their freedom and citizenship. At some future time, it may be that some other race will fall under the ban of race discrimination."

*Mr. Justice* **Bradley** delivered the opinion of the court:

These cases are all founded on the 1st and 2d sections of the Act of Congress, known as the Civil Rights Act, passed March 1, 1875, entitled "An Act to Protect all Citizens in their Civil and Legal Rights." 18 Stat. at L. , 335. Two of the cases, those against Stanley and Nichols, are indictments for denying to persons of color the accommodations and privileges of an inn or hotel; two of them, those against Ryan and Singleton, are, one an information, the other an indictment, for denying to individuals the privileges and accommodations of a theater, the information against Ryan being for refusing a colored person a seat in the dress circle of Maguire's theater in San Francisco; and the indictment against Singleton being for denying to another person, whose color is not stated, the full enjoyment of the accommodations of the theater known as the Grand Opera House in New York, "Said denial not being made for any reasons by law applicable to citizens of every race and color, and regardless of any previous condition of servitude." The case of Robinson and wife against the Memphis and Charleston R. R. Company was an action brought in the Circuit Court of the United States for the Western District of Tennessee, to recover the penalty of $500 given by the 2d section of the Act; and the *gravamen* was the refusal by the conductor of the Railroad Company to allow the wife to ride in the ladies' car, for the reason, as stated in one of the counts, that she was a person of African descent. The jury rendered a verdict for the defendants in this case upon the merits under a charge of the court to which a bill of exceptions was taken by the plaintiffs. The case was tried on the assumption by both parties of the validity of the Act of Congress; and the principal point made by the exceptions was, that the Judge allowed evidence to go to the jury tending to show that the conductor had reason to suspect that the plaintiff, the wife, was an improper person, because she was in company with a young man whom he supposed to be a white man, and on that account inferred that there was some improper connection between them; and the Judge charged the jury, in substance, that if this was the conductor's *bona fide* reason for excluding the woman from the car, they might take it into consideration on the question of the liability of the Company. The case is brought here by writ of error at the suit of the plaintiffs. The cases of Stanley, Nichols and Singleton, come up on certificates of division of opinion between the Judges below as to the constitutionality of the 1st and 2d sections of the Act referred to; and the case of Ryan, on a writ of error to the judgment of the Circuit Court for the District of California, sustaining a demurrer to the information.

It is obvious that the primary and important question in all the cases, is the constitutionality of the law; for if the law is unconstitutional, none of the prosecutions can stand.

The sections of the law referred to provide as follows:

"Sec. 1. That all persons within the jurisdiction of the United States shall be entitled to the full and equal enjoyment of the accommodations, advantages, facilities and privileges of inns, public conveyances on land or water, theaters and other places of public amusement; subject only to the conditions and limitations established by law, and applicable alike to citizens of every race and color, regardless of any previous condition of servitude.

"Sec. 2. That any person who shall violate the foregoing section by denying to any citizen, except for reasons by law applicable to citizens of every race and color, and regardless of any previous condition of servitude, the full enjoyment of any of the accommodations, advantages, facilities or privileges in said section enumerated, or by aiding or inciting such denial, shall for every such offense forfeit and pay the sum of $500 to the person aggrieved there by, to be recovered in an action of debt with full costs; and shall also, for every such offense, be deemed guilty of a misdemeanor and, upon conviction thereof, shall be fined not less than $500 nor more than $1,000, or shall be imprisoned not less than thirty days nor more than one year; *Provided,* That all persons may elect to sue for the penalty aforesaid, or to proceed under their rights at common law and by state statutes; and having so elected to proceed in the one mode or the other, their right to proceed in the other jurisdiction shall be barred. But this provision shall not apply to criminal proceedings, either under this Act or the criminal law of any State; *And provided, further*, That a judgment for the penalty in favor of the party aggrieved, or a judgment upon an indictment, shall be a bar to either prosecution respectively." Are these sections constitutional? The 1st section, which is the principal one, cannot be fairly understood without attending to the last clause, which qualifies the preceding part. The essence of the law is, not to declare broadly that all persons shall be entitled to the full and equal enjoyment of the accommodations, advantages, facilities and privileges of inns, public conveyances and theaters; but that such enjoyment shall not be subject to any conditions applicable only to citizens of a particular race or color, or who had been in a previous condition of servitude. In other words: it is the purpose of the law to declare that, in the enjoyment of the accommodations and privileges of inns, public conveyances, theaters and other places of public amusement, no distinction shall be made between citizens of different race or color, or between those who have and those who have not been slaves. Its effect is, to declare that, in all inns, public conveyances and places of amusement, colored citizens, whether formerly slaves or not, and citizens of other races, shall have the same accommodations and privileges in all inns, public conveyances, and places of amusement as are enjoyed by white citizens; and *vice versa*. The 2d section makes it a penal offense in any person to deny to any citizen of any race or color, regardless of previous servitude, any of the accommodations or privileges mentioned in the 1st section.

Has Congress constitutional power to make such a law?

Of course, no one will contend that the power to pass it was contained in the Constitution before the adoption of the last three Amendments. The power is sought, first, in the 14th Amendment, and the views and arguments of distinguished Senators, advanced whilst the law was under consideration, claiming authority to pass it by virtue of that Amendment, are the principal arguments adduced in favor of the power. We have carefully considered those arguments, as was due to the eminent ability of those who put them forward, and have felt, in all its force, the weight of authority which always invests a law that Congress deems itself competent to pass. But the responsibility of an independent judgment now thrown upon this court; and we are bound to exercise it according to the best lights we have.

The 1st section of the 14th Amendment, which is the one relied on, after declaring who shall be citizens of the United States, and of the several States, is prohibitory in its character, and prohibitory upon the States. It declares that "No State shall make or enforce any law which shall abridge the privileges or immunities of citizens of the United States; nor shall any State deprive any person of life, liberty or property without due process of law; nor deny to any person within its jurisdiction the equal protection of the laws." It is state action of a particular character that is prohibited. Individual invasion of individual rights is not the subject matter of the Amendment. It has a deeper and broader scope. It nullifies and makes void all state legislation, and state action of every kind, which impairs the privileges and immunities of citizens of the United States, or which injures them in life, liberty or property without due process of law, or which denies to any of them the equal protection of the laws. It not only does this, but, in order that the national will, thus declared, may not be a mere *brutum fulmen,* the last section of the Amendment invests Congress with power to enforce it by appropriate legislation. To enforce what? To enforce the prohibition. To adopt appropriate legislation for correcting the effects of such prohibited state laws and state Acts, and thus to render them effectually null, void and innocuous. This is the legislative power conferred upon Congress, and this is the whole of it. It does not invest Congress with power to legislate upon subjects which are within the domain of state legislation; but to provide modes of relief against state legislation or state action, of the kind referred to. It does not authorize Congress to create a code of municipal law for the regulation of private rights; but to provide modes of redress against the operation of state laws, and the action of state officers executive or judicial, when these are subversive of the fundamental rights specified in the Amendment. Positive rights and privileges are undoubtedly secured by the 14th Amendment; but they are secured by way of prohibition against state laws and state proceedings affecting those rights and privileges, and by power given to Congress to legislate for the purpose of carrying such prohibition into effect; and such legislation must, necessarily, be predicated upon such supposed state laws or state proceedings, and be directed to the correction of their operation and effect. . . .

And so in the present case, until some state law has been passed or some state action through its officers or agents has been taken, adverse to the rights of citizens sought to be protected by the 14th Amendment, no legislation of the United States under said Amendment, nor any proceeding under such legislation, can be called into activity; for the prohibitions of the Amendment are against state laws and acts done under state authority. Of course, legislation may and should be provided in advance to meet the exigency when it arises; but it should be adapted to the mischief and wrong which the Amendment was intended to provide against; and that is, state laws, or state action of some kind, adverse to the rights of the citizen secured by the Amendment. Such legislation cannot properly cover the whole domain of rights appertaining to life, liberty and property, defining them and providing for their vindication. That would be to establish a code of municipal law regulative of all private rights between man and man in society. It would be to make Congress take the place of the State Legislatures and to supersede them. It is absurd to affirm that, because the rights of life, liberty and property, which include all civil rights that men have, are, by the Amendment, sought to be protected against invasion on the part of the State without due process of law, Congress may, therefore provide due process of law for their vindication in every case; and that, because the denial by a State to any persons, of the equal protection of the laws, is prohibited by the

Amendment, therefore Congress may establish laws for their equal protection. In fine, the legislation which Congress is authorized to adopt in this behalf is not general legislation upon the rights of the citizen, but corrective legislation, that is, such as may be necessary and proper for counteracting such laws as the States may adopt or enforce, and which, by the Amendment, they are prohibited from making or enforcing, or such acts and proceedings as the States may commit or take, and which, by the Amendment, they are prohibited from committing or taking. It is not necessary for us to state, if we could, what legislation would be proper for Congress to adopt. It is sufficient for us to examine whether the law in question is of that character.

An inspection of the law shows that it makes no reference whatever to any supposed or apprehended violation of the 14th Amendment on the part of the States. It is not predicated on any such view. It proceeds *ex directo* to declare that certain acts committed by individuals shall be deemed offenses, and shall be prosecuted and punished by proceedings in the courts of the United States. It does not profess to be corrective of any constitutional wrong committed by the States; it does not make its operation to depend upon any such wrong committed. It applies equally to cases arising in States which have the justest laws respecting the personal rights of citizens, and whose authorities are ever ready to enforce such laws, as to those which arise in States that may have violated the prohibition of the Amendment. In other words, it steps into the domain of local jurisprudence, and lays down rules for the conduct of individuals in society towards each other, and imposes sanctions for the enforcement of those rules, without referring in any manner to any supposed action of the State or its authorities.

If this legislation is appropriate for enforcing the prohibitions of the Amendment, it is difficult to see where it is to stop. Why may not Congress with equal show of authority enact a code of laws for the enforcement and vindication of all rights of life, liberty and property? If it is supposable that the States may deprive persons of life, liberty and property without due process of law, and the Amendment itself does suppose this, why should not Congress proceed at once to prescribe due process of law for the protection of every one of these fundamental rights, in every possible case, as well as to prescribe equal privileges in inns, public conveyances and theaters? The truth is, that the implication of a power to legislate in this manner is based upon the assumption that if the States are forbidden to legislate or act in a particular way on a particular subject, and power is conferred upon Congress to enforce the prohibition, this gives Congress power to legislate generally upon that subject, and not merely power to provide modes of redress against such state legislation or action. The assumption is certainly unsound. It it is repugnant to the 10th Amendment of the Constitution, which declares that powers not delegated to the United States by the Constitution, nor prohibited by it to the States, are reserved to the States respectively or to the people.

We have not overlooked the fact that the 4th section of the Act now under consideration has been held by this court to be constitutional. That section declares "That no citizen, possessing all other qualifications which are or may be prescribed by law, shall be disqualified for service as grand or petit juror in any court of the United States, or of any State, on account of race, color or previous condition of servitude; and any officer or other person charged with any duty in the selection or summoning of jurors who shall exclude or fail to summon any citizen for the cause aforesaid, shall, on conviction thereof, be deemed guilty of a misdemeanor, and be fined, not more than $5,000." In *Ex parte Va.,* 100 U. S., 339 [XXV., 676], it was held that an indictment against a State officer under this section for excluding persons of color from the jury list is sustainable. But a moment's attention to its terms will show that the section is entirely corrective in its character. Disqualifications for service on juries are only created by the law, and the first part of the section is aimed at certain disqualifying laws, namely: those which make mere race or color a disqualification; and the 2d clause is directed against those who, assuming to use the authority of the State Government, carry into effect such a rule of disqualification. In the *Virginia Case,* the State, through its officer, enforced a rule of disqualification which the law was intended to abrogate and counteract. Whether the statute-book of the State actually laid down any such rule of disqualification, or not, the State, through its officer, enforced such a rule; and it is against such state action, through its officers and agents, that the last clause of the section is directed. This aspect of the law was deemed sufficient to devest it of any unconstitutional character, and makes it differ widely from the 1st and 2d sections of the same Act which we are now considering.

These sections, in the objectionable features before referred to, are different also from the law ordinarily called the "Civil Rights Bill," originally passed April 9,1866 [14 Stat. at L., 27], and re-enacted with some modifications in sections 16, 17, 18, of the Enforcement Act, passed May 31, 1870 [16 Stat. at L., 140]. That law, as re-enacted, after declaring that all persons within the jurisdiction of the United States shall have the same right in every State and Territory to make and enforce contracts, to sue, be parties, give evidence and to the full and equal benefit of all laws and proceedings for the security of persons and property as is enjoyed by white citizens, and shall be subject to like punishment, pains, penalties, taxes, licenses and exactions of every kind, and none other, any law, statute, ordinance, regulation or custom to the contrary notwithstanding, proceeds to enact that any person who, under color of any law, statute, ordinance, regulation or custom, shall subject or cause to be subjected any inhabitant of any State or Territory to the deprivation of any rights secured or protected by the preceding section, above quoted, or to different punishment, pains or penalties, on account of such person being an alien or by reason of his color or race, than is prescribed for the punishment of citizens, shall be deemed guilty of a misdemeanor, and subject to fine and imprisonment as specified in the Act. This law is clearly corrective in its character, intended to counteract and furnish redress against state laws and proceedings, and customs having the force of law, which sanction the wrongful acts specified. In the Revised Statutes, it is true a very important clause, to wit: the words "any law, statute, ordinance, regulation or custom to the contrary notwithstanding," which gave the declaratory section its point and effect, are omitted; but the penal part, by which the declaration is enforced, and which is really the effective part of the law, retains the reference to state laws, by making the penalty apply only to those who should subject parties to a deprivation of their rights under color of any statute, ordinance, custom, etc., of any State or Territory, thus preserving the corrective character of the legislation. R. S., secs. 1977, 1978, 1979, 5510. The Civil Rights Bill here referred to is analogous in its character to what a law would have been under the original Constitution, declaring that the validity of contracts should not be impaired, and that if any person bound by a contract should refuse to comply with it, under color or pretense that it had been rendered void or invalid by a state law, he should be liable to an action upon it in the courts of the United States, with the addition of a penalty for setting up such an unjust and unconstitutional defense.

In this connection it is proper to state that civil rights, such as are guarantied by the Constitution against state aggression, cannot be impaired by the wrongful acts of individuals, unsupported by state authority in the shape of laws, customs or judicial or executive proceedings. The wrongful act of an individual, unsupported by any such authority, is simply a private wrong, or a crime of that individual; an invasion of the rights of the injured party, it is true, whether they affect his person, his property or his reputation; but if not sanctioned in some way by the State, or not done under state authority, his rights remain in full force, and may presumably be vindicated by resort to the laws of the State for redress. An individual cannot deprive a man of his right to vote, to hold property, to buy and to sell, to sue in the courts or to be a witness or a juror; he may, by force or fraud, interfere with the enjoyment of the right in a particular case; he may commit an assault against the person, or commit murder, or use ruffian violence at the polls, or slander the good name of a fellow citizen; but, unless protected in these wrongful acts by some shield of state law or state authority, he cannot destroy or injure the right; he will only render himself amenable to satisfaction or punishment; and amenable therefor to the laws of the State where the wrongful acts are committed. Hence, in all those cases where the Constitution seeks to protect the rights of the citizen against discriminative and unjust laws of the State by prohibiting such laws, it is not individual offenses, but abrogation and denial of rights, which it denounces, and for which it clothes the Congress with power to provide a remedy. This abrogation and denial of rights, for which the States alone were or could be responsible, was the great seminal and fundamental wrong which was intended to be remedied. And the remedy to be provided must necessarily be predicated upon that wrong. It must assume that in the cases provided for, the evil or wrong actually committed rests upon some state law or state authority for its excuse and perpetration.

Of course, these remarks do not apply to those cases in which Congress is clothed with direct and plenary powers of legislation over the whole subject, accompanied with an express or implied denial of such power to the States, as in the regulation of commerce with foreign Nations, among the several States, and with the Indian Tribes, the coining of money, the establishment of postoffices and post-roads, the declaring of war, etc. In these cases, Congress has power to pass laws for regulating the subjects specified in every detail, and the conduct and transactions of individuals in respect thereof. But where a subject is not submitted to the general legislative power of Congress, but is only submitted thereto for the purpose of rendering effective some prohibition against particular state legislation or state action in reference to that subject, the power given is limited by its object, and any legislation by Congress in the matter must necessarily be corrective in its character, adapted to counteract and redress the operation of such prohibited state laws or proceedings of state officers.

If the principles of interpretation which we have laid down are correct, as we deem them to be, and they are in accord with the principles laid down in the cases before referred to, as well as in the recent case of U. S. v. Harris [ante, 290], decided at the last Term of this court, it is clear that the law in question cannot be sustained by any grant of legislative power made to Congress by the 14th Amendment. That Amendment prohibits the States from denying to any person the equal protection of the laws, and declares that Congress shall have power to enforce, by appropriate legislation, the provisions of the Amendment. The law in question, without any reference to adverse state legislation on the subject, declares that all persons shall be entitled to equal accommodations and privileges of inns, public conveyances and places of public amusement, and imposes a penalty upon any individual who shall deny to any citizen such equal accommodations and privileges. This is not corrective legislation; it is primary and direct; it takes immediate and absolute possession of the subject of the right of admission to inns, public conveyances and places of amusement. It supersedes and displaces state legislation on the same subject, or only allows it permissive force. It ignores such legislation, and assumes that the matter is one that belongs to the domain of national regulation. Whether it would not have been a more effective protection of the rights of citizens to have clothed Congress with plenary power over the whole subject, is not now the question. What we have to decide is, whether such plenary power has been conferred upon Congress by the 14th Amendment; and, in our judgment, it has not. . . .

It may be that, by the Black Code, as it was called, in the times when slavery prevailed, the proprietors of inns and public conveyances were forbidden to receive persons of the African race, because it might assist slaves to escape from the control of their masters. This was merely a means of preventing such escapes, and was no part of the servitude itself. A law of that kind could not have any such object now, however justly it might be deemed an invasion of the party's legal right as a citizen, and amenable to the prohibitions of the 14th Amendment.

The long existence of African slavery in this country gave us very distinct notions of what it was, and what were its necessary incidents. Compulsory service of the slave for the benefit of the master, restraint of his movements except by the master's will, disability to hold property, to make contracts, to have a standing in court, to be a witness against a white person, and such like burdens and incapacities were the inseparable incidents of the institution. Severer punishments for crimes were imposed on the slave than on free persons guilty of the same offenses. Congress, as we have seen, by the Civil Rights Bill of 1866, passed in view of the 13th Amendment, before 14th was adopted, undertook to wipe out these burdens and disabilities, the necessary incidents of slavery, constituting its substance and visible form; and to secure to all citizens of every race and color, and without regard to previous servitude, those fundamental rights which are the essence of civil freedom, namely: the same right to make and enforce contracts, to sue, be parties, give evidence, and to inherit, purchase, lease, sell and convey property, as is enjoined by white citizens. Whether this legislation was fully authorized by the 13th Amendment alone, without the support which it afterwards received from the 14th Amendment, after the adoption of which it was re-enacted with some additions, it is not necessary to inquire. It is referred to for the purpose of showing that at that time, in 1866, Congress did not assume, under the authority given by the 13th Amendment, to adjust what may be called the social rights of men and races in the community; but only to declare and vindicate those fundamental rights which appertain to the essence of citizenship, and the enjoyment or deprivation of which constitutes the essential distinction between freedom and slavery.

We must not forget that the province and scope of the 13th and 14th Amendments are different; the former simply abolished slavery; the latter prohibited the States from abridging the privileges or immunities of citizens of the United States, by depriving them of life, liberty or property without due process of law, and from denying to any the equal protection of the laws. The Amendments are different, and the powers of Congress under them are different. What Congress has power to do under one, it may not have power to do under the other. Under the 13th Amendment, it has only to do with slavery and its incidents. Under the 14th Amendment, it has power to counteract and render nugatory all state laws and proceedings which have the effect to abridge any of the privileges or immunities of citizens of the United States, or to deprive them of life, liberty or property without due process of law, or to deny to any of them the equal protection of the laws. Under the 13th Amendment, the legislation, so far as necessary or proper to eradicate all forms and incidents of slavery and involuntary servitude, may be direct and primary, operating upon the acts of individuals, whether sanctioned by state legislation or not; under the 14th, as we have already shown, it must necessarily be and can only be corrective in its character, addressed to counteract and afford relief against state regulations or proceedings.

The only question under the present head, therefore, is, whether the refusal to any persons of the accommodations of an inn or a public conveyance or a place of public amusement, by an individual and without any sanction or support from any state law or regulation, does inflict upon such persons any manner of servitude, or form of slavery, as those terms are understood in this country? Many wrongs may be obnoxious to the prohibitions of the 14th Amendment which are not, in any just sense, incidents or elements of slavery. Such, for example, would be the taking of private property without due process of law; or allowing persons who have committed certain crimes, horse stealing, for example, to be seized and hung by the *posse comitatus* without regular trial; or denying to any person or class of persons the right to pursue any peaceful avocations allowed to others. What is called "class legislation" would belong to this category, and would be obnoxious to the prohibitions of the 14th Amendment, but would not necessarily be so to the 13th, when not involving the idea of any subjection of one man to another. The 13th Amendment has respect, not to distinctions of race or class or color, but to slavery. The 14th Amendment extends its protection to races and classes, and prohibits any state legislation which has the effect of denying to any race or class or to any individual, the equal protection of the laws.

Now, conceding, for the sake of the argument, that the admission to an inn, a public conveyance or a place of public amusement, on equal terms with all other citizens, is the right of every man and all classes of men, is it any more than one of those rights which the States by the 14th Amendment are forbidden to deny to any person? And is the Constitution violated until the denial of the right has some state sanction or authority? Can the act of a mere individual, the owner of the inn, the public conveyance or place of amusement, refusing the accommodation, be justly regarded as imposing any badge of slavery or servitude upon the applicant, or only as inflicting an ordinary civil injury, properly cognizable by the laws of the State, and presumably subject to redress by those laws until the contrary appears?

After giving to these questions all the consideration which their importance demands, we are forced to the conclusion that such an act of refusal has nothing to do with slavery or involuntary servitude, and that if it is violative of any right of the party, his redress is to be sought under the laws of the State; or if those laws are adverse to his rights and do not protect him, his remedy will be found in the corrective legislation which Congress has adopted, or may adopt, for counteracting the effect of state laws, or state action, prohibited by the 14th Amendment. It would be running the slavery argument into the ground, to make it apply to every act of discrimination which a person may see fit to make as to the guests he will entertain, or as to the people he will take into his coach or cab or car, or admit to his concert or theater, or deal with in other matters of intercourse or business. Innkeepers and public carriers, by the laws of all the States, so far as we are aware, are bound, to the extent of their facilities, to furnish proper accommodation to all unobjectionable persons who in good faith apply for them. If the laws themselves make any unjust discrimination, amenable to the prohibitions of the 14th Amendment, Congress has full power to afford a remedy, under that Amendment and in accordance with it.

When a man has emerged from slavery, and by the aid of beneficent legislation has shaken off the inseparable concomitants of that state, there must be some stage in the progress of his elevation when he takes the rank of a mere citizen, and ceases to be the special favorite of the laws, and when his rights, as a citizen or a man, are to be protected in the ordinary modes by which other men's rights are protected. There were thousands of free colored people in this country before the abolition of slavery, enjoying all the essential rights of life, liberty and property the same as white citizens; yet no one, at that time, thought that it was any invasion of their personal *status* as freemen because they were not admitted to all the privileges enjoyed by white citizens, or because they were subjected to discriminations in the enjoyment of accommodations in inns, public conveyances and places of amusement. Mere discriminations on account of race or color were not regarded as badges of slavery. If, since that time, the enjoyment of equal rights in all these respects has become established by constitutional enactment, it is not by force of the 13th Amendment, which merely abolishes slavery, but by force of the 14th and 15th Amendments.

On the whole we are of opinion, that no countenance of authority for the passage of the law in question can be found in either the 13th or 14th Amendment of the Constitution; and no other ground of authority for its passage being suggested, it must necessarily be declared void, at least so far as its operation in the several States is concerned. . . .

*Mr. Justice* **Harlan** dissenting:

The opinion in these cases proceeds, it seems to me, upon grounds entirely too narrow and artificial. I cannot resist the conclusion that the substance and spirit of the recent Amendments of the Constitution have been sacrificed by a subtle and ingenious verbal criticism. "It is not the words of the law but the internal sense of it that makes the law; the letter of the law is the body; the sense and reason of the law is the soul." Constitutional provisions, adopted in the interest of liberty, and for the purpose of securing, through national legislation, if need be, rights inhering in a state of freedom, and belonging to American citizenship, have been so construed as to defeat the ends the people desired to accomplish, which they attempted to accomplish, and which they supposed they had accomplished by changes in their fundamental law. By this I do not mean that the determination of these cases should have been materially controlled by considerations of mere expediency or policy. I mean only, in this form, to express an earnest conviction that the court has departed from the familiar rule requiring, in the interpretation of constitutional provisions, that full effect be given to the intent with which they were adopted.

The purpose of the 1st section of the Act of Congress of March 1, 1875, was to prevent race discrimination in respect of the accommodations and facilities of inns, public conveyances and places of public amusement. It does not assume to define the general conditions and limitations under which inns, public conveyances and places of public amusement may be conducted, but only declares that such conditions and limitations, whatever they may be, shall not be applied so as to work a discrimination solely because of race, color or previous condition of servitude. The 2d section provides a penalty against any one denying, or aiding or inciting the denial, to any citizen, of that equality of right given by the 1st section, except for reasons by law applicable to citizens of every race or color and regardless of any previous condition of servitude.

There seems to be no substantial difference between my brethren and myself as to the purpose of Congress; for, they say that the essence of the law is, not to declare broadly that all persons shall be entitled to the full and equal enjoyment of the accommodations, advantages, facilities and privileges of inns, public conveyances and theaters; but that such enjoyment shall not be subject to conditions applicable only to citizens of a particular race or color, or who had been in a previous condition of servitude. The effect of the statute, the court says, is, that colored citizens, whether formerly slaves or not, and citizens of other races, shall have the same accommodations and privileges in all inns, public conveyances and places of amusement as are enjoyed by white persons; and *vice versa*.

The court adjudges, I think erroneously, that Congress is without power, under either the 13th or 14th Amendment, to establish such regulations, and that the 1st and 2d sections of the statute are, in all their parts, unconstitutional and void.

Whether the legislative department of the government has transcended the limits of its constitutional powers, "Is at all times," said this court in *Fletcher* v. *Peck,* 6 Cranch, 128, "a question of much delicacy, which ought seldom, if ever, to be decided in the affirmative, in a doubtful case. . . . The opposition between the Constitution and the law should be such that the judge feels a clear and strong conviction of their incompatibility with each other." More recently in *Sinking Fund Cases,* 99 U. S., 718, we said: "It is our duty, when required in the regular course of judicial proceedings, to declare an Act of Congress void if not within the legislative power of the United States, but this declaration should never be made except in a clear case. Every possible presumption is in favor of the validity of a statute, and this continues until the contrary is shown beyond a rational doubt. One branch of the government cannot encroach on the domain of another without danger. The safety of our institutions depends in no small degree on a strict observance of this salutary rule."

Before considering the language and scope of these Amendments it will be proper to recall the relations subsisting, prior to their adoption, between the National Government and the institution of slavery, as indicated by the provisions of the Constitution, the legislation of Congress, and the decisions of this court. In this mode we may obtain keys with which to open the mind of the people, and discover the thought intended to be expressed.

In section 2 of article IV. of the Constitution it was provided that "No person held to service or labor in one State, under the laws thereof, escaping into another, shall, in consequence of any law or regulation therein, be discharged from such service or labor, but shall be delivered up on claim of the party to whom such service or labor may be due." Under the authority of this clause, Congress passed the Fugitive Slave Law of 1793, establishing a mode for the recovery of fugitive slaves, and prescribing a penalty against any person who should knowingly and willingly obstruct or hinder the master, his agent, or attorney, in seizing, arresting and recovering the fugitive, or who should rescue the fugitive from him, or who should harbor or conceal the slave after notice that he was a fugitive.

In *Prigg* v. *Commonwealth of Pennsylvania*, 16 Pet., 539, this court had occasion to define the powers and duties of Congress in reference to fugitives from labor. Speaking by *Mr. Justice Story* it laid down these propositions:

That a clause of the Constitution conferring a right should not be so construed as to make it shadowy, or unsubstantial, or leave the citizen without a remedial power adequate for its protection, when another construction equally accordant with the words and sense in which they were used, would enforce and protect the right granted;

That Congress is not restricted to legislation for the execution of its expressly granted powers; but, for the protection of rights guarantied by the Constitution, may employ such means, not prohibited, as are necessary and proper, or such as are appropriate, to attain the ends proposed;

That the Constitution recognized the master's right of property in his fugitive slave and, as incidental thereto, the right of seizing and recovering him, regardless of any state law, or regulation, or local custom whatsoever; and,

That the right of the master to have his slave, thus escaping, delivered up on claim, being guarantied by the Constitution, the fair implication was that the National Government was clothed with appropriate authority and functions to enforce it.

The court said: "The fundamental principle, applicable
to all cases of this sort, would seem to be that when the end
is required the means are given, and when the duty is enjoined the ability to perform it is contemplated to exist on
the part of the functionary to whom it is intrusted." Again:
"It would be a strange anomaly and forced construction to
suppose that the National Government meant to rely for
the due fulfillment of its own proper duties, and the rights
which it intended to secure, upon state legislation, and not
upon that of the Union. *A fortiori,* it would be more objectionable to suppose that a power which was to be the same
throughout the Union, should be confided to state sovereignty which could not rightfully act beyond its own territorial limits."

The Act of 1793 was, upon these grounds, adjudged to be
a constitutional exercise of the powers of Congress.

It is to be observed from the report of *Priggs' Case* that
Pennsylvania, by her Attorney-General, pressed the argument that the obligation to surrender fugitive slaves was on
the States and for the States, subject to the restriction that
they should not pass laws or establish regulations liberating
such fugitives; that the Constitution did not take from the
States the right to determine the *status* of all persons within
their respective jurisdictions; that it was for the State in
which the alleged fugitive was found to determine, through
her courts or in such modes as she prescribed, whether the
person arrested was, in fact, a freeman or a fugitive slave;
that the sole power of the General Government in the
premises was, by judicial instrumentality, to restrain and
correct, not to forbid and prevent in the absence of hostile
state action; and that for the General Government to assume primary authority to legislate on the subject of fugitive slaves, to the exclusion of the States, would be a
dangerous encroachment on state sovereignty. But to such
suggestions this court turned a deaf ear, and adjudged that
primary legislation by Congress to enforce the master's
right was authorized by the Constitution.

We next come to the Fugitive Slave Act of 1850, the constitutionality of which rested, as did that of 1793, solely
upon the implied power of Congress to enforce the master's rights. The provisions of that Act were far in advance
of previous legislation. They placed at the disposal of the

master seeking to recover his fugitive slave, substantially the whole power of the Nation. It invested commissioners, appointed under the Act, with power to summon the *posse comitatus* for the enforcement of its provisions, and commanded all good citizens to assist in its prompt and efficient execution whenever their services were required as part of the *posse comitatus*. Without going into the details of that Act, it is sufficient to say that Congress omitted from it nothing which the utmost ingenuity could suggest as essential to the successful enforcement of the master's claim to recover his fugitive slave. And this court, in *Ableman* v. *Booth*, 21 How., 506 [62 U.S., XVI., 169], adjudged it to be "in all of its provisions fully authorized by the Constitution of the United States."

The only other case, prior to the adoption of the recent amendments, to which reference will be made, is that of *Dred Scott* v. *Sandford*, 19 How. 399[60 U.S., XV., 663]. That case was instituted in a Circuit Court of the United States by Dred Scott, claiming to be a citizen of Missouri, the defendant being a citizen of another State. Its object was to assert the title of himself and family to freedom. The defendant pleaded in abatement that Scott—being of African descent, whose ancestors, of pure African blood, were brought into this country and sold as slaves—was not a *citizen*. The only matter in issue, said the court, was whether the descendants of slaves thus imported and sold, when they should be emancipated, or who were born of parents who had become free before their birth, are citizens of a State in the sense in which the word "citizen" is used in the Constitution of the United States.

In determining that question, the court instituted an inquiry as to who were citizens of the several States at the adoption of the Constitution, and who, at that time, were recognized as the people whose rights and liberties had been violated by the British Government. The result was a declaration by this court, speaking by *Chief Justice Taney*, that the legislation and histories of the times and the language used in the Declaration of Independence, showed "That neither the class of persons who had been imported as slaves, nor their descendants, whether they had become free or not, were then acknowledged as a part of the people, nor intended to be included in the general words used in that instrument;" that "they had for more than a century before been regarded as beings of an inferior race, and altogether unfit to associate with the white race, either in social or political relations, and so far inferior that they had no rights which the white man was bound to respect, and that the negro might justly and lawfully be reduced to slavery for his benefit;" that he was "bought and sold, and treated as an ordinary article of merchandise and traffic, whenever a profit could be made by it;" and that "this opinion was at that time fixed and universal in the civilized portion of the white race. It was regarded as an axiom in morals as well as in politics, which no one thought of disputing, or supposed to be open to dispute; and men in every grade and position in society daily and habitually acted upon it in their private pursuits, as well as in matters of public concern, without for a moment doubting the correctness of this opinion."

The judgment of the court was that the words "people of the United States" and "citizens" meant the same thing, both describing "the political body who, according to our republican institutions, form the sovereignty and hold the power and conduct the government through their representatives;" that "they are what we familiarly call the 'sovereign people,' and every citizen is one of this people and a constituent member of this sovereignty;" but, that the class of persons described in the plea in abatement did not compose a portion of this people, were not "included, and were not intended to be included, under the word 'citizens' in the Constitution;" that, therefore, they could "claim none of the rights and privileges which that instrument provides for and secures to citizens of the United States;" that, "on the contrary, they were at the time considered as a subordinate and inferior class of beings, who had been subjugated by the dominant race, and whether emancipated or not, yet remained subject to their authority and had no rights or privileges but such as those who held the power, and the government might choose to grant them."

Such were the relations which formerly existed between the government, whether national or state, and the descendants, whether free or in bondage, or those of African blood, who had been imported into this country and sold as slaves.

The 1st section of the 13th Amendment provides that "Neither slavery nor involuntary servitude, except as a punishment for crime, whereof the party shall have been duly convicted, shall exist within the United States, or any place subject to their jurisdiction." Its 2d section declares that "Congress shall have power to enforce this article by appropriate legislation." This Amendment was followed by the Civil Rights Act of April 9, 1866, which, among other things, provided that "All persons born in the United States, and not subject to any foreign power, excluding Indians not taxed, are hereby declared to be citizens of the United States." 14 Stat. at L., 27. The power of Congress, in this mode, to elevate the enfranchised race to national citizenship, was maintained by the supporters of the Act of 1866 to be as full and complete as its power, by general statute, to make the children, being of full age, of persons naturalized in this country, citizens of the United States without going through the process of naturalization. The Act of 1866, in this respect, was also likened to that of 1843, in which Congress declared "That the Stockbridge Tribe of Indians, and each and every one of them, shall be deemed to be and are hereby declared to be citizens of the United States to all intents and purposes, and shall be entitled to all the rights, privileges and immunities of such citizens, and shall in all respects be subject to the laws of the United States." If the Act of 1866 was valid in conferring national citizenship upon all embraced by its terms, then the colored race, enfranchised by the 13th Amendment, became citizens of the United States prior to the adoption of the 14th Amendment. But, in the view which I take of the present case, it is not necessary to examine this question.

The terms of the Thirteenth Amendment are absolute and universal. They embrace every race which then was, or might thereafter be, within the United States. No race, as such, can be excluded from the benefits or rights thereby conferred. Yet, it is historically true that that Amendment was suggested by the condition, in this country, of that race which had been declared, by this court, to have had—according to the opinion entertained by the most civilized portion of the white race, at the time of the adoption of the Constitution—"no rights which the white man was bound to respect," none of the privileges or immunities secured by that instrument to citizens of the United States. It had reference, in a peculiar sense, to a people which (although the larger part of them were in slavery) had been invited by an Act of Congress to aid in saving from overthrow a government which, theretofore, by all of its departments, had treated them as an inferior race, with no legal rights or privileges except such as the white race might choose to grant them.

These are the circumstances under which the Thirteenth Amendment was proposed for adoption. They are now recalled only that we may better understand what was in the minds of the people when that Amendment was considered, and what were the mischiefs to be remedied and the grievances to be redressed by its adoption,

We have seen that the power of Congress, by legislation, to enforce the master's right to have his slave delivered up on claim was *implied* from the recognition of that right in the National Constitution. But the power conferred by the Thirteenth Amendment does not rest upon implication or inference. Those who framed it were not ignorant of the discussion, covering many years of our country's history, as to the constitutional power of Congress to enact the Fugitive Slave Laws of 1793 and 1850. When, therefore, it was determined, by a change in the fundamental law, to uproot the institution of slavery wherever it existed in the land, and to establish universal freedom, there was a fixed purpose to place the authority of Congress in the premises beyond the possibility of a doubt. Therefore, *ex industria,* power to enforce the Thirteenth Amendment, by appropriate legislation, was expressly granted. Legislation for that purpose, my brethren concede, may be direct and primary. But to what specific ends may it be directed? This court has uniformly held that the National Government has the power, whether expressly given or not, to secure and protect rights conferred or guarantied by the Constitution. *U.S.* v. *Reese,* 92 U. S., 214 [XXIII., 563]; *Strauder* v. *W. Va.,* 100 U. S., 303 [XXV., 664]. That doctrine ought not now to be abandoned when the inquiry is not as to an implied power to protect the master's rights, but what may Congress, under powers expressly granted, do for the protection of freedom and the rights necessarily inhering in a state of freedom.

The 13th Amendment, it is conceded, did something more than to prohibit slavery as an *institution*, resting upon distinctions of race, and upheld by positive law. My brethren admit that it established and decreed universal *civil freedom* throughout the United States. But did the freedom thus established involve nothing more than exemption from actual slavery? Was nothing more intended than to forbid one man from owning another as property? Was it the purpose of the Nation simply to destroy the institution, and then remit the race, theretofore held in bondage, to the several States for such protection, in their civil rights, necessarily growing out of freedom, as those States, in their discretion, might choose to provide? Were the States against whose protest the institution was destroyed, to be left free, so far as national interference was concerned, to make or allow discriminations against that race, as such, in the enjoyment of those fundamental rights which by universal concession, inhere in a state of freedom? Had the 13th Amendment stopped with the sweeping declaration, in its 1st section, against the existence of slavery and involuntary servitude, except for crime, Congress would have had the power, by implication, according to the doctrines of *Prigg* v. *Commonwealth of Pennsylvania,* repeated in *Strauder* v. *West Virginia,* to protect the freedom established and, consequently, to secure the enjoyment of such civil rights as were fundamental in freedom. That it can exert its authority to that extent is made clear, and was intended to be made clear, by the express grant of power contained in the 2d section of the Amendment.

That there are burdens and disabilities which constitute badges of slavery and servitude, and that the power to enforce by appropriate legislation the 13th Amendment may be exerted by legislation of a direct and primary character, for the eradication, not simply of the institution, but of its badges and incidents, are propositions which ought to be deemed indisputable. They lie at the foundation of the Civil Rights Act of 1866. Whether that Act was authorized by the 13th Amendment alone, without the support which it subsequently received from the 14th Amendment, after the adoption of which it was re-enacted with some additions, my brethren do not consider it necessary to inquire. But I submit, with all respect to them, that its constitutionality is conclusively shown by their opinion. . . .

I am of the opinion that such discrimination practiced by corporations and individuals in the exercise of their public or *quasi* public functions is a badge of servitude, the imposition of which Congress may prevent under its power, by appropriate legislation, to enforce the 13th Amendment; and, consequently, without reference to its enlarged power under the 14th Amendment, the Act of March 1, 1875, is not, in my judgment, repugnant to the Constitution.

It remains now to consider these cases with reference to the power Congress has possessed since the adoption of the 14th Amendment. Much that has been said as to the power of Congress under the 13th Amendment is applicable to this branch of the discussion, and will not be repeated.

Before the adoption of the recent Amendments, it had become, as we have seen, the established doctrine of this court that negroes, whose ancestors had been imported and sold as slaves, could not become citizens of a State, or even of the United States, with the rights and privileges guaranteed to citizens by the national Constitution; further, that one might have all the rights and privileges of a citizen of a State without being a citizen in the sense in which that word was used in the national Constitution, and without being entitled to the privileges and immunities of citizens of the several States. Still further, between the adoption of the 13th Amendment and the proposal by Congress of the 14th Amendment, on June 16, 1866, the statute books of several of the States, as we have seen, had become loaded down with enactments which, under the guise of Apprentice, Vagrant, and contract regulations, sought to keep the colored race in a condition, practically, of servitude. It was openly announced that whatever might be the rights which persons of that race had as freemen, under the guarantees of the national Constitution, they could not become citizens of a State, with the privileges belonging to citizens, except by the consent of such State; consequently, that their civil rights as citizens of the State depended entirely upon State legislation. To meet this new peril to the black race, that the purposes of the nation might not be doubted or defeated, and by way of further enlargement of the power of Congress, the 14th Amendment was proposed for adoption.

Remembering that this court, in the *Slaughterhouse Cases,* declared that the one pervading purpose found in all the recent amendments, lying at the foundation of each and without which none of them would have been suggested, was

> the freedom of the slave race, the security and firm
> establishment of that freedom, and the protection
> of the newly made freeman and citizen from the
> oppression of those who had formerly exercised
> unlimited dominion over him

—that each amendment was addressed primarily to the grievances of that race—let us proceed to consider the language of the 14th Amendment.

Its first and fifth sections are in these words:

> SEC. 1. All persons born or naturalized in the
> United States, and subject to the jurisdiction
> thereof, are citizens of the United States and of the
> State wherein they reside. No State shall make or
> enforce any law which shall abridge the privileges
> or immunities of citizens of the United States; nor
> shall any State deprive any person of life, liberty, or
> property, without due process of law; nor deny to
> any person within its jurisdiction the equal protec-
> tion of the laws. . . .

> SEC. 5. That Congress shall have power to enforce,
> by appropriate legislation, the provisions of this ar-
> ticle.

It was adjudged in *Strauder v. West Virginia*, 100 U.S. 303, and *Ex parte Virginia*, 100 U.S. 339, and my brethren concede, that positive rights and privileges were intended to be secured, and are, in fact, secured, by the 14th Amendment.

But when, under what circumstances, and to what extent may Congress, by means of legislation, exert its power to enforce the provisions of this amendment? The theory of the opinion of the majority of the court—the foundation upon which their reasoning seems to rest—is that the general government cannot, in advance of hostile state laws or hostile state proceedings, actively interfere for the protection of any of the rights, privileges and immunities secured by the 14th Amendment. It is said that such rights, privileges and immunities are secured by way of *prohibition* against state laws and state proceedings affecting such rights and privileges, and by power given to Congress to legislate for the purpose of carrying *such prohibition* into effect; also, that congressional legislation must necessarily be predicated upon such supposed state laws or state proceedings, and be directed to the correction of their operation and effect.

In illustration of its position, the court refers to the clause of the Constitution forbidding the passage by a State of any law impairing the obligation of contracts. That clause does not, I submit, furnish a proper illustration of the scope and effect of the 5th section of the 14th Amendment. No express power is given Congress to enforce, by primary direct legislation, the prohibition upon state laws impairing the obligation of contracts. Authority is, indeed, conferred to enact all necessary and proper laws for carrying into execution the enumerated powers of Congress and all other powers vested by the Constitution in the Government of the United States or in any department or officer thereof. And, as heretofore shown, there is also, by necessary implication, power in Congress, by legislation, to protect a right derived from the National Constitution. But a prohibition upon a State is not a *power* in *Congress* or *in the National Government*. It is simply a *denial* of *power* to the *State*. And the only mode in which the inhibition upon state laws impairing the obligation of contracts can be enforced, is, indirectly, through the courts, in suits where the parties raise some question as to the constitutional validity of such laws. The judicial power of the United States extends to such suits for the reason that they are suits arising under the Constitution. The 14th Amendment presents the first instance in our history of the investiture of Congress with affirmative power, by *legislation*, to *enforce* an express prohibition upon the States. It is not said that the *judicial* power of the Nation may be exerted for the enforcement of that Amendment. No enlargement of the judicial power was required, for it is clear that had the 5th section of the 14th Amendment been entirely omitted the judiciary could have stricken down all state laws and nullified all state proceedings in hostility to rights and privileges secured or recognized by that Amendment. The power given is in terms, by congressional *legislation*, to enforce the provisions of the Amendment.

The assumption that this Amendment consists wholly of prohibitions upon state laws and state proceedings in hostility to its provisions, is unauthorized by its language. The first clause of the 1st section — "All persons born or naturalized in the United States, and subject to the jurisdiction thereof, are citizens of the United States, and of the State wherein they reside" — is of a distinctly affirmative character. In its application to the colored race, previously liberated, it created and granted, as well citizenship of the United States, as citizenship of the State in which they respectively resided. It introduced all of that race, whose ancestors had been imported and sold as slaves, at once, into the political community known as the "People of the United States." They became, instantly, citizens of the United States, *and* of their respective States. Further, they were brought, by this supreme act of the Nation, within the direct operation of that provision of the Constitution which declares that "The citizens of each State shall be entitled to all privileges and immunities of citizens in the several States." Art. 4, sec. 2.

The citizenship thus acquired, by that race, in virtue of an affirmative grant from the Nation, may be protected, not alone by the judicial branch of the government, but by congressional legislation of a primary direct character; this, because the power of Congress is not restricted to the enforcement of prohibitions upon state laws or state action. It is, in terms distinct and positive, to enforce "the *provisions of this article*" of Amendment; not simply those of a prohibitive character, but the provisions — *all* of the provisions — affirmative and prohibitive, of the Amendment. It is, therefore, a grave misconception to suppose that the 5th section of the Amendment has reference exclusively to express prohibitions upon state laws or state action. If any right was created by that Amendment, the grant of power, through appropriate legislation, to enforce its provisions, authorizes Congress, by means of legislation, operating throughout the entire Union, to guard, secure and protect that right.

It is, therefore, an essential inquiry what, if any, right, privilege or immunity was given, by the Nation, to colored persons, when they were made citizens of the State in which they reside? Did the constitutional grant of state citizenship to that race, of its own force, invest them with any rights, privileges and immunities whatever? That they became entitled, upon the adoption of the 14th Amendment, "to all privileges and immunities of citizens in the several States," within the meaning of section 2 of article 4 of the Constitution, no one, I suppose, will for a moment question. What are the privileges and immunities to which by that clause of the Constitution they became entitled? To this it may be answered, generally, upon the authority of the adjudged cases, that they are those which are fundamental in citizenship in a free republican government, such as are "common to the citizens in the latter States under their constitutions and laws by virtue of their being citizens." Of that provision it has been said, with the approval of this court, that no other one in the Constitution has tended so strongly to constitute the citizens of the United States one people. *Ward* v. *Maryland*, 12 Wall., 418; *Corfield* v. *Coryell*, 4 Wash. C. C., 871; *Paul* v. *Va.*, 8 Wall., 168; *Slaughter-House Cases*, 16 Id., 36.

Although this court has wisely forborne any attempt, by a comprehensive definition, to indicate all of the privileges and immunities to which the citizen of a State is entitled, of right, when within the jurisdiction of other States, I hazard nothing, in view of former adjudications, in saying that no State can sustain her denial to colored citizens of other States, while within her limits, of privileges or immunities, fundamental in republican citizenship, upon the ground that she accords such privileges and immunities only to her white citizens and withholds them from her colored citizens. The colored citizens of other States, within the jurisdiction of that State, could claim, in virtue of section 2 of article 4 of the Constitution, every privilege and immunity which that State secures to her white citizens. Otherwise, it would be in the power of any State, by discriminating class legislation against its own citizens of a particular race or color, to withhold from citizens of other States, belonging to that proscribed race when within her limits, privileges and immunities of the character regarded by all courts as fundamental in citizenship; and that, too, when the constitutional guaranty is that the citizens of each State shall be entitled to "all privileges and immunities of citizens of the several States." No State may, by discrimination against a portion of its own citizens of a particular race, in respect of privileges and immunities fundamental in citizenship, impair the constitutional right of citizens of other States, of whatever race, to enjoy in that State all such privileges and immunities as are there accorded to her most favored citizens. A colored citizen of Ohio or Indiana, while in the jurisdiction of Tennessee, is entitled to enjoy any privilege or immunity, fundamental in citizenship, which is given to citizens of the white race in the latter State. It is not to be supposed that anyone will controvert this proposition.

But what was secured to colored citizens of the United States—as between them and their respective States—by the national grant to them of state citizenship? With what rights, privileges or immunities did this grant invest them? There is one, if there be no other: exemption from race discrimination in respect of any civil right belonging to citizens of the white race in the same State. That, surely, is their constitutional privilege when within the jurisdiction of other States. And such must be their constitutional right, in their own State, unless the recent Amendments be splendid baubles, thrown out to delude those who deserved fair and generous treatment at the hands of the Nation. Citizenship in this country necessarily imports at least equality of civil rights among citizens of every race in the same State. It is fundamental in American citizenship that, in respect of such rights, there shall be no discrimination by the State or its officers, or by individuals or corporations exercising public functions or authority, against any citizen because of his race or previous condition of servitude. . . .

My brethren say, that when a man has emerged from slavery, and by the aid of beneficent legislation has shaken off the inseparable concomitants of that state, there must be some stage in the progress of his elevation when he takes the rank of a mere citizen, and ceases to be the special favorite of the laws, and when his rights as a citizen, or a man, are to be protected in the ordinary modes by which other men's rights are protected. It is, I submit, scarcely just to say that the colored race has been the special favorite of the laws. The Statute of 1875, now adjudged to be unconstitutional, is for the benefit of citizens of every race and color. What the Nation, through Congress, has sought to accomplish in reference to that race, is—what had already been done in every State of the Union for the white race—to secure and protect rights belonging to them as freemen and citizens; nothing more. It was not deemed enough "to help the feeble up, but to support him after." The one underlying purpose of congressional legislation has been to enable the black race to take the rank of mere citizens. The difficulty has been to compel a recognition of the legal right of the black race to take the rank of citizens, and to secure the enjoyment of privileges belonging, under the law, to them as a component part of the people for whose welfare and happiness government is ordained. At every step, in this direction, the Nation has been confronted with class tyranny, which a contemporary English historian says is, of all tyrannies, the most intolerable, "For it is ubiquitous in its operation, and weighs, perhaps, most heavily on those whose obscurity or distance would withdraw them from the notice of a single despot." Today, it is the colored race which is denied, by corporations and individuals wielding public authority, rights fundamental in their freedom and citizenship. At some future time, it may be that some other race will fall under the ban of race discrimination. If the constitutional Amendments be enforced, according to the intent with which, as I conceive, they were adopted, there cannot be in this Republic, any class of human beings in practical subjection to another class, with power in the latter to dole out to the former just such privileges as they may choose to grant. The supreme law of the land has decreed that no authority shall be exercised in this country upon the basis of discrimination, in respect of civil rights, against freeman and citizens because of their race, color or previous condition of servitude. To that decree—for the condition of servitude. To that decree—for the due enforcement of which, by appropriate legislation, Congress has been invested with express power—every one must bow, whatever may have been, or whatever now are, his individual views as to the wisdom or policy, either of the recent changes in the fundamental law, or of the legislation which has been enacted to give them effect.

For the reasons stated I feel constrained to withhold my assent to the opinion of the court.

# WASHINGTON LAFAYETTE CLAYTON, *OLDEN TIMES REVISITED*

## *(1906)*

Washington Lafayette Clayton (1836–1921) was born in Jefferson, Alabama, but migrated with his family to Itawamba County, Mississippi, during the 1840s. He lived in Fulton and later moved to Tupelo, in Lee County, working as a circuit-riding lawyer with a keen eye for detail and local color. Early in the twentieth century, Clayton published several autobiographical articles in the *Tupelo Journal* chronicling the social history of northeastern Mississippi during Reconstruction. His historical memory of the period conforms to what historian David W. Blight termed "the white supremacist vision" of the Civil War era, which "by the turn of the century delivered the country a segregated memory" of the conflict "on Southern terms." Clayton, for example, portrayed the freedmen as gullible, ignorant, ungrateful, yet wily. He believed that carpetbaggers, scalawags, and ex-slaves betrayed his fellow white Mississippians. Military rule and self-assertion by the freedpeople were odious, he recalled. The blacks, in his opinion, "kept moving from bad to worse." In his final article, Clayton detailed the nonviolent means whites employed to trick and intimidate black voters. "This took place throughout the state," he said, seemingly with pride, "and the Republican party was put out of business in Mississippi."

When the war of 1861 had closed and the survivors of the army returned to their homes, they found many changes had taken place in their absence, and especially was this noticeable in the border land of the country. In the first place, all property in slaves was destroyed, and the supply of horses and mules had been reduced very much. Such a thing as a good saddle horse or a good wagon mule could not be found, unless they had been hidden out, and this was a very dangerous thing to do. Some enemy or slave would be almost sure to point out the hiding place of the stock, and if the enemy came, he took them, and if the friend happened along, he impressed them for service, and in either event, the stock was gone and the owner none the better off, as the scrip given by the friend proved of no more value toward the last than the want of it by the enemy. To the everlasting credit of the negroes it must be said that they were so far loyal to their owners as a general thing that they remained at home and worked faithfully, and in many instances had the care and possession of the entire interests of their master's farms and stock, and were ever ready to do and suffer whatever might be required for the interest of their owners.

After the war in all the thinly settled slave districts, like North Mississippi, they still remained at home and finished the crops before they were turned loose as free. I have often thought that as the slaves assembled round the cabin hearths in the days succeeding the close of the war and before the time of their final release, they had wonderful reasonings among themselves as to what would be the outcome of the war to them. You must remember that they could neither read nor write, and only in a few instances had anyone explained to them that Lincoln had issued his proclamation freeing them, and as we went on with our work as formerly, they must have endeavored often to peer into wonderland to find what it would bring to them. And yet how cautious they must have been, because of the fear of punishment. They had not yet learned that they were no longer in fear of the Patrolers if they failed to carry a pass from their owners, and consequently had not moved about much. I remember very well that our slaves were just as obedient and worked as well during the making of the crop of 1865 as they had ever been and done. So one morning after the crop was completed, I said to my father, "Father, I think we had better tell our negroes they are free and have a right to go where they please." He agreed it was the course to take, and we called them up and told them of their right to go or remain as they might choose, and that they were as free as we were, and I think we might have added, a little freer. And I assure you that the white women had the cooking to do that day, and many women who had never made a biscuit or fried ham and eggs, were forced to look into cookbooks to learn that which seemed to have come to the old black mammy by instinct.

But I want to tell you it did not take a lifetime for the poor ignorant negroes to learn the extent of their freedom and their rights thereunder. When they ascertained the fact that they had a right to stand and listen to a white man talk, and none dare molest or make them afraid, they took advantage of every opportunity to listen and to learn. And when the reconstruction measures were passed by Congress, they were not long in learning that the bottom rail was on top. I remember and shall never forget the wonderful influence any worthless carpetbagger had on them to the exclusion of all advice any of us might give. Some irresponsible fellow put it into their heads that every slave was to be given forty acres of land and a mule from the lands of the former slave owners, and having once taken root, it spread through the land of the South, and was generally believed.

Once upon a time one of these slick friends of the former slaves, and who had such wonderful influence over them, taking advantage of the ignorance and confidence of an old time darkey, meeting him on his former master's plantation, informing the old ex-slave that he was one of the men whom the government had appointed to measure off the aforesaid forty acres and give him a deed to it, and that another man would be round soon to assign and deliver him his mule with which to work it. So with glad heart and ready hand the old negro assisted the pretended official in making the measurement. When that was done, the old man wanted his deed, which was readily written and delivered on the payment to the swindler of $8.75, being all the money the old man had. Some days after this the old negro seemed more independent than usual, and began putting on airs of ownership when his former master said to him, "Dick, what's the matter with you? For some time you have been putting on airs like you owned the place." "Yes, sar, I does own part of de place." "How's that? What do you mean, you old fool?" "Well, sar, de guberment man jist comed round and measured me off my forty acres offen your land, and gived me a deed to it." Much astonished, but knowing some fraud had been practiced upon the old darkey, the owner asked to see the deed. Thereupon the old man handed out his supposed deed for the inspection of his former master, and the present landlord, and when held up to the light of intelligence, the old man was dumbfounded to hear the words read, "As Moses lifted up the serpent in the wilderness, so have I lifted this old darkey out of eight dollars and seventy-five cents. Selah!" It was said long, long time ago that "a fool and his money are soon parted," and this is especially true where gross ignorance and unbounded confidence [are] on one side and unscrupulousness on the other. But I have thought of all the villains known to mankind it is he who abuses the confidence reposed in him, and swindles under the guise of friendship. It puts me more in mind of the kiss with which our Saviour was betrayed than any with which I can compare it.

It was some years before the old darkey ceased saying, "Masser" when addressing a white man. Old Uncle Jim Hussey, a fine old time darkey, who lived and died near Mooresville in Lee county, Mississippi, kept up the habit of calling his old friends Masser till the time of his death. There was another peculiarity about Uncle Jim which I do not think applies to any other ex-slave in all this country, and that is that he always under all circumstances voted the Democratic ticket. In the darkest days of Mississippi, when the colored population marched to the polls in solid phalanx and voted in columns for the Republican party, Uncle Jim always from the very beginning and as long as he voted, put in his vote for the Democrats. He always said that as the colored people were living with the whites and largely dependent upon them, it did seem to him that what was to the interest of one race must be equally so for the other, and that as the white people were the more intelligent, it stood to reason that they would advocate and vote for those principles which would make for their betterment and consequently for the best interests of all.

He was a fine old character, as polite as a Chesterfield, and as kind hearted as any man I have ever met, white or black. He thought nothing of taking off his hat and bowing graciously to anyone whom he met from pure politeness.

But those kind are becoming fewer and fewer every year. If we had more such men as Uncle Jim, and fewer of the worthless and law-breaking class, the country would be better off.

Just what was heaped upon a proud and noble people here in the South after the war, none will ever know after this generation passes off the stage of action. We cannot write so succeeding generations can appreciate what we endured. The truth is that the South was settled by the chevaliers of England and their descendants, a proud and loyal people. In addition to this, they raised up what their enemies call a slave aristocracy, but which we thought of as agricultural kings, who lived on their plantations, surrounded by their slaves, managed generally by overseers, and dispensed hospitality like princes. Then we had the smaller slave-holders, nestled here and there amid these greater slave owners, and hoping to be larger owners of both slaves and land in the future, the most of those who did not own slaves hoped to do so some time in the future. There were really few of them of the renting class who aspired to no better situation in the financial world. The master owned his slaves, and when he said to one, "go," he went, and when he said to another, "do this," he did it. No questions were asked, but unquestioning obedience was the rule of the master. Not only this, but even those who did not own slaves, felt no hesitance in commanding them when about them as if they did own them. But when the reconstruction measures were enforced, all these ex-slaves were allowed to vote and hold office, while all the whites who had held any office, civil or military, in the United States, or in the different states, were disfranchised. As a general thing it was the custom to elevate to office our most intelligent and accomplished men; and so take the number who had held office, from the old men of eighty and the young men of twenty-one and all the way between, and there was a mighty host of our best men who could neither vote nor hold office under these infamous measures. Consequently, the negroes, just from the plow and the hoe, and having no learning, and in most instances no intelligence, took the offices and went to the capitals, to make laws for us. If a man is in bondage and has no desire for freedom and liberty of action and no aspirations for higher and loftier things, he may not suffer much from his condition, and especially when he has a kind and considerate master. But a proud, noble and intelligent people, like those of the South, to be subjected to such treatment as we received just after the war, was enough to cause more suffering and did cause more suffering than our slaves ever endured, mental suffering being so much worse than bodily suffering.

I myself was in Jackson, Mississippi when the legislature was in session during the seventies, and while there were not as many negroes then in the legislature as there had been, they very largely predominated. The Legislative Hall looked like a great dark cloud with a small white rift at the edge of it. You know I suggested some time back that it was quite probable that the negroes, just after the war, and before they were actually told by their owners that they might go free, had many whispered talks as to what the war would bring to them, being still under fear of their old owners.

The people of the South had seen much of sorrow and death during the war, and had been beaten and overpowered by numbers and forced to submit. Her brave and chivalrous sons were resting beneath the soil of the many battlefields on which they had sustained Her honor, or their bones were bleaching Her plains, where no friendly eye ever saw their forms after they fell. The military power of the United States, dotting town and hamlet, held the survivors in subjection. We were thus held beneath the rod and afraid to make a move for our release. You can understand, when you are told that many men came down from the North to lead these ignorant slaves and fatten on the South, why the Jews so much hated one of their own race who became a tax collector under the Roman Empire, to whom they were subjected in the time of our Saviour's sojourn on earth. Men will have to be different to what they now are before they can quietly and placidly see their enemies take their sustenance, make the laws by which they are to be governed and appoint over them their former slaves to execute such laws. Nothing restrained our people during those reconstruction days but the fear of the military power.

I remember very well how intense the feeling was against one, Flood, who was chief of the Registration Board at Fulton, where I then lived. That always was a white county, and it was almost impossible to restrain the boys from doing him some personal injury. He was a shrewd, unscrupulous adventurer, who came here, not to serve his country, but himself, and who ingratiated into the confidence of the negroes, and but for the fact that he feared the consequences of his conduct, would have remained there to try for office. But when the election was over by which the military constitution was adopted, he had seen enough to indicate to him that he might do better somewhere else. During the first campaign for the adoption or rejection of the constitution, which had been submitted to the people for ratification or rejection, I took a part in the speech making in opposition to the adoption. There were several features of that constitution which were so objectionable, that it failed of the necessary vote. Then the military authorities, who were in charge of the entire South, and who had all power, eliminated certain of those objectionable features, and the constitution for Mississippi was again submitted, with those features left off, and thus carried.

In that first campaign Eugene Whitfield ran for Congress on the Republican ticket, and was opposed by a little fellow from the North, who ran for the same office, but now opposed the adoption of the constitution, and whom I suspect was here after the "loaves and fishes," as well as Flood. His name has passed out of my mind. I remember to have made a speech at old Ryan's Wells, north of Fulton, during this campaign, and in which Whitfield and his opponent also spoke. There was a yankee driving Whitfield around over the campaign, against whom Whitfield's opponent seemed to have great feeling for some cause, and when he rose to make his speech in opposition to the constitution and Whitfield, I saw him place a cocked pistol in his hat behind where he stood to make his address, and I thought sure he was going to open in warm style on Whitfield. But when he began he said, "Gentlemen, I am not after Colonel Whitfield. He is a nice gentleman. But I am after his carriage driver." And from that he went for the carriage driver in the roughest manner I have ever heard anyone abused from the stump, but he opened not his mouth. It seems he was a Republican booster of Whitfield, and was carrying him through the campaign.

When we had defeated the first constitution, we really did not know whether to be sorry or glad. Those were perilous times, and we knew not what a day might bring forth. So while we were sure we had right yet, fearing what might be the next move of the powers at Washington, we were ill at loss. But it came out all right, and this is another illustration of the doctrine, "Do right and leave the consequences to God."

Many of us remember and will ne'r forget the days from 1865 to 1875, ten eventful years in the history of our Southland. Of course it is impossible to paint in true colors the events of those years. Being under military rule part of the time, and under military power all this time, which means the same thing as military rule practically, we could do nothing openly that would alleviate our condition. What we did in the way of relief measures had to be done on the sly. Young men were growing up who had never been in the war, but whose hands were itching to take hold of something by which they might signalize their entrance into life's arena by some action for the benefit and relief of their country and which might put a feather in their own caps that would in some degree look like they were worthy sons of worthy sires; and so they were ever ready to do anything which might be thought to even tend toward relief, and doubtless would have been guilty of many indiscretions but for the advice of older and wiser heads. But in the meantime the negroes kept moving from bad to worse, led on by unworthy and often trifling white men. Under these circumstances many devices were resorted to to checkmate their political moves. An old friend of mine, just before an election, happened to come into the possession of a Republican ticket. He showed it to some of the Democratic leaders in an adjoining county and they were delighted to get it, saying it was the very thing they had been endeavoring to secure for some time. You see, before the Democrats came into power and passed a law that no picture or device of any kind should be printed on any ballot by which it could be distinguished and that all ballots should be alike, the ignorant negroes knew their Republican ticket by the picture that headed it, and not by the names which were written thereon. You see how easy it was for the "leading politicians" on our side to duplicate the ticket, how easily these bogus tickets could be placed in the hands of the ignorant voters and how the count would show up on our side. Again, men did not scruple to take out the votes which were actually cast and substitute the Democratic ticket therefor, and ease their conscience by the thought that "all things are fair in war," and that the good of the country demanded this. Sometimes one means was used and sometimes others to accomplish such action. It was well known that the most of the leaders of the negroes, both white and black, were quite venal and ready for a bid in money to betray their party. By this means the ignorant voter was often deceived by his pretended friends, and made really to vote the Democratic ticket, when he thought he was voting for the other side. Sometimes the tickets were exchanged by the art of legerdemain, so to speak, and the innocent leader gave out the tickets which had been left in place of the genuine article. You see the picture was there all the same, and it was that by which they judged. But, after a few of such tricks had been played on them, they were more careful and some other scheme had to be resorted to. The rule of the black voter was always to line up in solid column at voting time. This was very distasteful to the white man. Many means were resorted to to break up this custom. Sometimes the whites came to the polls with their cannons on the ground, booming them once and awhile while the white men stood 'round, and some of them occasionally fired off pistols or guns. There was nothing said to the negroes about not voting as they might please, and no intimidation whatever, but all the same the cannons were boomed and guns and pistols fired, and the negroes ran off and left the polls and never came back to vote.

Finally, in 1875, the whites decided they had had enough of it, and it must stop in some way. It was managed differently in different places. In Lee county we had a meeting of prominent workers for the cause and it was decided that everybody should be on a committee to make a general and close canvass of the county one day before the election and press home to the negroes every argument we could to induce them to vote with us. I remember very well to have been in that canvass. We searched out the brother in black and told them one by one in as much as we could, and each squad of whites numbering as many as we well could, and one man talking for awhile and then another. Many agreed to vote with us, but said it in such a way that we knew very well that they did not mean it. Many others were mum. On the next day when the polls were opened the whites were much and early on the ground, and when the negroes came in they did not present that solid black phalanx of column they had formerly done. The truth is they had been informed that it was not good manners. The most of them, though, were very anxious to vote the Republican ticket. No violence was offered, but many whites would surround a negro voter and use all kind of arguments and persuasions to vote the Democratic ticket, and as each voter could be induced to cast his vote in that way, the entire white contingent would raise a yell that would have done honor to the old Rebel soldier's battle cry; and thus one by one the negroes were induced to fall into line, except a few who retired to the rear without voting at all. This took place throughout the state, and the Republican party was put out of business in Mississippi.

# EXTRACTS FROM *LAY MY BURDEN DOWN: A FOLK HISTORY OF SLAVERY*

## *(1945)*

Historical memory also lay at the heart of the stories about Reconstruction told by former slaves and collected by Benjamin Albert Botkin (1901–1975) in the 1930s. Botkin, one of America's foremost folklorists, directed the slave narrative program of the New Deal's Federal Writers' Project, which recorded more than two thousand interviews with ex-slaves aged seventy-five to one hundred five. He pioneered the use of ex-slave narratives to document slavery and emancipation. The former slaves recalled the joys of freedom, the success of finding work and gaining self-respect, and earning money. But many of their stories highlight the serious difficulties the blacks experienced making the transition from slavery to freedom—finding and reestablishing families and feeding, clothing, and sustaining themselves. As eighty-five-year-old Warren McKinney, a former South Carolina slave, put it: "Reconstruction was a mighty hard pull."

## HE SOLD HIS FIVE BOYS

. . . . I 'members day of 'mancipation. Yankees told us we was free, and they call us up from the field to sign up and see if us wanted to stay on with 'em. I stayed that year with the Moorings, then I bargain for land, but couldn't never pay for it. Turned loose 'thout nothing.

But they was a coal-black free-born nigger name George Wright had a floating mill right here on the 'Bigbee River, stayed at the point of the woods just 'bove the spring branch, and it did a good service. But he got in debt, and he sold his five boys. They was his own children, and he could sell 'em under the law. The names was Eber, Eli, Ezekiel, Enoch, and Ezra, and he sold 'em to the highest bidder right yonder front of the post office for cash. And Jack Tom was another free nigger here, and he bought some of 'em, and they others the white folks bought, and I never heard no complaint, and I seed 'em long as they lived. They was a heap of things went on. Some I likes to remember, some I don't. But I'd rather be free now. I never seed Mr. Lincoln, but when they told me 'bout him, I thought he was partly God.

## They Just Expected Freedom

They just expected freedom, all I ever heard. I know they didn't expect the white folks to give them no land 'cause the man what owned the land bought it hisself 'fore he bought the hands what he put on it. They thought they was ruined bad enough when the hands left them. They kept the land, and that is about all there was left. What the Yankees didn't take they wasted and set fire to it. They set fire to the rail fences so the stock would get out—all they didn't kill and take off. Both sides was mean. But it seemed like 'cause they was fighting down here on the South's ground it was the worst here. Now that's just the way I sees it. They done one more thing too. They put any colored man in the front where he would get killed first, and they stayed sorta behind in the back lines. When they come along, they try to get the colored men to go with them, and that's the way they got treated. I didn't know where anybody was made to stay on after the war. They was lucky if they had a place to stay at. There wasn't anything to do with if they stayed. Times was awful unsettled for a long time. People what went to the cities died. I don't know, they caught diseases and changing the ways of eating and living I guess what done it. They died mighty fast for awhile. I knowed some of them, and I heard 'em talking.

That period after the war was a hard time. It sure was harder than the depression. It lasted a long time. Folks got a lots now besides what they put up with then. Seemed like they thought if they be free they never have no work to do and just have plenty to eat and wear. They found it different, and when it was cold they had no wood like they been used to. I don't believe in the colored race being slaves 'cause of the color, but the war didn't make times much better for a long time. Some of them had a worse time. So many soon got sick and died. They died of consumption and fevers and nearly froze. Some near 'bout starved. The colored folks just scattered 'bout hunting work after the war.

## Then Came the Calm

When freedom come, folks left home, out in the streets, crying, praying, singing, shouting, yelling, and knocking down everything. Some shot off big guns. Then come the calm. It was sad then. So many folks done dead, things tore up, and nowheres to go and nothing to eat, nothing to do. It got squally. Folks got sick, so hungry. Some folks starved nearly to death. Times got hard. We went to the washtub—onliest way we all could live. Ma was a cripple woman. Pa couldn't find work for so long when he mustered out.

## I Got Along Hard
## After I Was Freed

I got along hard after I was freed. It is a hard matter to tell you what we could find or get. We used to dig up dirt in the smokehouse and boil it and dry it and sift it to get the salt to season our food with. We used to go out and get old bones that had been throwed away and crack them open and get the marrow and use them to season the greens with. Just plenty of niggers then didn't have anything but that to eat.

Even in slavery times, there was plenty of niggers out of them three hundred slaves who had to break up old lard gourds and use them for meat. They had to pick up bones off the dunghill and crack them open to cook with. And then, of course, they'd steal. Had to steal. That the best way to git what they wanted.

## Reconstruction Was a
## Mighty Hard Pull

I was born in Edgefield County, South Carolina. I am eighty-five years old. I was born a slave of George Strauter. I remembers hearing them say, "Thank God, I's free as a jay bird." My ma was a slave in the field. I was eleven years old when freedom was declared. When I was little, Mr. Strauter whipped my ma. It hurt me bad as it did her. I hated him. She was crying. I chunked him with rocks. He run after me, but he didn't catch me. There was twenty-five or thirty hands that worked in the field. They raised wheat, corn, oats, barley, and cotton. All the children that couldn't work stayed at one house. Aunt Mat kept the babies and small children that couldn't go to the field. He had a gin and a shop. The shop was at the fork of the roads. When the war come on, my papa went to build forts. He quit Ma and took another woman. When the war close, Ma took her four children, bundled 'em up and went to Augusta. The government give out rations there. My ma washed and ironed. People died in piles. I don't know till yet what was the matter. They said it was the change of living. I seen five or six wooden, painted coffins piled up on wagons pass by our house. Loads passed every day like you see cotton pass here. Some said it was cholera and some took consumption. Lots of the colored people nearly starved. Not much to get to do and not much houseroom. Several families had to live in one house. Lots of the colored folks went up North and froze to death. They couldn't stand the cold. They wrote back about them dying. No, they never sent them back. I heard some sent for money to come back. I heard plenty 'bout the Ku Klux. They scared the folks to death. People left Augusta in droves. About a thousand would all meet and walk going to hunt work and new homes. Some of them died. I had a sister and brother lost that way. I had another sister come to Louisiana that way. She wrote back. I don't think the colored folks looked for a share of land. They never got nothing 'cause the white folks didn't have nothing but barren hills left. About all the mules was wore out hauling provisions in the army. Some folks say they ought to done more for the colored folks when they left, but they say they was broke. Freeing all the slaves left 'em broke.

That reconstruction was a mighty hard pull. Me and Ma couldn't live. A man paid our ways to Carlisle, Arkansas, and we come. We started working for Mr. Emenson. He had a big store, teams, and land. We liked it fine, and I been here fifty-six years now. There was so much wild game, living was not so hard. If a fellow could get a little bread and a place to stay, he was all right. After I come to this state, I voted some. I have farmed and worked at odd jobs. I farmed mostly. Ma went back to her old master. He persuaded her to come back home. Me and her went back and run a farm four or five years before she died. Then I come back here.

## Who Was Freed by the War?

When I was a boy we used to sing, "Rather be a nigger than a poor white man." Even in slavery they used to sing that. It was the poor white man who was freed by the war, not the Negroes.

## Freedmen's Bureau

When freedom was on, Papa went to Atlanta and got transportation to Chattanooga. I don't know why. He met me and Mama. She picked me up and run away and met him. We went in a freight box. It had been a soldiers' home—great big house. We et on the first story out of tin pans. We had white beans or peas, crackers and coffee. Meat and wheat and cornbread we never smelt at that place. Somebody ask him how we got there, and he showed them a ticket from the Freedmen's Bureau in Atlanta. He showed that on the train every now and then. Upstairs they brought out a stack of wool blankets and started the rows of beds. Each man took his three as he was numbered. Every night the same one got his own blankets. The room was full of beds, and white guards with a gun over his shoulder guarded them all night long. We stayed there a long time—nearly a year. They tried to get jobs fast as they could and push 'em out, but it was slow work. Mama got a place to cook at—

Mrs. Crutchfield's. She run a hotel in town but lived in the country. We stayed there about a year. Papa was hired somewhere else there.

## I Got My Money, Too

I went down to Augusta to the Freedmen's Bureau to see if 'twas true we was free. I reckon there was over a hundred people there. The man got up and stated to the people: "You all is just as free as I am. You ain't got no mistress and no master. Work when you want." On Sunday morning Old Master sent the house gal and tell us to all come to the house.

He said: "What I want to send for you all is to tell you that you are free. You have the privilege to go anywhere you want, but I don't want none of you to leave me now. I wants you-all to stay right with me. If you stay, you must sign to it."

I asked him: "What you want me to sign for? I is free."

"That will hold me to my word and hold you to your word," he say.

All my folks sign it, but I wouldn't sign. Master call me up and say: "Willis, why wouldn't you sign?" I say: "If I is already free, I don't need to sign no paper. If I was working for you and doing for you before I got free, I can do it still, if you wants me to stay with you."

My father and mother tried to git me to sign, but I wouldn't sign. My mother said: "You oughta sign. How you know Master gwine pay?" I say: "Then I can go somewhere else."

Master pay first-class hands $15 a month, other hands $10, and then on down to $5 and $6. He give rations like they always have. When Christmas come, all come up to be paid off. Then he calls me. Ask where is me. I was standing round the corner of the house. "Come up here, Willis," he say. "You didn't sign that paper but I reckon I have to pay you too." He paid me and my wife $180. I said: "Well, you-all thought he wouldn't pay me, but I got my money too."

I stayed to my master's place one year after the war, then I left there. Next year I decided I would quit there and go somewhere else. It was on account of my wife. You see,

Master bought her off, as the highest bidder, down in Waynesboro, and she ain't seen her mother and father for fifteen years. When she got free, she went down to see 'em. Wa'n't willing to come back. 'Twas on account of Mistress and her. They both had childrens, five-six year old. The childrens had disagreement. Mistress slap my gal. My wife sass the mistress. But my master, he was as good a man as ever born. I wouldn't have left him for nobody, just on account of his wife and her fell out. . . .

I quit and goes over three miles to another widow lady's house, and make bargain with her. I pass right by the door. Old Boss sitting on the piazza. He say: "Hey, boy, where you gwine?" I say: "I 'cided to go." I was the foreman of the plow hands then. I saw to all the looking up, and things like that. He say: "Hold on there." He come out to the gate. "Tell you what I give you to stay on here. I give you five acre of as good land as I got, and $30 a month to stay here and see to my business.". . .

I say, . . . . "I can't, Master. It don't suit my wife round here. She won't come back. I can't stay."

He turn on me then, and busted out crying. "I didn't thought I could raise up a darky that would talk that-a-way," he said. Well, I went on off. I got the wagon and come by the house. Master say: "Now, you gwine off but don't forget me, boy. Remember me as you always done." I said: "All right."

I went over to that widow lady's house and work. Along about May I got sick. She say: "I going send for the doctor." I say: "Please ma'am, don't do that." (I thought maybe he kill me 'cause I left him.) She say: "Well, I gwine send for him." I in desperate condition. When I know anything, he walk up in the door. I was laying with my face toward the door, and I turn over.

Doctor come up to the bed. "Boy, how you getting on?" "I bad off," I say. He say: "See you is. Yeh." Lady say: "Doctor, what you think of him?" Doctor say: "Mistress, it 'most too late, but I do all I can." She say: "Please do all you can, he 'bout the best hand I got."

Doctor fix up medicine and told her to give it to me.

She say: "Uncle Will, take this medicine." I 'fraid to take it . 'Fraid he was trying to kill me. Then two men, John and Charlie, come in. Lady say: "Get this medicine in Uncle

Will." One of the men hold my hand, and they gag me and put it in me. Next few days I can talk and ax for something to eat, so I git better. (I say: "Well, he didn't kill me when I took the medicine!")

I stayed there with her. . . . . Next year I move right back in two miles, other side where I always live, with another lady. I stay there three year. Got along all right. When I left from there, I left there with $300 and plenty corn and hog. Everything I want, and three hundred cash dollars in my pocket!

## AFTER FREEDOM

Right after freedom, my father plaited baskets and mats. He shucked mops, put handles on rakes, and did things like that in addition to his farming. He was a blacksmith all the time, too. He used to plait collars for mules. He farmed and got his harvests in season. The other things would be a help to him between times.

My father came here because he thought that there was a better situation here than in Georgia. Of course, the living was better there because they had plenty of fruit. Then he worked on a third and fourth. He got one bale of cotton out of every three he made. The slaves left many a plantation, and they would grow up in weeds. When a man would clear up the ground like this and plant it down in something, he would get all he planted on it. That was in addition to the ground that he would contract to plant. He used to plant rice, peas, potatoes, corn, and anything else he wanted too. It was all hisn so long as it was on extra ground he cleared up.

But they said, "Cotton grows as high as a man in Arkansas." Then they paid a man $2.50 for picking cotton here in Arkansas, while they just paid about 40 cents in Georgia. So my father came here. Times was good when we come here. The old man cleared five bales of cotton for himself his first year, and he raised his own corn. He bought a pony and a cow and a breeding hog out of the first year's money. He died about thirty-five years ago.

When I was coming along, I did public work after I became a grown man. First year I made crops with him and cleared two bales for myself at 12½ cents a pound. The second year I hired out by the month at $45 per month and board. I had to buy my clothes, of course. After seven years I went to doing work as a millwright here in Arkansas. I stayed at that eighteen months. Then I steamboated.

We had a captain on that steamboat that never called any man by his name. We rolled cotton down the hill to the boat and loaded it on, and if you weren't a good man, that cotton got wet. I never wetted my cotton. But just the same, I heard what the others heard. One day after we had finished loading, I thought I'd tell him something. The men advised me not to. He was a rough man, and he carried a gun in his pocket and a gun in his shirt. I walked up to him and said, "Captain, I don't know what your name is, but I know you's a white man. I'm a nigger, but I got a name just like you have. My name's Webb. If you call 'Webb,' I'll come just as quick as I will for any other name and a lot more willing. If you don't want to say 'Webb,' you can just say 'Let's go,' and you'll find me right there." He looked at me a moment, and then he said, "Where you from?" I said, "I'm from Georgia, but I came on this boat from Little Rock." He put his arm around my shoulder and said, "Come on upstairs." We had two or three drinks upstairs, and he said, "You and your pardner are the only two men I have that is worth a damn." Then he said, "But you are right; you have a name, and you have a right to be called by it." And from then on, he quit calling us out of our names.

# SOURCES OF THE TEXTS

1. "An Act for the Release of certain Persons held to Service or Labor in the District of Columbia," in *The Statutes at Large, Treaties, and Proclamations, of the United States of America from December 5, 1859 to March 3, 1863*, vol. 12, ed. George P. Sanger (Boston: Little, Brown and Company, 1863).

2. Abraham Lincoln, "Preliminary Emancipation Proclamation," in *The Collected Works of Abraham Lincoln*, vol. 5, ed. Roy P. Basler (New Brunswick, NJ: Rutgers University Press, 1953).

3. Abraham Lincoln, "Emancipation Proclamation," in *The Collected Works of Abraham Lincoln*, vol. 6, ed. Roy P. Basler (New Brunswick, NJ: Rutgers University Press, 1953).

4. Abraham Lincoln, "Proclamation of Amnesty and Reconstruction," in *The Collected Works of Abraham Lincoln*, vol. 7, ed. Roy P. Basler (New Brunswick, NJ: Rutgers University Press, 1953).

5. "Transcript of Wade-Davis Bill (February 15,1864)," U.S. National Archives & Records Administration, http://www.ourdocuments.gov/print_friendly.php?flash=true&page=transcript&doc=37&title=Transcript+of+Wade-Davis+Bill+(1864).

6. "By the President of the United States: A Proclamation," July 8,1864, http://www.ourdocuments.gov/print_friendly.php?flash=true&page=transcript&doc=37&title=Transcript+of+Wade-Davis+Bill+(1864).

7. "The Wade-Davis Manifesto," in *The Radical Republicans and Reconstruction, 1861–1870*, ed. Harold M. Hyman (Indianapolis, IN: Bobbs-Merrill, 1967), 137–47.

8. Henry Highland Garnet, "Let the Monster Perish," in *Lift Every Voice: African American Oratory, 1787–1900*, eds. Philip S. Foner and Robert James Branham (Tuscaloosa: University of Alabama Press, 1998).

9. "An Act to establish a Bureau for the Relief of Freedmen and Refugees," in *The Statutes at Large, Treaties, and Proclamations, of the United States of America from December 5, 1859 to March 3, 1863*, vol. 13, ed. George P. Sanger (Boston: Little, Brown and Company, 1866).

10. Abraham Lincoln, "Second Inaugural Address," in *The Collected Works of Abraham Lincoln*, vol. 8, ed. Roy P. Balser (New Brunswick, NJ: Rutgers University Press, 1953).

11. Charles Sumner, "Right and Duty of Colored Fellow-Citizens in the Organization of Government," in *The Works of Charles Sumner*, vol. 9 (Boston: Lee and Shepard, 1875).

12. Andrew Johnson, "Proclamation Establishing Government for North Carolina," in *The Papers of Andrew Johnson*, vol. 8, ed. Paul H. Bergeron (Knoxville: University of Tennessee Press, 1989).

13. Andrew Johnson, "Amnesty Proclamation," in *The Papers of Andrew Johnson*, vol. 8, ed. Paul H. Bergeron (Knoxville: University of Tennessee Press, 1989).

14. Emily Waters to Her Husband (July 16, 1865), in *Free at Last: A Documentary History of Slavery, Freedom, and the Civil War*, eds. Ira Berlin, Barbara J. Fields, Steven F. Miller, Joseph P. Reidy, and Leslie S. Rowland (New York: The New Press, 1994).

15. Thaddeus Stevens, "'Reconstruction,' September 6th, 1865, in Lancaster," in *The Selected Papers of Thaddeus Stevens*, vol. 2, eds. Beverly Wilson Palmer and Holly Byers Ochoa (Pittsburgh, PA: University of Pittsburgh Press, 1997).

16. "A Freedmen's Bureau Officer Reports on Conditions in Mississippi, 1865," in *Race and National Power: A Sourcebook of Black Civil Rights from 1862 to 1954*, ed. Christopher Waldrep (New York: Routledge, 2011).

17. "From Edisto Island Freedmen to Andrew Johnson," October 28, 1865, in *The Papers of Andrew Johnson*, vol. 9, ed. Paul H. Bergeron (Knoxville: University of Tennessee Press, 1991).

18. Andrew Johnson, "Message to Congress," in *The Papers of Andrew Johnson*, vol. 9, ed. Paul H. Bergeron (Knoxville: University of Tennessee Press, 1991).

19. "Amendment 13," in *The United States Government Manual 2003/2004* (Washington, D.C.: Office of the Federal Register, National Archives and Records Administration, 2003).

20. Carl Schurz, "Report of Carl Schurz on the States of South Carolina, Georgia, Alabama, Mississippi, and Louisiana," in Carl Schurz, *Report on the Condition of the South* (New York: Arno Press and the *New York Times*, 1961).

21. *Laws of the State of Mississippi passed at a Regular Session of the Mississippi Legislature held in the city of Jackson, October, November and December, 1865* (Jackson, MS: J. J. Shannon & Co., State Publishers, 1866).

22. Joseph S. Fullerton to Andrew Johnson, February 9, 1866, in *The Papers of Andrew Johnson*, vol. 10, ed. Paul H. Bergeron (Knoxville: University of Tennessee Press, 1992).

23. "Vicksburg, Miss., March 8, 1866," in John Richard Dennett, *The South as It Is: 1865–1866*, ed. Henry M. Christman (New York: The Viking Press, 1965).

24. Charles Sumner to the Duchess of Argyll, April 3, 1866, in *The Selected Letters of Charles Sumner*, vol. 2, ed. Beverly Wilson Palmer (Boston: Northeastern University Press, 1990).

25. "The Civil Rights Act of 1866" (April 9, 1866), *Statutes at Large* 14 (Thirty-ninth Congress), 27–30.

26. Benjamin C. Truman, "Relative to the Condition of the Southern People and the States in Which the Rebellion Existed," Senate Executive Document, No. 43, Thirty-ninth Congress, first session (Washington, D.C.: Government Printing Office, 1866).

27. Carl Schurz, "The Logical Results of the War," September 8, 1866, http://www.trip.net/~bobwb/schurz/speech/warresults.html.

28. Rhoda Ann Childs's Statement in *Free at Last: A Documentary History of Slavery, Freedom, and the Civil War*, eds. Ira Berlin, Barbara J. Fields, Steven F. Miller, Joseph P. Reidy, and Leslie S. Rowland (New York: The New Press, 1992).

29. George Fitzhugh, "Camp Lee and the Freedman's Bureau," *De Bow's Review* 2, After War Series (October 1866): 346–55, in *The Causes of the South: Selections from De Bow's Review 1846–1867*, eds. Paul F. Paskoff and Daniel J. Wilson (Baton Rouge: Louisiana State University Press, 1982).

30. Frederick Douglass, "Reconstruction," *Atlantic Monthly* 18 (December 1866): 761–65.

31. "President Johnson's Message," December 3, 1866, in Edward McPherson, *The Political History of the United States of America During the Period of Reconstruction* (1871; reprint, Bedford, MA: Applewood Books, [2009]), 144–47.

32. Claude August Crommelin, *A Young Dutchman views Post–Civil War America: Diary of Claude August Crommelin*, trans. Augustus J. Veenendaal Jr. (Bloomington: Indiana University Press, 2011).

33. Henry Latham, *Black and White: A Journal of a Three Months' Tour in the United States* (1867; reprint, New York: Negro Universities Press, 1969), 262–79.

34. "An Act to Provide for more efficient Government of the Rebel States" [First Reconstruction Act] (March 2, 1867), *Statutes at Large* 14 (Thirty-ninth Congress), 428–29.

35. Anonymous, "Untitled," *Charlottesville Chronicle*, March 6, 1867, in *The Reconstruction Era: Primary Documents on Events from 1865 to 1877*, ed. Donna L. Dickerson (Westport, CT: Greenwood Press, 2003).

36. "The Prospect of Reconstruction," *The Nation* 5 (March 14, 1867): 212–13.

37. "Impeachment from a Legal Point of View," *The Nation* 5 (March 14, 1867): 214–15.

38. "Congress and the Constitution," *The Nation* 5 (March 28, 1867): 254.

39. "The Prospect at the South," *The Nation* 5 (March 28, 1867): 254–55.

40. "Land for the Landless," *The Nation* 5 (May 16, 1867): 394–95.

41. John Forsyth, "The Argument of Numbers," *Mobile Advertiser and Register*, June 27, 1867, and W. W. Screws, "Why Oppose a Convention?" *Montgomery Daily Advertiser*, June 28, 1867, in *The Reconstruction Era: Primary Documents on Events from 1865 to 1877*, ed. Donna L. Dickerson (Westport, CT: Greenwood Press, 2003).

42. "The Freedmen," *The Missionary Reporter of the A.M.E. Church* 1 (July 1867): 4–5.

43. Thaddeus Stevens, "Reconstruction," July 9, 1867, in *Congressional Globe*, Fortieth Congress, first session, in *The Selected Papers of Thaddeus Stevens*, vol. 2, eds. Beverly Wilson Palmer and Holly Byers Ochoa (Pittsburgh, PA: University of Pittsburgh Press, 1997).

44. "The Negro's Claim to Office," *The Nation* 5 (August 1, 1867): 90–91.

45. "Samson Agonistes at Washington," *Harper's Weekly* (August 24, 1867): 544.

46. George Fitzhugh, "*Cui Bono?* — The Negro Vote," *De Bow's Review* 4, After War Series (October 1867): 289–92, in *The Causes of the South: Selections from De Bow's Review 1846–1867*, eds. Paul F. Paskoff and Daniel J. Wilson (Baton Rouge: Louisiana State University Press, 1982).

47. "The Virginia Election," *The Nation* 5 (October 31, 1867): 354.

48. "What Shall We Do with the Indians?" *The Nation* 5 (October 31, 1867): 356.

49. Andrew Johnson, "Third Annual Message," in *The Papers of Andrew Johnson*, vol. 13, ed. Paul H. Bergeron (Knoxville: University of Tennessee Press, 1996).

50. J. T. Trowbridge, *A Picture of the Desolated States; and the work of Restoration, 1865–1868* (Hartford, CT: L. Stebbins, 1868).

51. Cornelia Hancock to Philadelphia Friends Association for the Aid and Elevation of the Freedmen, January 1868, in *South After Gettysburg: Letters of Cornelia Hancock, 1863–1868*, ed. Henrietta Stratton Jaquette (1937; reprint, New York: Thomas Y. Crowell, 1956).

52. Francis L. Cardozo, "Break up the Plantation System," in *Lift Every Voice: African American Oratory, 1787–1900,* eds. Philip

S. Foner and Robert James Branham (Tuscaloosa: University of Alabama Press, 1998).

53. "The Impeachment," *New York Times*, February 24, 1868, in *The New York Times Complete Civil War, 1861–1865*, eds. Harold Holzer and Craig L. Symonds (New York: Black Dog & Leventhal, 2010), 453.

54. S. A. Atkinson, "The Supreme Hour Has Come," *Athens Southern Banner*, March 13, 1868, in *The Reconstruction Era: Primary Documents on Events from 1865 to 1877*, ed. Donna L. Dickerson (Westport, CT: Greenwood Press, 2003).

55. "Karinus," Letter to the Editor—"Equal Suffrage in Michigan," *Hillsdale Standard*, March 17, 1868, in *The Reconstruction Era: Primary Documents on Events from 1865 to 1877*, ed. Donna L. Dickerson (Westport, CT: Greenwood Press, 2003).

56. "This Little Boy Would Persist in Handling Books Above His Capacity. And This Was the Disastrous Result," *Harper's Weekly* (March 21, 1868): 192.

57. Thaddeus Stevens, "Speech on Impeachment Trial of Andrew Johnson," April 27, 1868, *Congressional Globe*, Fortieth Congress, second session, supplement 320, in *The Selected Papers of Thaddeus Stevens*, vol. 2, eds. Beverly Wilson Palmer and Holly Byers Ochoa (Pittsburgh, PA: University of Pittsburgh Press, 1997).

58. "The Result of the Trial," *The Nation* 6 (May 21, 1868): 404.

59. "Republican, at Chicago, May," in Edward McPherson, *The Political History of the United States of America during the Period of Reconstruction* (1871; reprint, Bedford, MA: Applewood Books, [2009]), 364–65.

60. Carey Styles, "Not Our 'Brother,'" *Atlanta Constitution*, June 24, 1868, in *The Reconstruction Era: Primary Documents on Events from 1865 to 1877*, ed. Donna L. Dickerson (Westport, CT: Greenwood Press, 2003).

61. "Amendment 14," in *The United States Government Manual 2003/2004* (Washington, D.C.: Office of the Federal Register, National Archives and Records Administration, 2003).

62. Henry McNeal Turner, "I Claim the Rights of a Man," in *Lift Every Voice: African American Oratory, 1787–1900*, eds. Philip S. Foner and Robert James Branham (Tuscaloosa: University of Alabama Press, 1998).

63. "Remarks of William E. Mathews," *The Missionary Reporter of the A.M.E. Church* (January 1869): 9–11.

64. Ulysses S. Grant, "President Grant's Inaugural Address, March 4, 1869," in Edward McPherson, *The Political History of the United States of America During the Period of Reconstruction* (1871; reprint, Bedford, MA: Applewood Books, [2009]), 416–17.

65. Lydia Maria Child, "Homesteads," *National Anti-Slavery Standard*, March 28, 1869, in *A Lydia Maria Child Reader*, ed. Carolyn L. Karcher (Durham, NC: Duke University Press, 1997).

66. "Amendment 15," in *The United States Government Manual 2003/2004* (Washington, D.C.: Office of the Federal Register, National Archives and Records Administration, 2003).

67. Frederick Douglass, "At Last, at Last, the Black Man Has a Future: An Address Delivered in Albany, New York, on 22 April 1870," in *The Frederick Douglass Papers: Series One: Speeches, Debates, and Interviews*, vol. 4: 1864–1880, eds. John W. Blassingame and John R. McKivigan (New Haven, CT: Yale University Press, 1991).

68. Carl Schurz, "Enforcement of the Fifteenth Amendment," in *Speeches, Correspondence and Political Papers of Carl Schurz, vol. 1: October 20, 1852–November 26, 1870*, ed. Frederic Bancroft (New York: G. P. Putnam's Sons, 1913).

69. "An Act to Enforce the Right of Citizens of the United States to Vote in the Several States of This Union, and for Other Purposes," in *The Statutes at Large, Treaties, and Proclamations, of the United States of America from December 1869 to March 1871, and Treaties and Postal Conventions*, vol. 16, ed. George P. Sanger (Boston: Little, Brown and Company, 1871).

70. *Proceedings of the Ku Klux Trials at Columbia, S.C., in the United States Circuit Court, November Term, 1871* (1872; reprint, New York: Negro Universities Press, 1969).

71. Hiram R. Revels, "Abolish Separate Schools" in *Lift Every Voice: African American Oratory, 1787–1900*, eds. Philip S. Foner and Robert James Branham (Tuscaloosa: University of Alabama Press, 1998).

72. Robert Brown Elliott, "The Amnesty Bill," in *Congressional Globe*, Forty-second Congress, first session, March 14, 1871, in *Black Congressmen During Reconstruction: A Documentary Sourcebook*, ed. Stephen Middleton (Westport, CT: Praeger, 2002).

73. "An Act to Enforce the Provisions of the Fourteenth Amendment to the Constitution of the United States, and for Other Purposes," in *The Statutes at Large, Treaties, and Proclamations, of the United States of America from March 1871 to March 1873*, vol. 17, ed. George P. Sanger (Boston: Little, Brown and Company, 1873).

74. Charles Stearns, *The Black Man of the South, and the Rebels; or, The Characteristics of the Former, and the Recent Outrages of the Latter* (1872; reprint, New York: Kraus, 1969).

75. "The Man with the (Carpet) Bags," *Harper's Weekly* (November 9, 1872): 880.

76. James S. Pike, *The Prostrate State: South Carolina Under Negro Government* (1874; reprint, New York: Harper & Row Publishers, 1968).

77. Robert Brown Elliott, "The Civil Rights Bill," in *Lift Every Voice: African American Oratory, 1787–1900,* eds. Philip S. Foner and Robert James Branham (Tuscaloosa: University of Alabama Press, 1998).

78. John Mercer Langston, "Equality Before the Law," in *Lift Every Voice: African American Oratory, 1787–1900,* ed. Philip S. Foner and Robert James Branham (Tuscaloosa: University of Alabama Press, 1998).

79. James T. Rapier, *Congressional Record,* Forty-third Congress, first session, June 9, 1874 (Washington, D. C.: Government Printing Office, 1874), 4782–84.

80. "An Act to Protect All Citizens in Their Civil and Legal Rights," in *The Statutes at Large, Treaties, and Proclamations, of the United States of America from December 1873 to March 1875,* vol. 18, ed. George P. Sanger (Boston: Little, Brown and Company, 1875).

81. "The Negro Spirit," *Charleston* (SC) *News,* reprinted in *New York Times* (July 21, 1876), 2.

82. Carl Schurz, "Hayes versus Tilden," August 31, 1876, http://www.trip.net/~bobwb/schurz/speech/hayesandtilden.html.

83. Thomas Wentworth Higginson, "Some War Scenes Revisited," *Atlantic Monthly* 42 (July 1878): 1–9, in Thomas Wentworth Higginson, *Army Life in a Black Regiment and Other Writings* (New York: Penguin Books, 1997).

84. D. H. Chamberlain, "Reconstruction and the Negro," *North American Review* 128 (February 1879): 161–73.

85. *Civil Rights Cases* (1883), in *Cases Argued and Decided in the Supreme Court of the United States, October Terms, 1881, 1882, 1883, in 106, 107, 108, 109 U.S.* (Rochester, NY: Lawyers Co-operative Publishing Company, 1886).

86. Washington Lafayette Clayton, *Olden Times Revisited: W. L. Clayton's Pen Pictures,* ed. Minrose Gwin (Jackson: University Press of Mississippi, 1982).

87. *Lay My Burden Down: A Folk History of Slavery,* ed. B. A. Botkin (1945; reprint, Athens: University of Georgia Press, 2000).

# ENDNOTES

1. See Guy Gugliotta, "New Estimate Raises Civil War Death Toll," *New York Times*, April 3, 2012, D1. The 750,000 figure derives from recent research by the demographic historian J. David Hacker. See Hacker's "A Census-Based Count of the Civil War Dead," *Civil War History* 57 (December 2011): 307–48. The number of civilian casualties in the war remains understudied and undetermined.

2. Eric Foner, "The Civil War in 'Postracial' America," *The Nation*, October 10, 2011, 24.

3. Abraham Lincoln, "Second Inaugural Address," March 4, 1865, in Roy P. Basler, ed., *The Collected Works of Abraham Lincoln*, 8 vols. (New Brunswick, NJ: Rutgers University Press, 1953), 8:333.

4. Lincoln, "Last Public Address," April 11, 1865, in ibid., 401, 403.

5. Catherine Ann Devereux Edmondston diary, December 16, 1865, in Beth G. Crabtree and James W. Patton, eds., *"Journal of a Secesh Lady": The Diary of Catherine Ann Devereux Edmondston, 1860–1866* (Raleigh, NC: Division of Archives and History, Department of Cultural Resources, 1979), 721.

6. Steven Hahn, *The Political Worlds of Slavery and Freedom* (Cambridge: Harvard University Press, 2009), 52–53. Also see 85.

7. John Stauffer, "Fighting the Devil with His Own Fire," in Andrew Delbanco, *The Abolitionist Imagination* (Cambridge: Harvard University Press, 2012), 78.

8. In 1963 James P. Shenton edited a volume of more limited scope. See *The Reconstruction: A Documentary History: 1865–1877* (New York: G. P. Putnam's Sons, 1963).

9. Robert D. Reid, review of Walter Lynwood Fleming, *Civil War and Reconstruction in Alabama*, and Fleming, *Documentary History of Reconstruction*, in *Journal of Negro History* 35 (October 1950): 455.

10. Eric Foner, *Reconstruction: America's Unfinished Revolution, 1863–1877* (New York: Harper & Row, 1988).

11. Gregory P. Downs, "A Palace That Will Fall upon Them: Reconstruction as a Problem of Occupation," *Reviews in American History* 39 (March 2011): 118–26.

12. Foner, *Reconstruction*, xxii.

13. Ibid., xxiii.

14. For a partial listing, see Eric Foner, *Freedom's Lawmakers: A Directory of Black Officeholders During Reconstruction* (New York: Oxford University Press, 1993).

15. Albion W. Tourgée quoted in Richard Nelson Current, *Those Terrible Carpetbaggers: A Reinterpretation* (New York: Oxford University Press, 1988), 376.

16. Richard Franklin Bensel, *Yankee Leviathan: The Origins of Central State Authority in America, 1859–1877* (Cambridge: Cambridge University Press, 1990).

17. Edward L. Ayres, "Civil War, Emancipation, and Reconstruction," in Gary W. Reichard and Ted Dickson, eds., *America on the World Stage: A Global Approach to U.S. History* (Urbana: University of Illinois Press, 2008), 131.

18. W. E. B. Du Bois, *Black Reconstruction in America: An Essay Toward a History of the Part Which Black Folk Played in the Attempt to Reconstruct Democracy in America, 1860–1880* (1935; reprint, New York: Atheneum, 1973), 30.

19. Eric Foner, "Foreword," in David A. Lincove, comp., *Reconstruction in the United States: An Annotated Bibliography* (Westport, CT: Greenwood Press, 2000), xiii–xiv. Lincove's work is a definitive reference work, annotating more than 2,900 articles, books, and dissertations on Reconstruction.

20. Foner, *Freedom's Lawmakers*, xxv.

21. Foner, *Reconstruction*, 61.

22. James M. McPherson, "In Pursuit of Constitutional Abolitionism," in Alexander Tsesis, *The Promises of Liberty: The History and Contemporary Relevance of the Thirteenth Amendment* (New York: Columbia University Press, 2010), 30.

23. Foner, *Reconstruction*, 181.

24. Foner, *The Fiery Trial: Abraham Lincoln and American Slavery* (New York: W. W. Norton, 2010), 240–43.

25. Foner, *Reconstruction*, 142-43.

26. Catherine Ann Devereux Edmondston diary, December 16, 1865, in Crabtree and Patton, eds., *"Journal of a Secesh Lady,"* 721.

27. Steven Hahn, *A Nation Under Our Feet: Black Political Struggles in the Rural South from Slavery to the Great Migration* (Cambridge, MA: Belknap Press of Harvard University Press, 2003), 158.

28. Stephen Kantrowitz, "Reconstruction Era, 1865–77," in Michael Kazin, ed., *The Concise Princeton Encyclopedia of American Political History* (Princeton, NJ: Princeton University Press, 2011), 434.

29. Hahn, *A Nation Under Our Feet*, 235.

30. Hans L. Trefousse, *Historical Dictionary of Reconstruction* (Westport, CT: Greenwood Press, 1991), 42-43.

31. Foner, *Reconstruction*, 230.

32. Ibid., 272.

33. As historian Michael Fitzgerald has made clear, the oft-confusing disfranchisement clause of the Military Reconstruction Acts disqualified from voting only those persons who had held public office before the war and who then sided with the Confederates, along with some high-ranking Confederate officials. Their status remained to be determined by state constitutions that were yet to be revised. According to Fitzgerald: "The Military Reconstruction Acts did not apply the ironclad oath on the whole Southern white electorate. It temporarily excluded from registering and voting for the new constitutions those barred from office under the proposed Fourteenth Amendment." Fitzgerald notes that contemporaries judged that the act disfranchised roughly between five and ten percent of the South's white males. See Michael Fitzgerald, "Disunion" Blog on NYTimes.com, February 4, 2011.

34. Hugh Davis, *"We Will Be Satisfied with Nothing Less": The African-American Struggle for Equal Rights in the North During Reconstruction* (Ithaca, NY: Cornell University Press, 2011), 116.

35. Foner, *Reconstruction*, 277.

36. Nicholas Lemann, "Reversals," *The New Yorker*, July 30, 2007, 28.

37. Hahn, *The Political Worlds of Slavery and Freedom*, 142.

38. Foner, *Reconstruction*, 421.

39. Ibid., 523.

40. Hahn, *A Nation Under Our Feet*, 312.

41. Trefousse, *Historical Dictionary of Reconstruction*, 50.

42. William Garrott Brown, review of James Ford Rhodes, *History of the United States from the Compromise of 1850 to the Final Restoration of Home Rule in the South in 1877*, in *American Historical Review* 12 (April 1907), 681.

43. Trefousse, *Historical Dictionary of Reconstruction*, 50.

44. Hahn, *A Nation Under Our Feet*, 441.

45. Kantrowitz, "Reconstruction Era, 1865–77," 434.

# ON SHATTERED GROUND

*A Civil War Mosaic, 1861-1865*

### Edited and with an Introduction by Eileen and Roger Panetta

This anthology of documents traces the American Civil War from its root causes in the antebellum period to the major battles and events of the war and on through the assassination of President Lincoln. With original documents ranging from newspaper articles and pamphlets to songs and personal letters written by participants and observers, the documents featured in this anthology capture the wide spectrum of individuals—from statesmen to citizens, generals to solders, abolitionists to slaves, and journalists to artists—who all felt the profound effects of the American Civil War. What emerges is a powerful portrait of the first modern war—one that reached into the homes and lives of the average American in new and powerful ways.

# THE CIVIL WAR
## *A History*

by

## **Harry Hansen**

Presented in one comprehensive volume, this is the Civil War as it really was—the forces and events that caused it, the soldiers and civilians who fought it, and the ideas and values that are its legacy today.

Available wherever books are sold or at
signetclassics.com

**facebook.com/signetclassic**

# READ THE TOP 20
# SIGNET CLASSICS

SIGNETCLASSICS.COM
FACEBOOK.COM/SIGNETCLASSIC